TRETHURGY

Excavations at Trethurgy Round, St Austell: Community and Status in Roman and Post-Roman Cornwall

Henrietta Quinnell (formerly Miles)

with contributions by Justine Bayley, Stuart Blaylock, Sarnia Butcher, Caroline Cartwright, PJ Casey, Rob Ixer, Helen Keeley, JG MacDonnell, Peter Marshall, Jennifer Price, Richard Reece, Rosemary Robertson, S Staines, Carl Thorpe, Sue Watts, and DF Williams

To the memory of Patricia Brierley, née Carlyon,
a great friend to whose extensive knowledge
of Cornwall in the Roman period I owe so much.

Cover illustrations:
Front Cover: *Aerial photograph of the excavations.*
Reproduced by permission of the Royal Naval Air Station, Culdrose.
Back Cover: *Trethurgy bowl.* Photo: *Adam Sharpe*

Frontispiece: Colour reconstruction of the Round during Stage 6. Illustration Rosemary Robertson

Contents

List of Tables iv
List of Figures iv
List of Plates vi
Preface viii
Acknowledgments ix
Addresses of contributors xi
Summaries: English, French, and German xii

1 Introduction: general background, methodology, and presentation 1
1.1 Location 1
1.2 Geology and soil 1
1.3 Circumstances of the excavation 3
1.4 Excavation method 5
1.5 Report presentation 7

2 Site stratigraphy 9
2.1 Summary of the site chronology 9
2.2 Period 1 10
2.3 Period 2. The Old Land Surface and possible field system 10
2.4 Construction of the Period 3 Enclosure 10
2.5 Period 4 activity between the Construction of the Enclosure and of the Round 13
2.6 Period 5 Round Earthworks 15
2.7 Period 5 Round: the Central Area 23
2.8 Period 5 Round: Structure V 23
2.9 Period 5 Round: Structure U, possible byre 25
2.10 Period 5 Round: House Z 29
2.11 Period 5 Round: Structures between House Z and Rampart, Area Q 35
2.12 Period 5 Round: Structure Y 38
2.13 Period 5 Round: House X 38
2.14 Period 5 Round: Structure E 44
2.15 Period 5 Round: Structure G 46
2.16 Period 5 Round: House D 48
2.17 Period 5 Round: House A 50
2.18 Period 5 Round: House T 60
2.19 Period 5 Round: Area R 63
2.20 Period 6 Medieval use 66
2.21 Period 7 16th-century field enclosure 66
2.22 Period 8 Post-Medieval use 66

3 Metalworking and metal finds 67
3.1 Coins 67
3.1.1 Coins from the excavation *PJ Casey* 67
3.1.2 Some background on Roman coinage in Cornwall *Richard Reece* 67
3.2 Brooches *Sarnia Butcher* 70
3.3 Other copper alloy objects 72
3.4 Silver *Justine Bayley* 73
3.5 Tin ingot *Justine Bayley* 73
3.6 Slags and other metallurgical finds *Justine Bayley* 73
3.7 Schorl *Rob Ixer* and *JG McDonnell* 73
3.8 Discussion of the tin ingot and non-ferrous metalworking 74
3.9 Iron artefacts 76
3.10 Ironworking 83

4 Romano-British and early Post-Roman glass vessels and objects *Jennifer Price* 85
4.1 Composition and dating of the glass assemblage 85
4.2 Supply and use of glass 85
4.3 Distribution of glass within the site 86
4.4 The Romano-British vessel glass 86
4.5 Early Post-Roman vessel glass 87
4.6 Objects and window glass 89
4.7 Glass catalogue 90

5 The pottery with contributions by *DF Williams* 93
5.1 The assemblage and its study 93
5.2 The quantification of the assemblage 97
5.3 Continental and Mediterranean imported wares 98
5.4 British wares with province-wide distribution 104
5.5 British regional wares 104
5.6 Cornish gabbroic ware 108
5.7 Medieval and Post-Medieval pottery with *Carl Thorpe* 127
5.8 Baked clay 128

6 Stone artefacts 129
6.1 Materials used 129
6.2 Bowls and mortaria 130
6.3 Weight 139
6.4 Mould and mould cover 142
6.5 Slate discs 142
6.6 Net sinkers 142
6.7 Whetstones 142
6.8 Rubbing and polishing stones 143
6.9 Spindle whorls 143
6.10 Discs or counters 144
6.11 Shale bracelets and the use of shale 144
6.12 Querns and mortars 145
6.12.1 Rotary querns with *Sue Watts* 145
6.13 Unmodified stone 152

7 Flint and quartz 153
7.1 Quantity and distribution 153
7.2 Source and typology 153
7.3 Lithic assemblages in the St Austell area 156

8 Environmental data 157
8.1 Bone, antler, and shell 157
8.2 Soils *S Staines* 157
8.3 Soil phosphate analysis *Helen C M Keeley* 159
8.4 Pollen 159
8.5 Charcoal *Caroline Cartwright* 159
8.6 The potential for the study of plant macrofossils 160

9 Radiocarbon dating, phasing, and chronology 161
9.1 Radiocarbon determinations *Peter Marshall* 161
9.2 Phasing and chronology 165

10 The architecture of the large oval buildings 183
10.1 The archaeological data for large oval buildings 183
10.2 Other oval buildings in Cornwall 186
10.3 The problems posed by the archaeological data 189
10.4 Possible architectural solutions for large oval buildings *Stuart Blaylock* 190
10.5 Brief comment on the implications of the proposed reconstructions 201

11 Structures other than the large oval buildings 203
11.1 Rectangular timber building X1 203
11.2 Four-posters E1, E2 and Structure E3 203
11.3 Irregular rectangular stone structure T5 204
11.4 Large oval structures X2 and X3 204
11.5 Small oval timber building D1 205
11.6 Sub-circular stone buildings 205
11.7 Small, irregular oval buildings 205
11.8 Buildings with ancillary platforms 206
11.9 Structures with dump walls 207
11.10 Lines of posts 207
11.11 Paired postholes 207
11.12 Structure G - shrine or store? 208
11.13 Structure U1, a possible byre 209

12 Trethurgy Round - commentaries on themes and problems presented by the data 211
12.1 Rounds and small enclosures - definitions, frequency, and function 211
12.2 The Trethurgy landscape until the 2nd century AD 214
12.3 Cornwall and the *Civitas Dumnoniorum* 215
12.4 The building of the Period 5 Round and the character of its enclosure 217
12.5 The grooves on Entrance paving [188] and the use of vehicles 220
12.6 The population of the Round 221
12.7 The Round and its landscape in the initial, 2nd-century AD Stages 221
12.8 The Round in its later Stages during the Roman period 225
12.9 The colour reconstruction of the Stage 6 Round 228
12.10 Middens, manure, and the survival of artefacts 229
12.11 Living in an oval house 231
12.12 Crafts and the production of artefacts within the Round 232
12.13 Trade, exchange, and taxation; contact with a wider world 234
12.14 Religious and ritual activity 236
12.15 The Round and its regional context in the 5th century AD 238
12.16 The Round and its regional context in the 6th century AD 240
12.17 End note: the move away from rounds 243

Appendix 1 Context details 245

Appendix 2 Radiocarbon dates from Roman and Post-Roman Cornwall *Peter Marshall* 263

Bibliography 277

Index *Susan Vaughan* 291

List of Tables

Table 3.1	Details of coins	68
Table 3.2	Analysis of Cornish coin hoards and single finds	69
Table 3.3	Analysis of Cornish coin hoards by date	69
Table 3.4	Slag descriptions and identifications	74
Table 3.5	Available weights of dateable tin ingots	75
Table 3.6	Distribution of ironwork across the Round.	77
Table 5.1	References to principal publications of ceramic assemblages from Roman Cornwall	93
Table 5.2	Analysis of the ceramic assemblage by main context and fabric groups	94
Table 5.3	Minimum vessel counts, excluding small sherds of unidentified fabrics	96
Table 5.4	Sherd and weight counts for 'Other Roman/Post-Roman fabrics'	97
Table 5.5	Percentages of the ceramic assemblage for major fabric groups	98
Table 5.6	Diameters of Type 4 jar rims	112
Table 6.1	Cornish stone weights as multiples of suggested Roman and Celtic standards	140
Table 6.2	Details of unmodified pebbles	151
Table 7.1	Distribution of flint across the site	153
Table 7.2	Analysis of the flint assemblage	153
Table 8.1	Details of soil phosphate analysis	158
Table 8.2	Details of identified charcoal	158
Table 9.1	Radiocarbon age determinations	162
Table 9.2	Suggested chronology of the Period 3 Enclosure, Period 4, the Period 5 Round, and subsequent Periods	164
Table 9.3	Artefacts and radiocarbon determinations relevant to site chronology	164
Table 10.1	Details of large oval buildings	183
Table 11.1	Details of possible large oval timber structures	204
Table 12.1	An attempt to indicate the dates at which excavated rounds were occupied	212
Table 12.2	Details of changing structural and population patterns through the suggested Stages of the Round.	222

List of Figures

Frontispiece	Colour reconstruction of the Round during Stage 6	
Fig 1	Location maps	2
Fig 2	Location of the Round at Trethurgy	4
Fig 3	Layout of detailed excavation plans and section lines	5
Fig 4	Period 3 Enclosure	6
Fig 5	Period 5 Round: composite plan	7
Fig 6	Key to site plans and sections	8
Fig 7	Sections through the Earthworks	11
Fig 8	Details of Periods 3/4 Enclosure features in Areas P and O	12
Fig 9	Periods 3/4 Structure N and Period 5 Round Stage 1 to 3 features in Areas N and Q	14
Fig 10	Entrance plans	18
Fig 11	Entrance sections	19
Fig 12	Sections p-pp, q-qq, Areas N and Y	21
Fig 13	Structure V plan	23
Fig 14	Section g-h across Structure V	24
Fig 15	Phase plan of Structure V2	24
Fig 16	Structure U1, the byre, and U2 plan	26
Fig 17	Sections i-j-k across Structure U and the Earthworks	27
Fig 18	Phase plans of Structures U1 and U2	28
Fig 19	House Z1 plan	30

Fig 20	House Z2 plan	32
Fig 21	Section n-o across Houses Z1 and Z2	33
Fig 22	Plan of structural sequence in Area Q	34
Fig 23	Section l-m across Area Q	35
Fig 24	Structure Y plan	37
Fig 25	House X plan	39
Fig 26	Section r-rr across House X	40
Fig 27	Sections of hearth pits	41
Fig 28	Phase plans of House X1 and X4	43
Fig 29	Structures E and G, plans	45
Fig 30	Sections t-tt and u-uu across Structure G	47
Fig 31	House D plan	48
Fig 32	Section v-vv across House D	49
Fig 33	Phase plans of House D1 and D4	49
Fig 34	House A1 plan	51
Fig 35	Sections w-ww and x-xx across House A	52
Fig 36	Phase plan to show features of House A1a	52
Fig 37	Houses A2 and A3 plan	53
Fig 38	Phase plans of House A2 and House A3	54
Fig 39	Houses T1, T2, and T3 plan	57
Fig 40	Phase plans of House T2 and T3	58
Fig 41	House T4, plan	59
Fig 42	House/Structure T5, plan	59
Fig 43	Section y-yy across House T sequence	60
Fig 44	Area R earlier features	62
Fig 45	Area R later features	64
Fig 46	Brooches	70
Fig 47	Tin ingot	72
Fig 48	Iron objects M4-M6	79
Fig 49	Iron objects M7-M19	80
Fig 50	Iron objects M20-M24	82
Fig 51	Glass vessels and window glass	90
Fig 52	Glass objects	92
Fig 53	Non-gabbroic pottery, P1-28. Oxfordshire, White ware import, Phocaean Red Slip ware, Late Roman Amphorae, E ware, BB1, South Devon, P24 Medieval	100
Fig 54	Gabbroic wares P29-54	113
Fig 55	Gabbroic wares P55-73	115
Fig 56	Gabbroic wares P74-94	116
Fig 57	Gabbroic wares P95-100	119
Fig 58	Gabbroic wares P101-5	120
Fig 59	Gabbroic wares P106-30	122
Fig 60	Gabbroic wares P131-47	126
Fig 61	Trethurgy bowls in elvan S1-S3	132
Fig 62	Trethurgy bowls in elvan S4-S6	133
Fig 63	Cornish mortars in elvan, S13 weight in kaolinised granite	134
Fig 64	Unfinished elvan Cornish mortar	135
Fig 65	Bronze bowl from Nijmegen (after Mutz 1972), a possible prototype for the Trethurgy bowls	136
Fig 66	Trethurgy bowl in greisen from Richborough	138
Fig 67	Stone mould S14; mould cover S15; slate disc S16; net sinker S17; whetstones S18-23, S22 made on a broken weight; rubbing stones S24-6	141
Fig 68	Spindle whorls and small discs	143
Fig 69	Shale bracelets	144
Fig 70	Upper rotary quern S42	145

Fig 71	Upper rotary quern S43	146
Fig 72	Upper rotary quern S44	147
Fig 73	Upper rotary quern S45	148
Fig 74	Upper rotary querns S46 and S49	149
Fig 75	Sections through lower rotary querns S47, S48, and S49	150
Fig 76	Flints, F1-F16	154
Fig 77	Flints, F17-F25	155
Fig 78	Probability distributions of radiocarbon determinations based on simple radiocarbon calibration	163
Fig 79	Probability distributions of radiocarbon determinations based on simple radiocarbon calibration and further chronological modelling	163
Fig 80	The Round Stage 1, suggested structures *c* AD 150-175	168
Fig 81	The Round Stage 2, suggested structures *c* AD 175-210	169
Fig 82	The Round Stage 3, suggested structures *c* AD 210-260	170
Fig 83	The Round Stage 4, suggested structures *c* AD 260-325	171
Fig 84	The Round Stage 5, suggested structures *c* AD 325-375	173
Fig 85	The Round Stage 6, suggested structures *c* AD 375-400	174
Fig 86	The Round Stage 7, suggested structures *c* AD 400-450	176
Fig 87	The Round Stage 8, suggested structures *c* AD 450-500	177
Fig 88	The Round Stage 9, suggested structures *c* AD 500-550+. General position of Post-Roman import wares indicated	179
Fig 89	The Round Stage 10, suggested structures ?AD 700 onward	181
Fig 90	Conjectural reconstruction of House Z2 from the south-east	195
Fig 91	Conjectural reconstruction of House Z2 in plan view	196
Fig 92	Conjectural reconstruction of House Z2 from the north-west	196
Fig 93	Conjectural reconstruction of structural details of House Z2	197
Fig 94	Conjectural reconstruction of House A1	198
Fig 95	Conjectural reconstruction of House T2	200
Fig 96	Probability distributions for radiocarbon dates for Roman and Post-Roman Cornwall	275
Fig 97	Probability distributions for radiocarbon dates for Roman and Post-Roman Cornwall (continued)	276

List of Plates

Pl 1	Aerial photograph of the Round, partly excavated, from the east, September 1973	1
Pl 2	Aerial photograph from the north to show hillslope position of the Round	4
Pl 3	The Period 3 Enclosure Bank on the east of the Round	12
Pl 4	Drain [917] within the Period 3 Enclosure Ditch	13
Pl 5	The Round Rampart on the west (northern part), stripped of Period 7 field hedge [236]	15
Pl 6	The Round Rampart on the west (southern part), showing the length stripped of Period 7 field hedge	16
Pl 7	Drain [199] beneath Round Rampart on north side of Entrance	16
Pl 8	Ditch terminal north of Entrance	16
Pl 9	Period 3 Enclosure gulley [459] passing beneath Round inner revetment [15] south of House T	17
Pl 10	Round inner revetment [15] in its highest surviving part, south-east of House T	17
Pl 11	The Entrance showing Stages 1-4 surface [215] and Stage 5 paving [188] in section	19
Pl 12	The Entrance with Stage 5 paving [188]; [521] on berms	20

Pl 13	Entrance paving slabs [188]	20
Pl 14	Entrance paving slab in [188] showing wear from opening of south gate-leaf	21
Pl 15	The Entrance: south gate posthole [201] and pivot hole [208]	21
Pl 16	North Rampart terminal by Entrance with surface [521] over berm and drain [199]	22
Pl 17	Structure V from south-west	24
Pl 18	North end of Structure V	25
Pl 19	South-east part of Structure U	29
Pl 20	House Z2, general view from north-east	31
Pl 21	House Z, west end	31
Pl 22	House Z2; slot [858] in paving [777]	35
Pl 23	Drain [910] in front of wall [911], Structure Q5	36
Pl 24	Area X, fragments of walling [680] from House X4	40
Pl 25	Area X, hearth pit [674] cut by posthole [692] on left side	42
Pl 26	General view of north-east part of House X	42
Pl 27	Structure X5	44
Pl 28	Shelf along upper side of Round, part of House A2 in foreground, House D4 and Structure E3 to rear	44
Pl 29	Paving [25] in Structure E3	46
Pl 30	Postholes from Structures E1/2	46
Pl 31	Structure G excavated, with backing [255] behind	47
Pl 32	Structure G from above	47
Pl 33	Structure G showing top of infill [77]/[256]	48
Pl 34	Features in Houses D2 and D4	50
Pl 35	House A2 with walling [65], interior excavated to reveal features of House A1	55
Pl 36	House A1b hearth pit [294] and associated stakeholes	55
Pl 37	South side of House A2	56
Pl 38	House A3 at early stage of excavation	56
Pl 39	Paving [7] with saddle quern in Area R	65
Pl 40	Area R looking south from Entrance	65
Pl 41	Trethurgy bowl S1	129
Pl 42	Trethurgy bowl S2	130
Pl 43	Trethurgy bowl S3	130
Pl 44	Inside of bowl S3	131
Pl 45	Trethurgy bowl S4	131
Pl 46	Trethurgy bowl from Calartha, St Just	136
Pl 47	Tin bowl from Treloy, side view	137
Pl 48	Tin bowl from Treloy, view from above to show flat-topped handles	137
Pl 49	Stone weight S13, side view	139
Pl 50	Stone weight S13, face view	139

Preface

The present report is inevitably deficient by the standards of the early 2000s as it describes an excavation undertaken within a framework of enquiry, and recorded to standards, current in the early 1970s. Immediately after the excavation, the then Department of the Environment agreed that the report should be published in the monograph series it was then sponsoring. The plans and sections were prepared in 1975/6 to the specifications for that monograph series and an initial draft written on the stratigraphy. At this stage basic work was also carried out on the pottery and on the stone artefacts: a series from each category was selected for special description and illustration and retained by the author, and the remainder of the pottery and stonework deposited with the Royal County Museum in Truro.

After 1976 little detailed work was done on the report until 1985/6, because of health problems and pressures of adult education work. In 1985/6 the author was granted two terms sabbatical leave by Exeter University, part of which was spent on Trethurgy. Reports on the other categories of finds (apart from the glass) were prepared, a series of radiocarbon determinations arranged, and a first draft attempted of the chronology and general discussion. After the sabbatical leave, there were difficulties in continuing, partly from pressure of other work, partly from those encountered by a single individual working alone on a substantial monograph.

In 1998 the author approached the Cornwall Archaeological Unit to explore the possibility that the organisation could support the report as one of its projects with funding from English Heritage. Peter Rose of the Unit was able to obtain agreement for this in 1999 and Jacqueline Nowakowski was appointed to work as Project Manager. She, together with the author, prepared a Project Design for English Heritage, which was given approval to proceed in 2000. The present report is the result of work carried out in 2000/1 with a little final revision in 2003.

During the final report preparation all sections were revised, including those previously contributed by specialists. Newly written sections were those on the glass vessels and the building reconstructions together with Chapter 12. The dates at which substantive work was done on different sections has been indicated. Every attempt has been made to produce a coherent account of the site and its finds but inevitably the result is uneven. Much of the data used was not recorded to modern standards and the absence of any detailed environmental information became an increasingly obvious lack as work proceeded.

The site is one of unusual importance, not in itself, but as the sole extensively excavated example of a settlement in Western Britain which spans the Roman and Post-Roman centuries. Its long-delayed publication is likely to be used as a standard reference for some time to come. It is hoped that the data presented will stand the test of time. The interpretations put forward, especially those of the detailed chronology, have been deliberately presented in a clear-cut way, to provide the basis for future analysis and discussion. It is hoped that these interpretations bring the site to life. Unlike the data, however, they are not intended to stand the test of time but to provide the basis for future thinking. They should not be quoted as definite.

Because of the importance of the site, the delay in publication has been unfortunate for scholars working on the area and periods concerned. I apologise to all who have been inconvenienced by the long hiatus between excavation and publication, forcing them to rely on brief interim account or replies to questions which were of necessity based on incomplete data.

All excavation reports are composite works. An attempt has been made to acknowledge the principal contributors but I would like again to express my thanks to all those involved, particularly those who, over the last four years, have done so much to ensure that the report finally appeared in print.

Henrietta Quinnell

Acknowledgments

Excavation

The principal acknowledgment goes to Peter Sheppard for drawing the site to my attention and pressing for its excavation. I am grateful to English China Clays Ltd (now Imerys) for permission to excavate and for much assistance, including the provision of accommodation and mechanical excavation equipment: special thanks due to W Gilmour of their Estates Department for all his help. The Cornwall Archaeological Society administered the finance provided by the Department of the Environment (DoE); the then Treasurer, the late Peter Trudgian, was of great assistance in the management of accounts. Members of the DoE Inspectorate of Ancient Monuments: Andrew Saunders, Geoff Wainwright, and Chris Young were extremely helpful, as was Colin Carpenter of their Plymouth Works Department. K Symons of Tavistock provided tools and equipment. Trevor Miles was responsible for the finds shed, with active assistance from Lesley Simpson. Linda Therkorn acted as Assistant Director: her contribution, both during the excavation and in post-excavation work, was invalauble. The other excavation staff are thanked for their hard work: Ian Burrow, Earl Godwin, the late Carol Layland, John McKiernan, Robert Milne, Jack Stevenson, Edna Thompson, and David Wardle. Over 100 volunteer excavators took part, too numerous to be thanked individually; their contribution, especially those from the Cornwall Archaeological Society organised by the then Secretary, the late Mary Irwin, was essential to the success of the excavation. The late Wendy Aldridge provided invaluable secretarial and administrative backup. Martin Fletcher, Ordnance Survey Archaeology Division, gave help with the surveying. Charles Thomas was a supportive visitor and arranged with the Royal Naval Air Station at Culdrose for a series of aerial photographs.

Post-excavation

Plans and sections were drawn by Linda Therkorn and Sandy Morris, finds by Lesley Simpson, Sandy Morris, Andrew Brown, Roger Penhallurick, Carl Thorpe, and Yvonne Beadnall. They have been prepared for publication by S Diment and J Brinkhoff of Technical Services, Cornwall County Council. Photographs of artefacts were taken by Peter Brierley who also made the best out of printing the author's excavation negatives. Specialist assistance has been provided by Peter Marshall (radiocarbon dating), Helen Keeley and Stephen Staines (soils), Caroline Cartwright (charcoal), Chris Caseldine (pollen), Justine Bayley, Rob Ixer, and Gerry McDonnell (aspects of metallurgy), John Casey and Richard Reece (coins), Sarnia Butcher (brooches), Jennifer Price (glass), David Williams, Paul Bidwell, the late Brian Hartley, and John Allan (pottery), Sue Watts (querns), Bill Manning and Fred Ferguson (ironwork), and by E Francis, Brian Selwood, and Roger Taylor (geology and petrography). The architecture of the oval houses has been considered by Stuart Blaylock, reconstruction drawings of the houses were developed by Rosemary Robertson, and Phil Bennett has provided valuable comments. The colour reconstruction drawing is by Rosemary Robertson. The French translation of the Summary is by Charlette Sheil-Small, and the German translation by Konstanze Rahn with the input from Sabine Wolfram. The Index is the work of Susan Vaughan. All the staff of the Royal Institution of Cornwall were extremely helpful: Angela Broome, the late Les Douch, Roger Penhallurick, and, especially during the final stages, Anna Tyacke. Carl Thorpe has been of great assistance in preparing the archive for storage and for comment on Post-Roman and later pottery.

I am indebted to the University of Exeter for sabbatical leave during which much of the first stage of the report was written. Much initial work on finds and records was carried out by Wendy Aldridge. Typing and word processing of initial drafts was done by Jean Hutchings, Sue Farrell, and Rose Woods. During the final report preparation Rob Iles, Ian Morrison, and Fachtna MacAvoy of English Heritage have provided advice and support. Peter Rose was responsible for the initiative which lead to report preparation becoming a Cornwall Archaeological Unit Project; he and Nicholas Johnson are thanked for their continued support. Many members of the Unit have provided help and advice, especially Steve Hartgroves, Peter Herring, and Andrew Young. My greatest thanks however go to Jacqueline Nowakowski who performed the arduous role of Project Manager, removed much of the administrative burden from my shoulders, and has been unstinting in help and advice. The presentation of the printed report was greatly assisted by copy editing by Peter Ellis and design work by the Technical Services of Cornwall County Council under Mike Tippett, especially Dave Taylor.

The report owes much to information from, or discussion with, a wide range of people at different times, in particular Paul Bidwell, Ewan Campbell, Jo Draper, Dawn Eldridge, Sandy Gerrard, Valerie Maxfield, Oliver Padel, Roger Penhallurick, E Southworth, and Charles Thomas; comment from Richard Reece and David Mattingly has provided insights for Chapter 12. Pat Carlyon Brierley, who worked extensively on material from Roman Cornwall, was a continuous support until her death in 2001 and this report is dedicated to her knowledge and enthusiasm, the best exemplar of amateur expertise.

My husband Norman Quinnell has been supportive throughout in a great variety of ways, not least in his faith in its eventual completion. The project predates our marriage and he will be as relieved to see its publication as I will.

The production of this report stretched over three decades and aspects have been discussed with numerous individuals who have provided advice, help, and encouragement. There are bound to be omissions amongst those named individually and to these in conclusion I ask for understanding and express my thanks.

Jennifer Price owes grateful thanks to Ewan Campbell for discussions on the Post-Roman glass from Trethurgy and for access to his unpublished report on the glass from Tintagel, to Henrietta Quinnell for unpublished information about glass finds in Devon and Cornwall in connection with her forthcoming report on the glass from Penhale Round, to Mark Taylor and David Hill for information about their experiments in window glass production, to Colin Haselgrove and Pam Lowther for unpublished information about Stanwick, and to Yvonne Beadnell for producing the drawings.

Stuart Blaylock would like to thank Henrietta Quinnell, Rosemary Robertson, Neil Holbrook, Francis Kelly, Steve Ottery, and Michael Baldwin for helpful discussion of aspects of the reconstructions. Phil Bennet read the draft text of the contribution in Chapter 10 and provided many useful comments based on his practical experience of the reconstruction of Iron Age buildings. Peter Reynolds was to have performed a similar role, but sadly had not done this by the time of his death. The many references to Reynolds' published research on the subject of structural reconstruction show how indebted to his work anyone attempting an exercise such as this must be.

Grant aid towards publication was made available from English Heritage.

Addresses of contributors

Dr Justine Bayley, Ancient Monuments Laboratory, English Heritage, Fort Cumberland, Fort Cumberland Road, Eastney, Portsmouth PO4 9LD

Stuart Blaylock, 1 Colebrooke Lane, Cullompton, Devon EX15 1EB

Sarnia A Butcher, Pilots Retreat, Church Road, St Mary's, Isles of Scilly TR21 ONA

John Casey, 112 Alberta Street, Kennington, London SE17 3RT

Dr Caroline Cartwright, Department of Scientific Research, The British Museum, Great Russell Street, London WC1B 3DG

Dr Helen Keeley, 28 Collins Road, Southsea, Hants PO4 9NZ

Dr Rob Ixer, 44 Elms Road, Sutton Coldfield, West Midlands B72 1JF

Dr Peter Marshall, Centre for Archaeology, English Heritage, Fortress House, 23 Savile Row, London W1S 2ET

Dr Gerry McDonnell, Department of Archaeological Science, University of Bradford, Bradford, W Yorks BD7 1DP

Professor Jennifer Price, Department of Archaeology, University of Durham, South Road, Durham DH1 3LE

Henrietta Quinnell, 9 Thornton Hill, Exeter EX4 4NN

Dr Richard Reece, The Apple Loft, The Waterloo, Cirencester, Glos GL7 2PU

Rosemary Robertson, Design for Archaeology, Wheal Daniel Cottage, North Hill, Chacewater, Truro, Cornwall TR4 8NW

Dr Stephen Staines, Kinnagrelly, Collooney, Co Sligo, Eire

Carl Thorpe, Environment & Heritage, Cornwall County Council, Kennall Building, Old County Hall, Truro, Cornwall TR1 3AY

Sue Watts, 1 Trinity Cottages, Cullompton, Devon, EX15 1PE

Dr David Williams, Department of Archaeology, University of Southampton, Highfield, Southampton, SO17 1BJ

Summary

Small enclosures, traditionally called rounds, were the principal settlement type in Cornwall from the Later Iron Age through the Roman centuries and continued into the Post-Roman period. The interior of Trethurgy Round near St Austell, covering c 0.2ha, is the first to be completely excavated and was occupied from the mid 2nd century to the 6th century AD. The report presents a definition of a 'round' as a settlement of local status and authority and attempts to disentangle functional usage from fieldwork terminology for which 'small enclosure' is more appropriate.

The earliest activity on the site was evidenced by a mainly Later Neolithic flint assemblage. There were slight traces of a late-prehistoric field system in one unit of which an Enclosure was built, probably for stock, in the 1st century BC. This Enclosure, housing a single insubstantial structure, was never completed and its earthworks were heavily eroded before those of the Round were built along their line.

The Round was enclosed by a Ditch and a Rampart revetted on both faces with stone; a single Entrance, central to the downhill side, was closed by a double-leaved gate. The Rampart and Entrance were maintained throughout occupation but the Ditch was disused by the 4th century. The interior contained five oval stone houses and a range of ancillary buildings, a four-poster granary, a byre, a probable shrine, and various stores and workshops. Not all these buildings were contemporary but the basic plan continued through the centuries, with houses rebuilt *in situ* and the same areas used for penning stock, storage, outside activities, and rubbish disposal. The changing use of the buildings formed a complex sequence, presented for simplicity as nine separate Stages, with major rebuilding allocated to the early 4th century. After 6th-century abandonment, the site was intermittently reused for stock and was enclosed in the present field in the 16th century.

The distinctive oval buildings are now recognised as the principal house form during the Roman period in Cornwall and their architecture is discussed with illustrations of possible reconstructions. For all categories of structures and artefacts found, summaries for use and context in Roman Cornwall are presented drawing on both published and unpublished data. The difficulties of providing firm chronology from the artefacts and radiocarbon determinations available are discussed for the site and for Roman Cornwall. Specific dates for the Stages of occupation are presented as a basis for modelling changes within the Round and its social background but should not be quoted as definitive. Thus it is proposed that maximum residential capacity was reached during the 2nd century and again in the late 4th; there was a gradual decline through the 5th century with a little increase in the 6th.

There was a little evidence for structured deposition but generally rubbish was systematically removed from the site so that artefacts recovered were sparse for the area excavated as is usual in Cornwall. A single midden not removed from a disused building provided the only large associated group of finds. The Round community was largely self sufficient, with non-monetary exchange networks used for most transactions. Coins were principally represented by a small 3rd-century hoard. Large bowls of local stone, termed 'Trethurgy Bowls', with handles copying those of metal tableware, were part of a distinctive tradition of stone artefact manufacture which included carved stone weights. Saddle querns and mortar stones continued in use alongside rotary querns. Tin was probably produced in the vicinity although not smelted in the Round; an ingot had been cached in the 4th-century midden. There was small-scale production of copper alloy and, probably, silver artefacts, and smithing of iron within the Round. About 90% of the pottery was of gabbroic fabric from the Lizard, the standard Romano-Cornish ware. A Type Series is proposed for its distinctive styles which loosely copy Romano-British trends. Gabbroic pottery production appears to have continued without noticeable change through the 5th century AD. Samian, South Devon, South East Dorset BB1, and Oxfordshire wares were present in small quantities, as was glass, generally from containers rather than tableware. Much of the samian had been curated for several centuries. A wide range of Post-Roman Mediterranean import wares and some glass vessels indicated that a settlement of some status continued into the 6th century.

The data from the excavation are used to demonstrate a distinctive local social structure and life style in Roman Cornwall, based on a mixture of indigenous traditions and ideas and techniques from the Roman world. There may have been an administrative unit to suit local conditions separate from that of the *Civitas Dumnoniorum* based in Exeter. Rounds were settlements of status and authority underpinning a society sufficiently stable to provide continuity into the early Post-Roman period.

Résumé

De petites enceintes, connues sous le nom traditionnel de 'rounds', représentaient le principal type de peuplement en Cornouailles à partir de la fin de l'âge de fer, pendant les siècles romains et jusqu'à l'époque post-romaine. L'intérieur du Round de Trethurgy, près de St Austell, d'environ 0,20 ha, est le premier qui a été complètement fouillé, et il avait été occupé du milieu du 2ème siècle au 6ème siècle. Le présent rapport présente une définition d'un 'round' en tant que peuplement d'importance et d'autorité locales, et s'efforce de séparer son utilisation fonctionnelle de la terminologie du travail sur le terrain pour laquelle 'petite enceinte' convient mieux.

Un ensemble de silex, datant principalement de la fin du néolithique constituait l'indice des activités les plus anciennes sur le site. Il y avait quelques traces d'un système de cultures remontant à la fin de la préhistoire et une enceinte avait été construite dans l'un des champs au 1er siècle avant J.-C., probablement pour le cheptel. Cette enceinte, contenant une seule structure peu solide, n'avait jamais été terminée et ses ouvrages de terre s'étaient déjà érodés avant la construction de ceux du Round suivant leur alignement.

Le Round était entouré d'un fossé et d'un rempart revêtu de pierre des deux côtés ; une seule entrée, au milieu du côté en pente descendante, était fermée par un portail à deux battants. Le rempart et l'entrée avaient été maintenus durant toute l'occupation du site mais l'utilisation du fossé avait cessé avant le 4ème siècle. A l'intérieur du Round, se trouvaient cinq maisons ovales et une rangée de bâtiments auxiliaires, un grenier à quatre poteaux, une étable, un autel probable, et divers entrepôts et ateliers. Ces bâtiments n'étaient pas tous contemporains mais le plan fondamental était resté le même au cours des siècles, les maisons étant reconstruites sur le même site et les mêmes endroits étant utilisés pour parquer le cheptel, pour le stockage, les activités extérieures et l'élimination des déchets. Le changement d'utilisation des bâtiments formait une séquence complexe laquelle, pour en simplifier la présentation, a été divisée en neuf stades séparés, avec une grande reconstruction attribuée au début du 4ème siècle. Après avoir été abandonné au 6ème siècle, le site fut réutilisé par intermittence pour le cheptel et devint partie intégrante du champ actuel au 16ème siècle.

Les bâtiments ovales caractéristiques sont dorénavant reconnus être la principale forme de maison au cours de la période romaine en Cornouailles, et leur architecture est évoquée, avec des illustrations de reconstructions possibles. Des résumés sont présentés concernant l'utilisation de toutes les catégories de structures et d'objets façonnés découverts ainsi que leur contexte dans la Cornouailles romaine, résumés qui s'appuient à la fois sur les données publiées et sur les données non publiées. Les difficultés liées à l'établissement d'une chronologie solide à partir des objets façonnés et des datations au radiocarbone déjà disponibles sont évoquées pour le site et pour la Cornouailles romaine. Des dates précises pour les stades d'occupation sont présentées comme base des changements de modèle à l'intérieur du Round et de son contexte social mais ne doivent pas être citées de façon définitive. On suggère donc que la capacité résidentielle maximale avait été atteinte au cours du 2ème siècle et, une fois de plus, à la fin du 4ème siècle, qu'il y avait eu un déclin graduel durant le 5ème siècle et une légère augmentation au 6ème siècle.

Il existait quelques indices de dépôts structurés mais, en général, les déchets avaient été systématiquement enlevés du site et on n'a donc retrouvé que peu d'objets façonnés par rapport au site fouillé, ce qui est habituel en Cornouailles. Un seul amas de débris qui n'avait pas été enlevé d'un bâtiment abandonné a fourni le seul grand ensemble associé de découvertes. La communauté du Round était largement autarcique, des réseaux d'échange non monétaires étant utilisés pour la plupart des transactions. Les pièces de monnaie étaient principalement représentées par un petit trésor du 3ème siècle. De grands bols de pierre locale, dénommés ' Bols de Trethurgy', équipés de poignées copiant celles de la vaisselle en métal, appartenaient à une tradition bien distincte de fabrication d'objets en pierre englobant des poids sculptés en pierre. L'utilisation de meules à bras et de mortiers avait continué en même temps que l'utilisation de meules rotatives. L'étain avait probablement été produit aux alentours mais il n'y avait pas eu de fonte à l'intérieur du Round ; un lingot avait été caché dans l'amas de débris du 4ème siècle. A l'intérieur du Round, il y avait eu production d'alliage de cuivre à petite échelle et probablement d'objets façonnés en argent et de fer forgé. Environ 90% de la poterie était de manufacture gabbroïque, en provenance du Lizard, la vaisselle romano-cornouaillaise typique. Une Série Type est proposée pour ses styles caractéristiques, libres copies des tendances romanobritanniques. La production de poterie gabbroïque semble avoir continué sans changement sensible pendant tout le 5ème siècle. De la céramique sigillée, des articles du Sud du Devon, du Sud-Est du Dorset BB1 et d'Oxfordshire étaient présents en petites quantités, et il y avait également du verre, provenant en général de récipients plutôt que de vaisselle. Une grande partie de la céramique sigillée avait été préservée pendant plusieurs siècles. Une grande variété de vaisselle post-romaine importée de la Méditerranée et quelques vaisseaux en verre indiquaient qu'un peuplement d'une certaine importance continua jusqu'au 6ème siècle.

Les données tirées des fouilles sont utilisées pour démontrer la présence d'une structure sociale et d'un style de vie local caractéristiques en Cornouailles romaine, basés sur un mélange de traditions autochtones et d'idées et de techniques provenant du monde romain. Il y avait peut-être une unité administrative adaptée aux conditions locales et séparée de celle du *Civitas Dumnoniorum* basé à Exeter. Les 'Rounds' étaient des peuplements d'importance et d'autorité fournissant les bases d'une société suffisamment stable pour fournir une certaine continuité jusqu'au début de la période post-romaine.

Charlette Sheil-Small

Zusammenfassung

Kleine, runde und befestigte Siedlungen - so genannte 'Rounds' - waren von der jüngeren Eisenzeit bis in die nachrömische Periode die vorherrschende Siedlungsform in Cornwall. Das *ca* 0.20 ha grosse Trethurgy Round in der Nähe von St Austell ist das erste, das vollständig ausgegraben worden ist. Trethurgy wurde von der Mitte des 2. Jh. n. Chr. bis ins 6. Jh. n.Chr. besiedelt.

Der Bericht bietet eine Begriffsbestimmung eines 'Round' als Siedlung von örtlichem Rang (status) und Machtbefugnis (authority) an und versucht den funktionalen Gebrauch von der Terminologie der Feldforschung zu trennen, für die "kleine Einfriedung" (small enclosure) angemessener ist.

Die früheste Begehung des Fundplatzes ist durch eine überwiegend spätjungsteinzeitliche Feuersteinansammlung belegt. Ausserdem zeigten sich schwache Spuren eines eisenzeitlichen Feldsystems, in dem in einem Abschnitt im 1. Jh. n.Chr. eine Einfriedung, vermutlich für Vieh, errichtet worden war. Diese Einfriedung, die ein einziges, wohl nicht überdachtes Gebäude aufwies, wurde niemals vollendet, und die Erdwälle waren stark erodiert bevor die Erdwälle des 'Round' auf ihrem Verlauf errichtet wurden.

Das 'Round' war umgeben von einem Graben und einem Wall, der auf beiden Seiten mit Stein verkleidet war. Der einzige Eingang, zentral auf der hügelabwärts gelegenen Seite, wurde durch ein zweiflügeliges Tor geschlossen. Wall und Eingang wurden während der gesamten Besiedlungsdauer instand gehalten, der Graben allerdings wurde vor dem 4. Jh. aufgegeben. Der Innenraum enthielt fünf ovale Steinhäuser und eine Reihe von Nebengebäuden, einen 4-Pfosten-Getreidespeicher, einen Stall, einen vermutlichen Schrein und verschiedene Lager- und Arbeitsräume. Nicht alle diese Gebäude bestanden gleichzeitig, aber der Grundplan wurde über Jahrhunderte beibehalten, indem Häuser an derselben Stelle wieder aufgebaut wurden und dieselben Bereiche für Viehpferche, Vorratshaltung, Aktivitäten im Freien und Abfall benutzt wurden. Die sich ändernde Nutzung der Häuser bildet eine komplizierte Abfolge, der Einfachheit halber als neun unterschiedliche Phasen dargestellt, mit einer grösseren Neubauphase im frühen 4. Jh.. Nach der Aufgabe des Round im 6. Jh. wurde das Areal des Fundplatzes wiederholt zur Viehhaltung genutzt, um schliesslich im 16. Jh. in das gegenwärtige Feld eingegliedert zu werden.

Die markanten ovalen Gebäude sind inzwischen als die wichtigste Hausform im römerzeitlichen Cornwall anerkannt. Ihre Bauweise wird in diesem Bericht mit Hilfe von Illustrationen möglicher Rekonstruktionen diskutiert. Der Gebrauch aller dokumentierten Baustrukturen und Funde sowie ihr Kontext im römerzeitlichen Cornwall werden zusammenfassend, unter Heranziehung von veröffentlichtem und unveröffentlichtem Material, vorgestellt. Die Schwierigkeiten, eine genaue Chronologie anhand der Funde und C14 Datierungen zu erstellen, werden für Trethurgy Round und für das römerzeitliche Cornwall diskutiert. Spezifische Daten für die Besiedlungsphasen sind als Grundlage eines Modells, das die Veränderungen innerhalb des 'Round' und ihres sozialen Hintergrundes darzustellen versucht, zu verstehen und sollten nicht als endgültig angesehen werden. So wird vorgeschlagen, dass die grösste Siedlungskapazität während des 2. Jh. und abermals im späten 4. Jh. erreicht wurde; mit einem allmählichen Rückgang im 5. Jh. sowie einem erneuten kleinen Anstieg im 6. Jh.

Es gab wenig Hinweise für eine "structured deposition", aber Abfall wurde im allgemeinen systematisch von der Anlage beseitigt, so dass Funde im Verhältnis zur ausgegrabenen Fläche gering waren, wie es in Cornwall üblich ist. Ein einziger Abfallhaufen, der nicht von einem aufgegebenen Gebäude entfernt worden war, barg die einzige grössere zusammengehörige Gruppe von Fundstücken. Die Gemeinschaft von Trethurgy Round war weitgehend autark und nicht-monetäre Tauschsysteme wurden für die meisten Transaktionen verwendet. Münzen werden überwiegend durch einen kleinen Hort aus dem 3. Jh. repräsentiert. Grosse Schalen aus örtlichem Stein, sogenannte 'Trethurgy Bowls', deren Griffe die von metallischer Tafelware nachahmen, waren ein Teil der charakteristischen Tradition der Herstellung von Artefakten aus Stein, wie z. B. Gewichte. Schiebemühlen und Steinmörser blieben neben Drehmühlen in Gebrauch. Zinn wurde vermutlich in der Nähe produziert, aber nicht im 'Round' geschmolzen; ein Barren war im Abfallhaufen des 4. Jh. versteckt. Kupferlegierung wurde in kleiner Auflage hergestellt, ebenso Silbergegenstände, und Eisen wurde vor Ort geschmiedet. Etwa 90% der gefundenen Keramik ist aus Gabbroischem Ton, der auf dem Lizard ansteht, und stellt die gängige Romano-Britische Ware dar. Eine Typologie für seine charakteristischen Stilarten wird vorgeschlagen, die in etwa Romano-Britische Trends nachahmt. Die Herstellung von Grabboischer Tonware scheint ohne erkennbare Veränderungen durch das 5. Jh. hindurch angehalten zu haben. Terra sigillata, South Devon, SE Dorset BB1 und Oxfordshire Ware waren in kleinen Mengen vorhanden, ebenso Glas, überwiegend eher von Behältnissen als von Tafelgeschirr. Der Grossteil der gefundenen Terra sigillata war über mehrere Jahrhunderte hinweg (von den Bewohnern des Trethurgy Round) aufbewahrt worden. Eine grosse Bandbreite von nachrömischem Import aus dem Mittelmeer und einige Glasgefässe deuten an, dass die Siedlung eine gewisse Bedeutung bis ins 6. Jh. behielt.

Das Material der Ausgrabung wird dazu benutzt zu zeigen, dass es im römerzeitlichen Cornwall sowohl eine markante lokale Sozialstruktur als auch Lebenstil gab, die auf einer Mischung aus einheimischen Traditionen sowie Ideen und Techniken aus der römischen Welt basierten.

Es ist möglich, dass es eine Verwaltungseinheit gab, die unabhängig von der *Civitas Dumnoniorum* in Exeter örtlichen Gegebenheiten angepasst war. 'Rounds' waren Siedlungen von Rang (status) und Machtbefugnis (authority), die eine Gesellschaft stützten, die in sich gefestigt genug war, Kontinuität bis in die frühe nachrömische Zeit zu gewährleisten.

Konstanze Rahn

1 Introduction: general background, methodology, and presentation

1.1 Location

The Round at Trethurgy was a small univallate enclosure situated 4km north-east of St Austell town, but within its parish, on the edge of the Hensbarrow (St Austell) granite at SW 0347 5563 (Fig 1, Pl 1). It lay near the bottom of a gentle east-facing slope at about 170m OD, across a slight valley (Fig 2, Pl 2) from the modern village of Trethurgy. It is probable that this valley may have carried a small stream before extensive recent disturbance of the area for mineral workings. The valley is an upper branch of a small drainage system, the streams of which now reach the sea at Par. The topography of the coastline here has changed considerably over the last millennium, and the valley may once have been tidal 2km above Par, within 3km of the Round. The open sea in St Austell Bay is within sight of the Round, some 4km due south.

The name of the present settlement of Trethurgy derives from *tre* (farmstead, estate) and *doferghi* (otter) (Padel 1985, 86, 223), although the latter element probably derived from a personal name. This is first recorded c AD 1200 as *Tredheuergy* (Gover 1948, 388) and was part of the manor of Treverbyn (Hammond 1897).

1.2 Geology and soil

The granite bedrock beneath the Round is covered by a head deposit of granite lumps of varying sizes in a matrix of yellowish gravelly loam, known in Cornwall as 'rab' or 'growan'. This head was formed under periglacial conditions and blankets the lower slopes of the St Austell granite much more extensively than is indicated on current published geological maps. The

Pl 1: Aerial photograph from the east, September 1973; the upper, west, part of the site has been largely excavated, the lower part still shows later features. Reproduced by permission of the Royal Naval Air Station, Culdrose

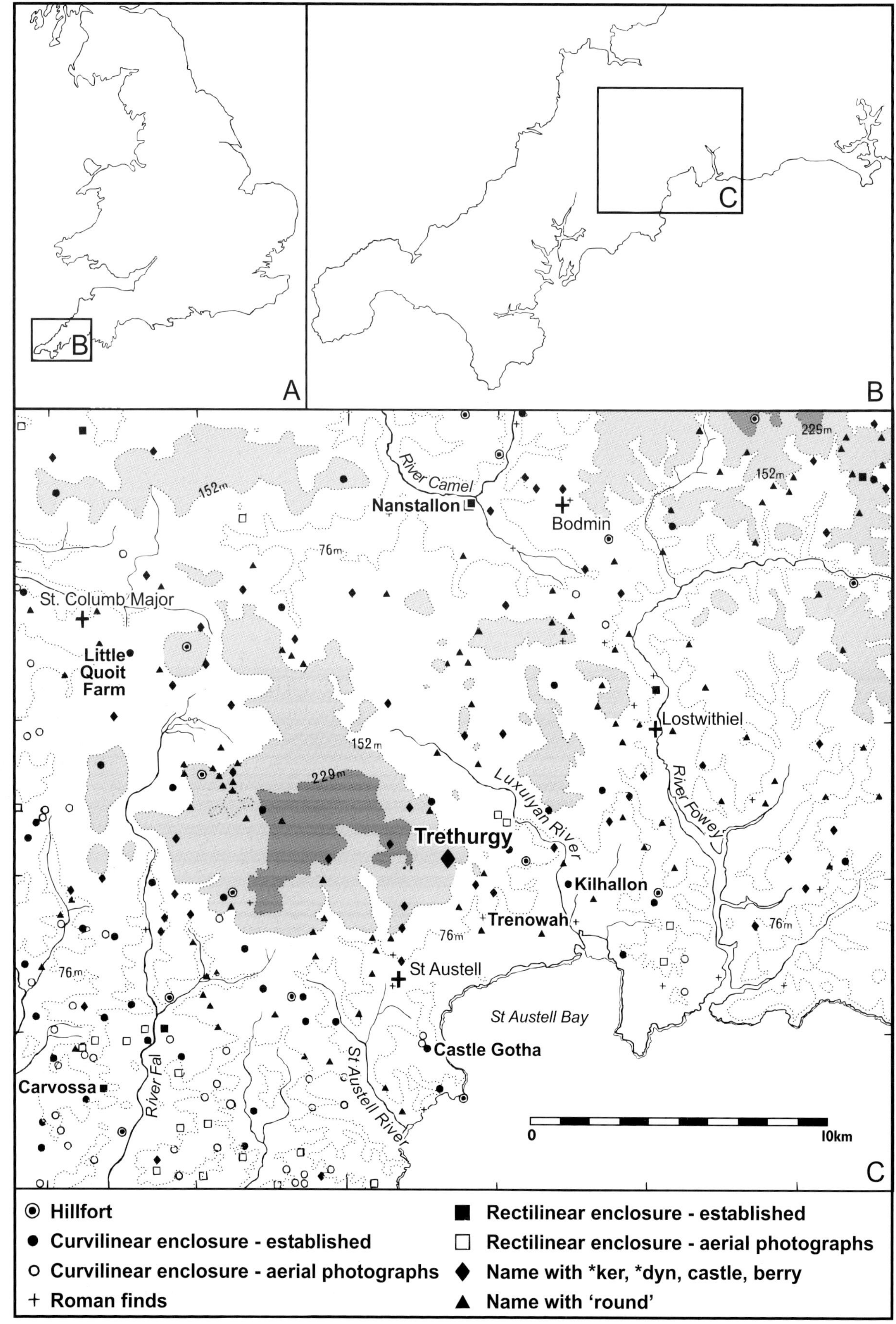

Fig 1: Location maps. All symbols may indicate rounds except 'hillfort' and 'Roman finds'.
CCC © Crown copyright. 100019590, 2004

soil is a loamy brown podzol of the Moretonhampstead series (Section 8.2).

The aureole of the St Austell granite contains a rich variety of metalliferous lodes. An iron lode runs north-south 30m east of the Round and erosion along its line has caused the small former stream valley above which the Round is situated (Fig 2). This iron lode consists of very high quality red haematite (Collins 1912, 130), which was worked between 1847 and 1871 as Wheal Ruby with an adit 80m long (Fig 2) (*ibid*, 245); the waste dumps from Wheal Ruby are still visible just north of the Round. Wheal Ruby and other workings along the lode have affected the local water table (E Francis pers comm). The nearest source of water to the Round today is a small stream 200m to the south. The granite aureole also contains lodes bearing tin, copper, and silver. The erosion of the former has lead to the formation of 'tin grounds' in the local valleys (Fig 2).

1.3 Circumstances of the excavation

Small univallate enclosures, known traditionally in Cornwall as rounds, occur in some numbers in the St Austell area (Fig 1). The nearest extant site to Trethurgy is that at Restineas 1km to the south-east at SW 0446 5511. Before the excavation of Trethurgy, the date range of these sites was thought to be limited to the Later Iron Age and Roman periods. The known density of small earthworks in the area has been greatly increased over the past 40 years by fieldwork initiated as part of the parish check-list programme sponsored by the Cornwall Archaeological Society and continued by the Cornwall Archaeological Unit (formerly the Cornwall Committee for Rescue Archaeology). The National Mapping Programme which started a comprehensive study of aerial photographs in 1994, and is still (2003) ongoing, has added further to the number of enclosures known (see Chapter 12). Appropriate usage of the term 'round' is discussed in Section 12.1.

Most of the work on parish check-lists in the St Austell area was carried out by Peter Sheppard in the late 1960s and early 1970s. Trethurgy Round was discovered by Peter Sheppard in 1971 who noted the name 'Gears' for Field 4366 in the 1840 St Austell Tithe Map Apportionment. 'Gears', and variants, in Cornish place-names derives from **ker* (Padel 1985, 50) and usually indicates a former earthwork enclosure or fortification. Field 4366 on the Tithe Map had suggestive bulges on its south and west sides and a dashed line within the field possibly indicating the position of the former east side of an earthwork. Inspection of the field confirmed the presence of a small enclosure, its bank on the south and west incorporated in the current field system, that on the north and east almost levelled but still visible. The site was listed as Round 2 in the St Austell check-list (Sheppard 1972).

Trethurgy Round at the time of its discovery lay in an area designated for a new waste tip for china-clay working, the construction of which involved the stripping of all the topsoil from the area of the Round and the digging of an extensive drainage system. Peter Sheppard brought the site to the attention of the author, to whom the Ancient Monuments Inspectorate of the then Department of the Environment made funds available for a trial excavation in 1972. This trial work confirmed the site as a round or enclosed settlement with a probable date range of 2nd to 6th centuries AD. As the interior of no round had, or still has, been completely stripped, the Inspectorate of Ancient Monuments funded full excavation of the interior in 1973, which took place in two parts, from July to early September and from October to early November. The owners English China Clays Ltd, now Imerys, gave generous help with equipment and accommodation. The Cornwall Archaeological Society sponsored the work by administrating finance, and valuable assistance was given on site by a number of their members.

The Round proved to be a univallate enclosure 56m by 48m internally (0.2ha), sloping down from 175m to 109m OD, a drop of 1:8. Its Bank survived to a maximum height of 1.5m on the west and south, where it has been incorporated in current field hedges. Elsewhere it had been levelled or eroded to as little as 0.3m. Before excavation there was no surface indication of the Ditch, or of the Entrance which proved to be central to the downhill side. The structures in the interior had been badly plough damaged. On the uphill, west, side virtually all upstanding structures had been removed. Downhill, a stratigraphic sequence survived but its upper levels were badly disturbed.

The outline of the Round, including the eroded Bank on the east, showed on the RAF 1948 air photograph very clearly (CPE/UK 2521 3257). No outworks were visible on this or on the air photograph series held by English China Clays Ltd. There was no indication of any related field system, visible either on air photographs or on the ground. No fields adjacent to the Round have archaeologically suggestive names in the Tithe Apportionment. Partly for these reasons, partly through financial constraints, no attempt was made to investigate the area outside the Round for indications of contemporary activity. Inadequate arrangements were made for investigating environmental data from the site, the excavation taking place before wet sieving of soil samples became standard practice. An interim report and a popular account were published in 1973 (Miles and Miles

Pl 2: Aerial photograph from the north to show hillslope position of the Round, September 1973. Reproduced by permission of the Royal Naval Air Station, Culdrose

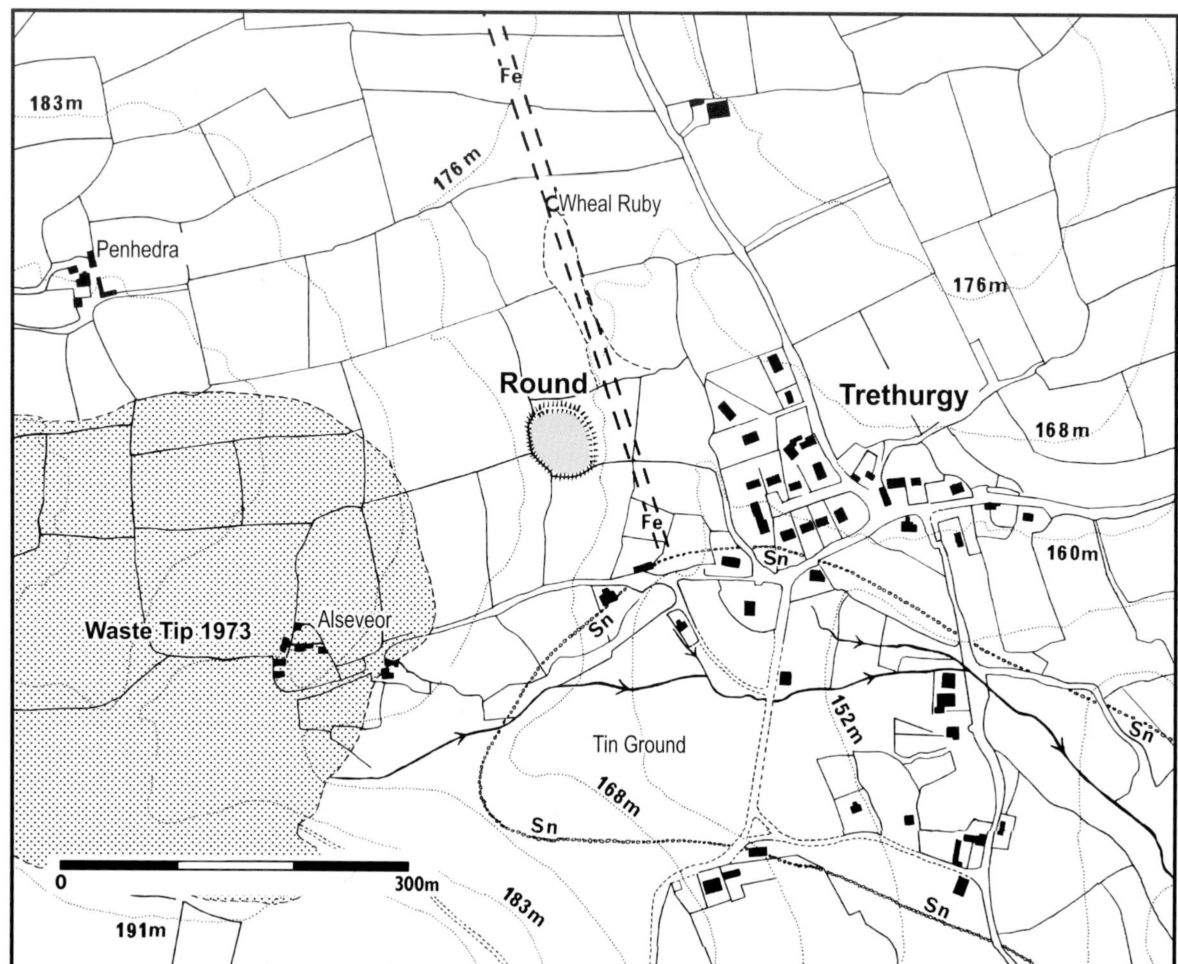

Fig 2: Location of the Round at Trethurgy. Sn indicates edge of adjacent tin ground, Fe position of iron lode.
CCC © Crown copyright. 100019590, 2004

1973a; 1973b) and aspects of the excavation were discussed in a review of Cornwall in the Iron Age and Roman periods (Quinnell 1986). The excavation demonstrated that Trethurgy Round had been occupied during the 2nd to 6th centuries AD. The extension in date into the Post-Roman period and the discovery of a wide range of different types of buildings has caused the limited range of published information about the site to be widely quoted in a general way eg by Todd (1987) and Hingley (1989). The author, well aware of the problems caused by the delay in production of the full excavation report, has contributed details as accurately as was feasible when requested eg by Alcock (1995). However it must be stressed that this final excavation report presents data which differ substantially from that either previously published by the author or by other authorities using the sources available to them.

The site of the Round today lies beneath the edge of a landscaped china clay waste dump. This is screened by a band of trees which run approximately along the position of its former east side.

1.4 Excavation method

The initial 1972 trial excavation consisted of a 1m wide trench running downhill across the centre of the presumed site; ploughsoil was mechanically removed. The trench, situated immediately south of the central baulk on Figs 4 and 5, located the Entrance. In the area of the Entrance and also for 10m at the opposite, uphill, west side of the Round, the trial trench was widened to 3m and excavated down to the top of surviving structures. A small machine cut confirmed the presence of a Ditch just north of the Entrance.

In 1973 ploughsoil was removed from the whole interior by a tracked back-actor machine. A central baulk was left, and, initially, two shorter baulks running from it to the north-west and south-east at right-angles to the line of the Bank. An additional baulk in the south sector was left over a modern pipe trench which ran right across the site (Pl 1). After the removal of ploughsoil, all work was carried out by hand. This ploughsoil removal showed that most of the Round interior was covered by granite rubble. After a little cleaning of this, the outlines of the main

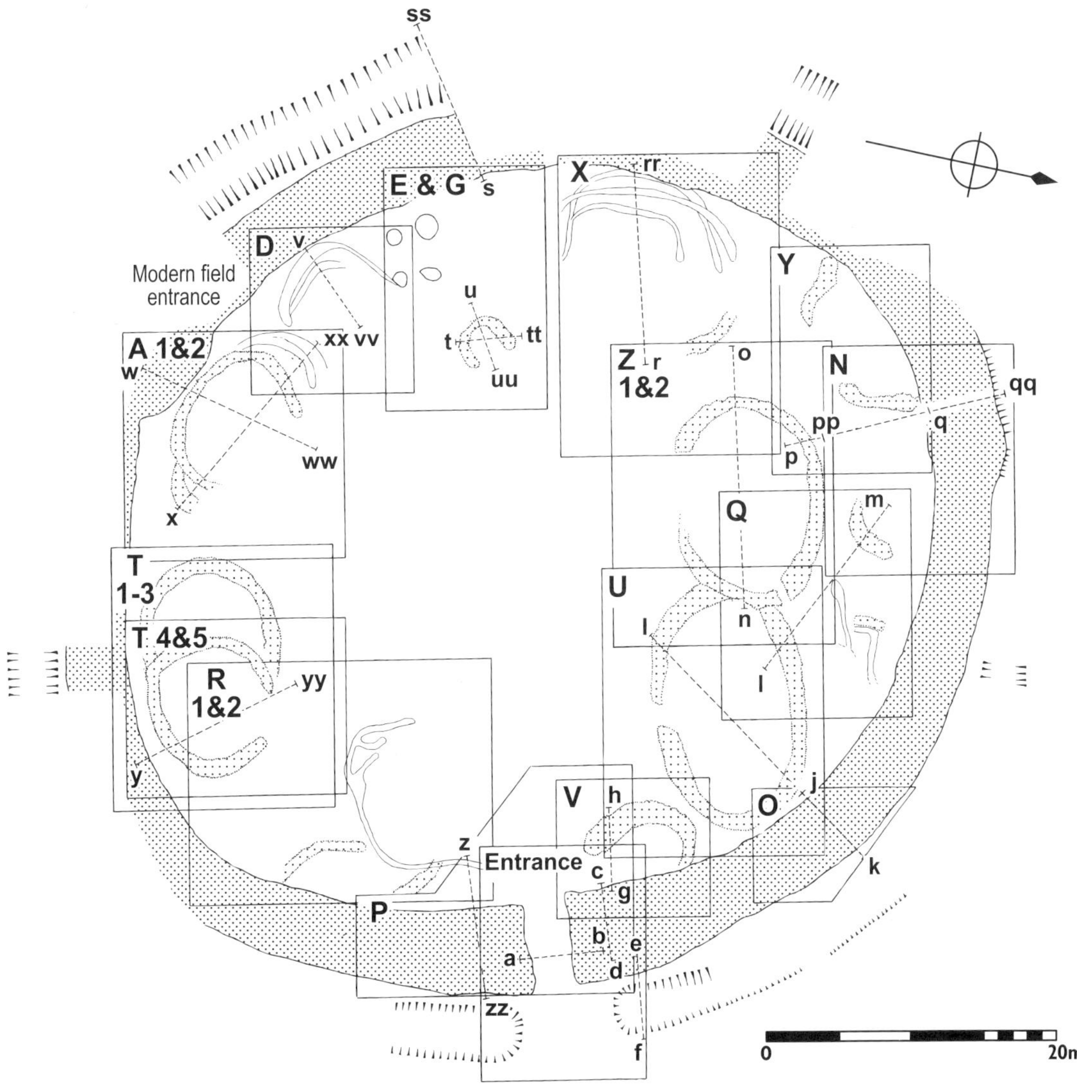

Fig 3: Layout of detailed excavation plans and section lines

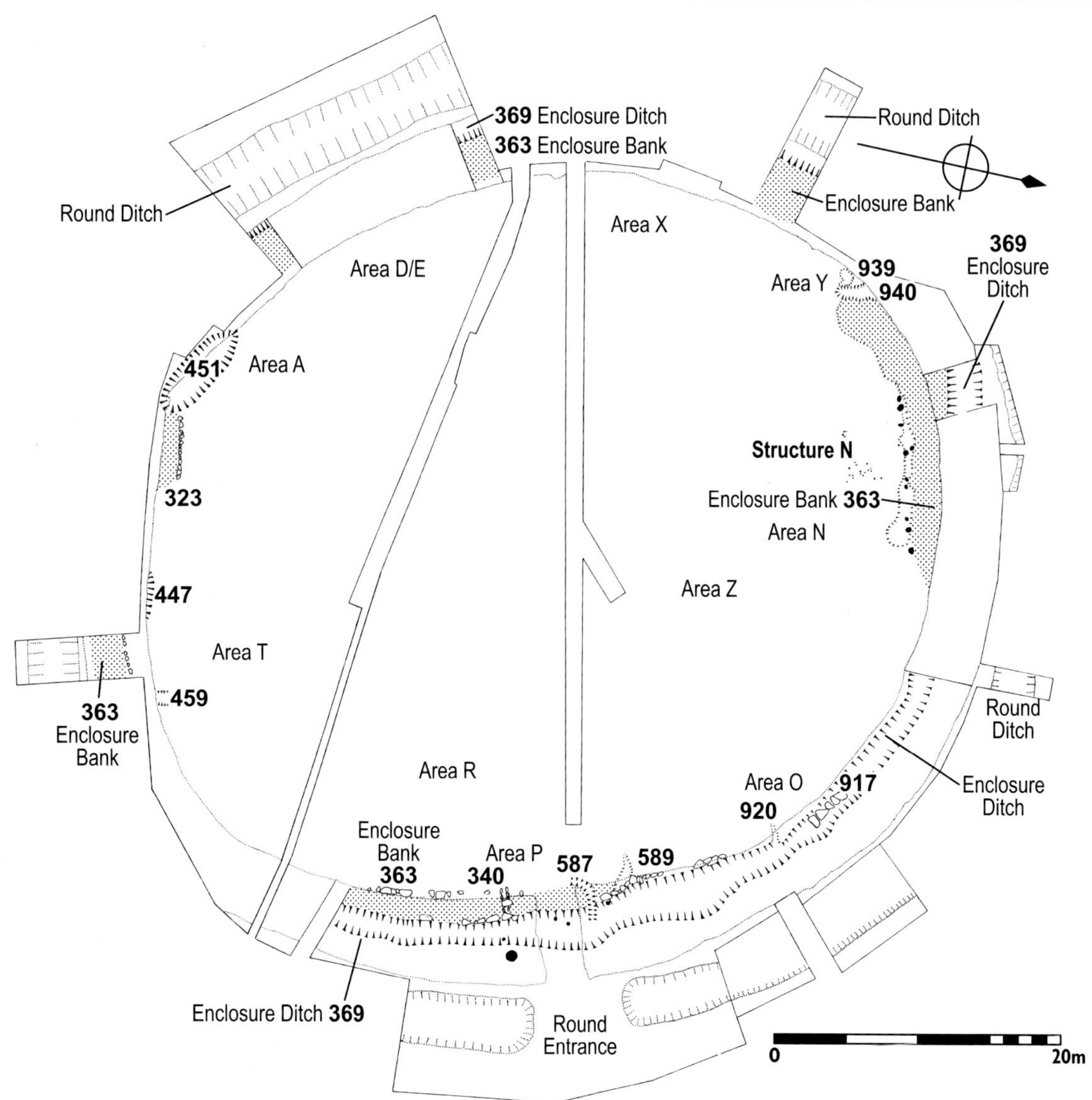

Fig 4: Period 3 Enclosure; some Period 4 activity

structures became clear and dictated the positions of section lines which were mostly set out along the probable long axes of structures. Layers were usually sectioned along the lines laid out, and spot heights taken, before complete removal. The published sections are compiled from the sections of layers drawn on site and profiles drawn after excavation was completed. Areas which appeared to contain structures were given letters as they were identified, starting with A in the south sector and working back from Z in the north. Where structures were confirmed, they were labelled House A, Structure E etc. The capital letters such as A used in Fig 3 both indicate Structures and Areas surrounding the Structures so labelled. (Some area letters initially assigned such as B and C proved not relate to structures and these letters were dropped from the published report for simplicity.) All internal features were completely excavated or dismantled except for the walls of House A1, House T1, and Structure U.

The remains of the field hedge were cleared manually from a length of bank on the west of the Round (Pl 6). The lynchet which had formed outside this section of bank was removed from the underlying Ditch beyond by machine. The remaining Ditch silts in this area were excavated manually, as were those in three other sections and lengths either side of the Entrance. The full extent of the excavation, including the location of Ditch sections, is shown in Figs 3 and 4.

The site code used was TGY. A single series of context numbers was used, ranging from [1] up to [967]. These were allocated in blocks as different areas were excavated and were marked on records inside circles. Separate context numbers were not given to interfaces or cuts for pits or postholes. Available context numbers were increased by adding A, B, etc as suffixes eg [56A]. This was done to enable either different fills in features or closely adjacent features to be given sequential numbers. It is stressed that context numbers with alphabetic suffixes should be regarded as independent; there is no stratigraphic relationship implied between eg [56], [56A], and [56B].

Plans were generally recorded at 1:20 and sections at 1:10. The finds from each day's excavation of each context were given a 'bag number'. The bag number series ran separately from 1 to 990 and was marked on finds inside a rectangle. The finds register recorded the context from which each bag number had come and identified which category of finds such as iron or Roman coarsewares were present. The bag numbers were linked back to contexts on a card index. The purpose of providing the bag numbers separate to those for contexts was to allow the identification of areas of intrusion or of incompetent excavation. In retrospect the bag number system was an unnecessary complexity, the results from which did not justify its use. A limited system of recording small finds in triangles was also used, limited because of the small number of distinctive artefacts found; these were recorded under the relevant bag number in the finds register.

Excavation revealed a series of structures around the perimeter of the Round with a central open space (Fig 5; Pl 1). The stratigraphic sequence was complex; many structures had been rebuilt on the same site several times, but the contemporaneity of different phases of the various structures was often difficult or impossible to establish. The Round had been built over an earlier, unfinished, earthwork, identified in this report as the Period 3 Enclosure.

1.5 Report presentation

In the basic stratigraphic description (Chapter 2) the earthworks are first discussed, and subsequently the structures around the interior described in an anti-clockwise direction. A key for the detailed plans is given in Fig 3. Activity on the site is divided into eight Periods, of which Period 3 represents the unfinished Enclosure and Period 5 the Round. In Chapter 9 buildings and features within the Period 5 Round are divided into Stages 1 to 10, which are presented as plans in Figs 80 to 89. The Periods and Stages are referred to in the stratigraphic description where appropriate.

Descriptions have been kept to a minimum. Where a description of a soil or fill is not given, this was of the gritty mid-brown soil most common on the site. Small

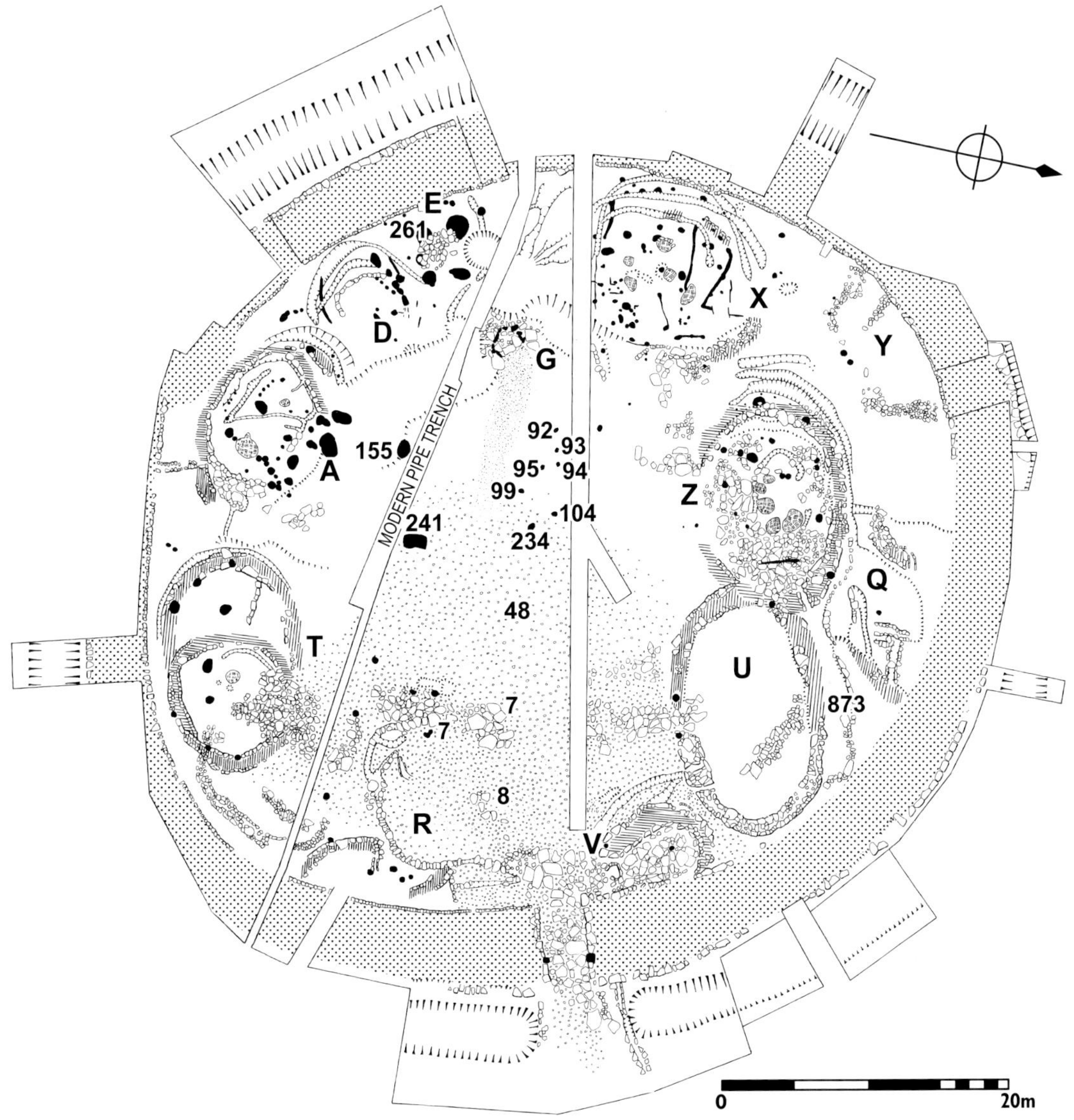

Fig 5: Period 5 Round: composite plan. Features are only numbered if they do not appear on other plans

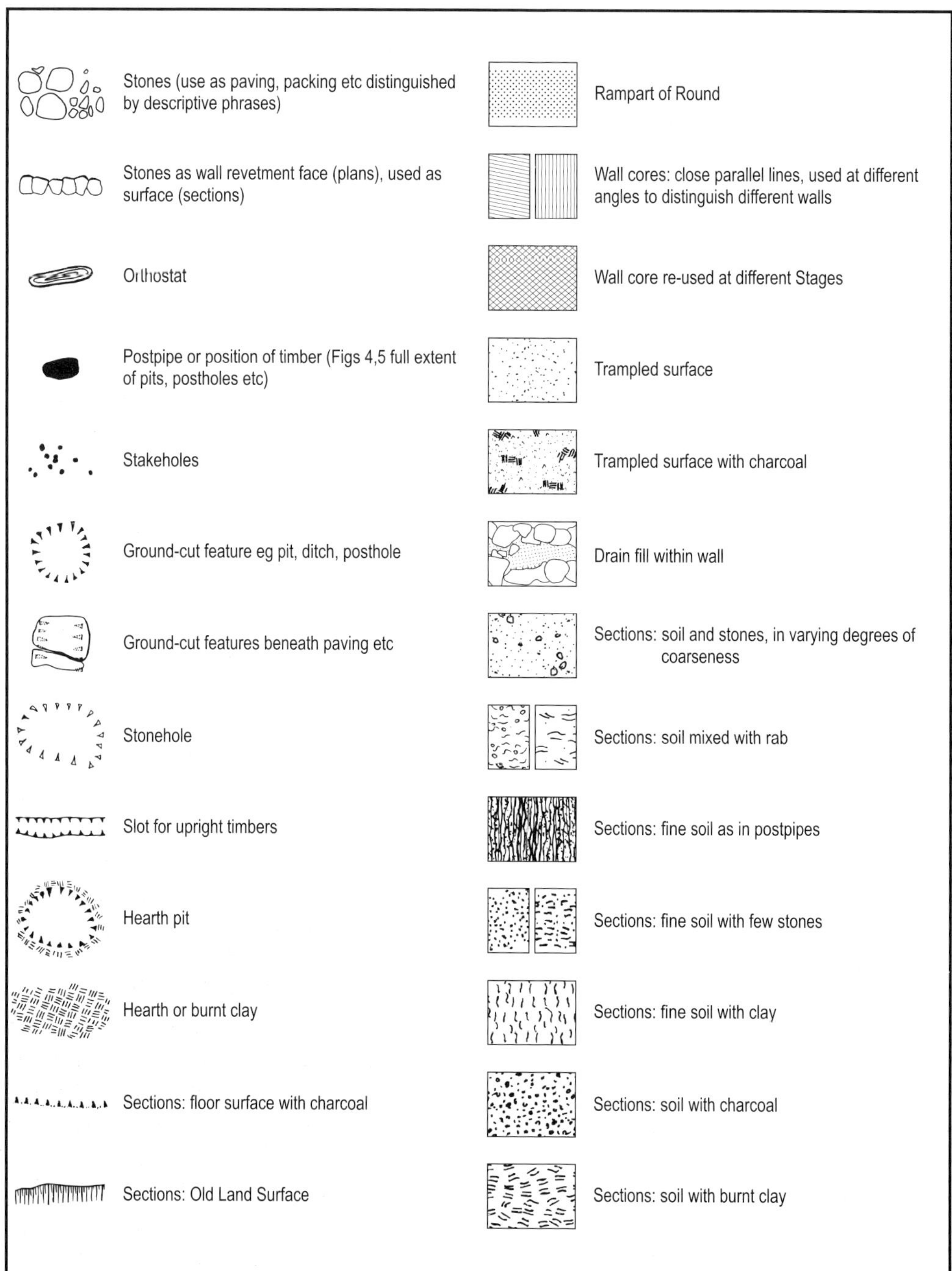

Fig 6: Key to site plans and sections

surfacing stones up to *c* 0.1m are described as cobbles, larger pieces as paving; both types were of granite. A key to conventions used in illustrations is given in Fig 6. Context numbers given during the excavation have been retained, somewhat simplified, in the report. Separate parts of rubble spreads, wall lines, Ditch fills and surfaces, were frequently given different context numbers at the start of their excavation but one context number has been used in publication and the records annotated accordingly.

The finds have been grouped and stored under the context numbers used in this publication.

A Context List in numerical order, giving all numbers used in this report, is given in Appendix 1. This is intended as an index to assist use of the report and references the principal illustrations on which a context appears. The Context List also includes depths where not given in Chapter 2, suggested Period or Stage allocations, and details of associated finds.

The finds and records have been deposited at the Royal Cornwall Museum, River Street, Truro by kind permission of Imerys. The records have been microfilmed on the National Monuments Register of the Royal Commission on Historic Monuments England, now English Heritage.

2 The site stratigraphy

2.1 Summary of the site chronology

The difficulties in dealing with the stratigraphy and in understanding the overall sequence on the site have been discussed in Chapter 1, and the detailed reasons for the phasing and dating of the sequence are presented in Chapter 9. The term 'Period' is used for major developments which have been clearly demonstrated to be cohesive and sequential. The term 'Stage' is used for subdivisions of activity in the Round. The successive Stages divide up a (probable) continuous sequence to provide an impression of what the Round may have consisted of at various times in its development, but the reasons for allocating buildings and features to each Stage are varied and in many cases alternatives would be acceptable. The basis for the division into Stages is therefore of a different kind to that for the successive Periods. It must be stressed that the dates assigned to the Stages are only tentative and the chronology that they present should not be taken as firm, but rather as a 'best fit' interpretation. The term 'Phase' is used for developments within structures, including the enclosing earthworks.

The stratigraphy is presented in successive Periods. Most of this relates to the Round, Period 5, first the Rampart, Ditch, and Entrance and then each Area inside running anti-clockwise around the interior, with cross references where appropriate to Stages.

Period 1 Activity associated with a flint scatter, possibly starting in the Mesolithic but mostly Later Neolithic. Also covers any use of the site before Period 2.

Period 2 Agricultural activity causing slight lynchets preserved within the Old Land Surface beneath the Round. Probably late 1st millennium BC.

Period 3 Enclosure with irregular, unfinished bank and ditch, beneath, and on the line of, the Round's earthworks. The Enclosure was apparently sited within a Period 2 field. Possibly late 1st century BC.

Period 4 Several slight timber structures were built in the Enclosure which was used for farming; the presence of animals resulted in erosion of its earthworks. A small quantity of artefacts was deposited which probably derives from a focus of settlement elsewhere. Covers the 1st century AD and continues until the construction of the Round.

Period 5 The Round, with a suggested construction date of *c* AD 150.

Stage 1 c AD 150-175. Oval Houses A1 and Z1, the latter with adjacent Structure Q1; unfinished oval House T1, four-poster E1 and rectangular timber structure X1, paired postholes [462A] and [462C] etc in R; Ditch silting begins.

Stage 2 c AD 175-210. Provision of buildings increases to provide maximum residential capacity. Oval Houses A1 and Z1 continue, the latter with adjacent Structure Q2; oval House T2 built and small timber oval House D1; four-poster E1 and rectangular timber Structure X1 continue; new paired postholes in R; Ditch silting continues.

Stage 3 c AD 210-260. Minor alterations. Oval Houses A1, Z1, and T1, and four-poster E1 continue, Structure Q3 built adjacent to Z1, oval House X2 built to replace rectangular X1, small oval rebuilt as D2, new paired postholes in R; Ditch silting continues.

Stage 4 c AD 260-325. Major alterations involving the rebuilding of Houses A1 and Z1, Structure Q5 built, four-poster rebuilt as E2, D3 postline replacing small House D2, oval House T altered to T3, an irregular building with adjacent platform [13], oval House X2 continuing, scrappy walls and hearths instead of paired posts in R; Ditch silt nearly fills terminals. A possible hiatus in use of the Round may occur at the end of this Stage.

Stage 5 c AD 325-375. All structures rebuilt. Rampart and Entrance remodelled with paving extending into interior; Ditch terminals cobbled over; oval byre U built and oval Houses A2 and X3 and small oval Houses T4 and D4; four-poster rebuilt as E3, hearths in Area Y; drains and scrappy walls in R.

Stage 6 c AD 375-400. Houses A2, T4, D4, X3 continue. New oval House Z2 built; byre U goes out of use and midden [932/801] deposited; shrine Structure G built, and Structure Y abutting Rampart; scrappy drains and walls continue in R; further activity in Q.

Stage 7 c AD 400-450. Residential capacity shrinking with only Houses A2, Z2, and X3 continuing. T and D out of use; shrine G continues, as does Structure Y; Structure V1 built by Entrance and Structure U2 built over midden; use of walls and drains in R continues as does some use of Q; new cobbles [520] over Entrance terminals.

Stage 8 c AD 450-500. Minor changes, residential capacity again shrinking. House X3 out of use; A2 and Z2 continue as does shrine G, Structure Y, and Structure U2; Structure V2 and T5 built; some continued use of Structures in Q and R.

Stage 9 c AD 500-550+. Some major rebuilding, especially oval House X4. House Z2 continues but timber A3 built over/into A2; V2 and Structure Y continue, Structure T6 built; shrine G infilled towards end and buildings in general decline leading to abandonment of the Round as a residence.

Stage 10 c AD 700 onward. Reuse as stock fold, with new gates in Entrance. Scrappy walls and drains in R; sumps and paving in V; small enclosure X5 built against Rampart.

Period 6 Agricultural use of the Round from the 11th to the 16th centuries.

Period 7 Incorporation of the Round into the present field system, involving the levelling of its east side, probably during the 16th century.

Period 8 Periodic agricultural use of the site since its incorporation into the present field system, with some robbing of stone.

2.2 Period 1

No features can be linked to the Late Neolithic flints, nor were there concentrations which might indicate areas of activity. While it is possible that small postholes without any relationship to later Period features could be of this date, the absence of flint in fills makes any further discussion pointless.

2.3 Period 2 The Old Land Surface and possible field system

The Old Land Surface (OLS) [371] was best preserved beneath the Period 3 Enclosure Bank [363] (sections s-ss, z-zz, Fig 7). Where protected only by the Period 5 Round Rampart [390] its zoning was less clear, and it gradually became undetectable in the unprotected strip inside the Round in Area R (Fig 44). The OLS was studied in a number of sections through Bank [363] and Rampart [390]. In sections on the uphill part of the site, behind Houses A and Z and Structure E, its profile differed from that in those downhill (Fig 7).

In the downhill section (z-zz, Fig 7, location Fig 3) the OLS was podzolic. The upper horizon, 0.15m thick, was grey-brown and humic, with small fragments of parent granite scattered evenly throughout. The base of this horizon was irregular but clear cut. Beneath was a narrow eluvial light grey-buff horizon surviving no more than 0.05m thick. This passed downward into a bright orange-brown band up to 0.2m thick, which gradually merged into the light orange-buff rab beneath.

In the uphill section (s-ss, Fig 7, location Fig 3) the upper horizon was similar in make-up but thinner, usually about 0.1m, with the same clear cut but irregular base. The eluvial zone was not present. Directly beneath the upper humic horizon was the bright orange-brown band, usually about 0.1m thick, which merged with the lighter coloured rab beneath it.

In all sections the nature of the upper humic horizon, with its even scatter of granite-derived fragments, suggested recent disturbance rather than long-maintained turf cover or woodland. The sharp break at its base would be consistent with the disturbance associated with regular cultivation. On the 1:8 slope, on which the site lay, soil creep would be rapid if cultivation continued for any length of time. This would account for the removal of the eluvial horizon on the uphill part of the site, part of the process of negative lynchet formation. No plough marks, nor any patterning, was observed in the irregularities at the base of the humic horizon, but the soil profiles suggest agricultural use, presumably ploughing, for some time before the construction of the Period 3 Enclosure. Nothing which could be interpreted as an associated field boundary was found, but the nature of, and differences in, the OLS on the upper and lower sides of the site would be consistent with the presence of slight lynchets running along the contour of the slope. A sample from OLS [371] beneath the Period 3 Enclosure Bank proved positive for phosphates, suggesting some use by animals.

Posthole [207] was the only feature sealed by OLS [371]. This lay in Area P outside the Period 3 Enclosure Ditch and south of the Round Entrance (Fig 8). It was 0.2m deep and had a possible postpipe with charcoal apparently relating to *in situ* burning. This latter produced radiocarbon determination UB-3254 of 360-1 cal BC at 95% confidence, the earliest date from the site (Section 9.1). This date corroborates the evidence for activities predating the 1st century AD.

2.4 Construction of the Period 3 Enclosure

The Period 5 Round Rampart survived well on the west and south but had been deliberately levelled on the north and east. Throughout, it had been built over the remains of an earlier, eroded, and possibly unfinished univallate enclosure of similar area, c 0.2ha. This earlier Enclosure, referred to as the Period 3 Enclosure (Figs 4, 7, 8), could only be thoroughly investigated on the east where the Round Rampart was low and could be easily stripped off. Where the Period 3 Enclosure Bank [363] had remained exposed on the inside of the Round Rampart, it had been completely eroded almost everywhere. The Period 3 Enclosure Ditch [369] survived well on the east and north but to the west had been largely cut away by the Round Ditch.

The Period 3 Bank [363] was built over OLS [371] from which the turf had not been stripped. The Bank was about 2m wide and survived to a maximum height of 0.5m. It was built of layers of soil and redeposited rab tamped flat, revetted to front [366] and rear [373]

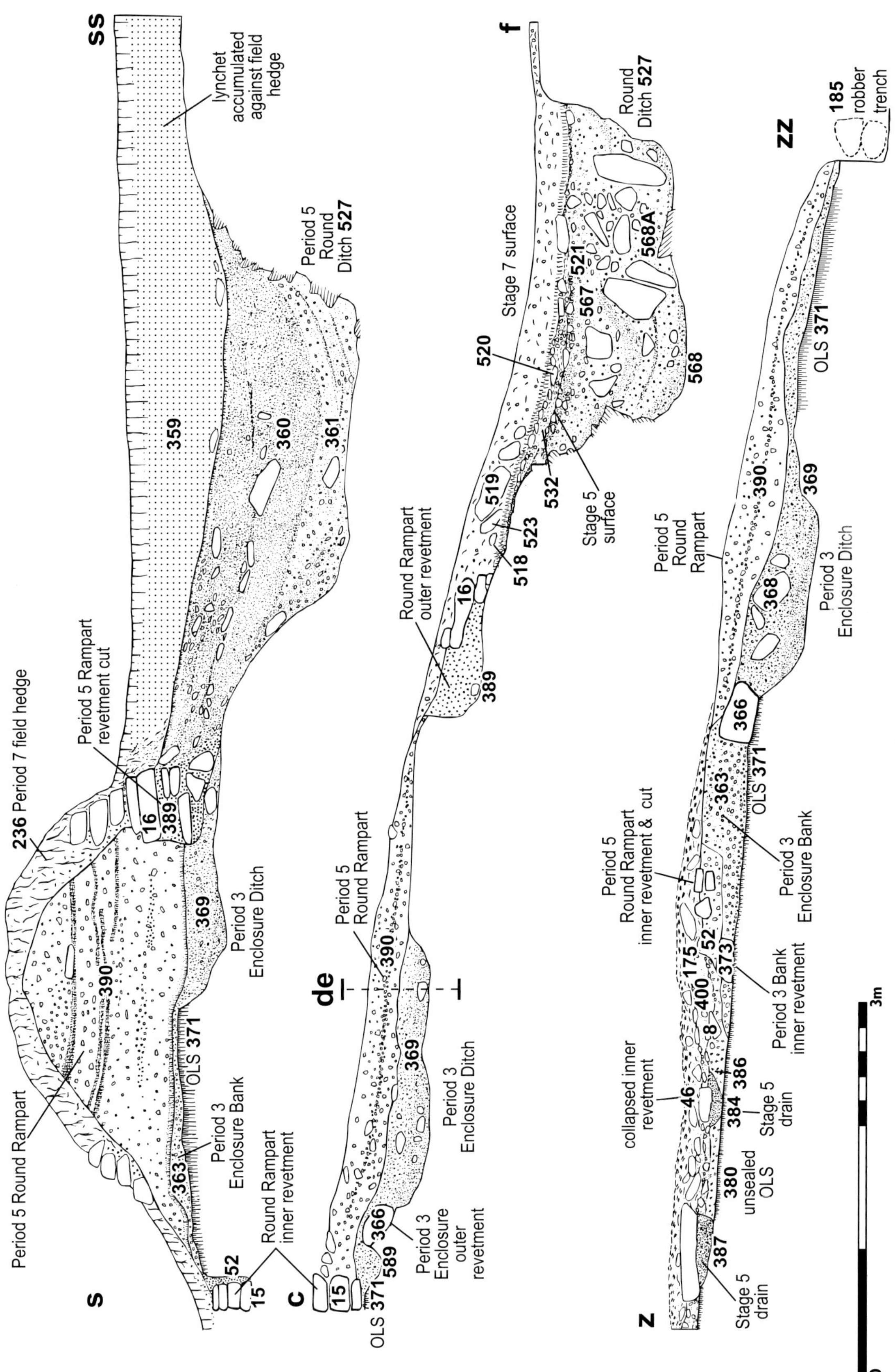

Fig 7: Sections s-ss, c-d/e-f, z-zz through the Earthworks

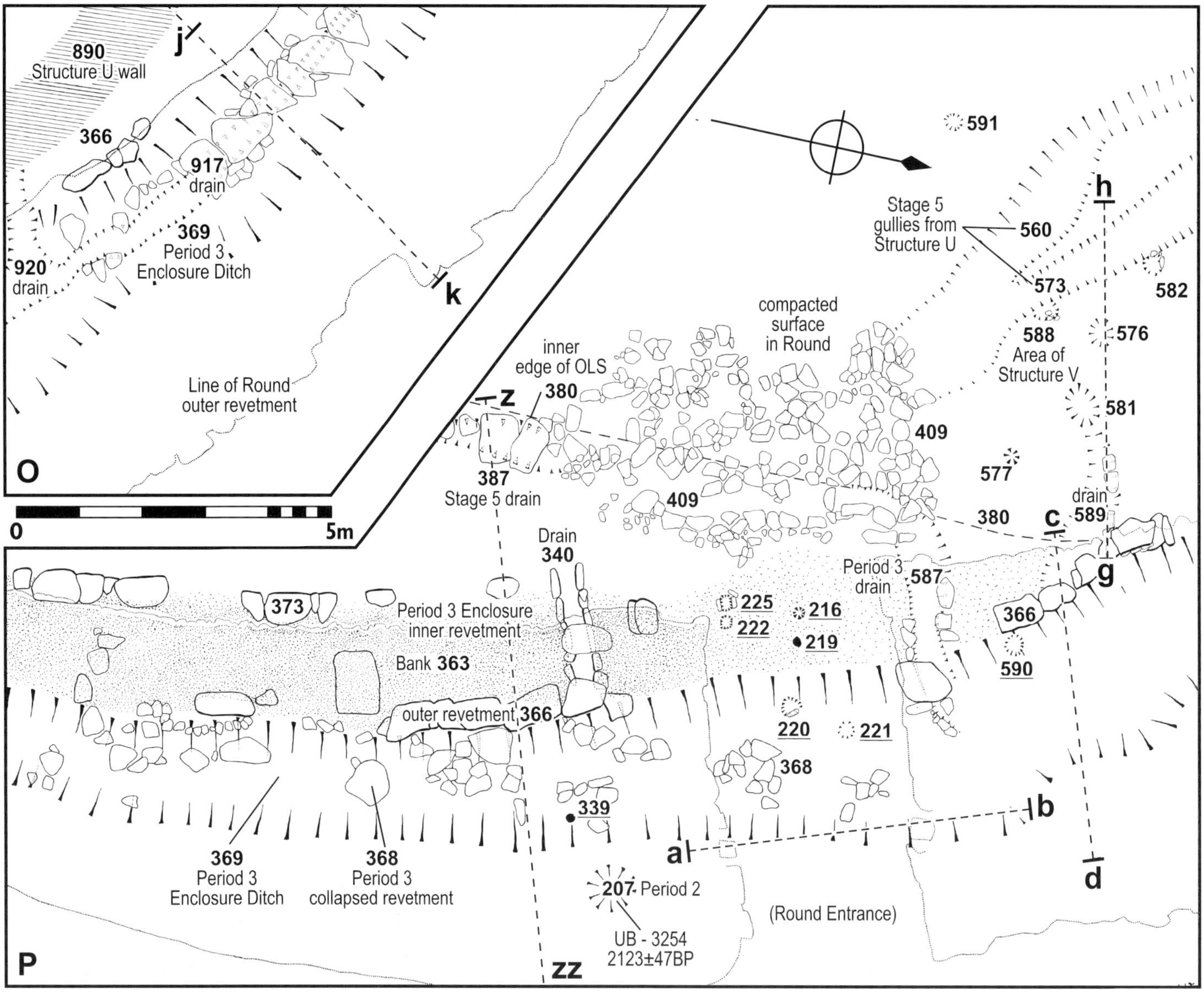

Fig 8: Details of Periods 3/4 Enclosure features in Areas P and O. Period 4 contexts cut into Period 3 earthworks underlined

Pl 3: Period 3 Enclosure Bank on the east of the Round. The Period 5 Round inner revetment [15] is still in position above the Period 3 Enclosure inner revetment [373]; the Period 3 Enclosure Ditch with collapsed revetment material [368] shows on the right. View from south. 2m scale

with granite blocks set directly on OLS [371] (Fig 8). No more than two courses survived *in situ* but up to five courses of the outer revetment had slumped forward [368] into the Ditch in places (Pl 3). The Bank's surviving circuit was irregular in detail. A length of bank [323], revetted by [322], found behind House A (Fig 34), was apparently off line, but as this partly underlay the Rampart of the Round it seems reasonable to assign it to the Period 3 Enclosure as a surviving remnant of [363]. A gap to the north-west (found beneath later Structure Y) may have been an original entrance as the Bank widened here as though to form terminals. In this area the position of Bank [363] was largely detected by a ridge of subsoil without a distinctive OLS. The material of the Bank, here labelled [780] (Fig 12), had been subsequently spread to form a continuous layer running several metres into the interior and across into the Ditch [369]; no definite *in situ* bank material was detected.

The Ditch [369] was irregular and flat bottomed (see also Fig 9), 1.5 to 2.5m wide and 0.5 to 0.75m deep. It was filled with gritty silt, normally grey and gleyed. For *c* 5m on the north-east in Area O (Figs 8, 17) it was only *c* 0.1m deep. Here a slot 0.2m deep was dug in its base to accommodate drain [917] with orthostatic sidestones and capstones (Fig 8; Pl 4); the drain had either never been completed or had been later removed. In the north-west section (section q-qq, Fig 12) the Ditch and its fill differed from the remainder of the circuit investigated. The Ditch was, exceptionally, *c* 4m wide. Its inner lip, with stoneholes [946] and [964] (Fig 9), was covered by [945], a layer of redeposited rab. Layer [945] had the appearance of bank material thrown down into Ditch [369] which had been locally cut too wide. It was overlain by silt [944] which underlay spread bank material [780]. The Ditch was filled, above [780], by grey silt [943A], but it still formed a distinct depression here when the Rampart of the Round was built. Elsewhere Ditch [369] had silted nearly to its top before being covered by the Round Rampart.

Pl 4: Drain [917] within the Period 3 Enclosure Ditch. Part of wall [890], Structure U, shows on the left. View from east. 2m scale

A number of drains or gullies had apparently been intended to drain through the Enclosure Bank into the Ditch. The best preserved was [340] (Fig 8) which had sidestones and capstones constructed at the same time as the outer revetment [366]. Gulley [587] to its north was more ruinous — or less complete; it ran out from beneath a stone spread [409], some of which may have been initially laid in Period 3 (Area R, Section 2.19). Drain [589] a few metres to the north of [587] was contiguous with revetment [366]. A further drainage channel [920] (Fig 8), with no surviving stonework, ran into the end of drain [917] set in the bottom of the Ditch. All these drains had some grey silt in their bases and were infilled above with redeposited rab and soil. Gullies [447] and [459] (Fig 39; Pl 9), found on the south-east side of the Round under House T, were filled with grey silt and ran back under the Round Rampart; these were probably also Period 3 drains. Another gulley [940] (Fig 24), found on the north-west side beneath Structure Y, was also silt-filled and appeared to drain towards Ditch [369]; gulley [940] was sealed by the spread bank material [780], as was the adjacent pit [939] (Fig 24).

2.5 Period 4 activity between the construction of the Enclosure and of the Round

2.5.1 Features intermediate between the Enclosure and the Round

A group of postholes in Area P, shown underlined on Fig 8, had been cut into the eroded Period 3 Enclosure Bank and Ditch but were covered by the Round Rampart — [339], [225], [222], [216], [219], [220], [221], and [590]. These were all small, *c* 0.1-0.15m deep, except [220] at 0.25m deep. Posthole [225] preserved the position of a square post; the remainder were much ruined. The group of six in the Round Entrance might have been connected with temporary barriers during its construction in Period 5, but [339] and [590] definitely fell chronologically between the Enclosure and the later Round.

In the area of House A the worn hollow filled with [451] had eroded in the Period 3 Enclosure Bank, subsequently causing instability to the Round Rampart (Figs 34, 35).

2.5.2 Structure N and features within the Period 3 Enclosure

Because of the difficulty of demonstrating contemporaneity with the Period 3 Enclosure, the fills of all features such as drains and Ditch are assigned to Period 4, as are structures within its earthworks.

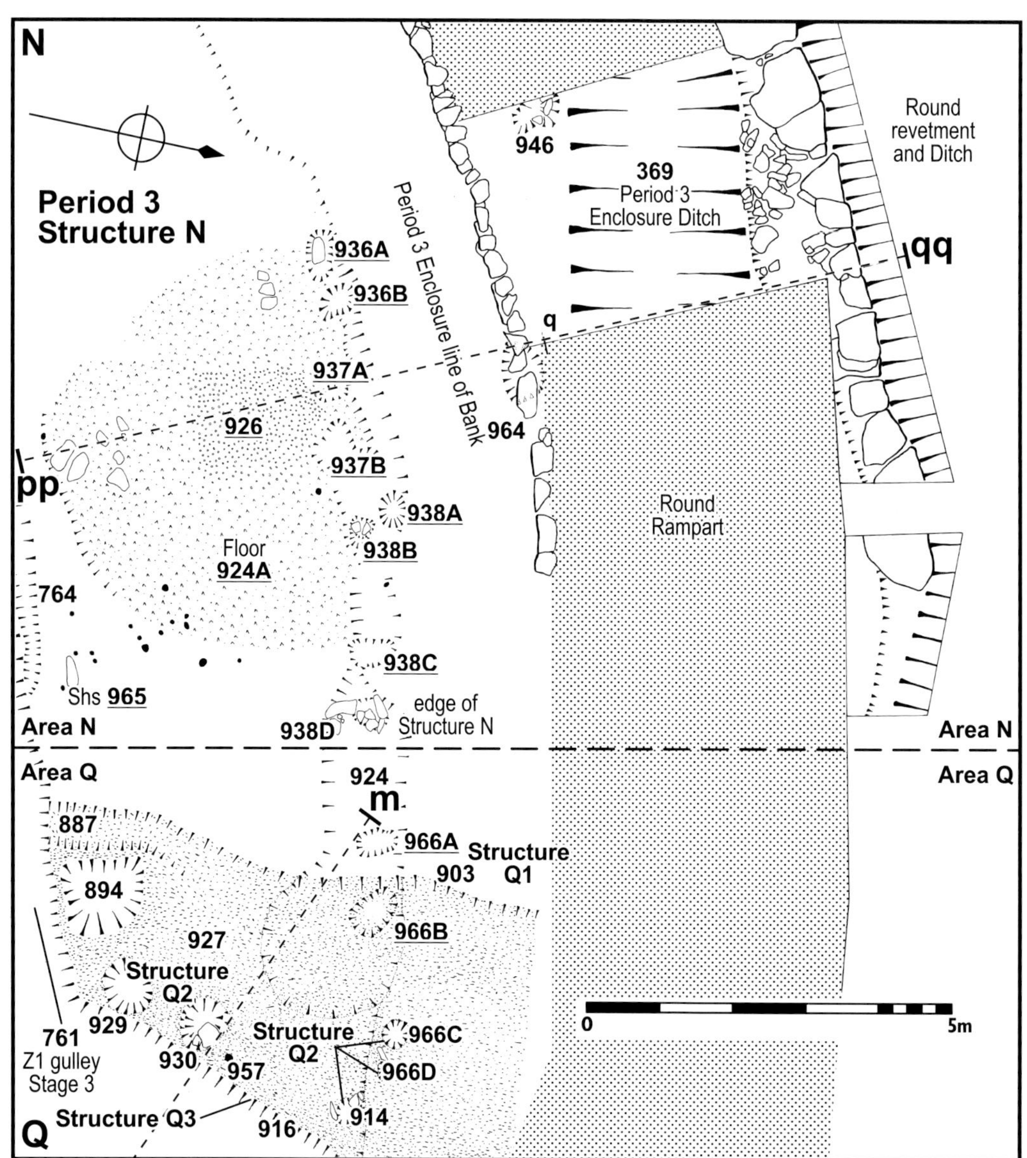

Fig 9: Periods 3/4 Structure N (contexts underlined) and Period 5 Round Stage 1 to 3 features in Areas N and Q

Only on the north-west in Area N, where spread Enclosure Bank material [780] provided stratigraphic distinction, was definite occupation predating the Period 5 Round identified within the Enclosure (Figs 9, 12). In other Areas some postholes and features predating the earliest structures inside the Round could relate to the Period 3 Enclosure; such features are described with the structures they predate.

The position of the Enclosure Bank in Areas N (Fig 9) and Y (Fig 24) was represented by a 20m long ridge of subsoil eroded on its inner edge. For the eastern 10m this edge also formed one side of gulley [924]. This gulley was up to 0.3m deep, filled with brown silty soil, and ended to the east with an enlargement 1.2m across, which was cut through by levelling [903] (Section 2.11.1) in Stage 1 of the Round. Structure N had ten postholes (Fig 9) set in or adjacent to gulley [924]-[936A], [936B], [937A], [937B], [938A], [938B], [938C], [938D], [966A], and [966B]. These were between 0.2m and 0.25m deep, much damaged with no postpipes detectable. South of gulley [924] and the posthole line, the subsoil had been slightly levelled and was much worn as [924A] for an area 5m across; the south side of the worn and levelled surface [924A] was parallel to [924] but was only distinguishable for 3m. Surface [924A] is interpreted as a worn floor including flat stones and a group of stakeholes [965], and a patch of trampled black soil [926]. The character of Structure N represented by these features is not clear, although it was evidently much used. Its area was covered over by [925], orange-brown soil mixed with redeposited rab which underlay the spread Enclosure Bank [780].

A group of postholes in Area P (Fig 8) was sealed beneath Round Stage 5 cobbles [557] below Structure V — [591], [588], [582], [576], [577], and [581]. These again were all *c* 0.2m deep and much damaged; [588] and [582] were later cut by gulley [573] of Structure U. These features were early in the sequence and could be contemporary with the Period 3 Enclosure, or belong to Period 4 activity or to the early Stages of the Round.

Pl 5: Round Rampart on the west (northern part), stripped of Period 7 field hedge [236], showing dry stone walling of outer revetment [16] with Round Ditch [527] in foreground; complete section through Rampart on left and view across the north part of Round in early stages of excavation. View from south-west. 2m scale

2.5.3 General comments on the Period 3 Enclosure and its use in Period 4

The Enclosure can never have been intended to have been as substantial as the later Round. Its Bank [363] and Ditch [369] contained gulley features and the residual remains of Structure N of uncertain form and function. All this evidence was poorly preserved. The insubstantial nature of the Bank [363], and the absence of any revetments especially on its west side, could suggest that it was never entirely completed or that it had been severely eroded and damaged by later phases of activity. Limited evidence for ditch silts such as [944] suggest either that the Ditch was not open for long or was regularly cleaned out. Drainage was clearly a concern given the number of drains identified running through the Bank, such as [587] and [340] on its east side. Remnant bank material survived in situ on the west and east sides but on the north-east had been spread [780]; this spread may indicate deliberate levelling. As no evidence for soil formation was found beneath it, the denudation resulting in [780] may have occurred quickly and have been accelerated by animal trampling. Samples from Ditch silt proved positive for phosphates and were consistent with the use of the Enclosure by stock (Section 8.3.2).

2.6 Period 5 Round earthworks

The Rampart survived to a maximum height of 1.5m on the west and south of the Round where it had been incorporated in recent field boundaries (Figs 2, 7; Pl 5); elsewhere it had been denuded to c 0.3-0.5m. It was generally about 4m wide. The length incorporated in the field hedge south-west of the Round was stripped of recent levels, the Rampart sectioned at either end, and the Ditch completely cleared (Pls 5, 6). The denuded Rampart was stripped for 50m on the east of the Round, and sections cut through the earthworks on the north-west, north and south.

2.6.1 The Rampart

The Rampart [390] was built along the general line of, and over, the eroded Period 3 Enclosure earthworks, which suggests that these were still visible (Pls 7, 8). These had not developed any detectable soils, which may indicate only a short lapse of time, as may the use of Period 3 Bank revetment stones as a foundation for the Rampart revetment in places. At the base of the Rampart in some stretches (section s-ss, Fig 7) a layer of turves was placed upside down. The bulk of [390] was redeposited rab with some small stones, carefully tamped in level layers. Towards the

Pl 6: Round Rampart on the west (southern part), showing the length stripped of Period 7 field hedge [236]; Ditch [527] partly excavated. View from south. 2m scale

Pl 7: Drain [199] beneath Round Rampart on north side of Entrance; Rampart material partly removed to show cover stones. Surface [521] shows outside Rampart revetment [16]. View from east. 2m scale

top of the higher surviving parts were level layers of turves. The larger stones dug from the ditch had been separated from the rab for use in the revetments. After

Pl 8: Ditch terminal north of Entrance. Surface [520] over unexcavated Ditch, [521] on berm. View from south. 2m scale

the Rampart material was deposited to a height of around 0.6m, a cut [389] was made in places to seat the outer revetment [16] (section s-ss, Fig 7). A similar cut [52] for the inner revetment [15] was found to be discontinuous. This constructional sequence was logical because a quantity of ditch material had to be excavated before adequate stone for the revetments was amassed. In places either side of the Entrance, the remnants of the Period 3 Enclosure Bank outer revetment [373] were used as a base for the inner revetment [15] (section z-zz, Fig 7). Smaller blocks were used for the inner than for the outer revetment. The inner revetment was neatly built and survived up to ten courses high, a maximum of 0.75m, where protected by soil accumulation on the south-east of the site (Pls 9, 10). The inner revetment was more or less vertical, the outer sloped inwards at about 70°. Blocks up to 0.75m long were used in the outer revetment and were carefully interlocked but not coursed (Pl 5).

There were some irregularities in the Rampart construction. In the south section [390] was initially dumped in a bank 3.5m wide and then thickened to 4.5m before the revetments were built. Adjacent to House A (Figs 34, 35), a worn hollow on the line of the inner revetment had removed the Enclosure Bank. This hollow (see Period 4 above) was filled in with [451], dark silty soil (with only a single run of rab) which had the appearance of redeposited ditch silt,

Pl 9: Period 3 Enclosure gulley [459] passing beneath Round inner revetment [15] south of House T. View from north. Scale 0.5m segments

Pl 10: Round inner revetment [15] in its highest surviving part, south-east of House T. View from north-west. Scale 0.5m segments

perhaps derived from the Enclosure Ditch (section w-ww, Fig 35). Inner revetment [15] was apparently built over [451] but only a clump of stones [452] survived. Subsequently in Stage 5 a layer of rab [446] was deposited over [451], covering the surviving end of the inner revetment. Layer [446] extended up to the rear wall [65] of House A2, and formed a distinct bulge in the Rampart (Figs 35, 37). It seems probable that the infill [451], and the hollow beneath it, had caused the inner edge of the Rampart to collapse and the resultant depression was infilled when House A2 was built in Stage 5. On the south-east of the Round the inner edge of the Rampart was also strengthened during Stage 5 with rab [398] revetted by [397] (Figs 41, 43), when House T4 was built. No other rebuilding of the Rampart was noted.

The Rampart revetments had begun to collapse while the Round was in use. Large stones from the outer revetment were found in the upper part of the secondary ditch silts [360]. The inner revetment tumbled as rubble [46] in Area R in a period of disuse between Stages 9 and 10 (section z-zz, Fig 7; Pl 40). In Area X during the same disuse between Stages 9 and 10 (Figs 25, 26; Section 2.13.5) the inner revetment collapsed, causing the Rampart to bulge outwards. The Rampart generally continued to stand about 1.5m high until the 16th century.

With the 16th-century field enclosures, the Rampart on the west and south-west was made into a field hedge by refacing it with stone on either side and heightening it [236]; modern growth of bushes on the hedge had caused much disturbance along its top. The remainder of the Rampart was levelled, its material presumably incorporated in the new field hedges. After the Post-Medieval field enclosures, ploughing uphill to the west caused a lynchet [359] 1m thick outside the field hedge incorporating the Rampart (section s-ss, Fig 7).

2.6.2 The Ditch

The Ditch [527] was extremely irregular (Fig 7, Pl 5), varying in width between 3m and 5m and in depth between 0.8 and 1.5m. It was flat bottomed, but its profile everywhere was uneven due to the hollows left by the removal of large granite blocks from the head and the protrusion of still larger blocks around which the finer material had been scraped away. Primary silt [361] was generally 0.3 to 0.4m thick, mainly yellow-brown gritty deposits mixed with runs of humic material. Secondary silts [360] were up to 1m thick and consisted of an even mixture of dark silt and rab-derived materials. A soil surface gradually stabilised on the top of the secondary ditch silts. The more elaborate sequence in the terminals by the Entrance is dealt with below.

2.6.3 The Entrance

The Rampart widened to Entrance terminals (Fig 10) 6m across, revetted with stones up to 1m in length. To the north, revetment [187] was bonded with revetments [15] and [16] on either side of the Rampart, but, to the south, the junctions of [182] with

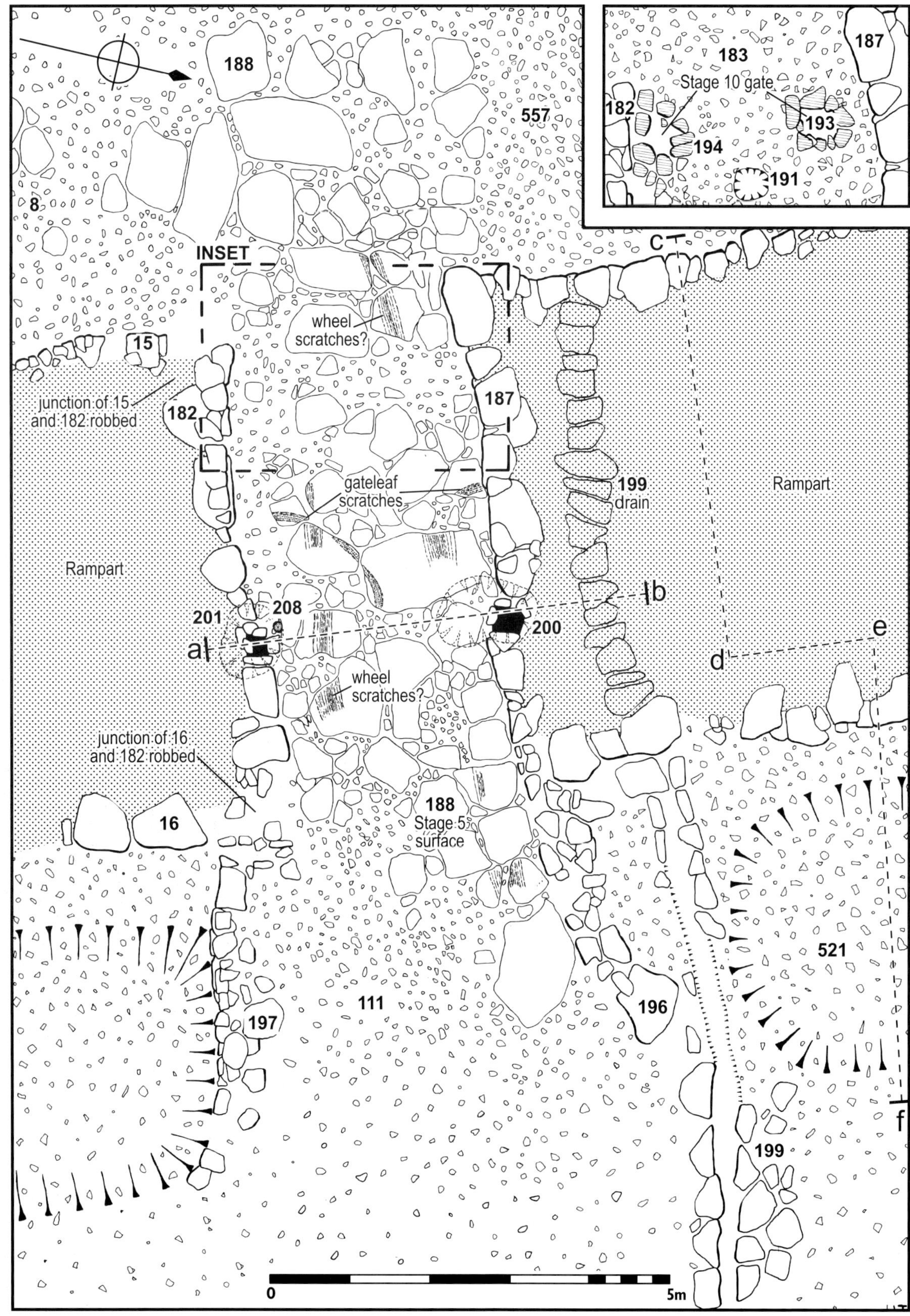

Fig 10: Entrance plans

[15] and [16] had been robbed out. The bank material [390] already *in situ* had been trimmed back to provide seating for the [182] revetment, and the gap remaining after the latter was put in position was tightly packed with rubble and soil [205]. On the north side of the Entrance, the Rampart material originally stopped 2m short of the entranceway itself and drain [199] was constructed, bonded with the inner and outer revetments, to provide drainage through the Rampart (Pl 7). This was stone-lined and capped and set within a trench 0.35m deep cutting through the Period 3 Enclosure Bank and Ditch (Fig 11, Pl 7). Drain [199]

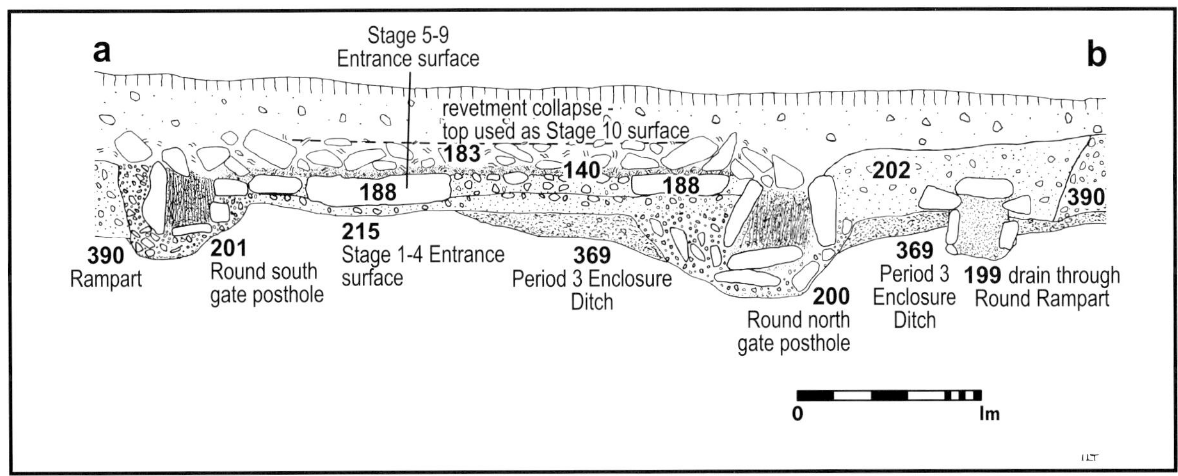

Fig 11: Entrance sections

continued for 6.6m outside the northern terminal although its capping stones, and some of its sidestones, no longer survived. It was infilled with fine dark soil throughout its length. The north Rampart terminal was built up as [202] over drain [199] at the same time as its revetment [187] was constructed.

Rough walls [196] and [197], up to three courses high, continued the lines of the terminal revetments across the Ditch causeway to shield the ends of the Ditches. In the unrobbed junction to the north, [196] appeared to have been bonded with the Rampart revetment [16].

The Entrance revetments survived up to three courses high, defining an entrance passage 6m long by 2.75m wide which expanded to 3m inside the gateposts (Fig 10). A double-leaved gate had opened inwards; the inner part of the Entrance expanded to form slight recesses against which the leaves could fold back. The settings for both gateposts consisted of post pits [200] and [201], dug before the revetments were erected. They cut through the silt of the Period 3 Ditch and their upcast was scattered over its top beneath the Entrance paving. The post pits had been dug too large and were partly backfilled and levelled with large stones before wooden gateposts were set in them and tightly packed around with stones (Fig 11). It is possible however that a replacement phase was missed (see below). Both posts appear to have been of rectangular section 0.22m by 0.16m set 0.35m deep. The packing of the south hole [201] survived intact and gave the dimensions for the posts (Pl 15). The stones in the north hole [200] had partially collapsed. Both sockets were filled with fine dark soil. The intact condition of the packing stones in both holes is probably consistent with the posts having rotted *in situ* rather than with these having been withdrawn at some late stage.

The revetments, [182] and [187], had been constructed after the erection of the gateposts, as they and the backing to the revetments,[202], [205], partly covered the gatepost pits. The passageway was then surfaced with [215], small cobbles mixed with rab and soil (section a-b, Figs 11, 80; Pl 11). These were much worn on their surface. Layer [215] did not extend outside beyond the entrance passage but stretched c 3m into the interior to merge into [409] (Fig 8), a stone spread in a slight hollow. This latter contained several rough channels and was probably a soak for drainage. It possibly included stones laid in Period 3 but was mainly functional during the Period 5 Round as, later in Stage 5, drains [387], [560], and [573] were dug to run into it (see Fig 8).

Pl 11: Entrance showing Stages 1-4 surface [215]; Stage 5 paving [188] in section. View from outside, from east. 2m scale

Pl 12: Entrance with Stage 5 paving [188]; [521] on berms. View from outside, from east. 2m scale

Pl 13: Entrance paving slabs [188]. View from outside, east. 2m scale

During Stage 5, the Entrance (Fig 84; Pls 12, 13) was resurfaced with [188] (Fig 10), large granite blocks with smaller pieces in the interstices. These rested directly on [215] except in places where a little rab was used as bedding (see Fig 11). Layer [188] projected beyond the Entrance and was continued across the causeway between walls [196] and [197] by smaller stones [111] which themselves gradually faded out. In the interior, the [188] surface was continued by cobbles [557] beneath Structure V (Fig 14) and cobbles [8] in Area R (Fig 45), indicating that this extensive resurfacing of the Interior was contemporary with the repaving of the Entrance, in Stage 5 (Fig 84).

Within the Entrance, surface [188] incorporated a small setting [208] 0.17m north-west of the south gatepost [201]. Setting [208] was 0.1m deep, lined with tightly packed small stones and much worn (Pl 15). It appears to have formed the pivot socket for the south gate-leaf. The partial collapse of packing stones around the north gate posthole [200] may account for no equivalent being found here. It is quite possible that gateposts were replaced when [188] was laid in Stage 5, or indeed subsequently. The raising and relaying of paving slabs may not have been detected during excavation. Replacement of the gateposts would account for the slabs in the postholes, well above their bases (Fig 11). Replacement holes were not detected

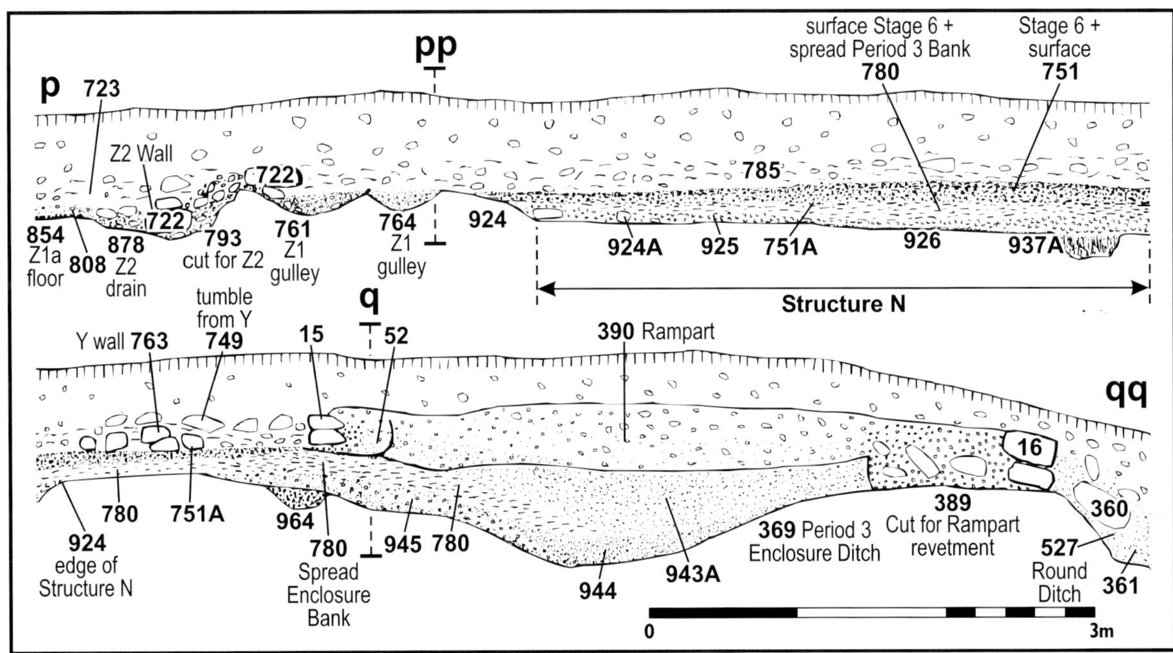

Fig 12:Sections p-pp, q-qq, Areas N and Y

Pl 14: Entrance paving slab in [188] showing wear from opening of south gate-leaf. View from east. Scale 2p coin

Pl 15: Entrance south gate posthole [201] and pivot hole [208]. View from east. 0.3m scale

during the excavation. The gate appears to have operated throughout the 300+ years of the site's occupation, which makes it likely that the gateposts would have been renewed. Squared posts could have been dropped into slightly recut sockets without disturbing the Entrance revetments and packed from their outer sides.

Paving [188] was very worn. Arcs of scratches had been formed by the double leaves of the gates as they swung inwards; each leaf would have been about 1.4m wide (Pl 14). The survival of these gate-arc scratches, on paving which was very worn, suggests that the gates were operational until a late stage in the occupation of the site. There were also slight scratched or worn

Pl 16: North Rampart terminal by Entrance with surface [521] over berm and drain [199]. View from east. Scale 50 cm segments

grooves parallel with the passageway, probably wheel tracks. These appeared to belong to two separate sets, about 1.4m and 1.6m apart respectively. As with the gate-arc scratches, the 'wheel grooves' should also belong to a late phase in the use of the Entrance (Fig 10).

The Ditch terminals may have been kept clean for a while as only a small amount of primary silt ([568], section e-f, Fig 7; Pl 8) accumulated before a mass of large stones and rabby soil [568A] was pushed into the north terminal from the outer lip. The source of this material was unclear, but its result was to narrow the ditch and make it shallower. The [568A] infill extended in the north Ditch terminal for the whole length excavated. There was a similar but less substantial infill [213] in the south Ditch terminal. In both terminals secondary silts [567], containing much dark soil, then accumulated almost up to the Ditch top. These silts contained many large stones and may incorporate episodes of infill. A layer of cobbles [521] was then spread over the Ditch terminals and the berm, right up to the outer Rampart revetment, drain [199] (Pl 16), and causeway walls [196] and [197]. There were sparse patches outside the Ditch. Surface [521] was very worn. With the settling of Ditch silts, the portion of cobbles [521] (Pls 7, 8) over the Ditches sank, breaking away from those on the berm; soil [532] washed into the resulting hollows. A second layer of cobbles [520] (Pl 8) was laid to level up the top of the Ditch. This was more patchy than the earlier [521] but had also been very much worn. The lower cobbling [521] was probably contemporary with later Entrance resurfacing episodes during Stage 5; the upper, [520], belonged to a later period, perhaps Stage 7 (section e-f, Fig 7).

Soil [523] accumulated over upper cobbles [520] and, beyond the Ditch, on [521], which still formed the surface on the berm. Soil [523] sealed parts of causeway walls [196] and [197] and drain [199], which were all now ruinous, and was continuous with soil [140], accumulating up to 0.05m thick over the Entrance paving [188]. Soil [140] (Fig 11) was in turn continuous with [400] in the south part of the Round (see Areas R and T). This extensive soil spread [523]-[140]-[400] in its entirety represents an interval when the whole of the site was disused, between Stages 9 and 10. As, but largely after, soil [140] formed, the Rampart revetments became ruinous, giving rise to a level of rubble [183] in the Entrance, which sealed the gate postholes. Outside, the outer Rampart revetment slumped as rubble [519] causing some Rampart material [518] to collapse. Inside the Rampart, collapsed revetment material such as stones [46] (Area R) was contemporary with the collapse represented by [183] in the Entrance. The collapse of revetments and the accumulation of soil together indicate an abandonment event at the end of Stage 9.

Subsequently the site was reoccupied in Stage 10 and the top of [183] in the Entrance was used as a surface. Some spreads of cobbles were laid on [183] and outside over the revetment collapse. A new gate was constructed in post-settings [193] and [194] (Fig 10, inset). These were indefinite features *c* 0.4m deep, their packing stones difficult to distinguish from rubble [183] into which they were set. A pit [191], 0.4m deep, was cut at some stage adjacent to the postholes; its base and sides had some clay lining and were fire-reddened; its fill contained charcoal, iron-smithing slag and burnt clay (Table 3.4). Pit [191], assigned to Stage 10, may be connected with iron-smithing (Fig 10, inset).

This upper surface in the Entrance was covered only by dark soil (not given a separate context number), which spread over the denuded Rampart and up into the ploughsoil. A robber trench [185] for the outer Rampart revetment was traced for a least 5m along the south terminal (section z-zz, Fig 7, but not on plan).

2.7 Period 5 Round: the Central Area

The space in the centre of the Round had been roughly levelled (Fig 5), involving the removal of up to 0.7m of head subsoil on the slope below Structure G, and a number of projecting stones had been taken out. This left a shelf 8-9m wide along the top of the Round, on the west and south-west upon which Structures X, E, D and A were built (Pl 28). Most of the central area was surfaced with patchy cobbles [48], which were most continuous on the east where they spread down to [409] inside the Entrance and to [173] in Area R. Cobbles [48] probably represented many minor phases of resurfacing.

A group of probable postholes seemed to form a cluster — [92], [93], [94], [95], [99], [104], and [234] (Fig 5), and [783] and [784] (Fig 25). These should perhaps be interpreted as the remnants of fencing or of paired post-structures rather than of more regular buildings. There were two larger isolated postholes, [241], recut once with packing stones in both phases, and [155] with packing stones over a layer of charcoal on its base. All these postholes have been omitted from the Stage plans as chronological indicators are lacking.

2.8 Period 5 Round Structure V

Structure V (Figs 13, 14) was constructed against the inside of the Rampart north terminal, and was rebuilt or altered several times. Its first phase was founded on cobbling [557] and abutted Structure U and so postdated both these Stage 5 features. Its first phase is assigned to Stage 7, its last phase to Stage 10.

2.8.1 Structure V1

In its first phase Structure V (Stage 7) survived only as an arc of scrappy walling [538] between 1m and 1.8m wide, set directly on cobbles [557] and abutting Structure U. Its east side was formed by inner Rampart revetment [15], giving a maximum internal width of 4.5m. Most of its north end was probably formed by the walling of U [890] and the remainder by walling, now removed, across the narrow gap between U and the Rampart; the maximum internal length may have been *c* 12m. There need not have been a roof. The entrance gap to the south was 3.2m across. The Stage 5 cobbles [557], over which the Structure was built, appear to have formed the floor, on which a layer of soil [548] accumulated; there were no internal

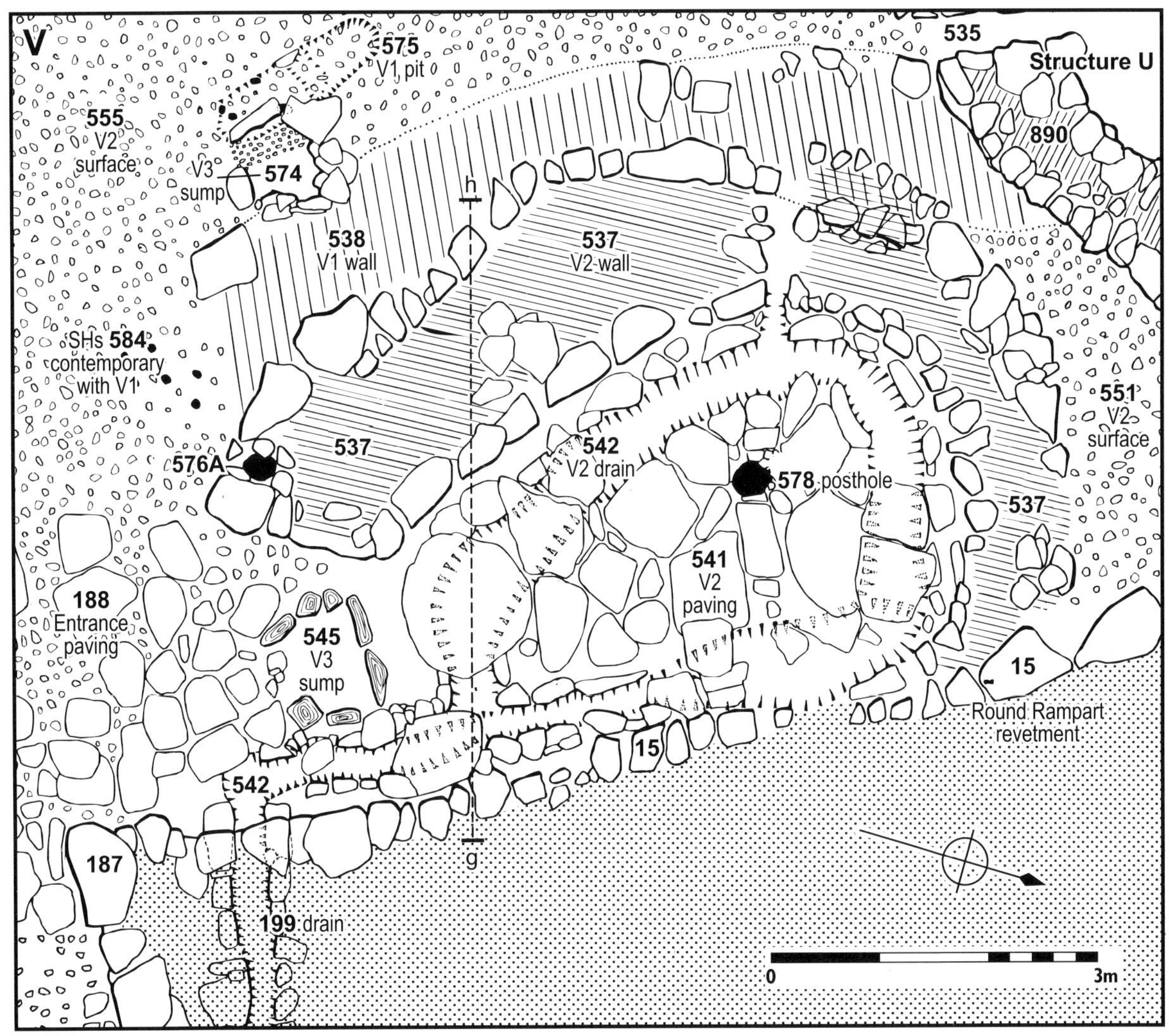

Fig 13: Structure V plan

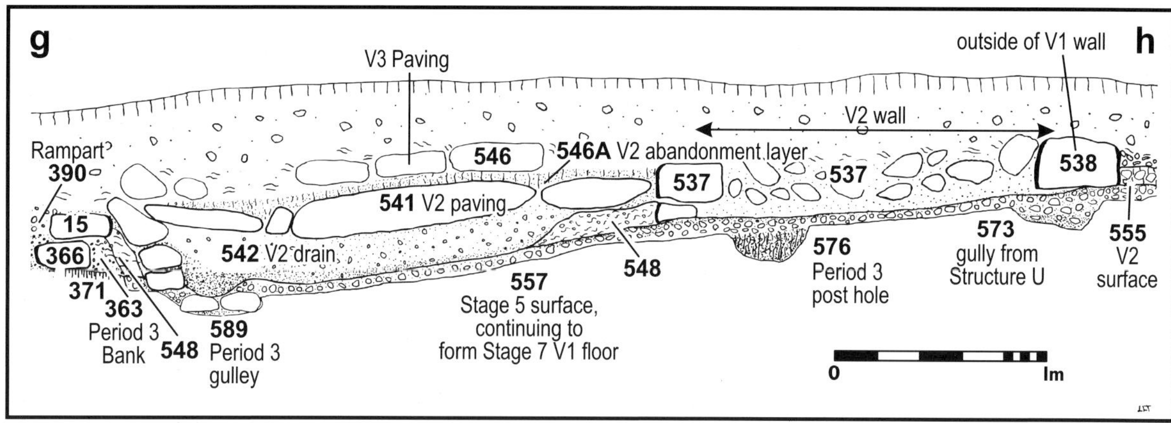

Fig 14: Section g-h across Structure V

features. Wall [538] was much eroded, or robbed away, and most of its external face was missing (section g-h, Fig 14).

Outside, to the west and possibly contemporary, was pit [575], 1.6m across and 0.6m deep. This was cut into cobbles [557], on which trampled upcast lay, and covered by later cobbles [555] (see below). Patches of charcoal and traces of burning were found around the edge of pit [575], with a setting of small cobbles adjacent to its east lip. The central part of its base was 0.3m deeper than the remainder, and four stakeholes were set to one end. Its fill was of fine dark, rather clayey, soil. A group of six stakeholes [584] were in a similar stratigraphical position to [575].

2.8.2 Structure V2

Structure V was rebuilt in Stage 8 as an oval structure 6m by 3m internally (Fig 15). Its new wall [537], between 1.2m and 2m wide, had been set into soil [548] and incorporated the former inner face of [538] as its outer side (Pl 17). This suggests that Structure V1 was much eroded before rebuilding. Wall [537] formed the west and north sides, curving round to abut the Rampart revetment which was again used as the east side. The entrance at the south was a 3m gap between wall [537] and the Rampart. A single posthole [576A] was set into the wall terminal. The interior was paved with large granite blocks [541] surrounding off-centre posthole [578], 0.3m deep, which may have supported a roof. A drain [542] ran around the interior beneath the paving (Pl 18). This was *c* 0.25m deep and filled with dark silt. Its edges were partially lined with orthostats, and it fed into [199] which ran under the north Rampart terminal (see above). Its capstones and sidestones had subsequently been removed at the north end and at the junction with [199], and the drain here had been filled with rubble. Outside, a new layer of cobbles [555] was laid, which were spread north-west to the entrance paving [528] of Structure U and south to

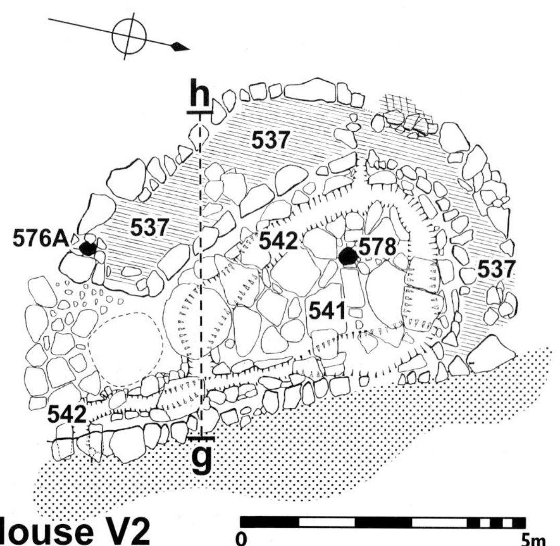

Fig 15: Phase plan of Structure V2

Pl 17: Structure V from south-west. Some V3 paving slabs [546] over V2 paving [541]; V1 wall [537] in foreground, Rampart fully excavated in background. 2m scale

Pl 18: North end of Structure V, V2 paving [541], drain [542], posthole [578]; core of V2 wall [537] removed; V1 wall [538] in background. Structure U top right. View from east. 2m scale

merge with the edges of the Entrance paving [188]; cobbles [551] were laid to the north (Fig 13) in the triangle between V2, U, and the Rampart.

2.8.3 Structure V latest phases

The latest levels of V were extensively disturbed by the plough. The interior appears to have been repaved, as a few paving blocks [546] survived at a high level both inside and outside the doorway (Fig 14). Paving [546] was separated from the main paving [541] by a dark soil level [546A] (Fig 14). Soil [546A] represented disuse and/or abandonment and was part of the same episode as, and continuous with, soil spread [140]-[523]-[400] (see above) which relates to a phase of disuse between Stages 9 and 10. Paving [546] belonged to the later reoccupation in this part of the site during Stage 10. The rough stone filling of drain [542], after the removal of capstones and sidestones at its junction with Rampart [199], was worn on its surface and formed a continuous level with upper paving [546] (Pl 17). This paving [546] was contemporary with stone-lined pit [545], 0.8m by 0.6m by 0.5m; the interstices between the sidestones were tightly packed with rab and the bottom was covered with iron pan. Its fill was of dark brown soil. The top of its lining stones were roughly on a level with the upper flags [546] (Fig 13). The function of [545] is not clear. It may have formed a sump for drainage, as the earlier drain [542] was now out of use. A second pit [574], similar to the suggested sump [545], was found just west of V, though only surviving 0.4m deep. Surface [546] had been cut into the upper cobbles [555]. These late features may be grouped for convenience as Structure V3 (Fig 89).

2.9 Period 5 Round Structure U, possible byre

No building was found in the area of Structure U until Stage 5. The main Structure, U1, possibly a byre, was built in that Stage contemporary with surface [557]. A midden, [932/801], accumulated within it during Stage 6, and a small structure U2 reused its east end in Stage 7.

2.9.1. Structure U1

Structure U in the north-east of the Round (Figs 16, 17, 18) was built in a levelled area, which removed many earlier features; the edge of this levelling [951] truncated the sequence relating to Stages 1-4 in Area Q (Fig 22). Its west end overlay House Z Stage 4 paving [949] and soil [808] which had accumulated on it. Its wall [890] sealed stakeholes [961] and [960], and posthole [963].

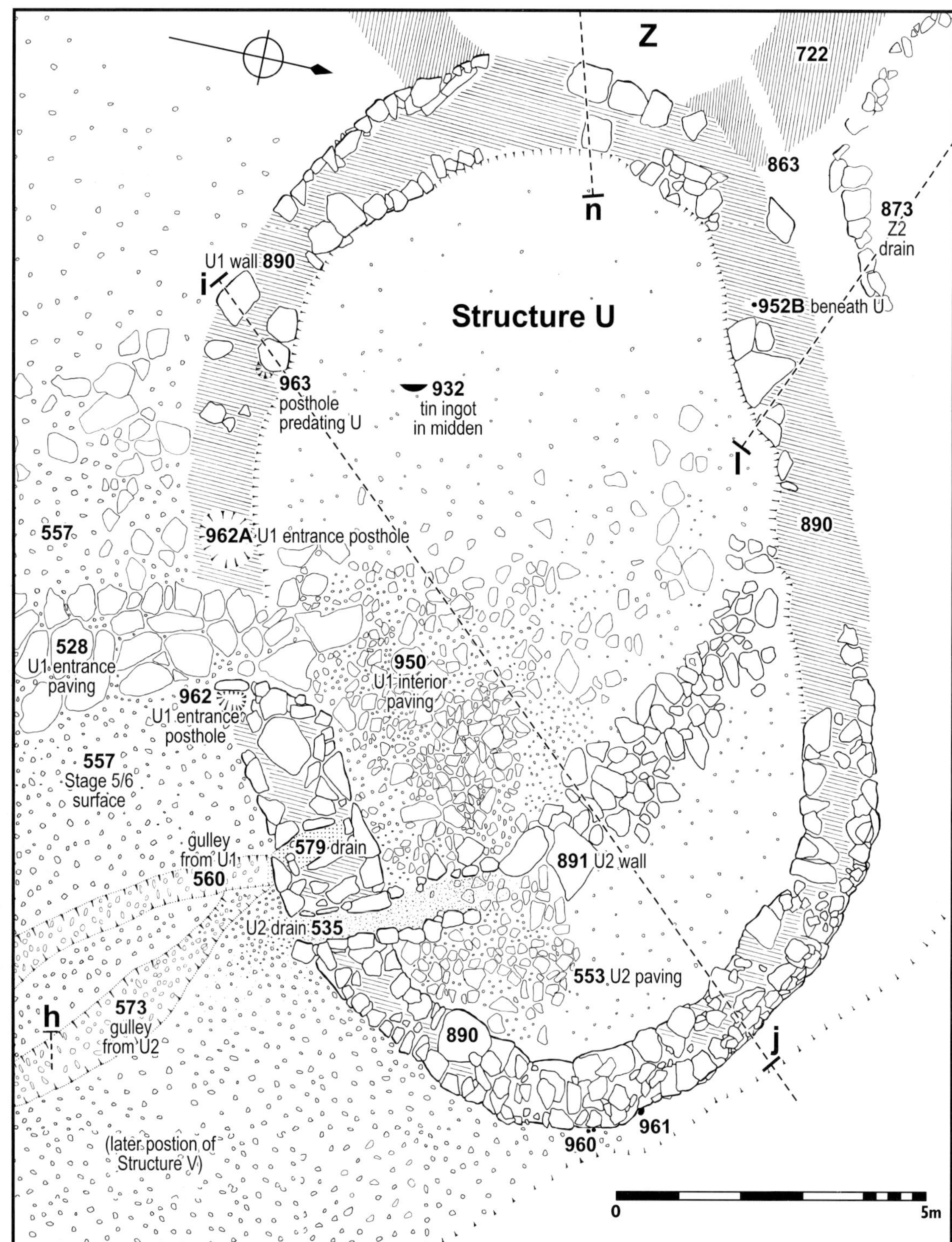

Fig 16: Structure U1, the byre, and U2 plan

The building (Fig 16) was oval in plan, 14m by 8m internally, with its long axis set down the slope. Its wall [890], between 1m and 2m wide, was a core of rubble and earth faced on both sides by granite blocks. It survived up to eight courses, 0.5m high, on the east, downhill side, but uphill all stonework had been removed (by ploughing) from long stretches. The entrance was almost centrally placed in the south wall, with a width of at least 1.5m, that of the threshold paving [528] which was noticeably worn. Walling west of the entrance did not survive but that to the east was several courses high and incorporated posthole [962], 0.15m deep, whose shape suggested that it may have held a semi-circular post *c* 0.4m across. The posthole may have supported one side of the door-frame, and was possibly paired with [962A], 0.10m deep, another posthole lying 2m to the east, in which case the original entrance would have been 2m wide.

The interior of U (Pl 19) had been slightly levelled and holes where rocks had been dug out back-packed with rab and small stones. A patchy paving [950] was laid directly on the levelled rab, extending the

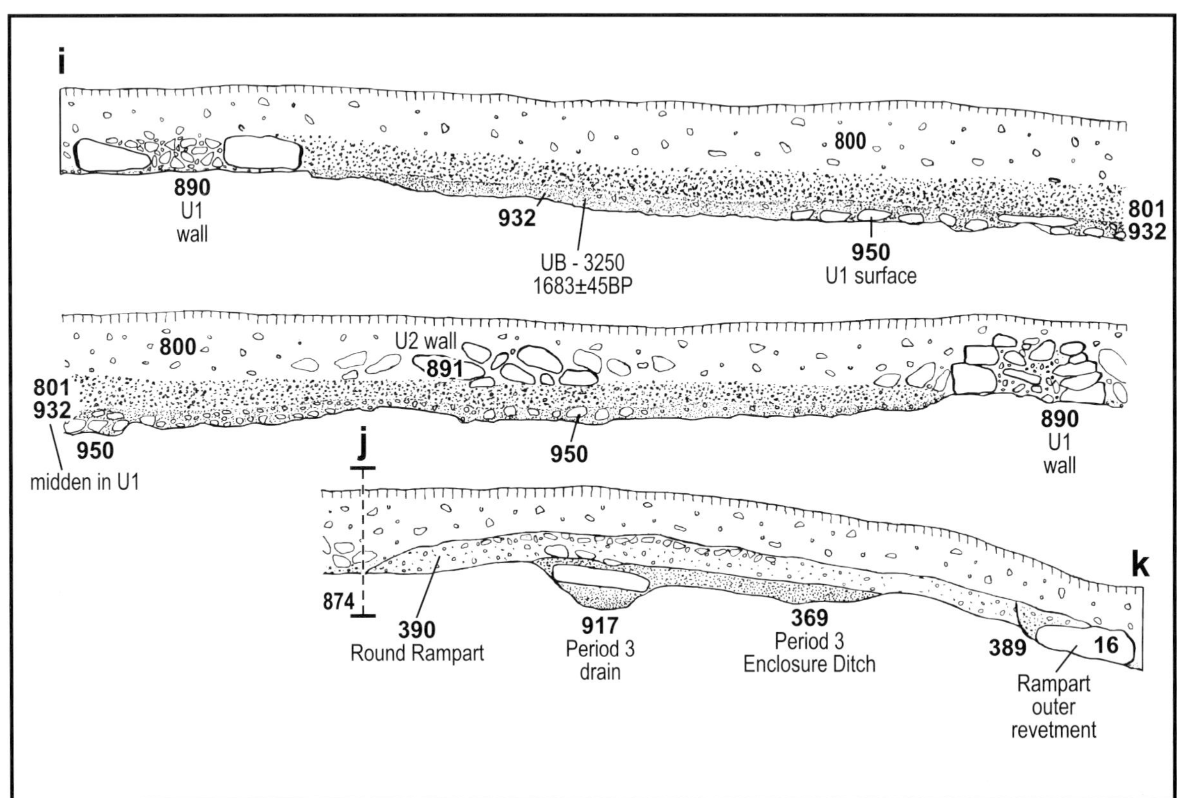

Fig 17: Sections i-j-k across Structure U and the Earthworks

threshold paving [528] into parts of the interior. Paving [950] was also worn. In the unpaved areas, the rab had been eroded leaving small stones projecting to form an irregular surface. There were no hearths or internal features. The interpretation of Structure U as a byre is discussed below (Section 11.13). It is assumed that Structure U was completed and roofed, but, in the absence of internal features, this cannot be demonstrated with certainty.

A drain [579] (Pl 19), lined with orthostats and 0.45m wide, was constructed integrally with the wall south of the entrance; its capping did not survive. There was no inlet from the interior. Externally it fed into gulley [573] up to 0.15m deep and, at a later stage, into [560] up to 0.2m deep, both of which had a silty fill mixed with stones indistinguishable from the surrounding cobbles [557]. These gullies fed into drain [199] beneath the north Rampart terminal (Section 2.6.3).

Structure U is assigned to Stage 5. Cobble surface [557], set directly on dirty rab, had been laid up against its wall [890]. Cobbling [557] formed an extension of the Entrance repaving [188] and its surface was continuous with [528], the Structure U entrance paving. West of [528] it merged with the sparse surfacing [48] in the centre of the Round. Its irregularity made it difficult to detect patchings. It is probable that cobbling [557] was laid contemporary with the early gulley [573] which acted as a soak with a stone fill, and that the later gulley [560] was cut through it and again filled with stone to form a simple soakaway.

2.9.2 Midden [932/801]

Over the initial worn internal surface of Structure U a compact soil [932] accumulated. This was c 0.1m thick, almost black and greasy with much charcoal, and contained the greatest concentration of pottery found on the site. Layer [932] passed gradually upward into a paler soil [801], 0.15-0.2m thick, which also contained many artefacts. These layers were contained within the interior of Structure U soil but did not extend as far as the Entrance. They probably represent a period of disuse in which the Structure became partly ruinous, as, in places, the soil spread a little over the line of the wall. Midden [932/801] appears to represent a continuous deposition of debris, which had contained a lot of ash and which may be referred to as a midden. It is assigned to Stage 6 and provided the only large assemblage of artefacts on the site. Layer [932] produced radiocarbon determination UB-3250 of cal AD 240-440 at 95% confidence (Section 9.1).

2.9.3 Structure U, later use

After midden [932/801] had accumulated, the lower, eastern, end of Structure U was rebuilt, in Stage 7, as Structure U2 (Figs 16, 17, 18). A roughly piled stone bank or wall [891], 0.4m high, cut across the easternmost 3m of wall [890], which was presumably rebuilt, to form a crude semi-circular structure. This later structure had an entrance gap 1.8m wide with rough paving [553]. Drain [535] (Pl 19) had been cut through wall [890]; it appeared to have been

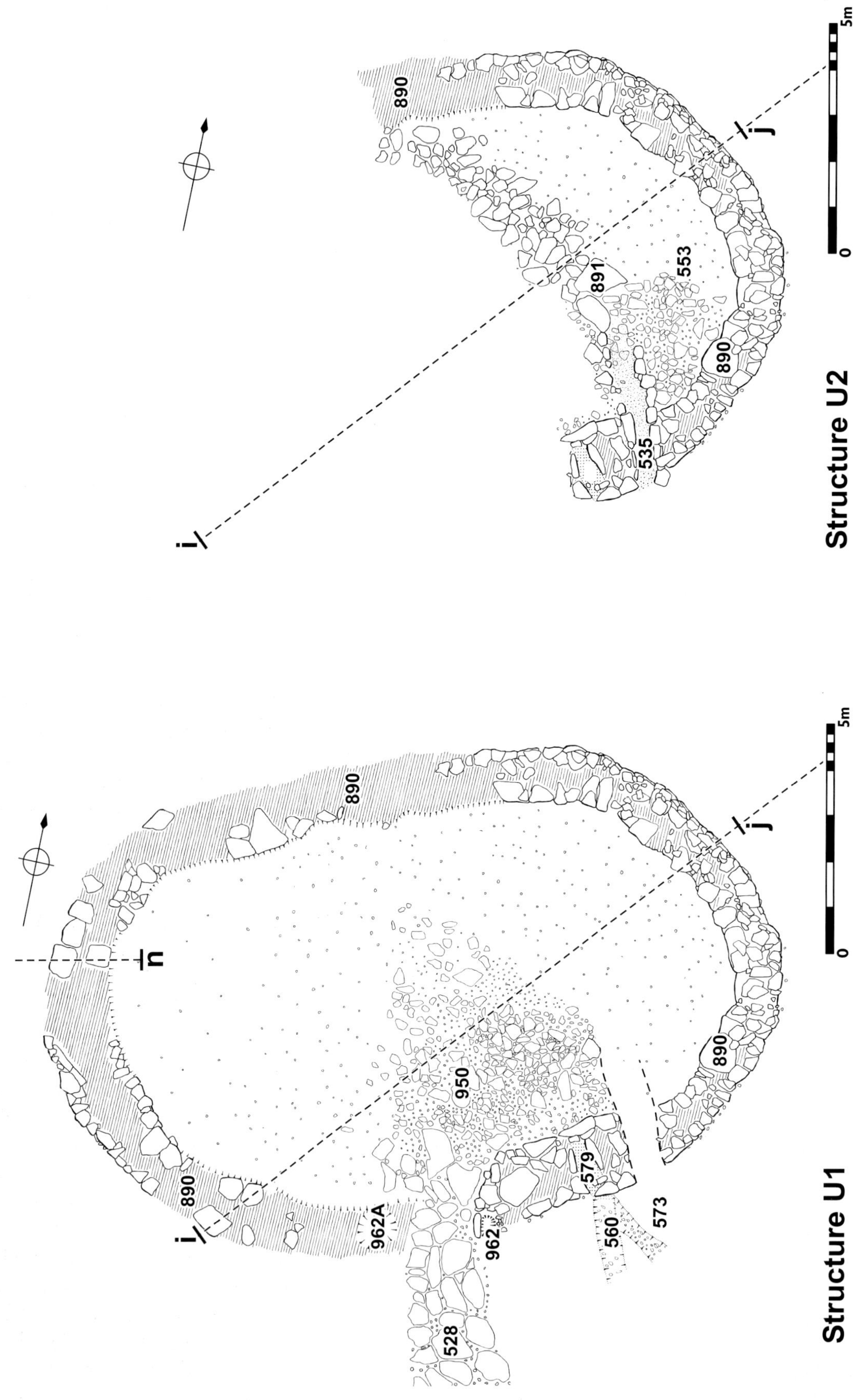

Fig 18: Phase plans of Structures U1 and U2

Pl 19: South-east part of Structure U showing internal surface [950], gullies [535] and [579] outside; soak/surface [409] exposed behind Rampart; Structure V removed. Entrance entirely excavated top left. View from north. 2m scale

constructed together with wall/bank [891] and to have run across the entrance to Structure U2. The capstones of drain [535] had been removed but they would have been level with paving [553].

Subsequently, perhaps during Stage 9 or the Stage 9/10 hiatus, wall [891] collapsed, leaving a tumble of stones in the east part of U. Ploughsoil [800] over Structure U contained a large number of finds, probably derived from disturbance of midden [932/801].

2.10 House Z

House Z lay on the north side of the Round, well away from the Rampart; the intervening space was taken by structures in Area Q. It had two distinct phases; Z1 could be divided into subphases Z1a Stages 1-3 and Z1b Stage 4, whilst Z2 belonged to Stages 6-9. There appears to have been no building here while Structure U1, immediately to its east, was in use during Stage 6.

2.10.1 House Z1

For House Z1 (Figs 19, 21; Pls 20, 21) a complex sequence of features, assigned to Stages 1-4, was recorded. Its floor was covered by soil [808] which accumulated during a period of disuse, and its east end was cut away, in Stage 5, by the levelling for the building of Structure U. The sequence of features in House Z1 can be related to the ancillary sequence in Area Q to its north. The features are described here in basic detail. The arguments for chronological division will be rehearsed in the discussion on site chronology (Section 9.2).

House Z1 was defined on its uphill, west, side by three drainage gullies, presumably successive (Pl 21). That furthest downhill [761] underlay the north and west parts of House Z2 wall [722]. It was irregular, up to 1m wide and 0.3m deep, and filled with a mixture of redeposited rab and dark brown silt, charcoal-flecked, with a fair quantity of pottery. At its east end it ran out into, and may have been contemporary with, the levelling cut [916] in Area Q (Section 2.11.3). Gulley [761] cut through gulley [764] to its west (section p-pp, Fig 12). This was of similar irregularity and dimensions, but its fill was less dark and contained less pottery and organic debris. Gulley [765], 0.2m wide, uphill and west of [764] had no stratigraphic relationships. It was in general similar to the other two gulleys but its fill contained even less organic debris and was lighter in colour. It is suggested that [765] was the earliest of the gullies and that this was twice replaced, each time further downhill. Gulley [765] is assigned to Stage 1, [764] to Stage 2, and [761] to Stage 3.

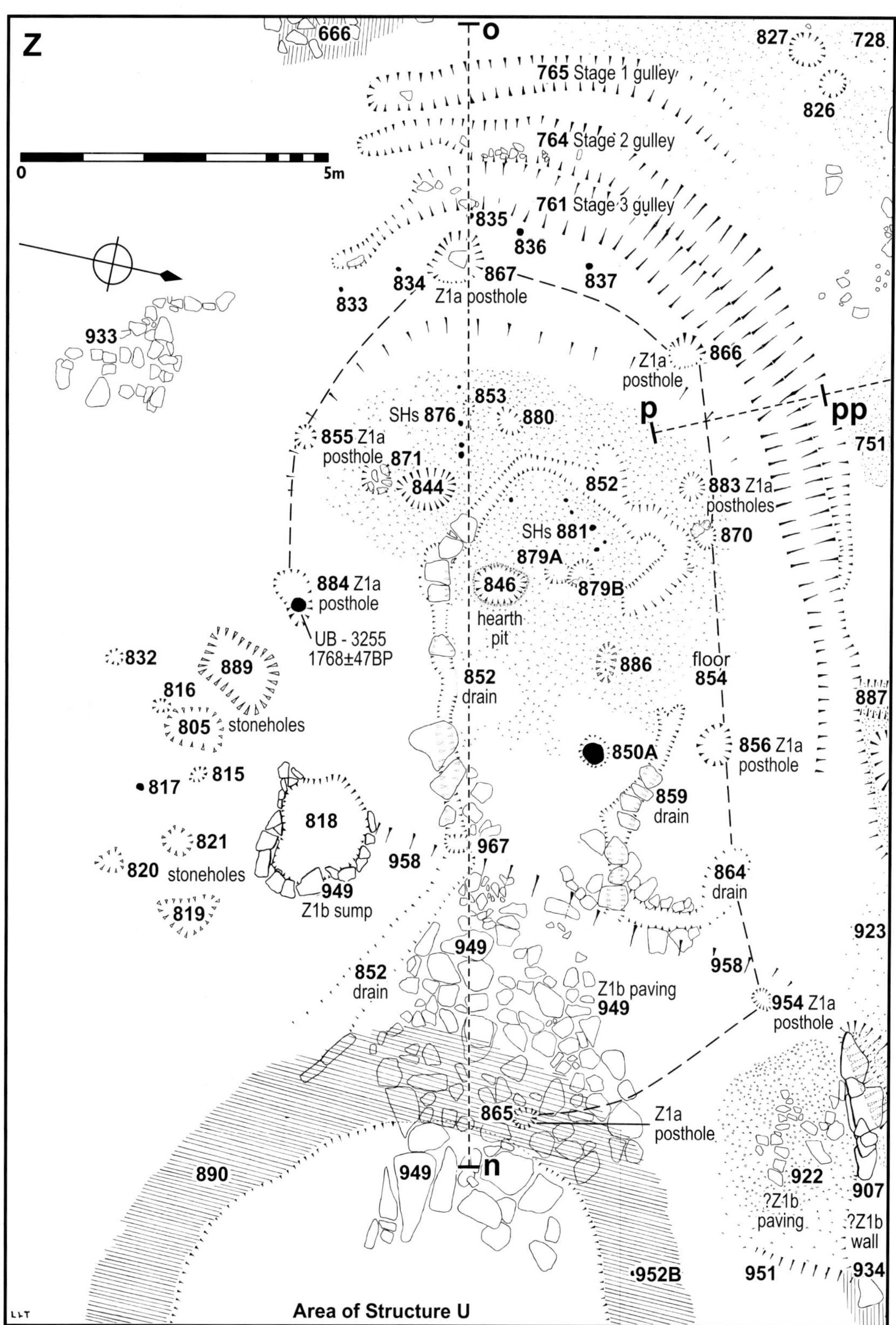

Fig 19: House Z1 plan

The site had been prepared by the removal of a number of large stones from the rab whose holes had been packed with a soil and rab mixture ([805], [819], [820], [821], [886], and [889]).

The dimensions of House Z1 cannot be accurately established as no wall survived and its east side was truncated by Structure U but 16m by 7m is a minimal estimate. House Z1 may have had at least two structural phases, referred to as Z1a and Z1b (Section 9.2.6). Postholes [884], [855], [867], [866], [883], [870], and [856] form a reasonably regular curve inside the east and north of the House and may have been related to an inner wall face, as in House T2. Postholes [954] and [865], although less regularly placed, might continue this curve on the north-west and west. All these postholes had an identical packing

Pl 20: House Z2, general view from north-east; position of House X in background. 2m scale

Pl 21: House Z, west end; Z1 gullies [764], [761]. Z2 wall [722] collapsed into interior as [723]. View from north. 2m scale

of rab and stones; depths are given in the Context List. Of these, postholes [866] and [867] were sited too close to gulley [761] to allow much thickness of wall; the postholes may have belonged to Z1a, Stages 1-3, when gulleys [764] and [765] were in use. Postholes [871], [853], [880], [879A], [879B], and [850A] form an inner, less even, curve and just possibly may have held roof supports. If not they must have been for internal fittings as must [844] and [967]. Posthole [884] produced radiocarbon determination UB-3255 of cal AD 130-400 at 95% confidence (section 9.1). Postholes [832], [815], [816], and [817] probably lay outside the building to the south. Of all Z1 postholes only [850A] and [884] had defined postpipes and the only recut was [879B] replacing [879A].

The interior of House Z1 was divided into two parts, both levelled *c* 0.1m into the hillside at their west end. The uphill part had been floored by tamped redeposited rab [854], 0.03-0.05m thick, which survived only patchily; it had a smooth surface in places. Three drains [852], [859] and [864] (Fig 19) had been cut *c* 0.2m deep beneath the floor. Their capstones, worn on the surface, survived only for short distances. The drains were filled with dark-brown silt. Drain [852] continued down through the lower, east part and [859] probably did so originally; this area was much disturbed by drain [863] of the later phase, Z2.

There was no hearth but [846] was a central hearth pit. This was 0.8m by 0.6m by 0.1m deep. It was lined with hard yellow clay and lumps of charcoal; its lower fill was fine red-brown soil, the upper part clay soil burnt bright orange. There were two groups of stakeholes [876] and [881] in floor [854]. Paving [933] just outside House Z to the south-west could not be related to any phase in the building.

The east, downhill part, defined on its upper side by levelling cut [858], accumulated soil [948] upon it (Fig 21), possibly relating to Z1a. It is probable that [907] (Figs 19, 22) formed part of the Z1b wall in Stage 4, thus representing an extension. This was paved with [949], of small worn blocks, over soil [948], of which paving [922], abutting wall [907] to the north, may have been a continuation. Layer [949] also extended

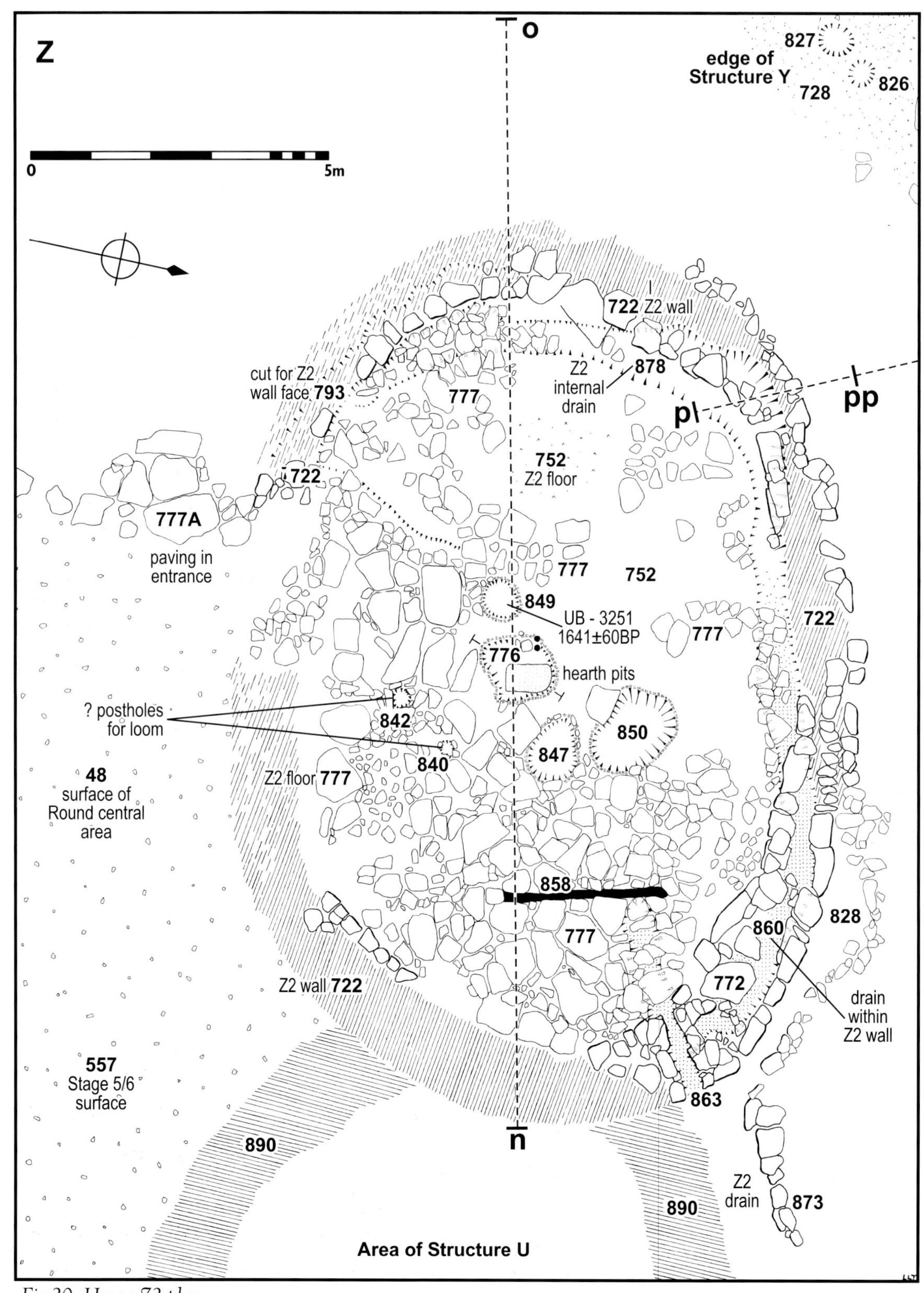

Fig 20: House Z2 plan

to [818], a stone-lined drainage sump 0.40m deep filled with small stones (Fig 19).

Both parts of House Z1 were covered by dark-brown soil [808], up to 0.2m thick, which contained much domestic debris (Fig 21). To the west it filled the uphill levelling cut but did not continue beyond to seal the gulleys [761] to [765]. On the north-east in Area Q, [808] rested up against the top of wall [907] sealing rubble collapse [907A]. It only survived as a distinguishable layer where it was sealed by House Z2 stonework. Its accumulation presumably represents a gap in the structural use of this part of the site, during Stage 5.

2.10.2 House Z2

House Z2 (Figs 20, 21; Pl 20) was constructed after the west end of Structure U had become ruinous, as Z2 floor [777] incorporated part of [890], the east wall of Structure U. Its construction is assigned to Stage 6 and it appears to have had a long life, probably until Stage 9.

The House, about 12m by 8m internally, was set with its long axis down the slope. It had been much damaged by ploughing, most of the south wall being removed and the west, uphill part of interior paving [777] disturbed. Its external wall [722] had stone facing either side of a rubble and earth core; it widened from c 1m to 1.5m around the exit for drain [863] (Fig 20). On the uphill end, a cut [793] in the rab provided a seating for its inner face; the outer face was set at a higher level and partly overlay the Z1 gulley [761] which had caused slumping. The inner edge had also slumped on the north-west, into the internal drain [878] (section p-pp, Fig 12). The possibility that wall [722] incorporated part of an earlier wall, from House Z1, is discussed in the section on chronology (Section 9.2.6). The entrance, about 2m across, was west of centre in the south side, where remnant paving [777A] survived across the wall-line and outside the building. The interior had been paved with large granite blocks [777], bedded in places with a small amount of grey clay [861]. These blocks were much worn. From the number of blocks lying scattered in the base of plough soil over the west, uphill end and the position of the surviving paving *in situ*, it is probable that most of the interior was originally paved, although in places the top of the underlying soil [808] may have been used as floor [752] (section n-o, Fig 21). At the east end, the paving had been set to leave a distinct slot [858], which presumably had held a timber (Pl 22). Slot [858] was 2.4m long, 0.1m wide and between 0.2m and 0.3m deep. To the south were two postholes [840] and [842], both 0.20m deep, set in paving [777]. These would have been of appropriate size and spacing to have held a loom.

Within the interior, careful provision had been made for drainage. A soak drain [878] ran along the inside of the wall in the uphill part. This was filled with

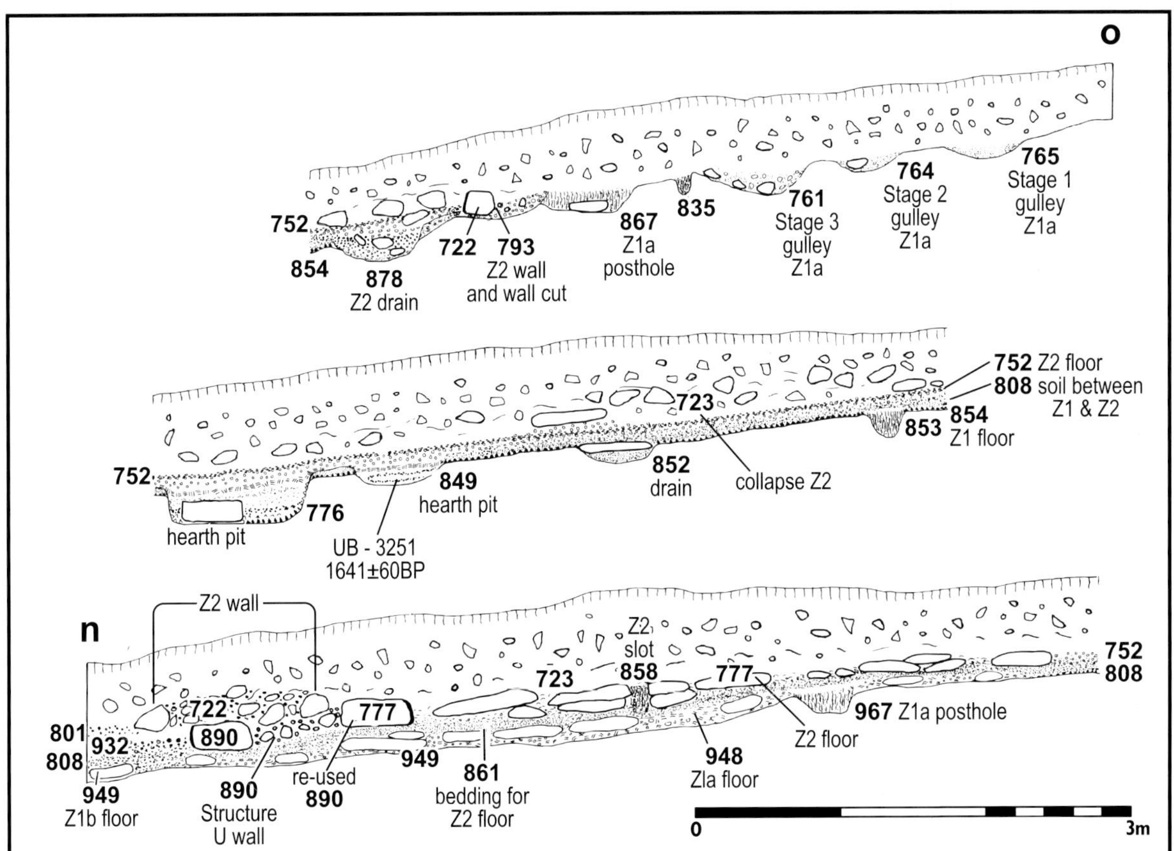

Fig 21: Section n-o across House Z

stones and dark soil, 0.2m deep. It led beneath the north wall which, in its east part, had been specially constructed to incorporate it. Drain [878], where built into wall [722], was distinguished as context [860]. A second drain [863], cut into underlying Z1 levels and rab directly east of slot [858], was capped by floor paving [777]; it was filled with stones and dark soil. A stone-lined channel had been provided for drain [863] through wall [722], and drain [860] joined it in this channel. Downhill, outside House Z2, drain [863] fed into drain [873] built against the outer wall of Structure U for *c* 12m (Fig 5) down almost to the Rampart. However, the junction between exterior drain [873] and the rampart revetment was eroded. A rough drain [828], external to the north wall of House Z2, also led into drain [873].

Four hearth pits [776], [849], [847], and [850], were set in paving [777] in the centre of the building, and may be presumed to have been successive. Possibly the earliest [776] (Fig 27), 1m square and 0.37m deep, was lined with hard-packed rab into which a large stone was set. There was 0.03m of charcoal on the lining around the stone with 0.05m of mixed charcoal and dark soil above. Dark soil with rab lumps filled up the pit over the stone but the very top was covered with a clay layer incorporating charcoal burnt orange-red; there were two stakeholes in this clay. It appears that pit [776] was first used as a hearth pit and subsequently as a hearth at floor level. The second hearth pit [849] was circular, 0.6m across and 0.15m deep; this produced radiocarbon determination UB-3251 of cal AD 250-560 at 95% confidence (Section 9.1). It was filled with fine dark soil incorporating a band of charcoal and again had a top layer of burnt orange clay. Hearth pit [847] was more irregular, 0.8m by 1m and 0.3m deep. Its edge was burnt orange-red around the top; it was filled with dark soil and charcoal. The final hearth pit [850] was also irregular, 1.6m by 1m and 0.25m deep. Its sides were partly lined with rab and were heavily burnt around the top. It was infilled with dark soil, charcoal and stones, some of which were burnt.

A brown soil [723] mixed with some wall tumble covered the undisturbed parts of House Z2 and a

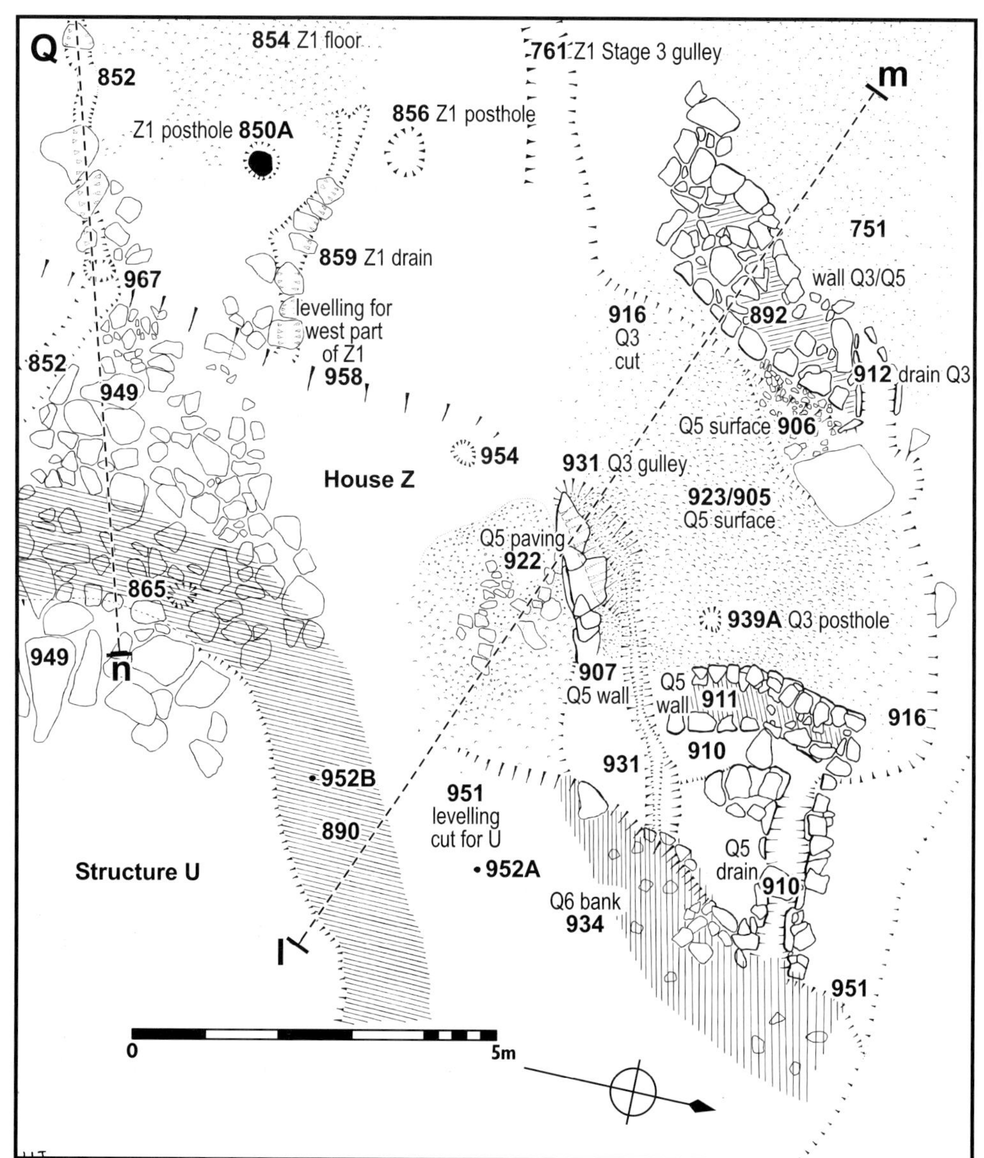

Fig 22: *Plan of structural sequence in Area Q*

Pl 22: House Z2; slot [858] in paving [777]; wall [722] with drain [860] in foreground, rubble over external drain [828] in immediate foreground. View from north. 2m scale

similar soil mixed with stones of varying sizes covered the remainder (Pl 21); these deposits relate to the abandonment of the House.

2.11 Structures between House Z and the Rampart, Area Q

Levels and structures in this area (Figs 9, 22, 23) survived in a fragmentary state because a sequence of levelling had left remnants of the earlier phases only at the west, uphill, end. All activity described below postdated the Rampart of the Round and the earliest part of the sequence truncated the eroded Period 3 Enclosure Bank [780] (Section 2.5.2) and Period 4 Structure N. It is probable that the structures here were not houses but small ancillary buildings, which used the Rampart as their north side. The structures described as Q1 to Q6 are therefore of a different kind to those so far discussed and are incomplete because of levelling cuts associated with successive phases. Structures Q1 to Q5 were contemporary with House Z1, Q6 with House Z2.

2.11.1 Structure Q1

A cut [903] for an area of levelling (Figs 9, 23), 0.2m deep, cut away Period 3 Bank [780] and Structure N but extended as far as the Rampart of the Round, which it appeared to postdate. Gulley [887], 0.15m deep and filled with brown soil, continued the

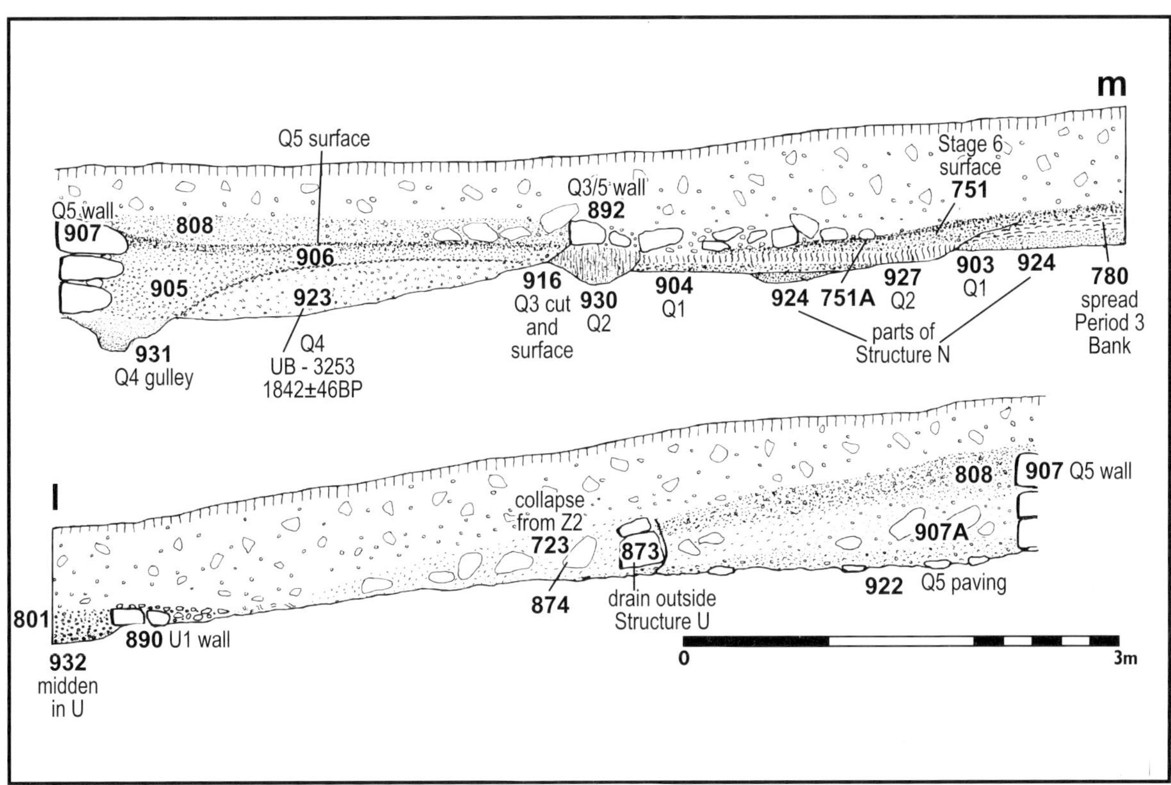

Fig 23: Section l-m across Area Q

line of cut [903] until truncated by gulley [761] associated with a late phase of House Z1. The levelled area defined by [903] (Stage 1) had a worn base but no structure could be associated with it. Its east edge was cut away by [916] (Section 2.11.3). The levelled area was covered by [904] (Fig 23), a gritty yellow-brown soil, with [927], a more clayey soil, above. Q1 is assigned to Stage 1.

2.11.2 Structure Q2

A group of postholes [894], [929], [930], [914], [966C], and [966D], and stakehole [957], were set into the compact surface of [927]. These appeared to form a rough line between House Z and the Rampart. This postline was covered over by soil [751] which had been gradually accumulating over soil [780] to the west (see Structure Y, Section 2.12). The line is assigned to Stage 2.

2.11.3 Structure Q3

Wall [892] (Figs 22, 23), built over some accumulation of soil [751], roughly followed the postline [894]-[914] beneath [751] and may have initially formed a freestanding division. Drain [912], lined with orthostats on either side, was constructed with wall [892] and allowed for drainage through it. The cut for the levelled area [916] followed the outer face of [892] and appeared contemporary to it; the edge of the latest Z1 gulley [761] appeared to be continuous with cut [916]. The base of [916] was slightly worn with a solitary posthole [939A] set in it. Cut [916] and its worn base was sealed by layers [905] and [923]. Wall [892] and levelled area [916] are assigned to Stage 3.

2.11.4 Structure Q4

A dump [923] of mixed materials, rab, white sand, white clay, burnt clay lumps, and charcoal, lay on the base of cut [916]; this was delimited to the south by a narrow gulley [931] 0.2m deep with a grey-brown silt fill (section l-m, Fig 23). Layer [923] produced C14 determination UB-3253 of cal AD 70-330 at 95% confidence (Section 9.1). Gulley [931] appeared to continue the line of Z1 levelling cut [958] which seated paving [949]; it was truncated to the east by levelling cut [951]. Structure Q4 appeared to have consisted of wall [892] with a platform [923] in front of it, drained by gulley [931]. It is assigned to an early part of Stage 4.

2.11.5 Structure Q5

Both the dump [923] and the gulley [931] were covered by another dumped soil [905] and revetted by walls [907] and [911] to form a level platform running east from wall [892]. This soil [905] formed the base of a hard, probably trampled, surface between these three walls, with a small patch of cobbles [906] upon it adjacent to wall [892] (Fig 22). Wall [907] may have formed part of the Z1 walling in Stage 4. Structure Q5, consisting of walls [907], [911], and earlier wall [892], appeared to have been an irregular rectangle between House Z1 and the Rampart, which would have formed its north side. Drain [910] had been built with coursed stones, not orthostats, against the outer, east side of wall [911] (Pl 23), and turned at right-angles downhill; this was truncated by later cut [951]. Some capstones survived in places on drain [910]. The junction of [907], [911], and [910] was almost totally eroded. Structure Q5 is assigned to a late part of Stage 4.

Paving [922] lay to the south of wall [907], probably originally continuous with paving [949] in House Z1b (Stage 4); the area was disturbed by later drain [873]. Paving [922] was covered by soil [808], a continuation of the soil over House Z1, again containing much domestic debris. Adjacent to wall [907], and partly over its stub, soil [808] merged with tumble [907A]. Structure Q5 appears to have gone out of use at the end of Stage 4, at the same time as

Pl 23: Drain [910] in front of wall [911], Structure Q5; rab core of wall [911] removed. View from east. 2m scale

House Z1. Wall [892] was not covered by soil [808]; it projected up to the base of ploughsoil and remained in use for some time, possibly until Stage 6.

2.11.6 Levelling cut [951] postdating Q5

The external features of Structure Q5 and soil [808] were cut away to the east by the slight levelling cut [951] (Fig 22), which from its position and stratigraphy related to clearance for the building of Structure U in Stage 5. Soil [874] (Fig 23) which accumulated on the base of this cut, associated with stakeholes [952A] and [952B], was only a little lighter than soil [808] postdating House Z1. Soils [808] and [874] are typical of the normal hillwash deposit on the site. It is probable that soil deposition started with the first use of the Round, continued during the disuse of Z1 as [808] and subsequently during the use of Structure U as [874], so that, by the time of the construction of House Z2 and its external drains, there was a gentle but smooth and continuous slope between Structures U and Z and the Rampart.

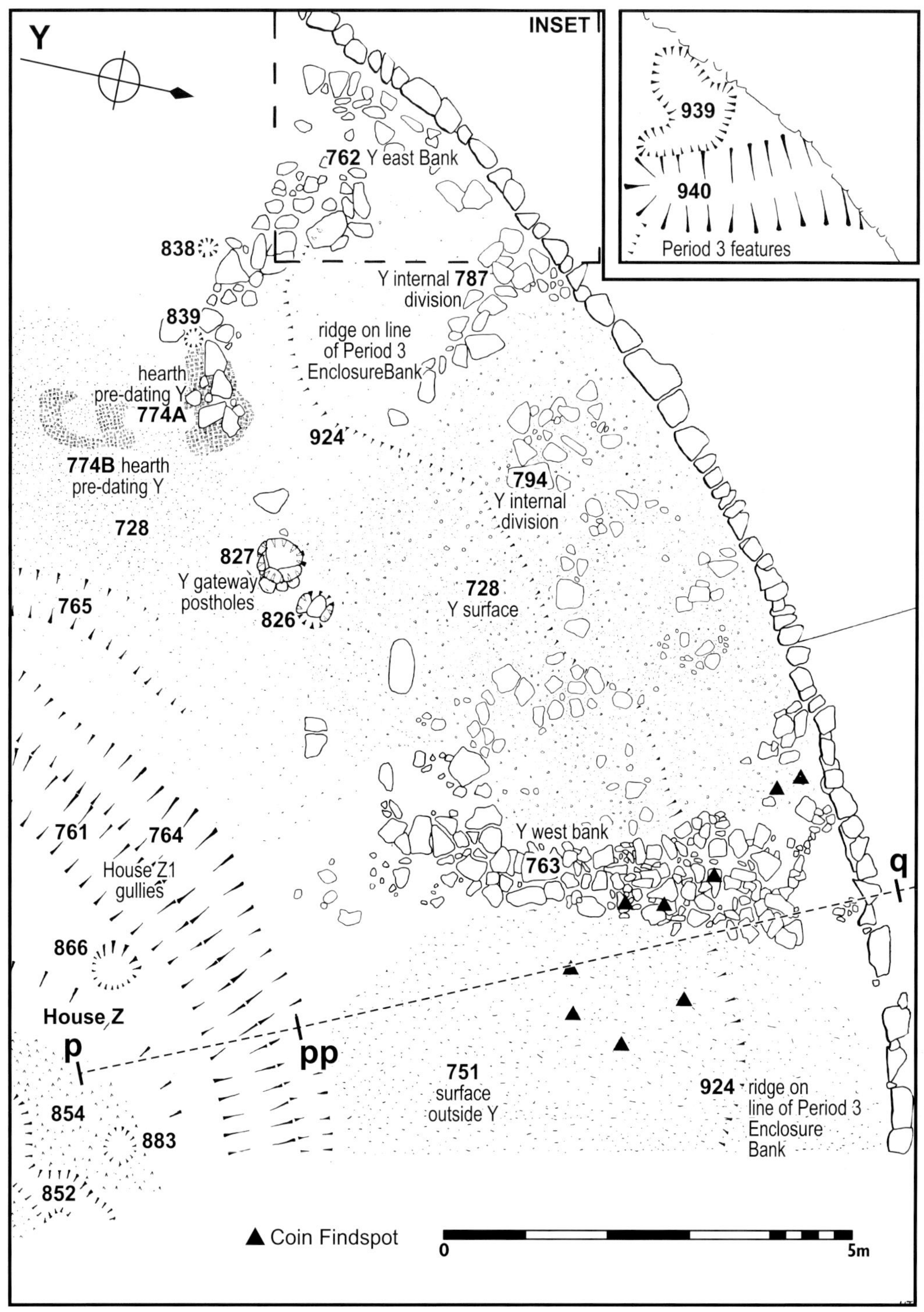

Fig 24: Structure Y plan

2.11.7 Structure Q6

In the east part of Area Q lay [934] (Fig 22), a rough rubble and soil bank 2m wide and up to 0.3m high. It was set over the slope formed by soil [874]/[808] (see above). Although the bank did not survive as far south as House Z2 or its external drain [873], it appears probable from its stratigraphic position that it formed a division between Z2 and the Rampart. It is the latest surviving feature in the area, although wall [892] may also have survived this late (see above). Bank [934] may be tentatively assigned to Stage 6 onward and is referred to as Structure Q6.

2.12 Structure Y

The area (Fig 24) north-west of House Z appears to have been little used during the early stages of the Round. Soil [751A] (Fig 12) gradually formed inside the Rampart. The soil spread east, to be truncated by cut [916] relating to Structure Q3 (Section 2.11.3), and south and west towards the areas of X and Z. However the soil, never more than a few centimetres thick, did not preserve a sufficiently distinctive character for relationships with these structures to be determined. Areas of burnt clay [774A] and [774B] represent open hearths laid on soil [751A] predating the construction of Y (Fig 24). Postholes [838] and [839], both 0.15m deep, may have been associated; both were outside the surviving surfaces of Structure Y. Six coins, a small mid 3rd-century AD hoard (Section 3.1.1), were found in soil [751A], three sealed by the east wall [763] of Structure Y. Another coin was found in [728] (the surface of Structure Y) and two more in the overlying soil [785]. These three coins are of similar date and condition to the other six and formed part of the scattered hoard. Their positions indicate considerable disturbance and movement of soils in this area.

Structure Y was a rough enclosure, 4m by 8m, built against the Rampart, on top of soil [751A] (Fig 24; Pl 24). Its stone and soil banks, [762] and [763], survived up to 0.5m high; no postholes were found within them. As found, the entrance gap was c 4m wide but may have originally been narrower as the banks diminished in height away from the Rampart and may have been eroded. A pair of postholes, [826] 0.3m deep and [827] 0.1m deep, apparently centrally positioned, may have formed part of a gateway. Compacted surface [728] covered the interior of Y but spread beyond the entrance; the top of packing stones in [826] and [827] were level with [728]. This surface had formed on the top of soil [751A] and was contained by banks [762] and [763]. A similar surface [751] ran east outside Structure Y to link with wall [892], suggesting that Y was in use while at least [892], part of Structure Q3, was still standing. In the interior of Y two rough heaps of stone and earth, [787] and [794], interrupted surface [728] and would appear to be eroded remnants of internal fittings or divisions. The construction of Y is assigned to Stage 6.

Brown soil [785] accumulated within Structure Y over surface [728]. It contained tumbled runs of stone [749] (section p-qq, Fig 12) which appear to have derived from the slow collapse of the structure. Tumble [749] survived best against the Rampart; the outer area had been much plough damaged.

2.13 House X

The area of House X (Figs 25, 26, 28; Pl 24) in the west, uphill part of the Round, had suffered much from plough erosion except immediately adjacent to the Rampart. House X was situated on the platform along the east side of the Round defined by the cut for levelling of the interior of the Round. The rab subsoil here contained virtually no stone and enabled the detection of very slight features.

The House had been multi-period and was probably used through all Stages of the Round. The scraps of walling which survived, [666] and [669] on the east, [680] to the west, could all have belonged to one phase, presumably the latest, in which the axis of the House ran north-south; gulley [743] provided appropriate outer drainage on the uphill side. The other gullies, [665] and [734], appear to have belonged to structures with their axes in the other direction, east to west. Of these [665] is the earlier. Gulley [734] was overlain by the scrappy walling [680] of the suggested last phase. This gives a feasible sequence of gulley [665] and its associated structure, then gulley [734] and lastly [743] and the walling. However, it is probable that the earliest structure here was built entirely of timber. There was a greater concentration of postholes here than elsewhere on the site, but in no case did a posthole cut through a gulley. Postholes are only referred to below where they are relevant to the stratigraphic sequence or to the layout of structural phases in X.

2.13.1 House X1

Slots [652], [731], and [685] appeared to have been early in the stratigraphic sequence. These slots, the only ones found in the Round except for [168] and [292] in House D, were irregular, c 0.1-0.25m deep, with compact fills of back-packed rab and occasional stones and possible post-sockets; slot [685] appeared to postdate postholes [720] and [725]. They were all aligned east-west and all three became shallower at their east ends, from which lengths may have been

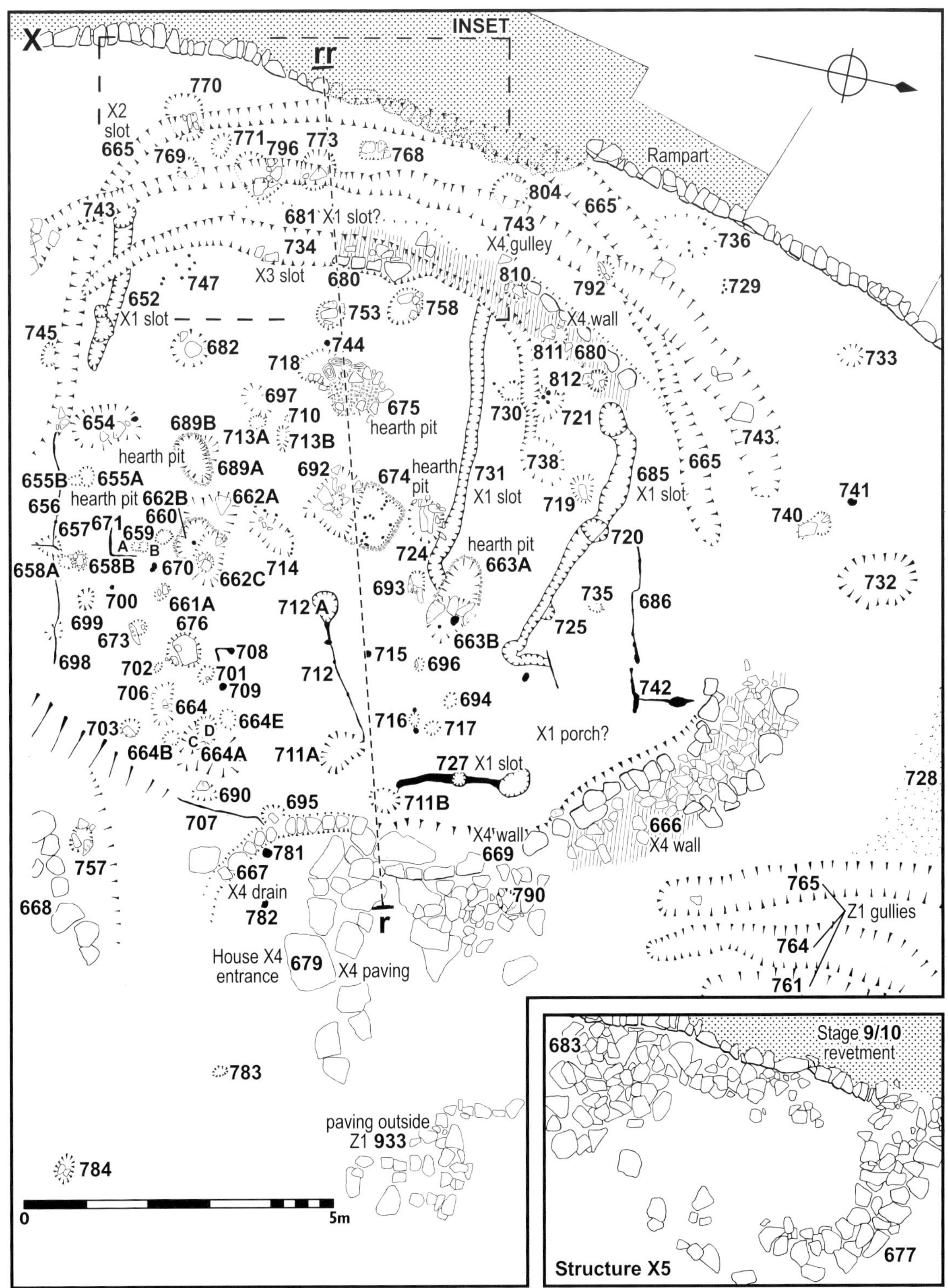

Fig 25: House X plan

removed by subsequent wear and erosion. These three slots may be interpreted as parts of a timber building, X1 (Fig 28). Slot [652] may have formed its south side and [685] its north, while its west side may have been formed by [681] (predating [734]). The latter slot was a shallow, irregular linear feature in the back-packed rab fill of which three defined post-sockets were located [810], [811], and [812]. Slot [727] may have formed part of the east side; its north end is symmetrical with the projection north from slot [685], suggesting a possible porched entrance. The south-west part of the suggested House X1 had not survived well, but a number of the smaller postholes such as [699] or [703] could be surviving remnants. The structure would have been c 8m square with an internal wooden division represented by slot [731]. It

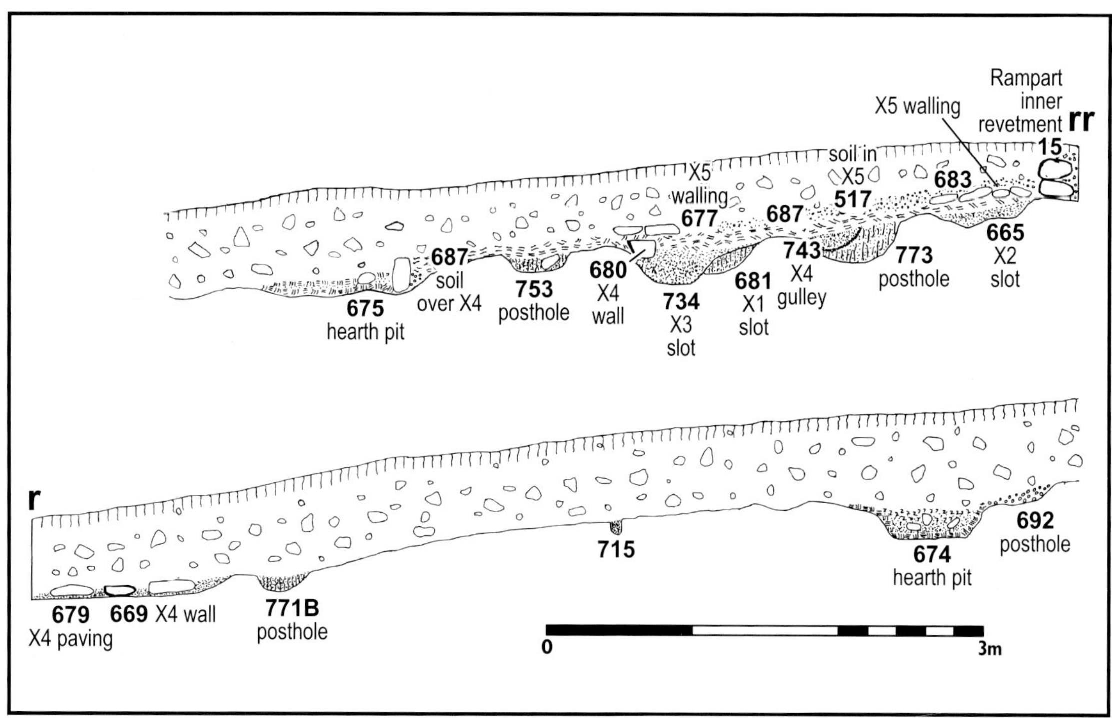

Fig 26: Section r-rr across House X

Pl 24: Area X, fragments of walling [680], [666], from House X4 on left and right in mid picture, hearth pit [674] in foreground. Structure Y in background. View from south. 2m scale

is possible that some of the postholes such as [796] and [773] cut by later gulley [743] could have formed an annex to the west. The timber House X1 is suggested as primary in this area of the Round and may belong to Stage 1.

2.13.2 Houses X2 and X3

Gulley [665], 0.3m deep, contained a charcoal-flecked fill of mixed dark soil and rab, which appeared as packed infill, not silt. It was cut through by gulley [734], 0.3m deep, which had a fill with much rab mixed in, with posthole [738] positioned at its north-west end. Both 'gulley' [665] and 'gulley' [734] could have been structural. It is not possible to relate any particular features to the structures of which these 'gullies' may have formed the uphill side, but the numerous postholes in the interior of the house allow for the incorporation of a range of substantial structural timbers. 'Gulley' [665] may have formed part of an oval timber House X2 aligned east-west down the slope, with its east side close to the Rampart; it is tentatively assigned to Stages 3-4. It was replaced by House X3 represented by a similar but smaller 'gulley' [734], again on an east-west alignment but set further down the slope leaving a 2m gap between it and the Rampart; it is assigned to Stages 5-7.

2.13.3 House X4

The House was remodelled on a north-south axis. Gulley [743], 0.2m deep, had the usual drainage fill of dark silty soil; it may have continued south of the main baulk as one of shallow gulleys [119], [120], and [120A] (Fig 29). The suggested House (Fig 28) it surrounded was oval, about 8m by at least 11m, and stone-walled with [666], [669], and [680] as surviving fragments; as usual walls were faced on both sides with stones and had an infill of rab, soil, and smaller stones. On the east, downhill side, walling [666] and [669] were set into the top of the levelling cut for the Round interior. The edge of the levelling cut indicated the oval shape of the House, even where walling had disappeared; this may have been recut to seat the walling. Walling [680] on the west side only survived where it had sunk into the fill of earlier features [734] and [681]. A length of stone-capped drain [667], 0.2m deep, ran out downhill through the east wall, possibly through the House entrance. Its capstones were worn. Fragmentary but worn paving [679] fringed the outer, downhill, side of the House, and contained posthole [790]. This paving extended into the probable entrance; it may originally have been continuous with [933] to the east and [668] to the south and have linked Houses X and Z. This paving was set in a brown soil [678], similar to the other hillwash deposits on the site; soil [678] spread to the north to merge indistinguishably with soil [751A] in Y, and did not provide relationships for features in this area ([732], [733], and [740]). Sherds of Late Roman 1 (Bii) amphora both in walling [666] and in gulley [743] suggest that House X4 is very late in the sequence on the site; it is assigned to Stage 9.

2.13.4 House X hearth pits and other features

There were five hearth pits, [662B], [663A], [674], [675], and [689B]. Of these, [662B], [663A], and [674] were cut through by postholes, the other two, [675] and [689B] postdated earlier features. The hearth pits are allocated, tentatively as for all features in X, to the Stage plans (Figs 80-88) on the basis that those cut through by other features are likely to be earlier than those which are cut by them.

Hearth pit [662B] was oval, 1.1m by 0.8m by 0.3m deep, cutting posthole [662A] and cut by posthole [662C]. Its upper edge was burnt and there was a layer of charcoal and ash on its base with yellow clay over it; the upper part was infilled with brown soil.

Hearth pit [663A] appeared to truncate the earlier slot [731] (associated with timber House X1). Pit [663A] was 1.4m by 0.8mm by 0.2m deep, with its

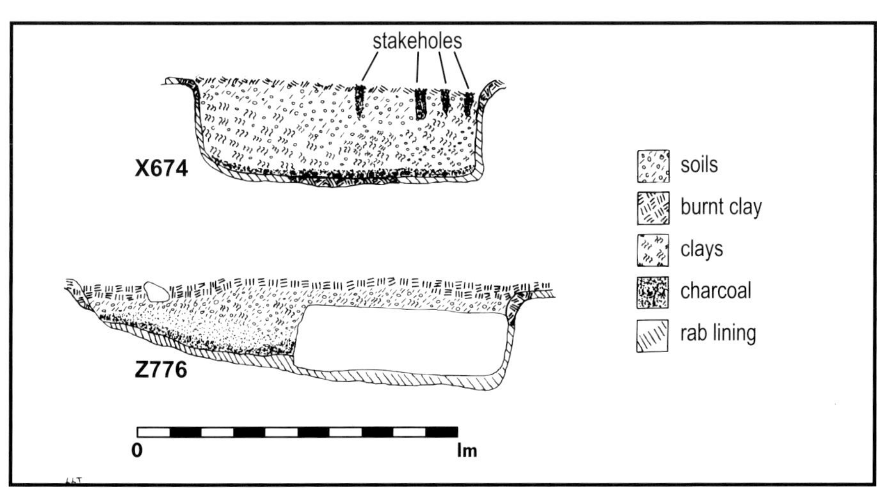

Fig 27: Sections of hearth pits. For position of [674] in House X see Fig 25, for [776] in House Z see Fig 20

Pl 25: Area X, hearth pit [674] cut by posthole [692] on left side. View from east. Scale 0.5m segments

upper edge burnt orange and filled by brown soil and charcoal; posthole [663B] cut [662A].

Hearth pit [674] (Fig 27, Pl 25) was rectangular, 0.8m by at least 1m and 0.3m deep, and cut through by posthole [692]. It was lined with redeposited rab, fire-hardened throughout but only burnt orange around the top. There was charcoal on the base of this lining, and the pit was infilled with brown soil mixed with lumps of rab varying in colour from yellow to (burnt) orange. The top of the fill appeared to have been burnt *in situ* with twelve stakeholes detectable in this burnt top. Posthole [692], cutting [674], contained a quantity of burnt and fire-blackened stones apparently used as post packing.

Hearth pit [675] lacked the burnt edge and was only 0.07m deep; it was irregular, 0.95m across and cut posthole [718]. Some stones were set upright around its edge. It was filled with brown soil and charcoal with lumps of burnt clay on its top.

Hearth pit [689B], cutting posthole [689A], was 0.8m by 0.4m by 0.25m deep, with burning around its top. There was a layer of charcoal and brown soil on its base above which the fill contained both charcoal and burnt rab lumps.

A number of narrow slots may have held interior wooden fittings — [656], [661A], [671], [686], [707], [708], [712], and [742] (Fig 28). These were V-shaped in profile, up to 0.1m deep but only 0.03-0.05m wide, and filled with fine very dark soil (Pl 26). In places they appeared to widen to distinct stake-sockets. They appeared to have first been cut by the tip of a spade and then widened out by ramming stakes in the grooves formed by the spade cuts. Slot [656] could be

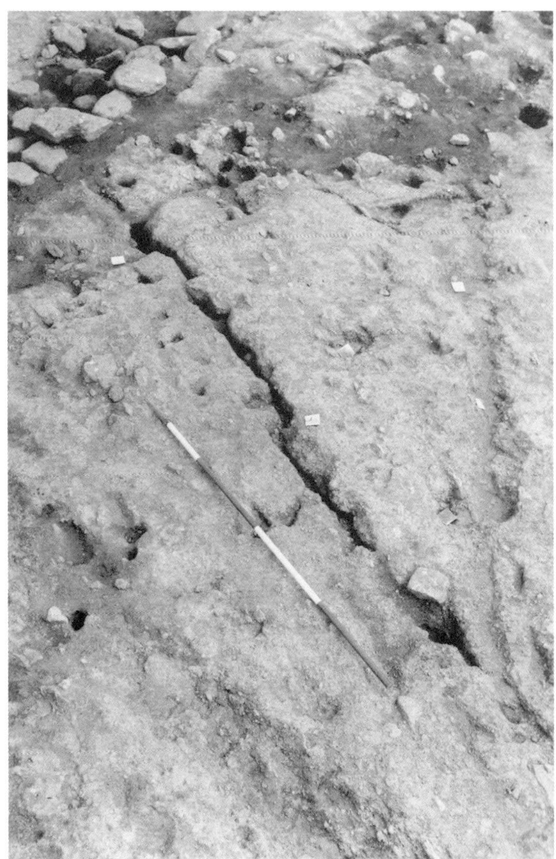

Pl 26: North-east part of House X, narrow slot [686], walling [666] House X4 top left, slot [685], unexcavated, to the right. View from north-west. 2m scale

traced across postholes [657] and [698]. Similar narrow slots were only otherwise found within and adjacent to Houses D and A where the rab subsoil was similarly stonefree. (However, if present, they should have been detectable in the laid rab floors of Houses Z and T.)

2.13.5 Structure X5

After House X4 ceased to be used, brown soil [687] accumulated over its site. Part of the Rampart inner revetment, its base weakened by gulley [665], had slumped forward over soil [687] (shown dotted in Fig 25). Structure X5, a small enclosure, (Fig 25, inset; Pl 27), 2m by 4m internally, had then been built, upon soil [687], with rubble and soil banks [677] and [683] against the Rampart. These banks were much disturbed by ploughing and were only three or four stones high. No associated surface or feature could be detected. The enclosure was infilled by a brown soil [517]. Downhill from Structure X5, soil [687] was not a distinctive layer and faded upwards into the base of ploughsoil. Structure X5, postdating House X4 of Stage 9, is assigned to Stage 10 and represents a reuse of the Round after some lapse of time; its function is unclear.

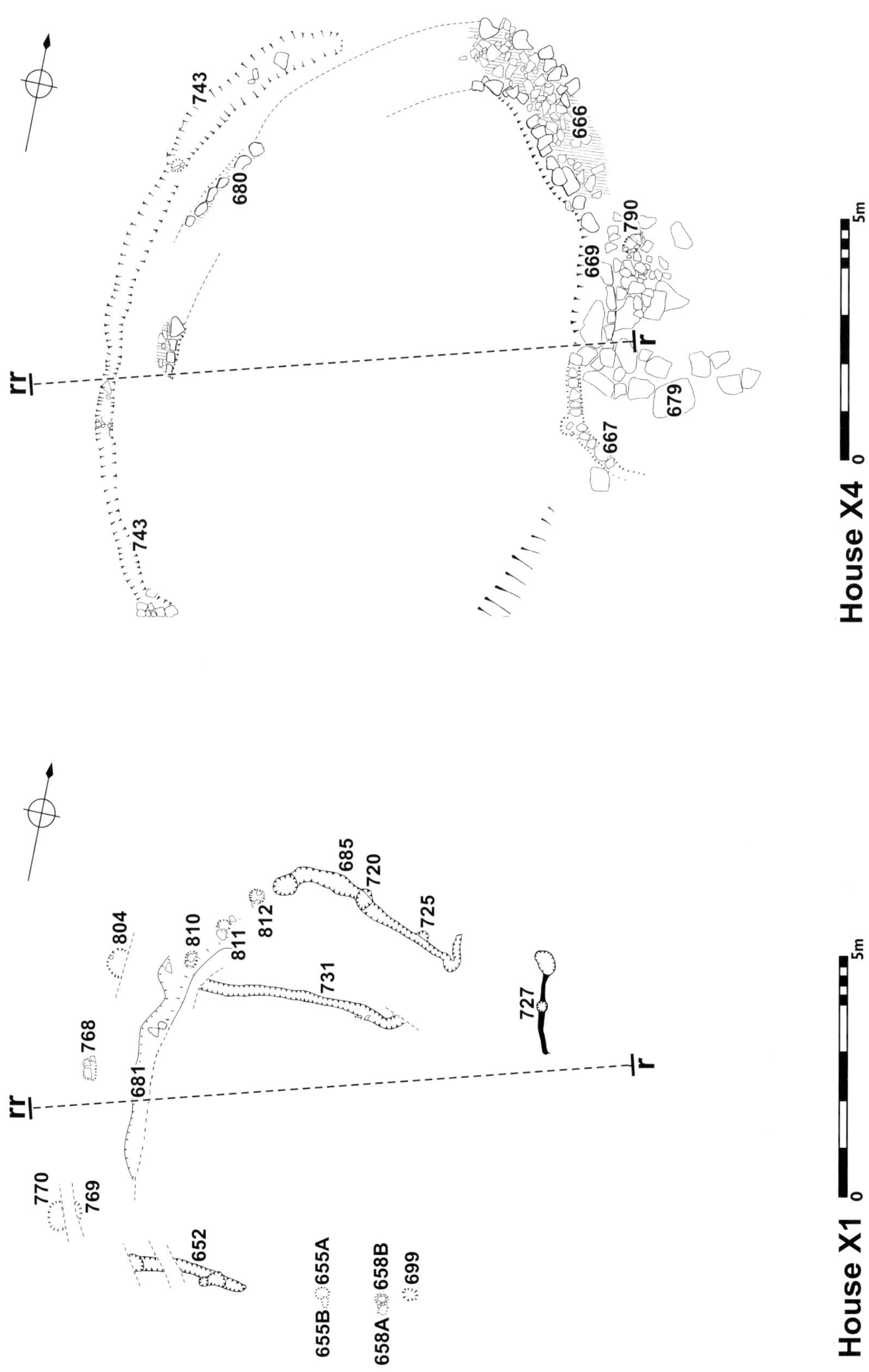

Fig 28: Phase plans of House X1 and House X4

Pl 27: Structure X5 with dump walls [677]/[683]. View from north. 2m scale

Pl 28: Shelf along upper side of Round; gulley [100], House A2, in foreground, House D4 and Structure E3 to rear. View from south. 2m scale

2.14 Structure E

This Structure (Fig 29) was situated adjacent to the Rampart on the ledge along the west, uphill, side of the Round (Pl 28). It was of three phases, each a simple rectangle.

2.14.1 Structure E1

The earliest phase of Structure E was set in four substantial roughly circular post pits, [282], [268], [145A], and [26] (Pl 30), each *c* 0.7m deep. The packing for all pits was of hard, mixed soil, rab and stones. Only [282] had a surviving postpipe filled with soft brown soil, 0.46m across and 0.65m deep. The post in [268] set 0.5m deep appeared to have been pulled out. Posthole [320A], 0.2m deep, was either earlier than, or related to, this phase as it was cut by posthole [320], 0.2m deep, which was partly covered by cobbles [310] of the subsequent phase. Structure E1 had no detectable floor surface. The relationship between post pit [26] and the end of gulley [153] of House D was not determinable. Structure E1 would have been *c* 3 by 2.4m and is assigned to Stages 1-3.

2.14.2 Structure E2

During the next phase all four post pits were recut, probably in Stage 4, as smaller oblongs whose rab and soil packing contained more stones; [321], [268A], [145B], and [26A] were all *c* 0.6m deep. Centre to centre these defined an area 2.6m by 2.0m. Post pit [268A] contained a postpipe 0.3m across and 0.5m deep but the other posts appeared to have been pulled out. The packing of the west pits [321] and [268A] was overlain by sparse but worn cobbles in brown soil [319], which covered the interior of Structure E2 where preserved under the later paving [25]. Structure E2 is assigned to Stage 4.

2.14.3 Structure E3

An area of paving [25], surviving 3m by 2.5m, was laid over cobbles [310] and sealed the earlier postholes [321] and [268A] (Pl 29). These paving stones were worn and their original extent uncertain, but their west edge, best protected by subsequent soil accumulation from erosion, was very regular. It is therefore possible that the paving was laid within a structure built on ground sills, and, since this west

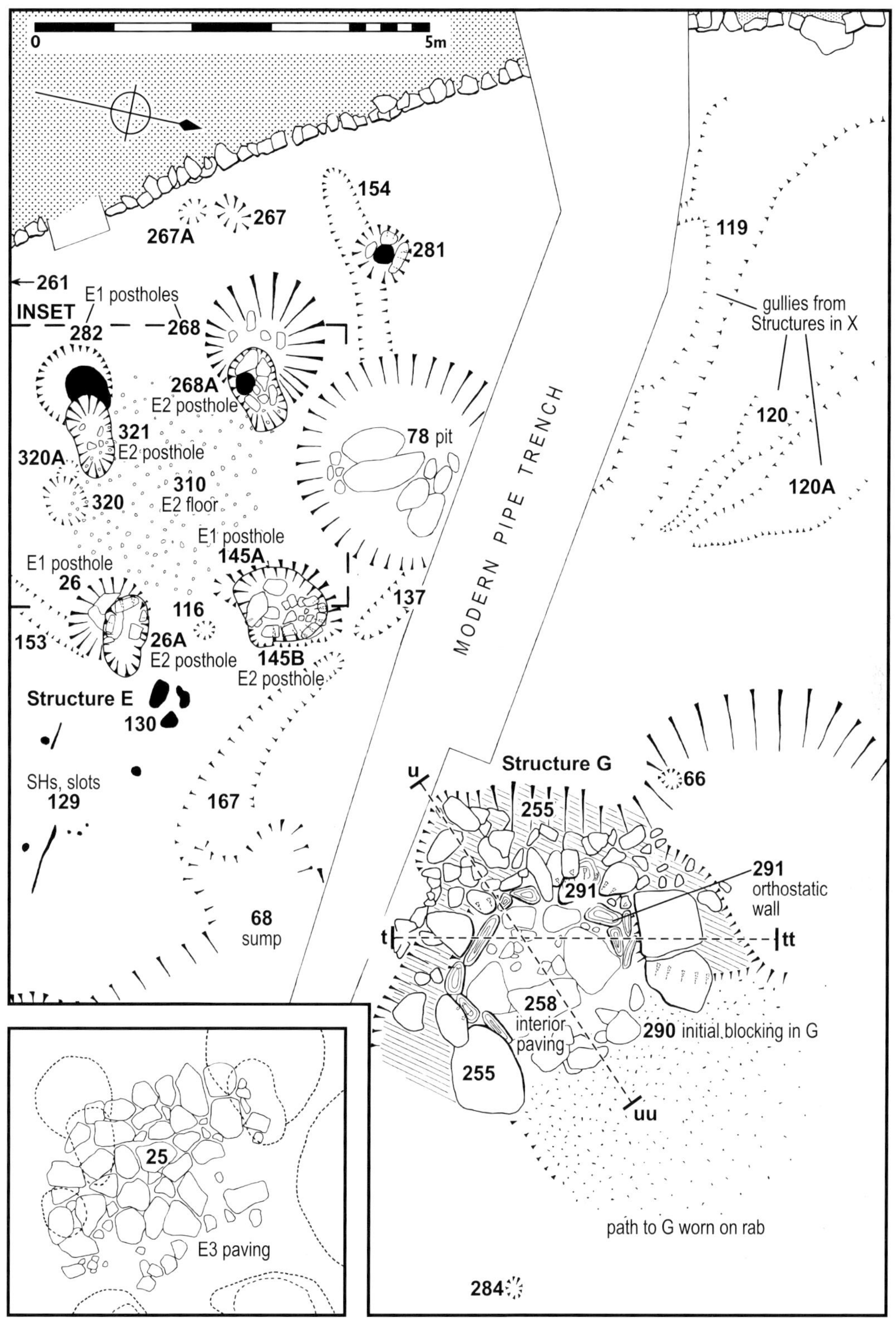

Fig 29: Structures E and G plans. Postholes of Structure E2 distinguished by line around top

edge is on the axis of the previous structures, this may have been related in function. Structure E3 would therefore have measured internally 3m north to south and at least 2.5m east to west. Paving [25] and the suggested Structure E3 may be of Stage 5.

2.14.4 Features in the area of Structure E

Pit [78] (Fig 29; Pl 30), just north of Structure E, was an even circle 2.6m across and 1m deep. There was a small amount of silt on its base, above which the fill of brown soil contained many large stones, including a saddle quern, which may have been deliberately buried. Gleying had caused the lower part

Pl 29: Paving [25] Structure E3; posthole [26] from Structure E2 in foreground, pit [78] in background. View from south. 2m scale

Pl 30: Postholes from Structures E1/2: [26]/[26A]-[145A]/[145B]-[268]/[268A]-[282]/[321] partly excavated. House D in background, pit [78] in foreground. View from north. 2m scale

of the fill to become grey and this gleying implies that the pit was uncovered so that some waterlogging occurred. It is placed so that it avoids the large Structure E1 postholes, or the latter avoid it. A possible interpretation might be that this pit, unique in size and shape on the site, was in some way related to the use of E1. This positioning and the deliberate burial of a quern stone might relate to the latter's functions as a grain store (Section 11.2). The dripping of water from the roof of the sequence of E structures would account for the gleying. This interpretation would attribute the pit to an early Stage, rather than to Stage 6 as suggested in Chapter 9 and on Fig 85.

Gullies [154] and [137], both *c* 0.2m deep with brown silty fills, had been cut by pit [78] (Fig 29). Gulley [137] may be a continuation of [119] to the north of the baulk. A continuation to the south [as 167] appeared to drain into [68], a stone-filled hole which may have acted as a sump filled with rab-mixed soil and rubble.

The varied character of the remaining postholes in the area precludes their grouping into possible structures. Posthole [281], with a postpipe, cut gulley [154]. Postholes [267], [267A], and [116] (Fig 29), [261] (Fig 5), [262] and [263] (Fig 31) are all small, generally similar to [320A]. Some may have held timbers for small fenced areas using the Rampart as their west side.

2.14.5 Levels over Structure E

A brown soil [11] accumulated on the ledge over Structure E and sealed all detected features. This was up to 0.3m thick against the Rampart but faded on the edge of the ledge, and so did not cover Structure G. Soil [11] spread north over [119] and [120] and would appear to be the equivalent of soil [687] over House X. To the south it spread over House D. Over E and D there were occasional clumps of stone in the make-up of soil [11] which appeared to be slip from the Rampart revetment, much disturbed by the plough (not shown on plan). The development of soil [11] may have taken place from Stage 6 onwards, when both Structures E and D were out of use.

2.15 Structure G

This was a polygonal structure (Figs 29, 30; Pls 31, 32), 1.8m by 1.5m, defined by orthostats. Situated north-west of Structure E, it was set within a scoop cut, with a level base, into the hillslope to a maximum depth of 1.5m. The scoop was part of a wide shallow levelling (Fig 5) which, on its uphill edge, was coincident with the ledge along the west of the Round. The base of the scoop was covered to a depth of *c* 0.1m with [258A] (Fig 30), mixed brown soil and rab containing a distinct patch of quartz sea sand, about a double handful in quantity, and some slate fragments. A rough semi-circle of orthostats [291] up to 0.6m high was then set onto soil [258A] and the scoop

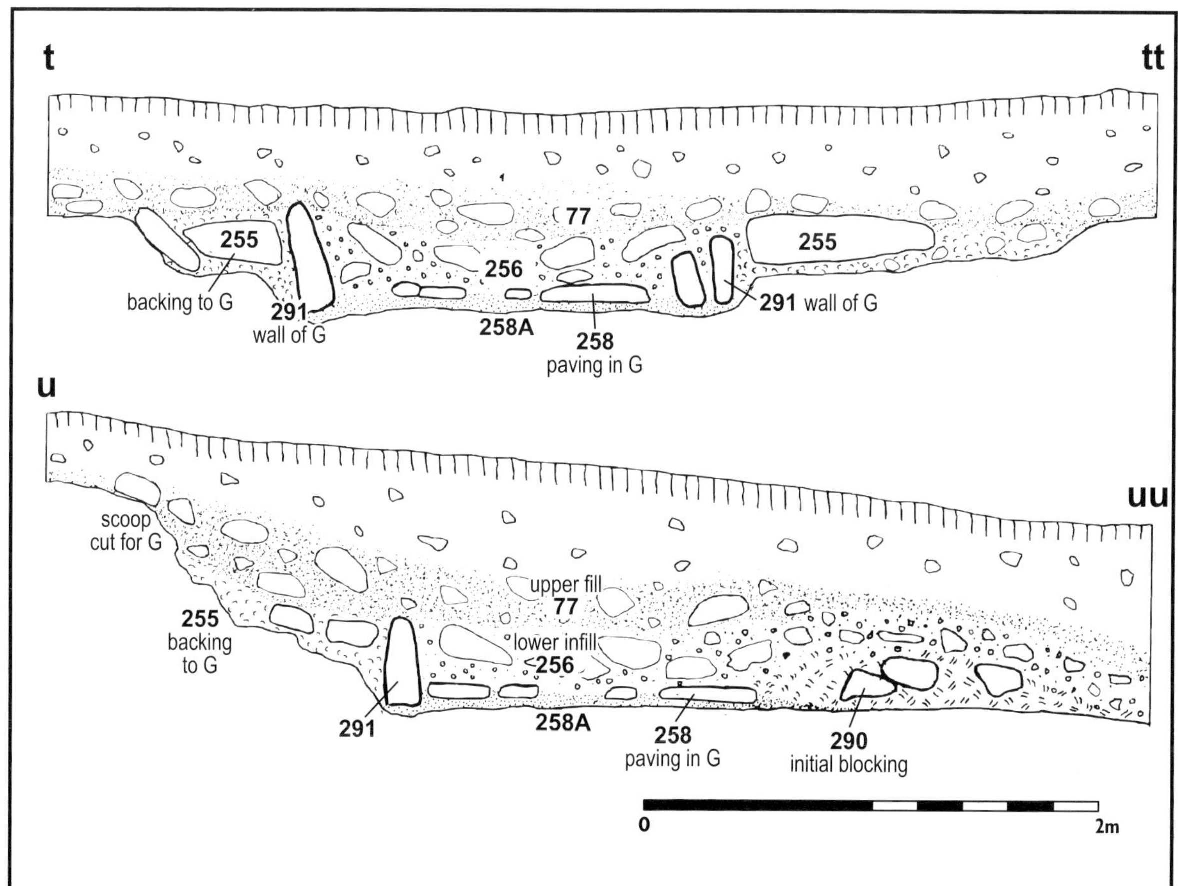

Fig 30: Sections t-tt and u-uu across Structure G

Pl 31: Structure G excavated, with backing [255] behind. View from east. 2m scale

Pl 32: Structure G, view from above. 2m scale

behind them filled with rubble [255]; some of the stones were very large, with brown soil in the interstices. The interior of the semi-circle was paved with [258], which was slightly worn. A worn path several centimetres deep and 3m wide led up to the Structure (Fig 5). Subsequently the entrance had been blocked with piled stones [290]. Structure G was then infilled with a dump of stones and soil [256] to the top of the orthostats and blocking. The whole of the scoop, including the lobe to the north, was then infilled with rubble and darker soil [77] to form a smooth slope obliterating the former levelling scarp (Pl 33). This fill was also found over paving [668] outside and downhill of House X4 (Fig 25). The surface of [77] was compact and worn. A solitary posthole [66] was sealed beneath [77]. Posthole [284] which lay 1m to the east may have been associated with G although no stratigraphic association was found. The reasons for assigning Structure G to Stage 6 and its blocking to Stage 9 are complex and set out in Chapter 9.

Pl 33: Structure G showing top of infill [77]/[256]. View from east. 2m scale

2.16 House D

House D (Figs 31, 32, 33; Pl 34) was situated to the south of Structure E on the ledge along the west side of the Round. There was no surviving walling, but the presence of rab flooring, drains, a possible hearth, and internal timber fittings allows interpretation as a house. The sequence of features suggests that this had several phases. The phasing given below cannot be proven, but is the simplest interpretation of the evidence. Comparison with the other Houses indicates that the drains with capstones [136] and [232] were probably internal and the surrounding silt-filled gulley [153] probably external.

2.16.1 House D1

The earliest phase may be represented by the narrow slot [292] with a probable return [168] some 5m to the north, both *c* 0.2m deep and filled with light-brown soil. These may have held upright timbers as neither their width nor their fill are consistent with drainage. Slot [292] was cut away by gulley [153] and by drain [232]; it faded out at both south and north ends. Its return [168] was also cut by [153]: to the west

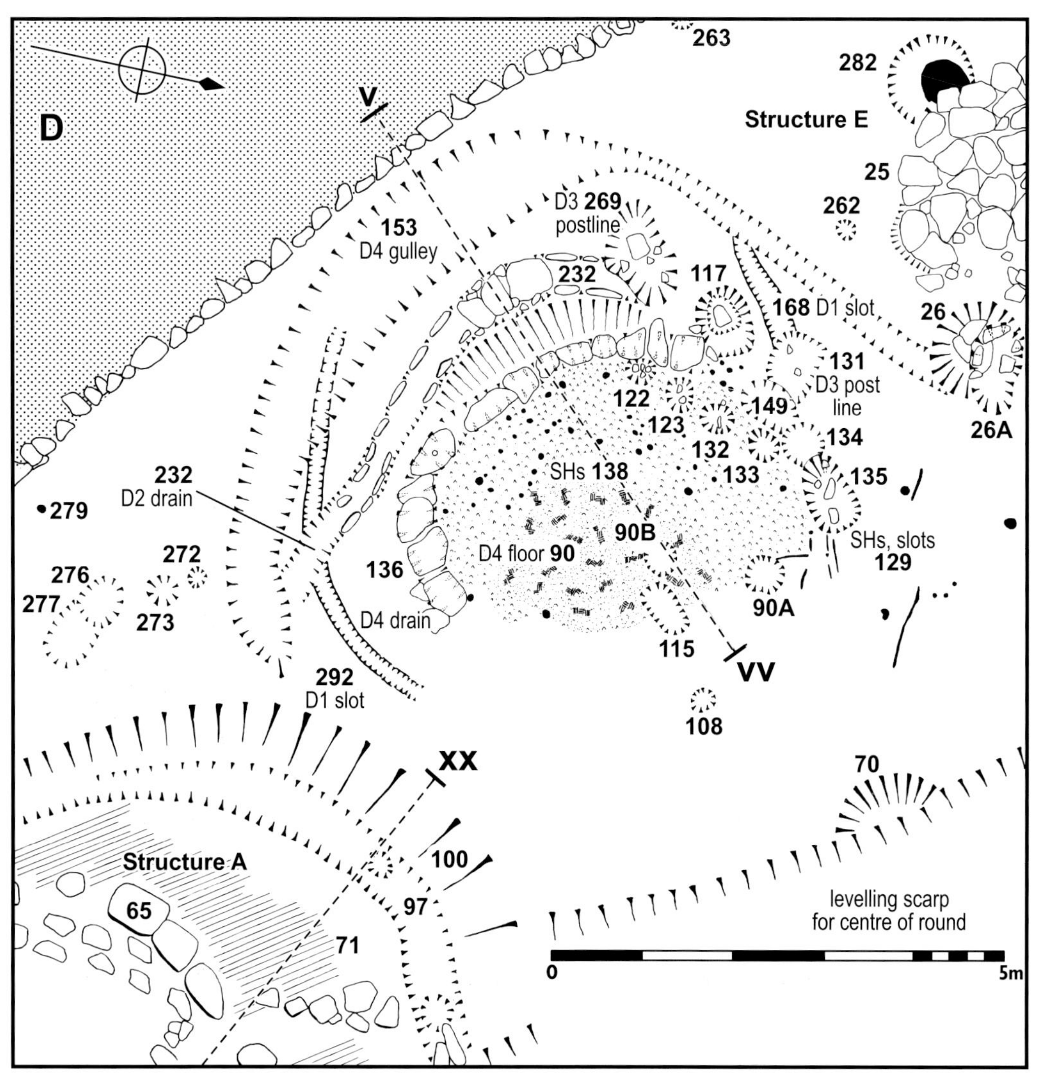

Fig 31: House D plan

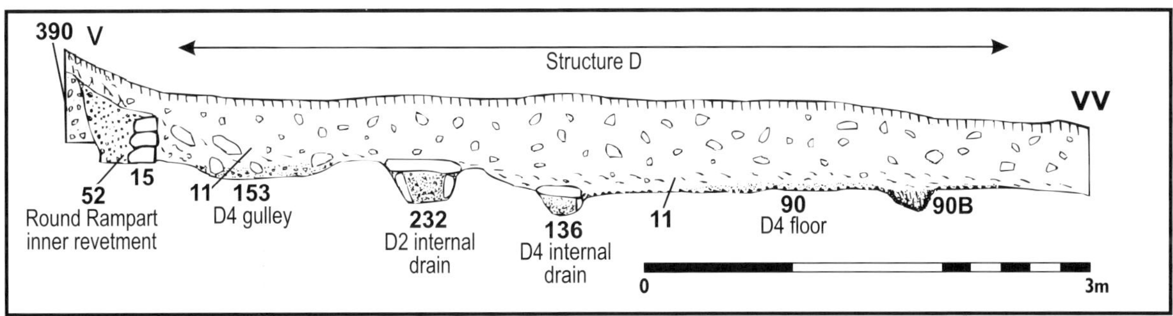

Fig 32: Section v-vv across House D

its relationship with posthole [131] was indeterminate. No features can be related to [292] — a fact explained by the subsequent levelling of much of the area it enclosed. House D1 would have been an irregular oval 6.7m across and is assigned to Stage 2.

2.16.2 House D2

The next phase was probably that with drain [232] which was later than slot [292]. This drain was *c* 0.3m deep, its channel stone-lined and capped and filled with dark soil. Few of its capstones survived *in situ*. It had acted as a soak drain as its bottom was level. It became shallow and faded out at either end, its relationship with gulley [153] indeterminate but cut to the north by posthole [269]. The structure, House D2, to which [232] related was presumably stone-walled in the absence of timber settings. Its interior would have been approximately level with the [232] capstones and thus largely cut away. It may belong to Stage 3.

2.16.3 Structure D3

A line of three postholes [269]-[117]-[131] may represent the next structure in the area. Posthole [269] cut drain [232] and the positions of the other two suggest that they formed a line with it. Posthole [131] was cut by [149] which belongs to the subsequent House D4 associated with floor [90]. Posthole [269], 0.35m deep, and [131], 0.20m deep, had a soil and rab packing with the posts withdrawn; [117], 0.35m, had a stony fill, again after the post had been withdrawn. This line of postholes may have formed the north side of a lean-to type structure about 3m long; any related features to the south would have been removed by levelling associated with D4. The D3 postline is assigned to Stage 4.

2.16.4 House D4

The last phase probably involved internal drain [136], with associated levelling, and external gulley [153]; a stone wall could have been set in the space between (Pl 34). The gulley [153], up to 0.3m deep, was irregular as though it had been much cleaned and its fill of very dark silt suggested a late phase (compare gullies in House Z — Section 2.10.1). The internal drain [136] was 0.2m deep, stone-lined and capped and filled with dark soil. It became shallow and disappeared at either end and must have acted as a

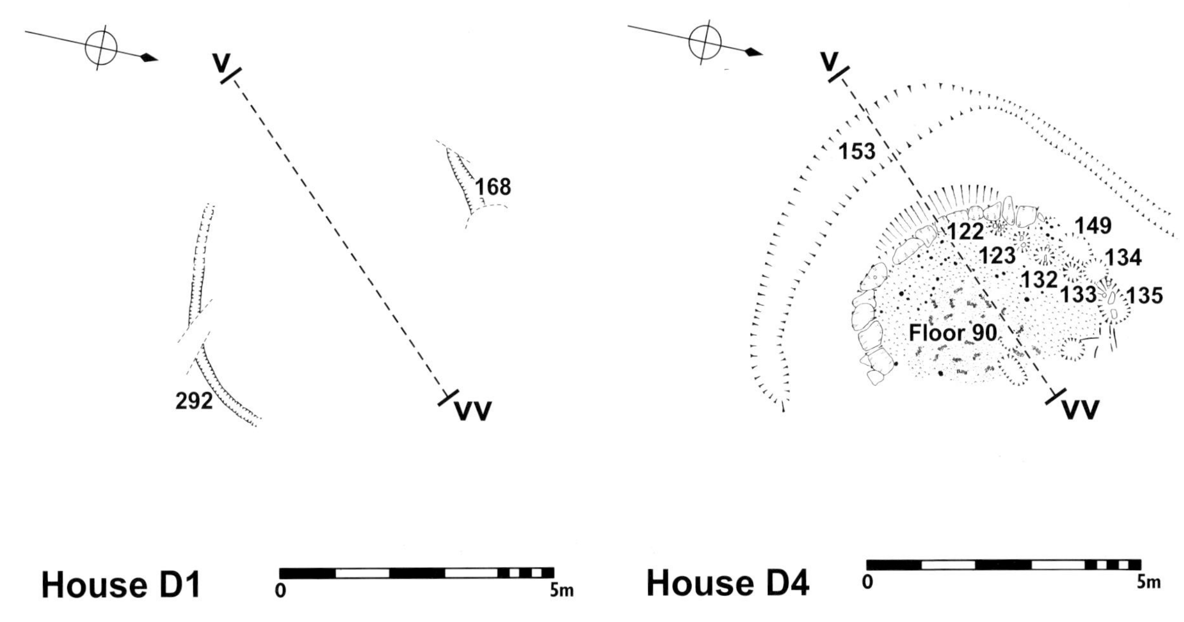

Fig 33: Phase plans of House D1 and House D4

soak-drain as it had no appreciable fall. One of its capstones was a slate slab 0.45m by 0.42m by 0.07m with a roughly worked hole 0.03m across in its centre. The capstones of [136] were embedded in the rab of floor [90], so the two were contemporary. Drain [136] delimited an area levelled 0.2m into the slope, on the clean, unworn base of which rab floor [90] had been laid up to 0.1m thick. It is presumed that the inner edge of the suggested stone wall of this phase would have been situated along the top edge of this levelling cut, on analogy with Houses A and Z. House D4 would then have been *c* 4m across and no more than 6m long, assuming the levelling scarp to the east was in its present position. Floor [90] had been lightly burnt in one area and was scattered with charcoal; there was no hearth pit. It was eroded to the east. The floor contained many contemporary or subsequent features, presumably for internal fittings. The line of postholes [122], [123], [132], and [133], from which the posts had been removed, had been set within floor [90] as one edge of [122] passed partly under a capstone of drain [136] contemporary with the floor. Postholes [135] and [149] were not sealed by floor [90] and may relate to it; their posts had been withdrawn; [135] cut posthole [134]; [149] cut D3 posthole [131] but its relationship with [134] was indeterminate. Probable postholes [115] and [90A] and the clay-lined pit [90B] cut through floor [90]. There were numerous groups of small stakeholes in the interior [138], and three larger ones [129] to the north beyond floor [90] with some vestigial narrow slots similar to those in House X. House D4 may have been in use for some time and is assigned to Stages 5 and 6.

2.16.5 Features around and over D

A group of shallow probable post-sockets were situated south of House D — [272], [273], [276], [277], and [279]. These had no physical relationship with D.

The levelling scarp along the west of the site truncated a shallow pit [70] filled with dark soil, which could have been a tree hole. Loose soil rab lumps and stones [14] appeared to be the result of erosion along the scarp, until it had become infilled and presented a smooth slope; it was not noticeably worn on its surface. This fill [14] could not be related to the deliberate fill of Structure G because of the modern pipeline which cut through this part of the site.

House D was covered over by a continuation of the soil [11] which accumulated over Structure E and which, it is suggested, did not begin forming until Stage 6 (Section 2.14.5). At the north end layer [11] was about 0.2m thick adjacent to the Rampart but thinned to the south because of disturbance connected

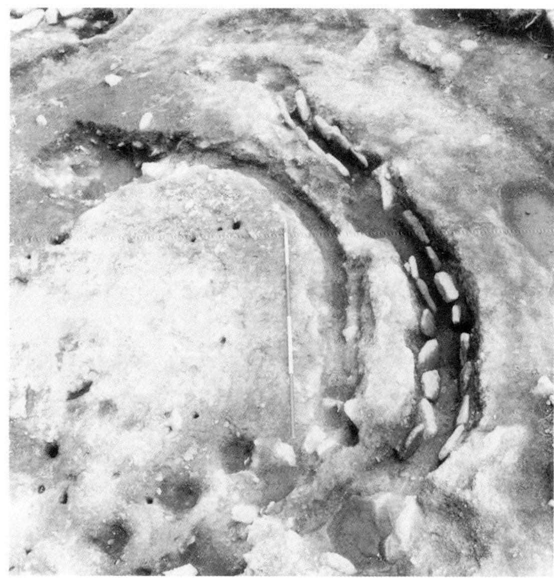

Pl 34: Internal drain [136], House D4, with cover slabs removed and associated floor [90]; drain [232] from House D2 and external gulley [153] House D4 to right. View from north. 2m scale

with the modern field entrance, and to the east because of ploughing. The plough had cut into the subsoil, removing the east part of floor [90] and any related features. The surviving thickness of protective soil over D suggests that the absence of any stone walling is due to removal of stone for later buildings, not to plough disturbance. If so, the building sequence in D terminated some time before the disuse of the Round, consistent with the suggested end date around Stage 6.

2.17 House A

House A (Figs 34-8; Pl 35) was situated to the south-east of House D and at a slightly lower level. The House had three distinct structural phases, A1, A2, and A3, the first of which may be divided into subphases A1a and A1b. House A2 was smaller than A1 but its floor was at a higher level, so that its walls and flooring sealed most of the features associated with the earlier phase.

An entranceway to the modern field had opened directly above House A and activity associated with it had worn down the Rampart adjacent to it. Despite this, internal stratigraphy survived well on the uphill side, but downhill, on the north-east, had suffered badly from erosion.

2.17.1 Features preceding House A

A few features predate A 1 — [341] a probable posthole sealed by House A1 wall [33] (Fig 34); [318] 0.4m deep, a pit with rab fill over a layer of charcoal under A1 floor [311]; posthole [87] beneath the wall

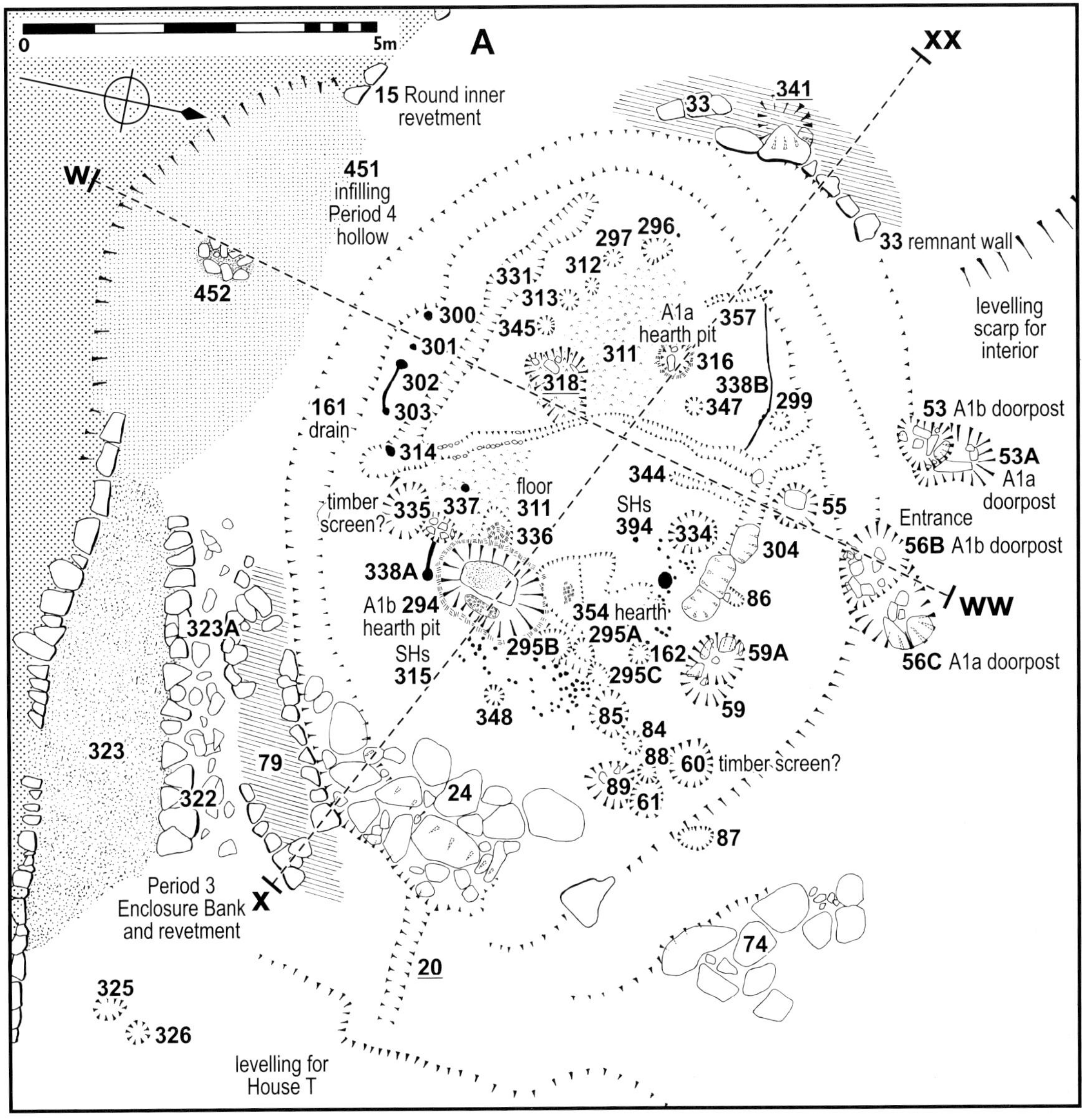

Fig 34: House A1 plan. Features of Period 3/4 underlined

line of A1; and gulley [20] truncated by A1 drain [161]. Other early features may have been removed or truncated by House A1 levelling. Some, if not all, of these features may belong to the Period 3 Enclosure.

2.17.2 House A1

House A1 had been about 11m by 8m internally. Its walling (Figs 34, 35, 36) had been set into rubble [323A] deriving from the Period 3 Enclosure Bank. A short length of wall on the south [79] possessed both faces, but to the north only inner face [33] survived. The interior had been levelled down to 0.2m below wall [33], on the uphill side of the House, and this levelling scarp continued east to the doorway posthole [53]. East of the doorway the line of the wall is probably represented by a scarp below the floor of the House, into which the inner face of the wall would have been set (as in X). Wall [33] incorporated a waterworn slate boulder 0.52m by 0.37m by 0.11m. The entrance may have been framed by posts in [53A], 0.45m deep, and [56C], 0.50m deep, 2m apart, with posts withdrawn. These lay on the suggested A1 house wall-line. Posthole [53A] was recut by [53], 0.38m deep, and [56C] by [56B], 0.35m deep, the posts again probably withdrawn. If these postholes have been correctly interpreted, A was the only house within the Round with evidence for a ground-set timber door-frame. The replacement of the doorposts suggests both some considerable length of use for House A1 and some structural refurbishment. It may be appropriate to consider A1 as having two sub phases, A1 and A2.

A soak drain [161], 0.15m deep, had been dug around much of the interior. Capstones survived as part of paving [24] but the drain itself was not stone-lined. A network of shallow drains *c* 0.1m deep, [331], [314], [344], [304], and [357], all appeared

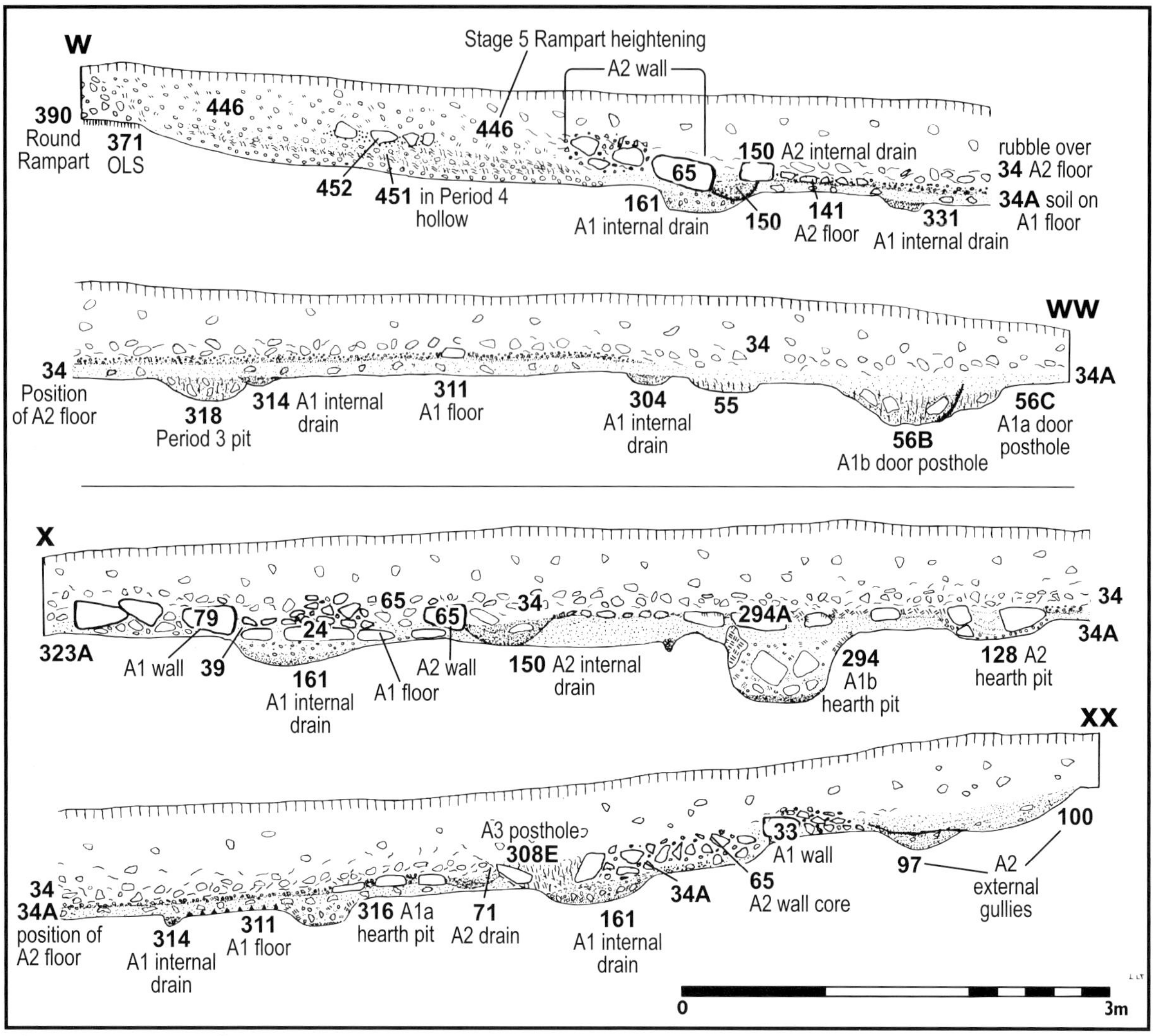

Fig 35: Sections w-ww and x-xx across House A

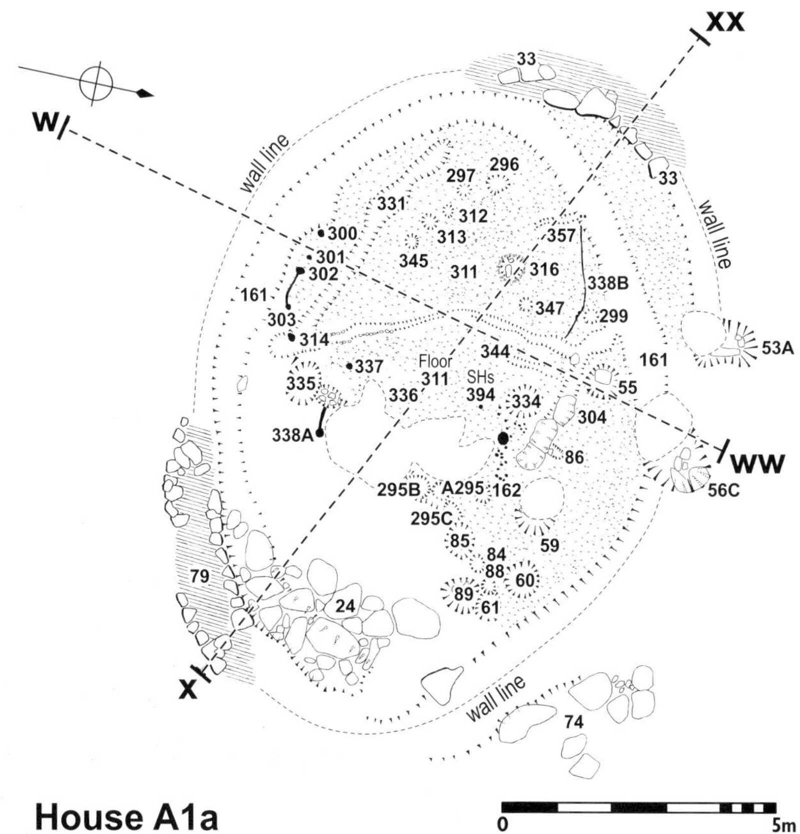

Fig 36: Phase plan to show features of House A1a

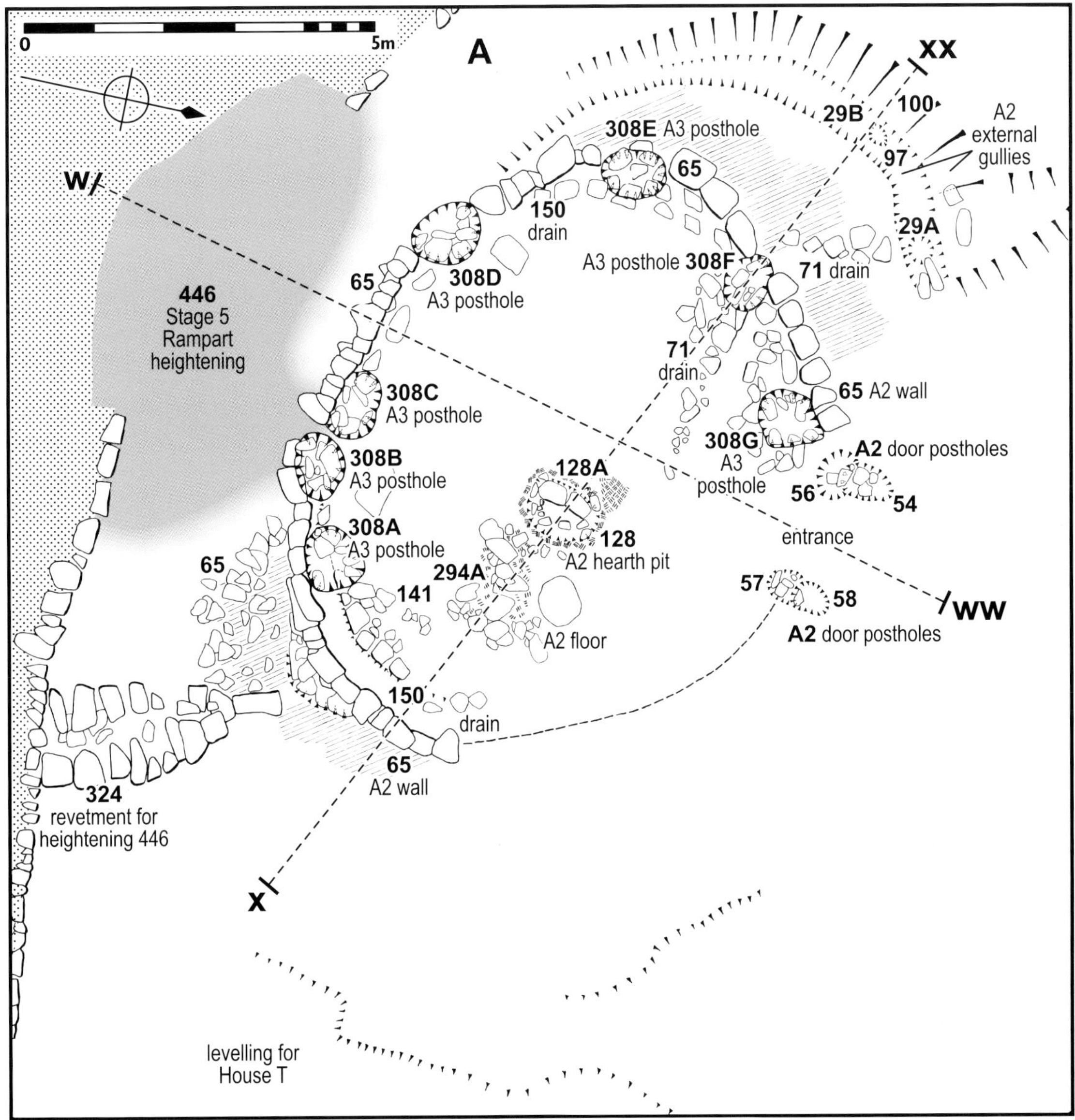

Fig 37: House A2 and A3 plan

contemporary with the main drain [161], and contained similar fills. Drain [314] had some small surviving sidestones and [304] some capstones. The uphill part of House A1 had been floored with tamped rab [311], which only survived patchily. The lower part had paving [24], much worn, most of which had been later removed. A drop of *c* 0.10m along the line of features [335]-[88] may originally have been cut as seating for this paving.

Features [335]-[88] along the line of the drop appear to have been postholes with their posts withdrawn. These divided into two groups on size. The larger group — [335] 0.35m deep, [85] 0.15m deep, [60] 0.18m deep, [61] 0.1m deep, and [89] 0.20m deep, were all *c* 0.6m across. The smaller group — [88] 0.2m deep, [84] 0.12m deep and [295A], [295B], and [295C] *c* 0.15m deep, were all about 0.3m in diameter. Of these, [295B] and [295C] appear to have been set at the same time, and [88] of the smaller series cut [61] of the larger group. All these postholes had a brown soil fill with many stones. They may have held a timber screen dividing the floor into two areas. They appear to predate the hearth pit [294] complex and to belong to House A1a.

The hearth pit [316], circular, 0.4m across and 0.2m deep, was situated on the east side just north of the entrance; it may belong to House A1a. It had been burnt around its upper edge which was formed by floor [311] and contained charcoal scattered in its fill of brown earth and stones.

A line of five postholes was found in the east of floor [311] — [345] 0.15m deep, [313] 0.1m deep, [312] 0.1m deep, [297] 0.27m deep, and [296] 0.05m deep. The remaining postholes made no obvious pattern. Of these, [347], [299], and [162] were all small in size, while [55], [334], and [59] (with a recut [59A]) were larger. There were a large number of stakeholes and short lengths of slot, two of which, [338A] and [338B], were of the very narrow kind found in X and D. The protection of the House A1 floor by later levels preserved evidence for the best

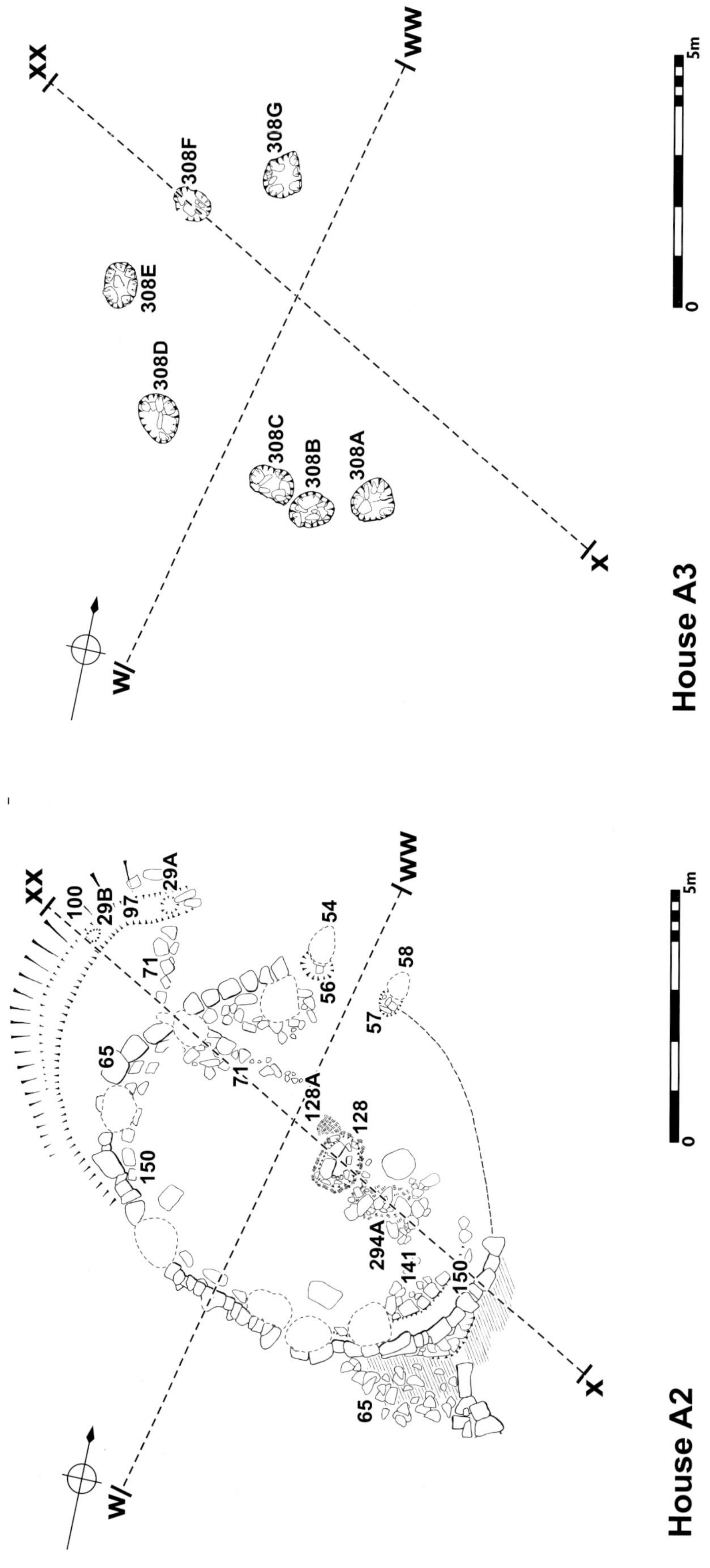

Fig 38: Phase plans of House A2 and House A3

Pl 35: House A2 with walling [65], interior excavated to reveal features of House A1. View from south-west. 2m scale

range of internal timber fittings found in any of the houses.

Hearth pit [294] was 1.6m by 1m by 0.6m (Pl 36) and lay across the drop in floor level and was associated with surrounding hearths [354], [336], and [337]. It position across the line of the suggested timber screen held in postholes [335] to [60] indicated that it was unlikely to be contemporary with it and the stratigraphic evidence, although not clear cut, suggested that [294] was later than the screen postholes on either side of it. Hearth pit [294] may therefore belong to House A1b. It was slightly burnt around its top, and had been lined with clay, most of which had been subsequently removed. A patch still adhered half-way down its nearly vertical south side; heavily burnt, it projected outwards which suggested that there may have been a clay structure built into the pit (section x-xx, Fig 35). A large stone on the base was slightly charcoal-smeared. The fill of [294] was of stones with some brown earth and charcoal. Hearth [336] was a patch of burnt clay in a shallow depression to the north-west, hearth [354] to the north a broader scoop with a small patch of burnt clay on its base. Hearth [337] to the west, 0.15m deep, was a small pit, its soil fill containing charcoal and lumps of burnt clay. The mass of stakeholes [315] north-east of [294] were situated in a slight (?worn) hollow in the rab. If the

Pl 36: House A1b hearth pit [294] and associated stakeholes, with posthole [335] from House A1a beyond; wall [65] and drain [150] of House A2 on left. View from north-east. 2m scale

drop in level along the [335]-[88] line is correctly interpreted as a cut for paving [24] to be set into, either these stakeholes were subsequent to the removal of this paving or else the paving was never laid in this area.

Externally a patch of worn paving [74] was set in a slight cut north-east of the suggested A1 wall-line.

House A1 appears to have become ruinous at the end of its life. Its main structural wall disappeared on the south and became fragmentary elsewhere with rubble [39] accumulating against the face in places where this survived. Soil with a few stones [34A] accumulated on the floor.

The division of House A1 into two structural phases, reflected by the recutting of the door-frame postholes and the two hearth pits, is explored further in Section 9.2. House A1a is assigned to Stages 1-3, House A1b to Stage 4. The ruinous state of the House relates to the possible hiatus in the use of the Round at the end of Stage 4.

2.17.3 House A2

House A was rebuilt as A2 (Fig 37; Pl 35); this was smaller than A1, about 8.5m by 6.5m internally, and little evidence for internal features survived. Its wall [65] had been set over the infill of A1 [34A] and revetted a rubble core which sealed the surviving fragments of the A1 wall. Its inner wall face survived virtually complete, except where removed by plough erosion on the north-east. Any outer face would have been set at a higher level and did not survive. A short length of wall [324] connected wall core [65] to the Rampart and acted as revetment to the build-up of material on its west uphill side. Soil and rubble [446] were dumped behind the House, where the Rampart had collapsed over Period 4 hollow [451], and ran up to wall [65] which seems to have acted locally as additional Rampart revetting.

The House A2 doorway, positioned to the north of its east side, may have been defined by postholes [56] 0.2m deep, and [57] 0.25m deep, 2m apart. Both were subsequently recut, [56] by [54], 0.20m deep, and [57] by [58], 0.15m deep. These postholes lay on the A2 wall-line but layer [34A] separating A1 and A2 was thin here and relationships were not clear. Posts had been withdrawn.

The A2 floor had been some 0.15 to 0.2m higher than that in A1. A patch of paving [294A] survived in its centre, set in clay, and may have been a flat hearth as it was heavily burnt. Adjacent to it was hearth pit [128] 0.3m deep, the stone lining of which was burnt; its fill was of brown soil with charcoal. To its north-west was a burnt clay patch [128A]. These features had been placed on [34A], the accumulation in the interior of House A1. Drain [150] had been constructed around the interior (Pl 37). On the south-east, downhill, side [150] was a gulley *c* 0.15m deep cutting into [34A]; its inner edge had been faced up with stone, bonded in with some rubble levelling [141] in the interior. In its uphill part, drain [150] was built up entirely above [34A] within this levelling [141]. On the south-east an outlet had been constructed to drain through the wall face. To the north-west, drain [71] had been constructed with the wall, to provide an outlet through it, and survived some way into the interior. No capstones survived on these drains. The proximity of [150] to the wall face had to some extent protected it from erosion. As no good interior floor surface survived except for the hard hearth surface [294A], few internal features were detected.

Pl 37: South side of House A2, wall [65], drain [150] partly excavated; paving [24] from House A1 partly showing in background. View from west. 2m scale

Pl 38: House A3 at early stage of excavation; posthole [308F] in foreground. View from north-west. 2m scale

Two drainage gullies, [97] and [100] with the usual brown silt fills, around the north-west of the exterior of the building appear to belong to A2. For much of their distance, they ran along the line of the A1 wall, removing it; the extreme east stone of this earlier wall [33] had been dislodged by gulley [97]. The first gulley [97] was 0.3m deep; two sockets *c* 0.1m deep in its base [29A] and [29B] may have been either stone removal holes or timber settings. The second gulley [100], a recut of [97], was much broader and only *c* 0.15m deep. Its fill contained clumps of stone.

House A2 is tentatively assigned to Stages 5-8. It became ruinous, capstones were removed from its drains and gaps formed in its walls. Its site was then infilled with soil and rubble [34], which was badly plough disturbed on its north-east side.

2.17.4 House A3

Seven postholes [308A] to [308G] *c* 0.25m deep were set into [34], the infill of House A2 (Pl 38). Three, A, C, and G, were set against the A2 wall cutting down into drain [150]. The others cut the wall-line, which must have been ruinous at the time. (No postholes were found on the north-east of the House because of plough erosion.) House A3 was *c* 7m by 5m. It may either have been entirely of timber or may have utilised parts of wall [65] still standing. No internal features were found. A3 is tentatively assigned to Stage 9 but it could have been later.

Some rubble and soil infilled the scarps on the downhill side of the House and covered paving [74] but neither this infill or the paving could be phased with any certainty.

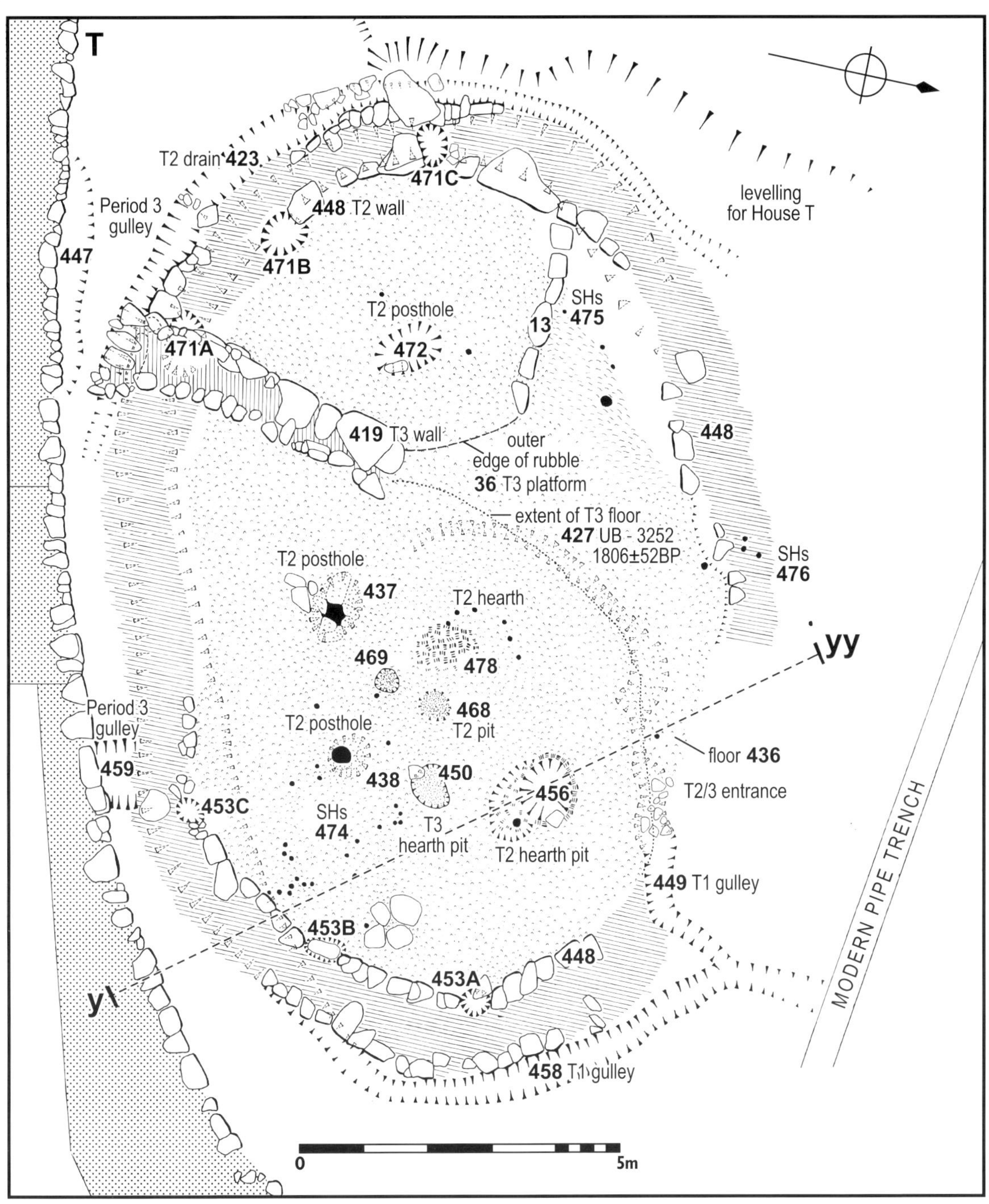

Fig 39: House T1, T2, and T3 plan. Features in heavy outline relate to T3

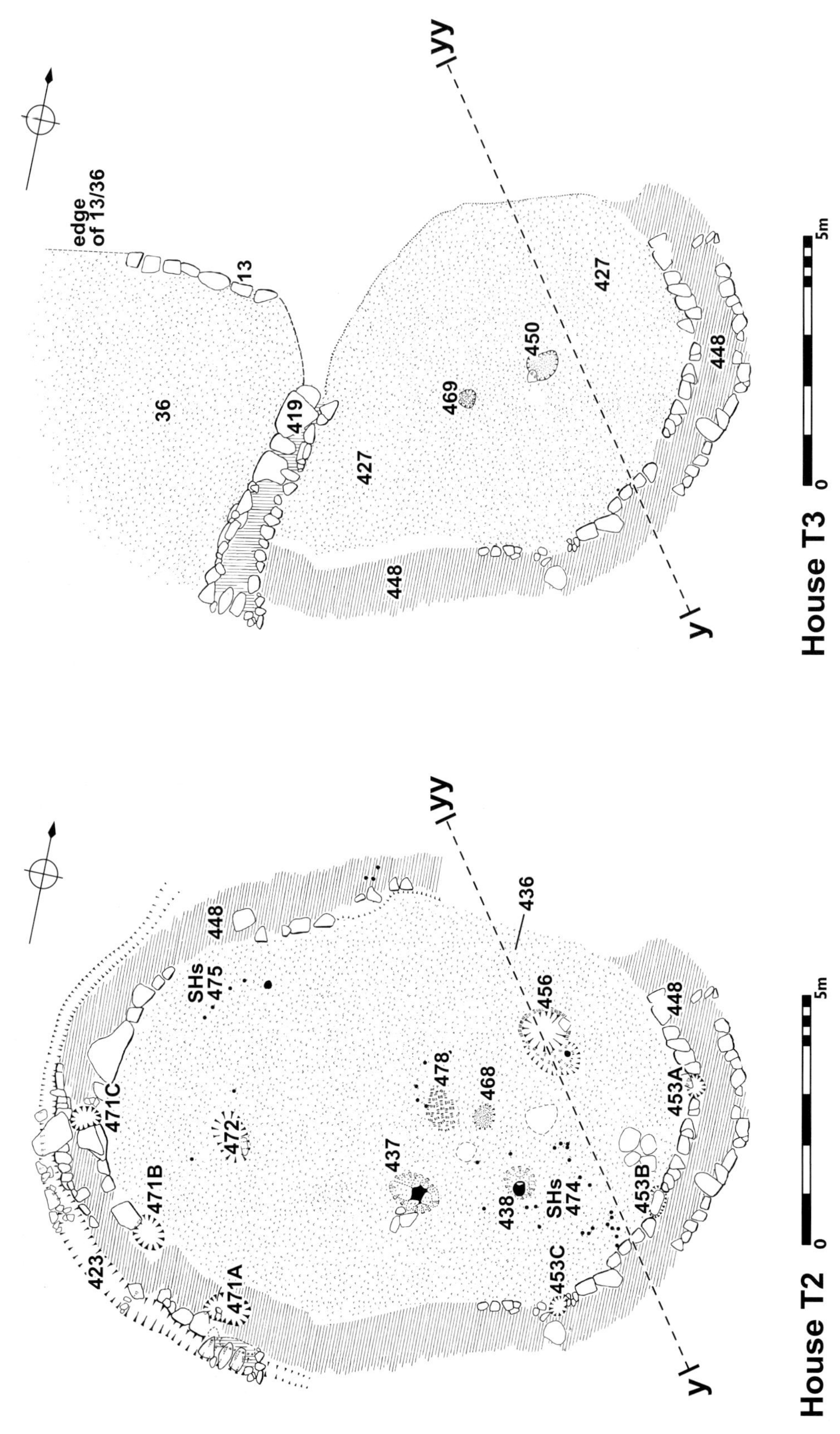

Fig 40: Phase plans of House T2 and House T3

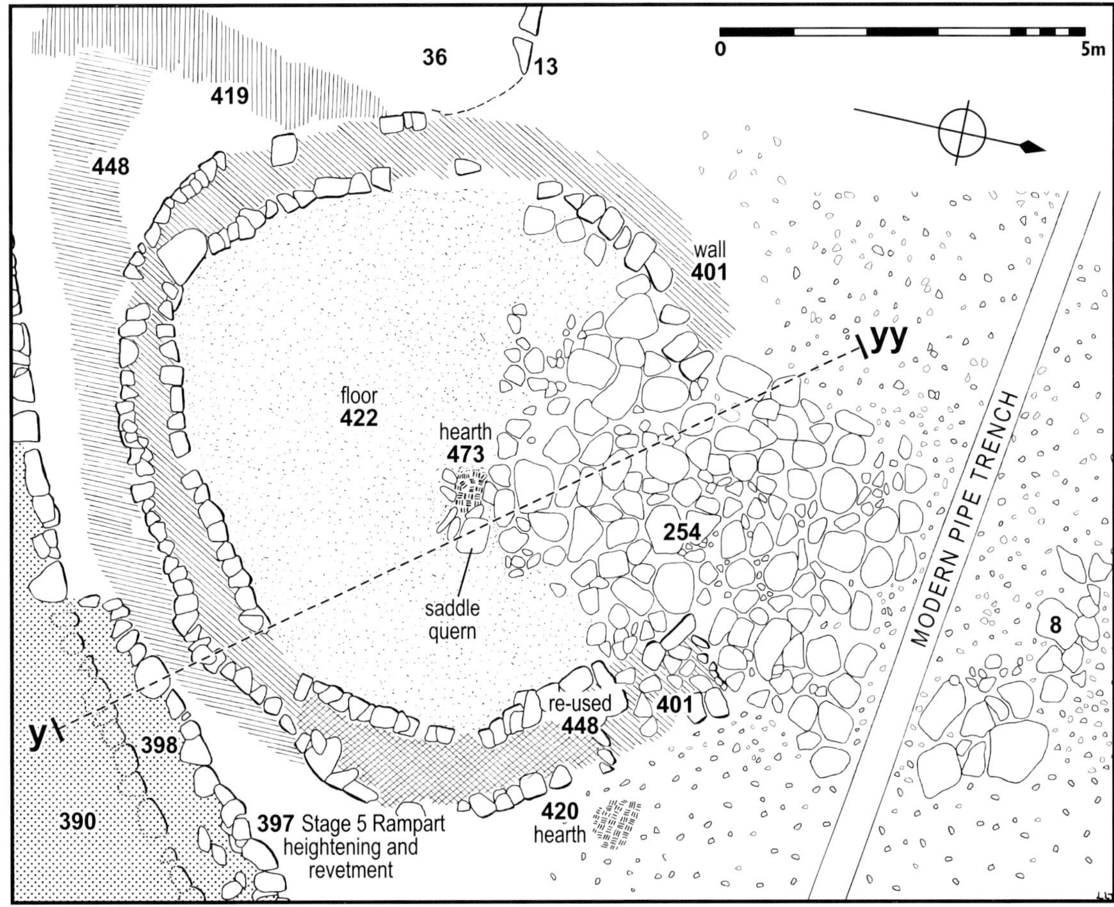

Fig 41: House T4 plan

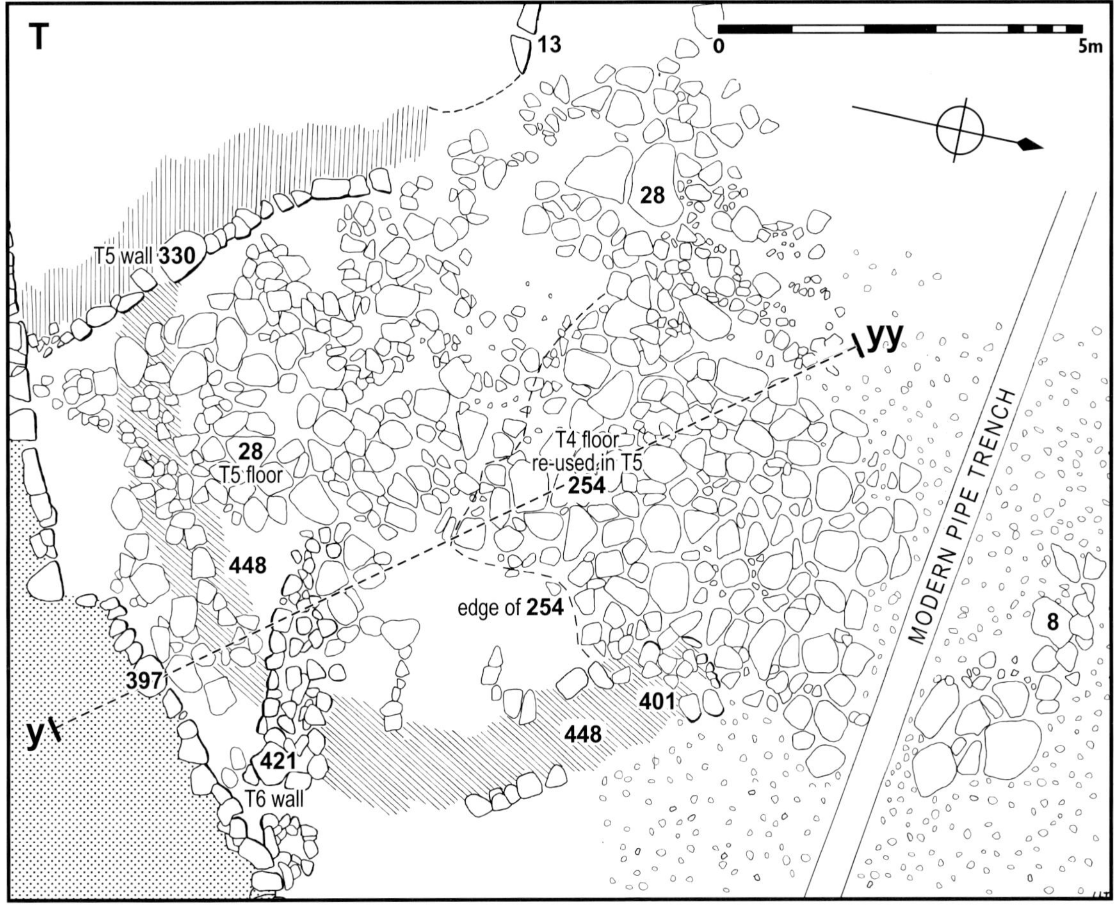

Fig 42: House/Structure T5 plan

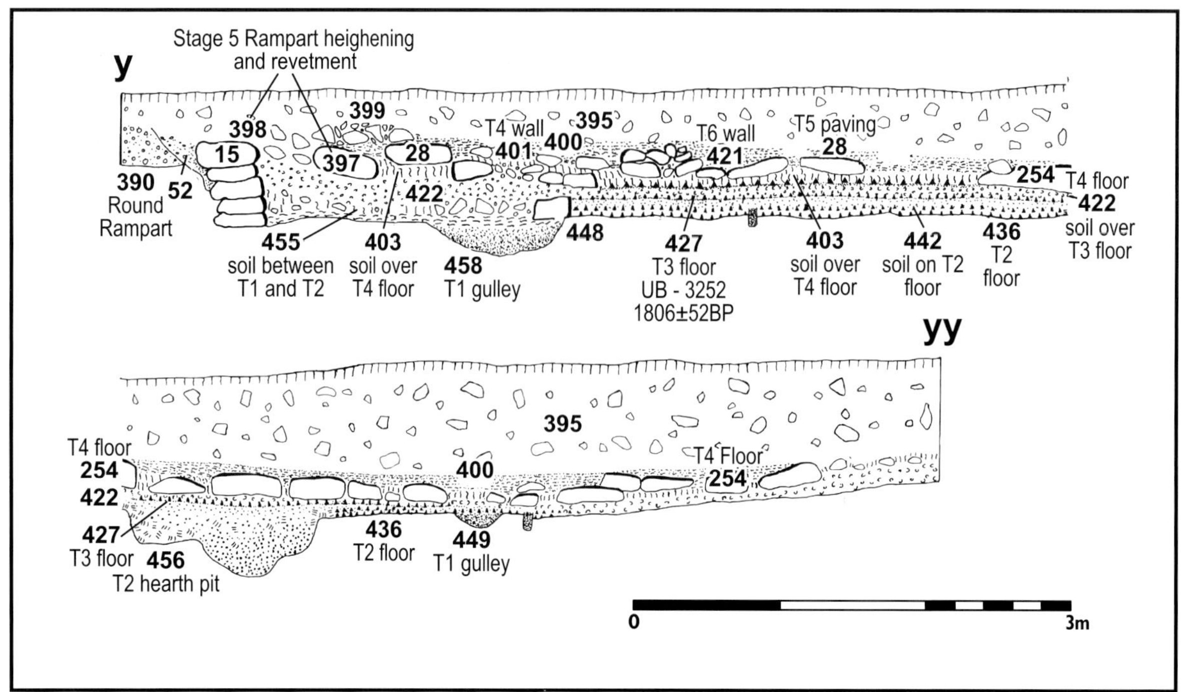

Fig 43: Section y-yy House T

2.18 House T

House T (Figs 39-43) was situated in the south-east of the Round, in a downhill position where soil wash collected against the Rampart revetment. This soil interleaved the various structural phases, T1 to T6, allowing them to be clearly distinguished and, in the later stages, provided some protection against plough damage. House T had therefore the clearest structural sequence in the Round.

The site for the House was cut almost level, leaving a scarp up to 0.3m high on the west uphill side. Postholes [325] and [326], both 0.15m deep (Fig 34), were set within the levelled area 3m south-west of House T but had no other relationships. The OLS [371] (see Area R, Section 2.19), projecting beneath the Rampart and distinguished as [380], gave out just east of T and may have been removed during the preparation of the site. Gullies [459] and [447] (Fig 39) beneath the Rampart belong to the Period 3 Enclosure (Section 2.4)

2.18.1 House T1

A gulley [458] 0.2m deep defined an oval area 13.5m by 8m across, and was joined by a second, [449] 0.15m deep, running out from the interior of the oval. Both had silted up gradually. Gulley [458] faded out at both ends. There was no structure associated with these gullies; if any walling had existed, it had been entirely removed. There were also no internal features, with the possible exception of stakeholes [476] sealed beneath the T2 wall (Fig 39). Gulley [449] was sealed beneath the T2 floor [436]. Dark soil [455], a southward extension of the lower soil [386] in R (Section 2.19.1), accumulated over the west part of the silted-up gulley [458]. The gullies, perhaps interior and exterior drains for a house never completed, are assigned to Stage 1.

2.18.2 House T2

House T2 (Figs 39, 43), again oval in shape, had been *c* 12m by 8.5m internally and had been built over soil [455] sealing T1. The T2 wall [448], with stone facings edging an earth and rubble core, survived several courses high to the east, where it had been reused in later phases, but elsewhere was scrappy. Six postholes — [471A], [471B], [471C], [453A], [453B], and [453C] — were set *c* 2.5m apart in the inner wall face in two groups at either end of the building, penetrating up to 0.2m into the rab beneath. Their packing stones appeared to form part of the rubble wall core, and so it is assumed that these postholes were contemporary with the wall; posts had been withdrawn. There was no trace of further holes along the sides of the House.

The interior of T2 was floored with mixed rab and soil [436], tamped hard over the levelled rab. The latter had been scraped clean, as soil [455] did not survive inside the wall-line. Floor [436] was *c* 0.05m thick over most of the interior but deepened to *c* 0.1m on the east, downhill side. Its edge on the north-east marked the line of the vanished inner wall face. The doorway was presumably in this sector of wall (Section 10.4.5). There was a little soil [442] on floor [436].

Hearth [478], a patch of burning 1m across with an arc of stakeholes to the north-west, was nearly central to floor [436]. A hearth pit [456], 0.4m deep, had burning around its upper edge. Both it and the adjacent 0.1m deep scoop had fills of brown soil with charcoal, as did pit [468] 0.15m deep. Two similar postholes, [437] and [438], with pipes 0.3m across and 0.25m deep, were 2m apart. Feature [472], 0.3m deep, was probably also a posthole but very much damaged. The only remaining features on floor [436] were groups of stakeholes [474] and [475] and four flat stones placed together at the east end. Soil [442] up to 0.05m thick was found over most of floor [436].

Drain [423] was cut around the outside of the west, uphill part of the House. This had had a stone lining which was ruinous. The channel was c 0.3m deep, filled with dark silt, had no outfall and probably acted as a soakaway. House T2 may have been built in Stage 2 and continued into Stage 3.

2.18.3 House T3

House T2, which had become ruinous at its west end, was remodelled as T3 (Figs 39, 43). Wall [419] formed a new west side, but the eastern part of T2 which was still extant was used for the remainder of the structure. T3 was therefore an irregular building about 7m across, floored with tamped rab [427] 0.05m thick. Only the south part of wall [419] survived and floor [427] faded out on the north so that the precise plan of T3 is uncertain. Pits [450], 0.3m deep, and [469], 0.2m deep, with soil and charcoal fill, possibly hearth pits, were the only features detected in floor [427] and assigned to this phase.

The former west end of T2 had collapsed, the resultant rubble infilling drain [423]. The rubble was spread as [36] to form a rough platform west of, and adjacent to, wall [419], revetted with a facing of stones [13]. The platform spread from wall [419], incorporating the lowest courses of the west wall [448] of T2, and extended to infill the levelling scarp west of the building. Some stones on the top of the platform had been much worn. There is no evidence as to whether platform [13]/[36] was roofed over or was open. House T3 therefore was very different in its irregular shape to its oval predecessor T2 and had two components, the House and the raised platform [36]/[13] to the west. The T3 complex is assigned to Stage 4.

Grey clayey soil [422] spread across the stub of wall [419], the south part of the T2/3 [448] wall-line and floor [427], but rested most thickly against the Rampart revetment. Soil [422] appeared to have been continuous with soil within the build-up over [386] in R (Section 2.19.1) suggesting a period of disuse between T3 and T4.

2.18.4 House T4

House T4 (Figs 41, 43) was oval or sub-rectangular in shape, about 8m by 7m. Wall [401] was constructed on top of soil layer [422] on the south, west, and north, but T2/3 wall [448] was reused on the east. A short length of the new wall [401] was built onto the north end of [448], to form one side of a doorway about 3m wide. This doorway was paved through with paving [254], bedded in patches of grey clay, which stretched some distance both inside and outside the House. A clay hearth [473], with stones — including a worn saddle quern — set on edge around, lay on the inner edge of paving [254], beyond which the surface of underlying soil [422] had been used as the floor. Outside, the paving formed a continuous surface with [7]/[8] in R (Section 2.19.2). A hearth [420] — simply the burnt top of soil [422] — was situated east of T4, amidst the scattered cobbles which appeared to be a continuation of the paved surface [254] in this area. House T4 is assigned, on the basis of the paving link with surface [8], to Stage 5, and may have still been in use in Stage 6.

The Rampart had been strengthened at this stage by constructing a new length of revetment [397], on soil [422], with an infill dump of mixed brown soils [398] behind it.

West of House T4, soil [429] accumulated over the T3 platform [13]/[36] against the outer face of wall [401]. This soil contained patches of charcoal and occasional lumps of burnt clay. It appears to have formed without a break with [422] beneath it, but the latter was not mixed with debris from hearths.

2.18.5 Structure T5

Wall [401] of House T4 (Fig 42) became ruinous, and was perhaps levelled. A dark soil layer [403] accumulated over the ruined wall [401] and over the south part of the T4 interior, running out over the edge of paving [254]. This soil may have accumulated during Stage 7. A wall [330] was then built over soil [403] running straight north-west from the Rampart. This had a face surviving only on the east, downhill side, revetting a rubble core. The paved surface [254] was extended by rather scrappier paving [28] which spread up to the Rampart and to wall [330]. Layer [28] also extended the paved surface to the north-west, where its edge in line with the wall face of [330] suggested that this may have continued 5m into the interior. Layer [330]/[28] may have formed an open paved area c 10m by 8m rather than a roofed building during this phase. This structure is assigned to Stage 8.

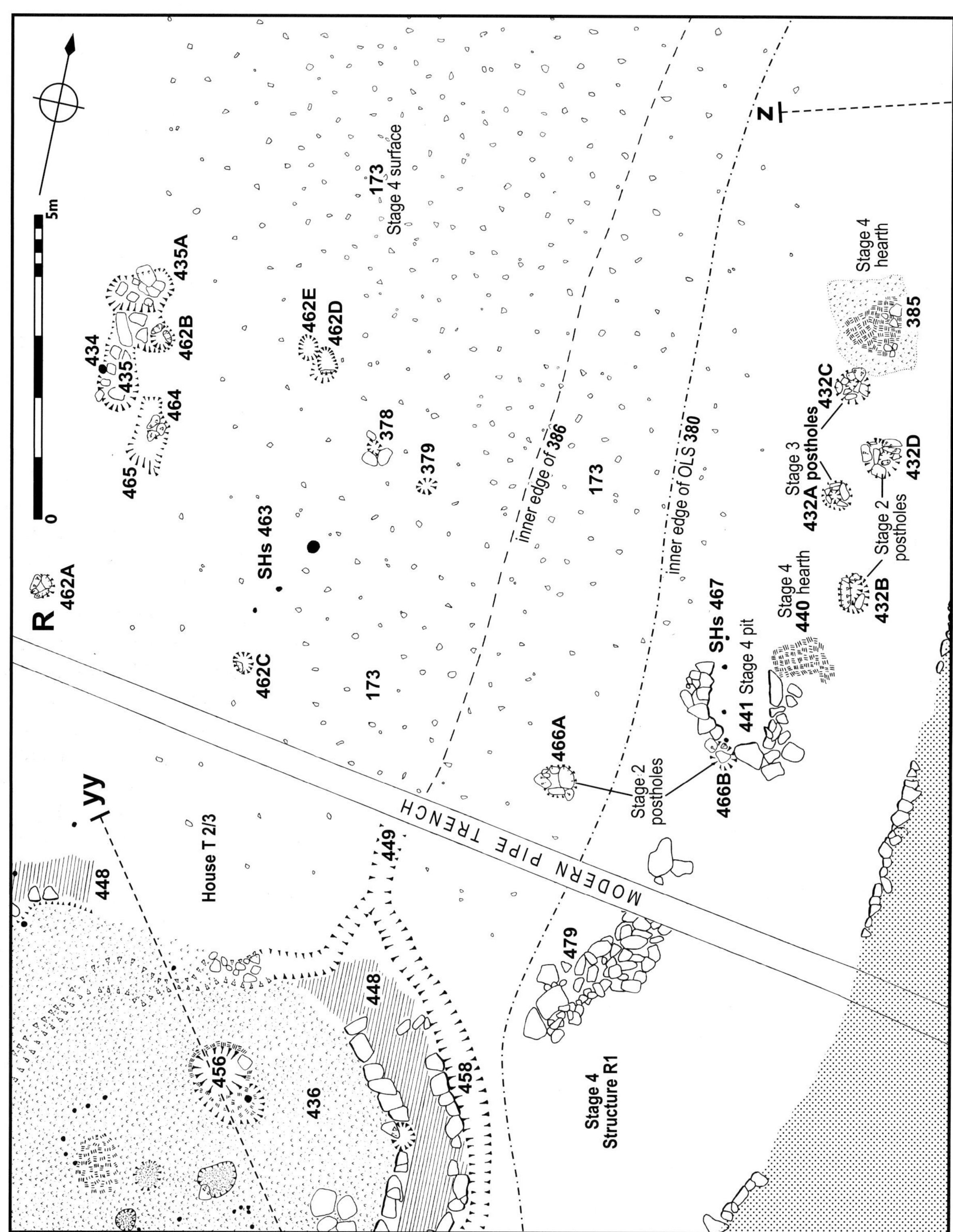

Fig 44: Area R earlier features

2.18.6 Structure T6

Later, dump wall [421] (Fig 42) was constructed (see also Fig 45). This was composed of steeply piled stones with a rough face evident in places on its south side. Wall [421] was built over soil [403] and probably over paving [28] but this was scrappy. It had suffered much from plough erosion away from the Rampart, but the surviving part ran parallel to the Rampart for 6m into Area R (Fig 45), and then curved gradually inward at both ends; it had originally formed a rough (? unroofed) enclosure, T6, at least 8m by 3m. The structure associated with wall [421] is assigned to Stage 9.

A layer of brown soil [400] accumulated over the T5 floor after wall [421], T6, had began to become ruinous. On this rested tumble [399], both from wall [421] and from the Rampart revetment. Further brown soil [395] over this tumble had been much disturbed and was effectively the base of plough soil. The soil [400] continued through Area R and into the Entrance as [140]. It and some of the Rampart collapse accumulated during the phase of abandonment between Stages 9 and 10.

2.19 Area R

Area R extended from House T to the Entrance. It contained a scrappy series of postholes and walling set within soil levels which gradually accumulated against the Rampart. Few of these could be recognised as coherent structures. Surface [7]/[8], which continued the resurfacing of the Entrance in Stage 5, spread across the Area and provided a clear distinction between the earlier and later Phases.

2.19.1 Area R earlier phases

The OLS [371] (Fig 44) beneath both the Period 3 Enclosure Bank and the Round Rampart spread for a distance of some 5m into the interior in this Area and was distinguished as [380]. On this, stones [409] (Fig 8) formed a surface just inside the entrance, but otherwise there was no definite horizon separating [380] from soil accumulations above it, and it cannot be regarded as sealed. After the Round Rampart was built, soil [386], dark grey and gleyed, gradually accumulated against it (section z-zz. Fig 7). This soil was up to 0.25m thick and spread across 8m of the interior right up to House T. It built up outside Houses T1-3, its top a continuation of soil [422] which formed over the T3 site. A sparse scattering of cobbles [173] (Stage 4) spread across the top of soil [386].

All features shown on Fig 44 were sealed by the paving [7]/[8] and soil [9] beneath it. These were difficult to place in sequence as they were not interconnected. The apparent sequence is based on the depths within [386] at which they were found. There were no features located beneath [386] which could be assigned to Stage 1. Postholes [466A] and [466B], [432B] and [432D], all *c* 0.2m deep, appeared at the lowest depth and are assigned to Stage 2. Slightly higher were a similar pair [432A] and [432C], perhaps of Stage 3. Higher again were dump wall [479] of Structure R1, stone-lined pit [441] 0.25m deep, and hearths [440] and [385], which may relate to activity in Stage 4. Beyond the extent of soil [386], phasing of features was not stratigraphically possible within Stages 1-4. Pits [435], [435A] and [465] were similar, *c* 0.40m deep, and evenly packed with rubble. Posthole [464] cut [465] and stakehole [434] cut [435]. Stakeholes [463] and postholes [462A], [462B], [462C], [462D], [462E], [378], and [379] had no relationships and so could not be interpreted as parts of coherent structures.

2.19.2 Area R later phases

Some soil [9] accumulated over cobbles [173] and the features described above in a phase of disuse between Stages 4 and 5, before surface [7]/[8] (Fig 45) was laid in Stage 5. Surface [7] consisted of paving which became very worn (Pl 39). It included a saddle quern worked on both faces and a mortar stone with a worn round depression, both apparently *in situ*. A drain complex marked by features [415], [414], [387], and [384] seemed designed to drain from the paved area into the existing soakaway [409] located just inside the Entrance (Fig 10), and consisted of unlined gullies up to 0.20m deep filled with dark silt. Surviving capstones formed a continuous surface with paving [7]. Drain [10], with sidestones but no capstones, did not appear to have formed part of this system although it had been cut from the same level. The surface beyond paving [7] consisted of small cobbles [8] which stretched behind the Entrance to continue as [557] beneath Structure V, and overlay [409]. This paving is assigned to the major restructuring in Stage 5.

Against the Rampart in the north-east corner of R, cobbles [8] appeared to be contained on the south by wall [396]. This, at right-angles to the Rampart, had a surviving face only on its south side and appeared to have been built together with drain [384] which ran beneath it. Wall [396] was probably contemporary with wall [375], the two forming Structure R2 against the Rampart which was 10m by 4m in area. Structure R2, as it was contemporary with paving [8], belongs to Stage 5 and may have existed until Stage 7.

Structure R2 became ruinous and was largely removed as soil [400] accumulated in this area of the Round and spread out over the edge of cobbles [8].

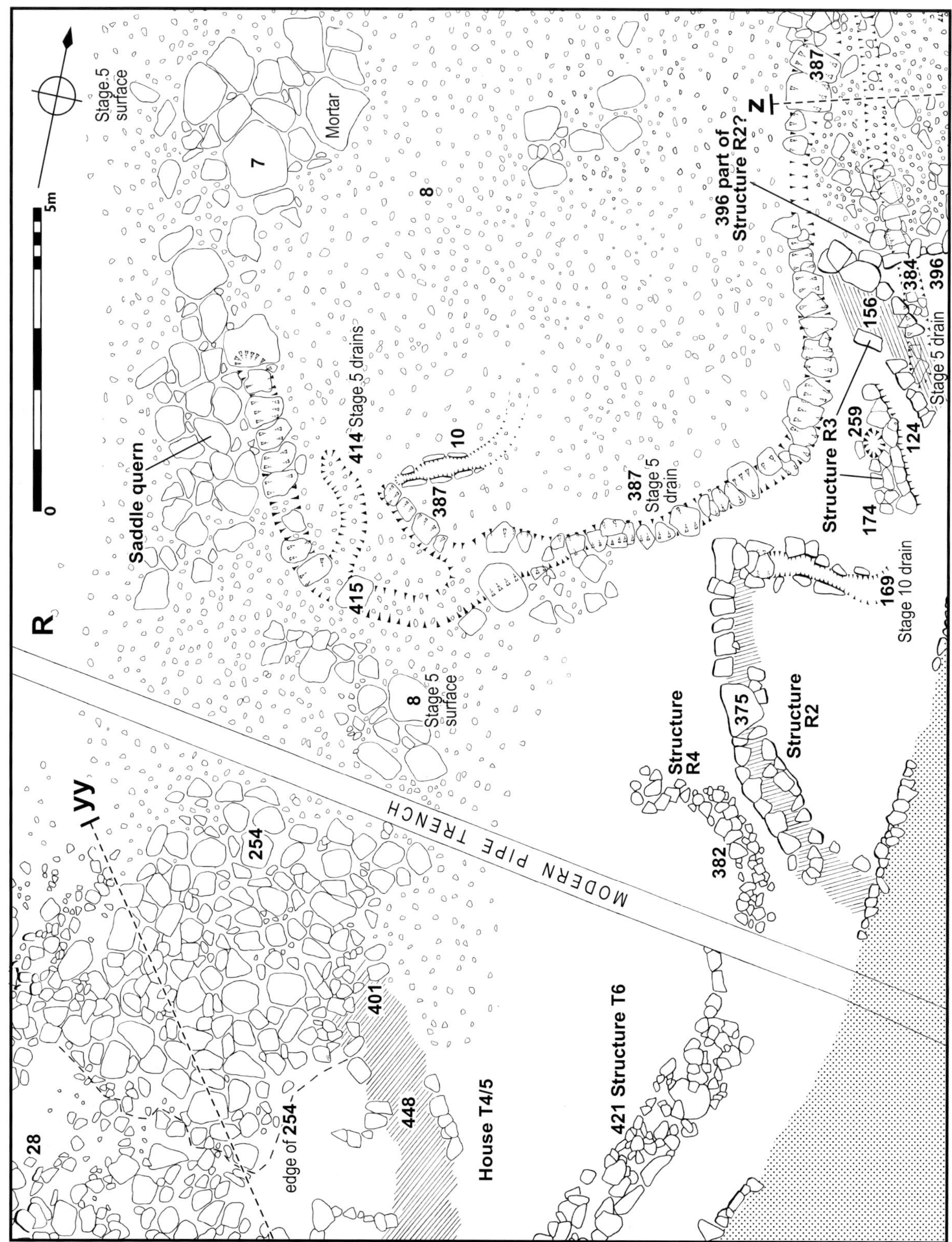

Fig 45: Area R later features

Scatters of stone within [400] suggested that the Rampart revetment was collapsing during its formation. Scattered cobble patchings [175] (section z-zz, Fig 7) were laid as soil [400] accumulated, perhaps during Stage 8, but because these were so scrappy the soils in [400] below and above the cobbles were not separable. Layer [175] may have been no more than worn patches of stone tumble and the surface may have gradually risen as both soil and stone accumulated. The amount of rubble from the revetment increased above [175] especially towards the Entrance (Pl 40) and formed a distinct layer [46] (continuous with [183] in the actual Entranceway), which eventually covered the site of Structure R2 over soil [400] and extended in a band parallel to the Rampart around to the site of House T. This rubble [46], in the top of soil [400], accumulated in the disuse of the site between Stages 9 and 10.

Pl 39: Paving [7] with saddle quern in Area R. View from north. Scale: saddle quern 0.6m in length

Set into rubble [46] was a short length of wall [156]; this had a stone-lined drain [124] to its south associated with a patch of worn paving [174] and a posthole [259] 0.15m deep; these are described as Structure R3. A second stone-lined drain [169] without any associated structure was also set into [46]. Dump wall [382], Structure R4, was built on top of soil [400] and was thus subsequent to Structure T6 [421] and Structure R2 [396]/[375]. Structure R4 wall [382] may have been contemporary with Structure 3, or may have been earlier or later. All these features were much plough damaged and were only covered by the bottom of ploughsoil. They are assigned to Stage 10 but if not contemporary, may represent scrappy reuse over many centuries.

Pl 40: Area R looking south from Entrance. Revetment collapse [46] and [183] overlapping paving [8]. 2m scale

2.20 Period 6 Medieval use

This Period covers agricultural use of the Round through the Medieval and early Post-Medieval periods and is represented only by a little pottery in surface levels. The robbing of some of the building walls and rampart revetments, such as [185] near the Entrance, may have taken place.

2.21 Period 7 16th-century field enclosure

The Round was incorporated into the present field system, probably during the 16th century AD (Section 9.2.8). The now eroded Rampart on the west and south was built up into hedge bank [236] with substantial stone revetments to front and rear (section s-ss, Fig 7). Presumably the east and north sections of the Rampart were levelled during this Period.

2.22 Period 8 Post-Medieval use

This Period covers the use of the site since its incorporation into the present field system, and is only represented by a little pottery, presumably lost during agricultural activity. There may have been some robbing of stone from Round structures or from the revetments of its Rampart.

3 Metalworking and metal finds

3.1 Coins

3.1.1 Coins from the excavation *PJ Casey*
(text written 2001)

The coins appear to comprise a single isolated find C10, a billon (copper/silver alloy) Antoninianus, and a scattered hoard of orichalcum (ie brass) sestertii, C1-9, derived from the reigns from Trajan to Commodus, in the area of Structure Y. Of these, six came from 751A (three sealed beneath the wall of Structure Y, Fig 24) and the remainder from 785, the soil over the Structure. The varying positions indicate the amount of disturbance in soil levels in the area; the hoard must have been buried in layer 751A and that layer considerably disturbed before the erection of Structure Y. The isolated find, C10, came from House A, from infill deposits [34] of a transitional phase between Houses A2 and A3 (Table 3.1).

The condition of the coins is suggestive of considerable circulation and the hoard falls into a well-established pattern of such finds which, whilst comprising coins of the 2nd, were almost certainly deposited in the middle of the 3rd century. The monetary background can be briefly sketched. Intermittent supply of lower value denominations characterised coin supply to Britain in the pre-Flavian period, thereafter bulk supplies were furnished on a regular basis, possibly connected to the raising of military pay in the reign of Domitian. Very large numbers of sestertii, and its fractions, flowed into the province in the reigns of Trajan, Hadrian, and Pius. From the middle of the reign of Marcus Aurelius this flow ceased, issues of Commodus and his successors are very scarce in British contexts. However sufficient coins had reached the provincial currency pool to provide for a circulating medium for the next half century.

Declining purchasing power in the post-Severan period pushed the sestertius to the fringes of the coin use pattern, probably resulting in the coins achieving a scrap value higher than their purchasing value. It is in this context that we may view such hoards as that from Trethurgy. Attempts to revive the denomination by Trajan, Decius and Postumus, who issued an extensive range of double sestertii overstruck on extremely worn Trajanic, Hadrianic, and Antonine specimens, met with little success. In the light of these data a *terminus ante quem* of AD 260 may be advanced for the Trethurgy hoard.

3.1.2 Some background on Roman coinage in Cornwall *Richard Reece*
(text written 2001)

This short summary depends on two earlier pieces of work that gathered together most of the available information. Alison Pritchard summarised the Roman coins found in Cornwall and the Plymouth area, both hoards and site-finds, in an undergraduate dissertation of 1983 (Pritchard 1983). Professor Anne S Robertson worked for most of her life on an inventory of coin hoards from Roman Britain which has just been published (Robertson 2000). It is, in effect, an outsider's summary of published evidence. There is a good deal of unpublished material now on record, of which a preliminary draft of this summary, together with Robertson's recent publication of hoards, has highlighted the importance. It is hoped that there may soon be an up-to-date study of all available material which will certainly change details and may well alter some of the broader interpretative themes presented here. In what follows, I have checked the two accounts of the coin hoards by Robertson and by Pritchard and they agree well. This is an excellent compliment to Alison Pritchard and suggests that her lists of site-finds may be accepted with confidence.

The hoards are most easily discussed by periods during which the coinage remained fairly constant (Table 3.2). In the table very rough totals for single finds are given in the same periods. Table 3.3 gives the name and number of each hoard according to the Robertson Inventory. The hoards known for Cornwall can be compared with those known for the whole of Britain and some deductions are possible. The Cornish hoards in general are nearly 2% of the total. For the earlier period when hoards are well known in other parts of Britain such as East Anglia none are yet known in the county. The two hoards from the period of stable currency between AD 69 and 192 are a little below average, but for the early 3rd century the two local hoards form a notable proportion of the total 85 known. This proportion rises for AD 238 to 260 when hoards are low over most of Britain. Fourteen Cornish hoards in the next period are overtaken by 530 British hoards so that the share drops to just over average and stays there till AD 348. The hoards of the later 4th century are not well represented.

There is one further point which can be made concerning the hoards up to AD 260. Three of the five earlier hoards are probably of bronze coinage (St Just,

No	Context & SF	Issuer	Denomination	Type	Reference	Date	Condition
C1	751A, SF115	Trajan	Sesertius	Obv. [IMP CAES NERVAE TRAIANO AVG GER DAC PM TRP COS V PP-SC] Rev. [SPQR OPTIMO PRINCIPI-SC]	519	103-11	EW/EW
C2	751A, SF113	Trajan	Sesertius	Obv.— Rev.—	—	98-117	EW/EW
C3	751A, SF114	Hadrian	Sesertius	Obv. [IMP CAESAR TRAIANVS HADRIANVS AUG] Rev. [PONT MAX TR POT COS II-SC ADVENTVS AVG]	547	118	EW/EW
C4	785, SF 2	Hadrian	Sesertius	Obv. [HADRIANUS AVG COS III PP] Rev. —	754/61	134-8	EW/EW
C5	785, SF101	Faustina I	Sesertius	Obv. — Rev. [AETERNITAS-SC]	as 1103A	141-61	EW/EW
C6	751A, SF111	Faustina I	Sesertius	Obv. [DIVA AVG]VSTA [FAVSTINA] Rev. —	as 1108	141-61	EW/EW
C7	751A, SF110	Faustina I	Sesertius	Obv. [DIVA FAVSTINA] Rev. [AETERNITAS-SC]	1127	141-61	EW/EW
C8	785, SF3	Faustina II	Sesertius	Obv. [FAVSTINA AVGVSTA] Rev. [IVNO-SC]	1645	161-76	EW/EW
C9	751A, SF112	Commodus	Sesertius	Obv. [M CO]MMO[DVS ANTONINVS AVG] Rev. [PROV DEOR TR P VI IMP III] COS III [PP]-SC	312a	180-1	VW/VW
C10	34, SF1	Tetricus I	Antoninianus	Obv. [IMP C TETRICVS]AVG Rev. [PAX] AVG	copy of 100	270-3	SW/SW

Table 3.1: Details of coins. Reference to Mattingly and Sydenham 1923-94. Condition: EW - Extremely worn, details are reduced to near invisibility; VW - Very worn, details are eroded but portrait and legends are still legible; SW - Slightly worn, all details are visible, wear confined to highest points

Date	Cornwall: hoards	Britain: hoards	Cornish hoards as percentage of British	Single finds in Cornwall	Percentage of total Cornish single finds by date
to AD 41	0	18	0	8	4.4
AD 41 to 69	0	37	0	12	6.6
AD 69 to 192	2	322	0.6	55	30.2
AD 192 to 238	2	85	2.3	10	5.5
AD 238 to 260	2	36	5.6	3	1.6
AD 260 to 296	14	530	2.6	44	24.2
AD 296 to 348	9	294	3.1	27	14.8
AD 348 to 364	1	119	0.8	7	3.8
AD 364 to 411	3	280	1.1	16	8.8
Total dated	33	1721	1.9	182	-
Undated	10	273	-	-	-

Table 3.2: Analysis of Cornish coin hoards and single finds

Wendron, and Mawgan-in-Meneage) and only two (Camborne and Polperro) are certainly of silver coins. Constantine has both bronze and silver, but Gare, buried around 270, has a few silver coins with over a thousand bronze coins mainly of the 2nd century. This concentration on bronze coinage is rather different from the usual hoard buried in Britain up to around AD 260 which contains silver denarii. Bronze however is a feature of hoards of similar date on the continent buried in France and Spain.

The later 3rd-century hoards which are made up of very base silver radiate coins are part of a general western-European pattern. Since they occur in roughly equal proportions in places where there were undoubted barbarian invasions, such as north-east Gaul, as well as places where there were few if any troubles, such as Aquitaine, they cannot be used as an index of unrest or disaster. Two gold coins of the latest 4th century at Lanyon and the hoards of silver coins of similar date at Zennor and on Samson in the Isles of Scilly fit well into the British pattern of hoarding and do not need special comment.

Into this context the hoard from Trethurgy fits perfectly. The date range and the inclusion of only bronze coinage adds to the earlier suggestion that early bronze hoards are a feature of the South West and makes the interpretation of earlier uncertain reports as bronze more probable.

In the survey made by Pritchard, single finds and site-finds of Roman coins follow a rather different

AD 69 to 192	St Just in Penwith [220], Wendron [298]
AD 193 to 238	Mawgan-in-Meneage [378], Camborne [417]
AD 238 to 260	Polperro, Lansallos [436], Constantine [451]
AD 260 to 296	Sharrow Point [468A], Gare [530], Lostwithiel [559], Breage [607], Ludgvan [608], Mawnan [609], Morvah [610], Sennen [611], St Michael Carhayes [742], Sancreed [765], Hayle [790], Perranarworthal, Carnon [791], East Cornwall [792], Malpas, St Clement [823]
AD 296 to 348	Budock [997], Camborne [1033], Gwinear [1110], Morvah [1111], Redruth [1133], Condurrow, St Anthony-in-Meneage [1134], Stithians [1135], Tywardreath [1136], Mullion [1163]
AD 348 to 364	St Just in Roseland [1360]
AD 364 to 411	Lanyon, Madron [1501A], Zennor, Towednack [1521], Samson, Scilly Isles [1522]
Undatable	Lanhydrock [1694], Gwinear [1714], Morval [1715], near Padstow [1716], Redruth [1717], Redruth [1718], Treryn [1719], Nanskeval, St Mawgan-in-Pydar [1887], St Paul [1888], Stratton [1889]

Table 3.3: Analysis of Cornish coin hoards by date; numbers follow Robertson (2000)

pattern from the hoards. Any numerical summary will be unbalanced by the coins from sites such as Nanstallon and Magor which overwhelm the casual losses and the few finds from less prolific sites. Since a fort such as Nanstallon has a history of occupation and coin loss determined by events well outside the county, those coins probably ought to be considered apart from other chance losses in future analyses. After a substantial number of finds from the 1st and 2nd centuries, most of which are bronze coins, there is a drop in the early 3rd century. This follows the general British pattern of site-finds rather than the Cornish pattern of hoards. The high point of hoarding in the late 3rd century is not equalled by single coin loss, but site-finds are slightly better represented than hoards in the later 4th century. All these points depend on small numbers of coins so that a few new discoveries could turn peaks into troughs and vice versa. The coins do exist, they can be turned into percentages, but the comments made about them have to emphasise the small size of the sample and the temporary nature of any commentary.

This summary makes the single site-find from Trethurgy totally in place. If a coin is found that is later than AD 200, the chances given by Table 3.2 are that it will be a radiate coin. This is indeed the case.

3.2 Brooches *Sarnia Butcher;*

alloy identification *Justine Bayley*

(text written 2001)

3.2.1 The finds

Fig 46

M1 From [932], lower midden in Structure U, Stage 6. Surviving length 51mm. Leaded bronze. A very heavy brooch with exceptionally thick rounded bow. The foot and most of the catchplate are missing. The crossbar is plain with an open curved back which must have held a spring: there is no lug for attachment but as the ends of the crossbar are broken it is possible that there was an axial rod. There are two copper alloy rivets through the upper bow and it seems likely that these held some form of crest which might have had a loop for the chord, especially as there is a notch in the back of the head where a wire may have passed.

This appears to belong to the 'Dolphin' type: numerous versions exist of these rather plain brooches whose main characteristics are the T-shape with wide crossbar and heavy rounded head to the bow. The pin attachment is either a hinge or a rather inefficient method of holding a spring, which is consequently

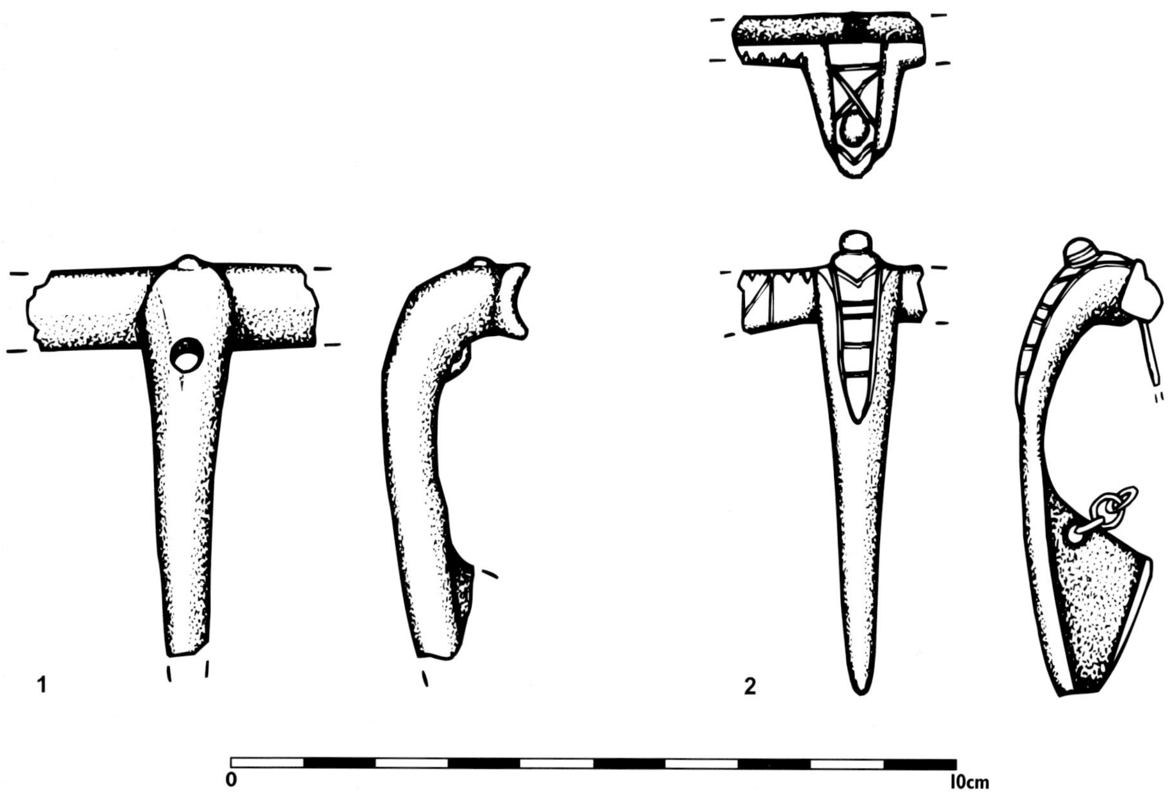

Fig 46: Brooches. Drawing L Simpson/C Thorpe. Scale 1:1

often missing. This stage appears in the mid 1st century AD and the general type occurs in most parts of Roman Britain in the latter half of the 1st century.

M2 From [11], soil over Structures D and E. Length 58mm. Leaded bronze. A T-shaped brooch with pin hinged on a rod housed in a semi-cylindrical moulding behind the crossbar. Both ends of the crossbar are broken. The strongly arched bow carries heavy moulded decoration on the head in the form of a raised crest with a series of grooves, a diagonal cross and a small knob. Justine Bayley informs me that the crest is probably part of the main casting and that the knob is not a separate rivet. The back of the bow is recessed behind the decorated area and the bow tapers to a plain foot. The triangular catchplate is perforated by one small round hole; when the brooch was drawn this still carried three loops of a fine chain which probably linked another brooch.

A group of similar though not identical brooches occurs in South West Britain: two from Mount Batten, Plymouth (Cunliffe 1988, fig 34, nos 72 and 73); others from Rock, Cornwall (Haverfield 1924, fig 5, no 12), Wookey Hole, Somerset (Branigan and Dearne 1990, no 3.1), Ilchester, Somerset (Leach 1982, fig 115, no 1), Bradford Peverel, Dorset (Hull forthcoming, 3813), and Dorchester (Hull forthcoming, 9025). None of these is from a dated context; typologically this group shows features of the very numerous 'Colchester derivative' brooches which developed in the second half of the 1st century.

3.2.2 Discussion

It is noticeable that a 1st-century date is suggested for both the brooches found at Trethurgy while other evidence establishes that the main occupation of the site begins later. This may be explained by a consideration of the characteristics of Roman-period brooch-finds in Britain generally.

Brooches are most common in the period mid 1st to early 2nd century AD in Britain. It seems that the pre-Roman fashion for wearing them continued, at first with standard types manufactured on the Continent such as the Aucissa and Hod Hill, and that British metalworkers soon began producing quantities of one-piece sprung brooches of the Colchester and 'Nauheim-derivative' types, usually made of brass. The next stage was of rather simple brooches echoing the Colchester shape but made with a separate spring or a hinge, perhaps necessitated by the use of leaded bronze, an alloy unsuitable to the drawing-out of the spring from a single strip of metal (Bayley 1985a; Bayley and Butcher forthcoming). Brooches such as those described under M1 were part of this general production, which probably went on in various parts of the country. In the South West the same general shape continued to be made, usually with rather limited decoration. Where analysed, these south-western brooches are nearly always shown to be made of heavily leaded bronze. The main production centre seems to have been in the Mendips, presumably to be associated with the newly opened lead mines: the evidence for this lies in the distribution of the brooches and the discovery of moulds for some of the types at Compton Dando in that area (Bayley 1985b).

The dating evidence for all these types shows that they were widespread in the later 1st and early 2nd centuries; however they are often found in later contexts and it is the interpretation of this which must now be considered. Part of the difficulty lies in the nature of the dated contexts: after the 1st century, when the campaigns of the Roman army left a number of sites with only short periods of occupation, most British sites show settlement over lengthy periods. When a 1st-century brooch turns up in a 2nd-century or later context, it is often difficult to know whether it has continued in use or whether it is simply redeposited rubbish. In the more Romanised parts of Britain it is probably the latter, since other types of brooch were developed in later centuries: eg the knee and crossbow types, though none were so numerous as the earlier types. However in Cornwall very few of these occur, so that it looks as if the use of brooches was not so general as to encourage either trade or local manufacture and those who owned one of the earlier brooches may well have kept them.

The Cornish evidence can be summarised as follows. The two largest groups of brooches known from Cornwall are those from St Mawgan-in-Pydar (Threipland 1956, 69-72) and Carvossa (Carlyon 1987, 123-7), both with 16 brooches, including two penannulars from each site. Both contain a mixture of south-western types and others found in Britain generally and in both the majority are 1st-century types, though Carvossa had a Continental plate brooch (No 23) which might be as late as AD 200+. Otherwise there are only one or two brooches from any known context (about 20 altogether) and many of these are of the simple 1st-century types to which the Trethurgy brooches belong. The one brooch found at Magor, a rare Roman-style building for Cornwall, was one of these (O'Neil 1933; 1934; the brooch is in the RCM, Truro). Again some of these single finds were of clearly non south-western types — eg the shoe-sole brooch from Kilhallon (Carlyon 1982, fig 5.1).

While future finds could well alter the picture, it seems from the present evidence that the use of brooches continued into the Roman period in Cornwall but that only a few individuals used them after the early years of the 2nd century AD: those found in later contexts seem most likely to have been preserved deliberately, whether in use or otherwise.

The picture is completely different for the Isles of Scilly, where the hundreds of brooches found at Nornour range from the second half of the 1st century through to the first half of the 3rd century or later (Dudley 1968; Butcher forthcoming). Here the most likely explanation is that the brooches were offerings at a shrine and the implications of this for Cornwall also need consideration: whether the few brooches from later contexts there were preserved for more than their everyday usefulness.

3.3 Other copper alloy objects

The only other objects of copper alloy (not illustrated) were a small globule, apparently a casting by-product, [11], soil over Structures D and E; fragments of a bracelet, extremely corroded, 0.08 internal diameter, simple circular cross-section 6mm, [852] House Z1 drain; two sheet fragments, probable covering of large studs, [519] revetment collapse over Ditch and [800] soil over Structure U.

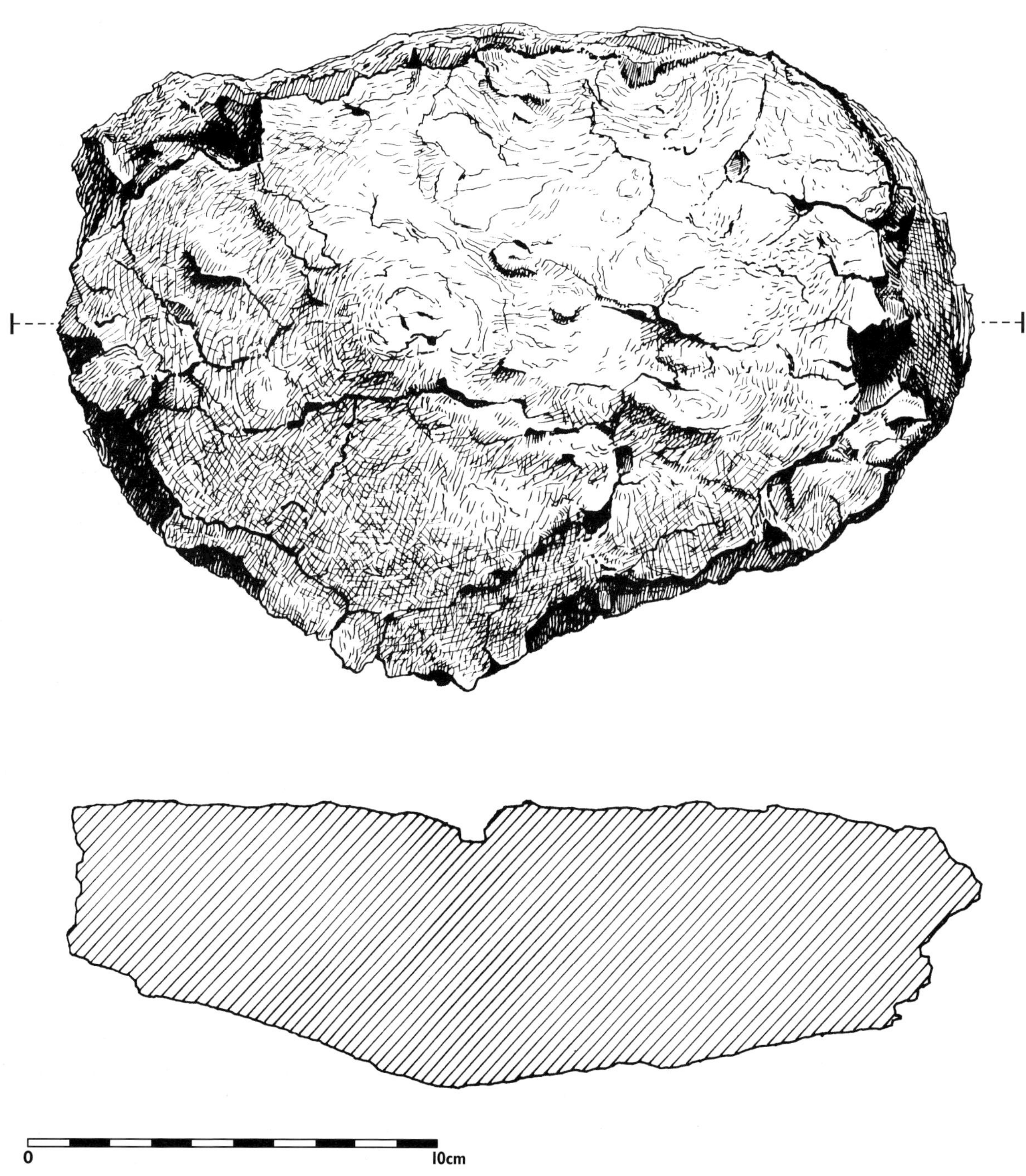

Figure 47: Tin ingot. Drawing R Penhallurick. Scale 2:3

3.4 Silver *Justine Bayley*

(text written 1986, updated 2001)

Two small fragments (not illustrated) from [11] soil over Structures D and E, with a rough underside and a smooth but slightly channelled upper surface, suggested waste material from casting: weights 4g and 2g. The silver (AM 777859) was qualitatively analysed by X-ray fluorescence (XRF). The major element present was silver but minor amounts of copper, zinc, lead, and gold were also detected. The composition of both pieces was similar. The metal appears to have been spilt on an uneven surface while molten.

3.5 Tin ingot *Justine Bayley*

(text written 1986, updated 2001)

Fig 47

M3 Tin ingot [932] lower midden in Structure U (Fig 16). The tin ingot (AM 777408) was originally roughly circular and plano-convex in shape. The thinner outer portion has broken up into blocky lumps as it corroded leaving a central piece which measures about 220x150mm and has a maximum thickness of 75mm. The weight of the main piece is about 7kg while the fragments weigh about 5kg. It is not possible to estimate accurately the original weight of the ingot as much of the tin is now present as tin oxide, which increases the apparent weight, while not all the pieces that have fallen off the ingot may have been retrieved which would reduce the apparent weight. A fragment of the ingot was analysed by XRF but the only elements detected apart from tin were iron and manganese, both almost certainly in the adhering soil. The analysis agrees with those quoted by Tylecote (1962, 66) who notes that tin ingots are usually better than 99% tin. The metal would have been obtained by smelting cassiterite (tin oxide) at a temperature of around 600°C (Tylecote 1962, 63).

3.6 Slags and other metallurgical finds *Justine Bayley*

(text written 1986, updated 2001)

The slags (AM Nos 777381-407) were examined and individual identifications are given in Table 3.4. The total weight was only a few kilogrammes.

The two largest groups of material were hearth lining and smithing slag. The hearth lining was red fired clay that had become vitrified on one surface from contact with the fire. The pieces were of various thicknesses indicating differing firing intensities. There is nothing in the hearth lining to associate it with a particular process but the presence of the smithing slag suggests that these hearths were used by blacksmiths working iron. The smithing slag is the sort of material one would expect to find on any settlement where small-scale ironworking was carried out, presumably to meet the local demand. Much of this slag had attached pieces of charcoal or impressions of charcoal, the remains of the fuel used in the hearth where the iron was being heated.

The other slags are fired clay (AM 777397 and 777400), vitrified clay (AM 777394) which is just clay that has been overheated, schorl (see below) (AM 777390-91), a piece of brick or tile with a vitrified surface (AM 777387) which may have been built into a hearth and vitrified like the hearth lining, and one piece of iron slag with a rather different structure to the rest (AM 777385). It appears to have been more fluid than the rest of the slag and maybe even to have run a little. This sort of structure is more usually associated with iron smelting where temperatures are higher than in smithing operations but in this case it was probably just the product of a smithing hearth where the temperature obtained was higher than normal.

The total quantities of slag were small and almost certainly only represent small-scale working, not a large industry.

3.7 Schorl *Rob Ixer* and *J G McDonnell*

(text written 1986, updated 2001)

Amongst the slags and other residues examined by Justine Bayley were two specimens (AM 777390-1) that resembled slag but required further investigation to identify them.

A powder sample for X-ray diffraction analysis, and polished specimens for microscopy, were prepared. Both reflected light and scanning electron microscopy were used, the latter including semi-quantitative chemical analysis.

The analyses showed the specimens not to be slags and so it was supposed that they were natural materials but possibly altered, eg due to partial smelting by man.

Therefore, a thin section was prepared, and along with a polished specimen they were examined by one of us (RI). The specimens were identified as schorl ($NaFe_3Al_6(BO_3)_3\ (Si_6O_{18})(OH)_4)$) one of the tourmaline group of minerals and a common accessory phase in Cornwall often associated with cassiterite (SnO_2) in tin ores. Where the two minerals occur together in a tin ore it is necessary to separate them in order to produce a concentrate that is suitable for smelting. The presence of both schorl and a tin ingot (M3, AM 777408) on the site would suggest that tin smelting had occurred on, or very close to, the site.

Context	AML No	Hearth lining	Smithing slag	Other
[363] Period 3 Enclosure Bank	777381	+		
[323] Period 3 Enclosure Bank behind A	777393		+	
[371] OLS beneath Round Rampart	777397			Black, fired, coarsely gritted clay lump?
[390] Round Rampart	777382		+	
[390] Round Rampart	777399	+		
[205] Cut for revetment of south Rampart terminal	777384		+	
[568] Primary Ditch silt	777383		+	
[532] Soil over cobbles [521] over Ditch terminal	777387			Piece of brick or tile with vitrified surface
[183] Entrance, Stage 9/10 rubble	777385			Iron slag that has ?flowed
[191] Pit Stage 10 in Entrance	777386		+	
[191] Pit Stage 10 in Entrance	777407	?		
[542] V2, drain	777400			?Iron object and coarsely gritted burnt daub
[932] U, lower midden	777388			(No sample in bag)
[808] Q, soils Stages 4/6	777389		+	
[517] Structure X5 soil	777401	+		
[666] X4, Stage 9 walling	777390			Schorl (see Section 3.7)
[77] G, upper infill	777391			Schorl (see Section 3.7)
[255] G, backing to Structure	777392		+	
[34] between A2 and A3	777402	+	+	
[471C] T2 posthole	777404	+		
[427] T3 floor	777405	+		
[36] Stage 4+ platform adjacent T3	777394			Vitrified clay
[422] Soil between T3 and T4	777395		+	
[403] Soil over T4	777396		+	
[395] Soil over T	777403	+		
[7] R, Stage 5+ paving	777398		+	
[175] R, patching of paving [8]	777406	+		

Table 3.4: Slag descriptions and identifications

Note: the failure to identify the mineral initially from the chemical analysis and the X-ray diffraction pattern was due to the inability of the scanning electron microscope to detect the element Boron (B), thus resulting in a search through Na/Fe/Al silicates, rather than Na/Fe/Al/B silicates.

3.8 Discussion of the tin ingot and non-ferrous metalworking

The Trethurgy ingot was found in the base of midden [932/801] within Structure U. Its total weight would have been around 12kg and it seems unlikely that such a quantity of tin was deliberately discarded. The date of the midden may be late 4th century AD (Stage 6), though this date is by no means firm. The ingot may have been cached during the midden's deposition or inserted later; it may therefore date to the late 4th, to the 5th century, or even later. The nature of midden [932/801] made it impossible for small intrusive holes to be detected.

The oval shape and plano-convex cross-section of the ingot are generally similar to those of other Cornish ingots from the late prehistoric to early Medieval periods (Tylecote 1986, fig 21). Of these the earliest, probably the only example of pre-Roman date, is that from Castle Dore (Royal Cornwall Museum; Beagrie 1983, 107)). The fragmentary ingot from St Mawgan-in-Pydar (Threipland 1956, 76; Tylecote 1978, 50) is very early in the Roman period. The ingot from Par Beach, St Martin's, Scilly, was dated by the excavator *c* 300 AD (Tylecote 1966, 33). The Carnanton ingot is the only example with probable formal Roman stamps but these are not clearly identifiable and do not provide a close date (Warner 1967; Beagrie 1985). (The ingot from Trereife, Madron, with raised letters on its surface, considered at one time to be of Roman date, is now generally accepted as Post-Medieval, the letters possibly referring to the East India Company - Penhallurick 1986, 236.) The ingots from Porthmeor, which also produced some 'doubtful tin slag', (Hirst 1937, 65) and Chun (Leeds 1926, 238) may be of late-Roman date but that from Porthmeor could be easily be 5th century and that from Chun any period up to the 8th century. Plano-convex ingots were certainly produced in the Post-Roman period and it is probable that the amount of tin working between AD 400-1100 has been underestimated. A group of four ingots was found in 1974 at Prah Sands, Germoe, exposed in a palaeosol on the beach; wood from the palaeosol has a C14 date (HAR-962); which calibrates to AD 630-890 at two sigma, a date supported by archaeomagnetic dating (Biek 1994, 61). From stream works at Boscarne there is a C14 date of AD 635-1045 at two sigma (UCR-1469) for one of two wooden shovels in possible association with an ingot (Penhallurick 1986, 210-2). Penhallurick (*ibid*, 225-36) has assembled from early records a considerable list of plano-convex ingots from Cornish stream works which may well be of prehistoric to pre-Norman date. A recent find of 44 ingots, mostly of the plano-convex type, has been made off the South Devon coast at Bigbury and interpreted as the result of a probable 6th-century AD wreck (Fox 1995). The Trethurgy ingot falls at the heavy end of this series though many of the stream work finds are of similar or greater weight (Table 3.5).

No tin slag was found at Trethurgy but cassiterite pebbles were found in [517] Stage 10 Structure X5, Stage 10 soil over V [524], and Stage 4 soil [905] in Structure Q5, while schorl fragments were found in Stage 9 walling [666] in House X4 and Stage 9 upper infill [77] in Structure G. The contexts of this material together with the probable Stage 6 date of the ingot may tentatively suggest tinworking during the later centuries on the site. It is presumed that actual smelting took place away from the site, near the tin ground and the sources of fuel used. Tin ground, or stream tin, lies along the stream which runs through Trethurgy village (Fig 2) within 100m of the Round and this could have been the source of the cassiterite pebbles. It is generally considered that most tinworking during the Roman and Post-Roman centuries used cassiterite pebbles extracted from tin ground (Gerrard 2000). The schorl fragments come from the sides of a tin lode (see Section 3.7). It is just possible that they indicate the working of lodes, perhaps more likely that they had eroded from a lode into surface soil from which they had been collected. A series of tin lodes intrude in the higher parts of the St Austell granite 3km north of Trethurgy.

Bigbury smallest	0.50kg
Castle Dore	0.54kg
Prah 1	3.85kg
Prah 2	1.86kg
Prah 3	1.90kg
Prah 4	1.91kg
Porthmeor	1.08kg
Chun	5kg
Trethurgy	12kg
Bigbury largest	12.95kg
Carnanton	17.67kg

Table 3.5: Available weights of datable ingots (approximate only, because of corrosion)

Any prehistoric or Roman period workings in the tin grounds have become obscured by later fluvial deposits, peat growth, and later workings. Penhallurick (1986, 173-224) has demonstrated that all pre-Medieval artefacts found in later workings came from the level of the tin ground and not above it; a concentration both of pre-Medieval artefacts and of plano-convex ingots occurs in the St Austell area. More recently Gerrard (2000) has produced a summary of tin extraction and production in Britain; the available evidence varies in quantity and quality but overall presents a picture of extensive use of the tin resources of South West Britain from the prehistoric period onward, in which those of the St Austell area were obviously extensively used over a long period.

There is no evidence for the degree of control exercised over the production of tin on the fringes of the Roman Empire. It is presumed that there would have been increased demand in Britain during the 3rd and 4th centuries AD because of the greater use of pewter, quite apart from Empire-wide needs relating to the decline of mines in Iberia and increased quantities of tin in coinage. It appears probable that Medieval Cornish mining laws were based, at least in part, on pre-Norman Cornish customary law (Pennington 1973, 13). General studies of pre-Roman land-use and social structure now make it plain that most aspects of life and land were more ordered than was once supposed (eg Lloyd Jones 1984, 176). In pre-Roman, Roman, and Post-Roman Cornwall (and indeed Devon) the extraction of tin may have been governed by local rules, and traditional rights to this in particular areas may have been held by communities as part of their resources. Such rules may well have been respected by the official Roman administration, and have been comparatively unaffected by its cessation; the use of local laws in Roman Britain is further addressed in Section 12.3. Quite possibly local landholders took out licenses as *conductores* to work metals within their traditional rights; such licenses would have allowed them to legitimately sell tin. The Trethurgy ingot may thus, whether 4th century or later, have been produced within a framework of local custom on mineral extraction. The Trethurgy ingot and other Cornish plano-convex ingots were not stamped because they never reached any market where stamps were required. Such ingots may have circulated within Cornwall through local exchange networks.

Several sites have evidence for some connection with tinworking in the Roman period. The small hillfort at St Mawgan-in-Pydar (Threipland 1956) produced apparent tin slag from a number of different structures with a possible smelting hearth in Hut A. Tin may have been worked on site but the one analysis published indicates that material interpreted as slag was actually tin (*ibid*, 76) and among this 'slag' is the ingot fragment referred to above (Tylecote 1978, 50). The other possible smelting site is indicated by the furnace found at Chun Castle (Leeds 1926, fig 6; Tylecote 1962, fig 11). This obviously postdates the main Iron Age occupation of the site and has been connected with finds of Post-Roman grass-marked ware (Thomas 1956). However, amongst the finds from the area of the furnace in the Royal Cornwall Museum, is gabbroic pottery of Roman date. Indeed Leeds' (1926, fig 8) illustration of the pottery includes a number of forms now well recognised as Roman. It is quite possible that the Chun furnace is of this period. Tylecote (1986, 43) has questioned the interpretation of the Chun furnace, and suggested that, if connected with metallurgy, it may have been for crucible melting. If so, the Chun evidence would be consistent with that for the rest of Cornwall — off-site smelting but some on-site working and finishing. The other sites to have produced cassiterite pebbles and small quantities of tin slag, possibly metallic tin, are Carn Euny (Borlase 1870, 167) and Chysauster (Hencken 1933, 270), and in both off-site smelting is indicated. The only location where there may have concentrated production of tin artefacts may be the enclosure at Killigrew, Trispen, during the 2nd and 3rd centuries AD (Cole forthcoming).

Tin smelting was taking place in the vicinity of Trethurgy Round with mould S14 and mould cover S15 suggesting some artefact manufacture on site; the Stage 8 contexts for these pieces are broadly consistent with the suggested late date of the ingot, cassiterite, and schorl. The two small pieces of cast silver and of copper alloy, unfortunately effectively unstratified, suggest that these metals were also worked. The St Austell district is rich in these metals (Dines 1956, 27) and lodes of both copper and silver occur 2-4km away. Small-scale artefact production in non-ferrous metals is common on Cornish rounds of Roman date. At Castle Gotha round (Bayley 1982) a range of different copper alloys were worked on a small scale; finds also included a mould for a brooch and a cassiterite pebble. The Carvossa enclosure also had limited evidence for working copper alloy and lead with a high tin content (Carlyon 1987, 128-9), and a greisen mould fragment (*ibid*, fig 12, no 6). The unenclosed coastal site of Duckpool in North Cornwall also was a focus for the melting and casting of lead, pewter, and copper alloy during the 4th century AD (Ratcliffe 1995, 113). Duckpool, Castle Gotha, and Carvossa are the only Roman sites in Cornwall to have produced evidence for copper alloy production, even on a small scale, although the army worked silver at Nanstallon (Fox and Ravenhill 1972, 108). A lead ingot from the round at Reawla (Appleton-Fox 1992, 118), the only metallurgical find from the site apart from iron, adds to the pattern of small-scale metalworking.

3.9 Iron artefacts

3.9.1 General comment and discussion

The assemblage consists of c 489 objects (Table 3.6), heavily corroded because of the acid soil conditions. Of these, 244 were nails, many broken, and 115 were hobnails. The nails were generally small, the median size of complete ones 45mm. There were six pieces of plate, ie sheet iron which might have come from objects such as cauldrons, and 14 pieces of strap, many apparently deliberately cut rather than broken. The collection was examined by WH Manning in 1986 who advised on procedure and provided some general comments. Of the 110 objects, only those with some apparent indications of form beneath the corrosion were selected for X-ray. The objects individually numbered and drawn are those for which X-rays showed sufficient metal present for cleaning to be attempted. Cleaning was restricted to the minimum needed to establish artefact shape. The drawings, except for M4 and M5 where corrosion had flaked cleanly from the metal throughout, have combined data from the X-rays with that from the selective cleaning. All artefacts will originally have been larger than their drawings indicate, and thinned cutting edges especially may have been lost through corrosion.

Location	Identified Objects	Nails	Hobnails	Strap frags.	Plate frags.	Objects not identified	Totals
Period 3/4 Enclosure	M18 cleat	3	-	1	-	2	6 + 1
Rampart		4	1	1	-	1	7
Entrance area	M6 binding	9	-	2	-	5	16 + 1
Ditch fills		4	1	-	-	2	7
Soil [9]	M11 cooking pan, M15 pivot, stud as M19	3	-	-	-	2	5 + 3
Structure V1		10	1	-	-	2	13
Structure V2		11	-	-	-	3	14
Structure V3 +	M5 punch	10	2	-	-	3	15 + 1
U1 wall [890]		2	-	-	-	1	3
U midden [801]/[932]	M7 slicker, M9 pin, M10 candlestick (soil over), M12 handle, M16 loop, loop as M17, cleat as M18, M22 spearhead (soil over), M24 fork	96	59	8	-	17	180 + 9
Structure Q3		5	-	-	-	2	7
Structure Q5		3	-	-	-	-	3
House Z1		7	1	2	3	3	16
Soil [808]	M4 stock, M13 knife, stud as M19, M23 cleaver	1	7	-	1	3	12 + 4
House Z2	M8 rake prong	17	4	-	-	7	28 +1
Structure Y		2	-	-	-	-	2
Structure X5		6	-	-	-	-	6
Structure G [255]	M17 loop	2	19	-	-	4	25 +1
Structure G infill	cleat as M18, M21 ferrule	5	1	-	-	-	6 +2
E Pit [78]	M20 ring	-	-	-	-	-	+1
Soil [11] in E		8	-	-	-	-	8
Area D		1	-	-	-	1	2
House A1	M19 upholstery stud(2)	6	-	-	-	9	15 +2
House A2	M14 knife, loop as M17	9	6	-	2	2	19 + 2
[34] over A2	loop as M17	3	3	-	-	-	6 +1
House T2		-	-	-	-	1	1
House T3		4	-	-	-	3	7
House T4		-	-	-	-	1	1
Between T4 & T5		2	-	-	-	1	3
Structure T5+		11	10	-	-	6	27
Totals	29	244	115	14	6	81	460 +29

Table 3.6: Distribution of ironwork across the Round

Small items such as needles will not have been recognised and may have been included among the nails. Some of the illustrated artefacts such as the pan, M11, and the knives, M13 and M14, have been deliberately chopped up as part of the recycling and smithing process.

The ironwork forms the largest group so far published from a Roman site in Devon or Cornwall with the exception of the Holcombe villa: there the assemblage, the overall size of which is not specified, included 34 objects with individual descriptions and 656 nails (Manning 1974, 144-7). The paucity of information in published reports is due more to the difficulties of identifying objects heavily corroded by the generally prevalent acidic soils than to scarcity of iron. Before the 1970s X-raying was not generally carried out, and since its use has become common, high costs have limited the cleaning of badly corroded ironwork. At Goldherring round and courtyard houses, excavated 1958-1961, 70 iron fragments, not X-rayed, were too corroded for identification except 13 nails, a hook and a knife (Guthrie 1969, 27). At Carvossa rectangular earthwork, excavated 1969-1971, around 90 objects were recorded but, despite X-rays, could not be identified (Carlyon 1987, 128). At Reawla round, excavated 1987, 78 objects were recovered but not X-rayed, and 13 were identified as nails and about ten as possible blades, rods, or strips (Adkins and Adkins 1992, 114). At Little Quoit Farm, a round with evidence for ironworking excavated 1998, 56 objects were retrieved from samples of extensive iron slag of which, with X-rays and cleaning, 14 were identified as artefacts such punches, joiners' dogs, and an upholstery stud (Quinnell 2003a). These examples provide some indication of the amount of ironwork present on Cornish sites and the difficulties of dealing with it. It will be apparent that the absence or rarity of a type, from individual sites or from Cornwall as a whole, can not be established and that the problems with corrosion and identification cause difficulties in discussing identified artefacts in the context of local comparanda. There has been less work on rural sites in Devon but the minimal amount of ironwork identified at the enclosure at Hayes Farm near Exeter (Simpson *et al* 1989, 17) indicates that the problems in Cornwall probably extend to the neighbouring county.

At Trethurgy the objects identified cannot be representative of the range of artefacts actually in use: apart from the problems with corrosion discussed above, artefacts were destroyed by the recycling of iron by on-site smithing, and others must have been taken away by the regular clearance of midden debris. The importance of the latter factor is shown by the high proportion of the assemblage which derives from midden [932/801] (Table 3.6), 96 out of 244 nails, 59 out of 115 hobnails, 8 out of 14 strap fragments and 27 out of 110 objects of which 10 could be identified and illustrated. Conversely the absence of any type is of no significance. For example small hooks, which could be used for pruning, reaping or the gathering of firewood (Manning 1985, 53-8), must have been indispensable tools: these occur in Cornwall at Carn Euny (Christie 1978, fig 52), St Mawgan-in-Pydar (Threipland 1956, fig 36), Duckpool (Quinnell 1995, fig 32) and Trevisker (ApSimon and Greenfield 1972, 350), but cannot be recognised in the surviving assemblage from Trethurgy. An overall picture of the iron artefacts in use in Cornwall during the Roman period will only gradually be built up as data from different sites accumulate.

The collection from Trethurgy is of interest as it shows Roman traditions adopted across a wide range of activities. The upholstery studs, M19, show influence on furniture, the rake prong, M8, on agriculture, the candlestick, M10, and the handled pan, M11, on domestic life and cooking. Even the hobnails reflect influence on clothing; these are not unusual on South West rural sites, occurring at Grambla (Saunders 1972, 52), Nornour (Dudley 1968, 25), Duckpool (Quinnell 1995), Penhale (Quinnell 1998/9) and Stoke Gabriel (Masson Phillips 1966, 25). The nails found were mostly small, under 50mm in length, appropriate for boxes, fittings, and furniture rather than structural use.

The ironwork is probably mainly Romano-British in date, but M5, M6, M8, M10, M21, and M22 together with two unillustrated 'Hod Hill' loops and a boot cleat similar to M18, could, on the chronology suggested, date to after AD 400. The collection therefore may also include artefacts of the Post-Roman period. The publications of Post-Roman ironwork assemblages from Cannington (Rahtz *et al* 2000), Cadbury Castle (Alcock 1995), Cadbury Congresbury (Rahtz *et al* 1992), and Dinas Powys (Alcock 1987) have been examined; where no comparanda are given for any of the possible Post-Roman objects from Trethurgy they appear not to be present at this group of sites. Recent work at Tintagel has so far produced only scanty and very corroded ironwork (Morris and Harry 1997, 72).

3.9.2 Descriptions of illustrated objects

Fig 48

M4 Smith's ingot or stock. [808] Stages 4/6 soil in Q. Length 245mm, width 50mm, thickness tapers from 26mm to 16mm: rectangular cross-section. Present weight 3.9kg, with *c* 1kg of corroded fragments. Tylecote (1986, tab 82) lists a number of examples with varying dimensions and weights. None have previously been identified from the rural South West.

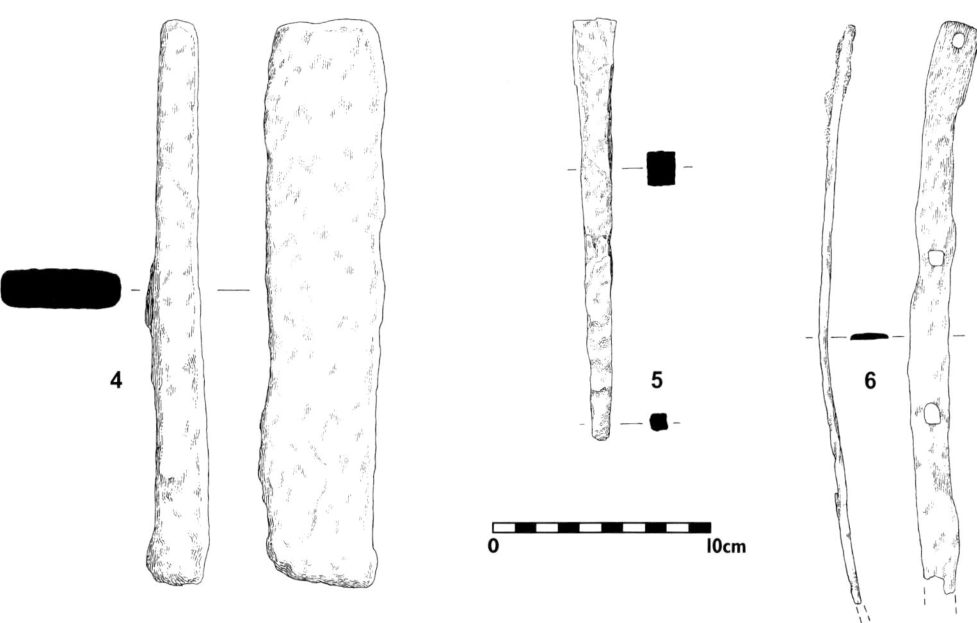

Fig 48: Iron objects M4-M6. Drawing S Morris. Scale 1:3

The presence of M4 strengthens the evidence for on-site smithing at Trethurgy.

M5 Square-sectioned punch for smithing. [524] Stage 10, latest soil in U. Length 182mm, thickness tapers from 20 to 7mm. Possible burring of top. A common Roman-British type (Manning 1985, 9); smaller versions now recorded in Cornwall at Little Quoit Farm (Quinnell 2003a, nos 2, 8, 11) and possibly at Reawla (Adkins and Adkins 1992, SF714, 114). Its context makes a Post-Roman date possible.

M6 Binding. [140] Stage 9/10, soil over Entrance Paving [188]. Curved, surviving length 25mm, 20mm wide, plano-convex section 3-5mm thick. Four squarish perforations. As Manning (1985, 142) remarks, it is not usually possible to identify the precise use of such a binding. Its context makes a Post-Roman date possible.

Fig 49

M7 Leatherworker's slicker? [801] Stage 6 upper midden in U. Width 52mm, thickness 7mm, both tangs broken; lower blunt edge may not be original. Small in size for suggested use (Manning 1985, 39) and the only possible example of the type so far recognised in Cornwall. M7 might however be a variant of a joiner's dog (cf Manning 1985, pl 61, no 52) similar to, though larger than, an example from Seaton (Silvester 1981b, fig 14, no 8).

M8 Rake prong? [723] Stage 9 or later collapse in Z. Tang broken; surviving length 60mm, width 15 mm, thickness 13mm. Roughly rectangular-sectioned point narrows to tapering tang. Back shows curve characteristic of rake prongs (Rees 1979, 485) which appear to be a Roman introduction into Britain. These are fairly common (Rees 1979, 737-40) though none has previously been recorded from South West Britain. Its context makes a Post-Roman date possible.

M9 Pin fragment. [932] Stage 6 lower midden in U. Round-sectioned shaft 6mm across flattening to form ring-head. Surviving length 55mm. Iron dress pins seem rare in Roman Britain, despite their frequency in the pre-Roman Iron Age; this may be because they are often ignored or confused with needles (Clarke 1979, 249). Ring-headed iron pins in Ireland continue through into the Early Christian period; a reasonable parallel to M9 is one from Lagore Crannog (Hencken 1950, 101, no 1585). There is as yet no other evidence to suggest the type also continued through the Roman period in South West Britain.

M10 Candlestick? [800] soil Stage 6 or later over U/disturbed top of midden [801]. One complete socket 65mm high, 13mm across rises from one corner of flat plate 64mm across; traces of a second on opposite corner; tang, broken, asymmetrically placed. Single socket candlesticks are the most common type; double socket forms are less frequent and of varying forms, cf that from Camerton (Wedlake 1958, fig 56, no 20). If M10 is correctly identified, it is the first recorded candlestick from rural sites in Cornwall and Devon. Its context makes a Post-Roman date possible; the suggested candlestick from Dinas Powys (Alcock 1987, fig 5.3, no 10) is of very different form.

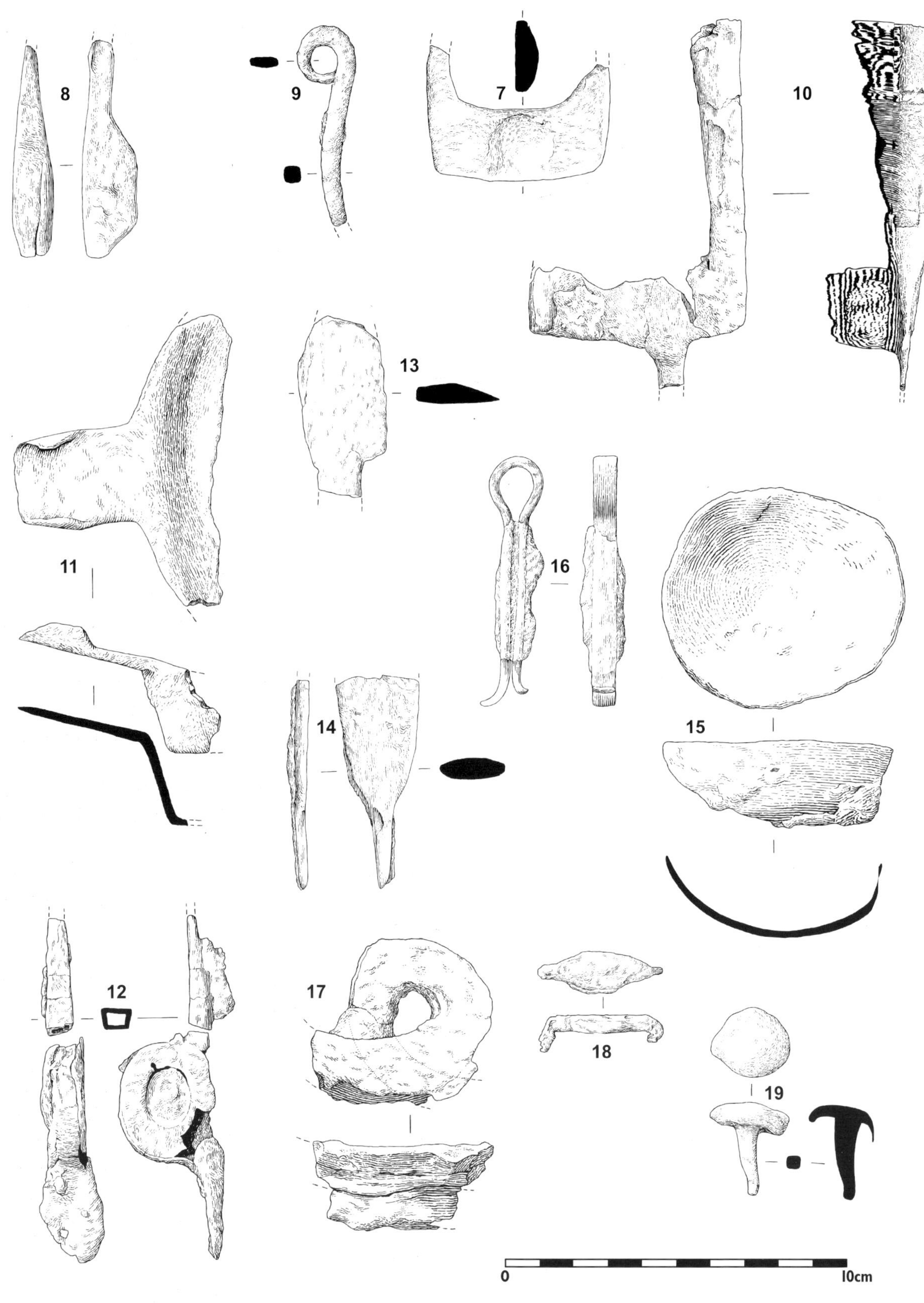

Fig 49: Iron objects M7-M19. Drawing S Morris. Scale 2:3

M11 Part of cooking pan. [9] Stage 4/5 soil on cobbles [173] in R. Depth of pan 23mm. Projecting handle flat with slightly incurved flanges; no indication of any holes for securing pivoted handle extension which would be usual with metal cooking pans; the flanged handle was probably intended to take a simple wooden extension. Insufficient circumference survives, because the object has been chopped up, to show whether pan was originally round or oval, and therefore to give diameter. Increasing numbers of these pans are now being identified from 3rd and 4th-century contexts in Britain (Manning 1985, 104). This possibly 4th-century example is the first published from Devon or Cornwall although a pan fragment, chopped to an almost identical shape, came from a 4th-century grave fill at Poundbury in Dorset (Davies 1987, fig 70, no 12).

M12 Handle for wooden tankard or similar vessel? [801] Stage 6 upper midden in U. Surviving length 98mm. Base flattened and rounded but no indication of any perforation; semi-circular handle-like projection 20mm across; broken upper end shows object hollow, square-sectioned above projection. The identification of the object as a tankard handle, possibly unfinished, is only tentative; there seem no exact parallels for M12. Possible tankard handles from the pre-Roman Iron Age settlement at Bodrifty, West Cornwall, were suggested (Dudley 1956, 29) but cannot now be identified.

M13 Knife. [808] Stage 4/6 soil in Q. Tip and tang broken, probably chopped off, width 27mm. The tang is centrally situated between the shoulder and the choil as in Manning's Type 16 (1985, 115, fig 28) which has a long chronology through the Roman period. Surprisingly knives are rare finds on South West rural sites. The only examples from Cornwall appear to be from St Mawgan-in-Pydar (Threipland 1956, fig 36), Goldherring (Guthrie 1969, 27), Duckpool (Quinnell 1995, 131, fig 32) and Little Quoit Farm (Quinnell 2003a, no 4).

M14 Knife. [141] Stage 5 levelling for House A2. Square-sectioned tang complete, blade broken. Width 28mm, thickness 7mm, no surviving sharp edge. Possibly Manning's Type 15 (1985, 115) with tang symmetrical to blade. Compare an example from Seaton (Silvester 1981b, no 6, fig 14).

M15 Pivot base? [9]Stage 4/5 soil on cobbles [173] in R. Circular, 60mm diameter, 22mm deep, 3mm thick. No indication of any projection or scar from handle, thus making identification as a ladle bowl unlikely. For pivot bases see Manning 1985, 127-8. None previously identified from rural contexts in Devon or Cornwall.

M16 Double-spiked loop. [932] Stage 6 lower midden in U. Overall length 75mm, width of bar forming loop 6mm, thickness 4mm. A common type (Manning 1985, 130). Intended for setting through timber, the bent-back ends securing it on the other side; it then formed a projecting loop into which hooks etc could be slipped. A similar loop, but with integral inset ring, was found at the Magor 'villa' (O'Neil 1933, 153).

M17 Part of 'Hod Hill' type double-spiked loop. [255] Stage 6 backing to G. Bar 25mm wide, 22mm thick, twisted to form loop with (originally) spiked ends in line but pointing in opposite directions; the spiked ends have now broken, or been chopped, off. Closely comparable to R51 from Hod Hill (Manning 1985, 131). Precise method of use uncertain but presumed to be an alternative to double-spiked loops for fixing a ring into timber. Number 13 from a 2nd-century context at St Mawgan-in-Pydar (Threipland 1956, fig 36) appears the only other example published from rural Devon and Cornwall.

At least three other similar loops from [34] Stage 8/9 infill in A, [100] Stage 7/8 gulley House A2, and [932] Stage 6 lower midden in U. The loop from [34] suggests that the form may continue into the Post-Roman period.

M18 Cleat. [920] drain through Period 3 Enclosure Bank. Length 34mm, width 12mm, thickness 5mm. Manning (1985, 131) suggests, on evidence from burials, that these small cleats were used on boot soles. An example from Seaton (Silvester 1981b, no 7, fig 14) is the only published parallel from rural Devon and Cornwall.

Others about 40mm long from [801] Stage 6 upper midden in U and [256] Stage 9 lower infill in G; the latter may be of Post-Roman date. Boot cleats occur at Dinas Powys (Alcock 1987, fig 5.4) and at Cannington (Rahtz *et al* 2000, 344, fig 234, nos 38, 72) although the latter may be of later Roman date.

M19 Upholstery stud. One of two from [55] Stage 1/4 posthole in House A1. Square-sectioned stem 25mm long, hollow domed head 20mm across.

Similar studs from [923] Stage 4 dump in Q4 and [9] Stage 4/5 soil in R. The four are examples of Manning's Type 8 nail (1985, 136, fig 32), the commonest form of upholstery stud. The only other such stud so far identified from rural sites west of Exeter is from Little Quoit Farm (Quinnell 2003a, no 6). They indicate the presence at Trethurgy of some items of sophisticated furniture.

Fig 50

M20 Ring. [78] Stage 6 large pit. Overall diameter 32mm, round section 5mm across. Within the size range of Manning's rings S18-48 (1985, 140); it is too small to have been the side-ring of a bit but could have been used in harness or tracery. Alternatively it may

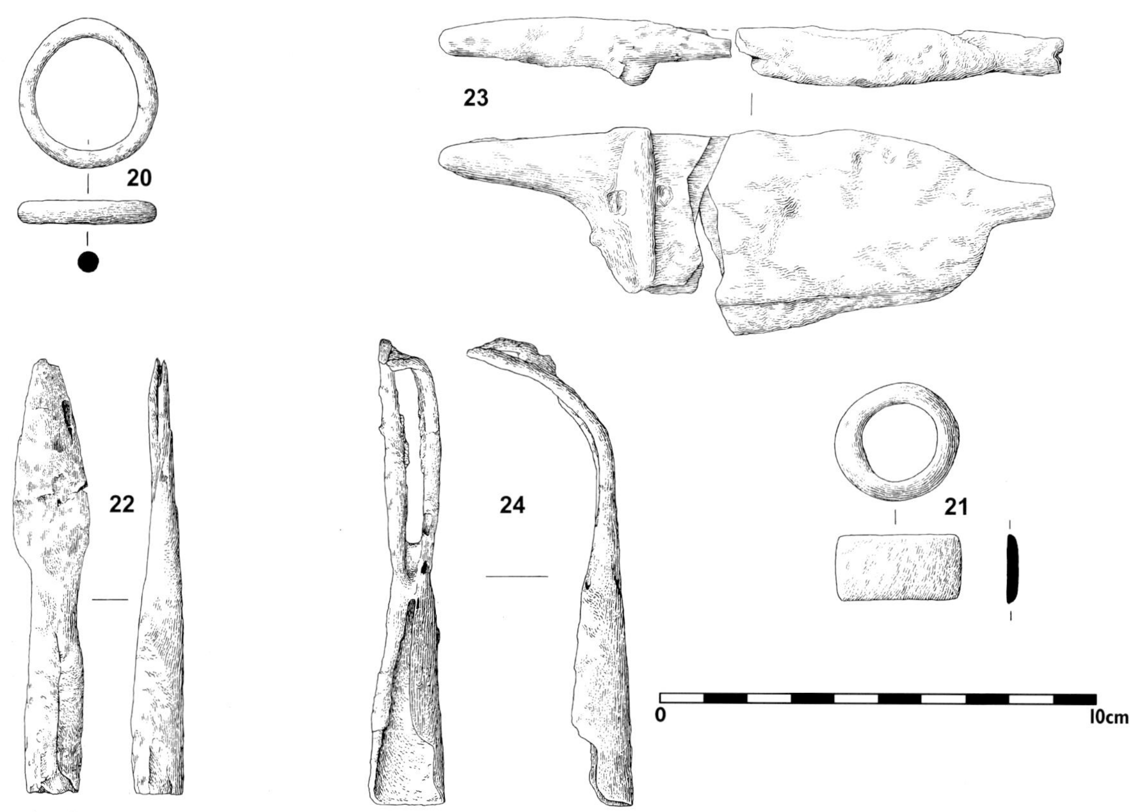

Fig 50: Iron objects M20-M24. Drawing S Morris. Scale 2:3

have been part of some domestic equipment such as a cauldron chain. Similar to the ring found inset in the double-spiked loop from Magor (O'Neil 1933, 153).

M21 Collar ferrule. [256] Stage 9 infill of G. Overall diameter 28mm, height 14mm, thickness 3mm. Similar to S84-94, collar ferrules from Hod Hill, the function of which was to prevent the splitting of the ends of wooden shafts (Manning 1985, 141). Context makes a Post-Roman date possible. There are two penannular collar ferrules from Cannington (Rahtz *et al* 2000, fig 233, nos 149, 58).

M22 Spearhead. [800] Stage 6 or later disturbed upper midden and soil in U. Overall length about 95mm, width of blade 17mm. Carefully made with weld just visible in socket. Flattish-sectioned blade, with slightly asymmetrical shape. In every way this conforms to Manning's Group 1A from Hod Hill (1985, 162) assigned to the mid 1st century and of military type. At Trethurgy the context suggests a 4th-century or later date. Spearheads appear extremely rare on non-military sites in Roman Britain, at any rate in those lowland, non-frontier areas with good preservation conditions. A variety of spearheads continued in use in Ireland and parallels to M22 may be found from Lagore Crannog (Hencken 1950, fig 29B) and Garyduff, Co Cork (Alcock 1971, fig 29, no 1). No examples survive from Dinas Powys (Alcock 1963) but two spearheads of similar size but less carefully made come from the Post-Roman site of Bantham, Devon (Fox 1955, fig 4). Cadbury Congresbury has two spearheads. One is very different to M22 but the other, B0719, is of similar size and a generally similar blade shape but has an open socket (Rahtz *et al* 1992, fig 86, 119); this was considered to have possible Anglo-Saxon affinities.

M23 Cleaver? [808] Stage 4/6 soil in Q. Artefact with apparent tang at either end, overall surviving length 135mm, width 45mm, too corroded to show whether either side had thinned to a cutting edge. Distinct ridge 5mm high across one end of blade. The suggestion that the object might be a variety of cleaver (cf Manning 1985, 120) comes from examples from Catsgore (Leech 1982, fig 83, nos 6-7) where the points of the blades are drawn out to exaggerated tips.

M24 Two-pronged fork. [801] Stage 6 upper midden in U. Overall length 105mm, length of socket 50mm, pronounced curve on fork tines which have bent towards each other and corroded together. It is difficult to find comparanda for this object, markedly similar to modern toasting and carving forks, from Roman Britain. It size suggests a domestic rather than an agricultural function.

3.10 Ironworking

An iron lode runs north-south within 100m of the site and consists, here within kaolinised granite, of remarkably pure haematite (Collins 1912, 244). This was profitably worked as Wheal Ruby during the 19th century. Occasional weathered fragments of haematite are found in topsoil in the area. Fragments of haematite were noted scattered evenly across the site, [9], [34](2), [55](2), [85], [386](2), [555](2), [567](2), [728], and [801], but these could have occurred naturally. The report by Justine Bayley (Section 3.6) indicates that no slag found derived from iron smelting. Iron is likely to have been smelted at specialist centres, possibly some way from the Round.

Only recently has it been established that iron in the Later Iron Age and Roman periods was generally smelted in shaft furnaces, which produced tap slag which has a distinctive appearance and composition (Bayley *et al* 2001), and not in bowl furnaces which produce circular lumps of slag plano-convex in profile. These plano-convex slag hearth bottoms are now recognised as diagnostic of smithing activity. This new research means that any statements about iron smelting and slags made before about 1990 are likely to be based on outdated information. In Cornwall only the rectangular earthwork at Carvossa has published evidence for iron smelting. A total of 36kg of iron slag was retrieved, some in association with hearths (Carlyon 1987, 127) and analysis indicated identified iron smelting slags. It is not known whether modern re-examination would confirm this identification. No specialist centre for iron smelting can yet be identified in Cornwall. It is likely that the majority of slags from Carvossa were from smithing and that plano-convex furnace bottoms were present (P Carlyon pers comm). Four furnace bottoms were found at the round at Reawla, together with a tuyère, but no actual smithing hearths were identified (Bayley 1992). Excavation of most Roman-period sites in Cornwall have produced small quantities of iron slag which can be interpreted as a by-product of smithing. The rounds at Carlidnack (Harris and Johnson 1976, 75), Trevisker (ApSimon and Greenfield 1972, 351), Castle Gotha (Saunders and Harris 1982, 147) and Goldherring (Guthrie 1969, 27) are all good examples. The situation mirrors that on rural sites elsewhere in Britain (Manning 1976, 152) where regular small-scale smithing is the norm. The only Cornish site which differs is the enclosure at Little Quoit Farm, St Columb Minor. Here large quantities of smithing slag, furnace bottoms, and iron pieces suggest production of iron objects on a scale larger than that needed by its inhabitants, a production interpreted as on a similar level to the household industries identified for potting (Quinnell 2003a). This interpretation would suggest that sites like Trethurgy had access to specialist smithing centres which would produce most new and complex artefacts and that on-site smithing would be confined to the production of simple objects, mending and alteration.

Table 3.4 lists smithing slag from 11 contexts at Trethurgy and hearth lining from another nine; small pieces of iron slag from two other contexts, [8] and [422], were not examined by Justine Bayley nor included in the Table. Hammerscale, a distinctive by-product of smithing, is not recorded. This may be because no wet sieving of large samples was carried out, a method which allows small fragments to be retrieved. It is unlikely that small corroded scraps of hammerscale would have been recognised during excavation unless they had occurred in concentrated groups. The wide range of contexts which produced smithing slag indicated that smithing was carried out throughout the use of the Round, and had occurred during Periods 3 and 4, as slag was present to be incorporated in the Period 5 Rampart.

Most of the iron was in small pieces and much had definitely been cut up (W Manning pers comm). The small size and reworking is consistent with the on-site smithing practices suggested, as is the smith's stock or ingot, M4 from soil [808] in Q. The only large group of artefacts, fragments, and nails was from midden [932/801], reflecting its general concentration of finds. Perhaps surprisingly, the midden did not produce smithing slag and there were no other indications that it had been the site of *in situ* smithing. Much of the iron in the midden may be from ash derived from the burning of broken-up wooden artefacts containing nails. No hearth, hearth pit, or burnt area was associated with smithing slag. The only feature which may be connected to *in situ* smithing was pit [191] (Fig 10) in the Entrance. This had cut through Entrance pavings from a high level and is assigned to Stage 10. Roughly circular, 0.4m across and 0.4m deep, it had a clay lining, burnt so that the material into which it was cut was reddened; its fill contained comminuted charcoal, smithing slag, and hearth lining. The date of pit [191] could be from any time subsequent to the final reorganization of the Entrance and may be the result of smithing within the shelter of the Entrance after regular occupation of the Round had ceased.

4 Romano-British and early Post-Roman glass vessels and objects

Jennifer Price

(text written 2001)

The excavations at Trethurgy produced 35 vessel fragments, five objects, and two pieces of window glass (Figs 51, 52). Of these, 27 vessel fragments, and the objects and window glass, were Roman, and six were certainly or probably early Post-Roman. Two Post-Medieval or modern fragments have not been studied.

4.1 Composition and dating of the glass assemblage

A minimum of seven vessels has been identified among the Roman glass, all of which are common finds in settlements in Britain in the 2nd and 3rd centuries AD. One is a good-quality colourless bowl or flask with abraded decoration (Gl 3/4), and the others are more ordinary bluish-green or greenish colourless vessels. One may be a drinking vessel (Gl 5) and the others, a jar (Gl 6) and at least four prismatic bottles and flasks (Gl 11/14, 15, 16, and 17), are household containers. The five objects, a finger ring and four beads (nos 18-22), are late Roman forms in use in Britain during the 4th century, and matt-glossy window glass (Gl 23/24) is found in many military and civil settlements from the 1st to late 3rd century.

The early Post-Roman fragments include two examples of pale yellow and yellowish-green decorated tablewares, a conical beaker with opaque white trails (Gl 1) and a conical bowl with abraded zones of motifs (Gl 2) which are comparable with vessels found at other settlements in western Britain in the 5th-7th centuries AD. The remaining pieces (Gl 7-10) which represent at least three closed vessels, probably flasks or unguent bottles, are more problematic. The glass colour, bluish-green with a grey tinge, is unlikely to be Romano-British and is rare in the early Post-Roman period. It has been difficult to find similar examples in settlements in western Britain although the find contexts indicate that they were deposited in the late Roman or early Post-Roman period, and they may be of more recent date.

4.2 Supply and use of glass

In total, a minimum of twelve vessels have been identified and assigned to the Roman and Post-Roman phases of occupation in the settlement. There are, however, considerable differences in the patterns of supply and use.

The Roman material indicates a very limited use of glass vessels. One possible drinking vessel (Gl 5) has been recognised, but with the exception of that and the colourless bowl or flask (Gl 3/4) and perhaps the jar (Gl 6), there is no evidence for the presence of glass tablewares. The remaining vessels reached Trethurgy because they were containers for foodstuffs, unguents, or medical preparations. Moreover, this glass reached the settlement over a fairly short period, probably only in the 2nd or early 3rd century.

To set this pattern of consumption in a wider context, it should be noted that a wide variety of glass vessels for serving and consuming food and liquid, such as beakers, bowls, cups, jars, and jugs, as well as containers and transport vessels, such as bottles, flasks, jars, and unguent bottles, were in use in Britain by the 2nd century AD. Some were probably imported, chiefly from elsewhere in the north-west provinces, and some were produced locally, in the glass workshops in or close to Romano-British towns and military establishments. However, the patterns of use of glass vary greatly between settlements of different status and in different geographical regions. Towns and legionary fortresses often have the widest range of forms (eg Cool and Price 1995, fig 13.3-4 for the forms present in Colchester between *c* AD 100 and *c* AD 230), while auxiliary forts and most rural settlements have much more limited assemblages.

Exeter, the Romano-British town closest to Trethurgy, shows a pattern of glass use comparable with other urban settlements in southern Britain during the 2nd/early 3rd century, although the quantity recorded is not very large, but other settlements in the South West have produced very few fragments. Patterns of use similar to or even more limited than that at Trethurgy have been recorded at rural sites elsewhere in Cornwall and the Isles of Scilly, such as Carvossa (Harden 1987), Kilhallon (Price 1982), Reawla (Adkins and Adkins 1992), Nornour (Charlesworth 1968), Halangy Down (Ashbee 1996, 73), and Penhale Round (Quinnell 1998/9) and this pattern is replicated at equivalent settlements at the margins of the Roman province in other parts of Britain, as in the northern frontier region (Ingemark 2000). It is arguable that the apparent dearth of glass may be misleading as the broken glass could have been recycled, but there is no evidence at Trethurgy for the production of glass objects, and it is perhaps more probable that little glass other than containers was available for supply to the settlement or that the inhabitants had a way of life which did not involve the acquisition of glass drinking vessels and other tablewares.

Small personal ornaments were readily portable items and the scatter of trinkets reaching the site towards the end of the Roman period presumably arrived through local trading networks in the South West. On the other hand, the presence of two fragments of window glass is interesting. Not only does this point to the existence of at least one building with a glazed window but it also raises questions about the origin of the pane as the risks of transporting a sheet of flat glass would have been considerable.

By contrast with the Roman period of occupation, when the glass reaching Trethurgy is likely to have been supplied by road from centres in southern Britain, the glass vessels of the early Post-Roman period indicate that the settlement, like others in Cornwall such as Tintagel (Harden 1956a, 70; Price 1982; Ewan Campbell pers comm) and perhaps Grambla (Saunders 1972) and Reawla (Adkins and Adkins 1992), was linked to the sea-borne trading networks between western Britain, continental Europe, and the Mediterranean region. At this time the inhabitants had access to high status imported tablewares comparable with those found at Dinas Powys (Harden 1963), Cadbury Congresbury (Price 1992), Cadbury Castle (Price and Cottam 1995), Whithorn (Campbell 1997), and other sites in western Britain.

4.3 Distribution of glass within the site

The distribution of the Romano-British vessel glass is concentrated in the midden in Structure U, conforming to the concentrations of other groups of artefacts on the site. Five of the seven vessels (Gl 3/4, 5, 6, 11/12, and 15) were found there, where they had presumably been deposited after the Structure had gone out of use. Two fragments from Houses T (Gl 13) and Z (Gl 14) also appear to come from one of the vessels (Gl 11/12) noted in Structure U, and House Z and the north Ditch terminal produced the remaining two vessels (Gl 16, 17).

The rest of the glass finds were more widely dispersed, and none came from Structure U. Among the objects, the finger ring (Gl 18) and the cubic square-sectioned bead (Gl 22) were found in House Z, and the other beads in soil over Structure E (Gl 21), beneath Structure V (Gl 19) and in soil in Area R (Gl 20). The two joining window glass fragments (Gl 23/24) came from House A and the Entrance, and the Post-Roman vessel fragments were found in House A (Gl 1, 8), Structure G (Gl 9), House T (Gl 2, 10), and House Z (Gl 7).

4.4 The Romano-British vessel glass

Four colourless convex body fragments, two with linear abraded decoration (Gl 3/4), were found in the midden, and the drain above the midden, in Structure U in contexts dated to the last quarter of the 4th century and first half of the 5th century. They were very similar in quality and form, and it is likely that they come from a single vessel, which was probably a convex bowl or flask, though it is not possible to identify the precise form from the surviving pieces. Convex colourless bowls and cups with wheel-cut and sometimes abraded linear decoration are found in Britain in mid and later 2nd-century contexts (Price and Cottam 1998a, 96-9, 124-6), although most of these were made in glass with fewer bubbles than the Trethurgy fragments. Fragments from colourless drinking vessels with wheel-cut and abraded lines have been found at Exeter (Charlesworth 1979, 224, nos 9-11, fig 70; Allen 1991, 227, nos 41-3, fig 95) and elsewhere in Cornwall and the Isles of Scilly, at Reawla (Adkins and Adkins 1992, 113, no 2) and at Halangy Down (Ashbee 1996, 73).

Abraded linear decoration is also found on cups and bowls in the 3rd and early 4th centuries, but many of these are made in greenish colourless rather than clear colourless glass. Another possible form is the convex-bodied flask with either a cylindrical neck or funnel mouth which was made in colourless and greenish colourless glass and has been recorded in 3rd-century and later contexts (Price and Cottam 1998a, 181-4). A cylindrical neck fragment, from a colourless convex-bodied flask or a bottle, is known in Exeter (Allen 1991, 228, no 58, fig 96).

The one possible bluish-green drinking vessel, Gl 5, came from the lower part of midden [932] in Structure U, a context dated to the last quarter of the 4th century. The piece is too small for any identification to be certain though it appears to come from a narrow straight-sided vessel, perhaps a cylindrical or conical beaker, and the colour, the thickness of the wall, and the absence of bubbles in the glass suggest that it belongs to the 1st to early 3rd century rather than later, but close parallels are scarce. It may belong to a small cylindrical cup with fire-rounded rim and tubular base ring. These were produced in large numbers in the later 2nd and early 3rd century, usually in colourless glass though some bluish-green examples are also known (Price and Cottam 1998a, 99-101). Colourless and bluish-green examples have been found in Exeter (Charlesworth 1979, 224, nos 19-20, fig 70; Allen 1991, 222, no 16, 227, nos 48-50, figs 94-5) and there is a colourless rim fragment from Kilhallon, Tywardreath (Price 1982, 163, no 1, fig 6).

Gl 6, which also came from midden [932] in Structure U in a context dated to the last quarter of the 4th century, is from a jar with a collar rim, although too little has survived for either the rim diameter or the shape of the body to be determined. Jars with vertical rims folded out and down to form a collar and either a square-sectioned body or a convex body are well known in the north-west provinces in the 1st and 2nd centuries AD and they were almost certainly produced in the region. They are common finds at settlements and in burials, as at Colchester (Cool and Price 1995, 106-9), Exeter (Charlesworth 1979, 227, nos 23-4, fig 70), and elsewhere in Britain (see Price and Cottam 1998a, 135-8, for discussion of these forms). Some of the examples with convex bodies are brightly coloured, but others are bluish-green, as are all the examples with square bodies. It is rather surprising that about two centuries appear to have elapsed between the production of this vessel and its deposition in the midden at Trethurgy, especially as the surviving fragment shows little signs of wear associated with long usage, except on the edge of the rim. However the quantity of 2nd-century samian in the midden, and the trend towards long periods of curation evidenced by 'status' artefacts in the Round, should be kept in mind (Section 5.3.1).

A minimum of three bluish-green prismatic bottles have been identified. The greatest quantity of fragments came from midden [932/801] in Structure U, where 15 pieces are so similar that they are likely to come from one specimen (Gl 11/12) which has a narrow neck , approximately 40mm in diameter, and a side approximately 75-80mm wide. Three other pieces, from the floor in House T2 (Gl 13), the drain in House Z1 (Gl 14), and unstratified, may also belong to this bottle. The other prismatic vessels are each represented by one body fragment; Gl 15, which was found in the midden in structure U, is noticeably thicker than the equivalent fragments from the first example, and Gl 16, from the late accumulation over the north terminal of the Ditch, appears to come from a much more substantial bottle than either of the others.

Square and other prismatic bottles were produced as transport vessels and containers for liquid and semi-liquid foodstuffs. They are extremely common throughout the western provinces from the middle of the 1st to the end of the 2nd century AD, and are found in virtually all settlements in Britain (see Cool and Price 1995, 179-99, and Price and Cottam 1998a, 194-202 for details of the production and distribution of prismatic bottles). These bottles frequently account for more than 50% of the vessel glass assemblages in towns and forts and are sometimes the only vessel glass found on rural sites

Unsurprisingly, large numbers of fragments of prismatic (square, hexagonal) and cylindrical bottles have been noted at Exeter (Harden 1952, 93, no 6; Charlesworth 1979, 227-8, nos 25-9, fig 71; Allen 1991, 224-6, no 31, fig 94), and cylindrical as well as square examples were noted at Carvossa (Harden 1987, 130, nos 97,112, 121), but otherwise, only prismatic bottles have been recorded in Cornwall, at Kilhallon (Price 1982, 164, nos 7-8), Tintagel (Ewan Campbell pers comm) and Penhale Round (Quinnell 1998/9, 85, fig 8). These vessels disappear soon after the end of the 2nd century, so the presence of a substantial part of an unworn bottle in midden deposits dated to the last quarter of the 4th century is remarkable. There are a few parallels for the late use of square bottles in the western provinces, as in Grave 1314 at Krefeld Gellep which contained a coin of Trebonianus Gallus (AD 251-253) (Pirling 1974, 19-20, nos 9-10, pl 20). However, if Gl 13/14 are indeed parts of the same vessel as Gl 11/12, the problem of the late date may largely be resolved, as these pieces came from 3rd to early 4th-century contexts.

The last Romano-British vessel (Gl 17), which is greenish colourless with a prismatic body, is represented by a body fragment from pit [818] in House Z1b assigned to Stage 4 (AD 275-325). The colour indicates that this is unlikely to be an ordinary prismatic bottle, and it may come from a square-sectioned flask with thick walls known as a Mercury flask. They are found in the north-west provinces in the late 2nd and early 3rd century, and occur in burials and on settlements in Britain, though much less frequently than bluish-green bottles (see Cool and Price 1995, 152-3, and Price and Cottam 1998a, 179-181 for discussion of the form).

4.5 Early Post-Roman vessel glass

The body fragment, Gl 1, was found in drainage gulley [100] around House A2, tentatively dated to c AD 400-500. It is a vessel of good quality, and the pale yellow colour and opaque white decoration indicate that it was almost certainly a conical beaker with fire-rounded rim and small rounded base. The fragment is too small for all elements of the decorative scheme to be certain, but they are likely to have included a closely wound fine spiral trail below the rim as well as broader trails dragged down to form loops on the body.

Vessels of this kind have been recorded at numerous settlements in western Britain and Ireland (see Campbell 2000, 39-43, Group D, for a recent survey). Other finds in the south-west peninsula include a fragment from Tintagel (Price 1987, 26, fig 8) and two other possible pieces, a pale yellow undecorated body fragment from Grambla (unpubl) and a blue rim fragment now lacking the opaque white spiral trail at Reawla (Adkins and Adkins 1992, 113, no 1, fig 23). In the Bristol Channel, similar pieces are known at Cannington (Price 2000a, 307-8, nos 105, 110, 114, 124, fig 206), Cadbury Congresbury (Price 1992, 141-3, nos 20-33, figs 97-8) and Dinas Powys (Harden 1963, 182-4, nos 24-30, 32-5, 47-93, fig 40), and others are known on sites along the South Wales coast and as far north as south-west Scotland. Many settlements have produced only one or two small fragments, but pieces of these beakers have also been found in larger numbers, and some, such as Cadbury Congresbury, Dinas Powys, and Whithorn (Campbell 1997; 2000) have produced reconstructable vessels, so it is no longer acceptable to discuss this glass as imported scrap.

Campbell (2000, 43-4) has pointed out that there are very close similarities between the Group D beakers found in western Britain and 6th-century and later finds in Aquitaine, particularly in and near Bordeaux (cf Foy and Hochuli-Gysel 1995, 163-5), which suggests that the British material has its origins in south-western France. He argues that the main phase of importation of these beakers is the 6th century. If the context of the Trethurgy fragment, drainage gulley [100], is really related to House A2, dated within the 5th century, this would be noteworthy. However the presence of Gl 1 in the gulley raises the possibility that the gulley could have been open contemporary with House A3, dated to the 6th century; it should also be noted that the gulley cannot be regarded as securely sealed.

The second tableware fragment, Gl 2, was found in abandonment phase [400] deposits over Structure T5, which are dated to the 6th or 7th century. It comes from the lower body of a yellowish-green truncated conical bowl; the complete vessel would have had a fire-rounded rim and a small concave base with a pontil mark (Price 2000b, 24-6). Vessels of this form are not present in late Romano-British contexts, but they are commonly found in Belgium, northern France, Aquitaine, southern France, Spain, and Portugal in the 5th and 6th centuries. Some undecorated, trailed, and mould-blown versions have been recorded in Saxon graves in south-east England, and undecorated and trailed examples belonging to different production traditions occur at settlements in western Britain, such as Tintagel (Ewan Campbell per comm), Cannington (Price 2000a, 308, no 111, fig 206), Cadbury Congresbury (Price 1992, 143, nos 34-8, fig 98), Dinas Powys (Harden 1963, 183-4, nos 31, 38, 42, 46, fig 40), Cadbury Castle (Price and Cottam 1995, 102, Gl 19-20, ill 7.1), and Whithorn (Campbell 1997, 307, nos 6-8, 48-50, figs 10.2,10.8).

The decoration on the Trethurgy bowl is unusual and distinctive. Parts of two horizontal rows of wheel-abraded or scratched decoration, with herringbone motifs above circular rings survive, and the intact vessel would presumably have had at least one more row below the rim. Its closest parallel is a fragment preserving the complete section of the bowl from an Anglo-Saxon burial at Holme Pierrepont, Nottinghamshire (Price 2000b, 24, fig 9.3, pl 7). This also has a row of rings above the base, a middle row containing a bird with a long tail, perhaps a peacock, and plants and other motifs, and a top row containing the letters ...S E M P E R... . An interesting point of detail is that the inscription is in retrograde, and thus was intended to be seen and read by the person looking inside from above, which implies that the bowl may have functioned as a drinking vessel. Fragments of two bowls with similar decoration are also known from Whithorn; one is greenish colourless with an abraded feature, perhaps a letter, below the rim, and the other is a pale yellow body fragment which appears to have a row of rings above the base, a middle row of running S-scrolls and part of an inscription (Campbell 1997, 300, nos 1, 3, fig 10.4).

Outside Britain, few examples of conical bowls with wheel-abraded decoration have been noted. One from Conimbriga in Portugal is nearly colourless and has two letters, perhaps ..A V .., below the rim (Alarcão *et al* 1976, 203, no 245, pls 44, 48). The other, without provenance, is pale green with a self-coloured spiral trail below the rim, a horizontal branch and floral frieze, and a row of herringbone motifs on the body and an eight-pointed star on the base (unpubl; British Museum GR 1970.6-3.1). Wheel-abraded motifs also occur on several other vessel forms in the Mediterranean region in the 5th-6th centuries (Price 2000b, 26), and small body fragments have occasionally been found in Britain, at Cadbury Congresbury (Price 1992, 139, nos 10-11, fig 97), Whithorn (Campbell 1997, 300, nos 2, 4-5, fig 10.4), and Traprain Law (unpubl).

Although conical bowls with wheel-abraded decoration have rarely been found in closely dated contexts, they are assumed to be more or less contemporary with other wheel-abraded vessels, and thus to belong to the 5th and 6th centuries. There is little doubt that they reached Britain from the Mediterranean region, and the distribution of the vessel form argues that they were produced somewhere in the western provinces, either in southern France or more probably in the Iberian peninsula.

As already indicated, Gl 7-10, the three closed vessels from 5th and 6th century — and in the case of Gl 10 probably early 4th-century — deposits, are difficult to set in context. The similarity of the colour and quality of Gl 8 and 9 suggest that they probably come from the same vessel, which may be a flask or jug, Gl 7 is also likely to be from a similar form or jug, and Gl 10, which has a very narrow body may be an unguent bottle. These are not common early Post-Roman forms, and the particular shade of bluish-green glass is also most unusual. Two yellowish-green convex-bodied vessels with necks are known at Tintagel (Price 1987, 25, no 8; Ewan Campbell per comm) but have not been recognised on other sites in western Britain, and the only other fragments which have features in common with the Trethurgy pieces are a small yellow concave base with a high central kick and pontil mark found at Whithorn which may come from a flask or small bottle (Campbell 1997, 309, no 64, fig 10.8) and a fragmentary small pale-green flask with a high kicked base and pontil mark from Llanelen, Gower (Campbell 1996, 127-8, fig 15a). Elsewhere in western Europe, small flasks with globular bodies have been noted in early 5th-century contexts in southern France (Foy 1995a, 195-6, nos 33-4, pl 6) and in 5th to 7th-century contexts in Italy (Sternini 1995, 260, 262, figs 18.33, 20.58), and a variety of flasks and jugs are known in 5th to 7th-century contexts in Spain (Gamo Parras 1995, 302-5, figs 1.1-3, 2.1-2, 3.1-5). Nonetheless, there is some uncertainty about these vessels, and it is possible that they could be of Post-Medieval date. None of the contexts from which they come can be regarded as securely sealed.

4.6 Objects and window glass

The ring fragment (Gl 18), which comes from the undecorated, plano-convex hoop which expands out towards the (missing) bezel, was found in a late 3rd to early 4th, or late 4th to early 5th-century context. No exact parallel for this piece is known, but apparently black glass finger rings, made in dark-green, yellowish-green or deep yellowish-brown glass, have been recorded in several Romano-British settlements. Examples are known from Exeter (Charlesworth 1979, 230 no 44, fig 71), Poundbury, Dorchester (Charlesworth and Price 1987, 109, no 9, fig 78), Great Witcombe villa, Gloucestershire (Price and Cottam 1998b, 91, nos 3-4, fig 26), Birdoswald (Price and Cottam 1997, 283, no 85, fig 193), and elsewhere. Almost all these rings appear to come from late deposits, and they were probably in circulation in the late 4th century. A recent survey of objects in use at the end of Roman Britain has included black finger rings (in glass and jet) as part of an assemblage of items which became popular towards the end of the 4th century and may have continued in use into the 5th century (Cool 2000, 50-6).

The three small globular beads, two translucent dark blue and one opaque blue (Gl 19-21), were found in 4th-century and later contexts. There is no evidence that these have been broken from wound segmented beads (Guido 1978, 91-3, fig 37, nos 1-2); the perforation areas are rounded and one end is slightly widened and distorted on each bead which suggests that they were made as wound globular beads. Guido (1978, 70, 169-72, Group 7iv) points out that these appear in the Late Iron Age-early Roman period, but many occur in late-Roman deposits, both in settlements and burials. A necklace from a context dated to c AD 380 or later in Room 14 at Great Witcombe villa consisted of 17 glass beads threaded on copper alloy links, including nine globular examples, six dark-blue and three opaque white, which were probably also made individually (rather than broken from segmented beads as stated in that report: Price and Cottam 1998b, 83-4, no 7, fig 23). Similar beads were found in the late-Roman settlement, the grave fills, and the Post-Roman settlement at Poundbury, Dorchester (Guido 1987, mf2 F6-7, nos 3-4, 15), and in Graves 100, 188, 199, 336, and 337 at Lankhills, Winchester (Guido 1979, 298-300). Single opaque blue and 'appearing black' examples were noted in Exeter (Charlesworth 1979, 230, no 47, fig 71; Allen 1991, 229, no 73, fig 96) and others in translucent dark-blue came from Nornour (Guido 1968, 27, no 62) and Halangy Down (Ashbee 1996, 72, no 2, fig 34.1).

The cube-shaped square-sectioned bead, Gl 22, was made in cloudy, almost opaque dark blue glass, though dark-green examples are also known. These beads occur in late-Roman contexts both in settlements and in burials. Seven blue examples came from Birdoswald, all but one in contexts postdating c AD 350 (Price and Cottam 1997, 273-5, nos 38-44, fig 185), four were recorded at Frocester Court, Gloucestershire in late 3rd, 4th-century and Post-Roman contexts (Price 2000c, 119, nos 105-7), two are known at Great Witcombe, one of which was part of the necklace mentioned above (Price and Cottam 1998b, 83-4, nos 7, 13, fig 23), and others formed part of late 4th-century necklaces at Lankhills, Winchester, and Poundbury, Dorchester (Guido 1978, 96, 212-5, fig 35, no 6).

The window glass fragments, Gl 23/4, come from one greenish matt-glossy pane which was made by pouring glass onto a flat surface and manipulating it into a rectangular shape (Mark Taylor and David Hill pers comm). Matt-glossy window glass was produced from the early 1st to around the late 3rd century, and was then replaced by cylinder-blown panes which were glossy on both surfaces, although some of the earlier panes continued in use into the 4th century, as in the Commandants House at South Shields fort (unpubl). Matt-glossy window glass was used in most military, urban, and high-status rural settlements, especially in the hot rooms of bath-houses and in residential buildings, where it served both to let light in and to keep heat in, but probably not to look through. In this connection, it is noteworthy that excavations in the legionary bath-house and basilica and forum in Exeter produced a large quantity of window glass (Charlesworth 1979, 229-30) but much less was found in other parts of the town (Allen 1991, 229). The panes were either set into wooden or metal frames and then inserted into the apertures or were fitted directly into the apertures secured with mortar; one of the fragments found in the bath-house, and basilica and forum retained a trace of mortar.

The presence of window glass, the first to be found in Roman Cornwall, is much more remarkable in a settlement such as Trethurgy where there was no sustained tradition of rectilinear buildings. Whether the large rectilinear timber structure House X1, dated to Stages 1-2 in the late 2nd century, is relevant here cannot be ascertained. It is just possible that one of the oval houses could have incorporated a small window, especially in the straighter long sides which are a feature of these houses in the 2nd and 3rd centuries. No information about the method of fixing the Trethurgy pane has survived and it is difficult to establish its original function, but the sharpness of the broken edges and the general lack of wear suggest that the fragments were not moved about very much after breakage and argue for their use on the site rather than importation as cullet. There is little evidence for the use of window glass in settlements of this kind, though a few instances have been been noted, as at Traprain Law in lowland Scotland (Ingemark 2000, 176), Cadbury Congresbury in Somerset (Price 1992, 138), and at Stanwick in North Yorkshire, where six matt-glossy fragments were found in the topsoil above a 1st-century roundhouse, but whether they come from the early house or from a later, as yet unidentified building nearby, is unknown (Colin Haselgrove and Pam Lowther pers comm).

4.7 Glass Catalogue

4.7.1 Vessels

Fig 51

Polychrome

Gl 1 [100], BN 109, SF9, House A2, late drainage gulley. ?Stages 7-8 AD 400-500 (but possibly earlier, see above). Body fragment, beaker. Pale yellow and opaque white. Straight side tapering in. Horizontal opaque white trail dragged down to form a loop, side slightly indented at point of loop. Few bubbles and black specks, otherwise good quality. No visible weathering, light scratches on outside surface. Present height 29.5mm. Thickness 1.2mm.

Incised Decoration

Gl 2 [400], BN 704, SF16, soil over Structure T5/6, period of abandonment. Stages 9/10 AD 500+, more likely to be 600+. Body fragment, bowl. Pale yellowish-green. Straight side, lower body tapering in, curving towards base edge. Two horizontal zones of abraded decoration; short diagonal lines arranged in herringbone pattern above small circular rings. Scatters of small bubbles, otherwise good quality. No visible weathering or wear marks. Present height c 21mm. Dimensions 37.5x33mm. Thickness 1.5-2.5mm.

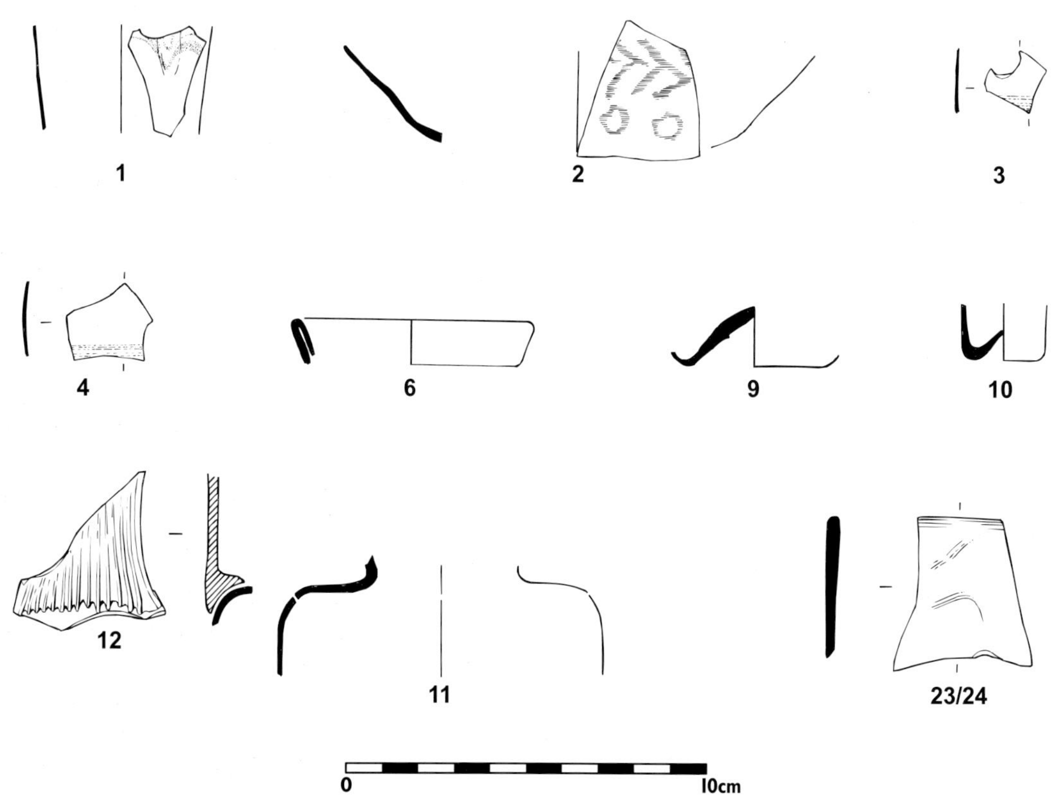

Fig 51: Glass vessels and window glass. Drawing Y Beadnall. Scale 1:2

Gl 3 [535], BN 268, Structure U2 drain. Stages 7/8 AD 400/500, but not well sealed. Body fragment from bowl or flask? Colourless. Wide convex side. Horizontal narrow and broad bands of abraded lines. Scatters of small bubbles. Dull. No wear marks. Dimensions 16.5x16mm. Thickness 1mm.

Gl 4 [801], BN 392, Structure U, upper part of midden. Stage 6 AD 375-400. Body fragment from bowl or flask? Colourless. Wide convex side. Horizontal narrow and broad bands of abraded lines. Scattered small bubbles. No visible weathering or wear marks. Dimensions 20.5x23mm. Thickness 1mm.

Also two undecorated body fragments: (a) [801], BN 620, Structure U upper part of midden. Stage 6 AD 375-400. Wide convex lower body fragment. Colourless. Scattered small bubbles, as BN 392. No visible weathering or wear marks. Dimensions 25x23mm. Thickness 1.2-1.5mm. (b) [932], BN 908, Structure U upper part of midden. Stage 6 AD 375-400. Convex body fragment. Colourless. Small bubbles, as BN 392 and BN 620. Slightly dull. No wear marks. Dimensions 13x10mm. Thickness 1mm

Bluish-green

Gl 5 [932], BN 859, Structure U; lower part of midden. Stage 6 AD 375-400. Body fragment, ?beaker. Bluish-green. Straight side, probably tapering in. Outside surface slightly uneven. No bubbles. No visible weathering. Dimensions 22.5x8mm. Thickness 1.5mm.

Gl 6 [932], BN 908, Structure U; lower part of midden. Stage 6 AD 375-400. Fragment of collar rim, jar. Bluish-green. Vertical rim, edge fire-rounded and bent out and down. Good quality, no bubbles. No visible weathering. Some wear on rim edge. Present height 12.5mm. Rim diameter *c* 65mm. Thickness 1.5mm.

Gl 7 [723], BN 297, House Z2 rubble collapse, not sealed. Stage 9 AD 500+. Neck fragment, flask or jug? Bluish-green with grey tinge. Cylindrical neck. Outside surface slightly uneven. Elongated bubbles throughout. No visible weathering. No wear. Dimensions 27x19.5mm. Thickness 2.3-3.3mm.

Gl 8 [34], BN 588, infill between House A2 and A3. Stage 8 AD 450-500. Neck fragment, flask or jug? Bluish-green with grey tinge. Cylindrical neck curving out slightly towards rim or body. Outside surface slightly uneven. Small elongated bubbles. No visible weathering. No wear. Dimensions 28.5x16mm. Thickness 1mm.

Gl 9 [77], BN 29, Structure G; upper fill. Stage 9 AD 500+ (not really sealed). Base fragment, beaker or flask? Bluish-green with grey tinge. Lower body tapering in, high pointed concave base. Pontil mark. Pimpled surface on edge of underside of base. Small bubbles. No visible weathering. Wear scratches on inside surface. Present height 17mm. Base diameter *c* 45mm. Thickness of lower body 1.2mm.

Gl 10 [36], BN 216, platform adjacent House T3. Stage 4 and later AD 260-325+. Body and base fragment, flask or unguent bottle. Bluish-green with grey tinge. Narrow cylindrical body, small, high, pointed concave base. Pontil bark on base edge. Small bubbles. No visible weathering. Wear scratches on outside surface, patches of wear on base edge. Present height 15.5mm. Body diameter 23.5mm.Thickness of body 1.5-2.5mm.

Bottles

Gl 11 [932], BN 925, Structure U, lower part of midden. Stage 6 AD 375-400. Twelve fragments, several joining, from neck, shoulder, and body of square bottle. Base of cylindrical neck with tooling marks, horizontal shoulder, parts of at least one flat side with 90° angles. No visible weathering; very clear, good-quality glass; mould marking on body fragments, clockwise spiral movement in glass visible on shoulder, probably from blowing body into mould. No wear marks. Neck diameter *c* 40mm. Width of shoulder *c* 18mm. Present height of largest piece 40mm. Width of body *c* 75-80mm. Thickness of body 1-3mm.

Gl 12 [800], BN 348, soil over Structure U, mainly disturbed top of midden. Not assigned to Stage. Shoulder and handle fragment, prismatic bottle, as BN 925. Curved shoulder and small part of vertical side, broad, straight, reeded handle applied to edge of shoulder. No visible weathering; shoulder and body made in clear, good-quality glass, small bubbles and black specks in handle. No wear marks. Present height 41mm. Maximum width of handle 41.5mm. Thickness (shoulder) 2.25mm, (body) 1.5mm.

Also three similar fragments: (a) [932], BN 908, Structure U; lower part of midden. Stage 6 AD 375-400. Body fragment, prismatic bottle, as BN 925 and BN 348. Flat side. Mould marking on outer surface. Good-quality glass. No visible weathering. No wear marks. Dimensions 30.5x18mm. Thickness 1.2-1.8mm. (b) [800], BN 575, soil over Structure U, mainly disturbed top of midden. Not assigned to Stage. Body fragment, prismatic bottle, as BN 925, 348 and 908. Flat side. Mould marking on outer surface. Good-quality glass. No visible weathering. No wear marks. Dimensions 11.5x5mm. Thickness 1.5-mm. (c) Unstratified, BN 929. Body fragment, prismatic bottle, as BN 925, 348, 908 and 575. Flat side. Mould marking on outside suface. Good-quality glass. No visible weathering. No wear marks. Dimensions 22.5x21.5mm. Thickness 2-2.5mm.

Gl 13 [442], BN 727, House T2, soil on floor. Stage 3 AD 210-260. Body fragment, ?prismatic bottle.

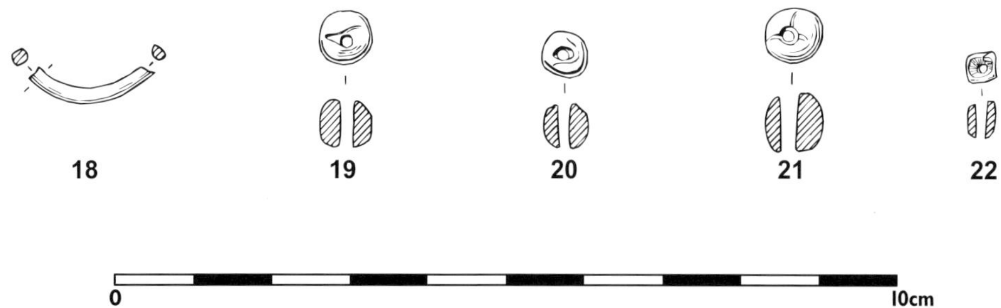

Fig 52: Glass objects. Drawing Y Beadnall. Full size

Bluish-green. Flat side. Good-quality glass, dimpled outside surface. No visible weathering. No wear marks. Dimensions 11.5x18mm. Thickness 1.5-2mm.

Gl 14 [852], BN 426, House Z1, drain. Probably sealed in Stage 4 AD 260-325. Upper body fragment, prismatic bottle. Edge of shoulder, flat side. Good-quality glass, small bubbles. No visible weathering. No wear marks. Dimensions 20x26.5mm. Thickness 1mm.

Gl 15 [801], BN 614, Structure U, upper part of midden. Stage 6 AD 375-400. Body fragment, prismatic bottle. Part of flat side. No visible weathering, pronounced mould marks on outer surface. Some usage scratches. Dimensions 22x16mm. Thickness 2-3mm.

Gl 16 [523], BN 118, soil over cobbles [521], north terminal of Ditch. Stage 9+ AD 500+. Body fragment, ? prismatic bottle. Pale bluish-green. Slightly concave side, apparently distorted by heat. Small bubbles. Dull, outside surface dimpled. Dimensions 10x24mm. Thickness 5mm.

Gl 17 [818], BN 432, House Z1b, pit. Stage 4 AD 260-325. Body fragment, prismatic bottle. Greenish colourless. Flat side. Small bubbles throughout. Dull, surfaces scratched. Dimensions 22x10mm. Thickness 2.5mm.

4.7.2 Objects

Fig 52

Gl 18 [793], BN 394, SF 109, cut for wall of House Z2. Stage 6 AD 375-400 or just possibly Stage 4 AD 260-325. Finger ring. Dark yellowish-green, appearing black. Fragment of D-sectioned ring, expanded at one end. Some wear on outside surface. Length of fragment 15.5mm. Internal diameter approximately 14mm. Height 2mm. Width 3-3.3mm.

Gl 19 [557], BN 709, SF 153, cobbling predating Structure V1. Stage 5 AD 325-375. Bead. Dark blue. Intact globular bead with flattened areas on the outside surface. Small perforation, widened at one end. Probably wound. No visible weathering. Height 6mm. Maximum width 7mm. Perforation 2-4mm.

Gl 20 [9], BN 710, SF 14, Area R soil accumulation between Stages 4 and 5 c AD 325. Bead. Opaque blue. Intact globular bead. Small perforation, widened at one end. Probably wound. Height 5mm. Maximum width 6.3mm. Perforation 1.5-4mm.

Gl 21 [11], BN 5, topsoil over Area E. Stage 9 AD 500+. Bead. Dark blue. Two joining fragments, complete globular bead. Small perforation, widened at one end. Probably wound. Height 7.4mm. Maximum width 7mm. Perforation 2-4mm.

Gl 22 [723], BN 271, collapse of House Z2. Stage 9 AD 500 onward. Bead. Dark blue. Intact square-sectioned bead. Small perforation, widened at one end. Probably wound and flattened. Height 4.4mm. Width 3.5mm. Perforation 1-3mm.

4.7.3 Window glass

Fig 51

Gl 23 [34], BN 64, joins [111], BN227, infill between Houses A2 and A3. Stage 8 AD 450-500. Edge fragment, cast window pane. Greenish. Thick rounded edge, top surface shiny and uneven, with two pressure points, bottom surface flat and dull, with dimples. Little visible weathering, some wear scratches on top surface, very worn on rounded edge. Dimensions 38x32.5mm. Thickness 2.4-4.2mm.

Gl 24 [111], BN 227, joins [34], BN 64, Entrance surface, later level. Stage 5 AD 325+, but not sealed. Fragment, cast window pane. Greenish. Top surface shiny, bottom surface flat, and dull with dimples. Little visible weathering, some wear scratches on top surface. Dimensions 15x17mm. Thickness 2-2.5mm.

5 The Pottery

with contributions by *DF Williams*

5.1 The assemblage and its study

5.1.1 Site conditions and the assemblage

Conditions on the site during and after the occupation of the Round caused difficulties in the study of its ceramics. The soil was acid and sherds tended to soften and abrade easily. Refuse appears to have been regularly removed from the site (Section 12.10) and only a small proportion of the pottery and other artefacts originally present remained. There was continual reuse of soil, to provide wall-core material and bedding and levelling for floors, so artefacts were moved around the site. Because of this reuse of soil, later contexts such as walls contain more pottery than early ones and early forms appear in late contexts. This is most clearly demonstrable with distinctive wares such as samian, but is relevant to all fabrics found. Very few contexts were completely sealed. All surfaces of soil and rab were liable to continuous trample and small-scale disturbance, and areas of paving could have been taken up and relaid in such a way as to be undetectable in excavation. The Round had been extensively ploughed, probably from the Medieval period onward, and ploughing can cause disturbance to a considerable depth as damage to upper stones may displace those beneath.

No context provided a securely sealed sizeable group. Only midden [932/801] contained a large assemblage and this may have suffered some disturbance. The few artefacts which are datable — the brooches and the coins — do not occur in contexts where they provide helpful associations and the radiocarbon dates (Section 9.1) provide only very broad indications for the date of the Round and of its finds. Dates for pottery types have therefore to be derived from other sites and from current overall understanding of the way in which ceramic forms changed in Cornwall during the Roman period. The pottery assemblage is however important in that it is the largest to be published in detail from Roman Cornwall, and the stratigraphic sequence, the Stages in the Round's occupation, provides a framework within which local ceramic typologies can be presented as a working model until such time as more reliable dating becomes available.

The principal comparable assemblages and their publication references are shown in Table 5.1.

Carn Euny	Elsdon 1978
Castle Gotha	Saunders and Harris 1982
Carvossa	Carlyon 1987; 1995
Carwarthen	Opie 1939; Carlyon 1995
Chysauster	Hencken 1928; 1933; Carlyon 1995
Duckpool	Quinnell 1995
Goldherring	Guthrie 1969
Kilhallon	Carlyon 1982
Magor	O'Neil 1933
Mulfra Vean	Thomas 1963
Nanstallon	Fox and Ravenhill 1972
Porth Godrevy	Fowler 1962
Porthmeor	Hirst 1937; Carlyon 1995
Reawla	Quinnell 1992
St Mawgan-in-Pydar	Threipland 1956
Shortlanesend	Harris 1980
Trebarveth T1	Serocold and Maynard 1949; Carlyon 1995
Trebarveth T3	Peacock 1969a
Trevisker	ApSimon and Greenfield 1972

Table 5.1: References to principal publications of ceramic assemblages from Roman Cornwall

5.1.2 Changing methodology of study 1976 - 2001 and the introduction of a Type-Series for Romano-British gabbroic pottery

The basic framework of the pottery report was established in 1976, seeking an approach which would adequately represent the assemblage, and explore its potential, given the scarcity of good sealed groups. Two factors were clear. The majority of the assemblage was in local gabbroic ware, for which there was no overall type-series available. The remainder included a wide range of fabrics ranging from Post-Roman Mediterranean imported wares to those then being recognised as distinctive at Exeter. A series of vessel forms was chosen for individual description and illustration to represent the range of the gabbroic assemblage. It was not intended that each illustrated vessel represent a distinct type, as the various jar and

General context	Gabbroic		BB1		S Devon		Other Roman/Post-Roman		Medieval/Post-Medieval		Total Roman/Post-Roman		Total all periods	
	Sherds	Weight	Sherds	Weight	Sherds	Weight	Sherds	Weight	Sherds	Weight	Sherds	Weight	Sherds	Weight
Period 3 EnclosureBank	2	26	-	-	-	-	-	-	-	-	2	26	2	26
Period 4	86	778	2	8	1	13	18	74	2	26	107	873	109	899
Round Earthworks	152	1928	7	72	6	64	47	406	58	634	212	2470	270	3104
Structure V1	22	80	-	-	-	-	2	26	-	-	24	106	24	106
Structure V2	193	1784	5	28	5	39	10	28	-	-	213	1879	213	1879
Structure V3	18	401	1	1	6	36	-	-	-	-	25	438	25	438
Soil over V	156	1887	3	12	6	41	20	74	23	173	185	2014	208	2187
Structure U1	72	716	8	67	5	52	3	263	-	-	88	1098	88	1098
Midden [932 / 801]	1321	24222	32	350	77	810	47	265	8	79	1477	25647	1485	25726
Soil over U	585	7834	26	207	21	217	26	135	120	1300	658	8393	778	9693
Pre-House Z	3	52	-	-	-	-	-	-	-	-	3	52	3	52
House Z1	224	3749	13	75	3	51	-	-	-	-	240	3875	240	3875
Between Z1/Z2	265	2995	7	35	12	221	4	26	1	3	288	3277	289	3280
House Z2	232	3118	26	153	3	31	1	2	1	4	262	3304	263	3308
Collapse Hse Z	225	2244	4	15	2	41	4	71	2	6	235	2371	237	2377
Soil over Z	99	1032	3	24	4	30	6	58	128	826	112	1144	240	1970
Q Stage 4	228	3513	5	41	2	13	-	-	-	-	235	3567	235	3567
Q Stage 5	15	112	1	5	-	-	-	-	-	-	16	117	16	117
Q Stage 6+	53	494	-	-	-	-	1	2	-	-	54	496	54	496
Soil over Q	72	1079	-	-	-	-	-	-	1	10	72	1079	73	1089
Pre-Structure Y	30	240	9	88	7	58	-	-	-	-	46	386	46	386
Structure Y	109	2625	10	62	-	-	36	227	19	88	155	2914	174	3002
Soil over Y	147	2095	8	24	5	20	3	6	1	8	163	2145	164	2153
House X1	1	30	-	-	-	-	1	1	-	-	2	31	2	31
House X4	9	53	-	-	-	-	9	25	-	-	18	78	18	78
Area X unphased	21	138	-	-	3	13	-	-	2	11	24	151	26	162

General context	Gabbroic		BB1		S Devon		Other Roman/Post-Roman		Medieval/Post-Medieval		Total Roman/Post-Roman		Total all periods	
	Sherds	Weight	Sherds	Weight	Sherds	Weight	Sherds	Weight	Sherds	Weight	Sherds	Weight	Sherds	Weight
Structure X5	15	141	11	116	3	23	7	64	23	192	36	344	59	536
Soil over X	12	249	-	-	-	-	-	-	-	-	12	249	12	249
Structure G	48	850	1	15	1	12	1	5	1	7	51	882	52	889
Structure G infill	19	263	1	3	2	17	21	111	10	145	43	394	53	539
Posthole [284]	1	5	-	-	-	-	-	-	-	-	1	5	1	5
Soil over G	11	133	-	-	1	18	6	33	57	702	18	184	75	886
Features, Area E	16	451	-	-	-	-	-	-	-	-	16	451	16	451
Structure D	4	38	-	-	-	-	3	7	-	-	7	45	7	45
Soil over D/E	127	2157	2	13	9	79	14	90	21	186	152	2339	173	2525
Pre-House A1	10	59	-	-	-	-	-	-	-	-	10	59	10	59
House A1	116	874	1	2	-	-	6	167	-	-	123	1043	123	1043
House A2	207	2721	4	66	-	-	12	55	-	-	223	2842	223	2842
Soil over A	129	1774	2	20	2	4	16	250	40	248	149	2048	189	2296
Structure T1	7	206	-	-	-	-	-	-	-	-	7	206	7	206
House T2	114	1562	2	8	2	6	10	75	-	-	128	1651	128	1651
House T3	146	1703	5	49	2	10	10	71	-	-	163	1833	163	1833
House T4	62	713	1	4	2	27	7	34	-	-	72	778	72	778
Late collapse in T and soil	113	1322	5	27	3	18	13	109	16	138	134	1476	150	1614
Structure T5	-	-	-	-	-	-	2	7	-	-	2	7	2	7
Soil over T	2	16	-	-	-	-	1	4	-	-	3	20	3	20
Area R OLS [380]	45	478	1	1	-	-	2	104	25	136	48	583	73	719
Area R Stages 1 - 4	235	3162	2	4	4	27	11	160	1	3	252	3353	253	3356
Area R Stage 5	146	1395	1	5	-	-	4	131	2	5	151	1531	153	1539
Area R Stage 8	35	537	-	-	-	-	7	13	-	-	42	550	42	550
Area R Stages 9 - 10	26	350	-	-	-	-	4	11	-	-	30	361	30	361
Soil over [46] R	10	94	-	-	-	-	2	5	-	-	12	99	12	99
Ploughsoil	208	2757	3	52	7	85	17	15	897	7997	235	2909	1132	10906
Field hedge [236]	-	-	-	-	-	-	-	-	1	8	-	-	1	8
Total	**6204**	**87235**	**212**	**1652**	**206**	**2076**	**414**	**3210**	**1460**	**12935**	**7036**	**94173**	**8497**	**107108**

Table 5.2: Analysis of ceramic assemblage by main context and fabric groups; 'Other Roman/Post-Roman' includes all fabrics of these dates not individually quantified ; weight in grammes

bowl forms display a considerable degree of overlap. Although some pieces selected were unique, more usually several were similar and that chosen for illustration provided the most complete profile and diameter. All other vessels with sufficient distinctive forms were then related to the numbered illustrated sequence. This provided the basis for a tentative minimum vessel count, based on rims, or, in some cases, other distinctive parts of the vessel. The presence of each vessel form, and also of each fabric, was recorded in the Context List Appendix 1.

Samples both of gabbroic fabric and of those fabrics recognised as being distinctive but not local to Devon and Cornwall, such as black-burnished ware (abbreviated as BB1) and Post-Roman Mediterranean imports, were submitted in 1976 to DF Williams for petrographic comment. Dr Williams revised his contribution in 2000.

In 1985/6 the report was reworked. The occupation of the Round was divided into ten Stages which provided a potential sequence within which the ceramics could be considered. It was realised that the illustrated vessels in gabbroic fabric in fact could be divided into reasonably distinctive groups, those used in the sub-headings below. The study was aided by the work of PM Carlyon on a wide range of published and unpublished material. This desk-top publication, in initial (1985) and revised (1995) versions, assisted with comparanda; the study contains numerous illustrations of unpublished material. Carlyon divided types up into 47 Groups, which are referred to below where appropriate.

In 2001 the report was finally revised. This involved two major changes. The whole assemblage was quantified by sherd numbers and weight for each context to provide additional information on the amounts of each fabric present to that provided by the tentative vessel counts and to present the basic data which would allow the assemblage to be compared to others studied by modern methods. The second change was the addition of Type numbers to the groups of types which had already been distinguished for gabbroic fabrics. Type numbers have been assigned leaving gaps for distinctive groups which may still be defined. The Type numbers can be sub-divided in future to accommodate variations which are found to be significant. Dates for each Type are suggested in the light of current evidence. This dating and classification system for Roman-period gabbroic pottery is intended to provide a basis for future study and in no way is to be regarded as definitive. In particular it is hoped that a clearly set out series of dated types will provide a reference system against which sealed groups can in future be tested.

The treatment of the non-gabbroic fabrics has reflected the great changes which have taken place in the understanding of ceramics in South West Britain since initial work on the pottery in 1975. Substantial

Continental and Mediterranean Imported Wares	**Numbers**	**British Wares with province - wide distribution**	**Numbers**
Samian	14	Oxfordshire colour-coats	9
Lezoux colour-coat	1	**British Regional Wares**	
Unguentarium import	1	SE Dorset BBI	23
White Slip ware import	1	SW Dorset BB1	1
Phocaean Red Slip wares (A ware)	2	BBI copy	1
E ware	1	Exeter flagon fabric 451	1
Post -Roman coarse ware imports	2	Exeter Gritty Grey ware fabric 101	2
Amphora - Dressel 1	1	Exeter Micaceous Grey ware Fabric 125	1
Amphora - Dressel 20	1	South-Western Grey storage jars	1
Amphora - Gauloise 4	1	South Devon ware	30
Amphora - Palestinian	1	**Total**	60
Amphora - Bi	1		
Amphora - Bii	2	**Local Wares**	
Amphora - Biv	1	Gabbroic	450
Amphora - Bv	1		
Total	**31**	**OVERALL TOTAL**	**550**

Table 5.3: Minimum vessel counts, excluding small sherds of unidentified fabrics. Note: British nomenclature retained for Post-Roman imports

revision took place both in 1985/6 and in 2001. The author is much indebted to Paul Bidwell for help with identification and dating provided in 1986 for the non-gabbroic Roman material. Bidwell (1979) had developed a Fabric Number sequence for Exeter which is used here where appropriate. The publication of the Roman pottery from Exeter by Holbrook and Bidwell (1991) provides an invaluable basis for the region as a whole and especially for black-burnished wares and has been drawn on extensively here. The study of Post-Roman imported wares has been vigorously pursued by Charles Thomas especially in relation to the Tintagel assemblage. Professor Thomas, together with Carl Thorpe, examined in 2001 all the material not so far assigned to a recognised fabric and identified a number of Post-Roman imports new to Trethurgy. There still remain unidentified fabrics in the assemblage which may be expected to be recognised in the course of future research work.

5.2 The quantification of the assemblage

The assemblage consisted of 8496 sherds weighing 107,108g; of these 1460 sherds weighing 12,935g were Medieval or Post-Medieval and are considered briefly in Section 5.7. The Roman and Post-Roman assemblage consisted of 7036 sherds weighing 94,173g. This core assemblage is presented by sherd numbers and weights in broad context groups in Table 5.2, divided into gabbroic, South-East Dorset BB1, South Devon and other fabrics. Sherd counts presented a problem, especially for the non-local wares which had a tendency to fragment after excavation; numbers here should be regarded only as approximate. An attempt at minimum vessel numbers has been based on variations in rim form or other typological feature; fabrics without typological features have been assumed to represent only one vessel; these counts for all fabrics present are shown in Table 5.3. It is now well established (Orton *et al* 1993, 171) that, of the three ways the Trethurgy assemblage is measured, weight provides the most reliable indicator for use in comparison with assemblages from other sites. It is also now accepted that estimated-vessel-equivalent (eve) is far more reliable than the minimum vessel numbers presented here (*ibid*) but resources did not permit the time consuming calculations required. The figures for weight are therefore those which will be used in describing the assemblage. Trethurgy provides the first large assemblage from Roman Cornwall to be analysed with this degree of detail.

Details of the 'Other Roman' and 'Post-Roman' fabrics are shown in Table 5.4, and the percentage representation of the major fabric groups in the assemblage in Table 5.5.

Fabric	Sherds	Weight (g)
Samian	60	282
Lezoux	7	6
Unguentarium	1	10
White Slip ware import	13	76
Phocaean Red Slip wares (A ware)	8	20
E ware	1	7
E Mediterranean Fabric 1	1	3
E Mediterranean Fabric 5	1	4
Amphora - Dressel 1	1	34
Amphora - Dressel 20	19	860
Amphora - Gauloise 4	5	44
Amphora - Palestinian	22	138
Amphora - Bi	15	130
Amphora - Bii	47	219
Amphora - Biv	2	12
Amphora - Bv	12	323
Oxfordshire colour-coats	28	213
SW Dorset BB1	2	15
BBI copy	1	8
Exeter flagon fabric 451	3	24
Exeter Gritty Grey ware fabric 101	4	41
Exeter Micaceous Grey ware fabric 125	1	3
South-Western Grey storage jars	26	261
Unidentified amphora	37	451
Unidentified fabrics	71	165

Table 5.4: Sherd and weight counts for 'Other Roman/Post-Roman fabrics' to complement data presented in Table 5.2

	Gabbroic	All BB1	SE Dorset BB1	S Devon	Other
Whole assemblage Roman/Post-Roman					
Sherds	88.2	3.0	2.9	2.9	5.9
Weight	92.6	1.8	1.7	2.2	3.4
Minimum vessels	81.9	4.4	4.2	5.5	8.2
Contexts Stages 1- 4					
Sherds	93.3	2.4	2.4	1.1	3.2
Weight	94.8	1.1	1.1	0.6	3.5
Stage 6 midden [932 / 801] including soil over [800]					
Sherds	89.3	2.7	2.7	4.6	3.4
Weight	93.6	1.6	1.6	3.0	1.8
Stage 6 midden [932 / 801] without soil over [800]					
Sherds	88.7	2.2	2.2	5.2	3.9
Weight	94.5	1.4	1.4	3.1	1.0

Table 5.5: Percentages of the assemblage for major fabric groups; Stage 1-4 contexts and the Stage 6 midden included to cover any chronological variation

5.3 Continental and Mediterranean imported wares

5.3.1 Samian

About 60 sherds were found (not illustrated), mostly small and with surfaces abraded and damaged by the acid soil conditions. A minimum of 14 vessels is represented. The only concentration of sherds, 25 in [932/801] midden and ploughsoil over this in Structure U, reflects the main concentration of pottery on the site.

Dr 27 cup Sherds, probably of one vessel, [567] secondary silt in Ditch terminal, [175] patching on surface [8] in R, [46] revetment collapse in R. Central Gaulish, Hadrianic-Antonine.

Dr 37 bowls Sherds with very abraded ovolo decoration, probably from two separate vessels, [161] House A1 drain, [400] soil over House T6. Rim sherd, probably from a third vessel, [932] lower midden in U. Central Gaulish, Antonine.

Dr 18 dish Rim sherd, [11] soil over Structures D and E. Central Gaulish, Antonine.

Dr 18/31 dish Rim sherd, [28] paving House T5. Central Gaulish, Antonine.

Dr 31 dishes Sherd from wall/floor angle, [555] cobbles around V2. Rim sherd, [751] surface between Structure Y and wall [892]. Foot-ring, [255] Structure G, backing infill. Central Gaulish, Antonine.

Dr 45 mortaria Wall/floor angle sherds from [932] and [801] lower and upper midden in U; from a second vessel, [801]; from a third, [751] surface between Structure Y and wall [892]. All Central Gaulish, Antonine.

Walters Form 81 Wall sherd, soft but comparatively unabraded. Central Gaul, Les Martres-de-Veyre, almost certainly made *c* AD 110-145. [808] soil between House Z1 and Z2. (I am grateful to the late Brian Hartley for commenting on this sherd).

Spindle whorl fragment [723] soil over House Z2.

Unidentifiable sherds from [175], [256], [369], [395], [518] (2), [537], [555], [560], [728], [743], [780] (2), [801] (8),[808] (3), [905], [907A], [931], [932] (4), and ploughsoil (12 — of which 9 are from [800] over U).

Virtually every Cornish site reputed to have been occupied during the Roman period has produced some sherds of samian, whatever the suggested date of occupation. The sherds are usually in very poor condition, soils derived from killas being at least as hostile as those from the granite, notably at Nanstallon (Fox and Ravenhill 1972, 100). The only sites which do not appear to have produced samian are Carngoon Bank, Magor, Chysauster, Goldherring, and Trebarveth, T1 and T3.

A high survival value for samian may be presumed, either as individual vessels or as sherds. Much of the samian which has been commented upon or is available for examination appears to be Antonine in date. Most notable is the deposit at Kilhallon, a deposit in a ditch containing a wide variety of fabrics dumped around the middle of the 3rd century AD; the samian present (five vessels) ranged from Trajanic/Hadrianic through to AD 160-200. At Trethurgy the 25 sherds in midden [932/801] were deposited in the context which produced the earliest Oxfordshire ware sherds, Stage 6. It is possible that some of these sherds were not immediate breakages, but had been preserved in sherd form for some purpose. If the suggested date of Stage 6, AD 375-400, is at all accurate, samian was being deposited 200 years after its manufacture. A single sherd occurred in the Stage 9 infill of Structure G [256], which with its associated Post-Roman import sherds should date to the 6th (or even the 7th?) century Stage 9. The long survival rate for samian in Western Britain has been noted for 6th-century Cadbury Congresbury (Burrow 1979, 227; 1981, 120-33), Dinas Powys (Alcock 1963, 22-5), and at the late 4th-century site of Bradley Hill, Somerset (Leech 1981, 239). The use of samian for dating must therefore be approached with caution in western rural areas, especially where controls in the form of other dateable artefacts are absent.

5.3.2 Lezoux colour-coat sherds

Seven small thin sherds (not illustrated), probably from the same vessel, pink with grey zones towards surfaces, with internal and external dark metallic slip. Date range AD 150-250. (Identified by P Bidwell). From [801], [932] (2), [555], [46], and [560]. Stage 6 and later. It is possible that the first four of these sherds had been made into counters; all were roughly rectangular, three 60x14mm, one 30x14mm.

5.3.3 *Unguentarium*

Sherd from neck of *unguentarium* (not illustrated); gritted grey fabric with oxidised surfaces. Erosion of exterior has removed distinctive rilling and white slip. A continental import; examples occur at Exeter. (Identified by P Bidwell). Paving [8] in centre of Round.

5.3.4 White slipped ware import

Fig 53

P6 Beaker in fine white-buff, slightly sandy fabric; traces of brown slip now almost totally eroded; fabric not sourced but suggested by P Bidwell to be an import to Britain. Joining rim sherds from [400] soil over House T and from ploughsoil in A; body sherds from [801] midden in U, with remaining sherds from ploughsoil in the north-east area, [9], [403] (2), [422], [429] (2), and [395]. These contexts are widely distributed across the site and chronologically range from Stages 4/5 [9] to Stage 7 [403] providing a graphic illustration of the way in which material spread around the site. As with samian and Lezoux colour-coat, this unusual fabric might have been retained as sherds, but this seems unlikely because the pieces were scarcely abraded.

5.3.5 Phocaean Red Slip ware (formerly A ware/ Late Roman C)

Fig 53

P7 From [256] lower fill of Structure G, on floor [258].

P8 From [523] soil over upper cobbling in north Ditch terminal.

Three sherds similar to P8 from [907A] tumble from wall [907] in Q, and [77] upper infill in G. A further three sherds were identified subsequent to examination by DF Williams, from [11] soil over E, [785] and soil over Z (2), making a total of eight.

DF Williams comments:

'Four small friable sherds, some with signs of a red slip, which equate to Radford's Class 'A' ware (1956, figs 13 and 14) and John Hayes Late Roman C ware (1972, 323-70). This is a class of fine tableware which comprises bowls and dishes with a thin red slip, slightly darker than the paste, commonly with wall-sided rims and often decorated with rouletting. One of the Trethurgy sherds is a small section of a rim that may possibly belong to Hayes form 3 (*ibid*). Due to the smallness and state of preservation of the other three sherds it is difficult to identify with any exactness the forms involved. On the basis of kiln wasters found at ancient Phocaea, Late Roman C ware was later renamed by Hayes as Phocaean Red Slip ware (1980). A thin section of rim sherd P8 revealed inclusions of small quartz, flecks of mica, some grains of plagioclase feldspar and few fragments of lava. The area of Phocaea in western Turkey now considered to be a major production centre for what used to be termed Late Roman C ware (Hayes 1980) contains volcanic rocks and so the petrology of the Trethurgy sherd would fit in with the geology of the Phocaean area. However, not enough work has been done on the fabric of Phocaean Red Slip ware to make the identification of source positive. The remaining three sherds all appear to be of a slightly coarser fabric than that normally associated by the writer with Phocaean Red Slip ware. However, it is now clear that 'Phocaean Red Slip Ware' was not only made at Phocaea, but also at other sites in the region including Grynion, Pergamon, and Ephesos (Dr L Vaag pers comm) and this may well account for a certain variation in fabric noted here.'

Fulford (1989) has cogently argued that imports of Phocaean Red Slip ware found in western Britain and Ireland (together with accompanying Late Roman 1, 2, and 3 amphora — see below) probably arrived during the period between c AD 475-550.

Thomas (1981) lists five other sites from Cornwall with Phocaean Slip ware, of which Tintagel, as for all the Post-Roman imports except E ware, produced by far the largest quantity.

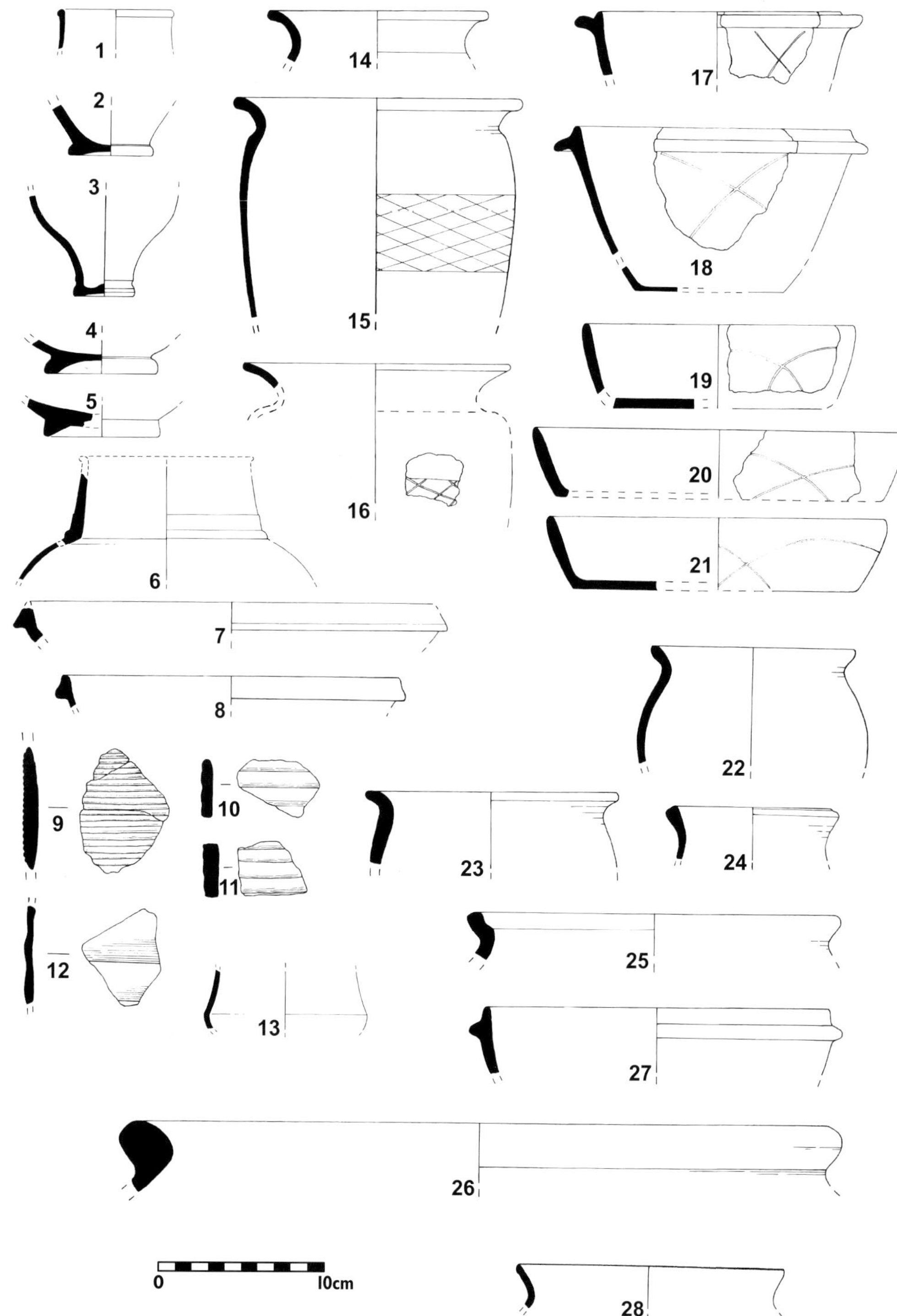

Fig 53 Non-gabbroic pottery. P1-5 Oxfordshire, P6 White ware import, P7-8 Phocaean Red Slip wares (A ware), P9-12 Late Roman amphorae (B ware), P13 E ware, P14-21 BB1, P22-3, 25-27 South Devon ware, P28 BB1 copy, P24 Medieval. Drawing L Simpson. Scale 1:4

5.3.6 Post-Roman imported E ware

Fig 53

P13 From [359], lynchet above the silted Ditch on the west of the site. A sherd of a carinated beaker (Thomas 1990, Form Eii) in characteristic heavily gritted buff fabric with a slightly reduced external surface (Peacock and Thomas 1967, fig 10d); these authorities suggest a source in the Charente-Inferieure and Gironde Departments of South West France, for which there now seems to be general agreement. E ware in general has a more westerly distribution than other forms of Post-Roman import wares; its date range in the British Isles is considered to start a little later than the amphorae and Phocean Red Slip wares, perhaps in the early 6th century and to continue rather later, into perhaps the early 8th (Thomas 1985, 195). In Cornwall the findspots concentrate in the

Isles of Scilly (Thomas 1981, 20; 1985, 195) but the fabric also occurs at Hellesvean, Gwithian, and the Kelsies, all on the North Cornish coast. The sherd from Trethurgy cannot be related directly to continued use of the Round but implies activity which may be as late as the 8th century somewhere in the immediate vicinity. (I am grateful to Euan Campbell for his discussion of this sherd.)

5.3.7 Post-Roman imported coarsewares

Possible small sherd of Eastern Mediterranean Sandy Cream ware (not illustrated), from Stage 5+ [8] surface in Area R; this is Post-Roman imported coarseware Fabric 5, of broadly 6th-century date. Possible small sherd of Eastern Mediterranean Red ware from gulley [743] in House X4; this is Post-Roman imported coarseware Fabric 1. Both fabrics occur at Tintagel (Thorpe 1997, 79) for which see description and further references. Identification by Charles Thomas and Carl Thorpe.

5.3.8 Amphora Dressel Type 1sp

A sherd from towards the base of an amphora (not illustrated), from [723], soil and collapse over House Z.

DF Williams comments:

'An amphora body sherd probably belonging to the Dressel 1sp form, in a hard, rough fabric, light red throughout, and quite clearly containing a large quantity of 'black sand'. It is not possible to say whether this sherd comes from the earlier Dressel IA form or the later 1B type. Both forms were predominantly made in Italy and normally carried wine. The 1A form was made from about 130 BC till around the middle of the 1st century BC, while the 1B form appears to have been made shortly before the beginning of the 1st century BC till the last decade of the century (Peacock and Williams 1986, Classes 3 and 4). The Trethurgy sherd is in a visually distinctive 'black sand' fabric — caused by dark-coloured grains of augite — which occurs in both the 1A and 1B forms. A thin section of the sherd shows an identical composition to Peacock's Fabric 2, with a provenance in the Bay of Naples area of Campania, southern Italy (1971a, 164-5; Peacock and Williams 1986, 87-8).'

As the sherd is not large enough for the form to be ascertained, a wide date range, from the mid 2nd century BC to late 1st century BC, is possible (Fitzpatrick 1985, 307). A group of Dressel 1 amphorae sherds have been recognised at the hillfort of Castle Dore, 7km east of Trethurgy (Quinnell and Harris 1985, 130) and at Carn Euny in West Penwith (Williams 1978, 406), while an unclassified probable pre-Roman piece has been described from the Rumps cliff castle in North Cornwall (Hawkes 1966). This material, including the Trethurgy sherd, have recently been re-examined by Fitzpatrick (forthcoming), who now considers that only a Carn Euny sherd is Dressel 1A, that the Trethurgy and Castle Dore sherds may belong to Dressel Types 2 to 4 within the Roman period, and that the piece from the Rumps may be either Roman or immediately Post-Roman. Implications are discussed further in Section 9.2.3.

5.3.9 Amphora Dressel Type 20

Seventeen sherds were present (not illustrated). Ten substantial sherds were examined by DF Williams, including part of a round-sectioned handle [161] and a chunk just above the basal spike [890]. These come from [890] wall core of Structure U, [801] upper midden in U, [161] drain House A1, [34] infill of House A2, ploughsoil over A (2), [471C] posthole House T2 wall, [9], and soil under paving [8] in R (2). The remaining sherds come from [314] House A1 drain, [723] collapsed wall in Z2, [808] soil between Z1 and Z2 (4), and soil over Q.

DF Williams comments:

'A handle and nine thick body sherds of the Baetican amphora form Dressel 20.

This is the most common amphora type imported into Roman Britain, though it is clear that it was already present in some numbers during the Late Iron Age (Williams and Peacock 1983). Dressel 20 amphorae were made alongside the banks of the River Guadalquivir and its tributaries between Seville and Cordoba in the southern Spanish province of Baetica, where they were used for the transportation of the local olive oil (Peacock and Williams 1986, Class 25). This type of amphora has a wide date range, from the Augustan prototype Oberaden 83 to the well known globular vessel which, with some typological variation, mainly to the rim form, was in use up to around the middle of the 3rd century AD (*ibid*). It is difficult to suggest a particular date within this period for the Trethurgy material.'

At Trethurgy the sherds are scattered chronologically from [471C], Stage 2, to [34], Stage 8/9. Baetican amphorae sherds, without precise dating, have also been recognised in Cornwall at St Mawgan-in-Pydar (Peacock 1971a, 180), at Castle Gotha (Saunders and Harris 1982, 143), and Carvossa (Carlyon 1987, 107).

5.3.10 Amphora ?Gauloise 4

From [523], soil over upper cobbles over Entrance terminals (2) and from ploughsoil above (not illustrated).

DF Williams comments:

'Three small sherds in a fairly fine-textured buff to pink fabric. These sherds may possibly belong to the thin-walled, flat-bottomed southern French wine amphora Gauloise 4 (Laubenheimer 1985). In Britain, Gauloise 4 is not found in contexts dating before the Boudican revolt. Gauloise 4 occurs in 1st to 3rd century AD contexts at Exeter (Holbrook and Bidwell 1991).'

5.3.11 Palestinian amphora

About 20 body sherds (not illustrated) from [728] surface in Structure Y, and a further sherd from the soil above [785], in a distinctive hard, white-gritted buff-brown fabric (identified by P Bidwell). These sherds did not appear much abraded. So far in South West England this material has only been otherwise identified in late 4th to early 5th-century levels at Exeter (Bidwell 1979, 133, table 10). Structure Y also produced a fair proportion of Post-Roman import wares on the site (Fig 88).

5.3.12 Late Roman 1 amphora (Peacock and Williams 1986, Class 44, British Bii)

Fig 53

Given problems with fragmentation, there appear to be between 40 and 50 sherds present, of which there are 30 broad-ribbed body sherds with slight variations in fabric, and a handle stub. A group comes from various levels in the Entrance indicating possible undetected disturbance — [219] posthole predating Entrance but cut into Period 3 Enclosure Ditch, top of Period 3 Enclosure Ditch [369] in entrance (2), soil among Entrance paving [188], P10 (and about four other sherds) from soil [140] over [188], and [183] rubble over soil [140] (5). Other contexts were soil [9] in R, [523] over Ditch terminal, soil [524] over Structure V with at least five sherds (some now comminuted) including the stub of a handle, [801] upper midden in U, P11 from surface [728] in Y, gulley [743] in X4, walling [666] in House X4, [256] lower infill of Structure G, and [77] upper fill of G (about 3).

In 2001 Charles Thomas and Carl Thorpe identified two possible sherds from [780] spread Period 3 Enclosure Bank and another two from [800] soil over U; further sherds were identified among Medieval material, from soil [9] in R, [65] wall of House A2, [517] in Structure X5, [785] soil over Y, and [800] soil over U (6).

DF Williams comments:

'With the exception of part of a handle from [524], the remainder of the material consists of small body sherds, some showing evidence of a wide ribbing. This material is in a hard, rough, sandy fabric, reddish-buff throughout, with some of the sherds displaying irregularly spaced horizontal ribbing (Peacock and Williams 1986, Class 44). A thin section examination of sherd P11 shows that in addition to grains of pyroxene and small pieces of cryptocrystalline limestone noted by Peacock in Late Roman 1 sherds from Glastonbury Tor (1971b), the fabric of the Trethurgy sherd also contains serpentine. This points to an origin in an area which has ultra-basic as well as sedimentary rocks. A heavy mineral analysis on the same sample produced an assemblage in which there were large numbers of diopside and enstatite. This suggests derivation from peridotite, an ultra-basic rock. The distribution of ultra-basic rocks in the eastern Mediterranean coastal area is not widespread. However, these rocks do outcrop in the two areas of the eastern Mediterranean where production sites for Late Roman 1 have been recognised, in south-western Turkey and south-western Cyprus (Empereur and Picon 1989; Williams 2001).'

Late Roman 1 amphorae have a wide distribution around the Mediterranean, Aegean, and Black Sea regions, as well as reaching Britain and northern Europe in small numbers (see Peacock and Williams 1986, for refs; Thomas 1981, for the British material). They date from the late 4th to the first half of the 7th centuries AD, reaching a peak in the later 5th and early 6th centuries AD (Fulford and Peacock 1984; van Alfen 1996; Williams 2001). The principal content is not known, although both olive oil and wine have been suggested (Williams 2001).

Thomas (1981) lists six contexts from Cornwall, again all near the sea, but unlike those for Late Roman 2 (Bi), include two sites in the Isles of Scilly; a recent findspot is St Michael's Mount (Thorpe 2000). Thomas (1993) provides a discussion of the context within which pottery was imported from the Mediterranean to Cornwall in the Post-Roman period.

At Trethurgy sherds from [256] and [77] in G, and [666] and [743] House X, come from good contexts and provide the main basis for the dating of these Stage 9 features to the 6th century AD; unfortunately the sherd from [65] A2 wall is not secure but should predate levelling for the A3 House.

5.3.13 Late Roman 2 amphora (Peacock and Williams 1986, Class 43, British Bi)

Fig 53

Fifteen sherds were identified, all with the distinctive narrow combing of this type illustrated by P9 from [77]. No uncombed sherds, rims, or bases were identified. The contexts were [360] secondary Ditch silts on west, [359] lynchet over Ditch on west (4), [728] surface Structure Y, [517] soil in X5, [77] upper fill of Structure G (5 including P9), [11] soil over Structure E, on [74] paving outside House A, and among revetment collapse [46] in R. In 2001 Charles Thomas and Carl Thorpe also identified a possible sherd from [28] paving in House T5.

DF Williams comments:

'This form has a globular body with a small basal knob, a short conical neck with a high everted rim and bowed handles from the shoulder to the neck. The upper part of the body contains deep horizontal grooves closely set together; these are normally straight but a wavy version, apparently later in date, also occurs. (For the complete form see Peacock and Williams 1986, Class 43.) All the Trethurgy material is represented by small body sherds in a fairly hard smooth fabric, pinkish-cream throughout, with a scatter of inclusions of white limestone, while a scheme of deep horizontal grooves set close together occurs on all of the Trethurgy material. A thin section was made of the sherd from [46] and studied under the petrological microscope. This showed a clay matrix containing small quartz grains, cryptocrystalline limestone and mica, with a little chert, plagioclase feldspar, and metamorphic quartzite. This agrees well with the description given by Peacock for his analysis of Late Roman 2 sherds from Glastonbury Tor (1971b).

Late Roman 2 amphorae are widely distributed around the Mediterranean seaboard and are also present in Roumania, Italy, and Istanbul as well as Britain, often found in association with Late Roman 1 (see Peacock and Williams 1986, for refs). The numbers found in the northern Aegean and Black Sea area may suggest a possible source in this region. However, a suspected kiln site for Late Roman 2 has been discovered near Kounopi on the Argolid (Munn 1985). With this in mind it is worth noting that at Athens there are coarse pottery forms in similar fabrics to Late Roman 2 amphorae, which may add weight to the idea of a reasonably local source (eg Robinson 1959, M226, M321, M371). Late Roman 2 amphorae occur in 4th-century AD contexts at Athens (Robinson 1959, M272), while at Carthage there is a noticeable increase in numbers there from about the middle of the 6th century AD (Fulford and Peacock 1984). With Late Roman 1 they also occur as part of the cargo on the early 7th-century AD Yassi Ada wreck (van Alfen 1996). The principal contents carried are unknown.'

Thomas (1981) lists nine contexts for Cornwall, none more than a few miles from the sea. As with the preceding type, recent finds have been made at St Michael's Mount (Thorpe 2000).

5.3.14 Late Roman 3 amphora (Peacock and Williams 1986, Class 45, British Biv)

Fig 53

Two sherds were found, P12 from [728] surface of Structure Y, the second from the underlying level [780] where it may be presumed intrusive.

DF Williams comments:-

'Two body sherds in a fairly hard, deep red or reddish-brown fabric, strongly micaceous, with a decorative scheme of broad shallow fluting. These two sherds almost certainly probably belong to the Late Roman 3 class of amphora. This is a comparatively thin-walled amphora with a slender neck, high rounded shoulder and tapering foot, and has a broad shallow ribbing covering most of the vessel (Peacock and Williams 1986, Class 45). This amphora form, with some distinctive typological changes, has a long tradition in the Mediterranean region and a widespread distribution. The earlier form has one strap-handle and first appears in the late 1st century AD (Lang 1955, 277-8; Panella 1973, 460-2). The later two-handled version is first found in late 4th-century AD contexts at San Vecchio in Rome (Annis 1975, 31, nos 1 and 2) and Carthage (Riley 1981). At Carthage there was a peak in numbers of Late Roman 3 during the Vandal period *c* AD 475, followed by a reduction until the 6th century AD when numbers increase again (Fulford and Peacock 1984). A source in south-western Turkey seems likely. The contents are unknown.

In Britain, the one-handled form generally occurs in late Roman or Post-Roman contexts (Peacock 1977; Thomas 1981). A complete example from Ospringe in Kent, however, was associated with a 2nd-century AD glass vessel, though this may have been an heirloom and a later date for the amphora is possible (Peacock 1997).'

Thomas (1981) lists four Cornish contexts (including Trethurgy) for the two-handled form but gives none for the earlier one-handled form.

5.3.15 Late Roman amphora, unsourced within Eastern Mediterranean (British Bv)

About 12 sherds of buff-coloured amphora (not illustrated) classified as British Bv by Thomas (1981). Over 200 sherds known from Tintagel (Thomas 1981, 15; Thorpe 1997, 78), the only other Cornish site at which it has been so far identified. Thorpe (*ibid*) comments on possible links with Peacock and Williams (1986) Class 34.

Seven sherds from [183] rubble in Entrance identified by Charles Thomas and Carl Thorpe; possible sherds also identified from [199] drain through Rampart, [422] soil between House T3 and T4, [386] soil in R (2), and [380] spread OLS in R.

5.3.16 Other amphorae

A total of 37 sherds were found in a number of fabrics which have not yet been identified (not illustrated).

5.4 British wares with province-wide distribution

These were represented solely by Oxfordshire ware of which *c* 28 sherds, many small and abraded, came from a minimum of nine vessels. As Oxfordshire wares had a wider distribution during the 4th century than in the 3rd (Young 1977, 239) it seems reasonable to assign the majority of the Trethurgy sherds to the later century. They are suggested to have reached Exeter just before the end of the 3rd century. Sherds of Oxfordshire bowls have now been recognised in Cornwall at Gwithian, Porthmeor, and Tintagel (Young 1977, 306), all of type C51 which is not definitely identifiable at Trethurgy. Reawla has nine sherds from two vessels, type C51 and C97. There is also a single sherd from Carvossa and a sherd from type C45 from Stencoose (Quinnell forthcoming a).

Fig 53

P1 Rim of beaker, fine buff fabric with brown slip on both surfaces. Identified by CJ Young as type C22, date range 240-400+ (Young 1977, 152, 291). Stage 9 [77] upper infill Structure G.

P2 Base and seven other sherds from beaker, darker slip than P1, type C22. Stage 6 [801] upper midden in Structure U; also three sherds from [932] lower midden in U, five sherds from [800] soil over U, one sherd from [723] soil over Z, and one sherd from [524] soil over V.

P3 Base of beaker, similar to P1, type C22. [800] soil over U. Two other bases of beakers came from [800] soil over U and Stage 6 [932] lower midden in U. A small sherd of indented beaker, presumably Oxfordshire and of the comparatively uncommon type C20 (Young 1977, 152-3) dating 270-400+, was from Stage 6 [801] upper midden in U.

P4 Base of mortarium, buff fabric, traces of orange-red slip, white trituration grits. Identified by C J Young as type C97 (copying samian form 45), date range 240-400+ (Young 1977, 173, 329). On Stage 10 [546] latest paving in Structure V, further sherd from [801] upper soil in U.

P5 Base of bowl in buff fabric with red slip within type range C109 to C117 (Young 1977, 335) from Stage 6/9 [728] surface in Structure Y. Three further sherds, probably from different bowls from Stage 6 [932] lower midden in U.

A sherd of white colour-coat mortarium, type WC7 date range 240-400+ (Young 1977, 122, 285) came from [395] soil over House T5. The remaining sherds were eroded and came from surface contexts; they may include New Forest material.

The earliest context with Oxfordshire ware is the lower midden [932] Stage 6, for which a possible date of AD 375-400 is suggested (Section 9.2). The concentration of sherds in midden [932/801] reflects the general artefact pattern on the site. Otherwise Oxfordshire wares come from disturbed or late contexts with a general distribution similar to that of Post-Roman import wares. P1 from G infill in Stage 9 suggests that some Oxfordshire ware may have been current in the 6th (or 7th centuries) AD.

5.5 British regional wares

5.5.1 Black-burnished ware - South-East Dorset BB1 and South-Western BB1

About 24 vessels are represented at Trethurgy.

DF Williams comments:

'The colour aimed at seems to have been ideally black, or dark grey, with the core of the vessel invariably the same colour as the surface appearance. The clay contains a very high amount of distinctive fairly well-sorted quartz sand, which in fracture, against a dark background, gives the impression of a 'cod's roe' appearance. All the pottery has received a characteristic burnishing treatment at the 'leather-hard' stage of manufacture. This has the effect of making the surface of the clay more compact, thereby reducing porosity. The burnishing appears to have been achieved mostly by freehand, and the short burnishing strokes are often clearly visible. The decoration, when present, consists of narrow shallow lines, sometimes rather loosely drawn. In the hand-specimen, the fabric of all the Trethurgy sherds appears virtually identical to black-burnished ware originating from the Wareham/Poole Harbour area of Dorset. To check this a heavy mineral analysis was undertaken on one of the sherds, P18, and this produced an assemblage which was characterised by a high tourmaline content. This agrees well with analyses on black-burnished ware vessels shown to have been made in the Wareham/Poole Harbour area and a similar origin is likely for the Trethurgy material (Williams 1977, Group I).'

Holbrook and Bidwell (1991) have studied the black-burnished ware from Exeter and published a type series. They refer to that manufactured in the Poole Harbour area as South-East Dorset BB1 (Exeter fabric 31) to distinguish it from a variant, Exeter fabric 40, thought to be made further west in Dorset and termed South-Western BB1. The dates for the type series from Exeter have been very closely argued and in some cases differ from those previously put forward by Gillam (1970; and see references in Holbrook and Bidwell 1991). While there are problems with the dates of some types at Exeter, it seems reasonable to use this study as the starting point for consideration of black-burnished ware from Devon and Cornwall and to conform to its terminology.

Fig 53

P14 Jar with out-turned rim. Generally comparable to Gillam (1970) Types 147 and 148 dated AD 290-370 and to Exeter Type 20 forms of late 3rd and 4th centuries. Stage 6 [255] backing to Structure G.

P15 Jar with out-turned rim and oblique lattice decoration with a scored line above it. Cf Gillam (1970) Types 147 and 148 dated AD 290-370. Comparable to Exeter Type 20.1a of the late 3rd and 4th centuries. Stage 9/10 [687] soil over House X preceding revetment collapse.

P16 As P15. Stage 6 [932] lower midden in Structure U. Further examples as P15 and 16 from Stage 6 [801] midden, Stage 6-9 [752] House Z2 floor, Stage 4+ [429] soil on Platform 13/36, soil over Z.

P17 Conical flanged bowl with intersecting arc decoration on exterior. Cf Gillam (1970) Type 228, dated AD 290-370, Exeter Type 45, dated from c 270 to the end of the Roman period. Stage 6 [932] lower midden in Structure U, also from Stage 9/10 [399] Rampart collapse.

P18 Conical flanged bowl, as P17 but with higher rim above flange. [751A] soil predating Stage 6 Structure Y. Further examples as P17 and 18 from Stage 4/5 [9] cobbles in R, Stage 8/9 [34] between House A2 and A3, Stage 4+ [36] platform, Stage 6+ [751] soil in Y, Stage 6 [801] midden, and Stage 4/6 [808] soil between House Z1 and Z2.

P19 Small plain-rimmed dish, intersecting arcs on exterior and base. Cf Gillam (1970) Type 329, dated AD 190-340, Exeter Type 59.3, dated mid 2nd century onward. Stage 6 [932] lower midden in U.

P20 Larger plain-rimmed dish. Comments as P19. Stage 9 [890] wall core of Structure U.

P21 As P20. Stage 6 [801] upper midden in U. Further examples as P19-21 from Stage 6 [722] House Z2 wall, [800] soil over U, Stage 4/6 [808] soil between Z1 and Z2, Stage 1/4[852] House Z1 drain, and Stage 4 [910] drain in Q.

A number of featureless South-East Dorset BB1 sherds were found in other contexts (see Context List and Table 5.2).

Two sherds from [751] external surface in Y and [399] revetment collapse in T appear to be from the same cooking pot with acute lattice decoration in South-Western BB1.

At Trethurgy the earliest jars with oblique lattice (P15 and P16) occur in [429] (Stage 4 or later) and [932/801] (Stage 6). The earliest conical flanged bowls occur in [36] (Stage 4) and then scatter regularly through the site. The site appears to have been in use for some time before these relatively late forms appear.

The limited quantity of BB1 material from Trethurgy would all be appropriate to a late 3rd and 4th-century date, with conical flanged bowls and cooking pots with obtuse lattice. Flat-rimmed bowls which tend to be later 2nd and early 3rd century are absent as are cooking pots with acute or right-angle lattice which cover much the same date range. South-East Dorset BB1 was the principal ceramic at Exeter during the 3rd and 4th centuries. South-Western BB1, the principal ceramic at Exeter during the 2nd century, probably ceasing production during the mid 3rd (Holbrook and Bidwell 1991, 93), is only represented by one vessel. Holbrook and Bidwell (1991, fig 25, appendix III) list Cornish sites with South-Western BB1 and these have a date range from the 1st to the mid 3rd centuries — St Mawgan-in-Pydar with an end date in the early 2nd century, Widemouth Bay mid 2nd century, Kilhallon mid 2nd to mid 3rd century, Castle Gotha ending sometime in the 3rd century, Carwarthen (unpubl) with a possible date range through and beyond the Roman centuries, and Carvossa mid 1st to 3rd century AD with about four times as much South-Western as South-East Dorset BB1. There has been no equivalent study of the occurrence of South-East Dorset BB1 in Cornwall. It occurs in some quantity at Porthmeor, a site occupied until at least the 5th century, and there is a substantial amount in an early 4th-century midden at Reawla.

The author's impression is that, among the older excavated assemblages and unpublished sites which mostly happen to belong to the 3rd to 5th centuries, conical flanged bowls in particular are of regular occurrence.

The pattern of BB1 finds from Cornwall has been suggested in general to mirror the situation in Exeter, with the late BB1 forms being more common than those of the earlier centuries (Quinnell 1986, 128). This was based on the minimum vessel count for Trethurgy giving 4.4% of the assemblage, linked to the fact that the forms present on the site were late 3rd and 4th centuries. Greater frequency in these centuries appeared to be supported by the minimum vessel count from Reawla (Quinnell 1992) of 8.5%. However it now appears premature to make general statements about the frequency of BB1 at different dates in Cornwall. Table 5.5 shows that the proportion of the assemblage by weight at Trethurgy is 1.8%, and that proportion is below 2% both in Stages 1-4, the late 2nd and 3rd centuries, and Stage 6, the later 4th century. Allen and Fulford (1996) have demonstrated that the pattern of distribution of BB1 is complex and heavily influenced by the proximity of sites to road or sea transport. Now, in 2001, it is necessary to accept that we do not yet have sufficient good-quality data to establish a reliable pattern of distribution in Cornwall and to note that the apparent preponderance of 3rd and 4th-century forms referred to above may simply be due, on other sites as at Trethurgy, to the fact that more pottery survives from late than from early contexts on these sites. This survival relates to site formation factors such as the reuse of soil in walls and levelling and may have nothing to do with the frequency of pottery at different dates.

It has not yet been established how late the production and distribution of South-East Dorset BB1 continued. A distinctive squat cooking pot, Type 21, appears at Exeter in the late 4th and very early 5th centuries while the equivalent, Type 18, occurs during that period at Dorchester and immediately adjacent sites (Woodward *et al* 1993). Holbrook and Bidwell in their discussion on Exeter (1991, 94) state that 'there is no evidence that the industry continued in production beyond the opening decades of the fifth century'. As the Exeter Type 21/Dorchester Type 18 cooking pots have been found so far in a limited area of Dorset and Devon, it appears at present as though coastal distribution of BB1 around Devon and Cornwall was gradually ceasing in the last decade or so of the 4th century.

5.5.2 Fabric imitating black-burnished ware

Fig 53

P28 Rim of jar in medium hard fabric containing fine micaceous sand. Black, burnished exterior. No known parallel in the South West (P Bidwell pers comm). Joining sherds from Stage 9 [743] gulley in X and Stage 10 [517] soil in X5.

5.5.3 Flagons, Exeter fabric 451

Base of flagon, red-buff fabric, slightly gritty, with external white slip (not illustrated). Possibly an Exeter product (fabric 451, Holbrook and Bidwell 1991, 143) where examples date to the 1st, 2nd, and 3rd centuries. Stage 5/6 [521] lower surface over Entrance terminals. Small sherd from neck of flagon Stage 6 [801] upper midden in Structure U. This flagon fabric has only otherwise been found so far in Cornwall at Carvossa.

5.5.4 Exeter Gritty Grey ware, Exeter fabric 101

Sherds from base angles of two different platters or bowls, and a dish rim of Type 23.1 (not illustrated). Slightly gritty grey fabric with dark-grey burnished exteriors. Possibly produced in the Exeter area from the 1st century until the early 4th (Holbrook and Bidwell 1991, 171). From Stage 6 [751] surface linking Structure Y with wall [892], from Stage 6 [932] lower midden in Structure U, and from ploughsoil. Kilhallon (Bidwell 1982, 159, fig 3, nos 19, 20 and other sherds) and Carvossa are the only other Cornish sites where this fabric has so far been recognised.

5.5.5 Exeter Micaceous Grey ware, fabric 125

Small grey ware sherd (Holbrook and Bidwell 1991, 163-5), very fine grit with a little mica (not illustrated). This fabric copies BB1 forms, probably produced in south-east Devon, and has a date range of late 1st to early 3rd centuries AD. From Stage 8 [555] external surface of Structure V2. This fabric has only so far otherwise been recognised in Cornwall at Kilhallon (Bidwell 1982, 159, fig 3, P21), Carvossa, and at Reawla.

5.5.6 South-Western Grey ware storage jars

A total of 26 body sherds were found in [11], [34], [34A], [77], [294], [687], [907A], and ploughsoil over House A and Structure G; all could come from one vessel (not illustrated). Soft gritty buff fabric with many inclusions apparently of rolled shale fragments. Storage jars in this fabric occur at Exeter (Holbrook and Bidwell 1991, 175-7) and are frequent in East Devon in the 3rd and 4th centuries (*ibid*, fig 69); they were probably manufactured at a number of centres in this area. An example occurred in the 3rd-century deposit at Kilhallon (Bidwell 1982, 160). The earliest Trethurgy contexts, Stage 4 [294] hearth pit in House A1 and Stages 4/5 [907A] wall tumble in Q, may suggest the vessel(s) was present by the 4th century.

5.5.7 South Devon ware

This distinctive fabric contains black mica and other granite-derived minerals. Sherds are mainly reduced grey but some surfaces are buff. Exteriors may be burnished and sometimes black-coated. The fabric tends to be friable and easily eroded. DF Williams examined the collection in 1976/7 and thin-sectioned P26. He comments:

'Hard, rough fabric, dark grey (Munsell 10YR 4/1) throughout, and with conspicuous inclusions of black mica scattered throughout the fabric. This sherd has a particularly distinctive appearance in the hand specimen and is easily recognisable. Examples of this fabric have come from 4th-century AD contexts at Stoke Gabriel, Devon (Masson Phillips 1966, 23), while a similar fabric (south-western micaceous?) has been recognised from 13th-century AD levels at Beere, Devon (Jope and Threfall 1958, 126). An origin on or near to a large granite formation seems likely, as the large quantity of mica present probably represents granite detritus.'

The sherds were examined by P Bidwell in 1985 and confirmed as Exeter fabric 5 (Bidwell 1979, 191). This is now known as South Devon ware (Bidwell and Silvester 1988) as its distribution indicates that it formed the major coarseware component of assemblages in South Devon, such as those at Clanacombe (Greene and Greene 1970) and Stoke Gabriel (Fox 1966). No production site has yet been found. A little of this ware was reaching Exeter during the late 1st and 2nd centuries, amounts increased in the late 2nd and 3rd centuries and became more significant in the 4th century (Holbrook and Bidwell 1991, 177-81); it also occurs in early 5th-century contexts. A type series has been established for Exeter. In Cornwall, South Devon ware has been identified from St Mawgan-in-Pydar, Carvossa, Porthmeor, Kilhallon, Magor, and Reawla (Holbrook and Bidwell 1991, fig 7), all forming less than 10% of the assemblage. At Duckpool on the North Cornish coast, South Devon ware forms over 90% of the assemblage, a proportion similar to that on sites in South Devon (Quinnell 1995). Identification as South Devon ware is reasonably certain when both forms and fabric can be compared. For some sites however it is possible that vessels made from a Cornish granitic source are present; St Mawgan-in-Pydar and Carn Euny both have forms representing variants of local Iron Age types. No work has yet been done to distinguish local Cornish source(s) from South Devon Ware. About 30 South Devon vessels are represented at Trethurgy, all of types present at Exeter. The fabric forms 2.2% of the assemblage by weight and increases from 0.6% in Stages 1-4 to 3% in the Stage 6 midden (Table 5.5). It has been suggested, as with BB1, that the main use of this material corresponds with the period of its greatest importance at Exeter, that is 4th century (Quinnell 1986, 129) but, as with BB1, more data is needed.

Fig 53

P22 Jar with simple out-turned rim, well burnished, Exeter Type 9.1. Stage 4/6 [808] soil between Houses Z1 and Z2. Also from [11] soil over E, Stage 8/9 [542] drain in V, Stage 7/8 [548] soil in V, Stage 9+ [723] soil in Z, Stage 6+ [751] surface outside Y, [800] soil over U, Stage 1/4 [852] Z1 drain, Stage 6 [932] midden, and soil over X.

P23 Jar with rather flatter out-turned rim, well burnished, Exeter Type 8.1. Stage 6 [801] upper midden in U (2).

P24 Not South Devon ware — see Section 5.7.

P25 Large jar rim with pronounced internal groove, Exeter Type 4.1. Stage 4/5 [9] soil beneath paving [8] in R, also from Stage 8 [555] surface in V.

P26 Large storage jar with heavy rolled rim, Exeter Type 1.1. Stage 4/6 [808] soil between House Z1 and Z2, also from Stage 6 [801].

P27 Flanged bowl, with slightly curved sides, Exeter Type 16.1b. Stage 6 [801] midden in U (4). Also from [11] soil over E, Stage 8 [555] surface in V, soil [800], Stage 4/5 [907A] tumble in Q, and Stage 6[932] midden.

P27A (not illustrated) Flanged bowl in a granitic fabric variant which has been fired to temperatures in excess of 1200° C (R Taylor pers comm); sherd found amongst Medieval material in the 2001 quantification exercise and may merit further study. From soil over G.

Forms not illustrated included a plain-rimmed dish, Exeter Type 17.1, from Stage 1/4 [852] drain in Z1, a jar with upright neck Exeter Type 7.1 Stage 8/9 [541] paving in V, body sherds with cordons Stage 9 [256] G infill, Stage 6 [751A)] soil beneath Y and with oblique lattice, and Stage 6 [722] Z2 wall. References to sherds without features are found in the Context List.

The earliest contexts (apart from Period 3/4 [920] disturbed by the levelling for Structure U) are Stage 4 [852] and [907A]; thereafter South Devon ware was scattered through the later Stages.

5.5.8 Other fabrics

About 70 small body sherds (not illustrated), in about 20 different fabrics (excluding amphorae), could not be identified. They had a fairly even chronological and spatial spread through the site. Their presence indicates the large proportion of pottery which must have been cleared from the Round during its use. The two most distinctive sherds are thin, micaceous, buff with burnished and rouletted dark grey exterior (from soil over Z). P Bidwell (pers comm) suggests they may not be British.

5.6 Cornish gabbroic ware

The majority of pottery from the site was macroscopically similar to the gabbroic fabrics which predominate on all Cornish Roman-period sites. The fabric formed 92.7% of the assemblage by weight, 88.1% by sherd count, and a minimum of 450 vessels was represented. These figures compare to 85.6% by sherd count from Reawla (Quinnell 1992) for an assemblage of some 2000 sherds, and 81.47% by sherd count from Carvossa for an assemblage of 8348 sherds (Carlyon 1987, 168). These three are the only sizeable published assemblages for which quantification has been attempted. The statement (Quinnell 1986, 129) that 'about 95% of all pottery from Roman Cornwall is gabbroic' may be a slight exaggeration.

5.6.1 Fabric, petrography, and sourcing

DF Williams examined a selection of this material and thin-sectioned 11 sherds; he comments:

'The colour of this pottery varies from buff to black; however, the consistent feature of the fabric is the high content of small white feldspar fragments which protrude through the surfaces. The majority of pottery from the site is clearly made from the same gabbroic clays derived from the Lizard and recognised by Peacock as being used for much Neolithic and Iron Age pottery in the South West (1969b; 1969c). Thin sectioning of P31, P33, P36, P44, P48, P60, P62, P97, P118, P122, and P124 confirm that the most prominent inclusions are made up of large angular grains of altered feldspar and fibrous aggregates of brown amphibole. The mineralogy so closely resembles Peacock's description of the gabbroic clays of the Lizard peninsula (*ibid*), that there seems little doubt that this material was also used for the Trethurgy pottery.'

The author's impression, based on later study of the assemblage, was that some sherds not examined by Dr Williams contain occasional inclusions such as quartz and fragments of shale or other rock, and that sometimes inclusions are slightly rolled or worn.

Most of the pottery is oxidised a light-brown throughout, but a few vessels are reduced and grey. The white feldspar grits usually show through the surfaces, which have been smoothed and sometimes burnished. These grits vary in size from 0.5mm to 2mm in size, although in some thick storage jars (eg P101) they can be 10mm. The fabric divides into three variants. 'Well-made' has a very compact body and is usually burnished; it may, often, be thin walled (eg P84). 'Standard' is rougher, with a less dense body, and more poorly finished surfaces; in this fabric cooking pots which have been long on the fire develop very friable surfaces; the 2001 quantification exercise showed a good deal of variation in finish and in size and range of inclusions. 'Standard' fabric is that found most generally on Cornish sites of the Roman period. 'Coarse' is the more heavily and largely gritted fabric used for storage jars (P101-5); it may be up to 15mm thick and is usually oxidised a red-brown.

The majority of vessels, whether jars, bowls or dishes have a black, originally burnished, coating. The majority of most Types also have sooted exteriors suggestive of cooking fires. The edges of sherds have frequently crumbled, on the shoulder or body for jars, near the base for bowls and dishes, and very few base sherds survived. It seems likely that repeated reheating caused the vessels to gradually crumble and break.

Since the identification of gabbroic fabrics and their probable Lizard source in 1969 there have been suggestions, notably by H Howard and S Sofranoff (in Mercer 1981, 179-81), that the range of minerals found in gabbroic pottery could occur elsewhere, specifically near Camborne, but possibly around other igneous rock areas. These have been summarised and refuted by Peacock (1988). A fieldwalking project was carried out by the Cornwall Archaeological Society 1978-83 to examine as much of the gabbro outcrop as was accessible to establish whether evidence for pottery manufacture survived. The results, negative with regard to ceramic production, were published by Smith (1987) accompanied by a paper by Quinnell (1987) summarizing work up to that date on gabbroic pottery and its source.

During the 1990s the author has been working with RT Taylor, a geologist with special expertise in Cornish igneous rocks, on gabbroic assemblages of all dates from Cornwall. Previous thin-section analysis had only addressed the question of whether a sherd was gabbroic and its source the Lizard. The new work involves looking at diachronic variations within gabbroic fabrics and has involved scanning of extensive groups of sherds under a x20 binocular microscope. This scanning has shown that variations do exist and are present in the period from the Later Iron Age to the immediate Post-Roman period. The variations relate to the range and size of inclusions, the former sometimes including non-gabbroic material. The most frequent non-gabbroic material is quartz sand which is likely to derive from the Crousa gravels which overlie the gabbro in places, but rock such as serpentinite and granite also occurs. Most of this work has been done as part of the assessment stage on two major projects, the A30 Indian Queen's bypass (Quinnell 1998) and Trevelgue cliff castle (Quinnell 2003b) but some analyses of assemblages are in press (Quinnell 1998/9). No attempt has been made to update the simple fabric analysis of the Trethurgy assemblage carried out in 1976 as these new gabbroic studies are still at a developmental phase.

It has become apparent that further detailed geological fieldwork on the Lizard is necessary. In 1999 Lucy Harrad of Oxford University commenced such fieldwork, linked to a detailed diachronic study of gabbroic pottery from the multi-period settlement at Bodrifty in West Penwith for a doctoral thesis; some initial results have been presented in the study of the assemblage from Atlantic Road, Newquay (Harrad forthcoming). More recently Dr R Ixer has embarked on two separate studies of gabbroic ceramics, one using transmitted reflected light petrography and polished thin-sections, the other portable X-ray fluorescence (pers comm). It is expected that the studies by Ixer and by Harrad, linked to those of Taylor and the author, will provide new insights into the chronological variations in gabbroic pottery and its sourcing.

The gabbroic pottery of any particular period is visually and tactually so similar that it appears a single fabric. It may be presumed that, whatever the source(s) of the pottery, the clays were selected to produce pottery which looked and handled in a similar way and, almost certainly the most important factor, could been used for cooking with the same reliability.

5.6.2 Gabbroic pottery from the Later Iron Age to the Post-Roman centuries - a summary view

Until the 1960s, work on Romano-Cornish pottery was confused because excavators found so little directly comparable to ceramics in the rest of Southern Britain. The white feldspar grits so typical of gabbroic fabric tended to be published as shell, despite acid soil conditions (Dudley 1956, 23). Roman period pottery, like that from Chun Castle (Leeds 1926, fig 8), had been published as Iron Age, and conversely the pottery from Trebarveth 3 (Serocold and Maynard 1949), in fact a largely 3rd century AD assemblage, was assigned to the Post-Roman period. References to 'sub-Roman' pottery of Trebarveth type confused publications during the 1950s. Working from this background, Thomas (1958, 23) identified the 'Gwithian Style' as a continuation of late-Roman forms into the early Post-Roman centuries. The main components of the Gwithian Style are platters and jars with distinctive rims which do not occur at Trethurgy. The chronology of the Gwithian Style and its relationship to the 5th to 6th centuries continuance of 4th century jars and bowls needs further elucidation: an English Heritage project for the publication of Gwithian commenced in 2003.

Fowler (1962) and Guthrie (1969), describing the assemblages from Porth Godrevy and Goldherring respectively, provide the first clear accounts of Romano-Cornish pottery, with dating which broadly still holds good today. They did not however recognise gabbroic fabrics. The first report to do so was that by Peacock (1969a) on Trebarveth, followed by the report on Trevisker by ApSimon and Greenfield in 1972, the year in which work at Trethurgy started. A range of reports has appeared as preparation of this report has progressed but most sites published have lacked the well stratified groups associated with datable material which are necessary for a clear understanding of the chronology of Roman-period gabbroic pottery. Carlyon (1995) assembled the material available up until 1985, both published and unpublished, and discussed its stratification and associations. The present report introduces a simple series of Type numbers which are intended as the basis for future study and reference.

Gabbroic fabric predominates in Cornwall from the South Western Decorated wares of the Later Iron Age, through the manufacture of Cordoned wares, to the production of Roman forms. This continuity suggests potting communities gradually modifying their products in response to new influences and needs but apparently not making much use, if any, of the potter's wheel. Gabbroic pottery, from the introduction of Cordoned ware onwards, is often described as wheel-made. Certainly the vessels in well-made fabric appear at first sight to be wheel-made, but on closer examination they reveal no features which could not be due to careful finishing. Most of the standard and coarse fabrics are all probably hand-made: some (eg P103) indicate clear traces of coil construction. It is possible that there was some use of the potter's wheel in the Late Iron Age and through the Roman period, but most vessels continued to be hand-made. A full study by xero-radiography is necessary to establish the extent to which the potter's wheel was used in gabbroic production. Hand-made pottery production on a large scale need occasion no surprise, in an area with a long local potting tradition. The much more prolific South-East Dorset BB1 industries of the Wareham/Poole region of Dorset produced only hand-made products (Swan 1984, 54) in an area of much more direct Roman influence and contact.

Cordoned wares were first identified in the report on Castle Dore (Radford 1951, 80) and dated to the closing decades of the Iron Age. Their full study by Threipland (1956) in the report on St Mawgan-in-Pydar provided a Type series which is still useful today. Threipland (*ibid*, 53) back-dated the start of Cordoned ware to the latter part of the 1st century BC on the grounds of refugee or trade influence after Caesar's conquest of Gaul. The initial date for Cordoned ware is still not firmly established. It is quite clear however that there are three phases in Cordoned ware, the first two of which were clearly marked out by Threipland. The first phase, which is probably entirely pre-Roman, consists of cups and bowls of Types F and G and the larger storage jars of Types H and J; there are also cooking pots which continue the upright-necked basic form of South Western Decorated ware but without decoration — Type D. The second phase starts sometime after the Roman Conquest of the South West. Types F and G disappear but large jars H and J continue as do upright-necked jars of Type D. These are joined by new styles which copy Roman imports but which suggest more profound changes. Dishes or bowls with externally grooved rims, Type R, provide, for the first time in the native ceramic repertoire, vessels for individual eating, and are the start of a series of such dishes which continue through the Roman period. At the same time as the Type R dishes were adopted, gabbroic potters began to experiment with a wide range of copies of beakers and jars, Types O, P, and Q, and with copies of samian. The gabbroic fabric used in this phase is generally still well made. The dates of the second Cordoned ware phase can not be more clearly established than the later 1st century AD until sometime in the 2nd century.

The third phase of Cordoned ware is not a distinct ceramic phase as such but a continuation of a general cordoned style through the Roman period and beyond. The smaller beakers of Types O to P and the one-off copies disappear but jars of Types H and J (Type 13) continue as do smaller jars with rolled rims and cordons (Type 11); Type R bowls (Type 19) continued for a while. Fabric is now standard rather than well-made. The continuation of the cordoned tradition through the Roman period was only recognised in the mid 1980s (Quinnell 1986) and carried with it the realisation that courtyard houses were linked to this and were of Roman rather than prehistoric date. It seems appropriate to describe this cordoned ware without an upper case C as it forms one group within the Roman period gabbroic tradition, a tradition which present evidence indicates continued into the 5th or 6th centuries.

The second phase Cordoned ware material ceases production at the same time as well-made fabric, at some date before the middle of the 2nd century. Well-made jars with upright necks (Type 1) are replaced by jars with slacker profiles made in standard fabric (Type 4). Type R bowls (Type 19) are found in standard fabric, as at Trethurgy. There would appear to be a long phase through most of the 2nd century in which Type R bowls occur alongside slack-profiled jars in standard fabric. Flat-rimmed bowls (Type 20) probably replace Type R bowls late in the 2nd century, together with flat grooved-rim bowls (Type 21) and plain-rimmed bowls (Type 23). Further changes occur early in the 3rd century. Small cordoned jars (Type 11) derived from St Mawgan Types P and Q disappear, shouldered jars with upright rims (Type 8) come in, as do bowls with upright or everted rims (Type 9). Large storage jars of cooking-pot shape (Type 16) begin to be made, alongside large cordoned ware jars (Type 13). The standard Type 4 everted-rim cooking pot is gradually increasing in diameter.

It has formerly (Quinnell 1986, 129) been argued that the bowl sequence followed general stylistic trends in finewares and metalwork, rather than copying directly South-East Dorset BB1 forms, because the bowls often have curved sides, a feature rare in BB1, and very seldom incised patterns, a common feature in BB1. It is now considered that the *rim forms* of BB1 bowls were the main factor to influence change, because these are copied very closely in gabbroic fabric and appear to be introduced in the same sequence as in South-East Dorset BB1. The proposed dating for the bowl rim forms is derived from that of South-East Dorset BB1 and, uncertain though this is, provides the main framework for the changes in gabbroic ceramic styles. It is suggested that this dating stands until it is either disproved or replaced by a more reliable system.

Flat-rimmed and flat grooved-rim bowls continue through the 3rd century until the former is replaced towards its end by the Cornish flanged bowl (Type 22) copying the rims of BB1 conical flanged bowls. The flat grooved-rim bowl (Type 21) probably continues through the 4th century alongside the Cornish flanged bowl, but the plain-rim bowl (Type 23) may go out of production early in the century. The diameter of slack-profiled jars continues to increase and their profiles have a tendency to get simpler. At some date in the early 4th-century shouldered jars with upright rims (Type 8) and bowls with upright or everted rims (Type 9) may cease production, as may the bowl with vertical, pierced, lugs or handles (Type 12). This then leaves a basic repertoire for the main part of the 4th century of the slack-profiled jar (Type 4), the Cornish flanged bowl (Type 22) and the flat grooved-rim bowl (Type 21), and storage jars both with cordons (Type 13) and of large cooking-pot form (Type 16). The Stage 6 [932/801] midden (suggested as later 4th century) contains just this mixture of Cornish flanged and flat grooved-rim bowls, slack-profiled jars, and large storage jars, some with cordons. This is the repertoire which may continue in production into the 5th or even 6th centuries.

This brief summary concentrates on the major Types, present at Trethurgy, and does not deal with the many variations which a scan of the literature or of Carlyon's (1995) summary reveals. It is intended to form a simple framework against which future assemblages can be assessed. Radiocarbon dates from Roman and Post-Roman Cornish sites are assembled in Appendix 2 and linked to the main ceramic Types discussed here. In general they provide support for the general trend of dates and for the continuance of later types into the Post-Roman period.

It appears probable, from a general study of Cornish material, that the standard of manufacture did decline through time and that most of the more roughly finished vessels are late in the sequence. It may be noted that recently recognised poorly worked 'Late Variant' gabbroic fabric on other sites (Quinnell 1998) appears 4th century and later and broadly contemporary with the general decline in production standards. (Some poorly made vessels do appear in the early Stages at Trethurgy.) At present there seems no way of separating 4th from 5th-century assemblages nor of establishing the terminal date for the production of gabbroic fabrics in the Roman tradition. A hiatus in the use of pottery has not been demonstrated. It is suggested below, under P148, that the subsequent grass-marked tradition may have had a variable start date, from the 6th to the 8th centuries. A later date supposes either a period with no ceramic production *or* the continuance of Roman gabbroic styles even later than suggested here, not a matter at present capable of resolution.

At Trethurgy itself, apart from the possible South Western Decorated P49 and Cordoned ware P143, the ceramics appear to start sometime towards the end of the second Cordoned ware phase. There are simple versions of Type 19 (Type R bowls) P106-9 and P140, the copy of a Dr 17 dish from Stage 2/3 [436] House T2 floor, the thin-walled copy P138 from Rampart collapse [9] and the base ring P83 from [386] Stage 1/4 soil in R. Jars with upright necks (Type 10, usually well-made (eg P29, P31-3) occur from the earlier Stages, which are gradually replaced by larger jars with slacker profiles and simple, out-turned rims (eg P45, 54) which are present from Stage 1 (Type 4). The ceramic sequence at Trethurgy appears to run through continuously from a date in the 2nd until the 5th or 6th century. Detailed arguments for the dating of the Stages are set out in Chapter 9.

5.6.3 Forms in gabbroic fabric

?South Western Decorated ware

Fig 54

P49 Two abraded sherds from a shouldered jar with band of roughly incised triangles. The fabric is standard gabbroic, less well-made than is usual for Iron Age forms, and the sherds were initially considered a variant of P48. However there is no parallel for this decoration on jars of the Roman period, but comparisons can be found amongst the range of South Western Decorated vessels in Cornwall, eg St Mawgan-in-Pydar (Threipland 1956, fig 14, no 11) and Killibury (Miles 1977, fig 40, no 6). Stage 6 [932] lower midden in U and soil over Y.

?Late Iron Age Cordoned Ware

Fig 60

P143 Thin-walled bowl with slightly out-turned rim, burnished exterior. Well made. Entirely typical of St Mawgan-in-Pydar (Threipland 1956) Type G carinated bowls. Stage 9+ [523], soil on upper surface over Entrance terminal of Ditch. Also from soil over Q.

Type 1 Jars with upright necks in well-made gabbroic fabric (P29-P34)

These, St Mawgan-in-Pydar Type D (Carlyon Group 1) and St Mawgan-in-Pydar Type M (Carlyon Group 10) which are very similar, represent the continuation of the basic local jar form from the pre-Roman Iron Age. Tend to occur on earlier Roman-period sites, Nanstallon (Fox and Ravenhill 1972, no 25), Trevisker (ApSimon and Greenfield 1972, no 50), Castle Gotha (Saunders and Harris 1982, nos 16, 18) Carvossa (Carlyon 1987, no 141) and Trebarveth T1, perhaps ceasing production in the first half of the 2nd century.

Fig 54

P29 Small jar with upright neck, well burnished, black-coated. Stage 1 [568] primary silt of Round Ditch. Also from Stage 1 [33], Stage 8 [175], Stage 7

Site	<130mm		130 - 170mm		>170mm		Total
St Mawgan-in-Pydar	63	37%	93	57%	11	6%	167
Carvossa	11	12%	58	62%	25	26%	94
Carwarthen	8	11%	23	30%	45	59%	76
Porthmeor	10	15%	15	23%	41	62%	66
Trethurgy	32	14%	51	23%	141	63%	224

Table 5.6: Diameters of Type 4 jar rims; those from Trethurgy include all examples of P44-P76; figures for the other sites supplied by P M Carlyon

[403], Stage 3 [442], Stage 7/8 [548], Spread Period 3 Enclosure Bank [780], Stage 4 [905], Stage 3/4 [948], and A ploughsoil. These tend to be early in the sequence on the site. Absent from Stage 6 midden [932/801].

P30 Jar with upright neck and globular body, rim only burnished and black-coated. Stage 2/4 [567] secondary Ditch silt by Entrance. Also from soil [11], Stage 9/10 [400], Stages 8/9 [541], Stage 8 [555], pre-Stage 6 [751], and Stage 4-6 [808]. Earliest context Stage 2/4 secondary Ditch silt, then scattered evenly through site.

P31 Jar with upright neck, sharply tooled rim. Stage 1 [568] primary silt of Round Ditch. Also from Stage 4 [905].

P32 Jar with upright neck, rounded out-turned rim. [363] Period 3 Enclosure Bank (2). Also from soil [11], Stage 1-4 [314], OLS [380] (2), Stage 9/10 [400], Stage 10 [524], and Stage 10 [546].

P33 Jar with upright neck, slightly beaded out-turned rim, black-coated. Stage 5/6 [153] House D4 gulley. Also from Stage 4/5 [9].

P34 Jar with upright neck and out-turned rim, less well-made than P31-3, black-coated. Stage 6 [932] lower midden in U. Also from Stage 7/8 [100], Stage 9 [256], Stage 9/10 [400], Spread Period 3 Enclosure Bank [780], soil [785], and Stage 6 [861].

Type 2 Jar with everted rim and globular body, well-made fabric (P30a)

Fig 54

P30a Jar with rim out-turned from globular body, upper part burnished. Carlyon Group 2. St Mawgan-in-Pydar Type O which is late 1st to early 2nd century. An earlier Roman period form, cf Nanstallon (Fox and Ravenhill 1972, no 23) and Trebarveth T3 (Peacock 1969a, 31). Stage 4 [923] dump between construction of walls [892] and [907], in Q.

Type 3 Small jars with everted necks, standard fabric (P35-P43)

Fig 54

These vessels are intermediate in form between jars with upright necks and slack-profiled, everted-rim jars (see below). Included in Carlyon Group 1, they are broadly St Mawgan-in-Pydar Group N which starts in the early 2nd century at latest. Production probably ends by the later 2nd century. The earliest Trethurgy context is [380] unsealed OLS and then Stage 3 [761].

P35 Simple rim, very poorly made, but has had black coating. Stage 3 [761] House Z1 gulley. Also from Stage 4 [722], Stage 4/6 [808].

P36 Simple rim, poorly made; appearance of rim groove produced in process of knife tidying of rim. Stage 6 [78] pit near Structure E.

P37 Simple rim, appearance of cordon produced by parallel grooves on neck. Presumably a variant of the Cordoned ware-derived forms such as P93. Precise parallels do not occur but see Trebarveth T1 (Serocold and Maynard 1949, fig 4, B5). Stage 8 [175] patching on surface [8], R. Also from spread OLS [380], Stage 6 [722], Stage 5+ [874], Stage 4/5 [907A].

P38 Simple rim, black-coated. Stage 6 [932] midden in U. Also from Stage 9 [723], Stage 6 [801].

P39 Simple out-turned rim, quite well-made, black-coated. Stage 9/10 [400] soil over House T5.

P40 Simple out-turned rim, incised groove on girth. Stage 5+ [874] soil in Q contemporary with Structure U. Also from Stage 4/5 [9], soil [11], Stage 4 /5 [422], and Stage 6/9 [728].

P41 Sharply out-turned rim, black-coated. Soil over A. Also from Stage 9/10 [399].

P42 Jar with upright neck, out-turned rim, well-made, black-coated. Possibly relates to P31-P34 group. Stage 8 [175] patching on surface [8], R.

P43 Thin-walled jar, out-turned rim. Stage 9 [723] collapse of House Z2.

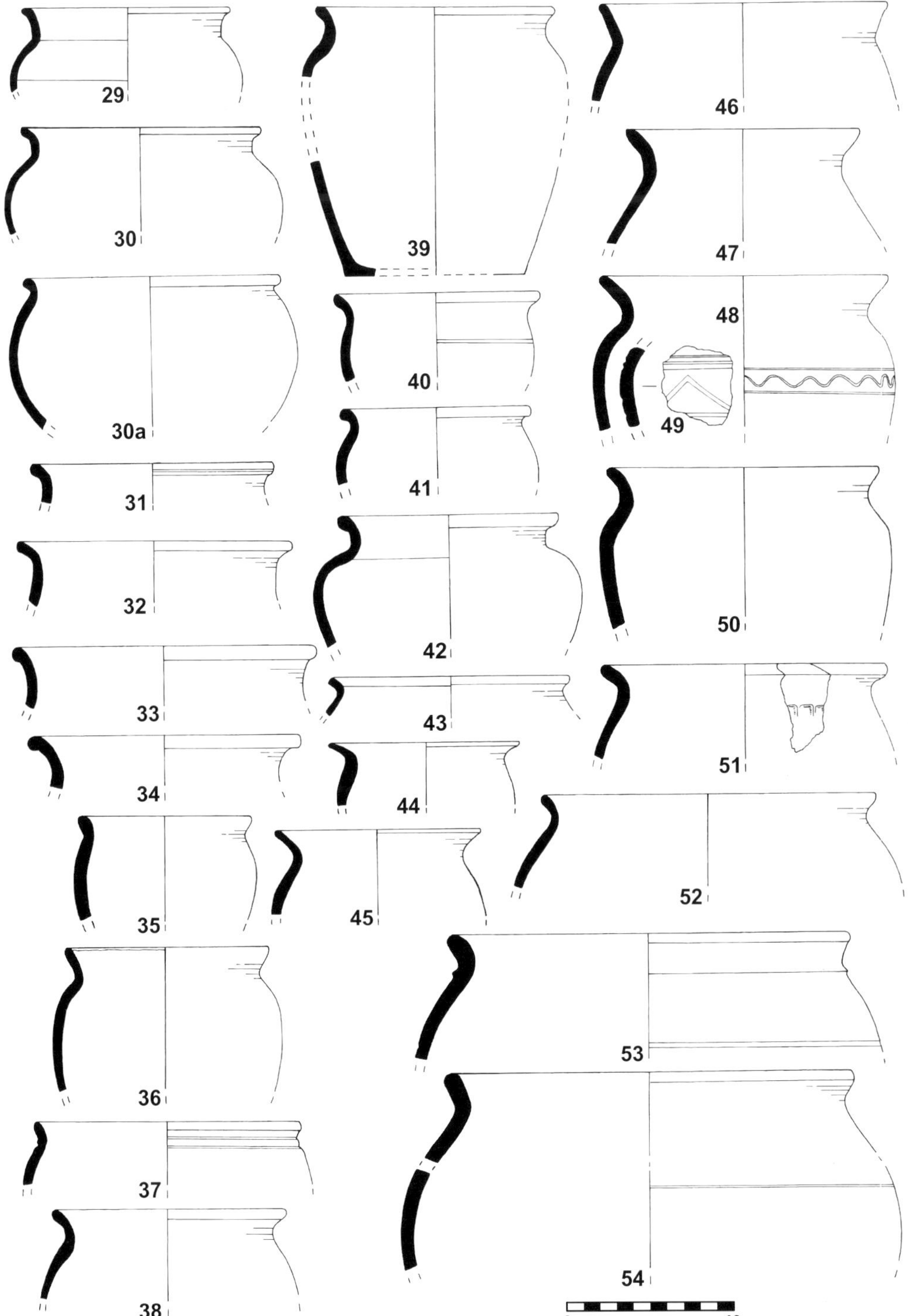

Figure 54:Gabbroic wares P29-54. P29-24 Type 1, P30a Type 2, P35-43 Type 3, P44-54 Type 4. Drawing L Simpson. Scale 1:4

Type 4 Jars with slack-profiled necks, standard fabric (P44-P70)

As the jars with upright necks become less frequent during the 2nd century, jars develop slack profiles with few distinguishing features and are mainly Carlyon Group 3. They are common on later Roman sites such as Porthmeor (Hirst 1937, fig 5, H, and unpublished material in Royal Cornwall Museum) and at Carwarthen, Roseland. There appears no way at present of subdividing these jars chronologically and they may have been made with no noticeable change of form from the mid 2nd to the 5th centuries. They do not appear to imitate features on jars in traded wares. In general on later Roman sites, jars appear to be of larger diameter than those of the 1st and 2nd centuries (Table 5.6). The category contains a good many variations and it is anticipated that it will need subdivision in future when full profiles are available for study.

The start date for slack-profiled jars is difficult to establish. They are not present, in the full slack-profiled form, at St Mawgan-in-Pydar. A few occur at Castle Gotha (eg Saunders and Harris 1982, fig 13, nos 23, 25), the date range of which probably did not extend beyond the 2nd, or early 3rd, century. No 6 at Shortlanesend comes from a site which, with radiocarbon dates, is later 2nd and early 3rd century (Appendix 2 and Harris 1980, 70). A start date in the mid 2nd century would work reasonably well with all the information currently available.

At Trethurgy the earliest, reasonably sealed, context was Stage 1 [458] (P60). Slack-profiled jars are common by Stage 4, are a major component of midden [932/801] in Stage 6, and occur in contexts of all later Stages. Their frequency in later Stages reflects the increase of pottery in later contexts.

Fig 54

P44 Straight out-turned rim. Soil over north-east of Round. Also from Stage 4+ [36], Stage 4 [722], Stage 6 [776], Stage 4/6 [808], Stage 8? [850], and soil over A and over Q.

P45 Straight out-turned rim, black-coated. Stage 6 [801] upper midden in U. Also from Stage 4/6 [808].

P46 Straight out-turned rim, very badly made, black-coated. Pre-Stage 6 [751A] soil predating Structure Y. Also from Stage 5/8 [65], Stage 8 [175], Stage 6 + [751].

P47 Similar to P46 but with straighter sided body. Stage 6 [801] and [932] midden in U. Also from Stage 5/8 [65], Stage 1/ 4 [386], Stage 4/6 [808], and Stage 4 [912].

P48 Jar with straight out-turned rim, black-coated, incised scribble on girth. Such girth scribbles are common on slack-profiled jars, eg Carlidnack (Harris and Johnson 1976, no 1), Porthmeor (Hirst 1937, fig 6) and Carwarthen. Stage 6 [932] lower midden in U. Also from Stage 5 [560], Stage 2/4 [567], Period 3 Bank spread [780], soil [800], Stage 1/4 [852], soil over Q.

P49 ?South Western Decorated ware (see above)

P50 Rim rather rounded, poorly made, black-coated. Stage 6+ [751] surface linking Structure Y and wall [892]. Also from Stage 7/8 [100] and Stage 7 [403].

P51 Sharply out-turned rim, black-coated; stamped decoration on shoulder. Soil over north-east of Round.

P52 Comparatively thin-walled. Stage 4 [910] drain associated with wall [911], Q. Also from soil [11].

P53 Rough tooled cordon on neck, groove on girth, black-coated. Simple girth grooves are quite common, eg Carvossa, Kilhallon (Carlyon 1982, P30), Porth Godrevy (Fowler 1962, fig 10, 7) and Carwarthen. It is possible that they sometimes form the top of a zone of decoration around the girth (Carlyon 1982, Kilhallon P32) but the absence of decorated body sherds at Trethurgy and elsewhere suggests that cooking pot girths were not commonly incised. Stage 4+ [36] rubble platform House T3. Also from Stage 3 [442], and soil over A.

P54 Girth groove; sufficient of the vessel survives to make it clear that this was not the top of a decorative zone around the girth. Stage 6 [861] bedding for House Z2 paving. Also from Stage 4/6 [808].

Fig 55

P55 Girth groove, black-coated. Stage 6 [801] upper midden in U. Also from Stage 6 [255], Stage 1/4 [386], Stage 10 [524], Stage 6/9 [728], and Stage 4 [923].

P56 Thick-walled. Stage 10 [546] latest paving Structure V. Also from Stage 8/9 [34], Stage 1/4 [161], Stage 1+ [199], Stage 6 [255], Stage 5/6 [521], Stage 9+ [723], soil [785] (2), and soil [800].

P57 Black-coated. Stage 6 [932/801] midden in U. Also from Stage 9+ [723], and Stage 6/9 [863].

P58 Girth groove. Stage 6 [801] upper midden in U. Also from Stage 8 [555], spread Period 3 Bank [780], Stage 4 [905], and soil over A.

P59 Incised scribble on girth below groove. Similar from Carlidnack (Harris and Johnson 1976, P1), Trebarveth T3 (Peacock 1969a, P6), Goldherring (Guthrie 1969, fig 14, 13), Carn Euny (Elsdon 1978, fig 60, 14, 15), Porthmeor (Hirst 1937, V.8 and V.9), and Carwarthen. Stage 4/6 [808] soil between House Z1 and Z2. Also from Stage 5+ [8] in R and Stage 9+ [723].

P60 Well-made, black-coated. Stage 6 [78] pit near Structure E. Also from Stage 9 [256], Stage 1 [458].

P61 Groove on outer edge of rim with row of small incisions below. Stage 6 [932] lower midden in U.

P62 Black-coated. Stage 7/8 [100] external gulley House A 2. Also from Stage 5+ [8], Stage 4/5 [9], and Stage 8/9 [34].

P63 Black-coated, fairly upright neck, incised lattice pattern on girth. This appears very much like copy of BB1 late 2nd-century jars with upright lattice (Holbrook and Bidwell 1991, 96). Incised girth lattice is unusual on gabbroic jars; exceptions are Porthmeor (Hirst 1937) V1.15, Goldherring (Guthrie 1969, fig 11, no 18), body sherds from Carwarthen. Stage 8 [175] patching on surface [8] in R.

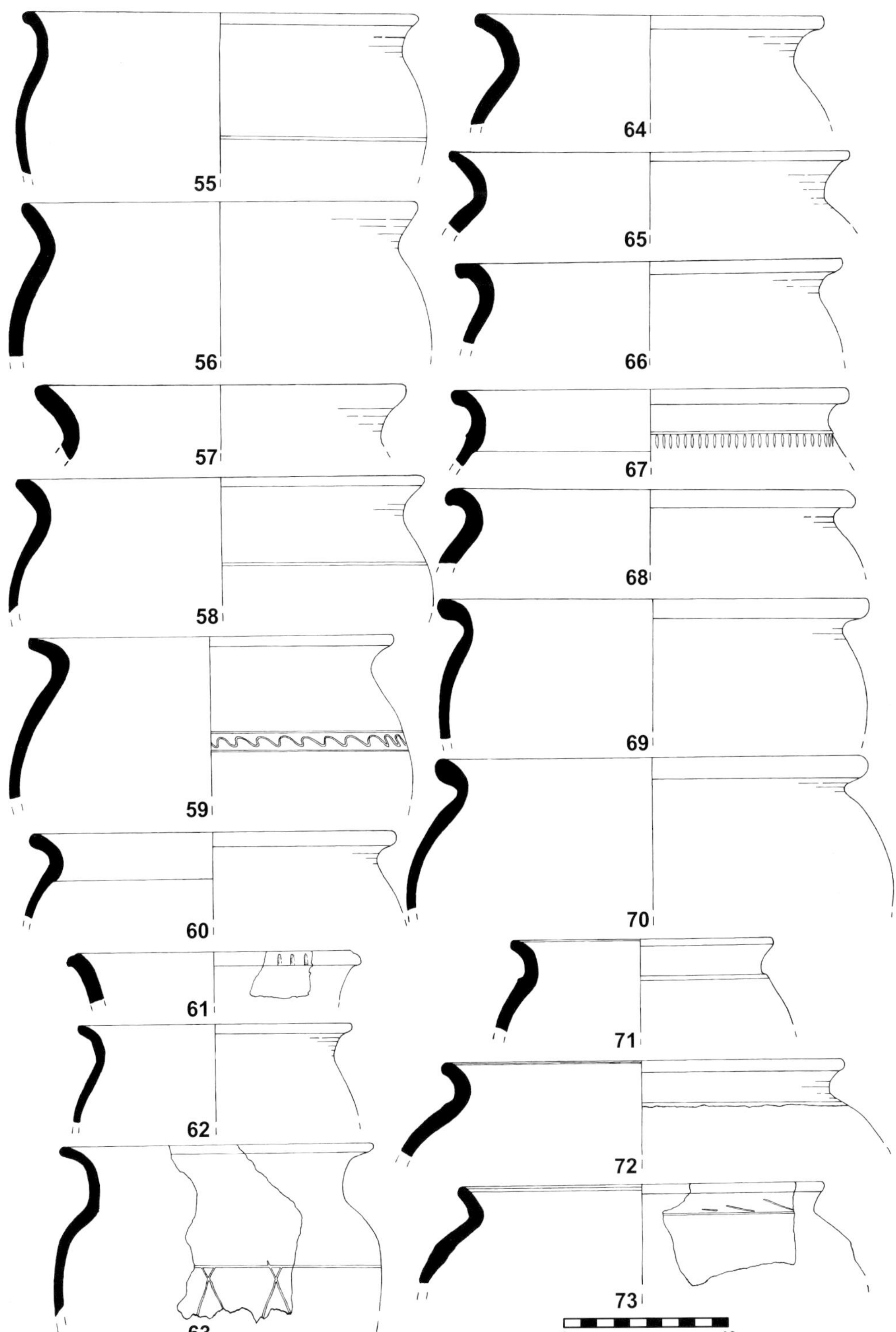

Fig 55: Gabbroic wares P55-73. P55-70 Type 4, P71-73 Type 6. Drawing L Simpson. Scale 1:4

P64 Thick-walled. Stage 5/6 [521] lower surface over Entrance terminals. Also from soil [785], and Stage 6/9 [863].

P65 Black-coated. Stage 6 [801] upper midden in U. Also from Stage 3 [442], Stage 8 [555], Stage 6/9 [722], Stage 4/6 [808], and Stage 8 [850].

P66 Flat-topped rim with possible shallow finger groove. Stage 6 [932] lower midden in U. Also from Stage 4 [818] and Stage 4 [905].

P67 Close-spaced stabbed incisions around the base of neck. Similar decoration on Carlidnack (Harris and Johnson 1976, P2), Porthmeor (Hirst 1937, fig 5.L), and perhaps Carwarthen. Stage 9+ [523] soil over upper surface over Entrance terminals. Also from Stage 8 [175], spread OLS [380], Stage 10 [524] (2), and Stage 1/4 [852].

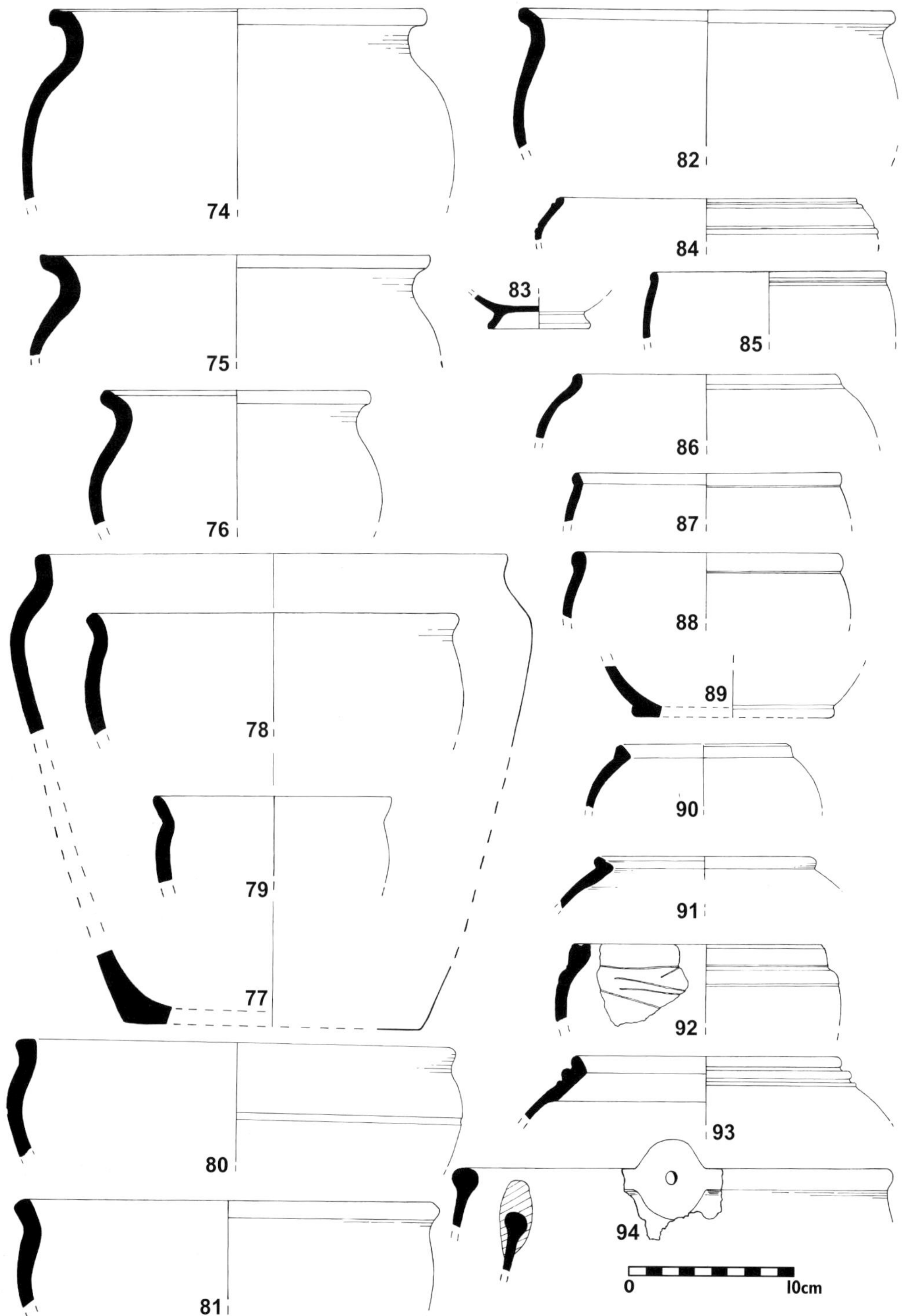

Fig 56: Gabbroic wares P74-94. P74-76 Type 6, P77-79 Type 8, P80-82 Type 9, P84-93 Type 11, P94 Type 12. Drawing L Simpson. Scale 1:4

P68 Black-coated. Stage 3 [761] external gulley House Z1.

P69 Thick-walled, black-coated. Stage 6 [932] lower midden in U. Also from Stage 1/4 [215], Stage 6 [255], Stage 6 +[751], and Stage 3 /4 [948].

P70 Thick-walled, black-coated. Stage 1/4 [386] soil in R.

Type 6 Jars, slack profiles, standard fabric, with rim-grooves or lid-seatings (P71-P76)

Rim-grooves occur on perhaps a third of vessels in the South Western Decorated pre-Roman tradition eg at Killibury (Miles 1977, figs 40-1) and, in more elaborate form, on Cordoned ware Type K at St Mawgan-in-Pydar. All the rim-grooves at Trethurgy are of the simplest form and probably represent a continuance of a local tradition. Most sites from the 2nd century onward have some vessels with these simple grooves, Castle Gotha (Saunders and Harris 1982, P13, P19, P20), Porth Godrevy (Fowler 1962, fig 10, 9) Trebarveth T3 (Peacock 1969a, P5) and Carwarthen. Trethurgy contexts are from Stage 4 onward.

Fig 55

P71 Narrow incised rim-groove, crude neck-cordon, black-coated. Stage 7/8 [100] external gulley House A 2. Also from Stage 5+ [8], Stage 1/4 [386], Stage 6 [932], and Stage 3/4 [948].

P72 Larger than P71 but otherwise similar. Stage 5 [950] surface associated with wall [907], Q. Also from Stage 6 [751], soil over X.

P73 Broad incised rim-groove, rough tooling on neck. Stage 1/4 [852] drain House Z 1. Also from Stage 8 [175], Stage 7 [403], and Stage 6/9 [722].

Fig 56

P74 Broad finger-groove on rim, black-coated. Stage 6 [932/801] midden in U. Also from Stage 4/5 [9], and Stage 4/6 [808].

P75 Thicker walled version of P74. Stage 6 [801] upper midden in U. Also from Stage 3/5 [422].

P76 As P74 but with slight incisions on edge of rim. Stage 6 [78] pit near Structure E. Also from Stage 8/9 [34], Stage 4 [56B], and Stage 8/9 [542].

Type 8 Jars, standard fabric, shouldered, with simple upright rims (P77-P79)

These, Carlyon Group 9, are not a common type in Cornwall, and do not occur at Carvossa or St Mawgan-in-Pydar. Similar forms from Porthmeor, Porth Godrevy (Fowler 1962, fig 11, 11), Castle Gotha (Saunders and Harris 1982, fig 13, no 24), and Trebarveth (Carlyon 1995, T1), and possibly Carn Euny (Elsdon 1978, fig 61, 15, 16), indicate a 3rd and 4th-century date range. At Trethurgy they first occur in [9]/[808] relating to the suggested Stage 4/5 hiatus (?early 4th century) and sparsely thereafter, although not in midden [932/801] (Stage 6).

Fig 56

P77 The rim and base, in large chunks, are of similar fabric and reconstruct to give a coherent jar profile, black-coated and burnished in its upper part but the base and upper part need not belong together and there appears no close parallel for the jar form. Stage 1/4 [386] soil in R. Also from Stage 4/5 [9].

P78 Jar with slightly out-turned rim, roughly made. Stage 7/8 [100] external gulley House A2. Also from Stage 8/9 [34].

P79 Black-coated. [785] soil over Structure Y. Also from soil [11].

Type 9 Bowls, standard fabric, with upright or slightly everted rims (P80-P82)

Included in Carlyon Group 9. These again do not appear common, and do not occur at Carvossa or St Mawgan-in-Pydar. Generally similar to Castle Gotha (Saunders and Harris 1982, P10, P24), Trebarveth T3 (Peacock 1969a, P25, 26), Goldherring (Guthrie 1969, fig 13, 23), Carwarthen, Porthmeor, Chysauster and Trebarveth T1 (many examples), comparisons best fit a 3rd and 4th-century date range. At Trethurgy they first occur in [808] relating to the suggested Stage 4/5 hiatus (?early 4th century) and sparsely thereafter, although not in midden [932/801] (Stage 6).

Fig 56

P80 Bowl with flat-topped slightly expanded rim, girth groove, black-coated. Stage 9/10 [183] rubble in Entrance below late gate. Also Stage 4/5 [907A].

P81 Bowl with flat-topped rim. Stage 4/6 [808] soil between House Z1 and Z2. Also from Stage 6/9 [728], soil [785].

P82 Bowl with simple out-turned rim, roughly made, black-coated. [785] soil over Structure Y.

Bowl with foot-ring (P83)

Fig 56

P83 Well made, thin walled, with out-turn on the base of foot-ring. Foot-rings appear to be both rare and early, the only good group being at St Mawgan-in-Pydar (Threipland 1956, nos 128-31); the Dr 29 gabbroic copy at Carvossa (Carlyon 1987, no 92) has a foot-ring as does the copy of a metal patera (nos 173-4), and no 42 from Trevisker (ApSimon and Greenfield 1972, fig 23). There is at least one from Porthmeor. The Carvossa, St Mawgan, and Trevisker material strongly indicate that foot-rings belong to the late 1st and early 2nd-century Cordoned ware phase in which innovation and copying were common. Stage 1/4 [386] soil in R. Also from Stage 6/9 [728].

Type 11 Small jars, standard fabric, rolled rims and/or cordons (P84-P93)

These jars relate to St Mawgan-in-Pydar Cordoned ware Type P of which Type Q with rim-groove is a variant (Carlyon Groups 18 and 24). At this site these

Types appear in later levels and date to the later 1st and early 2nd centuries. The slighter forms P84-89, with thin walls in fairly well-made fabric, only otherwise have been published from Carvossa and in a probable 2nd-century context at Reawla, the heavier variants P90-3 from Castle Gotha, Trebarveth, and Mulfra Vean. It might be argued from this that the sequence starts during the 1st century, continues through the 2nd and into the 3rd with the forms gradually getting heavier. These forms do not appear to continue on sites where occupation is later 3rd to 4th century, in contrast to the large jars similar to P95-100.

At Trethurgy P87 came from Period 3/4 Enclosure feature [924], otherwise most of the sealed contexts are Stage 4 or Stages 4/5. None came from midden [932/801] (Stage 6).

Fig 56

P84 Thin-walled jar with cordon produced by grooving. Similar at Carvossa (eg Carlyon 1987, no 150). Stage 1/4 [386] soil in R.

P85 Thin-walled, grooved below rim, black-coated and burnished. P85-7 compare Carvossa (Carlyon 1987, fig 5, no 148). Soil over House A.

P86 Grooved below rim. Stage 4 [427] House T3 floor. Also from Stage 5+ [8], Stage 3/5 [422].

P87 Rim bent outwards and grooved beneath, black-coated and burnished. [924] Periods 3/4 Enclosure gulley beneath Y.

P88 Groove below rim, burnished and black-coated. Stage 4 [931] gulley in Q.

P89 Base, with groove emphasizing projection around base angle, burnished. Base angles of this form only appear to occur with material of the late 1st to early 2nd-century phase of Cordoned ware eg St Mawgan-in-Pydar (Threipland 1956, nos 131-3), Castle Gotha (Saunders and Harris 1982, nos 48-9). Stage 7 [403] soil on House T4 floor.

P90 Sharply angled rim. Stage 4 [931] gulley in Q. Also from Stage 5+ [415].

P91 Out-turned rim, grooved beneath, with grooved lid-seating on top, typical St Mawgan Type Q in profile. Carvossa (Carlyon 1987, no 160), Castle Gotha (Saunders and Harris 1982, P45), Trebarveth T3 (Peacock 1969a, P23). Stage 10 [517] soil infilling X5. Also from Stage 9/10 [399].

P92 Deep rim groove, slight cordon formed by grooving on exterior; noticeable tool marks on interior. Stage 7/8 [100] external gulley House A2.

P93 Out-turned rim with applied cordon beneath, slighter ridge produced by tooling below. Compare Carvossa (Carlyon 1987, no 147), Castle Gotha (Saunders and Harris 1982, P38), Mulfra Vean (Thomas 1963, P19). Stage 9/10 [183] rubble in Entrance below late gate. Also from Stage 4/5 [9], Stage 4 [36], Stage 6+ [751A], and Stage 4/6 [808].

Type 12 Jar/bowl with rolled rim and vertical, pierced, lug (P94)

Fig 56

P94 Rolled rim, applied vertical lug, pierced through on line of rim. This form of lug (within Carlyon Group 45) occurs at St Mawgan-in-Pydar (Threipland 1956, no 23), at Carvossa (unpubl), Shortlanesend (Harris 1950, P1), Castle Gotha (Saunders and Harris 1982, P51), Trebarveth T1 (Serocold and Maynard 1949, A78, A9) and T3 (Peacock 1969a, P1 and P3), Reawla (Quinnell 1992, P63) and Goldherring (Guthrie 1969, fig 14, 26). It does not appear at Carwarthen or Porthmeor, perhaps disappearing *c* AD 300. Stage 10 [524] soil and upper disturbed levels, Structure V.

Type 13 Large jars, standard fabric, with rolled rims and/or cordons (P95-P100)

Jars with rolled rims P95-P98 continue the Cordoned ware tradition from St Mawgan-in-Pydar Type H, the standard Late Iron Age Cordoned ware jar; Carlyon Groups 22-3. These occur at Carvossa, at Shortlanesend dating to the late 2nd to early 3rd centuries, Castle Gotha with a terminal date in the 3rd century, and at Trebarveth T3 (Peacock 1969a, fig 20, 2, 10) where the material is likely to be 3rd and 4th centuries. They are common at Porthmeor, Carwarthen, and in the probable 3rd to 4th-century group from Carngoon Bank. They occur at Porth Godrevy and at Mulfra Vean where the ceramics are largely 4th century. Body sherds with cordons occur in a midden tentatively dated to the early 4th century at Reawla (Quinnell 1992, 103). It is difficult to find a Roman site in Cornwall of any date without large cordoned jar sherds. South Devon ware forms with similar rims and applied cordons were current in the 3rd and 4th centuries and occur at Trethurgy and elsewhere in Cornwall, especially at Duckpool (Quinnell 1995 for discussion). Large vessels strengthened by cordons, probably used as storage jars, appear to have been made throughout the Roman period by the two most westerly potting sources so far identified in South West Britain.

P99-100 have distinct applied cordons and P100 a neck-form which is not found in the pre-Roman Cordoned ware range. They tend to be fired oxidised red as P101-5. Some of the pieces, in particular P100, are unworn and in large chunks, although from unsealed soil contexts; it is possible these derive from

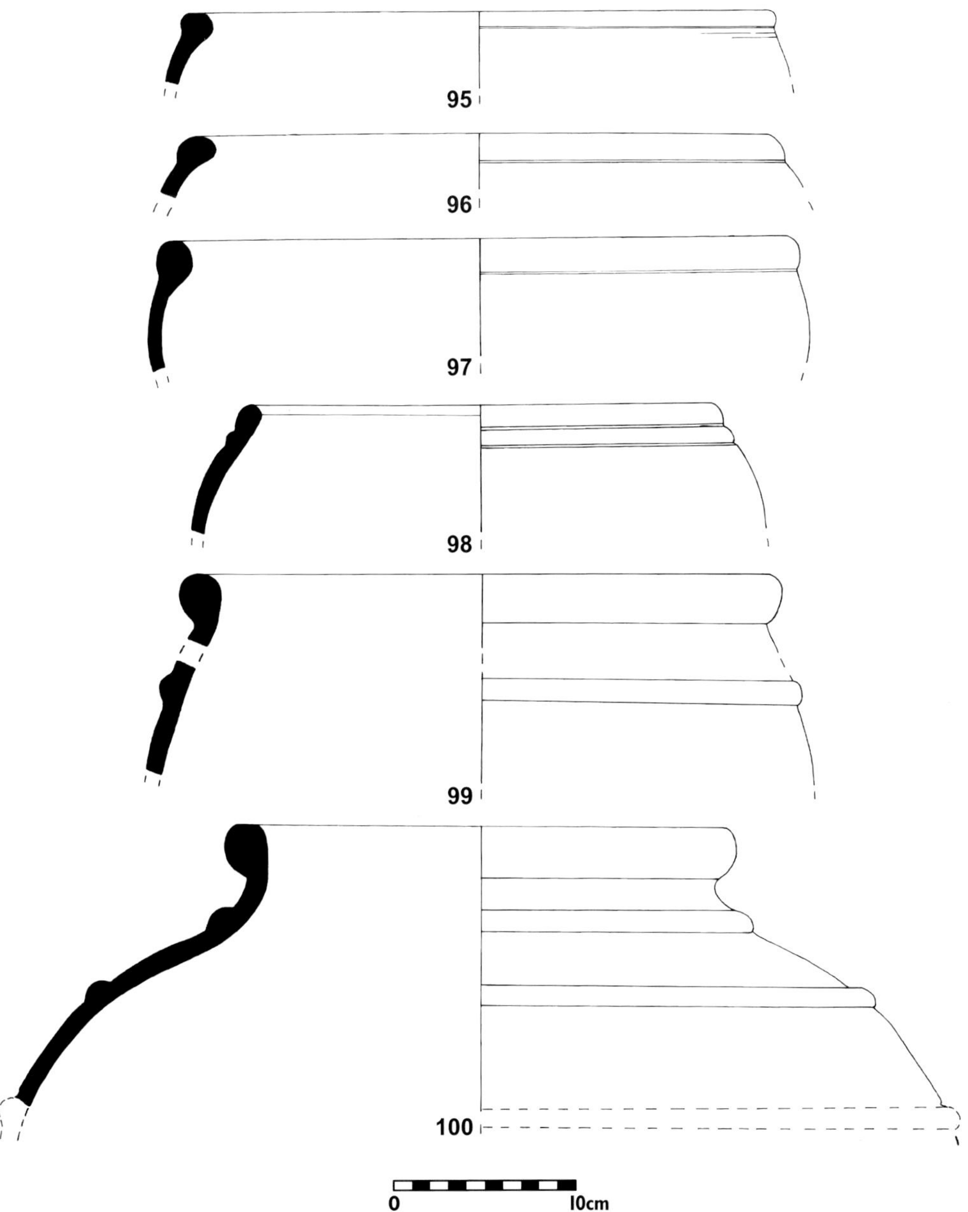

Fig 57: Gabbroic wares P95-100. All Type 13. Drawing L Simpson. Scale 1:4

the collapse of earlier features such as the Round Rampart. Stage 3 [442] provides the earliest context but there are examples in the Stage 6 [932/801] midden and a fair proportion of large pieces in unsealed late contexts.

Fig 57

P95 Simple rolled rim, roughly burnished. Stage 6 + [751] surface linking Structure Y and wall [892].

P96 Simple rolled rim emphasised by exterior groove. Stage 6 [801] upper midden in U. Also from Stage 5+ [8], Stage 9/10 [400], Stage 5 [560], Stage 6+ [751], Stage 6 [776], soil [785], and soil [800] (4).

P97 Rolled rim emphasised by broad groove beneath, burnished and black-coated, better made than others in this group. [785] soil over Structure Y. Also from soil [11].

P98 Rolled rim with cordon below formed by deep grooving, roughly burnished and black-coated. Soil over House A.

P99 Rolled rim, applied cordon on shoulder. Stage 9/10 [183] rubble in Entrance below late gate. Also from Stage 1/4 [314], Stage 3 [442], Stage 10 [524], Stage 6/9 [728], and Stage 4 [931].

P100 Heavy rolled rim above short upright neck, applied cordons, the scar for one remaining around girth, burnished. [11] soil over Structure E. Also from Stage 4/5 [9] and soil over A.

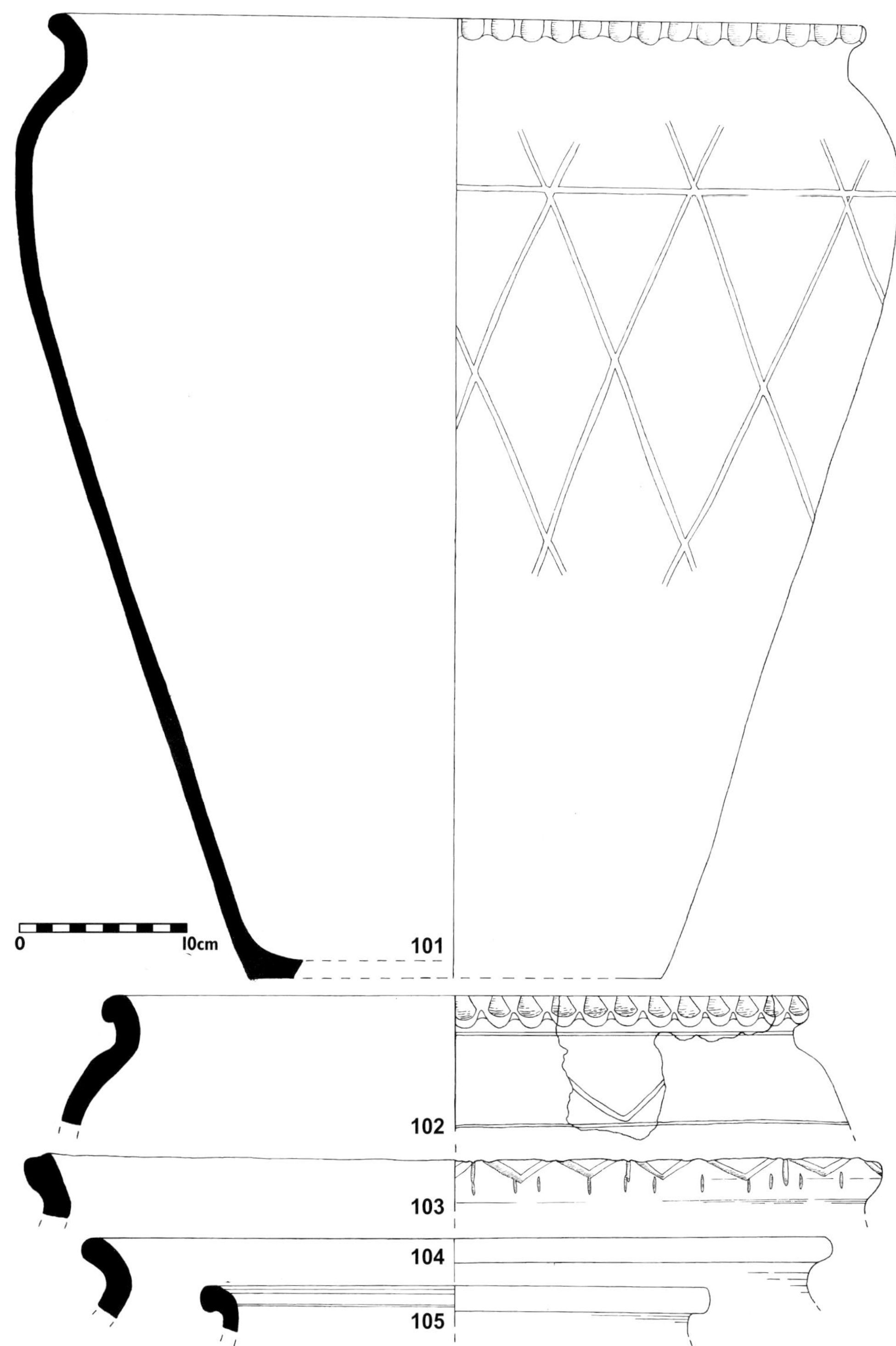

Fig 58: Gabbroic wares P101-105. All Type 16. Drawing L Simpson. Scale1:4

Type 16 Storage jars in coarse gabbroic fabric (P101-P105)

These coarsely gritted vessels tend to be fired in more oxidizing conditions and therefore to be more red in colour than other gabbroic pottery. Storage jars which are in shape enlarged versions of the basic cooking pot form become current in the West Country during the 3rd and 4th centuries, especially in South Western Grey storage jars with sherds present in Stage 4 and 4/5 contexts at Trethurgy (Section 5.5.6). They occur at Exeter (Bidwell 1979, 215-17) and at East Devon sites such as Holcombe (Pollard 1974, 135-7) and Seaton (Silvester 1981b, fig 13) but not apparently at the South Devon sites of Stoke Gabriel (Masson Phillips 1966) and Clanacombe (Greene and Greene 1970) where their place is taken by local South Devon versions. The gabbroic enlarged cooking pot storage jar (Carlyon Group 6) appears to have been adopted in Cornwall, alongside pre-existing cordoned styles, in the 3rd century and was probably in use into the 5th century. Their earliest context at Trethurgy is [761] Stage 3. They form a significant element in Stage 6 midden [932/801]. A radiocarbon determination from Penhale Round (Appendix 2; Quinnell 1998/9) is consistent with a 3rd-century introduction. The 3rd to 4th-century groups from Carwarthen and Porthmeor produce similar large roughly made jars (*pace* Carlyon 1995). The large jar (Guthrie 1969, no 6, fig 12) from Goldherring is also comparable, and examples have been found outside the main earthwork at Carvossa. There are sherds with a suggested deposit date of *c* 300 at Reawla (Quinnell 1992, P27) with a relevant radiocarbon determination (Appendix 2). Porth Godrevy produced body sherds only (Fowler 1962, fig 12, 1-4), as has Tintagel (unpubl) and it is probable that small sherds on other sites have not been detected.

Fig 58

P101 Large storage jar; profile from overlapping but not joining sherds. Rim decorated by finger-pinching at close-spaced regular intervals along its outer edge. Body decorated with a rough lattice pattern incised on wet clay. Thickness up to 15mm; small pieces could easily be mistaken for tile. Stage 6 [932] lower midden in U. Also from Stage 5+ [415], Stage 10 [524], Stage 8 [555], Stage 3 [761], soil [800] (2), Stage 6 [801] (6), Stage 4/6 [808], Stage 1/4 [852] (2), and Stage 5 [890]. Midden [932/801] probably contained sherds from some nine examples.

P102 Rim decorated with close-spaced indentations; part of incised lattice pattern around shoulder and girth survives. Stage 3 [761] external gulley House Z1. Also joining sherds from Stage 6 [932/801], and Stage 7 [403].

P103 Rim decorated with incised triangles along its top, vertical incisions along its outer edge. Very distinct coil structure. Joining sherds from Stage 6 [932/801] midden in U. Also from soil over House X.

P104 Simple rim with rough thumb marks under the outer edge. Stage 6 [932] lower midden in U. Also from Stage 5+ [8], Stage 8/9 [34], soil [800] (2), Stage 6 [801] (2), and Stage 1/4 [852].

P105 Roughly rolled back rim, with shallow grooves on interior; may relate to larger jars with lid seatings such as P74. [664A] posthole House X (not assignable to Stage).

Type 19 Bowls and dishes, standard fabric, with grooves and cordons below the rim (P106-P109)

These relate to St Mawgan-in-Pydar Type R, which was thought to be copied in the late 1st and early 2nd century from forms current in South and South East England. No such forms have yet been found as imports in Cornwall. P Bidwell (pers comm) comments that one or two possible prototype forms have been found in grey wares made during the legionary period at Exeter, but that they are not common. Vessels related to Type R, Carlyon Group 29, occur in large numbers at Carvossa, and Carlyon (1995) suggests that the main floruit of the type may be 2nd century. Examples occur at Goldherring (Guthrie 1969, fig 11, 19) and Trebarveth T1 (Serocold and Maynard 1949, fig 6), and some numbers on the 2nd to 3rd-century site at Killigrew (Quinnell forthcoming b). Variants, with grooved rims but no external cordons, occur at Castle Gotha (Saunders and Harris 1982, fig 15, 68-72) and at Carwarthen. No dishes in this class occurred at Shortlanesend, Kilhallon, or Reawla. If the sequence of bowl and dish forms in Cornwall was continuous, then Type 19 must have remained in production until the late 2nd century when Type 20 bowls were introduced (see below). At Trethurgy 12 examples come from the full range of chronological contexts, but none occurs in Stage 6 midden [932/801]; if these bowls ceased production in the late 2nd century then most of the Trethurgy examples were redeposited.

Fig 59

P106 Rim groove and exterior cordon; interior black coating. Stage 8 [555] surface around Structure V. Also from Stage 4/5 [9], and soil [11].

P107 Rim groove and exterior cordon; exterior black coating, well-made. [780] spread Period 3 Enclosure Bank beneath Structure Y. Also from Stage 8 [175], Stage 9/10 [400].

P108 Deep rim groove and exterior cordon; exterior black coating. Stage 5 [890] wall core of Structure U. Also from Stage 1/4 [386], Stage 9+ [723], and soil over Z.

P109 No rim groove but exterior cordon and black coating. Stage 9/10 [183] rubble in Entrance below late gate. Also from Stage 9/10 [399], Stage 7/8 [535].

Type 20 Bowls and dishes, standard fabric, with flat rims (P110-P113)

These vessels with simple out-turned rims are probably copies of flat-rimmed vessels in South-East Dorset BB1 which were current at Exeter during the late 2nd and early 3rd centuries (Holbrook and Bidwell 1991, 98). The subsequent introduction of the flat grooved-rim and the Cornish flanged bowl which also copy BB1 styles supports the probability of this influence on gabbroic forms. The adoption of bowls with external grooves and cordons in the late 1st

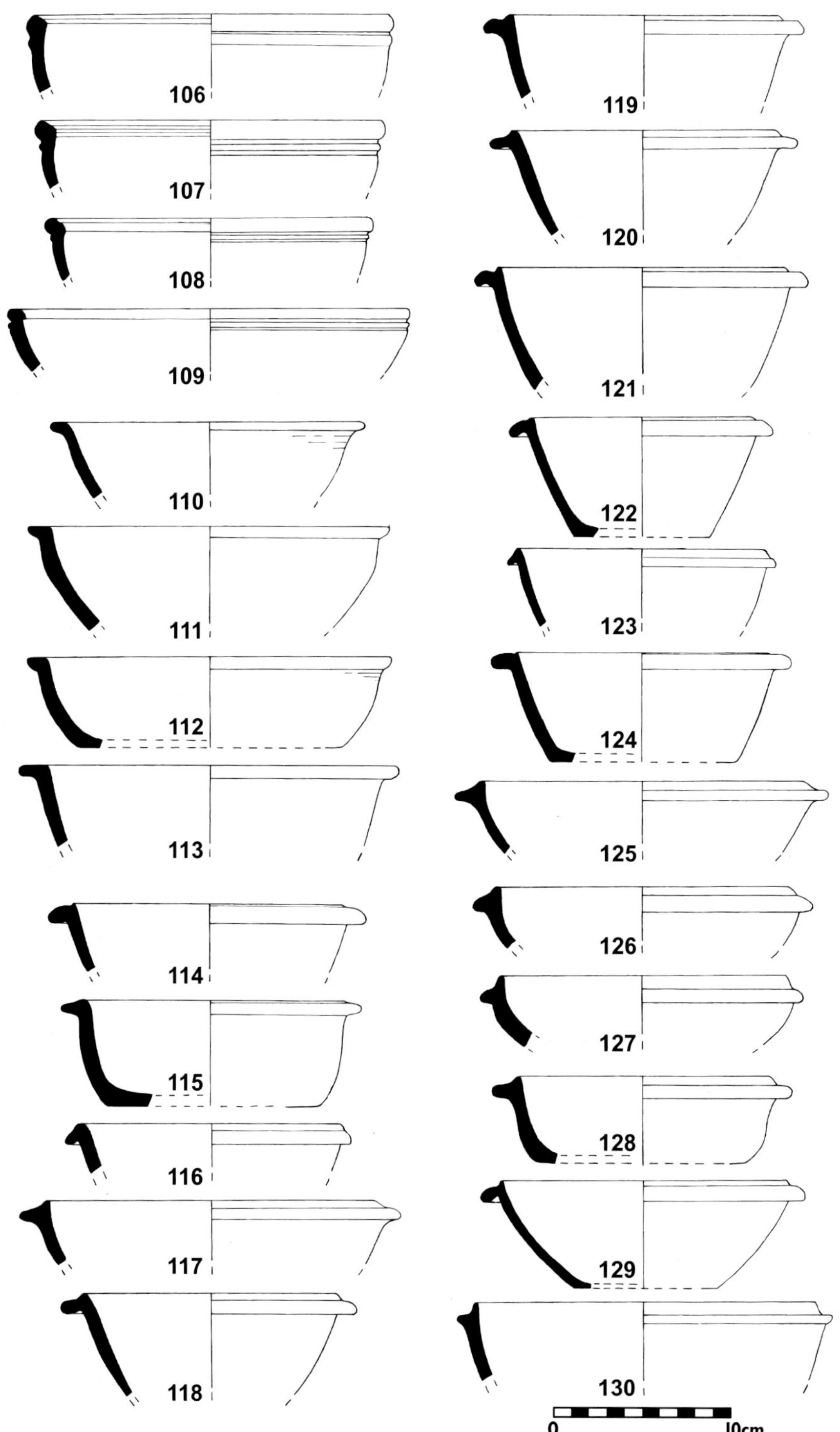

Fig 59: Gabbroic wares P106-130. P106-109 Type 19, P110-113 Type 20, P114-125 Type 21, P126-130 Type 22. Drawing L Simpson. Scale 1:4

century indicates new habits of eating requiring individual serving vessels. It seems reasonable to assume that this eating practice then continued through the Roman period. The flat-rimmed bowl is more practical than that with external cordons as it provides a surface on which to place inedibles like gristle. The date of its adoption can only be suggested as at some date during the late 2nd century but this fits the Cornish evidence in its present vague form. It is unclear whether it was replaced by the Cornish flanged bowl (Type 22) or continued to be made alongside it. The Trethurgy evidence suggests the former. Of 15 examples, the earliest context is [436] Stages 2-3, the latest of the sealed contexts is [808] Stages 4/5, and only one example occurs in midden [932/801]. These are Carlyon Groups 35-6; the shallower dish forms merge gradually into the deeper bowl forms without any clear distinction in gabbroic ware.

A Type 20 bowl occurs at the late 2nd to early 3rd-century site of Shortlanesend (Harris 1980, fig 30, no 7) with a range of consistent radiocarbon determinations (Appendix 2), several (Saunders and Harris 1982, nos 65, 65) at Castle Gotha and at Carvossa; the suggested 3rd-century group at Kilhallon has two (Carlyon 1982, nos 24-25), and one comes from a 2nd-century gulley at Trevisker (ApSimon and Greenfield 1972, no 31). Flat-rimmed bowls also appear on sites on which the pottery generally appears to be 3rd to 4th centuries, Chysauster (Leeds 1926, no 15), Carwarthen, and Porthmeor (unpubl examples in the Royal Cornwall Museum), Goldherring (Guthrie 1969, nos 19-21), at Trebarveth T1 (Serocold and Maynard 1949, fig 5) and Trebarveth T3 (Peacock 1969a, fig 20), and at Carn Euny (Elsdon 1978, fig 62, nos 28-32, 36, 38) but on these sites Cornish flanged bowls are more common. Overall the data from other sites supports a general date range of late 2nd to late 3rd century with some survival into the 4th.

Fig 59

P110 Black-coated. Stage 6 [932] lower midden in U. Also from Stage 4+ [36], soil [785], and Stage 4/6 [808].

P111 Black-coated. Stage 4+ [36] rubble platform House T3. Also from soil [11], and spread OLS [380].

P112 Well made, black-coated. Stage 2/3 [436] House T2 floor. Also from Stage 4/5 [9], and Stage 4+ [36].

P113 Black-coated. Stage 4/6 [808] soil between House Z1 and 2 (2). Also from Stage 6+ [751], Stage 4 [905], and soil over Q.

Type 21 Bowls and dishes, standard fabric, with flat grooved-rims (P114-P125)

The slight droop on the flange has been produced by pressing down the out-turned rim either with a finger tip or with a potter's tool. The type has no agreed terminology and is sometimes referred to as 'proto-flange' or nascent flange as it was seen (Gillam 1970, 70) as a precursor to the conical flanged bowl (see below). Holbrook and Bidwell (1991, 98) have demonstrated that the arguments for the gradual development of the conical flanged bowl from the flat-rimmed bowl cannot at present be substantiated and have used the simple descriptive term 'flat grooved rim' in their discussion of BB1 material from Exeter. This term is adopted here. In South-East Dorset BB1 flat grooved-rimmed bowls appear, on present evidence, to have been produced from the late 2nd to the late 3rd centuries. Their adoption into the gabbroic repertoire would be consistent with the adoption of other bowl and dish rim forms. As with other gabbroic bowls, the form shows a tendency towards curved, not straight walls. The initial date would then be towards the end of the 2nd century, perhaps around AD 200. It appears probable that bowls and dishes with flat grooved-rims continued to be produced alongside those with Cornish flanged rims; the distinction between the two rim forms is not always very clear. At Trethurgy about half of the *c* 33 examples come from Stage 6 midden [932/801], a very different number from the Type 20 flat-rimmed bowls for which an earlier terminal date is proposed. The earliest contexts, if the probable disturbed Periods 3/4 [780] is excluded, are [442] and [761] of Stage 3. Several examples predate the repaving in Stage 5. The form is Carlyon Group 38.

The data from other sites broadly support a date range of *c* AD 200 through the 4th century. It does not occur in the (admittedly small) late 2nd to early 3rd-century group from Shortlanesend or at Trevisker, but is present at Castle Gotha (Saunders and Harris 1982, nos 75-9 etc), Carvossa (Carlyon 1987, no 158, 161), Kilhallon (Carlyon 1982, nos 25-26) and at Porth Godrevy (Fowler 1962, fig 11, 7, 10). Number 68 comes from a probable early 4th-century context at Reawla (Quinnell 1992). The form occurs in some quantity at Porthmeor and Carwarthen (unpublished material in the Royal Cornwall Museum) clumping mainly in the 3rd and 4th centuries, and at Goldherring (Guthrie 1969, fig 13, 13-15 etc), and Trebarveth T1 (Peacock 1969a, fig 20, P20).

Fig 59

P114 Groove produced by narrow-ended tool, black-coated; well-made. Ploughsoil over Rampart, north-east of Round.

P115 Finger-groove, burnished but not black-coated. Soil over Q.

P116 Finger-groove, black-coated. Stage 3 [442] soil on House T2 floor. Also from Stage 4/5 [9], Stage 10 [524], and Stage 4/6 [808].

P117 Finger-groove, slight groove in interior, black-coated. Stage 6[801] upper midden in U. Also from soil [11] and Stage 9 [290].

P118 Deep finger-groove, black-coated. Stage 6 [801] (2) and [932] midden in U (several). Also from Stage 10 [524], Stage 8 [555], and spread Period 3 Bank [780].

P119 Deep finger-groove, black-coated, random scribbles on exterior. Stage 6 [801] upper midden in U.

P120 Deep finger-groove, black-coated. Stage 6 [801 / 932] midden in U, joining sherds.

P121 Flange bent downward, with narrow groove, burnished but black-coated. Stage 6 [932] lower midden in U. Also from Stage 4/5 [9] and Stage 1/4 [852].

P122 Flange bent downward, with deep narrow groove, black-coated; well-made. Stage 6 [801] upper midden in U.

P123 Flange bent outward with finger-groove, black-coated. Stage 6 [932] lower midden in U (several). Also from [801] soil over Q.

P124 Narrow groove, black-coated. Stage 3 [761] external gulley House Z1.

P125 Broad finger-groove, black-coated. Stage 6 [932] lower midden in U (several). Also from Stage 6 [255] and Stage 6 [801].

Type 22 Bowls and dishes, standard fabric, Cornish flanged rims (P126-P136)

In these vessels the rim projects upwards above the flange. In the past this rim form has often been described simply as flanged, especially when occurring in South-East Dorset BB1. Holbrook and Bidwell (1991, 98-9) have adopted 'conical flanged bowl' for the latter, a term which has the advantage of making a clear distinction from the less pronounced versions of 'flanged rims' which they now describe as 'flat grooved rims'. The author has, in the past, sometimes used the term 'conical flanged bowl' to describe bowls with this rim form in gabbroic ware, eg in the report on Reawla (Quinnell 1992). However the shape of the bowl in gabbroic fabric is often not conical but has a curved wall and a straight borrowing of the term appears inappropriate. It is proposed that the 'Cornish flanged bowl' be adopted for bowls in gabbroic fabric which have rim forms similar to those of conical flanged bowls in BB1. These are Carlyon Group 39. The conical flanged bowl in South-East Dorset BB1 was introduced *c* AD 270 and was current until the end of production in the early 5th century. On the assumption that this rim form in BB1 influenced gabbroic styles, adoption in the late 3rd century is quite possible and indeed likely. It certainly remains common in gabbroic assemblages as long as these were produced in the Roman tradition. There may be some earlier exceptions: bowls with rims of this type occur at various dates in different fabrics at Exeter and in the South West, for example the 2nd to 3rd-century example in South Western BB1 variant fabric 60 at Kilhallon (Carlyon 1982, no 18), and these may have been copied. However a late 3rd-century introduction of Type 22 Cornish flanged bowls provides a good fit to the current available data.

At Trethurgy, of some 24 examples, the earliest contexts are [948] and [905] in Stage 4, excepting the aberrant P135 in [685] of Stage 1. The two radiocarbon determinations (Table 9.3) might appear a little early but they are also relevant to the introduction of BB1 conical flanged bowls. Five occur in Stage 6 midden [932/801] for which a radiocarbon determination is consistent with late 4th-century dating. The late 3rd century onward dating for Cornish flanged bowls appears to fit the overall evidence from the Round.

Vessels with Cornish flanged rims do not occur at Trevisker, Shortlanesend, Castle Gotha, or Kilhallon (except in South-Western BB1). There are a few examples at Carvossa (Carlyon 1987, nos 164, 167). They are common amongst the unpublished material (Royal Cornwall Museum) from Carwarthen, Chysauster, and Porthmeor; they occur at Tintagel (Carlyon 1995, 76), Goldherring (Guthrie 1969, fig 12, 14), at Trebarveth T1 (Serocold and Maynard 1949) and T3 (Peacock 1969a, P13-15), Porth Godrevy (Fowler 1962, fig 11, 4, 14) and Carn Euny (Elsdon 1978, fig 63, 8-11c). They are present in the early 4th-century midden at Reawla (Quinnell 1992, nos 55, 61), and in a 4th-century dump in the ditch at Penhale which has an appropriate radiocarbon determination (Appendix 2; Quinnell 1998/9).

Fig 59

P126 Black-coated. Stage 6 [932/801], joining sherds midden in U. Also from [858], soil over Q.

P127 Distinctive curved wall. Stage 9/10 [399] revetment collapse over House T5.

P128 Black-coated. Stage 6+ [751] surface in Structure Y.

P129 Thick flange made by bending edge back under. [11] soil over Structure E. Also from Stage 9/10 [400].

P130 Black-coated. Stage 3 /4 [948] floor House Z1. Also from Stage 6+ [751], Stage 4 [905], and soil over Q.

Fig 60

P131 Black-coated. Stage 9+ [723] collapse of House Z 2. Also from Stage 4/5 [9].

P132 Flange made from added strip. Stage 6 [932] lower midden in U. Also from Stage 10 [524] and Stage 6 [801].

P133 Black-coated. Stage 9/10 [400] soil over House T5. Also from Stage 5+ [8] and Stage 9/10 [399].

P134 Black-coated. Stage 6 [932] lower midden in U. Also from Stage 7 [403], Stage 10 [546], and Stage 8 [555].

P135 Edge of flange decorated with vertical incisions; a scoop on top of the flange may be intended to imitate a mortarium spout. Possibly belongs with the copies of the Cordoned ware second phase. No exact parallels although an unpublished example from Carwarthen in the Royal Cornwall Museum has an indented edge to its flange. Stage 1 [685] slot of House X1.

P136 Very crudely made; flange decorated with alternate straight and curved (?fingernail) incisions; wall decorated with semi-circular incisions. No parallel known. An example from Goldherring (Guthrie 1969, no 3, fig 15) is probably a similar crudely made and decorated bowl. An unpublished non-gabbroic bowl from Tintagel is also somewhat similar but lacks the incised decoration. Stage 9 [77], upper fill of Structure G. The only gabbroic sherd from this context, which produced Post-Roman import sherds, and probably the only gabbroic vessel from the site which may be suggested as distinctively 5th to 6th centuries AD.

Other bowls, standard fabric (P137, P139)

Fig 60

P137 Crudely made, with slightly pinched-out rim. Unpublished parallels in Royal Cornwall Museum from Carwarthen and Porthmeor. Stage 1/4+ [360] secondary Ditch silt.

P139 Straight-sided bowl, with rounded rim. No precise parallels but cf Trebarveth T3 (Peacock 1969a, fig 20, nos 25-26) and Carn Euny (Elsdon 1978, fig 61, no 18). Stage 9+ [723] collapse of House Z2. Also from Stage 4/6 [808].

Bowl, dish, well-made fabric (P138, P140, P140A)

Fig 60

P138 Thin-walled, slight cordon below rim, black-coated on both surfaces. No immediate parallels but general appearance suggests a copy of some imported form in the late 1st to early 2nd century Cordoned ware phase. Stage 9 [46] collapse of Rampart revetment in R.

P140 Carinated dish with slightly out-turned rim and cordon on carination. Perhaps a copy of samian Dr 15/17, of the same broad date as P138. Closest parallel from Hillside Farm, Bryher, Isles of Scilly (Quinnell forthcoming e). Stage 2-3 [436] soil on House T2 floor.

P140A (not illustrated) Rim sherd probably copying Dr18, fine well-made fabric with a red, haematite-rich slip (R Taylor pers comm) which appears to imitate the finish on samian. Ploughsoil.

Type 23 Plain-rimmed bowls or dishes, standard fabric (P141, P142)

These simple bowls or dishes have slightly curved sides and plain rims. They look exactly like the South-East Dorset BB1 plain-rimmed forms which have a currency at Exeter from the mid 2nd century until the end of the Roman period (Holbrook and Bidwell 1991, 99-100) and it seems likely that the gabbroic forms copy these. However dishes with plain rims in other fabrics occur in Cornwall, such as a Gallo-Belgic platter from St Mawgan-in-Pydar (Threipland 1956, no 145), or a grey ware Exeter fabric 101 example from Kilhallon (Carlyon 1982, no 20). Plain-rimmed bowls do not occur at Carvossa, Shortlanesend, or Trevisker. The bowl at Castle Gotha (Saunders and Harris 1982, no 61) may be an early example. Goldherring in its late phase produces the largest group (Guthrie 1969, fig 14, nos 1-10); there are also examples from Porth Godrevy (Fowler 1962, fig 11, 6), Magor (O'Neil 1933, P7), Porthmeor (Hirst 1937, fig 5D) and Carwarthen but not Reawla. These sites suggest a 3rd to 4th-century date range, though a start in the late 2nd would be possible. They were not common in Cornwall compared to the flat-rimmed, flat grooved-rimmed, and Cornish flanged dish and bowl range. The earliest contexts at Trethurgy are Stage 4 [294], [910], and [923]; they do not occur in Stage 6 midden [932/801]. Their absence from the midden, and perhaps from the early 4th-century midden **148** at Reawla (Quinnell 1992) might indicate that the form does not extend much into the 4th century.

Fig 60

P141 Pronounced curve to wall. Stage 6+ [751] surface of Structure Y. Also from soil over A.

P142 Black-coated. Stage 4 [923] dump between construction of walls [892] and [907], Q. Also from Stage 8/9 [34], Stage 5/8 [128], Stage 4 [294], up to Stage 6 [751A], soil [800], and Stage 4 [910].

Type 26 Handled pitcher or flagon (P144)

Fig 60

P144 Flagon or pitcher with slight rim and stub of square-sectioned handle, standard fabric. Carlyon Group 45a. Handled vessels, with one or two handles, occur sporadically throughout the Roman period in Cornwall; St Mawgan-in-Pydar (Threipland 1956, fig 30, no 127), Carvossa (Carlyon 1987, nos 170-2), Trebarveth T3 (Peacock 1969a, fig 20, no 7) Porth Godrevy (Fowler 1962, fig 12, 11), Porthmeor (unpubl) and Goldherring (Guthrie 1969, fig 14).

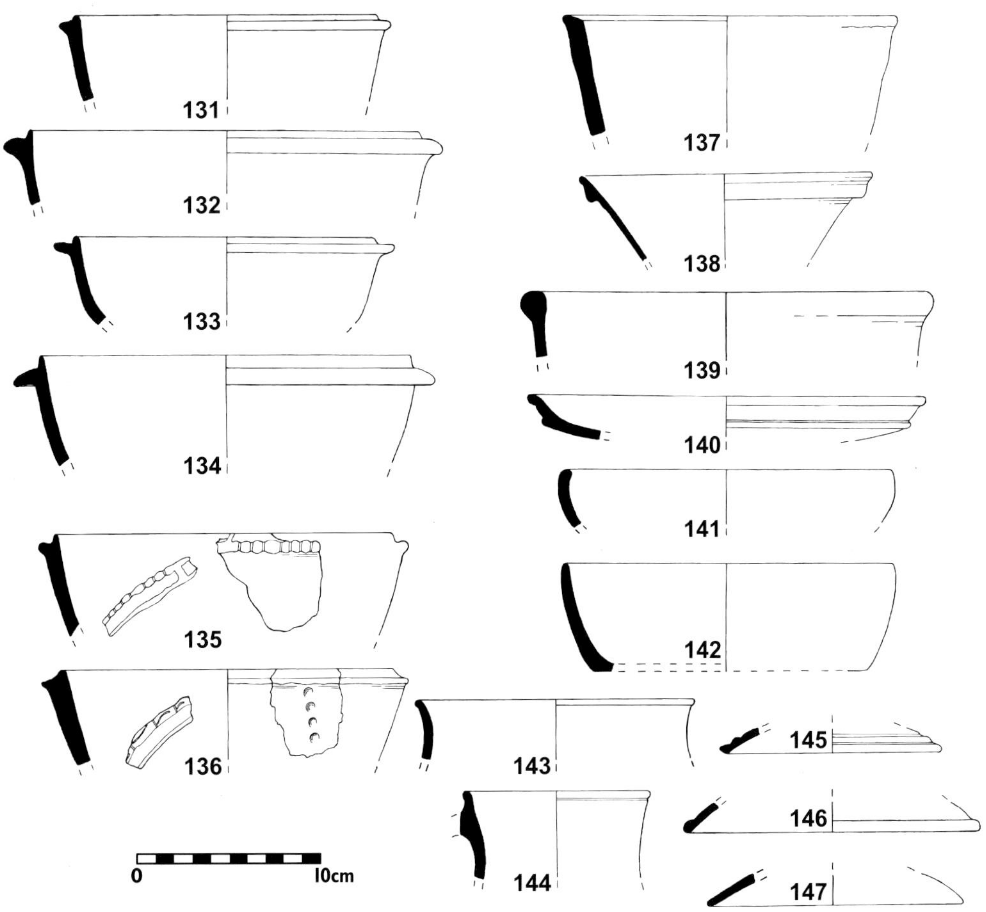

Fig 60: Gabbroic wares P131-147. P131-136 Type 22, P141-142 Type 23, P144 Type 26, P145-147 Type 28. Drawing L Simpson. Scale 1:4

Stage 4/6 [808] soil between House Z1 and 2 (2). Also from Stage 8/9 [542].

Type 28 Lids (P145-P147)

Fig 60

Lids occur occasionally throughout the Roman period from St Mawgan-in-Pydar (Threipland 1956, fig 36, nos 124-126), Carvossa (Carlyon 1987, no 140), Shortlanesend (Harris 1980, nos 19-20), Reawla (Quinnell 1992, nos 7, 39) and Carwarthen (unpubl, Royal Cornwall Museum). The examples from Trethurgy are similarly widely contexted; none are black-coated.

P145 Double groove on upper surface. Stage 2-3 [453C] posthole, House T2.

P146 Simple beaded edge. Stages 4/5 [422] soil between House T3 and T4.

P147 Slight groove around edge. [400] soil over House T5.

Grass-marked sherd

P148 Grass-marked sherd (not illustrated), probably from base of vessel. From ploughsoil in Q.

DF Williams comments:

'Hard, rough fabric, grey (Munsell 5Y 5/1) surfaces, dark-grey core. Impressions of grass or chaff can clearly be seen on the outside surface. A thin sectioning of the sherd showed that the grass impressions are confined to the outside surfaces only. Petrologically, the composition of the paste shows very little difference to that of the large gabbroic group, and so it seems reasonable to assume that the Lizard gabbroic clays were also used in this case. Similar grass-marked pottery from Cornwall and the Scilly Isles has previously been studied by Peacock (1975, 47) and also found to have been made of gabbroic clays. The petrological results suggest that the grass-marked pottery so far sampled was made at the same centre, or at least in the same area, as the bulk of the Roman coarse pottery at Trethurgy, and therefore that the tradition of making pottery from the Lizard gabbroic clays was a long one and continued from the Roman period (and before) well into the Post-Roman era.'

The date first suggested by Thomas (1968a) for the introduction of grass-marked pottery to Cornwall, *c* AD 600, has been questioned, and Hutchinson (1979, 86) has argued the case for the 8th century; her paper contains a comprehensive survey of grass-marked pottery finds in Cornwall until the late 1970s (1979, 91). Smith's discussion of the pottery from Carngoon Bank, Lizard (1980, 48) makes it clear that an 8th-century date would fit better with the other material from this site. Thomas (1985, 186), in the first detailed published comments on the material from the stratified site on Samson, Isles of Scilly, refers to grass-marked pottery possibly dating to the 7th and 8th centuries and occurring in a level lying over that which produced E ware. An 8th-century date fits with the sequence in Ireland, where E ware tends to predate grass-marked souterrain ware (eg Lynn 1982). However, as discussed above, there is no identified general hiatus in the use of pottery in Cornwall. If the later Roman tradition continued into the 6th century, then grass-marked styles may have gradually come in during that century to replace it. There may have been some local gaps in the use of ceramics and it may also be that the introduction of grass-marked styles occurred at slightly different times in different parts of Cornwall and Scilly.

Continuance of the use of gabbroic clay for the production of grass-marked pottery is now well established in Cornwall, although in areas such as the Isles of Scilly local granitic clays were used, indicating that, at some date in the Post-Roman period, gabbroic pottery ceased to be exchanged widely. However several gabbroic grass-marked sherds have been found in graves in the cemetery at Cannington in Somerset (Rahtz *et al* 2000, 258), showing that on occasion, gabbroic pottery was still travelling long distances at a date which may be 7th century or a little later. The Cannington material appears to be the only gabbroic grass-marked pottery so far found outside Cornwall.

Although only one definite grass-marked sherd was found at Trethurgy, the site was machine-stripped and the upper levels had been extensively damaged. This sherd could well be the only one recovered from a larger group.

5.7 Medieval and Post-Medieval pottery *Carl Thorpe* and *Henrietta Quinnell* (Text written in 2001)

Medieval and Post-Medieval material was bagged separately during the excavations but when the whole assemblage was reviewed in 2001 additional Medieval sherds were distinguished. All Medieval and Post-Medieval material was then rapidly scanned by Carl Thorpe to provide both dating for episodes of activity in the Round and information about the range of material which would be of use to future researchers. This note is a summary of the material present and is not intended as a full report. As ploughsoil was mechanically removed, only a small proportion of the pottery present was retrieved. Good recent coverage of the pottery briefly described below is provided by O'Mahoney (1989a; 1989b; 1994).

The Medieval and Post-Medieval material mainly came from contexts immediately beneath ploughsoil. A few contexts had one or two intrusive sherds of dates from the 10th to the 13th centuries — [8], [9], [678], [723], [751], [780], [793], [801], and [808]. These are most likely explained by disturbance connected with stone removal during ploughing. A group of contexts in the Entrance area produced an 11th or 12th-century Sandy Lane type base and rim, a small group of 13th to 14th-century material and a larger group of 17th to 19th-century sherds — [140], [183], [188], [215], [518], [523], [567], and robber trench [185] for Rampart revetment. Otherwise [380] in Area R produced a range of material from the 13th to the 20th centuries, and [728] in Y a single 13th-century sherd and some 17th to 19th-century material. The lower infill of G [255] contained a few 13th to 14th-century sherds and the upper infill [77] a quantity ranging from the 16th to the 20th century. Lynchet [359] over the Ditch outside the Round on the west contained a small quantity of 16th or 17th-century sherds.

Five sherds were of Sandy Lane type appropriate to the 10th to 12th centuries; one of these had possible grass-marking and another was gabbroic. There was a scatter of small sherds in Bunnings Park ware, most of which were 13th century, and a number in a variety of other fabrics which were probably Cornish. Lostwithiel ware was more common, a little as early as the 13th century, increasing in quantity until the 16th. There was a little St German's material. For the 17th and 18th centuries the predominant fabric was North Devon. The general pattern suggested an increase of deposition from at least the 13th century onwards ending with a little modern white ware. The collection was notable for its lack of imported material, for example no Frechen stoneware. Parts of pipe bowls and stems, all unstamped, of 17th to 19th-century types, were present, together with a little bottle glass. Two sherds are given special comment.

Fig 53

P24 Rim of jug, 13th-century Bunnings Park ware. From make-up of field hedge over Rampart. (Initially - in 1976 - identified as South Devon Ware).

P24A (Not illustrated) Part of a cresset lamp, including lip, in a wheel-made granitic fabric with heavy sooting on exterior. Parallels with Donyatt forms (Coleman-Smith and Pearson 1988, 258, fig 135, nos 16/1 and 16/2) suggest a 14th-century date. No other Medieval lamp appears to have been published from Cornwall. From [523], soil over Ditch by Entrance.

5.8 Baked clay

Fragments of baked clay, friable and very coarse with large granite grits, bright red to almost white in colour, were obviously from objects made locally. Several pieces have parts of a flattish, roughly smoothed surface, others have the impression of sticks. The fragments may have come from daub on walls, hearth linings or, possibly, loomweights although few pieces have much curve. Contexts were — [8] (2), [9] (1), [34] (1), [90] (2), [380] (2), [386] (3), [436] (6), [442] (2), [524] (1), [723] (2), [752] (9), [761] (2), [776] (4), [800] (5), [801] (9), [808] (1), [818] (3), [852] (1), [905] (15), [907A] (1), [910] (1), [923] (7), [932] (4), and soil over Z (3); these show a noticeable concentration in Area Q.

6 Stone artefacts

6.1 Materials used

Petrographical identifications were provided on site by E Francis, geologist with ECC. Those artefacts individually enumerated were described by Dr RT Taylor, then of the British Geological Survey, in the 1980s.

Most artefacts were of Cornish origin, generally within about 8km of the site. Only spindle whorl S28, probably from somewhere in the Midlands, and upper rotary quern S46, probably from South Wales, do not appear to have Cornish sources, apart from the artefacts of Kimmeridge shale. Most of those dressed into shape were of the even-textured cream-coloured rock, elvan, a local term for quartz porphyry or felsite, sometimes referred to as Pentewan stone. Elvan occurs in dykes from the latest phases of the igneous activity which produced the St Austell granite and has a wide distribution around the granite areas of Cornwall. (Quinnell 1993a, fig 1). It varies in hardness according to the degree of alteration since its intrusion and the softer types were chosen for artefact production. The majority of dykes have a similar mineral composition which impedes identification of specific sources. The closest recorded dykes to Trethurgy are between Roche and Belowda Beacon, about 8km north-west, and in the Polgooth/Sticker area, 6km to the south. Some artefacts are of greisen, which results from the alteration of granite during the final stages of cooling in which feldspar was replaced by quartz and mica. Greisen is softer than granite, finer in grain, and usually a silver or yellowish grey. Patches of greisen occur in the west edge of the St Austell granite and in the Tregonning/Godolphin areas. The texture of the greisen used for artefacts matches more closely those from the Tregonning/Godolphin and St Austell areas than those from the well-known occurrences at St Michael's Mount and Cligga Head (R Taylor pers comm). Both these easily worked rocks, elvan and greisen, were used for a distinctive Cornish range of carved artefacts during the Roman period which has been recognised since the excavations at Trethurgy (Quinnell 1993a).

River and beach cobbles and pebbles with a range of lithologies were selected for objects such as whetstones and polishing stones. Granite, either waterworn boulders or locally occurring blocks, was used for many larger items especially saddle querns. A small number of artefacts were made from Meadfoot slate, available immediately outside the St Austell granite.

Plate 41: Trethurgy bowl S1. Scale in cms. Photo: Peter Brierley

Plate 42: Trethurgy bowl S2. Scale in cms. Photo: Peter Brierley

Plate 43: Trethurgy bowl S3. Scale in cms. Photo: Peter Brierley

6.2 Bowls and mortaria

6.2.1 Bowl mortaria with projecting handles - 'Trethurgy bowls'

Parts of six, possibly, seven large bowls were found, all of elvan, with internal diameters ranging from 0.41m to 0.52m. Four (S1-4) had distinctive handles, consisting of a projecting horizontal lug with downward extensions. S1 was sufficiently complete to show that it had had only two opposed handles. Pieces of S2-4 are sufficiently large to show that four equally spaced handles were not possible. S5-7 are smaller fragments from bowls of the same size range as those with handles. All these bowls appear to have been used as mortars as their interiors are worn smooth; the smoothness increases towards the bases and in some cases wear had caused slight hollows. These large

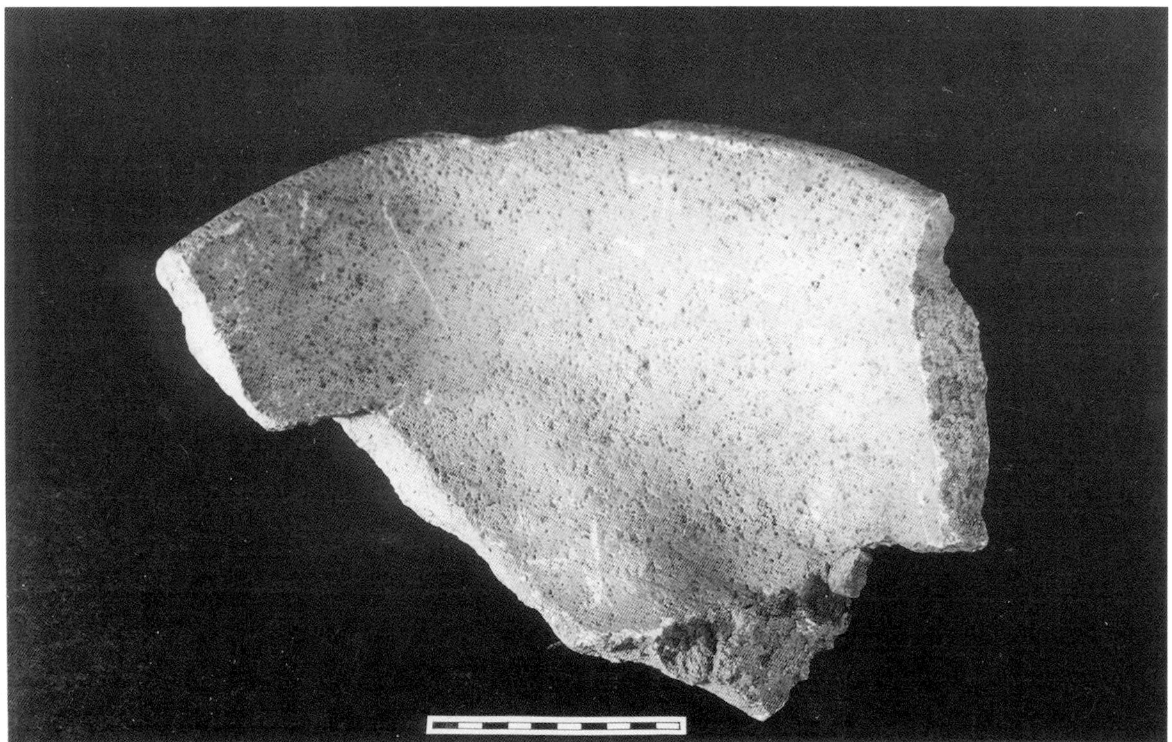

Plate 44: Inside of bowl S3. Scale in cms. Photo: Peter Brierley

Plate 45: Trethurgy bowl S4. Scale in cms. Photo: Peter Brierley

bowls with projecting handles were first recognised at Trethurgy and so have been termed 'Trethurgy bowls' (Section 6.2.4).

Fig 61

S1 (Pl 41) Two-handled bowl, externally chamfered rim, slight footring, internal diameter 0.49m. Four joining fragments, two from Stage 9/10 [399] Rampart collapse behind House T, one from Stage 9 or earlier [678] soil under paving [933] outside House X, and one from Stage 8/9 [34] infill between House A2 and A3.

S2 (Pl 42) Chamfered rim, one surviving handle, pronounced footring, internal diameter 0.44m. Single piece from Stage 8 [28] paving House T5.

S3 (Pls 43-4) Chamfered rim, part of one handle, pronounced angled footring, internal diameter 0.46m.

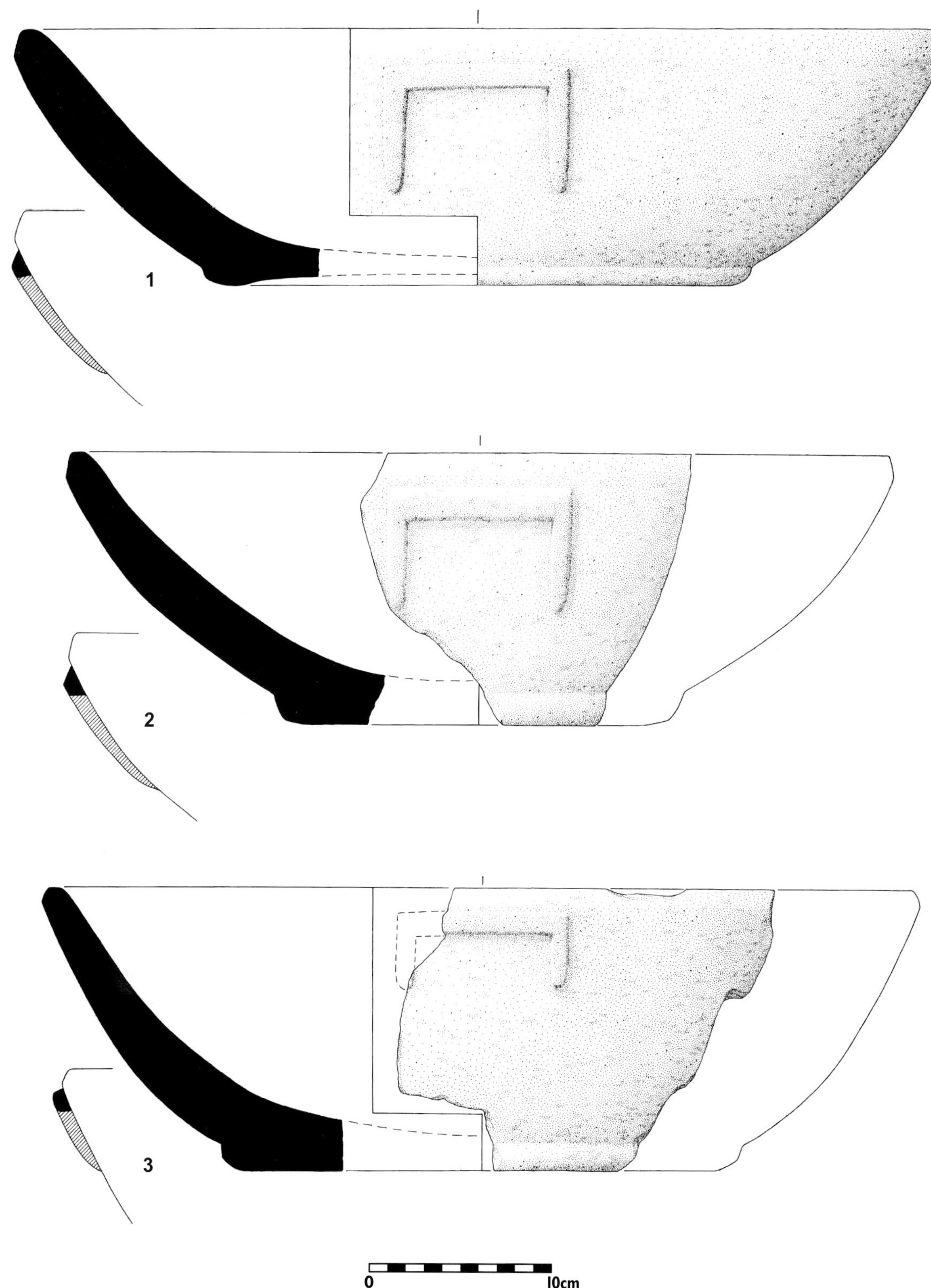

Fig 61: Trethurgy bowls in elvan S1-S3. Drawing S Morris. Scale 1:3

Very worn interior. Single piece used as packing stone in posthole [676] House X, not assignable to Stage.

Fig 62

S4 (Pl 45) Slightly projecting rim, part of one handle, no footring, internal diameter 0.52m. Joining fragments from Stage 4/6 [808] soil in Area Q, and from [785] soil over Y. A third fragment from [808] is almost certainly from S4.

S5 Almost rounded rim, no surviving handle, crudely worked footring, internal diameter 0.42m. From Stage 6 [255] backing to Structure G.

S6 Small fragment with rounded rim, internal diameter *c* 0.41m. From [360], secondary Ditch silt west of Round, not closely assignable to Stage.

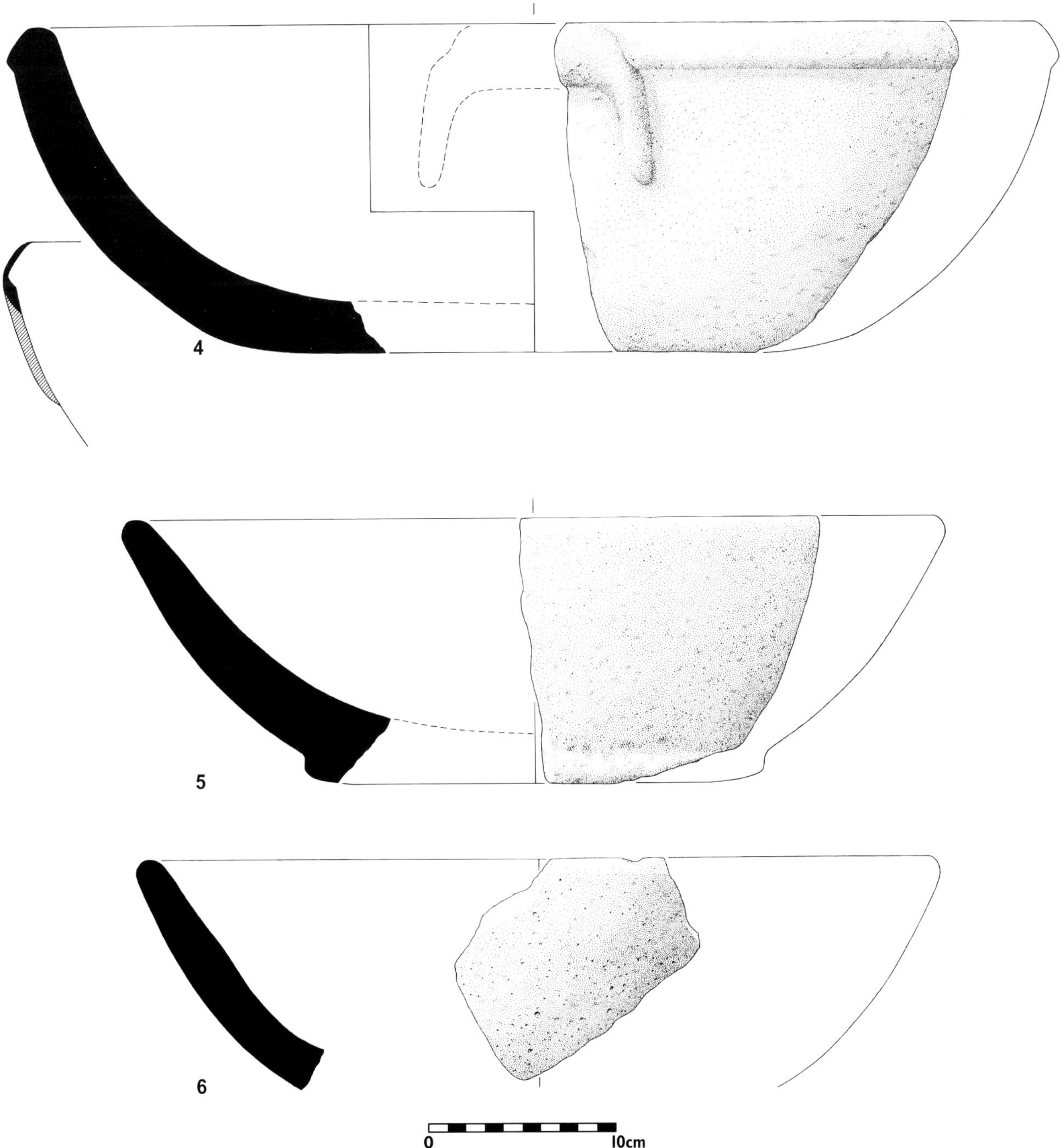

Fig 62: Trethurgy bowls in elvan S4-S6. Drawing S Morris. Scale 1:3

The only other Trethurgy bowl fragment found was a featureless piece from [808] soil between House Z1 and Z2.

A large number of the pieces found were substantial chunks with handles or other features. It is unclear whether this was due to retrieval methods, smaller fragments not being distinguished among rubble, or the retention on site of larger fragments because of their potential usefulness as building or packing stones. A disproportionate five out of 12 fragments had handles, suggesting that these were relevant either to retention or to recognition.

6.2.2 Cornish mortars

Four examples were found, together with an unfinished piece: all were of elvan. Cornish mortars are smaller in size than Trethurgy bowls, about 0.18m to 0.28m internally, have thicker walls in proportion to their size, and more complex rims. The form of these rims and the occasional survival of a single spout indicate that these mortars originated as copies of pottery mortaria. All interiors are worn smooth.

Fig 63

S7 Simple rim with external chamfer, footring, and grooved spout, internal diameter 0.25m. Sufficient survives for the presence of a single spout to be certain: a fragment from Kerris Vean with a single spout was reconstructed by Borlase (1872, 177) as a bowl with two opposed handles. Joining fragments from Stage 6 [932] lower midden Structure U and [800] soil over U.

S8 Rounded projecting rim which expands as though towards a spout before the break, internal diameter 0.26m. Exterior only worked smooth on upper part — a feature noted consistently on Purbeck marble mortaria (Beavis 1970). From topsoil (mechanical stripping).

S9 Straight-sided projecting rim with pronounced groove on its top, internal diameter 0.18m. From Stages 2/4 [567] secondary silt near Entrance terminal.

S10 Rounded projecting rim, internal diameter 0.27m. From [800] soil over U.

Fig 64

S11 Unfinished example; outline of a flat-topped rim and spout has been worked on the top of the stone by a square-ended chisel *c* 7mm wide; the exterior is also partly worked by a similar chisel. Broken along flaw in rock before completion. From [11] soil over D and E.

6.2.3 Trough

S12 Part of unfinished rectangular trough (not illustrated), 0.17m by at least 0.21m and 0.7m deep internally. Worked from an elvan boulder, exterior

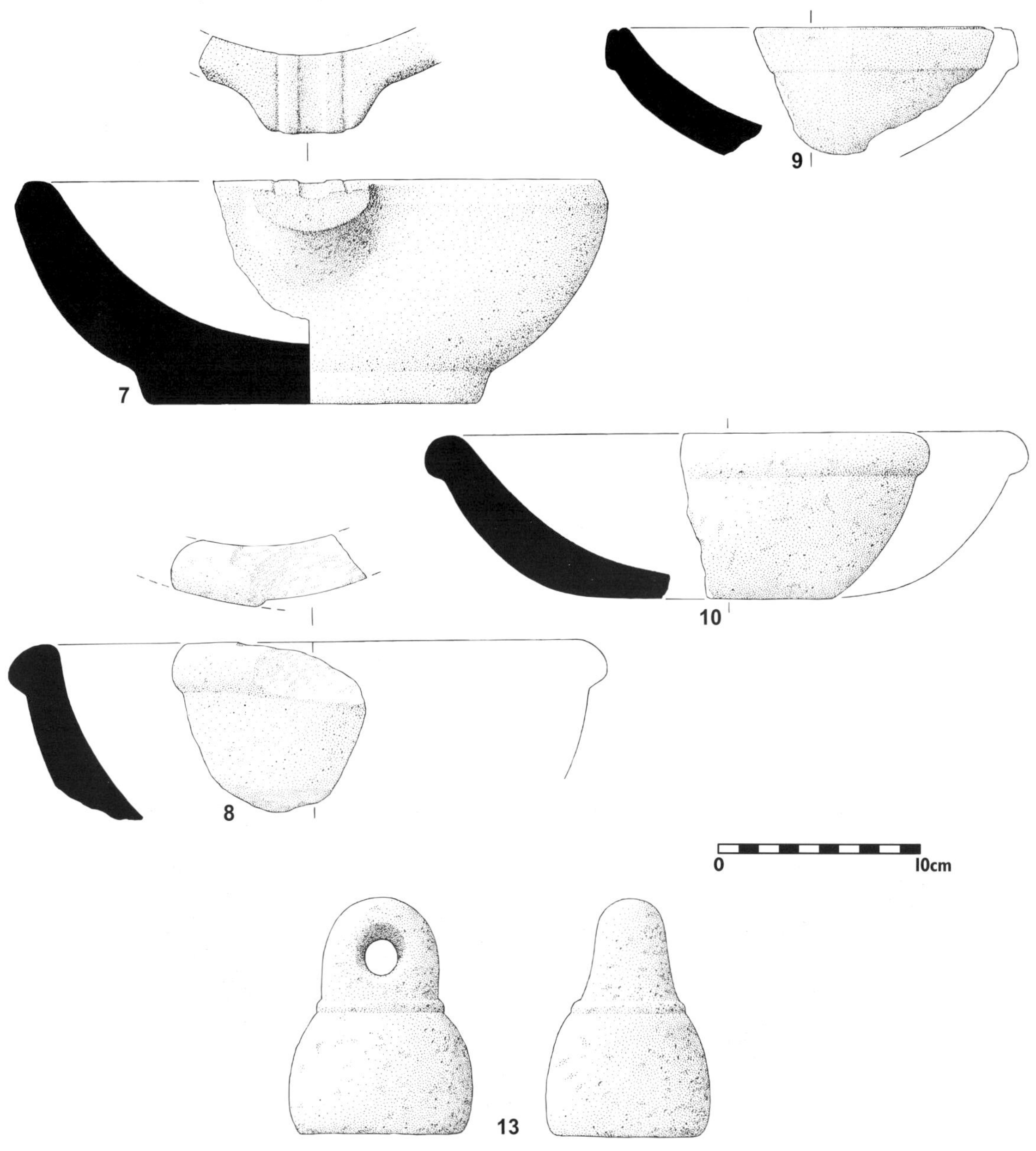

Fig 63: Cornish mortars in elvan, weight in kaolinized granite. Drawing S Morris. Scale 1:3

roughly pecked; the interior has long diagonal striations, possibly chisel marks. Split along line of weakness in the rock during manufacture. From Stage 10 [545], Structure V3.

The function of this trough is not known. It may have been intended as a 'trough quern', a variant of saddle quern with the interior lowered to prevent spillage which has been identified by Ashbee (1996, 106) at Halangy Down, St Mary's, Isles of Scilly.

6.2.4 Trethurgy bowls, Cornish mortars, and a tradition of stone artefact production

Mortaria of elvan and greisen have frequently been found on Cornish sites. A summary of those then known was published by Hirst (1936) but no further study had been carried out by 1973, the year in which Trethurgy was excavated. The variety of mortaria and other worked stone found at the site prompted a review by the writer (Quinnell 1993a) which identified

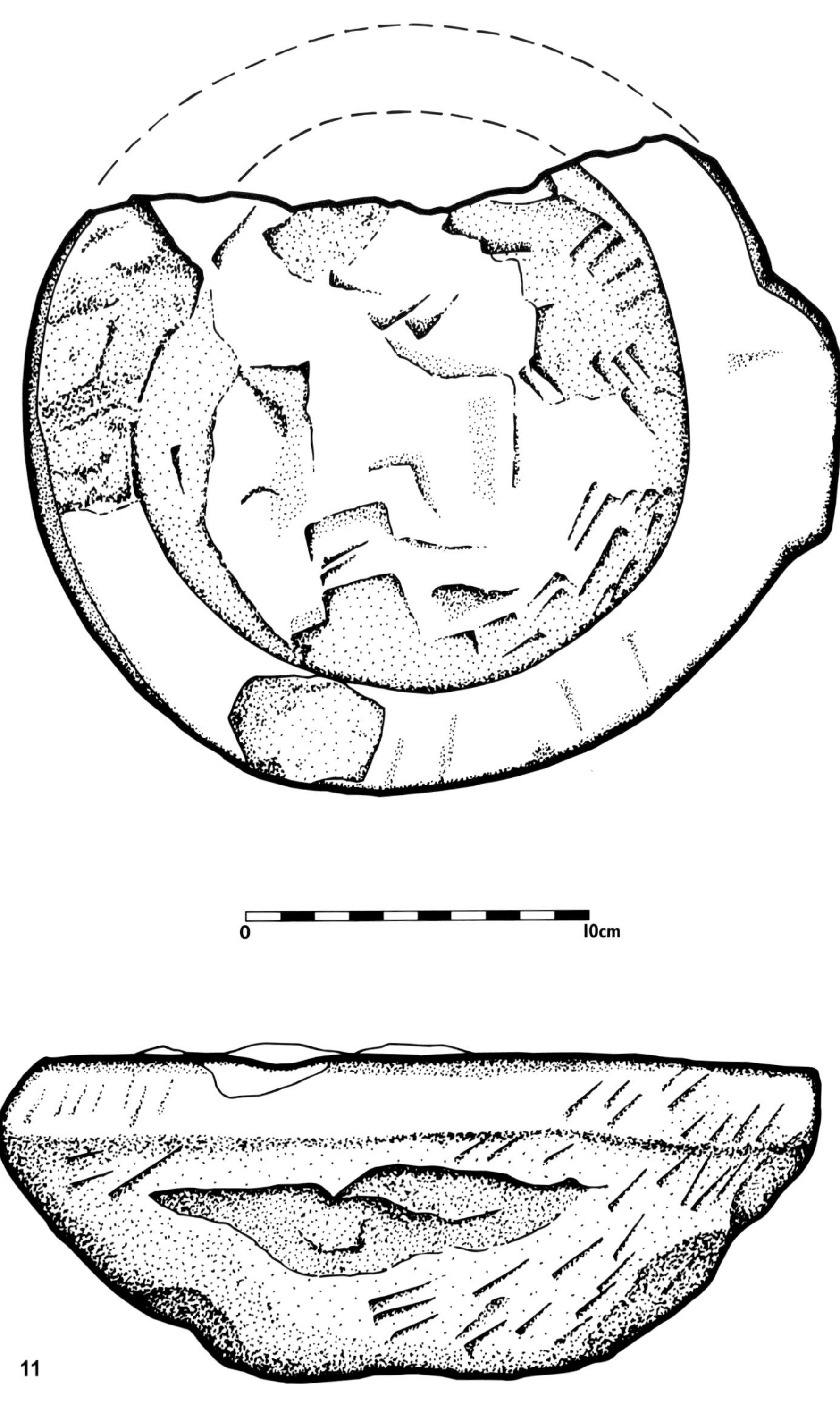

Fig 64: Unfinished elvan mortar S11. Drawing C Thorpe. Scale 1:2

Pl 46: Trethurgy bowl from Calartha, St Just. Scale in cms. Photo: Peter Brierley

a distinctive tradition of stone artefact production in Cornwall during the Roman period and the immediate Post-Roman centuries. This review included a gazetteer of all known Trethurgy bowls and Cornish mortars and supplies the references to examples referred to below. The only significant addition to those in the gazetteer is the handled rim fragment in elvan from the temple complex at Lydney (Casey and Hoffman 1999, fig 22, no 43).

The Trethurgy bowls from the eponymous site have a diameter of c 0.4m to 0.5m and four have distinctive handles carved in low relief. The date of their deposition as broken fragments ranges from the 4th to the 6th centuries. A fragment in greisen from Grambla, Wendron, had part of a handle and came from a bowl **c** 0.5m in diameter (C Saunders pers comm). A virtually complete greisen example, 0.53m in diameter with two opposing handles, was found at Richborough during the 19th century. It has been redrawn here (Fig 66) from the original publication (Roach Smith 1850, 104). A slight variant on the handle form occurs in a surface find from Calartha, St Just (Pl 46). As the diameter of these Trethurgy bowls is larger than of Cornish mortars, two fragments in greisen from Porthmeor, Zennor, may be assigned to this type. However a similar handle survives on half of a greisen bowl only 0.24m in diameter from St Agnes in the Isles of Scilly. The dates of the bowls from other sites are consistent, in so far as they are known, with the 4th to 6th-century range of the Trethurgy

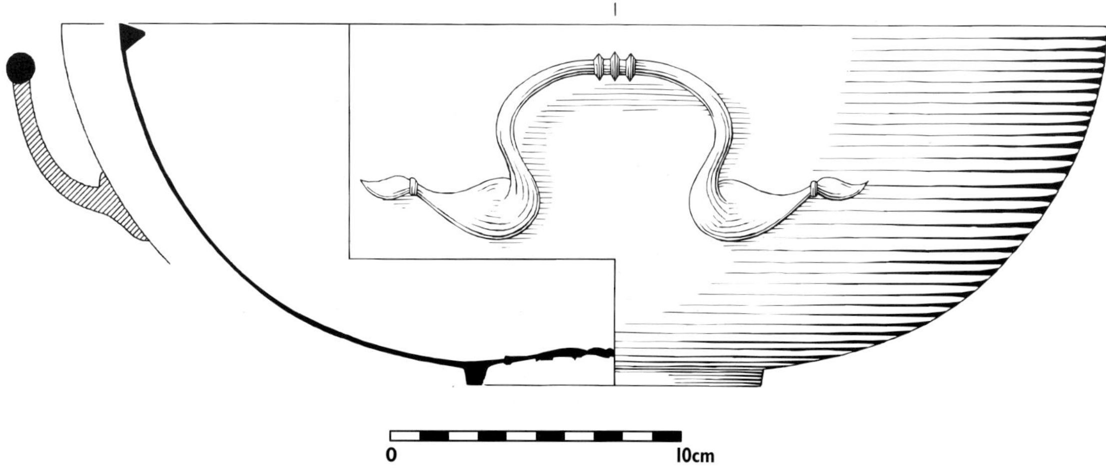

Fig 65: Bronze bowl from Nijmegen (after Mutz 1972), a possible prototype for the Trethurgy bowls. Drawing S Morris. Scale 1:3

deposition contexts. As the Trethurgy examples are all broken and redeposited — perhaps long after their original manufacture, the date range may tentatively be extended to begin during the, perhaps later, 3rd century. Their absence from the wide collection of finds at Carvossa, where occupation ended in the later 3rd century (Carlyon 1987), may support this late date.

The handles appear to be skeuomorphs of metal prototypes; while these project just far enough to provide some hand-hold, a functional handle developed as a separate local tradition might be expected to be more substantial. Metal prototypes may be found in the range of bronze bowls with fixed, upward projecting, handles known across northern Europe; an example from the Rhineland is shown in

Pl 47: Tin bowl from Treloy, side view. Scale in cms. Photo: Peter Brierley

Pl 48: Tin bowl from Treloy, view from above to show flat-topped handles. Scale in cms. Photo: Peter Brierley

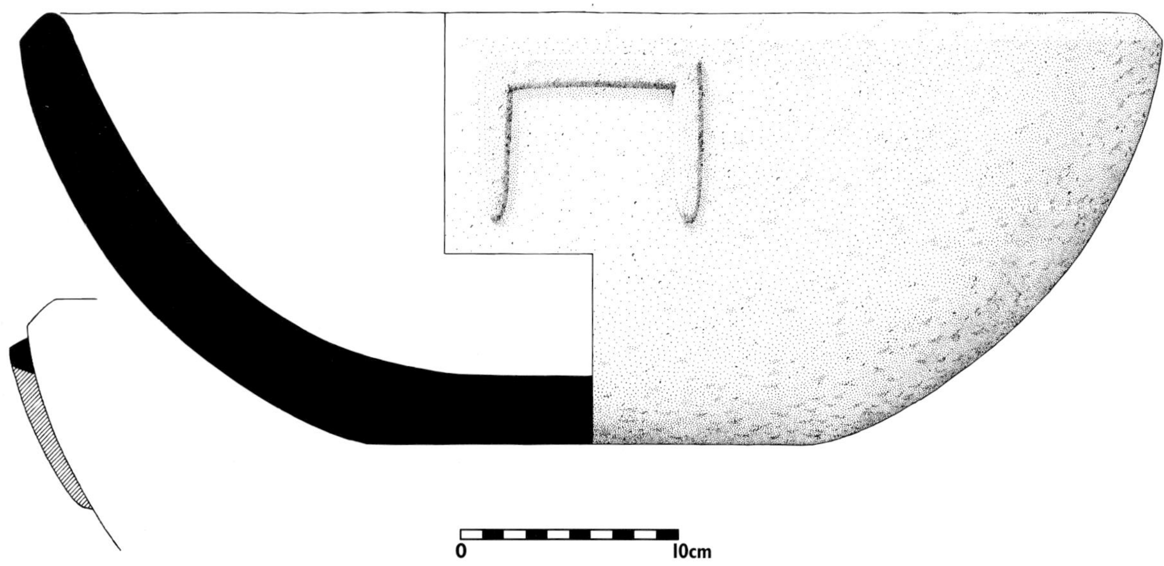

Fig 66: Trethurgy bowl in greisen from Richborough. Drawing S Morris (after Roach Smith 1850). Scale 1:3

Figure 65. Bronze vessels, apart from those used for cooking, are sparse in Britain. Eggers' (1966) survey shows only one, no 99 in the British Museum, with a generally comparable handle, and that one is both fragmentary and uncontexted. No pewter vessels with similar handles are recorded, but the Treloy tin bowl provide a remarkable comparison (Pls 47, 48) for the Trethurgy bowl handles. The Treloy tin bowl was found in 1830, apparently in association with a 3rd or 4th-century brooch in a tin working in St Columb Minor (Henwood 1874, 221; Penhallurick 1986, 200-2); it is now in the Royal Cornwall Museum. It is 0.35m in diameter. Its rim has been strengthened by rolling outwards, with handles soldered on to the rim top. This strengthened rim forms the securest position for the soldered handles. These project further than those on Trethurgy bowls and act as functional handles but their shape is very similar. The Treloy bowl appears so far to be an unique survival, but there are countless records of metal finds from tin working being smelted down (Penhallurick 1986, *passim*). If the association with the brooch date is accepted, the Treloy bowl dates to the later Roman period; it fits well within the wide range of British pewter and tin vessels which are generally of 3rd of 4th-century date (Wedlake 1958, 85 and gazetteer). Vessels such as the Treloy bowl may well have provided the prototype for the skeuomorphic handles on the Trethurgy bowls. It is however unclear whether the Treloy handles were entirely a functional development or were influenced by the form of handles on bronze bowls.

Cornish mortars are now known from at least 27 locations in Cornwall and three in Devon (Quinnell 1993a); some of the Cornish sites produced multiple finds and most sites of the Roman period in the county have produced at least one. Cornish mortars appear to copy pottery mortaria which were introduced into Cornwall by the Roman army and are found on sites occupied during the late 1st and early 2nd centuries, for example at Carvossa (Hartley 1987). Thereafter pottery mortaria are rare in the county. The presence of a Cornish mortar at Trevisker, probably abandoned sometime early in the 2nd century, suggests that stone copies had begun to be made by this date. Examples with elaborate grooved and beaded rims, which copy pottery mortaria, are early in the sequence from late 1st to early 3rd centuries. Simple rounded and chamfered rims are later, late 3rd through to 5th or 6th centuries. The Trethurgy examples fit well into this sequence. Bowl S9, with a pronounced rim groove, came from secondary Ditch silt [567], predating *c* AD 325 on the suggested Stage dating. The only other example with a good context was S7, with a simple chamfered rim, which came from midden [932/801], with a suggested Stage 6 dating of AD 375-400.

The regular adaption of mortaria from pottery to stone appears to be a feature of South West Britain. In Somerset, Ham Hill stone was occasionally used, at Catsgore (Leech 1982, 129) and Bradley Hill (Leech 1981, fig 28). A good copy with a spout in a red sandstone from South Somerset comes from a late 2nd-century context in Exeter (Holbrook and Bidwell 1991, fig 133, no 1). In Dorset, Purbeck marble mortaria were produced on a large scale (Eldridge 1978) and Burr Stone was also used (Beavis 1970). In both Cornwall and Dorset the development of stone mortaria may be connected to the unsuitability of the local potting clays. In Wales, by contrast, despite the presence of suitable rock, only occasional crude examples are found, eg at Caerau, Caern (O'Neil 1936, fig 7) and at Stackpole Warren, Dyfed (Benson *et al* 1990, 228).

The wear on both Trethurgy bowls and Cornish mortars produced smooth, and sometimes thinned, internal surfaces. Both types appear therefore to have been used for a process, presumably in food preparation, which involved a regular grinding motion, rather than pounding which leaves the surface rougher. No obvious implements — and pestles can be used for grinding — have been identified. If such implements were made of wood, long periods of usage are implied.

The production of stone artefacts was probably generally carried out on settlement sites, as indicated by the unfinished S11 Cornish mortar. However the review (Quinnell 1993a) indicated that greisen from the Tregonning area was extensively used and it is possible that more specialised production sites remain to be located. The inventive potential of this stone artefact production is further indicated by the skeuomorphic style of weight S13 (below) and other examples extending the range may be expected to be identified in the future. A greisen toggle is among the unpublished material from Grambla (C Saunders pers comm). Production appears to have been concerned very much with local consumption. Both greisen and elvan artefacts occur principally in Cornwall. While occasional examples are found in Devon, at Richborough (Fig 66) and in London, where a variant of a Trethurgy bowl with four projecting lugs is known from Pudding Lane, and more recently at Lydney, these are few compared to the quantity of Purbeck marble mortars found away from Dorset (Eldridge 1978) and are probably to be explained as incidental to trade in other items.

6.3 Weight

Fig 63

S13 Carefully worked weight (Pls 49, 50) of fine-grained kaolinised granite, base oval and slightly concave, roll around the neck, suspension loop with hour-glass type perforation and some wear; kaolinisation makes the granite relatively easy to work. Weight 882g. From [294], infill of House A1b hearth pit, Stage 4.

S13 is probably a mensuration weight as its elaborate shape indicates a more sophisticated purpose than controlling thatch or looms. No close parallels for its form are known but about a dozen carefully worked suspension weights of different shapes have been recorded from Cornwall, some from Roman contexts. A catalogue, with extensive illustrations, has now been published (Quinnell 1993a) and the weights discussed as part of the distinctive Roman-period Cornish tradition of stone artefact production which produced Trethurgy bowls and Cornish mortaria. Table 6.1 is reproduced from this article, with several additions which have since been found or recognised. The form of S13 is remarkably similar, though smaller in size, to that of some Roman bells from Usk (eg Manning 1995, fig 20, nos 4a-c). It may be regarded as a skeuomorph, in the same tradition of Cornish stone carving as the handles on the Trethurgy bowls. S22 (Section 6.7) appears to be a weight broken in manufacture and then used as a whetstone.

On the suggested Stage 4 dating the Trethurgy weight was deposited in the earlier 4th century. (S22,

Pl 49: Stone weight S13 side view. Scale in cms. Photo: Peter Brierley

Pl 50: Stone weight S13 face view. Scale in cms. Photo: Peter Brierley

	Weight (g)	Roman pound 327.45g	Celtic pound 309g	Celtic pound 638g
Gwithian	375+	-	-	-
Porthmeor	383	1.2	1.3	0.6
Killigrew S1	406	1.2	1.3	0.6
Killigrew S2	838	2.6	2.7	1.3
Reawla	680+	-	-	-
Trethurgy	882	2.7	2.9	1.4
Tregerthen 1	1106	3.4	3.6	1.7
Castle-an-Dinas 1	1370	4.2	4.2	2.2
Chysauster	1700+	-	-	-
Unlocated	1716	5.3	5.6	2.7
Bosence 1	1846	5.7	6.0	3.0
Tregerthen 2	1937	5.9	6.3	3.0
St Ives	2504	7.7	8.1	3.9
Bosence 2	6390	19.6	20.7	10.1
Castle-an-Dinas 2	7980	24.5	25.8	12.5

Table 6.1: Cornish stone weights as multiples of suggested Roman and Celtic standards: + indicates a broken weight. (For additions to the original table, Gwithian and Killigrew S1 and S2, see Quinnell 1993b, 45-6 and Quinnell forthcoming b respectively)

the possible roughout weight from Trethurgy used as a whetstone, was from a Stage 9 context.) All the other weights which have good excavated contexts belong to the 3rd or 4th centuries AD, with the exception of Gwithian for which a date range of 5th to 8th centuries is suggested (Quinnell 1993b). Nothing similar appears to be known from the Medieval or later periods.

These weights are unparalleled in Roman Britain. They may have been used with a balance, more likely as counterpoise weights for a steelyard beam. Weights in the Roman period may be made of lead, copper alloy, or stone. Balance weights were usually for small quantities, ounces, multiples of ounces or pounds, any rate as represented in Britain; a half ounce weight of this class was found at Nanstallon (Fox and Ravenhill 1972, 94, fig 18). Counterpoise weights usually have hooks, either in the metal of which they are made or inserted with lead fixing into the top of stone; the only weight of the latter type found in Cornwall is Killigrew S1 (Quinnell forthcoming b). A possible Roman-period lead weight from Maen Castle (Herring 1994, fig 10) is the only published example in metal from the county. A definite Roman lead weight, moulded around an iron core, has recently been excavated from a 4th-century AD context at Atlantic Road, Newquay (Quinnell forthcoming c) and another similar weight was found during ploughing together with a bronze steelyard in 1962 at Trenook Farm, Lelant (Royal Cornwall Museum 1990/102).

The use of stone weights for measurement is now established for the Iron Age of Southern Britain, but these either have inserted hooks or suspension knobs. Such weights have been discussed in relation to the large group from Danebury by Brown (1984). No such Iron Age weights have yet been recorded from Cornwall and a mensuration tradition surviving from the local Iron Age seems unlikely as the Roman-period weights have the unusual feature of integral stone suspension loops. The Cornish stone weights appear to be a local development, utilizing the skills which had evolved in the later Roman period for crafting stone artefacts and adapting weights with inserted metal hooks to those made entirely of stone. If the interpretation of these weights for mensuration is correct, it indicates the need for accurate records of commodities, whether for taxation or for exchange.

The pound (of 12 ounces) in use in the Roman Empire was 327.45g (*Oxford Classical Dictionary*), roughly three-quarters the modern pound of 457g. Surviving weights, even when marked with their intended value, rarely seem to have been accurate; that marked S (emis) or half pound from Richborough weighs 190.25g instead of 164g (Henderson 1949, 131). Intentional inaccuracy is hard to disentangle from weight change caused by wear, through metal corrosion or surface alteration of stone. The question of standards is further complicated by the likelihood that there were two different Celtic pounds in use. One of 309g was argued by Smith (1905) from British and German finds, the second of 638g put forward by Schwartz (1964) using data from Switzerland and adjacent areas (Quinnell 1993b for further discussion). The weights in Table 6.1 have been expressed as multiples of the Roman and the two Celtic pounds but no attempt has been made to fit the data to the

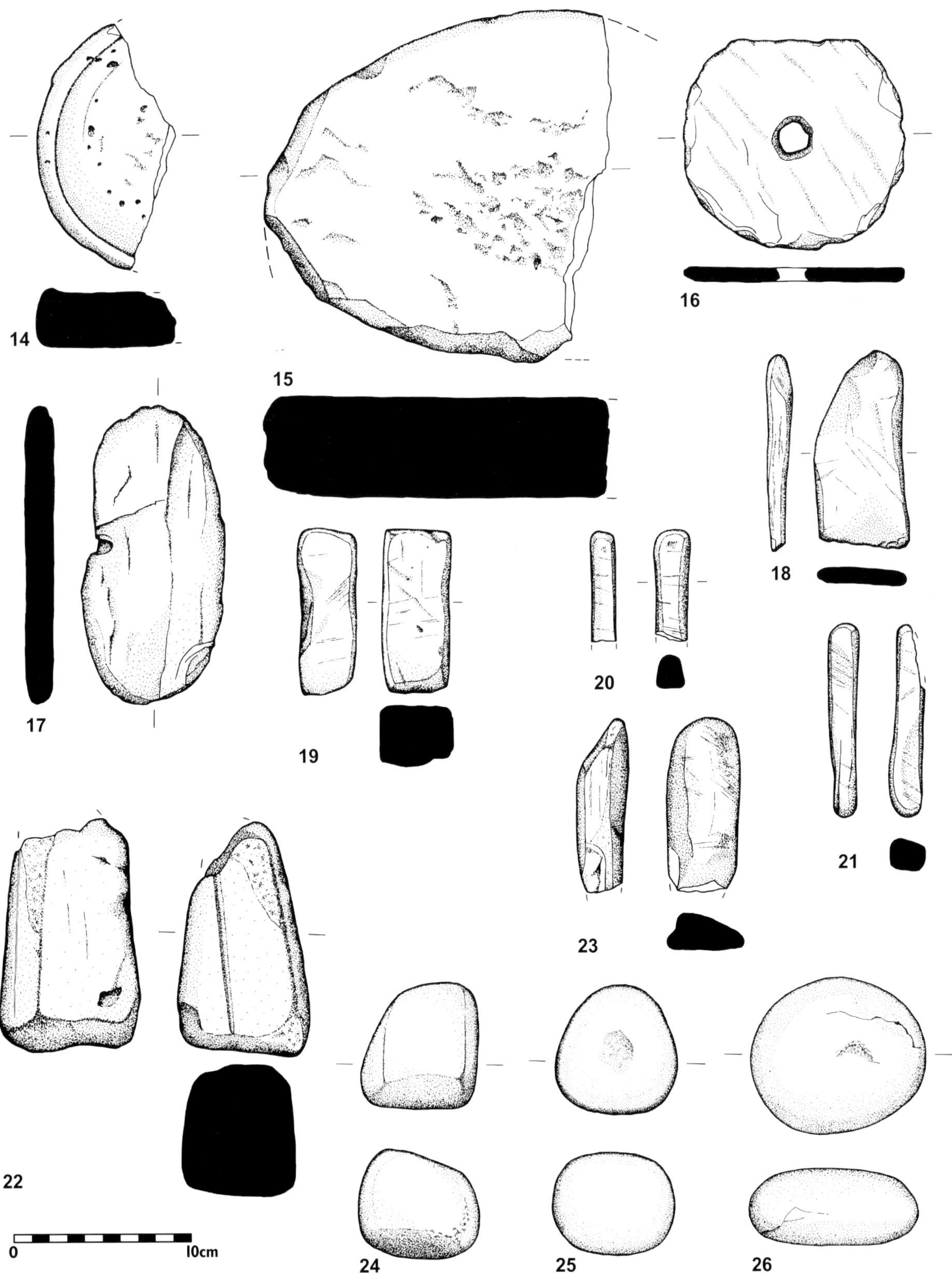

Fig 67: Stone mould S14; mould cover S15; slate disc S16; net sinker S17; whetstones S18-23, S22 made on a broken weight; rubbing stones S24-26. Drawing C Thorpe. Scale 1:3

suggested standards by statistical presentation because of the small size of the sample and the inherent inaccuracies of the measured weights as they survive.

6.4 Mould and mould cover

Fig 67

S14 Part of circular mould, in greisen almost certainly from Tregonning. Originally 140mm in diameter, with rim around flat central surface. Roughly worked, except for the smooth central surface. Some heat discolouration. Considerable wear on the broken edge. Possibly used with a cover for casting a flat circular plate. Stage 8 [555] surface outside Structure V2.

One part of a two piece greisen mould for a penannular brooch (Saunders and Harris 1982, fig 10, no 8) was found in the secondary ditch silt at Castle Gotha and a broken greisen piece (*ibid*, fig 10, no 9), possibly a mould for a flat rectangular plate, came from the earliest interior occupation levels. A complete two-piece greisen mould for a late-Roman pewter dish was found by William Borlase at Leswyn, St Just (Brown 1970). The only other moulds from the Roman period in Cornwall so far recognised are a granite fragment for a dish from Halangy Down, St Mary's, Isles of Scilly (Ashbee 1996, 102-3, fig 49) and an unpublished similar piece in elvan from Penhale Round (Nowakowski 1998, 5.2.10).

S15 Part of a flat slab *c* 400mm diameter, 57mm thick. One edge is evenly worked and appears to be an arc of a circle *c* 400mm in diameter; the second edge is rougher, the circular slab, after breakage, having been converted into an ellipse. One flat face has been worked very smooth and heat discolouration is detectable beneath this. S15 is interpreted as a mould cover, first circular and then reworked to an elliptical shape. From Stage 8 [175], patching of paving [8], [12].

Dr R T Taylor provides the following comments: 'This is probably a weathered mica lampropyre. The rock consists of large plates 1.2mm across of bleached biotite or related dark mica in a medium-grained matrix of soft (altered) pinkish feldspar and finer grained dark minerals (mica, chlorite). A little quartz is also present. Lamprophyres occur as scattered dykes in the Truro/Falmouth area and in the Newquay area. Unfortunately the available descriptions are difficult to match exactly with S15. The nearest continental source for such a rock would probably be Brittany. I have examined the dark wavy-looking patches of the flat surface under a binocular microscope. They have a shiny globular appearance in places and, although they are quite soft and not vitreous, could be the result of partial fusion.'

The closest parallel from Cornwall is the oval mould cover, found together with its mould, at Castle Pencaire, Germoe *c* 1853 (Rundle 1887, 361). This mould and cover, of Tregonning greisen, would have produced a metal plate 150mm by 110mm. The general shape and cross-section of the cover, although smaller and thinner, are very similar to S15. The Castle Pencaire mould and cover are not directly datable, but a very similar pair have been found in excavations at Dinorben hillfort, Clwyd, datable to the 4th century AD (Guilbert 1979, 187). Part of a possible greisen mould cover, a fragment of an oval *c* 140mm in diameter and 55mm thick comes from Carvossa (Carlyon 1987, fig 12, no 6).

6.5 Slate discs

Fig 67

S16 Thin disc of local slate from Meadfoot Beds, 130mm across with straight section worked on one side and irregularly chipped and worn central hole. Stage 8 [28], paving Structure T5. A further six discs, unperforated, were found, whole or fragmentary, from Stage 5+ [8], Stage 7+ [520], Stage 9 [723], [785] soil over Y, and ploughsoil; their sizes vary from 80mm to 120mm.

The usual interpretation of these discs is as pot lids; they occur frequently in pre-Roman Iron Age contexts eg The Rumps (Brooks 1974, fig 33) and on sites of the earlier Roman period as Castle Gotha (Saunders and Harris 1982, fig 11) and St Mawgan-in-Pyder (Threipland 1956, fig 37). They appear less common on later Roman sites, being absent from Porthmeor for example (Hirst 1937). If the interpretation as pot lids is correct, there may be a relationship with the increase in size of jars; these discs are suitable for the smaller jars found most frequently in the early-Roman period (Section 5.6.3, Type 4 jars).

6.6 Net sinkers

Fig 67

S17 Pebble of local slate, with notch cut in one side. [11], soil over Structure E. A broken example came from [934]. Net sinkers of this type are still in use in Brittany.

6.7 Whetstones

A total of 26 were recovered, mostly elongated pebbles on which facets had been worn by use as sharpening stones. Some are of granite, most pebbles of rocks which occur locally, on the beach or on stream beds within a few kilometres of the site. Those worked to a definite shape, or on which wear has produced marked facets, have been illustrated.

Fig 67

S18 Fine-grained local Devonian mudstone pebble with flattened sharpening facets along both edges and on both faces; made on broken pebble. Stage 1 + [360] secondary silt in Ditch.

S19 Granite piece, ground into a neat rectangular shape, three of the four long facets very smooth from use as whetstone. Stage 9+ [523] soil over upper surface in Entrance terminals.

S20 Broken fine-grained quartzite pebble, ground to rectangular section; flattened sharpening facets along edges; faces glossy. Stage 8 [555] surface associated Structure V2.

S21 Pebble of altered volcanic ash; heavily worn facets on three faces. Broken. [800] soil over Structure U.

S22 Fine-grained granite, worked as rough-out for a weight and broken across shoulder; pecking has slightly dished base. Subsequently used as whetstone with two adjacent surfaces worn smooth, one with a narrow sharpening groove. Stage 9 [678] soil under paving [933], outside House X.

S23 Pebble of local Devonian sandstone with triangular section; facets worn smooth by use on all three faces. Stage 9 [77] upper infill of Structure G.

6.8 Rubbing and polishing stones

A total of 26 pebbles had detectable signs of wear from rubbing and polishing. They may be presumed to have been used for a variety of purposes such as food processing, leather working, and cloth finishing. No detailed studies appear to have been carried out on the kinds of wear these activities would leave on rocks of different kinds. In some cases a fine, almost mirror-like, gloss is present. Most pebbles are oval, regular in shape, 100mm to 120mm across, and of fine-grained sandstone or quartzite, although granite and elvan were also used. The illustrated examples were selected as they display very noticeable wear traces. The rubbing stones were scattered evenly through the site. Such stones are universally found on sites of the Roman period in Cornwall eg Porthmeor (Hirst 1937, 65), Porth Godrevy where a very good range is illustrated (Fowler 1962, fig 14), and Reawla (Quinnell 1992) with a recent, detailed, discussion.

Fig 67

S24 Pebble of granite porphyry. Ground to a roughly cuboid shape with wear producing a very smooth surface on all faces. Stage 6 [932] lower midden Structure U.

S25 Pebble of fine-grained quartzite, ground to a curved triangular shape and worn to a high gloss all over. A small circular depression has been pecked in one face, perhaps to provide a grip. The high gloss on S25 and S26 is usually associated with the finishing of cloth. Stages 6-9 [863] House Z2 drain.

S26 Quartzite pebble worn to a very high gloss over almost all its surface; slight roughened patch for grip on both faces. Stage 9+ [723] collapse/soil over House Z2.

6.9 Spindle whorls of stone and pottery

Eight complete and four broken whorls were found; all the former are illustrated. Of these, eight were of various rocks and four of gabbroic pottery. In general, Roman-period spindle whorls in Cornwall are simple and undecorated compared to those of the Later Iron Age and 1st century AD; the rich decorated collection from St Mawgan-in-Pyder (Threipland, 1956, fig 38) compares sharply with Porthmeor where only one out

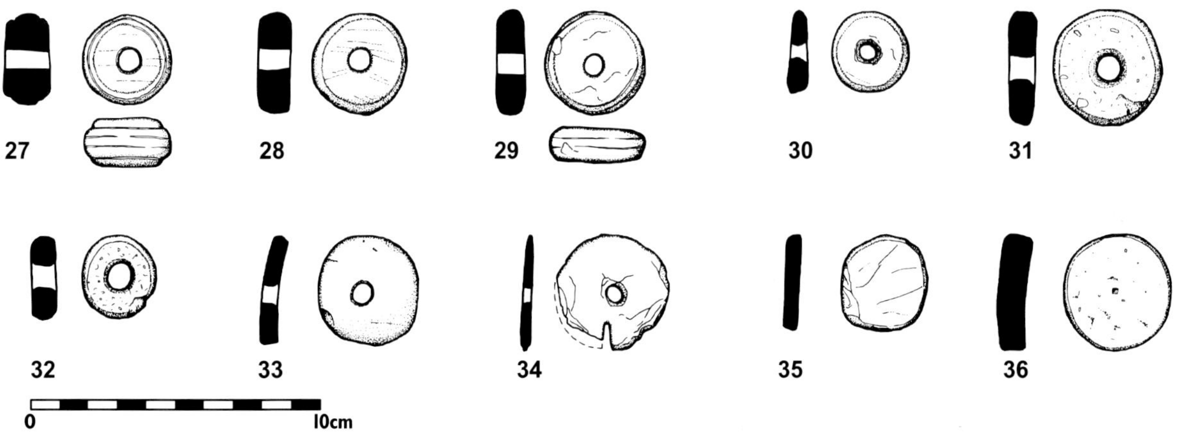

Fig 68: Spindle whorls and small discs. Drawing C Thorpe. Scale 2:5

of 29 was decorated (Hirst 1937, 63). Given the extent of the Trethurgy excavations, the number of whorls recovered appears small.

Fig 68

S27 Kimmeridge shale, 29mm diameter, cylindrical bore. Two sharply incised grooves and two slighter ones around girth. Damaged, weight 18g+. On Stage 4 platform [36], contemporary House T3.

S28 Open-textured sandstone, probably New Red Sandstone from somewhere in the Midlands, 32mm across, cylindrical bore, much worn. Weight 22g. Stage 6-9 [863] House Z2 drain.

S29 Slate from local Meadfoot Beds, 35mm diameter, hour-glass bore, slight grooves around girth, worn. Weight 19.5g. [11], soil over D and E.

S30 Slate from local Meadfoot Beds, 26mm diameter, cylindrical bore, slightly worn. Weight 6.5g. [785] soil over Structure Y.

S31 Gabbroic pottery, 40mm diameter, hour-glass bore. Weight 15g. Stage 9 [77] upper fill Structure G. Fragment of similar pottery whorl from[780] spread Period 3 Enclosure Bank.

S32 Gabbroic pottery, 27mm diameter, cylindrical bore. Weight 6.5g. Soil over House X.

S33 Gabbroic pottery, 37mm diameter, hour-glass perforation. Unworn. Weight 11g. Stages 2-3 [436] House T2 floor.

S34 Slate from local Meadfoot Beds, 37mm diameter. Rough perforation and worked notch. Weight 6g. [723] soil/collapse House Z2. Fragments of whorls of similar slate from [11], Stage 9+ [723], and [800].

6.10 Small discs or counters of stone and pottery

One imperforate disc of slate, one of samian, and three of gabbroic pottery, one broken, were found. These may be counters for games or possibly for use in some tally system; wear around the edges indicates that they are not unfinished spindle whorls. A detailed discussion of function, including possible use as weights, has been published by PJ Woodward (in Woodward *et al* 1993, 190-4). Such discs are not common on Cornish Roman-period sites; two were found at St Mawgan-in-Pyder (Threipland 1956, fig 38) and a number at Porthmeor (Hirst 1937, 63).

Fig 68

S35 Slate from local Meadfoot Beds, sub-rectangular, 31mm diameter. [780] spread Period 3 Enclosure Bank beneath Structure Y.

S36 Gabbroic pottery, 38mm diameter; small square depression in centre of one face possibly left by compass used to mark out shape. Stage 9+ [523] upper surface over Ditch terminals. A similar disc of gabbroic pottery came from [723] and a broken one from [800]. A rough disc trimmed around the raised centre of a samian dish of Dr31 or similar form, with the position of the potter's stamp just discernible, from [800].

6.11 Shale bracelets and the use of shale

Fragments of nine shale bracelets were found. Shale bracelets, presumably from the Kimmeridge district of Dorset, are not common in Roman Cornwall. Other occurrences are at Carvossa (Irwin 1987, fig 14), Grambla (Saunders 1972, 52), Chysauster (Hencken 1933, 259), Tregilders (Trudgian 1977, fig 47) and Penhale Round (Quinnell 1998/9). Four of the nine fragments at Trethurgy were deposited in contexts which should belong to the 5th or 6th centuries, indicating that the use, if not the manufacture, of shale bracelets may have continued after the Roman period.

The only other shale artefact from the site was the spindle whorl S27. A shale spindle whorl with a very simple biconical shape was found at Reawla (Quinnell 1992, 109, S3). The presence of both bracelets and whorls in shale continue a tradition from the Iron Age as at Castle Dore (Radford 1951, 70). Coastal contact with Dorset which provided South-East Dorset BB1 pottery may be linked to the presence of shale.

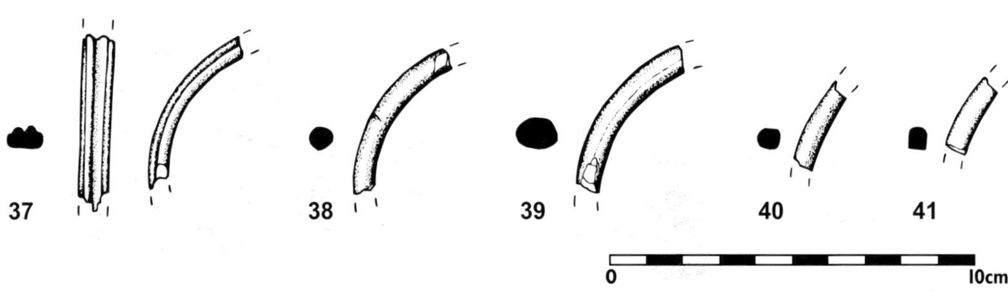

Fig 69: Shale bracelets. Drawing C Thorpe. Scale 1:2

Allason-Jones (1991, 271) comments on the large quantity of shale artefacts at Exeter which may be linked to the presence of this pottery, the predominant ware there in the 3rd and 4th centuries. The port site of Mount Batten, Plymouth (Cunliffe 1988, 72) has also produced shale including a roughout, suggesting artefacts may have been made there. However, even given the comparatively small amount of work carried out on Devon rural sites, shale objects of the Roman period appear rare in that county.

Fig 69

S37 Two fragments of the same bracelet, 80mm internal diameter, oval section, flattened facet on interior, deep central groove on exterior flanked by shallower grooves. [800] soil over Structure U.

S38 Pentangular cross-section, 70mm internal diameter. Stage 6 [801] upper midden Structure U.

S39 Flattened oval cross-section, 90mm internal diameter. [800] soil over Structure U. Fragment with similar cross-section but slightly smaller from Stage 6 [932] midden in U.

S40 Sub-rectangular cross-section, 90mm internal diameter. Stage 8 [555] surface outside Structure V2. Fragment of another bracelet from this context.

S41 Sub-rectangular cross-section, 100mm internal diameter. From Stage 9+ [723] soil/collapse House Z2. Fragment with similar cross-section but slightly smaller from Stage 5 [557] surface beneath Structure V, and another from Stage 9 [678] soil beneath paving in X.

6.12 Querns and mortars

6.12.1 Rotary querns *Henrietta Quinnell* and *Sue Watts* (text written 2001, revised 2003)

Nine upper and three lower stones were found, complete, or in fragments. All but two were of coarse-grained elvan. Rotary querns were introduced into Cornwall during the currency of South Western Decorated pottery and occur on sites such as Castle Dore (Radford 1951, 75) and the Rumps (Brooks 1974, 46, fig 37). The generally simple shapes in the

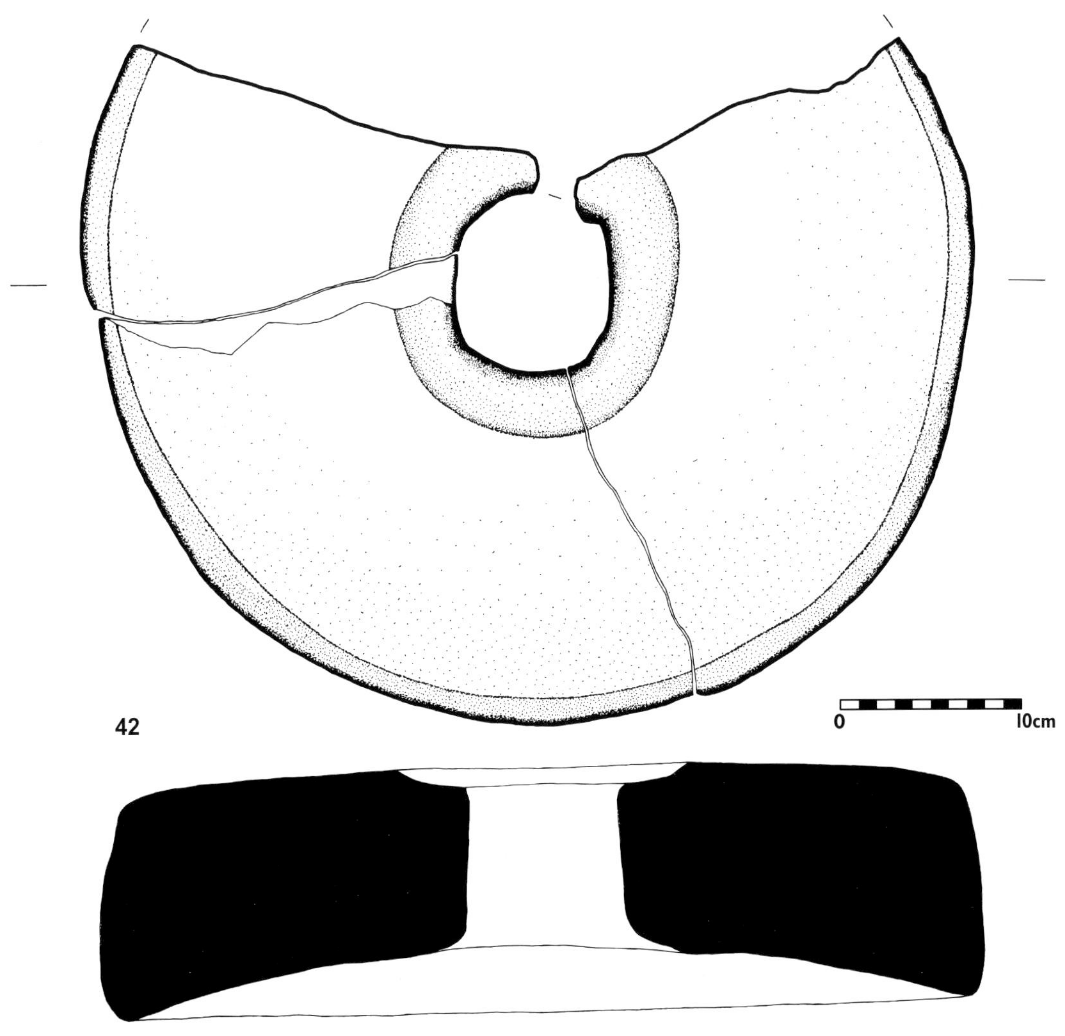

Fig 70: Upper rotary quern S42. Drawing C Thorpe. Scale 1:4

Roman period continue those current in the Later Iron Age, although a disc quern has been found at Penhale Round (Quinnell 1998/9). Rock available within a few kilometres was mostly used, generally granite or coarse-grained elvan. Greisen, either from Tregonning or St Austell, was the other rock often used. The use of Tregonning greisen presumably relates to the production of a range of artefacts in this rock, discussed above with reference to the Trethurgy bowls. If S49 is Tregonning greisen, its source was a distance of some 50km from the site, the furthest demonstrated for querns in Cornwall. Other greisen rotary querns come from Carn Euny (Christie 1978, 388) and Reawla (Quinnell 1992, 109), but as with S49, these can not be definitely sourced either to Tregonning or St Austell. The conglomerate S46 is the only quern of a non-Cornish rock so far recorded. Elvan was exploited for querns by the Roman army, evidenced at Nanstallon (Fox and Ravenhill 1972, fig 20, no 16), following the usual military practice of finding or

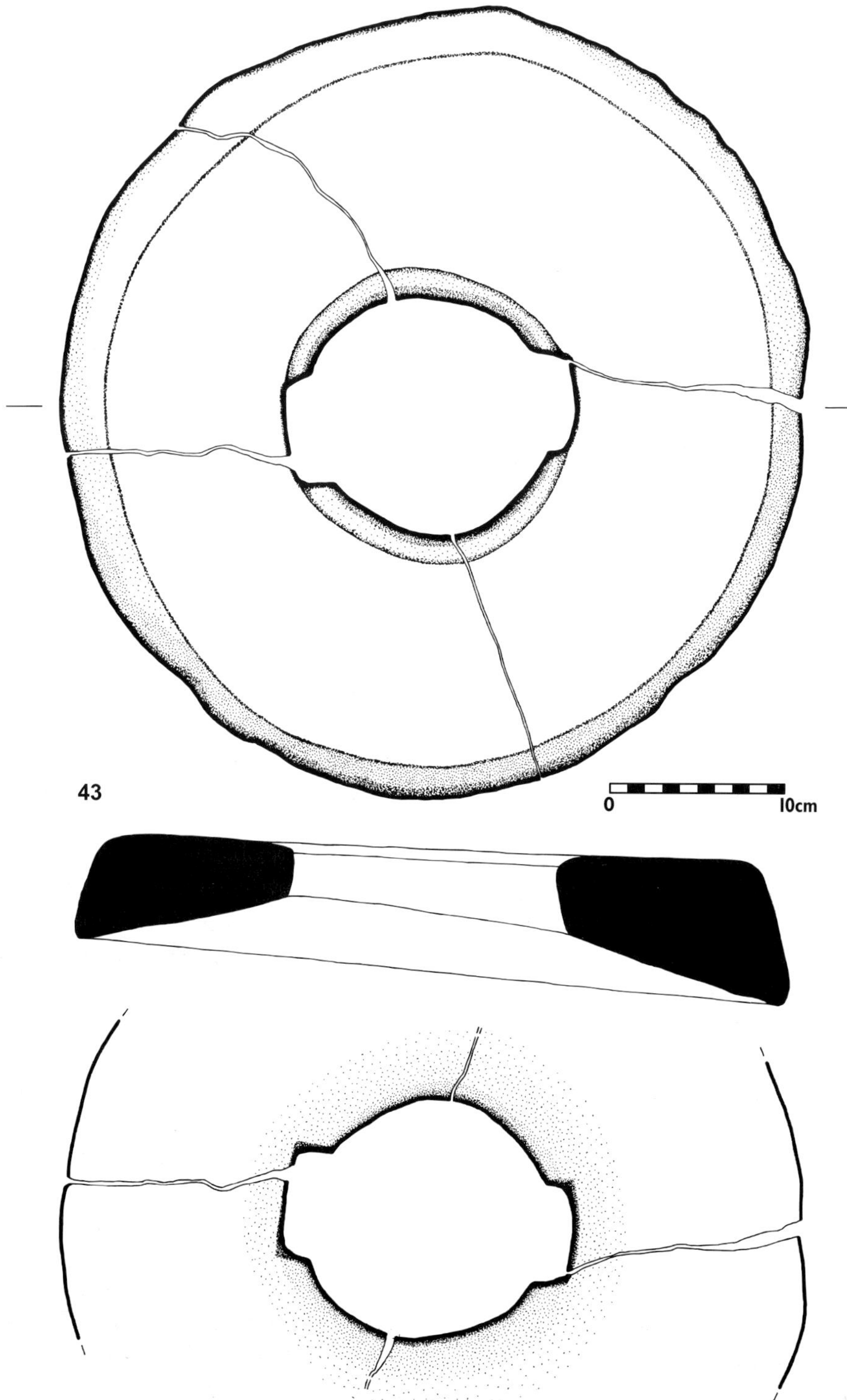

Fig 71 Upper rotary quern S43; lower view shows rynd chases in underside. Note that section goes through rynd and does not show shape of hopper. Drawing C Thorpe. Scale 1:4

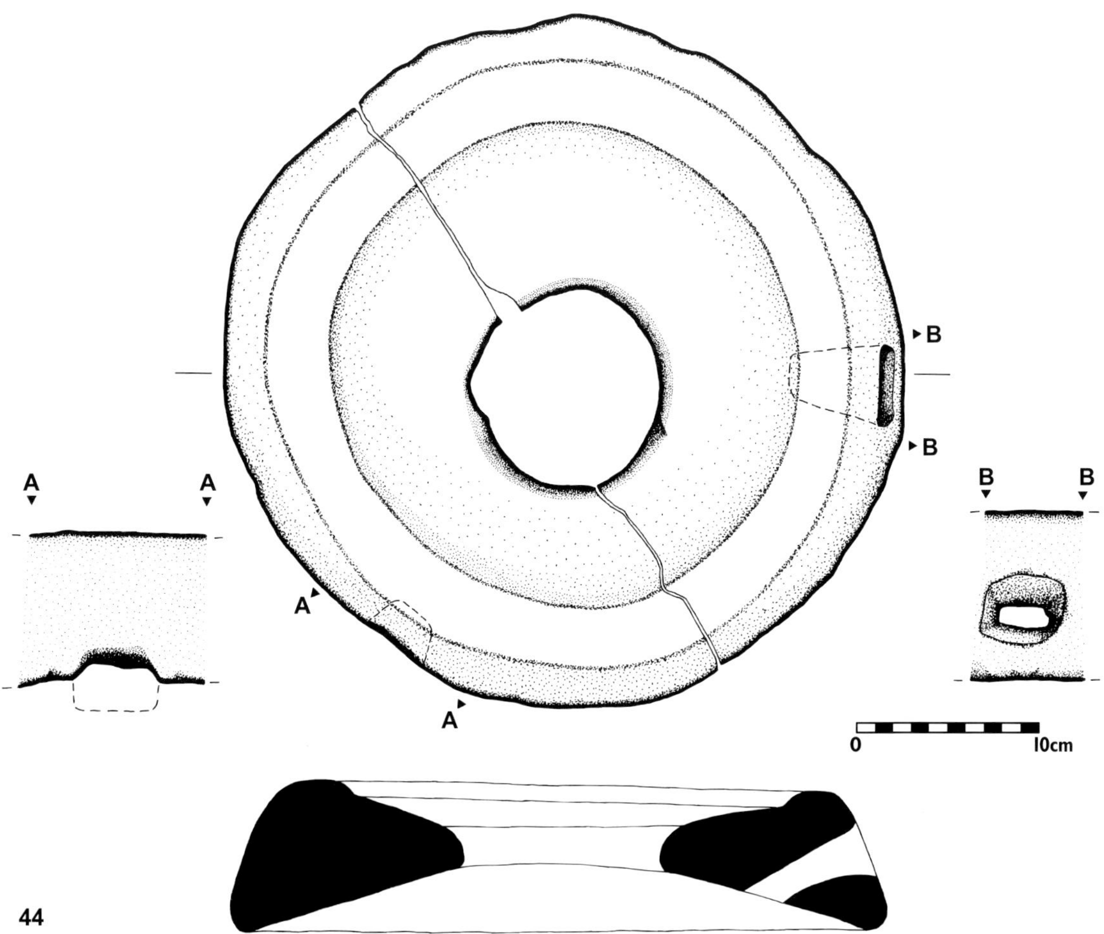

Fig 72: Upper rotary quern S44; A-A and B-B show parts of side of quern with handle sockets. Drawing C Thorpe. Scale 1:4

developing sources of supply locally. The choice of coarse-grained elvan at Trethurgy, where granite was available, emphasises the suitability of the rock, both for shaping and in use as querns. Its suitability for grinding relates to the quartz grains in the elvan which project from the fine-grained matrix; however the rock is soft and wears down quickly as the quartz grains gradually drop out, exposing fresh surface. As elvan naturally produces a myriad of cutting edges, it was not necessary to dress the grinding surfaces with a pattern of furrows, a practice often found on Roman querns. All of the stones have been used, shown by the concentric wear marks and/or glazing on the peripheries of the grinding surfaces.

Upper stones

Fig 70

S42 Part of upper stone, generally Roman in type, coarse-grained elvan, 490mm diameter, 125mm thick. Slight hopper around deep, regularly worked eye 85mm across. Its sub-rectangular shape might have held a fixture for a rynd. No handle socket in surviving parts. Concave grinding face. Fairly worn, broken across flaw in rock. Three joining fragments from Stage 6 [762] wall of Structure Y, [11] soil on scarped platform near Structure E and Stage 6 [255], backing to Structure G. Broken before the late 4th century.

Fig 71

S43 Upper stone of general Roman type, coarse-grained elvan, 420mm diameter, 80mm thick. Slight hopper runs up to the edge of the rynd sockets. The opposed rynd sockets show more clearly in the lower than the upper face either side of large (130mm) eye. No handle socket present. Unevenly worn concave grinding surface suggests that the stone may have been operated by a to-and-fro motion rather than complete rotation. Four joining fragments, their edges much abraded after breakage, two from extension of OLS [380] inside Round in R, others from Stage 6 [932] lower midden in Structure U and Stage 4-6 [808] soil between House Z1 and Z2. The pieces from[380] suggest S43 was broken early in the use of the Round, perhaps 2nd century.

Fig 72

S44 Upper stone, coarse-grained elvan, 370mm diameter, 95mm thick. Upper surface has ridge around large central hopper; eye 100mm across has no sockets for rynd but subrectangular shape may, as in S42, have held a fixture for this. Handle socket in side slopes obliquely inwards. Very heavy use has almost completely worn away one handle socket (A-A) and worn through end of a replacement (B-B). Concave grinding face. Two unabraded halves from [800] soil over Structure U and soil over Q. Undatable on context. The closest parallel to the ridge around the large central hopper is now in Abbey Gardens, Tresco (SMR PRN 7333); this has no definitive context on Tresco. However a quern from Danebury dating to the Middle Iron Age, although thicker, has a similar upper surface (Cunliffe 1984, fig 7.56, no 832).

Fig 73

S45 Half of upper stone, coarse grained elvan, 400mm diameter, 75mm thick. Upper surface has ridge around broad hopper. Eye 11mm across, with two generations of rynd chases in the lower surface; rynd chases in the underside of the stone are a Roman development and enabled the rynd to be tentered, taking the weight of the stone to alter the gap between the stones and so adjust the fineness of the meal. No handle mounting or socket survives. Groove around outer edge could have been for rope to hold handle although similar grooves occur on querns from Trevisker and Carn Euny which also have handle sockets (ApSimon and Greenfield 1972, fig 26B; Christie 1978, fig 49). Fairly worn. Concave grinding surface. Stage 8/9 [34] infill between House A2 and A3. Broken before *c* AD 500.

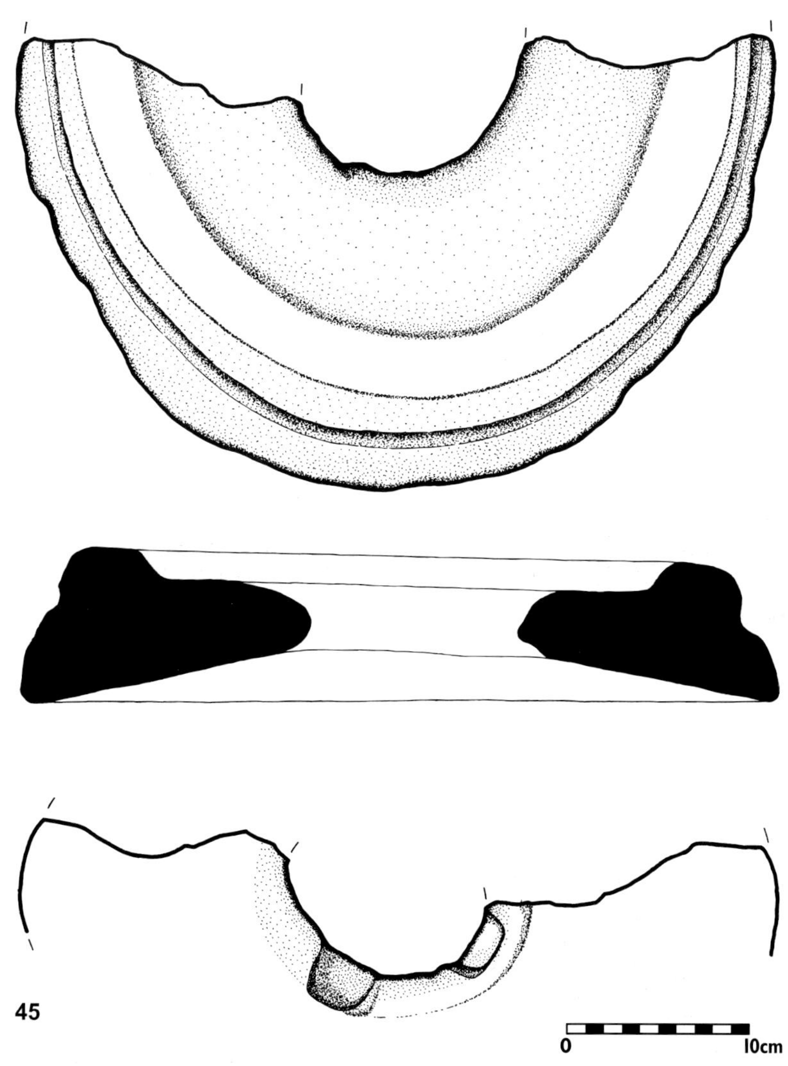

Fig 73: Upper rotary quern S45; lower view shows rynd chases in underside. Drawing C Thorpe. Scale 1:4

Fig 74

S46 Half of well-made upper stone, conglomerate, 390mm diameter, 45mm thick increasing to 95mm in collar forming hopper around the eye; eye 45mm across, possible part of socket for rynd truncated by fracture. No handle socket surviving. Grinding face slightly dished becoming more pronounced towards the eye, worn with no evidence of dressing. Technically quartz litharenite; clasts not sufficiently distinct to indicate a definite source. Possibly Carboniferous; rocks which are generally similar occur in the Pennant Sandstone Formation of the South Wales Coalfield (Drs B Selwood and M Thomas, University of Exeter, pers comm). Stage 5 [65] House A2. Broken by the early 4th century.

The collared shape of S46 is unique to Trethurgy and, so far, to Cornwall, appropriate for an imported piece. Curwen (1937, 44) first identified querns such as S46 as of 'projecting hopper type', dating these to the later Romano-British period. A 3rd to 4th-century date is supported by more recent work: Camerton 3rd-century examples (Wedlake 1958, 244), Vindolanda 3rd and 4th centuries (Welfare 1985), Ravenglass, Cumbria, 4th century (Potter 1979, 94-5), and Portchester 4th century and later (Cunliffe 1975, fig 144).

S49 Part of upper stone, greisen, 440mm diameter, 105mm thick. Much of upper surface dished to form hopper; no detectable rynd socket. Steeply sloping grinding face. Worn after breakage. Possibly sourced either to Tregonning or St Austell but not distinctively like either. Stage 6 [801] upper midden in Structure U.

Other upper querns fragments, all coarse-grained elvan (not illustrated): (1) upper stone as S45, Stage 9 [256] infill of Structure G (2) upper stone as S45, Stage 6 [801] upper midden in Structure U (3) upper stone, simple rounded profile, fragments from Stage 4 [429] soil on platform [13], Stage 4 [949] House Z1 paving, and Stage 2 [432B] posthole in R.

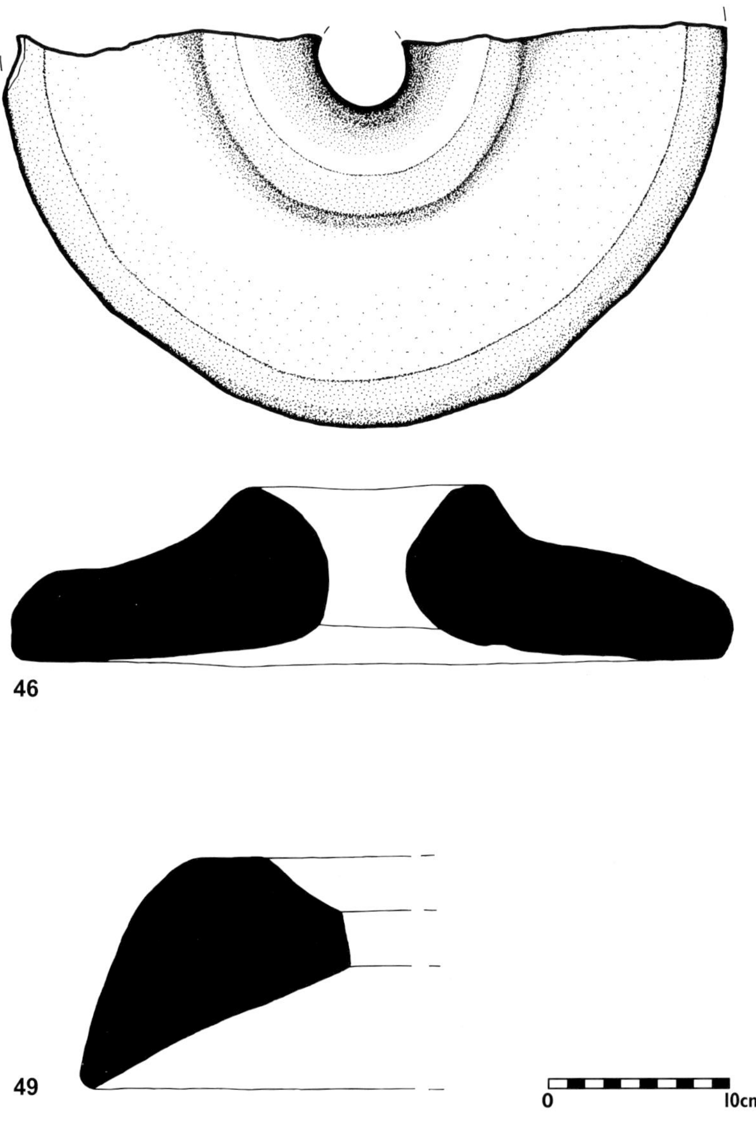

Fig 74: Upper rotary querns S46 and S49. Drawing C Thorpe. Scale1:4

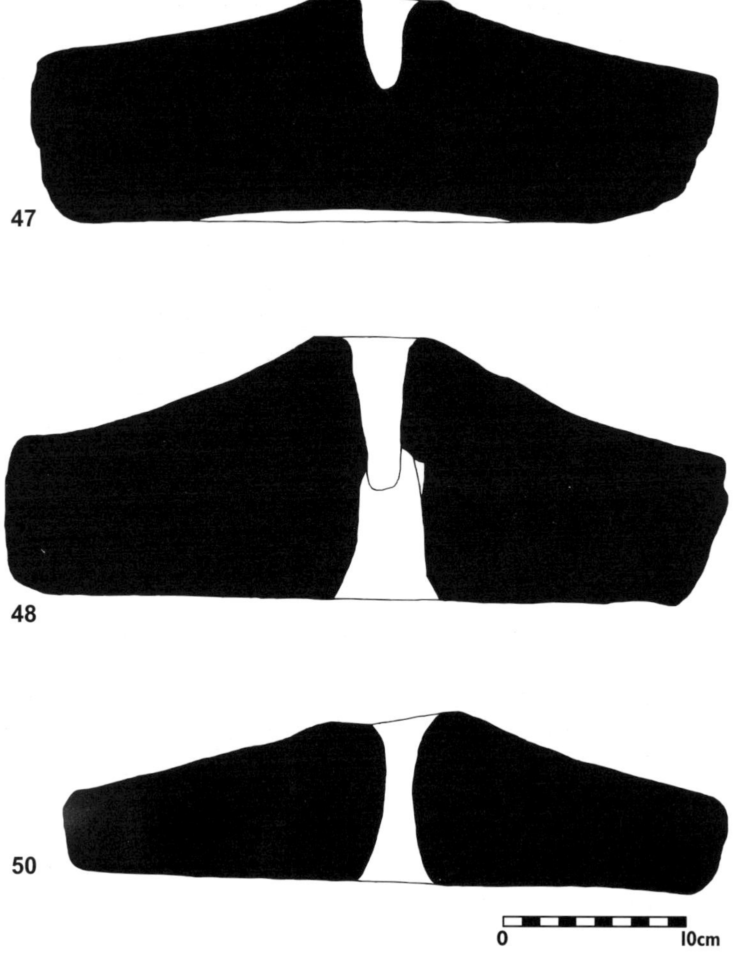

Fig 75: Sections through lower rotary querns S47, S48 and S50. Drawing C Thorpe. Scale 1:4

Lower stones

Fig 75

S47 Lower stone, coarse-grained elvan, 370mm diameter, 120mm thick at centre, 95mm at edge. Narrow conical pivot hole *c* 45mm deep. Edge and underside roughly worked, unevenly worn sloping working surface. [800] soil over Structure U.

S48 Part of lower stone, coarse-grained elvan, 390mm diameter, 140mm thick at centre, 85mm at edge. Worn sloping grinding surface. Conical spindle hole joins up with roughly worked circular socket on poorly dressed underside; the hole right through the lower stone potentially enables the upper stone to be tentered by means of a spindle projecting down to a movable lever beneath the lower stone. Stage 4/5 [907A] tumble from wall [907] in Q5. Broken by early 4th century.

S50 Lower stone, coarse-grained elvan, 350mm diameter, 90mm thick at centre, 48mm at edge. Sloping grinding surface. Complete perforation worked through from both surfaces as S48 but neater. Stage 6 [932] midden in U. Broken by late 4th century.

Comment

The rotary querns from Trethurgy are the largest group so far to be published from Roman Cornwall, and local Iron Age sites present few examples for comparison. In general in shape and proportions they reflect Roman styles, except perhaps for the thick upper stone fragment S49. S42 and S43 are of a general Roman type with flat tops and small hoppers, yet one has rynd sockets, the other not. S44 and S45, with the ridge around the edge of a shallow dished top which served as a hopper, may prove to be a local type, utilising the ease with which elvan could be carved. Again one has rynd sockets, in this case indicative of tentering, and the other not. Both S42 and S44 without rynd sockets have large sub-rectangular eyes which may hint at some local arrangement for supporting a pivot. S43 has no handle socket and others, more fragmentary, may not; only S44 had handle sockets. This seems unusual and may be connected with the nature of elvan which is soft and tends to fracture; a handle held in a band of iron, or perhaps of rope or leather, around the stone may have been more practical and the band have strengthened the stone. Overall the rotary querns show distinctive local adaptation of Roman styles and techniques which are found in so many other Cornish artefacts of the Roman period. The rotary querns present are not representative of the full range in use in Roman Cornwall, as a disc quern made from Tregonning granite was found at Penhale Round (Quinnell 1998/9), but nevertheless highlight the many forms of rotary quern utilised in the Roman period.

6.12.2 Saddle querns and riders

A total of 20 saddle querns were found (not illustrated), of which 12 were broken. More may have been present in walls which were not dismantled. All were made on blocks of local granite, many of which were waterworn. Sizes ranged from 65mm by 35mm by 20mm to 30mm by 25mm by 15mm. Most showed considerable signs of wear, which regularly left an oval depression consistent with a to-and-fro grinding, rather than a circular, grinding movement. Four had been used on both sides, including that set into paving [8] in R (Fig 45). The contexts occur fairly evenly through the site — [8] (2), [11], [28]/[473], [34] (3), [78], [256], [330], [387], [399], [432B], [458], [537], [722], [777], and ploughsoil (3).

Eleven oval quern riders, complete or in fragments, in elvan, granite, quartzite, and fine-grained sandstone came from the following contexts — set into [8] paving, [29], [56C], [175] (2), [453C], [723], [800], [801], [808], and [873].

The use of saddle querns alongside rotary querns continued throughout the Roman period in Cornwall, at least in areas where suitable stone was readily available. (The most extensively excavated sites are all in these areas.) The contexts from Trethurgy make it clear that the use of the two types of quern continued throughout the use of the site, into the 6th century. Both saddle querns and rotary querns occurred at Castle Gotha (Saunders and Harris 1982, 130) but there the saddle querns might have belonged to the, earlier, Iron Age occupation. Both also occurred at Carn Euny (Christie, 1978, 388) and saddle querns probably occurred there through the use of the site, well into the Roman period. Saddle querns, and the variant trough and saucer forms, were used alongside rotary querns at Halangy Down, Isles of Scilly (Ashbee 1996, 106-8); the published pottery indicates that activity on this site begins within the Roman period and continues through the early Post-Roman centuries. The most convincing case is Porthmeor, where the main occupation appears to be of the 3rd and 4th centuries with some continuation into the 5th and 6th centuries (Hirst 1937, 62); this site produced 14 saddle querns but only one of the rotary type.

The continuance of saddle querns alongside rotary querns during the Roman, and probably the Post-Roman centuries, occurs also in North Wales and Anglesey (eg Longley *et al* 1998, 232-4). Further east in Britain rotary querns generally replaced saddle querns during the Later Iron Age; there is not yet enough data for the situation to be clear for Devon. There is some evidence that, during the Post-Roman period, saddle querns were again used in some areas, for example at Cadbury Congresbury (Rahtz *et al* 1992, 113).

6.12.3 Mortar stone

The term 'mortar stone' is used to keep the distinction clear from the Cornish mortars described in Section 6.2.2. A granite boulder set in paving [8] (Fig 45) had a circular depression worn *c* 0.1m deep and 0.25m across in its surface. This depression had a concave base, the curve gradually changing to convex around the edge, and was the result of considerable wear. These worn depressions with a concave-convex profile are regularly found in courtyard house sites in West Cornwall. Usually found set *in situ* in paving, they were called stone basins at Chysauster (Hencken 1933, 276) and basin querns at Porthmeor (Hirst 1937, 62). An *in situ* example at Porth Godrevy (Fowler 1962, fig 7b, 56) was termed a 'boulder mortar'. All these concave-convex mortar stones are identical in size, shape, and wear to the ballauns found on early medieval ecclesiastical sites in Ireland (Edwards 1990, 116; personal observation by author). Similar mortar stones also occur in Roman and Post-Roman settlements in North Wales and Anglesey (Fasham *et al* 1998, 45).

Hencken (1933, 277) considered the soft granite of his stone basins inappropriate for grinding and suggested that these basins had been post-sockets, an idea which has proved remarkably enduring but which should now be abandoned. Examination by the author of the Chysauster stone basins or mortars indicates they all have wear appropriate for grinding. A recent

	<30mm	30 - 50mm	50 - 100mm	>100mm	Totals
White quartz	271	254	68	2	595
Other rocks	16	56	52	45	169

Table 6.2: Details of unmodified pebbles

survey by Watts (2003) has confirmed the presence of wear on Cornish mortar stones. At Carn Euny Christie (1978, 366) found a rubber inside one mortar stone and refers to others having been found in similar positions during 19th-century excavations by Borlase. The recent publication of Halangy Down courtyard settlement on Scilly clarifies matters. There Ashbee (1996, fig 50, no 1) illustrates a shallow, straight-sided circular granite depression which he interprets as a post-socket stone, clearly different in shape to all other mortars from the site.

6.12.4 General comment on cereal processing

Saddle querns, rotary querns, and mortar stones provide three different cereal processing artefacts, a variety accounted for by the range of cereals grown, by the diversity of food products which were prepared, and by the need to remove husks from hulled varieties; the subject has recently been explored by Watts (2003). All three may have been used for dehusking, although mortar stones appear to have been most efficient for this process. Grain is more efficiently dehusked when slightly damp. Watts suggests that mortars may be linked to an increased cultivation of oats; stone basins similar to mortar stones were recorded in the 1920s as still used until recent times for crushing oats (Hencken 1928, 160). A range of equipment allowed for flexible practice in an environment where grain may not always have been sufficiently dry to grind well in rotary querns. The variety of cereals grown is indicated by Scaife's (1998/9) work at Penhale Round; it is certain that there is a great deal more to be learnt amount the different varieties grown in different areas of Cornwall in the Roman and Post-Roman periods. A range of cereal-processing equipment must have been an advantage when optimum processing conditions could not be relied on, an advantage also evidenced across western parts of Britain, Wales, and in Ireland. The possibility that saddle querns, rotary querns, and mortar stones could have been used for grinding or pulverising materials other than cereals, such as metal ores, should also be kept in mind.

6.13 Unmodified stone

6.13.1 Amethyst

A lump of low-grade amethyst (not illustrated), pale in colour, was found in [723] soil/collapse of House Z2. Amethyst can occur in mineral lodes in the area. This piece could either have been naturally present in the soil over the site or brought in from elsewhere. The pale colour is common in veins in kaolinised granite, whereas deep colour is rare, and the colour therefore supports a local source (R Penhallurick pers comm).

6.13.2 Pebbles

A total of 764 pebbles (not illustrated) were found scattered throughout the site, 595 of white vein quartz and 169 of other rocks (Table 6.2). A few of the smallest, 10-20mm, had a very high gloss as though through repeated handling, exactly like the small pebbles found on barrow sites in the area (Miles 1975, 72). Those in the 30-50mm size range would be suitable for use as sling pellets: a clump of 36 of these was found on the scarped rab platform between Structure E and the Rampart. The larger pebbles may either also have been sling stones, or intended for use as rubbing stones. Small amounts of use will not leave recognisable traces of wear. The degree of rounding on most of the pebbles suggested a beach source, although some of the larger, more irregular, pieces may have come from a stream.

6.13.3 Slate

Small pieces of slate (not illustrated) were scattered throughout the site. Most have some iron-staining and tourmalinization, indicating an origin in the metamorphic aureole. They could be naturally present on site as similar fragments all over the Hensbarrow granite represent the remnants of overlying metamorphosed slates now weathered away. Some slate fragments at Trethurgy are of unaltered Devonian slate and not from the aureole. Pebbles of this slate occur in St Austell Bay, and water-worn facets on some pieces at Trethurgy suggest that they did come from the shore. There is no indication that slate was used for roofing.

7 Flint and quartz

7.1 Quantity and distribution

Only a small proportion of the assemblage originally present can have been retrieved as ploughsoil was removed mechanically. A total of 241 struck pieces was recovered, together with 16 flint pebbles and a quartz flake (Tables 7.1 and 7.2). The flint formed no concentrations and is therefore treated as a single group. The full extent of the scatter could not be established because adjacent fields were under grass. As there appeared to have been extensive agricultural use of the site with some lynchetting before the construction of the Round, many flints may have been moved from their original positions. None were found in any of the features which predated the Round.

7.2 Source and typology

A total of 107 pieces were cortical; of these 69 showed traces of pebble flint cortex and 38 the worn chalky cortex indicating nodular flint. About a third of the flint recovered appears to have come from a chalk source, possibly Beer in East Devon although recent research has demonstrated that chalk flint occurs at an extensive range of locations in Devon and traditional patterns of sourcing may need reconsideration (Newberry forthcoming). The pebble flint showed a variety of texture and colour. Flint pebbles occur in St Austell Bay. There are also 19th-century records of flint pebbles occurring in the 'tin ground' deposits in places in the valleys of mid-Cornwall (Henwood 1874, 215).

Area / Context	Flints
OLS [371]	3
Periods 3 /4	9
Round Ditch	24
Entrance	14
V	14
U	23
Q	5
Z	9
Y	15
X	7
E	2
D	-
G	2
A	15
T	10
R	22
Ploughsoil	84
Total	**258**

Table 7.1: Distribution of flint across the site

Pebbles	16
Unclassified chunks, chips	26
Cores — single platform	5
Cores — two platform	2
Cores — fragmentary	3
Flakes	67
Retouched flakes	28
Blades (L:B ratio >5:2)	9
Retouched blades	3
Flake or blade fragments	50
Retouched fragments	18
Transverse arrowhead	1
Arrowhead blank ?	1
Scrapers	18
Awls	4
Fabricator	1
Notched flakes	3
Choppers	3

Table 7.2: Analysis of the flint assemblage: total 258 pieces

Descriptions of illustrated pieces

Fig 76

F1 Transverse arrowhead of Green's chisel type (1980, fig 37); base broken. Good-quality dark-grey flint.

F2 Bifacially worked piece, possibly an attempt at a small lozenge/leaf arrowhead. Good-quality dark-grey flint.

F3 Large end scraper, chalk flint.

F4 End scraper, chalk flint; steep retouch continues down right edge; inverse retouch or heavy use on left side.

F5 End scraper on grey, probably pebble, flint.

F6 End scraper, good-quality dark-grey flint. Flat angle of retouch, pressure-worked. Some inverse working on left edge.

F7 End scraper, good-quality dark-grey flint. Broken; subsequent retouch on broken edge.

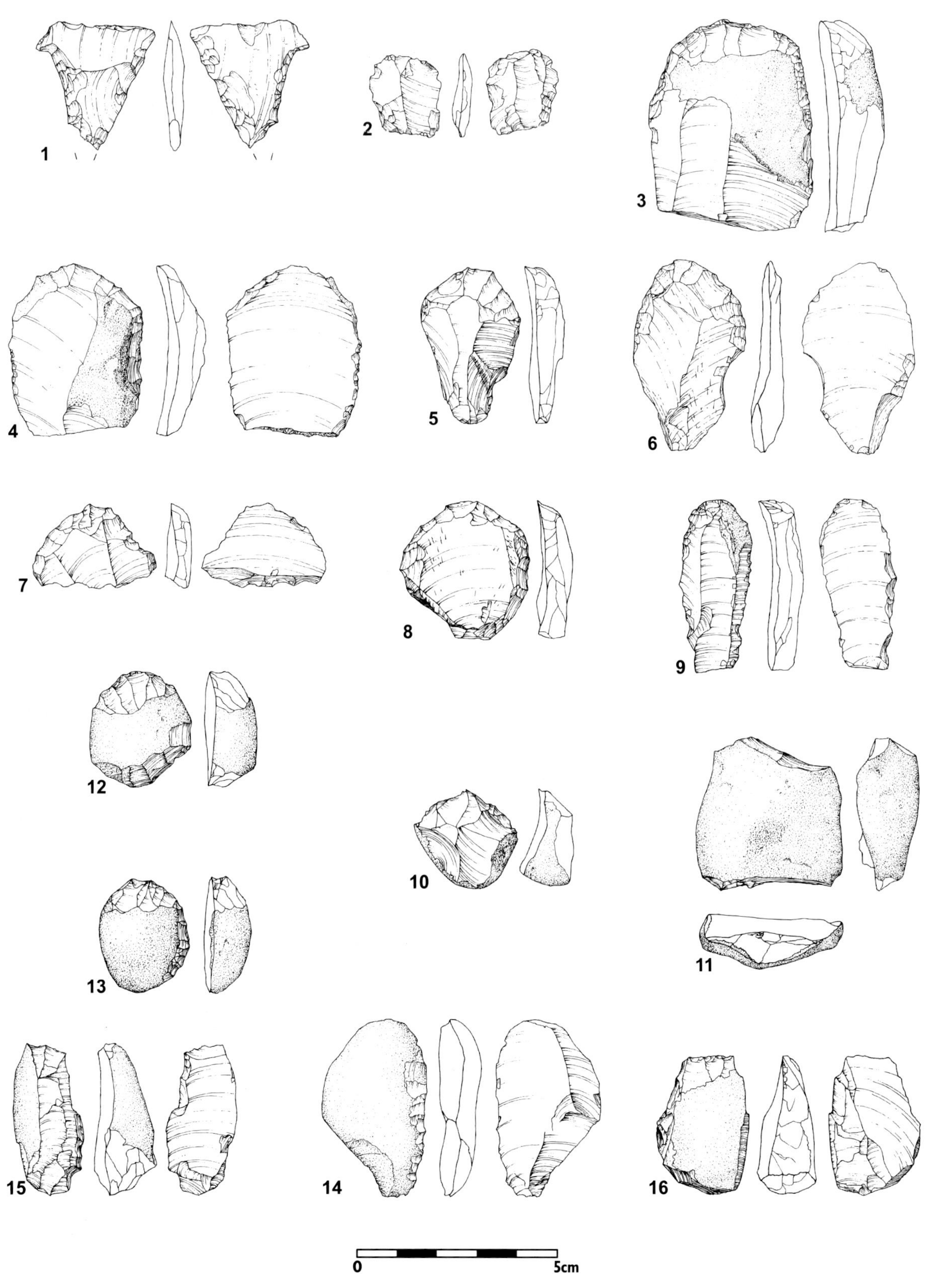

Fig 76: Flints. Drawing A Brown. Scale 2:3

F8 Scraper with retouch around 80% of perimeter. Chalk flint.

F9 End scraper on yellowish, chalk flint. Some inverse retouch on left edge.

F10 Rough scraper on grey pebble flint.

F11 Rough scraper on grey pebble flint. Proximal end broken, retouched as possible awl.

F12 Double-ended scraper on grey pebble flint.

F13 Scraper, end and right edge; grey pebble flint.

F14 Scraper on right edge, grey pebble flint. Rough attempt at bifacial working on left edge.

F15 Scraper on core trimming flake; some retouch on right edge. Grey pebble flint.

F16 Scraper on flake worked down as small core. Grey chalk flint.

Fig 77

F17 Awl on side of core trimming flake. Probably pebble flint.

F18 Awl made by fine pressure working on fracture surface of broken flake. Good-quality grey flint.

F19 Fabricator, triangular cross-section, end heavily worn. Broken. Probably pebble flint.

F20 Distal end of flake, good-quality flint, thinned by pressure flaking. Break retouched, ?knife edge or scraper. Notch worked by inverse retouch on tip.

F21 Notched flake; broken, retouch along right edge above notch. Good-quality grey flint.

F22 Notched flake, chalk flint. Retouch along entire right edge (except for later breaks).

F23 Chopper? Bifacially worked edge on flat buff flint pebble.

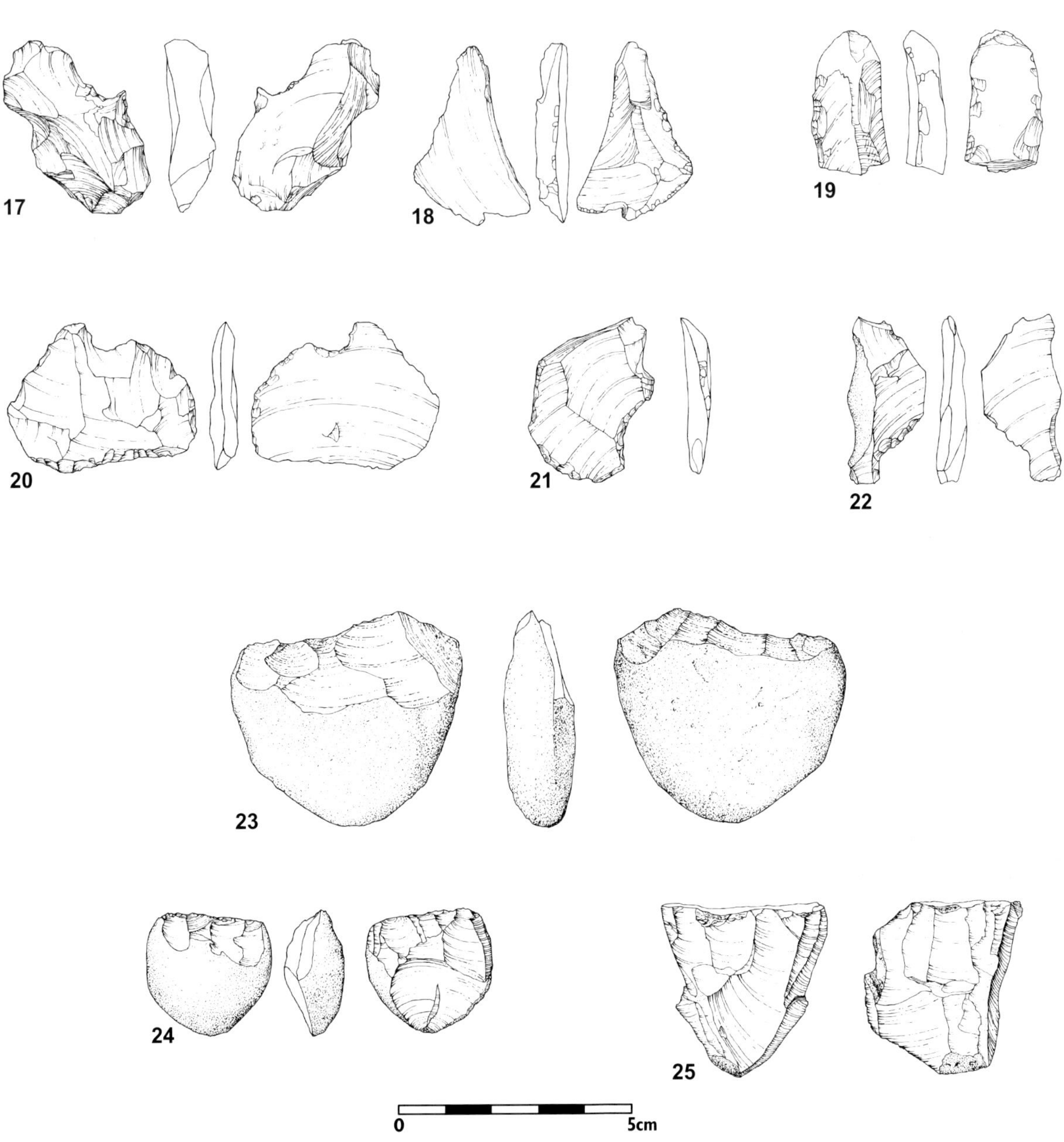

Fig 77: Flints. Drawing A Brown. Scale 2:3

F24 Chopper? Bifacially worked edge, heavily used, on grey flint pebble.

F25 Small single platform core worked around most of perimeter. Chalk flint.

The flints represent a wide date range. Some Mesolithic pieces may be present. The blades would not be out of place in a Mesolithic context and the scraper F10 could also be of this period. The choppers (F23, F24), and perhaps the narrow scrapers on core fragments (F15, F16), can be compared to examples from Constantine Island on the North Cornish coast (Norman 1977, fig 1). There these types form part of a distinctive, roughly-worked assemblage which is not closely datable, but which may have related to coastal food collecting activities. The presence of such elements at Trethurgy, fewer than three miles from the sea, is not surprising.

The use of nodular chalk flint is generally a feature of the Early Neolithic period (Tingle 1998, 94-8). F2 may well be Early Neolithic as may some of the blades and scrapers such as F3. However the chisel variety of transverse arrowheads such as F1 have been assigned by Green (1980, 114) to the Later Neolithic before barbed-and-tanged arrowheads became common. Most of the illustrated pieces, scrapers, fabricators, and notched flakes, as well as most of the debitage, appears to be of Later Neolithic type. The small 'thumbnail' scrapers (F12-13) occur regularly in assemblages of the Late Neolithic or Early Bronze Age (cf Stannon, Mercer 1970, 42). The Trethurgy assemblage may well span several millennia, from the Mesolithic through to at least the Late Neolithic. The area may well have been open space within woodland, visited, and perhaps expanded, by local communities over a long period of time.

7.3 Lithic assemblages in the St Austell area

Systematic fieldwalking has now taken place in several areas in Cornwall west of Trethurgy and has produced considerable, though varying, quantities of lithic material (eg Smith 1987). No major fieldwalking project has yet taken place in mid-Cornwall but many finds in the St Austell area are recorded in the Cornwall SMR. Numerous flints have been found in the unexcavated hillfort of Prideaux Rings, St Blazey (SX 059556) and scatters have been recorded at SX 0255 in St Austell parish and at SX 0446 5511 in adjacent St Blazey. Recent excavations at Trenowah, St Austell, SX 0450 5337, 2km south-east of Trethurgy, have produced a scatter of flints (Johns 2000); there were also pits producing an Early Neolithic sherd and radiocarbon determination (Johns forthcoming). Observation of a pipeline starting at Trebal on the north edge of the present Trethurgy village produced flints from Trebal itself down to St Blazey Gate (Jones 2001), most of the material appearing, on initial examination, to be Later Neolithic. Five barrows on the St Austell granite excavated during the 1970s produced flint assemblages; most of the flint had been introduced with the turves used in mound construction and range in date from the Mesolithic to the Early Bronze Age with Later Neolithic material predominating (Miles 1975a). These finds are all pointers to a Late Neolithic pattern of activity in the St Austell area which may have been as comparatively dense for its period as that of the Late Iron Age and Roman periods.

8 Environmental data

8.1 Bone, antler, and shell

Small fragments of bone, all too decayed to be identifiable, were found in [369] Period 3 Enclosure Ditch silt, [363] Period 3 Enclosure Bank, posthole [207] predating the Entrance paving, soil [386] in R, and [751] surface in Structure Y; [386] also produced antler. All these contexts were sealed to various extents from later disturbances, which may account for some degree of preservation. Burnt bone fragments were found in [568] primary Ditch silt and [907A] in Q.

Two dozen cockle-shells were found together in [360] secondary Ditch silt on the west of the site.

8.2 Soils *S Staines* (text written 1973)

The soils in the section through the Rampart and Ditch (section s-ss, Fig 7) were examined.

The site is on the St Austell granite at about 170m OD and the soils of the surrounding farmland are Moretonhampstead series, course loamy brown podzolic soils. Moretonhampstead soils are extensive on the lower, enclosed parts of all the granite uplands of England. They consist of a dark brown, finely structured sandy silt loam topsoil which overlies a strong brown or ochreous sandy silt loam or sandy loam subsoil. The subsoil rests on compact granitic gravel, locally known as 'rab' or 'growan'. The depth over the growan is often about 0.6m but there are both deeper and shallower soils, often as a result of historic soil erosion. There are numerous dry valleys on the granite which contain colluvium, the product of soil erosion from upslope. The colluvium usually consists of dark-brown sandy silt loam identical to surrounding topsoils.

On the site of Trethurgy Round a similar soil pattern is found. Over the main part of the Round there were shallow Moretonhampstead soils but the surrounding Ditch is filled with dark-brown sandy silt loam colluvium. The colluvium contained rounded quartz pebbles which looked as if they were strongly waterworn. This indicates a coastal source rather than a stream source.

The Old Land Surface was examined in places and was apparently the upper surface of the BC horizon, that is the compact, gravelly granitic head or rab.

Moretonhampstead soils are naturally well drained and acid. The soil naturally contains few free bases and liming is necessary for arable agriculture and reasonable grassland use. This is also likely to have been the case in Romano-British times.

Little work has been carried out on the vegetation history of Moretonhampstead soils although one profile has been examined for soil pollen on the margin of Dartmoor (Staines 1979). Here there was little evidence for heathland. A grass-hazel phase followed the original oak woodland and was subsequently followed by a grass-dominated vegetation. It is likely that woodland on Moretonhampstead soils was cleared later than on Hexworthy and similar soils which occur on the higher, unenclosed moors. It is possible that Moretonhampstead profiles developed under woodland and have changed little since woodland clearance, apart from deepening of the topsoil due to cultivation or in certain situations having suffered erosion due to agricultural activity. It is probable that most Moretonhampstead soils have changed little. They were probably reclaimed directly from woodland for agriculture and have been used agriculturally ever since although there must have been reversion to semi-natural grassland or scrub. Few buried, intact Moretonhampstead profiles have been examined and, as pollen preservation under agricultural conditions is poor, none of those used agriculturally has been examined for soil pollen.

The soils at Trethurgy during Romano-British times were probably little different from those found today. That is, they were moderately acid, medium to light textured, well drained soils. The natural fertility would have been low if woodland clearance had occurred, as is likely, sometime during the Bronze Age, but use of organic fertilisers and liming with sea sand would have raised the level of potential arable productivity.

On the assumption that the pebbles found on the site are coastal in origin then they may be evidence for liming with beach sand (the only local source of liming material) and/or for manuring with seaweeds. The latter is a practise that has gone on for many centuries in west Cornwall (see Bell 1981).

The relative shallowness of the soils within the Round and the accumulation within the Ditch section points to considerable erosion within the Round, presumably from cultivation after its abandonment.

Note: the above was written after the summer season in 1973 before the downhill section Fig 7, z-zz became available for study. The comments about the detailed makeup of the OLS in Section 2.3 were made from study of photographs during post-excavation by Henrietta Quinnell and Linda Therkorn.

Context	Sample No	Context description	Phosphate
369	888	Primary silt, Period 3 Enclosure Ditch	Positive
371	889	OLS beneath Period 3 Enclosure Bank	Positive
371	890	OLS beneath Period 5 Round Rampart downhill in R	Absent
371	891	OLS beneath Period 5 Round Rampart uphill	Absent
361	892	Primary silt Period 5 Round Ditch uphill	Absent
360	893	Secondary silt Period 5 Round Ditch uphill	Trace

Table 8.1: Details of soil phosphate analysis

Context	Context description	AML No	Charcoal
460	Published as [363] in Period 3 Enclosure Bank	777380	*Corylus* sp. 8g
207	Pit sealed by Round Rampart OLS	777349	*Fraxinus* sp. 83g *Ulex* sp. 25g
932	Midden with ?ashes in Structure U Stage 6	777361	*Ulex* sp. 17g *Calluna* sp. 1.5g
801	Midden with ? ashes in Structure U Stage 6	777353	*Fraxinus* sp. 3g *Ulex* sp. 6g
884	Posthole, House Z1 Stages 1-3	-	*Corylus* sp. 21g *Ulex* sp. 11g *Calluna* sp. 15g
849	Hearth pit, House Z2, Stage 7?	777359	*Fraxinus* sp. 11g *Corylus* sp. 10g
850	Hearth pit, House Z2, Stage 8?	777356	*Fraxinus* sp. 25g *Corylus* sp. 5g
923	Dump of material with ash, Area Q, Stage 4	777361	*Ulex* sp. 83g *Calluna* sp. 18g
663A	Hearth pit, House X, Stage 4	777369	*Ulex* sp. 15g *Calluna* sp. 13g
662B	Hearth pit, House X, Stage 5?	777367	*Fraxinus* sp. 42g *Calluna* sp. 22g
689B	Hearth pit, House X, Stages 6 & 7?	777368	*Fraxinus* sp. 81g
80	Published as [77], upper fill Structure G, Stage 9	777372	*Corylus* sp. 3g
316	Hearth pit, House A1, Stages 1-3	777373	*Ulex* sp. 5g
452	Stone setting with ? ashes behind House A1, Stage 1+	777354	*Fraxinus* sp. 28g *Corylus* sp. 23g *Crataegus* sp. 47g *Carpinus* sp. 8g
427	Floor, House T3, Stage 4	-	*Fraxinus* sp. 13g *Ulex* sp. 28g
379	Posthole, Area R, Stage 1?	-	*Corylus* sp.13g

Table 8.2: Details of identified charcoal

8.3 Soil phosphate analysis

Helen C M Keeley

(text written 1974, updated 2001)

8.3.1 Introduction

Detailed chemical analysis of soil phosphate was first developed as a tool in abandoned settlement analysis in the 1940s (Eidt 1984), when it was recognised that phosphorus (P) is one of the principle chemical additives caused by human settlement activities. However the difficulties of phosphate chemistry and the absence of relatively simple methods of its quantitative analysis held back advances in using soil P analysis until the 1960s, when public concern with pollution in the developed world led to more effort to improve the understanding of the retention of soil phosphate and methods of its detection. Human activity may result in additions of P (usually in the form of phosphate) to the soil, eg from faeces (domestic animal or human), ash, or bones. A simple ring chromatography field test was developed, using solutions of ammonium molybdate and ascorbic acid (Eidt 1984), which has been used extensively in archaeological investigations for many years with varying degrees of success (Keeley 1981; 1983) to detect human activity, such as animal stocking, adding fertiliser to agricultural soils and the decomposition of skeletal material.

The soils at Trethurgy were mainly coarse loamy brown podzolic soils of the Moretonhampstead series developed on granite (Section 8.2). These soils are naturally well drained and acid and thus relatively low in plant nutrients, including P. Six samples were tested for phosphate content, using the Eidt field method, to look for evidence of animal stocking in the Round.

8.3.2 Results and interpretation

The results are shown in Table 8.1. Only samples 888 and 889, from contexts relating to the Period 3 Enclosure, contained appreciable amounts of phosphate consistent with the use of the land by stock. The field beneath the Round may have been cultivated prior to its construction and subsequently come to be used as a centre for folding animals.

8.4 Pollen

Columns for analysis were taken through the OLS beneath both the Period 3 Enclosure Bank and the Round Rampart, but difficulties were experienced in finding a palynologist available to work on the material. When examined by Dr C Caseldine in 1980 the samples were found to be too degraded for reliable study. The acidity of the Moretonhampstead soil at Trethurgy makes it probable that a proper palynological study would have been productive.

8.5 Charcoal *Caroline Cartwright*

(text written 1988; revised 2000)

Charcoal was retrieved from 35 contexts (Table 8.2). In all cases this occurred where charcoal was noticed during excavation and lifted with varying quantities of soil. The excavation took place before the practice of bulk sieving from a large range of contexts became common. It only proved possible for English Heritage Ancient Monuments Laboratory to fund the identification of some charcoal samples when the possibility of obtaining radiocarbon determinations was being considered. Charcoal from the 16 contexts considered most likely to provide helpful determinations was therefore examined. During the process of microscopic assessment, identifiable charcoal fragments in every size category were picked out of their soil matrix for scientific identification and then reincorporated, in case there were minute fragments of charred material contained therein which might be required to 'bulk up' a C14 sample.

On archaeological sites, charcoal can fragment in a wide variety of size, condition, and friability as a result of the processes of burning, deposition, and post-deposition. It is vital, therefore, to avoid any selection of larger size fragments as this would result in an entirely unacceptable level of bias of the resultant quantification and interpretation of the charcoal taxa (ie trees and shrubs). The Trethurgy charcoal fragments were identified by means of standard techniques of optical microscopy using reflected (incident) light on a Leitz polarising microscope with darkfield capabilities and a range of objectives comprising magnifications from x20 to x1000. Each charcoal fragment was fractured (by hand) to expose transverse, radial-longitudinal and tangential-longitudinal surfaces for identification. Methods of expressing the relative proportions of the different trees and shrubs represented by charcoal have ranged from a simple presence/absence notation according to context through a variety of quantification methods which express the relative frequencies as percentages by weight in grams of a flotation or sieve sample (from a context) or as relative percentages according to volume of a standard sample (per context). The disadvantage of counting charcoal fragments as a basis for quantifying relative percentages is self-evident. Such a figure is simply an index of fragmentation. No quantitative method currently in use by charcoal specialists is entirely satisfactory, although expression of the relative proportions of taxa present through percentage by weight of the different wood charcoal taxa (in grams) can often provide a certain measure of inter-site comparability. In the case of the Trethurgy charcoal, however, given the fact that only certain contexts were sampled for charcoal, percentages of taxa would be fairly meaningless, so each taxon has been presented on Table 8.2 as a weight in grams where it occurs in the contexts sampled.

Ash (*Fraxinus* sp.), hazel (*Corylus* sp.), gorse (*Ulex* sp.) and heather (*Calluna* sp.) are consistently represented in the contexts sampled for C14 dating. Although this is not the entire amount of charcoal from the site, some observations may be drawn. For the most part, the hazel, gorse, heather, and hawthorn charcoal fragments from these samples derive from small roundwood lengths (twigs and small branches) with stem diameters commonly ranging from 4mm to 23mm. The ash charcoal (*Fraxinus* sp.), almost entirely found in hearth pits and pits, tends to derive from more mature timber for which no stem diameter is measurable. Ash occurs in 'chunk-like' fragments in remarkably good condition. It is not surprising that ash should have been selected for prime fuel as its properties of clean, steady, high burning may be observed time and again in domestic or kiln fires.

The small branches and twigs may be utilised for kindling or for stoking a domestic or industrial fire. Presumably the gorse, heather, hazel, and hawthorn were readily available in the surrounding environment. These not only make good kindling but can be used for hedging and stock enclosure fencing.

Context [452] is unusual as it contains the only occurrence of hawthorn and a small amount of hornbeam.

8.6 The potential for the study of plant macrofossils

The excavation of the Round took place before the practice of wet-sieving soil samples for the retrieval of plant macrofossils became established in the late 1970s. The study of this material from more recent excavations in Cornwall has been productive. Small quantities were identified from samples from Reawla Round (Straker 1992). These consisted of roughly equal quantities of emmer and spelt, some at least of which had been processed on site, a little hulled barley and some oats which might have been either cultivated or wild. Samples from Penhale Round were more productive (Scaife1998/9). Here spelt was the most common cereal but emmer and bread/club wheat (*Triticum aestivum* type) were also present, as were hulled barley and some oats which were considered cultivated from the size of grain. Again there was some crop processing in the Round. A few peas (*Pisum sativum*) were found. By contrast 5th and 6th-century deposits at the coastal site of Tintagel produced a predominance of oats, almost certainly cultivated, some barley and a little wheat which could not be more closely identified (Straker 1997); crops here may have been grown inland and imported to Tintagel partly cleaned. The predominance of oats is mirrored in 4th century and early Medieval deposits at Duckpool some miles further north up the coast (Straker 1995).

These few examples show something of the range of cultivated plants which might be grown in Roman and Post-Roman Cornwall, which might have been ground by the range of querns and mortars found at Trethurgy. It is to be expected that, as more work is done, local variations in crops will be related to topography and soil type and that there will be variations in the ways crops were processed at, and away from, settlement sites.

9 Radiocarbon dating, phasing, and chronology

9.1 Radiocarbon determinations

Peter Marshall
(text written 2001)

During work on the report in the mid-1980s it was decided to obtain a series of radiocarbon determinations to complement the chronological information provided by the artefacts, principally pottery, from the site. Dr H Keeley of English Heritage Ancient Monuments Laboratory arranged for Dr C Cartwright to identify charcoal from 16 contexts selected as potentially helpful for chronological information. D Jordan provided advice on sample selection; six determinations were arranged, selected from samples with more than 10gm of charcoal, two from the beginning of the occupation sequence (UB-3255, 3254) two from the middle (UB-3253, 3252) and two from the later Stages (UB-3251, 3250).

The six radiocarbon age determinations obtained on samples from Trethurgy were processed by the Queen's University, Belfast, Radiocarbon Research Laboratory in 1990 according to the methods outlined in Mook and Waterbolk (1985) and Pearson (1984).

9.1.1 Objectives

The principal aims of the dating programme were to:

i) provide a chronological framework for the development of the site,
ii) establish when oval houses, now accepted as the main structural domestic form in Roman Cornwall, start being constructed,
iii) establish when the use of oval houses finished,
iv) date the end of the formal use of the Round.

9.1.2 Sample selection

Prior to submission all the charcoal samples were identified. The majority of the charcoal was from small twigs and branches (stem diameters ranging from 4-23 mm), although UB-3251, UB-3253, and UB-3254 contained some *Fraxinus* sp. which derived from more mature timber.

9.1.3 Results

The results, given in Table 9.1, are conventional radiocarbon ages (Stuiver and Polach 1977), and are quoted in accordance with the international standard known as the Trondheim convention (Stuiver and Kra 1986).

9.1.4 Calibration

The radiocarbon determinations have been calibrated with data from Stuiver *et al* (1998), using OxCal (v3.5) (Bronk Ramsey 1995; 1998). The date ranges have been calculated according to the maximum intercept method (Stuiver and Reimer 1986), and are cited in the text at two sigma (95% confidence). They are quoted in the form recommended by Mook (1986), with the end points rounded outwards to ten years. The probability distributions (Fig 78) are derived from the usual probability method (Stuiver and Reimer 1993; Dehling and van der Plicht 1993; van der Plicht 1993). Those ranges printed in italics in this text are derived from mathematical modelling of archaeological problems.

9.1.5 Analysis and interpretation

A Bayesian approach has been adopted for the interpretation of the chronological data (Buck *et al* 1996) using the program OxCal version 3.5 (http://www.rlaha.ox.ac.uk/orau, Bronk Ramsey 1995; 1998). Such a methodology allows the results of the radiocarbon analyses to be combined with other information, such as stratigraphy, to produce realistic estimates of dates of archaeological interest. The algorithms used in the models described below can be derived from the structure shown in Figure 79. Estimated radiocarbon dates (Table 9.1) are presented throughout in italics.

In the analyses undertaken we have chosen to impose a uniform prior distribution on the spread of dates while assuming that the dated samples represent independent events and a random sample of a relatively constant level of human activity; see Bronk Ramsey (2000) for further details of its implementation. Such an approach has been used because, when radiocarbon dates are constrained by relative dating information, it has been shown that there is a danger that the posterior density distributions may be spread evenly across a plateaux in the calibration curve, irrespective of the actual age of the material dated (Steier and Rom 2000). This is due to the fact that the statistical weight of a group of measurements naturally favours longer overall spans.

Laboratory Number	Sample Number	Material	Context	Radiocarbon Age (BP)	$\delta^{13}C$ (‰)	Calibrated date range (95% confidence)	Estimated date range *(95% probability)*
UB-3250	TGY 932	Charcoal; *Ulex* sp. and *Calluna* sp. twigs and small branches	Midden in U Stage 6	1683 ± 45	-25.8 ± 0.2	cal AD 240 -440	*cal* AD *250 -440*
UB-3251	TGY 849	Charcoal: *Fraxinus* sp. (mature timber?) and *Corylus* sp. (twigs and small branches)	Hearth pit, House Z2 (Stage 7)	1641 ± 60	-25.2 ± 0.2	cal AD 250 -560	*cal* AD *240 -540*
UB-3252	TGY 427	Charcoal; *Fraxinus* sp. (mature timber?) and *Ulex* sp. (twigs and small branches)	Floor around hearth House T3 (Stage 4)	1806 ± 52	-25.3 ± 0.2	cal AD 80 -390	*cal* AD *80 -350*
UB-3253	TGY 923	Charcoal; *Ulex* sp. and *Calluna* sp. twigs and small branches	Area Q ash dump (Stage 4)	1842 ± 46	-25.3 ± 0.2	cal AD 70 -330	*cal* AD *150 -360 (94%) and cal* AD *370 -380 (1%)*
UB-3254	TGY 207	Charcoal; *Fraxinus* sp. (mature timber?) and *Ulex* sp. (twigs and small branches)	Pit sealed by Rampart OLS	2123 ± 47	-25.70 ± 0.2	360-1 cal BC	*350-320 cal* BC *(2%)* and *240 cal* BC - *cal* AD *10 (93%)*
UB-3255	TGY 884	Charcoal; *Corylus* sp. *Calluna* sp. and *Ulex* sp. all + twigs	Posthole in earliest phase of House Z (Stages 1-3)	1768 ± 47	-25.8 ± 0.2	cal AD 130 -400	*cal* AD *120 -330*

Table 9.1: Radiocarbon age determinations; charcoal identifications Section 8.5

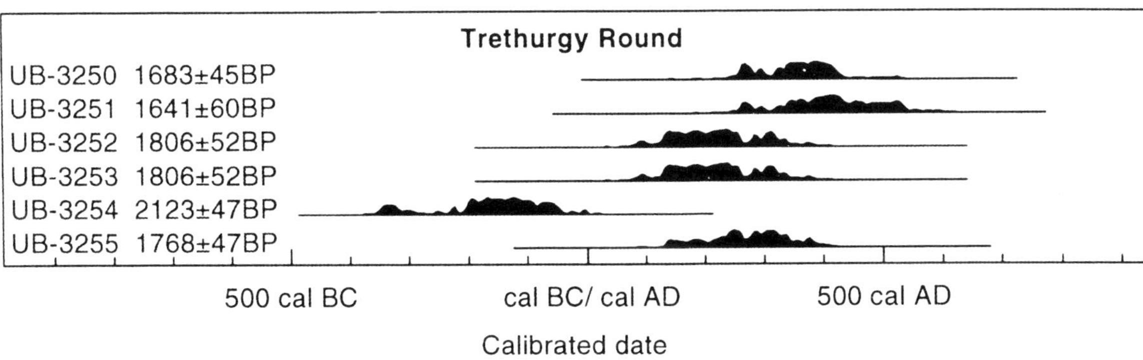

Fig 78: Probability distributions of dates from Trethurgy Round. Each distribution represents the probability that an event occurred at a particular time. These distributions are the result of simple radiocarbon calibration (Stuiver and Reimer 1993)

Figure 79 shows that the radiocarbon measurements are in good agreement with stratigraphy (A=94.7%). The contents of pit [207] (UB-3254) provide a *terminus post quem* for the construction of the Round. It is sealed by the OLS beneath the main Rampart and the sample comprised charcoal of *Fraxinus* sp. (mature timber?) and twigs and small branches of *Ulex* sp. The model shown in Figure 79 provides a *terminus post quem* for construction of the Round of *240 cal BC-cal AD 10 (93% probability)*.

UB-3255 from posthole [884] in the earliest phase of House Z (Stages 1-3) provides a *terminus post quem* for the end of House Z and the start of the main period of the Round occupation and use of oval houses. The charcoal probably relates to material incorporated during the use of the building (Bayliss 1999), as it is typical of 'fuel' species, ie twigs of *Corylus* sp., *Calluna* sp., and *Ulex* sp. *Ulex* sp. is often collected for fuel as it burns particularly efficiently, although it rarely grows to a size larger than twigs (Bayliss 1999). The *terminus post quem* is estimated at 2nd-4th centuries AD *(cal AD 120-330 at 95% probability)*.

UB-3252 comprised *Ulex* sp. and some *Fraxinus* sp. (mature timber?) from [427] an accumulation of trampled material in the floor around the hearth of House T3. It is assumed that the material represents a build up of material from the use of the structure and thus the measurement provides a *terminus post quem* for the disuse of House T3 (see Fig 79) *(cal AD 80-350 at 95% probability)*.

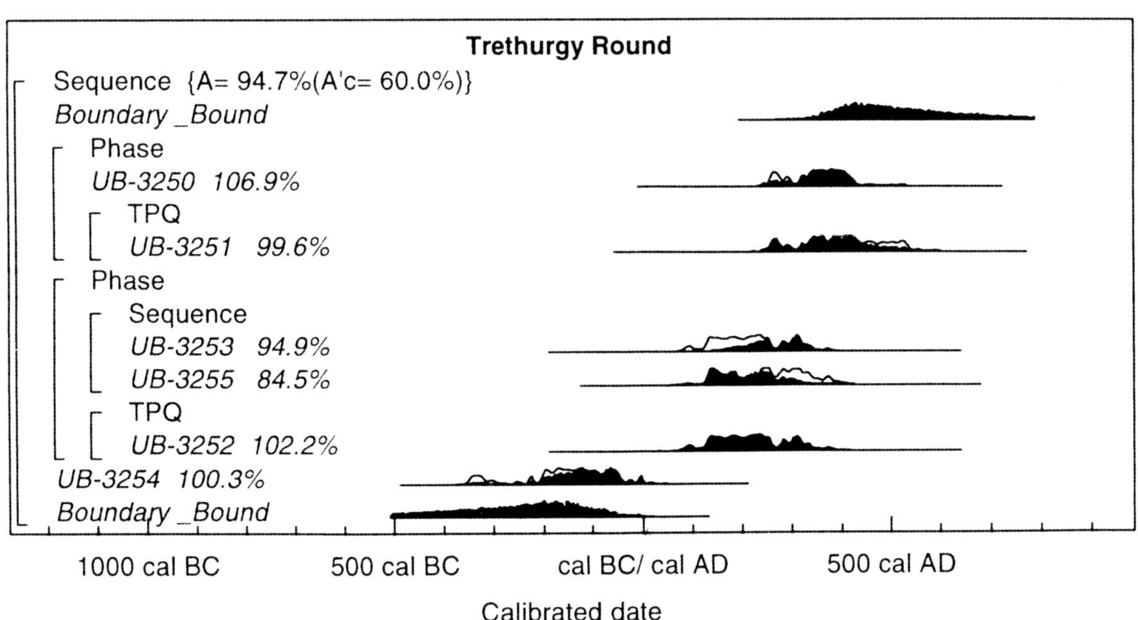

Fig 79: Probability distributions of dates from Trethurgy Round with additional chronological modelling. Each distribution represents the relative probability that an event occurs at a particular time. For each of the radiocarbon dates two distributions have been plotted, one in outline, which is the result of simple radiocarbon calibration, and a solid one, which is the estimated date based on the chronological model used. The large square brackets down the left hand side along with the OxCal keywords define the model exactly

Period	Suggested dating	Remarks
Period 3	late 1st century BC	Enclosure, not completed
Period 4	AD 1 - 150	Enclosure used for stock
Period 5	c AD 150	Round constructed
Stage 1	AD 150 - 175	Short duration
Stage 2	AD 175 - 210	Maximum residential capacity
Stage 3	AD 210 - 260	Minor alterations
Stage 4	AD 260 - 325	Major alterations
	possible hiatus	
Stage 5	AD 325 - 375	Major rebuild and paving
Stage 6	AD 375 - 400	Maximum capacity, midden [932/801]
Stage 7	AD 400 - 450	Residential capacity shrinking
Stage 8	AD 450 - 500	Residential capacity shrinking
Stage 9	AD 500 - 550+	Last residential rebuilding
	abandonment	
Stage 10	AD 700 - 1000	Re-use as stock fold
Period 6	11th to 16th century AD	Arable field, some stone robbing
Period 7	16th century AD	Incorporation in present field system
Period 8	16th to 20th centuries AD	Farmed, some stone robbing

Table 9.2: Suggested chronology of the Period 3 Enclosure, Period 4, the Period 5 Round, and subsequent Periods

Period 3 Enclosure	P32 in Bank [363]
Period 4	Samian in [369], S Devon [920], BB1 P87 [924]
Period 5 Round construction	UB-3254 *240 cal BC-cal AD 10* [207]
Stage 1	UB-3255 *cal AD 120-330* [884], P29 [33], P60 [458], P135 [685]
Stage 2	no useful secure finds
Stage 3	P102 + Type 16 sherds [761], S Devon [442]
Stage 4	UB-3252 *cal AD 80-350* [427], UB-3253 *cal AD 150-360* [923], P18 [36], [905] & [948] P130 (earliest contexts, BB1 conical flanged bowls and Cornish flanged bowls)
Stage 5	no useful secure finds
Stage 6	UB-3250 *cal AD 250-440* (95%) *cal AD 340-420* (68%) [932], P2 P3 Oxfordshire and midden ceramic assemblage [932/801]
Stage 7	UB-3251 *cal AD 240-540* [849]
Stage 8	no useful secure finds, no Post-Roman imports
Stage 9	Post-Roman imports [743] [666] [34] [256] [77], S1 [34] [678] [399]
Stage 10	E ware [359], grass-marked P148 soil over Z

Table 9.3: Artefacts and radiocarbon determinations relevant to site chronology

UB-3253 provides a *terminus post quem* for the overlying layer [905], which provides the earliest context on the site for a flanged bowl in local fabric. Identified during excavation as fresh 'ash-like' material, the deposit [923] from which the charcoal sample came formed part of a dump covered by layer [905]; ([923] and [905] are thought to have been deposited without any appreciable interval). The material, twigs and small branches of *Ulex* sp. and *Calluna* sp., is most likely to be a dump of *ex situ* hearth debris relating to the later use of House Z1 in Stage 4. The model suggests that UB-3253 (context [923]) dates to mid 2nd to the mid 4th century cal AD *(cal AD 150-360 at 94% probability; at 68% confidence cal AD 210-260 (29%) and cal AD 270-340 (39%))* and this would seem to support the idea that Cornish flanged bowls provide a *terminus post quem* date of AD 275.

The charcoal measured as UB-3251 was identified as *Fraxinus* sp. (mature timber?) and twigs and small branches of *Corylus* sp. It came from the contents of a 'hearth pit' — a distinctive type of pit in houses at Trethurgy with charcoal infill but burning only around the tops. The material relates to the use of the pit during the later phase of House Z — House Z2 — and is very unlikely to be residual or disturbed. Given that the bulk sample may represent charcoal fragments of a number of different ages, ie the *Fraxinus* sp. possibly comprises mature timber, the measurement only provides a *terminus post quem* for its context *(cal AD 240-540 at 95% probability)*.

UB-3250 the latest sample in the sequence comes from [932], a context at the base of a midden left to accumulate in the deserted Structure U. The midden was made up of a very black soil and contained large quantities of pottery as well as a rare tin ingot. If the interpretation of the deposit as an undisturbed midden is correct, it is unlikely that the charcoal is residual, as comprising twigs and small branches of *Ulex* sp. and *Calluna* sp. it most likely represents fuel debris. The estimated date of *cal AD 340-420 (at 68% probability)* agrees with the date for the context, later 4th century AD, assigned on the basis of a number of Oxfordshire ware sherds and other ceramics. This suggests that the assumption that the single Post-Roman amphora sherd in the upper part of the midden [801] is intrusive is correct.

9.2 Phasing and chronology

(Tables 9.2 and 9.3)

Table 9.2 provides a summary of dating suggested for Periods 3 to 8, while Table 9.3 details ceramics and radiocarbon determinations relevant to the chronology of the Period 3 Enclosure and the Period 4 Round. Throughout Section 9.2 estimated radiocarbon determinations are presented in italics.

9.2.1 Period 1 activity

Period 1 activity is defined by the range of lithics present which may span a long range from a date in the Mesolithic until the Early Bronze Age. The focus of activity is likely to have been in the Later Neolithic during the 3rd millennium cal BC (Chapter 7).

9.2.2 Period 2 activity

Period 2 activity is represented by the probable field system predating the Round and its cultivation. This activity could belong anywhere from the Middle Bronze Age until the construction of the Period 3 Enclosure.

9.2.3 The construction of the Period 3 Enclosure (Fig 4)

No features were identified predating the Period 3 Enclosure and only the pottery in the Bank [363] provides a *terminus post quem*. This pottery, all sherds of, or similar to, P32, is not closely datable, with a date range from the 1st century BC to the early 2nd century AD. Sherds from silting of the Ditch or infill of internal features may belong to the subsequent Period 4 as may early ceramics found in Period 5 contexts. Very tentatively it is suggested that the Period 3 Enclosure might have been constructed in the 1st century BC. The estimated date provided by pit [207] (UB-3254) *240 cal BC-cal AD 10 (93% probability)* cannot be directly related to the Period 3 Enclosure as it is only sealed by the OLS beneath the Round Rampart; it suggests activity at a rather earlier phase than that at which the Period 3 Enclosure was constructed.

9.2.4 Period 4 activity between the Enclosure and the Round

The unfinished Period 3 Enclosure, with some insubstantial buildings such as Structure N, was probably used for stock by the community living in the neighbourhood. The eroded state of the Period 3 earthworks and the complete silting of its Ditch suggest that the gap before the Round construction was of some duration. The Ditch [369] was everywhere sealed by the Round Rampart (except across the Entrance); the single eroded samian sherd it contained is unlikely to be intrusive and or to have been deposited before the 2nd century AD. Other, probably intermittent, use of the site in Period 4 is evidenced by the scatter of postholes such as [509]. This use may account for some of the pottery in Bank spread [780], and also for the smithing slag incorporated in the Period 5 Rampart and the pottery in its earliest structures.

Only the infill of Period 3 features [920] and [924] produced finds. These included P87, probably late 1st or early 2nd century, and a BB1 sherd and a South Devon ware sherd, not closely datable. The spread Period 3 Bank [780] beneath Structure Y contained a group of pottery which would be appropriate for the 2nd century but was subject to disturbance after the construction of the Round (Section 2.4).

Some ceramics from Period 5 contexts may be residual and relate to Periods 3 or 4. The Dressel 1sp amphora from [723] should date no later than the end of the 1st century BC, unless the alternative identification by Fitzpatrick as a Dressel 2-4 is correct (Section 5.3.8). The abraded South Western Decorated sherds P49 ([932] and soil over Y) are unlikely to have been made after the 1st century BC; P143 ([523] and soil over Q) belongs to the first Cordoned ware phase of 1st century BC to early 1st century AD and P83 [386], P138 [46], P140 [436], and P140A (ploughsoil), to the second Cordoned ware phase from the late 1st century to the early 2nd century AD (Section 5.6.2).

Some 150 years may well have elapsed between the construction of the Period 3 Enclosure and of the Round and this would appear appropriate for the amount of erosion of the earthworks of the former.

9.2.5 The construction of the Period 5 Round

The date for the construction of the Round cannot be established at all closely. The *terminus post quem* provided by pit [207] (UB-3254) beneath the Old Land Surface of 240 *cal BC-cal AD 10 (93% probability)* only provides a very broad indication. There is comparatively little pottery sealed in contexts early in the use of the Round, and none is of closely datable types.

The pottery assemblage from the Round as a whole may provide the most helpful guidance. Twelve out of the minimum 14 samian vessels are Antonine, only two possibly Hadrianic. Sherds were scattered throughout the full chronological range of contexts. A good proportion was found in the midden [932/801], which should be of 4th-century date and consequently samian may have been curated and retained. There is no black-burnished ware which need be earlier than the late 3rd century and generally the range of non-local fabrics is 3rd or 4th centuries. The gabbroic material may be more helpful, especially the sequence of bowl/dish forms. There are 12 with grooves and cordons below the rim P106-P110 (Type 19), probably manufactured from the late 1st until the late 2nd century. There are 15 flat-rimmed bowls P110-P113 (Type 20) probably manufactured from the late 2nd throughout the 3rd century, and 33 of the Cornish flanged form P126-P136 (Type 22) manufactured from the late 3rd century onward. Of these only the first, P106-110 Type 19, do not occur in midden [932/801], although they are residual in later soil spreads. Given that more pottery survives in late than in early contexts in the Round, the number of Type 19 bowls is striking, suggesting occupation starting well within their currency as the main bowl/dish form. A date of *c* 150 AD might be appropriate. By this date well-made gabbroic fabrics had largely been replaced by standard gabbroic. Less than 1% of the total gabbroic assemblage is well-made. Of these a number are Type 1 jars which were probably not made after the early 2nd century. Some of these, and some of the Type 19 bowls, may belong to Period 4, with the second-phase Cordoned ware discussed above. Some pottery is likely to have been brought to the site when occupation began. The date of AD 150 for Round construction appears to be the best fit for the data available, but the date could have been a generation earlier. Thereafter the Round continued in use, with possible occasional short gaps, until at least the currency of Post-Roman import wares *c* AD 500 or later.

9.2.6 The use of the Period 5 Round

Activity in the Round has been divided into ten Stages, a number arrived at by consideration of all the stratigraphic data for successive structural phases. The dating of these Stages has been derived from an assessment of their duration within the whole period of occupation between *c* AD 150 to post AD 500, assisted by data from ceramics and the cross links of broken stone artefacts. It has been decided to provided explicit dates for these Stages, to permit a clear interpretative biography of the site but it is stressed that the Stage dates are only 'best fits' to the data available and should not be quoted as definitive.

The stratigraphy on the east, downhill, side, being better preserved, allows the establishment of reasonable sequences. Broadly, House/Areas T, R, V, U, Z, Q and Y can be linked stratigraphically. Uphill, linking layers between A, D, E, G and X were lacking, although internal sequences could be established in all of them. For a sequence of chronological Stages, the data for the first group are comparatively firm. That for the second group has been assigned where it appears to fit best, but it must be stressed that the uphill sequences are fluid in relationship to each other and to much of the downhill sequence. The Stage plans should not be used as dogmatic statements of what the site was like at any particular time.

There is one stratigraphic link of great importance across the downhill side of the site. This is the contemporaneity of the repaving of the Entrance [188] with surfaces [557] and [8], the former being a continuation of Structure U and the latter of paving [254] of House T4. Stages 1-4 precede this surface link, Stage 5 is contemporary with the link, and Stages 6-10 postdate it.

Features such as the central group of postholes [92] etc (Fig 5) which had no relationships at all are not dealt with in the following discussion.

Obviously, the presentation of the site as a sequence of defined Stages suggests that rebuilding activity or periods of desertion were synchronous on different parts of the site. It is entirely possible that there was almost continuous activity, with rebuilding taking place at different times on different structures. The Stage plans would then present a misleadingly formalised picture of a fluid development. It must be stressed that the Stage plans are only an attempt to show approximately what the site was like at different stages of its development and that, as such, their presentation is preferable to making no attempt to visually disentangle the chronology of the Round. It is hoped that the data has been presented in sufficient detail to allow readers to formulate alternative Stage phasing.

Stage 1 (Fig 80)

Structures A, D, E, and X were all situated on the levelled shelf which was cut as a continuation of the seating for the inner Rampart revetment, and so were obviously subsequent to the construction of the Rampart. This shelf provided suitable locations for houses as there would have been little problem with drainage. House Z, in its earliest form, cannot be definitely demonstrated to postdate the Round, but this House, like the others, was rebuilt on the same site throughout the use of the Round, and its structural sequence links smoothly with subsidiary structures in Area Q which definitely postdated the Period 5 Rampart. The reasons for the siting of House Z are unclear; its area, though slightly sloping, is as level as is that beneath the later Structure Y adjacent to the Rampart. It may have been set inwards from the Rampart to provide for ancillary structures in the intervening space. T was the lowest lying of the Houses, with the disadvantage of potential drainage problems. House T1 consisted only of gulley [458], apparently a drain for a structure which was never built.

The basic layout of the Round allowed for four large houses in two pairs, A and T, and X and Z. While it cannot be demonstrated that A, X, and Z were all built at the same time, it is possible that provision was made for four families but that the fourth site, T, was not needed immediately. The initial planning of the Round allowed for activities other than House construction. Structure E lies almost exactly midway between A and X and may also have been an original feature; its large postholes contained no finds although the soil over the Structure came to contain a lot of artefact debris. Structure D appeared to have been inserted later, in the space between E and A, and in that case would not have been a primary building. The lower north-east corner was probably allocated for stock, as here the only drain, [199], was built through the Rampart. This drain was kept clear through the use of the Round. The later structures here, U and V, were connected with stock but their construction involved the removal of earlier features; except for postholes [576]-[591] (Fig 8) nothing is known of this area until Stage 5. The lower, south-eastern, Area R was left as open ground, with slight structures, on which soil wash gradually accumulated. It may have provided space for keeping agricultural equipment, as well as providing a good level surface for out-of-door activities.

The central area of the Round had a patchy cobbled surface [48] which presumably was used throughout the site's occupancy. Just inside the Entrance, rubble [409] (Fig 8), some of which may have been in position in Period 3, formed the surface during Stages 1 to 4, a sparse scattering of stones linking it with the initial Entrance paving [215]. Generally, extensive paving is not a feature until Stage 5; reasons may relate to climate, fewer animals being kept inside, or just a shortage of stone until more was garnered from the cultivation of nearby fields.

House Z1 (Fig 19) was chronologically complex. Its wall was totally removed at a later stage (probably Stage 5) except for fragment [907]. If the line of [907] is projected west it overlies drainage gulley [761], which cannot be a drainage feature directly connected with a primary wall, as it truncates an earlier gulley [764]. It seems probable that House Z1 was altered and enlarged in Stage 4; pre-alteration it is described as Z1a, post-alteration as Z1b. The best guess for the position of the Z1a wall in Stage 1 was that its outer edge lay immediately inside gulley [761], and that the wall-line incorporated some, at least, of postholes [884], [855], [867], [866], [883], [856], [954], and [865]. Postholes [867] and [866] were truncated by [793], which appeared to be infill of a cut for the Z2 wall (Stage 6) but which may have incorporated some earlier levelling. The Z1 rab floor [854] on the west

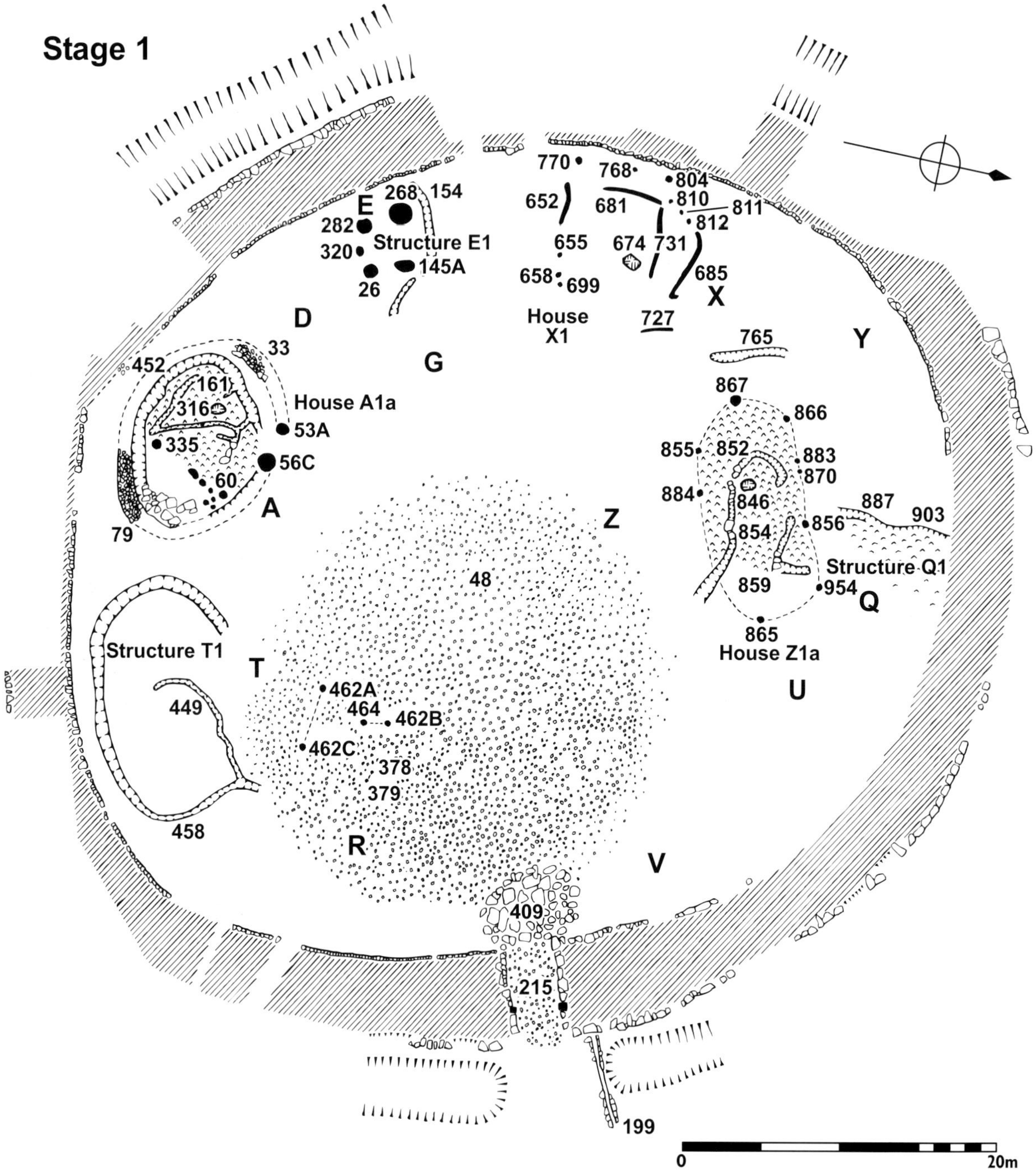

Fig 80: Stage 1 suggested structures c AD 150-175

with its associated drains did not undergo any detectable alteration; on the east, downhill side the rab subsoil was levelled and used as a floor during Stages 1-3 Z1a with soil [948] accumulating on it, beneath the Stage 4 paving [949] of Z1b. The evidence for Z1a in Stages 1-3 is scrappy — why for example is there only one hearth pit [846] for the whole of Z1 (Stages 1-4)? The Stage 1 exterior gulley for Z was probably [765], the earliest of the sequence and that with the least humic infill.

To Stage 1 in Q (Fig 9) should belong the earliest of the structural sequence, Structure Q1 levelling [903] with a worn surface (largely cut away in later Stages). There is no evidence for the form of structure it related to but this appears to have filled the space between Z1a and the Rampart.

In X (Fig 25) the earliest demonstrable features appeared to be slots [652], [681], [731], and [685] and possibly postholes such as [770]. House X1 to which they belonged was an irregular rectangle in plan, constructed, probably, entirely of timber. A series of postholes which could be primary have been added to the Stage 1 plan (Fig 28), together with a possible early hearth pit [674]. Because of plough damage, the elucidation of a detailed structural sequence in X is impossible.

In Stage 1 E1 (Fig 29) was a four-poster set in the substantial postholes [282]-[268]-[145A]-[26]. Gulley

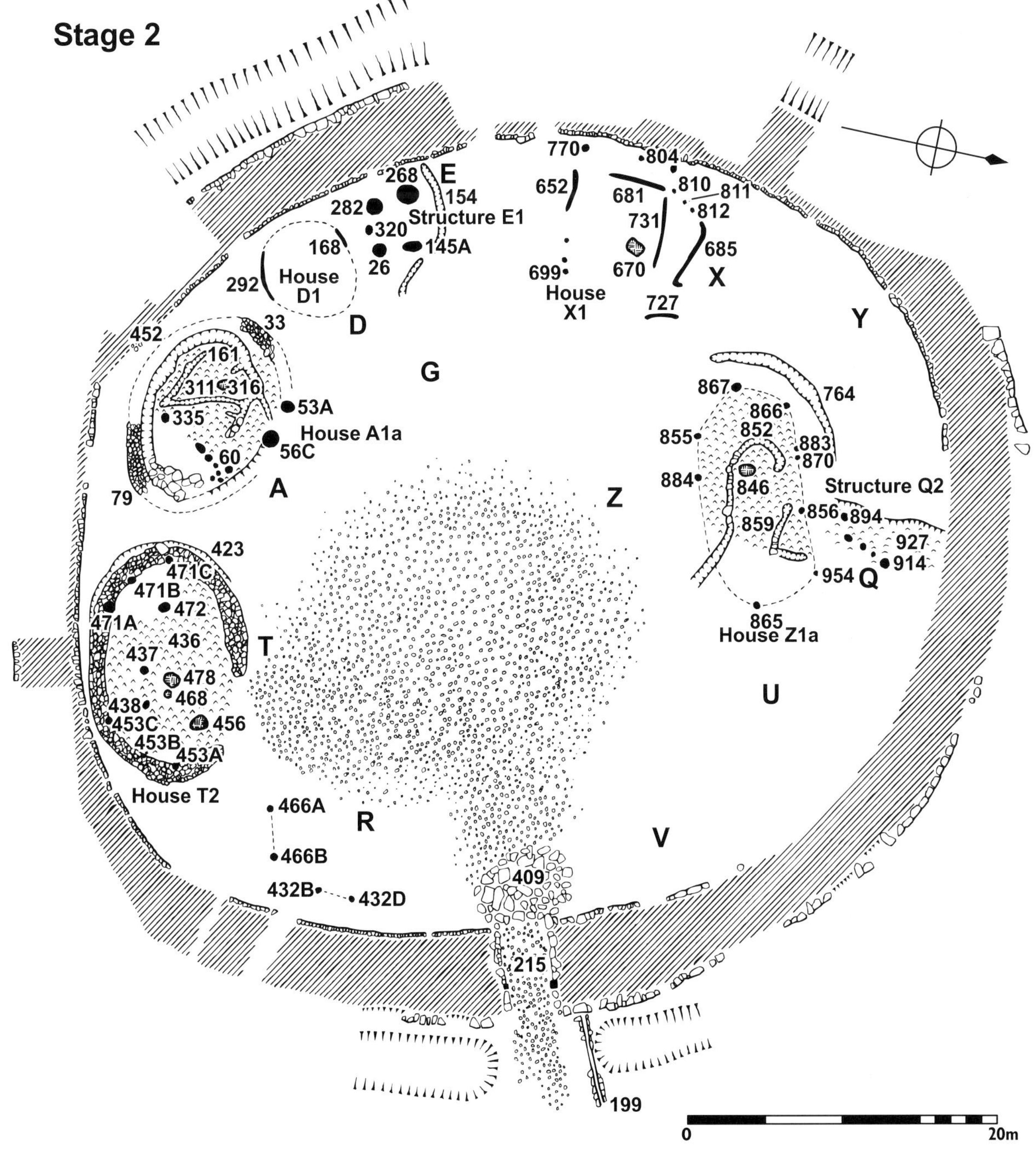

Fig 81: *Stage 2 suggested structures c AD 175-210*

[154] may have provided drainage at this or another early stage.

House A1 (Fig 34) had two clear structural episodes 1a and 1b, the later relating to the recutting of doorposts and the disturbance of the original paved floor [24]. House A1a in Stage 1 (Fig 36) had an internal drain [161] and doorposts [53A] and [56C]. A rab floor [311] with a network of drains on its uphill side was separated by a timber partition in posthole line [335]-[60] from paving [24] on the lower end. The remnants of its wall [33]/[79] were scanty.

In Area R the earliest features were paired postholes, possibly to be interpreted as drying racks. The posthole pairs shown in Stage 1 are [432B] and [432D], cut at a very early level in the soil wash sequence, and [462A]-[462C], [378]-[379], and [464]-[464B], which were inappropriately sited for later periods when House T was operational.

In Stage 1 the only contexts considered secure which producing finds were A [33] (P29), T [458] (P60), and X [685] (P135). P29 is an early jar form, P60 not closely datable while P135 is an unique hand-made piece possibly copying a 2nd-century mortarium. It seems appropriate from the structural evidence to suggest the duration of a generation for Stage 1, AD 150-175. The *terminus post quem* provided by UB-3255 from posthole [884] (Stages 1-3) in House Z1a is estimated *cal AD 120-320* (see Stage 3).

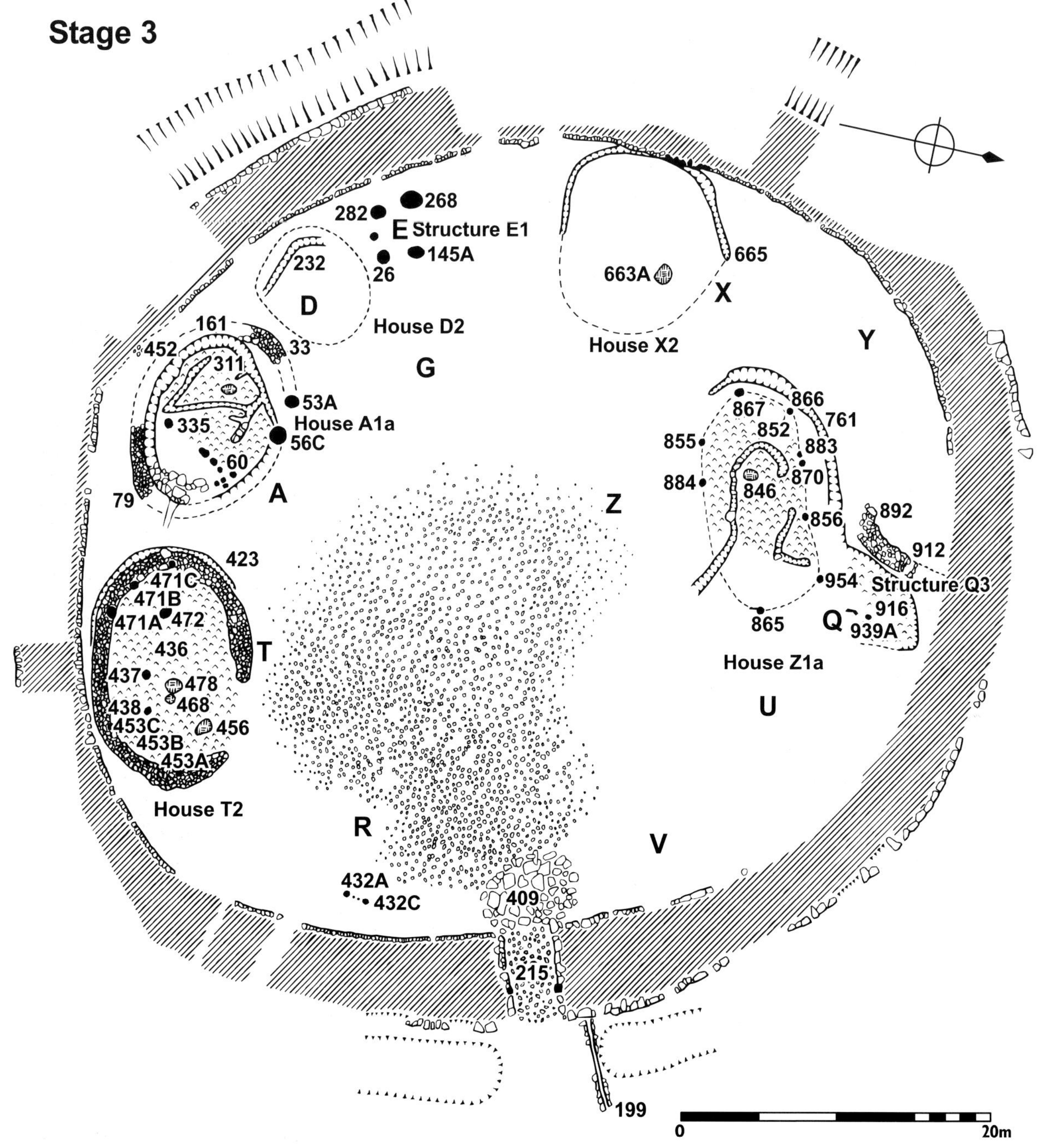

Fig 82: Stage 3 suggested structures c AD 210-260

Stage 2 (Fig 81)

This is suggested as a period of expansion, for with the addition of House T and Structure D, all house sites were in use. House T2 (Fig 40), the earliest proper structure on this site, may be assumed to have been an early addition because only a little soil [455] accumulated over the gulley of T1; also time must be allowed for rebuilding in Stage 4. D had a long structural sequence, delimited in area throughout by Structure E to its north, and should probably be interpreted as roughly contemporary with E. The small size of D suggests a 'squeezed-in' afterthought rather than a planned primary structure.

Outside House Z1a, gulley [764], with slightly more humic fill, replaced [765]; the ancillary Structure Q2 (Fig 9) incorporated postline [894]-[914] (over [927] which levelled up the earlier floor [903]). Soil [751A] started to accumulate behind Z and Q beneath later Structure Y. House X1 may have continued in its rectangular timber form; the evidence for the sequence here is unsatisfactory. The initial substantial posts in Structure E were unlikely to have needed rapid renewal.

The earliest feature in D was the narrow slot [292]/[168] (Figs 31, 33), largely destroyed by later levelling, apparently supporting D1, an oval timber

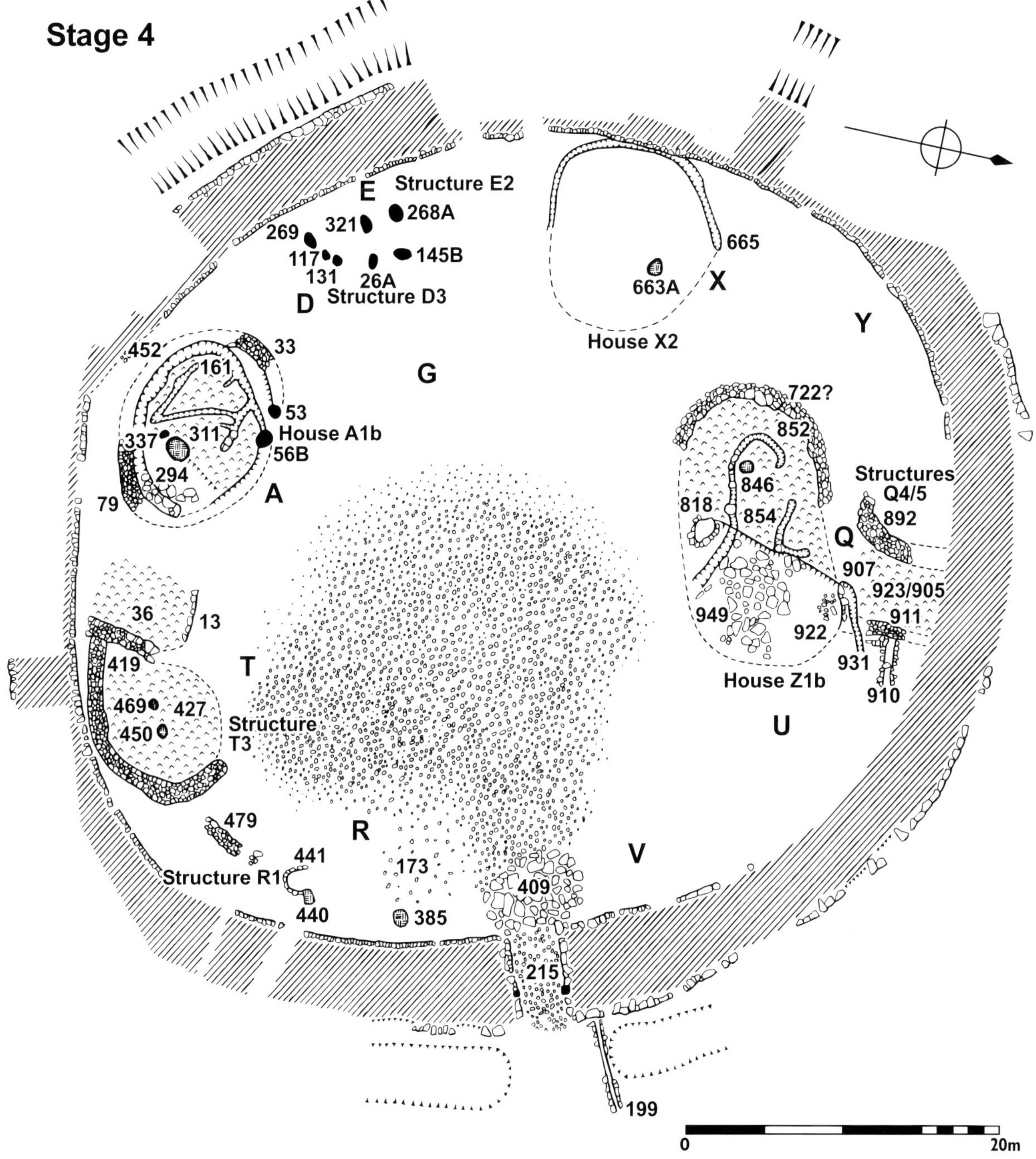

Fig 83: Stage 4 suggested structures c AD 260-325

structure *c* 6 m across. House A1a probably did not yet require alteration. The new building, House T2 (Fig 39), was a substantial stone-walled structure with a uniform rab floor [436], a hearth [478], and a hearth pit [456]. The wall incorporated postholes. In Area R, the timber structures of Stage 1 in the entrance area of House T may no longer have been used; nearer the Rampart, pairs [466A]-[466B] and [432B]-[432D] (Fig 44) were cut slightly higher in soil accumulation [386] than those suggested for Stage 1.

There are no diagnostic finds from sealed contexts suggested for this Stage, which may well have been longer than Stage 1. AD 175-210 might be suggested.

Stage 3 (Fig 82)

The Round continued to have its maximum residential capacity. Outside House Z1a the latest external gulley [761] was cut (Fig 19), which linked with the levelled area [916] and wall [892] of Structure Q3 (Fig 22). Wall [892] with drain [912] was substantial, linking House Z1a and the Rampart, and appeared to have had a long life, used in several successive Structures. Soil [751A] continued to accumulate behind wall [892] in Area Y. House X1 may have been altered from its initial rectangular plan. The next main stratigraphic feature was [665] (Fig 25). This had the broad profile of a gulley not a slot (Fig 26), but its fill was not of silt but of back-packed rab mixed with some stone and charcoal. It seems probable that this functioned as a slot supporting upright timbers. This structure, X2, will then have been an oval version of the stone houses used elsewhere on the site. Some of the numerous but unphased postholes in Area X may have been used in its construction. Structures A, E, and T may still have continued without major alteration. Perhaps the oval timber construction D1 of Stage 2 in D may have been replaced. Internal drain [232] (Fig 31) was the next feature in the sequence. The structure to which it belonged, D2, will probably have had a stone wall which was largely removed by later levelling. In Area R the latest pair of postholes was [432A]-[432C].

Gulley [761] accumulated pot sherds as it silted up. These included P102, which is suggested as mid 3rd century or later. This context is the earliest to produce a vessel of the large storage jar group (Type 16). House T2 appeared to have fallen into disuse at the end of the Stage, with posts pulled out and soil [442] accumulating on the floor. Soil [442] produced a South Devon ware sherd, the earliest sealed context to do so, apart from the doubtfully sealed Period 3/4 [920]. It may be relevant that South Devon ware and sherds of large storage jar P101 occur in secondary Ditch silt [567]. The Ditch may already have been largely infilled by this time. The *terminus post quem* provided by UB-3255 from posthole [884] (Stages 1-3) in House Z1a is estimated *cal AD 120-320*, a good *terminus post quem* for the end of House Z1a, as material from the posthole was probably derived from hearths within the House.

A date for Stage 3 spanning the middle of the 3rd century AD would be possible, perhaps rather longer than the preceding Stages to allow for some deterioration before the suggested rebuilding of the next Stage. AD 210-260 is suggested.

Stage 4 (Fig 83)

This Stage probably saw the first major phase of rebuilding in the Round. Z/Q, E, D, A, and T were all reconstructed; there were similarities in the rebuilding of Z and T as both had external revetted rubble platforms.

House Z was rebuilt on a larger scale as Z1b, so that its walling incorporated [907] (Figs 19, 22). This walling [907] formed a right-angle with wall [911] in Q which ran up to the Rampart and revetted make-up levels [923]/[905] against wall [892]; the platform so constructed was drained by [931] and [910] and is described as Structure Q4. In House Z1b it is just possible that the uphill end of wall [722] (Fig 20) was built at this Stage and subsequently reused; the plan shows an alteration in its nature at the point at which the Z2 (Stage 6) drain [878]/[860] runs through the wall. In any case the wall-line, if incorporating [907], will have been built over gulley [761] in Stage 4. Inside the House the lower part was paved with [949] and [922]; the gap between them (Fig 22) was caused by the later drain [873]. This paving sealed soil [948]. The downhill end of House Z1b was later truncated by Structure U, but the House must have been about 16m long. Behind House Z, Y appears still to have been open space with soil [751A] accumulating. The long continuance of this unbuilt area within the Round suggests it had some special function, possible a garden plot. The oval timber House X2 may have continued, perhaps for part of the Stage.

The four-post structure was rebuilt as E2, perhaps in this Stage, with slighter postholes [321]-[268A]-[145B]-[26A] (Fig 29). House A1a was rebuilt as A1b, with slighter postholes [53] and [56B] holding the door-frame, which may provide a tenuous link with the slight posts in the rebuilding of E. Other alterations to A, which may be grouped with the new door-frame, were the dismantling of the timber partition, with hearth pit [294] set on its former line (Fig 34) and the disturbance of the paving [24]. For Structure D, the next structural phase D3 was postline [269]-[117]-[131], which may either have been some form of drying rack or one side of a rectangular building, the south part of which was removed by later levelling.

House T was rebuilt (T3, Fig 40) on an irregular plan. Wall [419] was built out from the Rampart to form its west side, but the earlier wall [448] was reused for the remainder of the circumference. There was a new rab floor [427], with [450] and [469] which may have been hearth pits. West and uphill of House T3, a platform of rubble [36] ran back to the Rampart, revetted by [13]. Downhill, soil [386] continued to accumulate in Area R. There were several features on the surface of [386] which predated the Stage 5 paving. These were the dump wall [479] of Structure R1, hearths [385] and [440], pit [441], and cobble spreads [173].

Contexts in use, or sealed, in this Stage produced both BB1 conical flanged and gabbroic Cornish flanged bowls; BB1 conical flanged bowl P18 came from [36], and also from the unsealed level [751A], Cornish flanged bowl P130 from [905] and [948]. No earlier context produced these forms, which are dated from the late 3rd century onward. These flanged bowls provide one of the better chronological indicators on the site, and while their presence or absence should not be overstressed, they appear consistently in later Stages. The presence of these bowls in Stage 4 may suggest a date somewhere around AD 300.

Stage 4, if all the suggested alterations were contemporary, entailed a considerable restructuring of

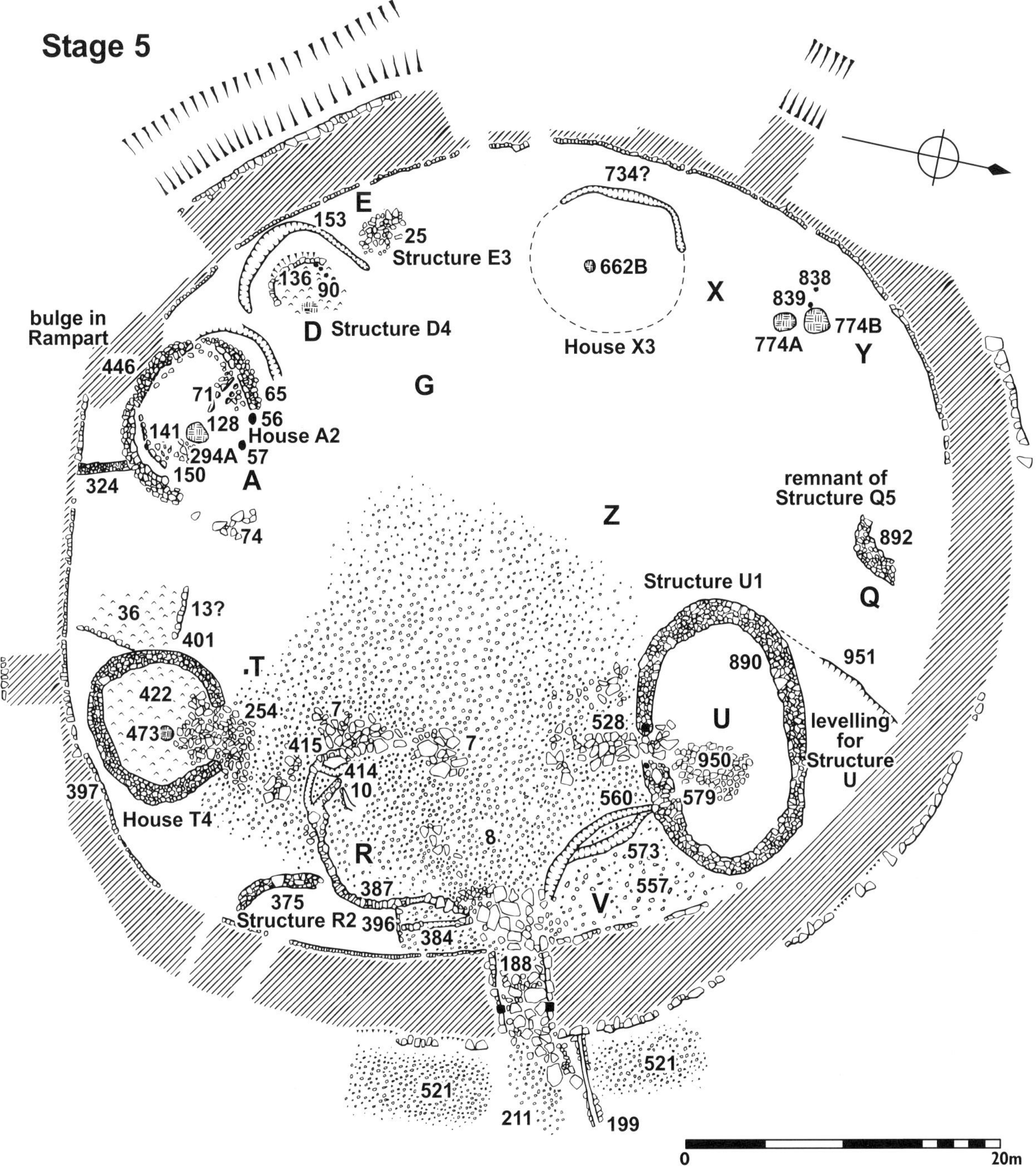

Fig 84: Stage 5 suggested structures c AD 325-375

the site, and it may have been of some duration. Subsequently there appeared to have been a phase of disuse before the major rebuilding of Stage 5. Structures Z, Q, A, T, and R all had some soil accumulation over Stage 4 contexts (conditions in D, E, and X did not allow such soil to survive). In Z/Q, soil [808] formed over floor [949]/[922] and wall tumble [907A] from wall [911]. Layer [34A] formed in House A. Soil [422] spread over House T3 and formed a continuous level with soil [9] in R. These soils could have formed very quickly. They contained a comparatively large quantity of pottery, providing the earliest context for the import P6 and for South-Western Grey storage jar sherds.

UB-3252 from [427], an accumulation of trampled material in the floor around the hearth of House T3, provides a *terminus post quem* for the disuse of the house and is estimated at *cal AD 80-350*. UB-3253 from context [923], estimated at 68% confidence to *cal AD 210-260 (29%)* and *cal AD 270-340 (39%)*, providing a *terminus post quem* for the overlying layer [905] containing Cornish flanged bowls, consistent with their introduction around AD 275.

Stage 4 may have been of some duration with a possible date range of AD 260-325.

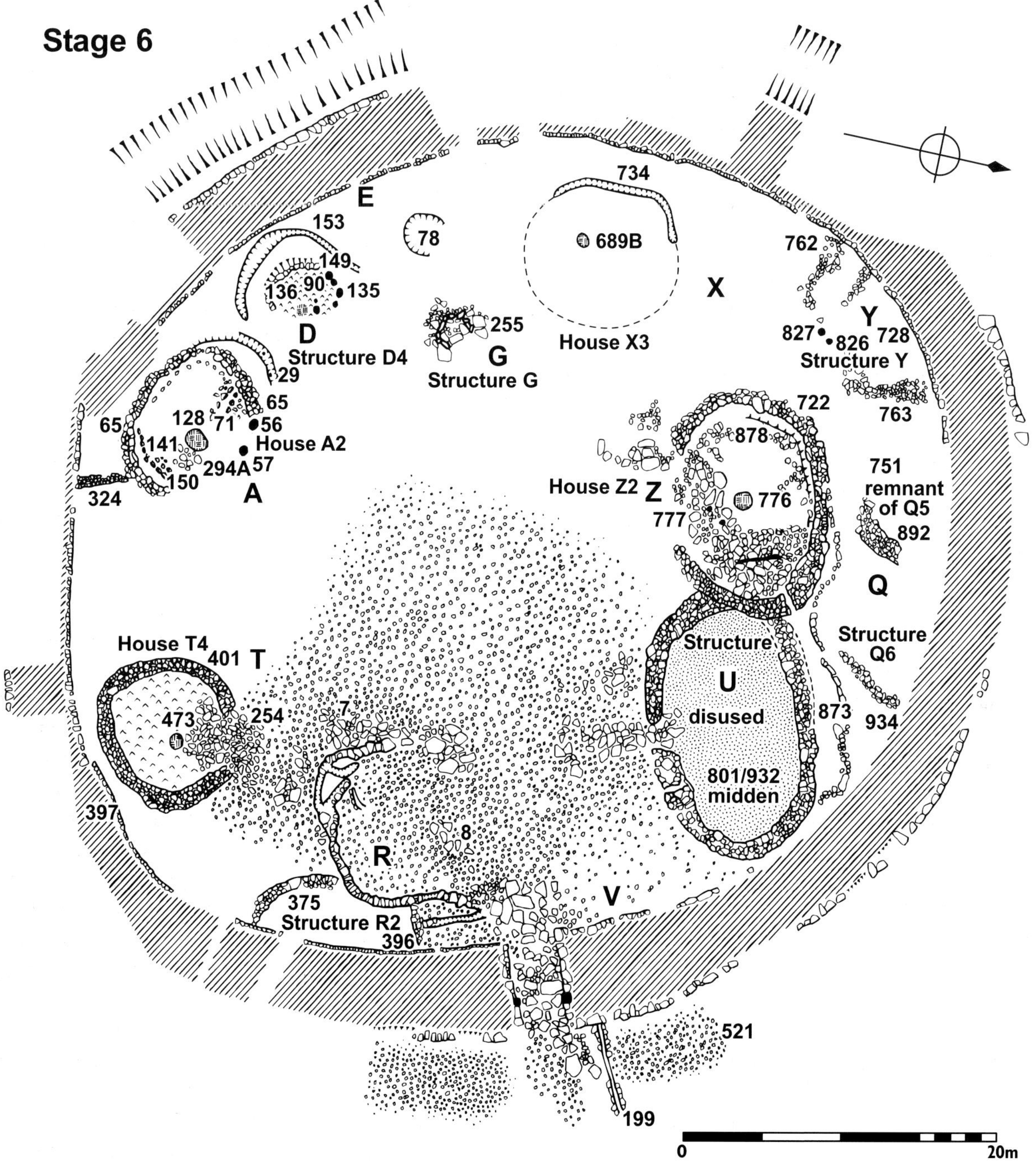

Fig 85: Stage 6 suggested structures c AD 375-400

Stage 5 (Fig 84)

The Entrance was restructured with the substantial paving slabs [188] laid and, probably, with the gateposts replaced. Outside, surface [521] over the Ditch terminals may be of this Stage, although subsidence had broken any stratigraphic connection. Inside the Round, paving [188] formed a continuous surface with [557], which was associated with Structure U and with [7]/[8] which was continuous with paving [254] in House T4. This Stage restructuring makes more use of good paved surfaces than those preceding it.

The construction of the byre, Structure U1 (Figs 16, 18), entailed clearance and levelling of the north-east corner of the site, delimited by cut [951]. Structure U had good entrance paving [528] which formed a continuous surface with [557], laid after the levelling of the area and which abutted the outside of the U1 wall [890]. Drainage gulley[573], succeeded by [560], ran out from U through surface [557] to exit through the Rampart drain[199]. House Z was out of use; U1 wall [890] ran over Z1b flooring [949] and soil [808] above it. Probably most of the Z1 walls were removed to build U, although [892] from Structure Q5 was still standing. If House X was rebuilt at this stage and not later, House X3 represented by ?slot [734] forms the next detectable structural phase; X3 is subject to the same interpretational problems as X2 (see Stage 3). Hearths [774A] and [774B] (Fig 24) beneath Structure Y may belong here.

Structure E3, the latest phase of Structure E represented by paving [25] (Fig 29) would be appropriate in a Stage when paving was so much used. Paving [25] reflected the outline of the earlier Structures E1 and E2 and so was unlikely to have been laid after any very long interval. The last phase of Structure D, D4 (Fig 33), is likely to have been contemporary with some structure in E because the D4 phase involved substantial levelling which respected E (Fig 31). After the interior of D4 was levelled, internal drain [136] was built with a rab floor [90] and a variety of internal features; outside was gulley [153].

The earliest phase of House A2 (Fig 38), postdating the 'disuse' soil [34A], may belong to Stage 5. It was smaller than House A1. Its wall [65] related to door-frame posts [56] and [57], with internal drains [150] and [71], flooring [141], and hearth pit [128]. Outside was drainage gulley [97], and wall [324] which ran back to the Rampart, revetting rubble behind it. The Rampart, weakened behind the House because it had been built over a silted hollow [451], was strengthened by dump [446] which ran right up to wall [65] of House A2.

House T4, its paving [254] continuous with Stage 5 paving [7]/[8], was again smaller than its predecessors (Fig 41). Its oval wall [401] incorporated part of wall [448] which survived from House T2. T4 contained a hearth [473]. The Rampart behind House T4 was strengthened by additional material [397] revetted by [398], consistent with the general tidying and strengthening of the Rampart in Stage 5, especially as seen in Area A and at the Entrance.

In Area R the large paving blocks of [7] were laid in the surface [8] and a complex of drains [415] and [387] were incorporated in [8] to keep this area dry. Structure R2, built against the Rampart, had walls [375] and [396] and a drain [384] linked to paving [8].

There was no distinctive dating material for Stage 5. A date AD 325-375 is suggested, to cover both any gap in occupation preceding Stage 5 and the Stage 5 rebuilding. There was considerable wear in Structure U, all of it of this Stage, and its external drain was recut on a different line, suggesting the Stage was of some duration.

Stage 6 (Fig 85)

Structure U1 went out of use and part of its wall was incorporated in House Z2, which was now built (Fig 20). The Z2 wall [722] may have been partly built over the line of House Z1b wall initially constructed in Stage 4. The interior was paved over most of its area [777] and there were four hearth pits, which suggest House Z2 may have been in use over a longish period. Outside, drain [873] was constructed round the stub of Structure U, but with no definite outlet. Bank [934] Structure Q6 (Fig 22) linking House Z2 to the Rampart belongs to this Stage or later, as it overlay soil infilling Stage 5 levelling for Structure U and some accumulation of soil [808]. Structure U itself was used as a midden [932/801]. As it is probable that rubbish was regularly collected for use as manure and removed from the site, the abandonment of this midden inside the Round may indicate some interruption in the usual activities in the Round.

House X3 may have continued. Structure Y may have been built at about this time. Its position suggests that it was constructed while House Z was standing. The base of wall [892] was still standing as surface [751] developed between it and Y, and its top became worn. The range of material from surface [728] inside Y includes Oxfordshire ware but also Post-Roman imported amphorae sherds, which indicates late activity here. It is quite possible that walls of dump construction could have been remodelled without leaving detectable traces. Wall [762] in Y contained part of quern S42, another piece of which was incorporated in Structure G. If Structure Y was not of Stage 6, it should belong to a later period. The coin hoard (Section 3.1) partly sealed beneath its wall has been given a *terminus ante quem* of *c* AD 260. While the taphonomic processes relating to the hiding of the hoard and its subsequent dispersal are not clear, the wide area of soil through which the coins were scattered suggests some gap between its deposition and the building of Structure Y.

Structure G may also have been built at about this time, although the presence of part of quern S42 in its backing [255], another part of which was built into Structure Y, is not a link that can be closely relied on. G has no stratigraphic links with other structures. It is unlikely to be primary; if it had been, the scarping on the shelf at the top of the site might be expected to have been cut to accommodate it. G in fact was built forward of this scarping, and the infill behind its orthostats contained dark soil and artefacts. Very early features on the site appear to have cleaner fills. There is also the possibility that if G had some storage function, it replaced E. The end date of E is uncertain; its latest stage has been assigned to Stage 5. The interior of G had a certain amount of wear, which,

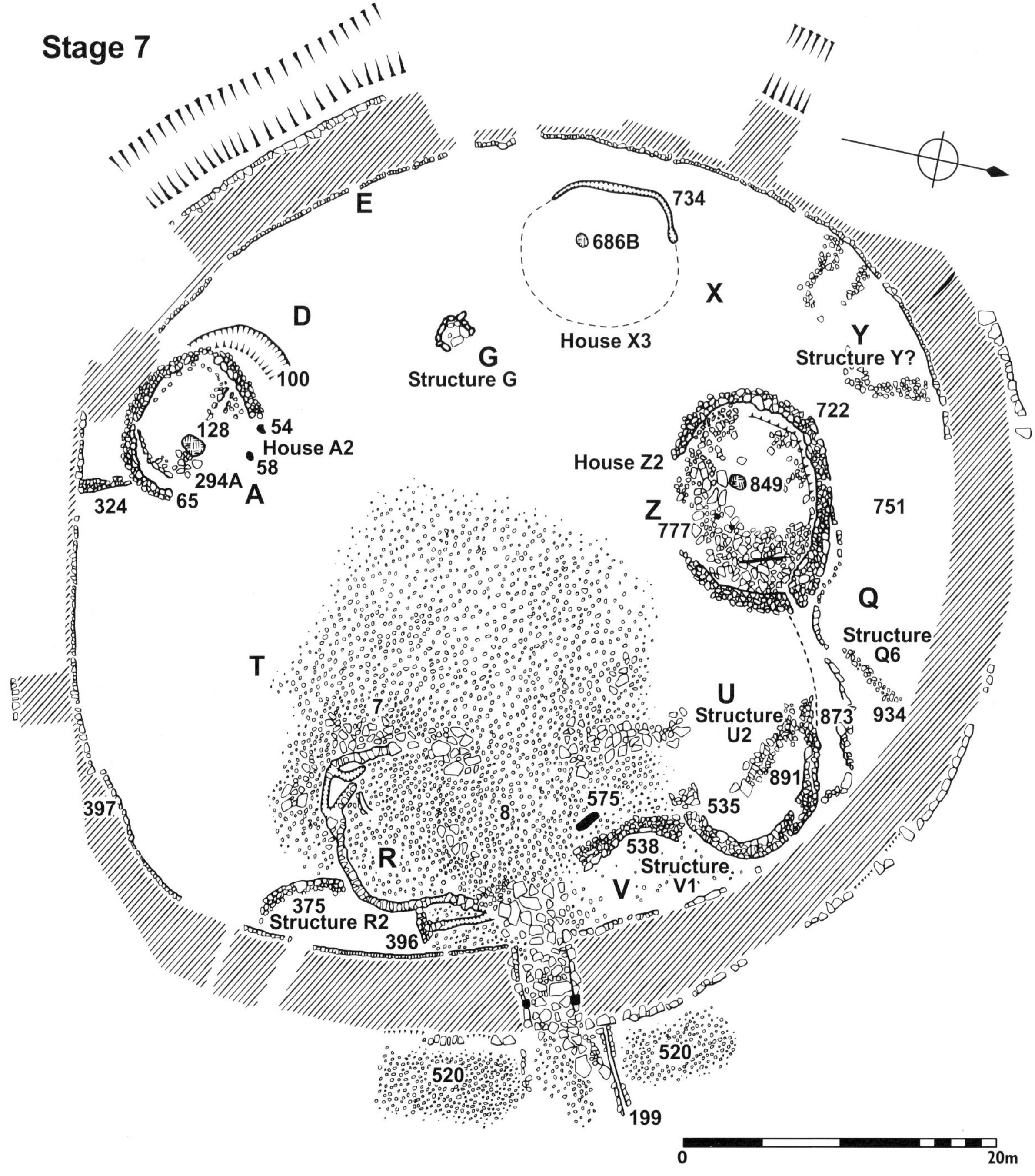

Fig 86: Stage 7 suggested structures c AD 400-450

given its restricted area, suggests a long phase of use. (The possibility that G was in fact a primary structure, rebuilt in Stage 6, is explored in Section 11.12.) Pit [78] seems to belong to a time when Structure E was not in use and may be Stage 6 or later.

The rebuilding of House Z may be explained by the need for more residential accommodation. If so, House D4, House A2 and House T4 may be presumed to have continued in use. Structure R2 may have had a long life because the next building in this area occurred much later, after House T5 had become ruinous. It is suggested that Stage 6 is fairly short, a period which saw some additional building to that of Stage 5 and also the deposition of the midden.

Midden [932/801] from Stage 6 provided the largest group of finds of any Stage in the Round. The midden contained BB1 conical flanged bowls and jars with oblique lattice but also a number of Oxfordshire ware sherds including P2 and P3. This is the earliest sealed context to produce Oxfordshire ware. If the dating sequence assigned to the Stages so far is followed, Stage 6 and the midden would belong to the late stage in the 4th century AD and AD 375-400 is suggested. This is perhaps rather late for the Oxfordshire ware which had probably been in use

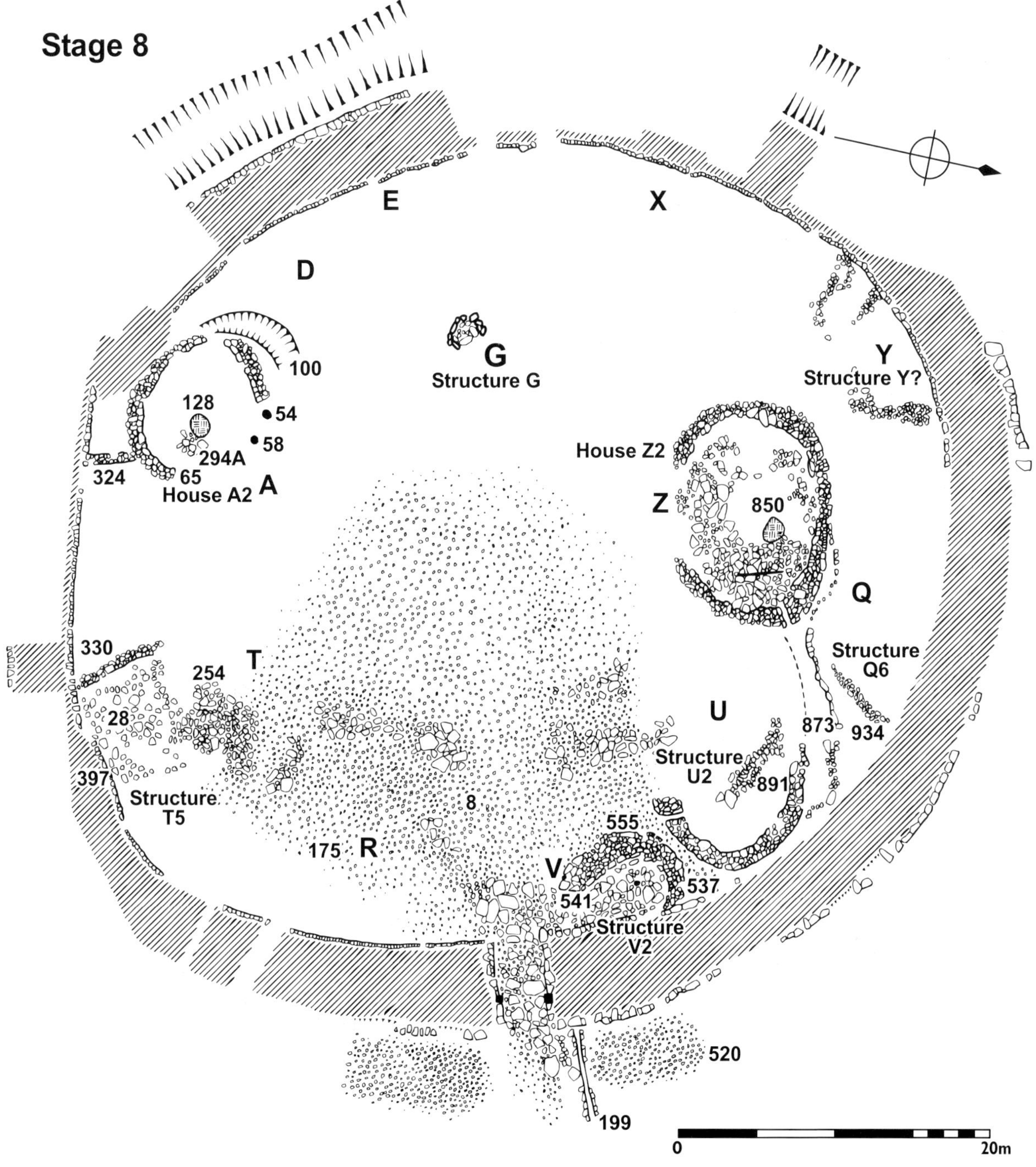

Fig 87: *Stage 8 suggested structures c AD 450-500*

locally since the late 3rd century and certainly later than dating proposed for midden dumps with Oxfordshire ware at Reawla (Quinnell 1992). However the author now considers that the Reawla dating may be a little early. There is also the consideration that finewares in the midden, whether samian, Oxfordshire, or other, tend to occur in the same state, small sherds rather abraded (see Section 12.10 for further discussion of the midden). The suggested dating also allows suitable time for Stages 7 and 8 before Post-Roman import wares appear in Stage 9; earlier dating for the midden and Stage 6 would lengthen these Stages. The dating assumes that the single Post-Roman amphora sherd in the upper midden [801] is intrusive; if this association were taken as real, the dating would be about a century later and the other Stages adjusted accordingly. The estimated date for the base of midden layer [932] (UB-3250) is *cal AD 250-440* at 95% confidence and *cal AD 340-420* at 68% confidence, good support for the late 4th-century dating of the midden. The *terminus post quem* provided by UB-3251 from hearth pit [849] in Z2 is estimated at *cal AD 240-540*. This hearth pit was assigned to Stage 7 in a random division of the group of hearth pits throughout the use of the House and the date is in broad accordance with the Stage 6 and later chronology proposed here.

Stage 7 (Fig 86)

The lower, eastern part of Structure U was rebuilt as U2 (Fig 18) with dump walling [891] and drain [535] over midden [932/801]. Structure V1, with its wall [528] (Fig 13) appeared contemporary with this rebuilding, as the new drain [535] in U2 was positioned to respect wall [528]. House Z2 continued, as it will be argued to have been in use until Stage 9. Structure Y also appears to have continued until Stage 9. Perhaps now wall [892] was pulled down and its stub incorporated into surface [751]. House X3 may have continued, as its last rebuilding belongs to Stage 9. Structure G was also still used, while behind it the area of Structure E began to accumulate soil and rubbish. The end date for Structure D4 is unclear but the general spread of rubble and rubbish in E continued over its site. House A2 was refurbished at some stage, the door-frame posts being recut as [54] and [58] (Fig 37). These, and the later gulley [100], may belong to Stage 7.

House T4 fell into disuse, its site accumulating soil [403] before its last rebuilding. It may not have been in use at this Stage. Structure R2 may have continued.

Outside the Round, the upper surface [520] over the Ditch terminals belonged to a Stage subsequent to Stage 5. Surface [520] became worn before soil accumulated in the disuse phase between Stages 9 and 10. It could belong to Stage 7.

There were few finds from contexts of this Stage. The suggested date is AD 400-450.

Stage 8 (Fig 87)

Structure V was rebuilt as V2, the wall [537] (Figs 13, 15) partly reusing the earlier wall [538]. Structure V2 was well-built with a paved floor [541] and internal drain [542]. The area outside was resurfaced with cobbles [551] and [555]. Structure U2 may have continued. House Z and Structure Y were also still in use. House X was rebuilt in the next Stage, Stage 9; it seems unlikely that House X3 would have lasted some 150 years, from Stage 5 onward, and the House site may have been out of use in this Stage.

House A2 in its refurbished form appears to have continued. The main problem concerns the second-phase gulley around the House, [100]. This produced Gl 1, the conical beaker fragment which is likely to be of 6th-century date (Section 4.5). There are various possibilities here. Gulley [100] may in fact belong to the subsequent Stage 9; its stratigraphic position is not entirely clear. Gl 1 could have been intrusive in the gulley, much of the surface of which was not securely sealed. Finally [100] and House A2 could have survived until the early part of the 6th century. On balance it seems likely that the top of [100] was still silting up in Stage 9 in the 6th century.

There was rebuilding over House T, after the disuse assigned to Stage 7. In T5 (Fig 42) the new wall [300] appeared to form part of an irregular rectangular enclosure which need not have been roofed; its interior paving [28] extended [254], which survived from T4, across to the Rampart. In Area R patchings [175] to surface [8] were laid after some soil [400] had accumulated and probably after Structure R2 was out of use.

The finds include a number of sherds from sealed contexts in T and V. These show continuation of late-Roman pottery forms, but no Post-Roman import wares. The Stage should probably be dated well into the fifth century, AD 450-500 would be appropriate, although, as Post-Roman import wares may well have been in circulation from *c* AD 475, the terminal date may be placed rather too late.

Stage 9 (Fig 88)

At this late Stage the arguments for contemporaneity and sequence of structures are based on increasingly fragmentary evidence. It has already been suggested that the site was less intensively used as the 5th century continued; therefore any rebuilding of different structures which can be detected may be sequential and not contemporary. Consideration of the later 5th century must include the significance of the Post-Roman import wares found. Although most were not firmly stratified, coming from plough-disturbed levels, they were scattered fairly evenly over the Round, including the Entrance area (Fig 88). This pattern suggests continued use of the Round as an occupied settlement, rather than casual visitation. While the dating of the Post-Roman import wares is still subject to adjustment, their introduction to Britain is considered broadly appropriate to the last quarter of the 5th century AD. Their deposition on the site may well be much later. Two sherds of Bii amphorae were found in features associated with the latest House in Area X, gulley [743] and walling [666]. While disturbance and intrusion cannot be disproved, it appears more likely that House X4 (Fig 28) was built at a date around AD 500, the first stone oval building in this Area and the latest to be constructed in the Round. Part of Trethurgy bowl S1 was found in [678] under paving outside X4, the others coming from Stage 9/10 rampart collapse in T and [34] preceding House A3.

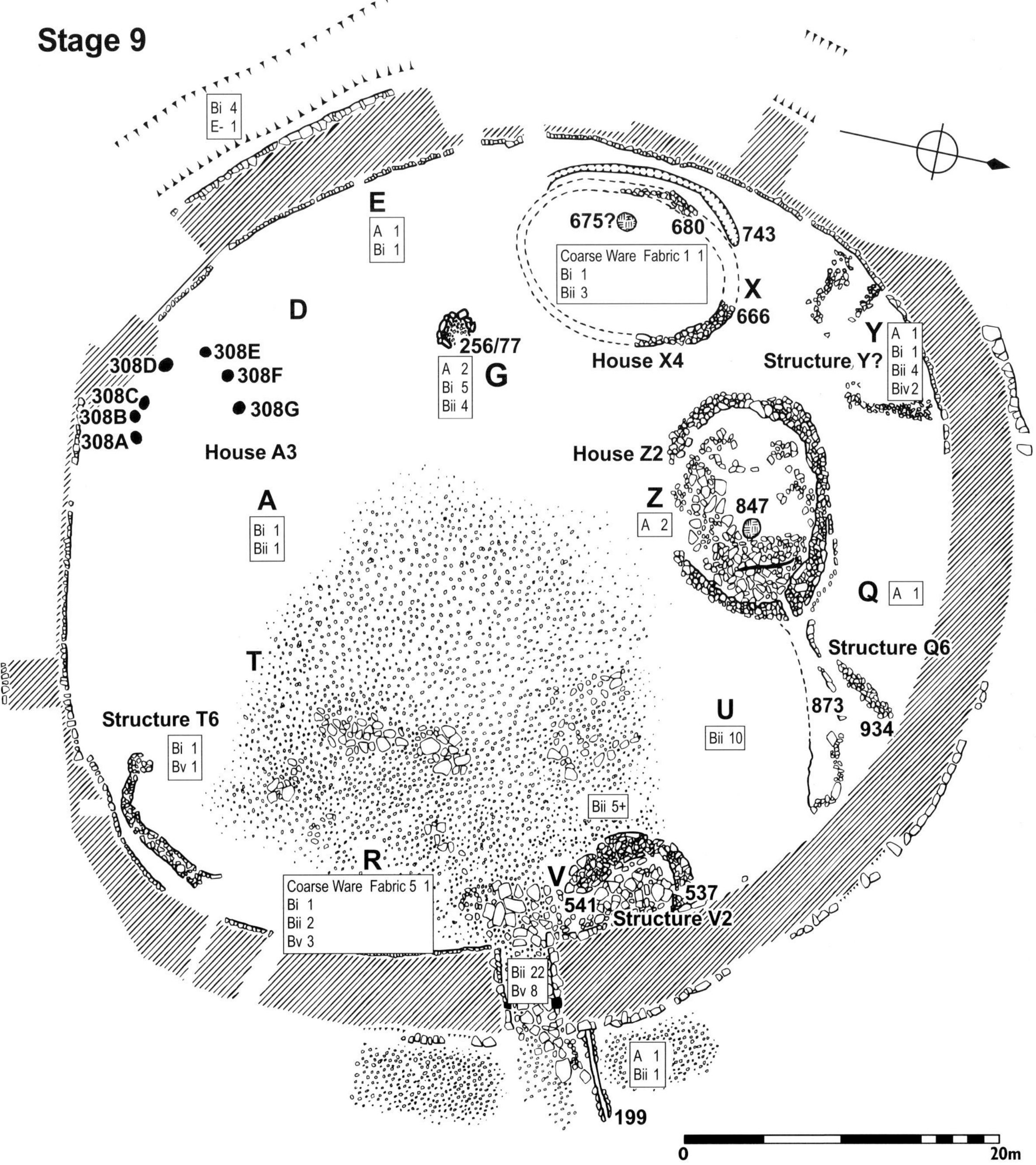

Fig 88: Stage 9 suggested structures c AD 500-550+. General position of Post-Roman import wares indicated, with Class A, B etc retained for brevity

Structure V2 with its substantial flooring [541] may have continued. Structure U2 was perhaps too insubstantial to have had a very long life. The end date for Z is difficult to establish; the fact that its wall-line remained virtually intact may indicate continuance, as it might have been expected to have been robbed for late rebuildings elsewhere. Structure Y had a group of Post-Roman import wares; this area of course might have been used for dumping rubbish, like that over Structure E. House A was rebuilt as A3 (Figs 37, 38), an oval formed by a series of postholes [308] set in rubble [34] which represented levelling of A2. Layer [34] contained a sherd of Bii amphora as well as part of bowl S1 referred to above. House T5 became disused and T6, dump wall [421], was built partly over its site. There were no definable structures at this Stage in Area R.

Structure G appeared to have been deliberately infilled, first with blocking [290] across its front, then with stone and soil layers [256] and [77]. This fill contained Post-Roman import wares and comparatively little late-Roman gabbroic material. This fill represents the latest sealed context on the site, and produced the unique decorated gabbroic flanged bowl P136. It is possible that this blocking related to a deliberate abandonment of the site, and the moving of the settlement elsewhere in the vicinity.

Across the lower part of the Round soil levels began to accumulate, presumably once the Round was no longer regularly occupied. These soil levels were [532] over the Ditch terminal surfaces, [140] in the Entrance, [400] in R and T, and [546A] in V. The spread of soil [687] over House X4 may be contemporary, while soil [11] continued to accumulate over Structure E. All these soil levels contained runs of stone from the collapse of the inner and the outer revetment [46], [399], and [519], with a substantial rubble level in the Entrance [183].

Active use of the site and rebuilding in Stage 9 may be assigned to AD 500-550. The blocking of G, the abandonment of the site and the gradual collapse of its Rampart may then date late in the 6th century AD or even later.

Stage 9 appears to be the latest during which the Round was used for regular human habitation. Its end appears to relate to the general shift from enclosed settlements to open hamlets of the *tre* type which took place from the 6th century AD and is discussed further below and in Sections 12.16 and 12.17.

Stage 10 (Fig 89)

After some collapse of rubble [183] in the Entrance, the Round was fitted with a new gate in postholes [193] and [194]. The Round may have been refurbished to serve as a stock fold for an adjacent community. The latest evidence for structures is assigned to Stage 10, suggesting that the enclosure formed by the Round was used for purposes other than arable farming. A scrappy series of structures postdated the beginnings of the Rampart collapse and the downhill soil accumulation [532]-[140]-[400]-[546A]; the Rampart collapse and soil accumulation suggest a gap in activity after Stage 9. Structure V appears to have still been standing. Within it, paving [546] and sump pits [545] and [514] were assigned to Phase V3. In Area R Structure R3 comprised wall [156], drain [124], paving [174], and posthole [259]; drain [169] may have been associated. Structure R4 was represented by dump wall [382]. These Structures are later than T6 assigned to Stage 9 because of the soil [140]/[400] which had accumulated over the latter and into which they are set. Uphill, Structure X5 was a small enclosure with dump walls [677]/[683] built over soil [687] over House X4. More late structures may have been ploughed away — the upper levels of House A had been particularly badly eroded. It is not known how much of Structures U and Z may have survived to be used as parts of buildings. The structures assigned to Stage 10 need not have been contemporary and were more probably for stock than for human habitation.

The grass-marked sherd P148 from soil over Z and the E ware sherd in lynchet [359] probably derive from settlement elsewhere in the immediate area. The Stage 10 stock fold, allowing some time for abandonment after Stage 9, may cover several centuries from around *c* AD 700. Activity within it may relate to the present settlement of Trethurgy. The foundation of *tre* settlements falls broadly within the period AD 500 to 1100 (Padel 1985, 223) but it is of course impossible to indicate whether the present Trethurgy was initially established as a new location by the last inhabitants of the Round.

9.2.7 Period 6 use of the Round

Some indication that the Round became a ploughed field is provided by the scattered contexts which had one or two intrusive sherds dating from the 10th to the 13th centuries: [8], [9], [678], [723], [751], [780], [793], [801], and [808]. These are most likely explained by disturbance connected with stone removal during ploughing. Contexts in the Entrance area produced a little 11th or 12th-century Sandy Lane material and a small group of 13th to 14th-century sherds. These suggest that the Entrance was being used, perhaps widened with some stone removed. There was a scatter of 13th to 15th-century material, generally not intrusive but in the soil over Structures. This may indicate regular activity and manuring of the Round when used as an arable field. The present Trethurgy was now in use, first recorded *c* AD 1200 (Hammond 1897). An RAF aerial photograph (CPE/UK 2521 3257) and the St Austell Tithe Map both indicate traces of a possible strip field system predating the present field pattern south-east of Trethurgy but growing, if fluctuating, population levels during Period 6, *c* AD 1000-1500, may have required more extensive areas of arable land. The detailed history of the area is likely to have been complex — Alseveor (see below and Fig 2) is a second small settlement 250m south-west of the Round first recorded in 1756 but of unknown origin (Cornwall County Record Office DDCN 2361).

9.2.8 Period 7 incorporation of the Round into the present field system

The date of the incorporation of the Round into the present field system cannot be established from documentary sources. The earliest map located which shows the field is the Ordnance Survey Field Drawing of 1813 (Cornwall County Record Office). In 1840 the Tithe Apportionment records the field, and some

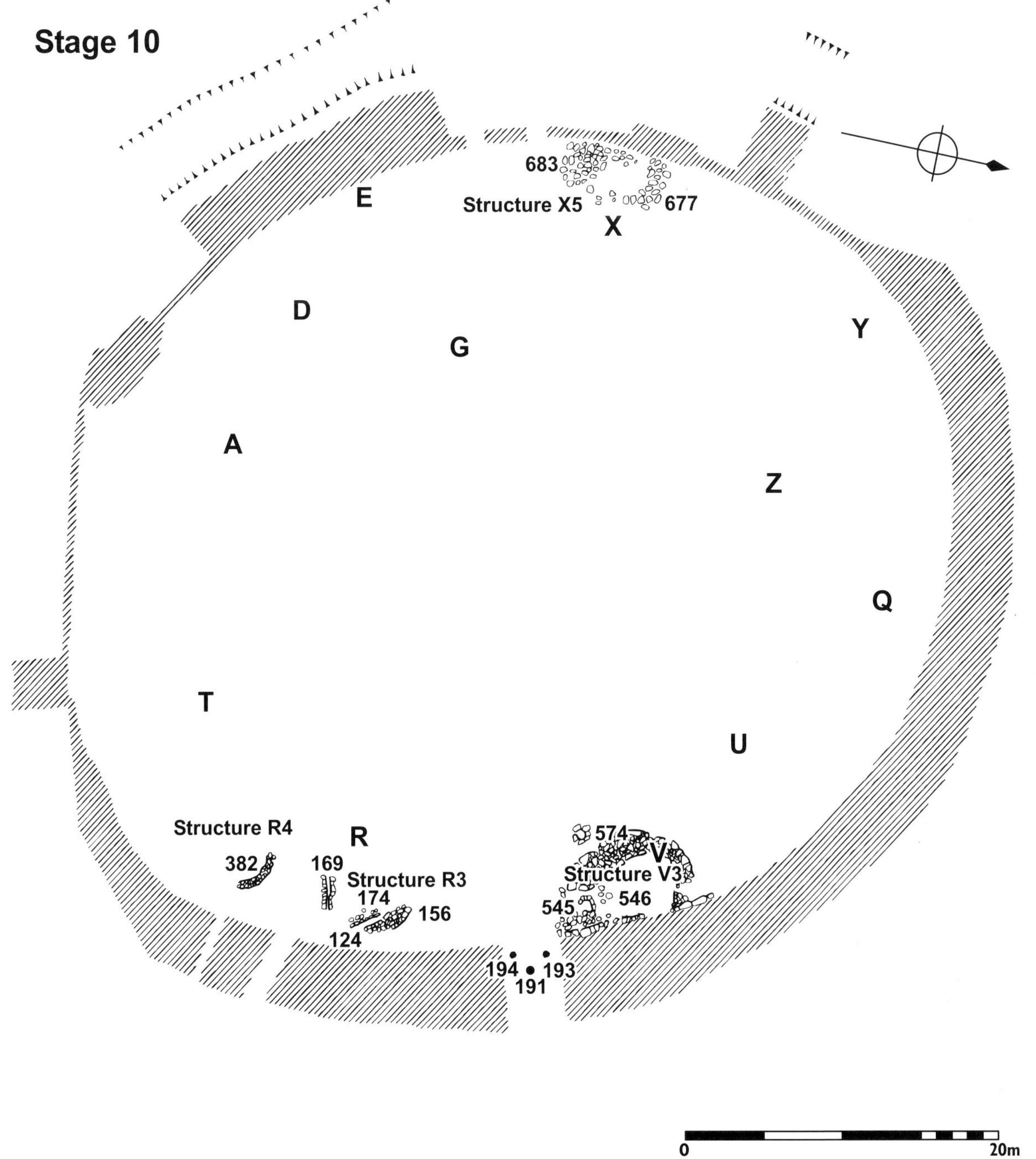

Fig 89: Stage 10 suggested structures relating to the reuse of the Round after its abandonment as a settlement ?AD 700 onward

adjacent, as owned by Samuel Roberts as part of the holding of Alseveor (Fig 2). The record of the tenement of Alseveor in 1756 noted above was in relation to tin bounds of ground which lay to its south; presumably most of the fields recorded in 1813 would have been enclosed by then.

The removal of a length of the present field hedge only produced the abraded 13th-century rim P24. Many more 16th to 17th-century sherds were found in soil over the Structures in the Round, and indeed in the Entrance area, than those of earlier centuries. If the field hedge had been built after *c* AD 1600, 16th-century sherds might be expected to have been included with the hedge make-up. A date in the 16th century AD is therefore tentatively suggested for the field hedge and the incorporation of the Round in the present field system. The RAF aerial photograph noted above shows subdivisions within several fields adjacent to the Round which were not present on the 1840 Tithe Apportionment Map. This suggests that the enclosure pattern in the area had been altered by the 19th century and therefore was of some antiquity. A 16th-century date for the present field system would conform well to the designation of the area as Anciently Enclosed Land (Herring 1998, 77, map). The lynchet [359] over the Round Ditch contained only a small quantity of 16th to 17th-century sherds so movement of soil by arable activity may have stabilised uphill from the Round before the present fields were established.

The construction of the present field hedges used considerable quantities of stone and soil. The levelling of the north and east sides of the Round would both have provided the material for these hedges and removed an impediment inside the new field.

9.2.9 Period 8 activity since incorporation of the Round into the present field system

Period 8 covers all activity subsequent to layout of the present field system in the 16th century. There is a quantity of pottery from the 17th to the 20th century. Robber trench [185] for Rampart revetment in the Entrance area contained material up to the 19th century, indicating an episode of substantial stone removal, possibly connected with the introduction of improved ploughs and the need for more even plough land. In Period 8 the Round was both used as arable land with related stone removal and also as pasture, pasture being the use recorded on the 1840 Tithe Map.

10 The architecture of the large oval buildings

10.1 The archaeological data for large oval buildings

10.1.1 Introductory comments

Until the excavation at Grambla, Wendron, in 1972 (Saunders 1972, fig 16) and Trethurgy in 1973, it was generally assumed that Roman structures in Cornwall, apart from the courtyard houses of West Penwith, continued the circular tradition of the Iron Age. The presence of large oval buildings was a surprise. Subsequent excavations and scanning of the literature and of unpublished surveys demonstrate that oval structures were the norm for Roman Cornwall and that this structural tradition was apparently unique to this area of Britannia. Trethurgy, despite its damaged state, provides the most extensive data for large oval structures and therefore the best basis for attempting to understand their methods of construction. Structures regarded as large oval buildings are U, Z1a , Z1b, Z2, X4, A1, A2, A3, and T2. All are interpreted as houses from the presence of hearths and/or hearth pits, except U1 which was probably a byre (Section 11.13). House A3 is included here, although small, because its postholes are set on the line of preceding House A2 and the amount of walling, if any, which survived to be used in conjunction with these is uncertain.

One preliminary observation may be pertinent. Few of the features described as postholes had clearly defined postpipes. Unless packing stones or pipes are shown on plan, the interpretation of any posthole must be regarded as uncertain.

10.1.2 Overall size and shape

Internal lengths ranged from 17m to 6.5m, with widths from 9m to 5.5m, and external lengths from 20m to 10.5m, with widths from 11m to 8.5m. Generally the sides in longer buildings such as U1 tended to be straight but were slightly curved in shorter buildings such as Z2. Plans were reasonably symmetrical and generally similar. A1, Z1a, and Z1b had an internal bipartite structure which differed in the upper and lower ends with some evidence for partitions between the two. Table 10.1 provides the basic data.

10.1.3. Degree of levelling

All structures except X4 were built with their length down the slope and levelled into it at their upper ends. None of the interiors was however horizontal, with drops along the length varying from 1m to 0.1m. Widths were generally fairly level because of the positioning of buildings across the slope. Only X4 was not levelled and, with its long axis set along the

	Internal length	Internal width	Floor area	Drop along length	Drop along width	Entrance width	Hearth pits	Hearths
U1	14m	8m	94m^2	c 0.4m	c 0.1m	2m	none	none
Z1a	16m	7m	120m^2	c 1.0m	level	n/a	846	none
Z1b	17m	9m	140m^2	c 1.4m	level	n/a	846	none
Z2	12m	8m	81m^2	c 0.9m-1.4m	level	2m	776, 847, 849, 850	none
X4	13m	8m	80m^2	c 0.1m	c 0.9m	2m	675	none
A1	11m	8m	80m^2	c 0.5m	c 0.1m	2m	294, 316	336?
A2	8.5m	6.5m	45m^2	c 0.4m	c 0.1m	2m	128	128?
A3	6.5m	5.5m	35m^2	c 0.3m	c 0.1m	n/a	n/a	n/a
T2	12m	8.5m	80m^2	c 0.2m	level	n/a	456	478

Table 10.1 Details of large oval buildings

slope, had a drop of 0.9m across its width. The interiors are assumed to have been intentionally left with slightly sloping floors after levelling, perhaps for drainage.

10.1.4 Height and nature of the walls

Most of the walls had been robbed or ploughed down to one or two courses, or had been removed altogether. The greatest surviving wall height was 0.5m in part of Structure U1. No wall survived in sufficiently good condition for its original upper surface to be identified. Where collapsed rubble was present in quantity, for example in House A2, this appeared consistent with walls about 0.5m high. However there was extensive Medieval and Post-Medieval stone robbing judging by the spread of pottery of these dates, although the only robbing trench identified related to the Entrance revetment. The surviving amount of rubble cannot be taken as an indicator of the amount originally present. It will be argued below that the walls were higher than 0.5m. There was no trace amongst layers of rubble or collapsed walling of sods or cob used to heighten the walls.

The walls varied between 1m and 2m in width. The inner and outer faces were roughly coursed with untrimmed granite pieces in a mixture of sizes, and the cores were tightly packed with small stones in a fine matrix. In the early Stages this matrix consisted of clean rab but, as the use of the site continued, the matrix gradually included more soil which darkened its colour. The change was presumably due to the difficulties of obtaining clean rab in later constructional phases. The technique of wall construction had been developed during the Middle Bronze Age for hut circles in granite areas and continued throughout the remainder of the prehistoric period.

10.1.5 Entrances

The width of entrances where data survived was remarkably standard at *c* 2m but there was considerable variation in construction. Ground-set pairs of postholes were most frequent. These were positioned on the outer side in U, the earlier use of A1 and the later use of A2, but on the inner side in later A1 and earlier A2. Single ground-set posthole [884] may have formed one side of the Z1 entrance. However there were no ground-set postholes in the entrances of Z2 and X4 and their width was determined by that of the paving across the wall-line — door-frames had been set within the wall structure. The method of constructing the door-frame could not have depended on a precise position with regard to the wall-line. No structure had any evidence for a porch.

10.1.6 External gullies and drainage

All large oval structures except A1 and Z1b had external gulleys around their uphill ends during Stages 1-4. These gullies may have served two purposes, firstly to contain drips from any eaves, secondly to divert surface water away from the buildings, in which the 1:8 slope down the interior of the Round would have assisted. The removal of some 0.7m of rab from parts of the interior left a shelf along the uphill, west side which would have facilitated drainage from Structures X, E, D, and A built upon it, and provided more of a 'sump' effect in the Round centre. Soil and rubble spreads such as [48] in the interior must have been planned to take downhill water seepage. The positioning of structures, especially Z set well inside the Rampart, may have been partly determined by considerations of drainage. The Entrance surface provided the main outlet for surface water as only drain [199] ran through the Rampart.

From Stage 5 there were fewer external gullies, none in U1, Z2, or T4, although Z2 had drain [873] down its north side. These buildings were all in areas which had accumulated soil and rubble uphill to act as soakaways and extensions to the central sump system. The two later buildings with external gullies, A2 and X4, were the uphill shelf inside the Rampart with little soil and rubble build-up. The more extensive use from Stage 5 onward of paving made with carefully set large slabs must have assisted drainage. Entrance paving [188] was continuous through [7]/[8] with [254] in T4 and [557] outside U1.

10.1.7 Internal drains

Most buildings had internal drains with slab coverings laid flush with floor surfaces. A1 and Z1 were similar with a network of internal drains which seeped into the make-up of their floors in their downhill ends. T2, and indeed the later T4, had no internal drains but the interior was unusually level. X had no provision for interior drainage until X4 in Stage 9. No house before Stage 5 had an outlet for internal drainage.

From Stage 5 most buildings were provided with drains running out through their walls, making use of the greater potential for external soakaway and general run off which was now present on the site. U1 had drain [579] constructed through its wall. Z2 had an outlet drain [863] set in its paved floor and running out through the wall. The only drainage in X4 was [695] which ran out through the entrance. A2 had provision with [71] for drainage through the upper House wall and the floor [34A]; the position of its outlet does not survive.

10.1.8 Interior floors

The floors in early Stages were generally of thin layers of tamped rab. This survived most extensively in [436] across T2. The upper parts of A1 and Z1 had also floors of tamped rab, [311] and [854] respectively, which survived only patchily, wearing down to incorporate parts of the natural rab surface. The lower parts of A1 and Z1 were paved above make-up levels connected with internal drainage discussed above.

From Stage 5 there was more use of paving. Z2 appears to have been completely floored with [777]. Paving [294A] may have covered A2 as surviving fragments occur at both ends of the House. X had been so extensively damaged by ploughing that no evidence for flooring survived but T4 had paving [254] across the half of the interior adjacent to the entrance.

10.1.9 Internal divisions

The most definite internal division was [858] in Z2 which appears to have held a timber screen set in paving [777] and separating off one-fifth of the interior at the lower end. The [858] screen was only 3m long, less than half the width of the House but positioned centrally. This division lay directly over [958] and [949] which marked the change in flooring in Z1 from rab to paving: some similar division may have been present in the earlier House.

The arrangement in Z2 is closely matched by that in A1 where postholes [335] to [60] and stakeholes [315] cut off the lower quarter of the interior. The features are best interpreted as having held some form of timber screen, frequently renewed. In both Z and A the partitioned end was that furthest from the door. The posthole and stakehole line in A1 marked a drop which provided seating for paving [24]. Hearth pit [294] cut across the suggested screen line, indicating that the partition was not present through the whole use of the House. The earlier House with the screen is distinguished as A1a, the latter, without the screen, as A1b. There was no indication of any partition in A2. The well-preserved floor of T2 provided no evidence for a screened-off end, and none of the eroded confused features in the interior of X can be interpreted as a partition across one end. An internal partition shielding the lower end of an oval building interior appears to have been an optional arrangement, rather than one which occurred regularly.

There may have been another form of internal screen in A1, set in the five postholes [296] to [345]; this would have been at least 2m long and divided off a 2m wide strip along the top, inner side of the House. Some similar screen division may be indicated by the line of four postholes in D4, [122] to [133]. Otherwise there are no obvious straight lines of post or stake holes in the Houses.

10.1.10 Hearths and hearth pits

Houses did not have hearths as a regular feature. Of all the buildings, not just the large oval houses, only A1, [336], A2, [128], T2, [478], and T4, [473] appear to have had hearths. The hearths in A1 and A2 were reasonably central but a little downhill of the door. Those in T were central but opposite the door. The poor survival of X prevents any comment about hearths but floors survived sufficiently well in both Z1 and Z2 for it to be certain that no hearths were present.

Hearth pits (see Section 12.11) are presumed to be a form of hearth in which fires were lit either in a pit or over the soft infill of a pit which provided seating for vessels. All the large oval buildings had hearth pits, except U1. In A1 hearth pit [316] is central and just uphill of the door and may belong to the same stage of use, A1a, as hearth [336] on the other side of the door. In A1b hearth pit [294] was set across the line of the former partition, and burnt clay areas such as [354] around it may have served as flat hearths. In T2 hearth pit [456] is closer to the doorway than contemporary hearth [478]. (Later T4 did not have a hearth pit.) In Z1 the centrally placed [846] appears to have served through the whole use of the building. By contrast a group of four hearth pits in Z2 — [776], [847], [849], and [850] — form a central group but there is nothing to indicate sequence; indeed several could have been in use together. The hearth pits assigned to X2 to X4 — [663A], [662B], [689B], and [675] — all cluster towards the centre of the house.

It may be noted that D, which in many ways appears a small variant of the large oval buildings, had no hearth or hearth pit. If provision for cooking is taken as an indicator of the function of a structure, the D building sequence was used differently from the main group of large oval buildings.

The broadly central placing of both hearths and hearth pits may have some relevance for the overall shape of the structures. It may be presumed that these would be placed where there was a good amount of headroom to allow movement in their vicinity and to allow smoke to rise up well above floor level.

10.1.11 The problem of roof support

No regular pattern of interior postholes can be found in the oval buildings which might relate to roof support. It is just possible that roof supports, either primary, or for secondary repairs, were set on stone pads, but some traces of such pads should have been noted in the well-preserved floor of T2.

Some large oval buildings have so few interior postholes that the weight of the roof must have been taken directly by the walls. U1, if ever finished, had no interior postholes, nor did Z2 which appears to have functioned as a roofed building for a long period, except for the small off-centre pair [840] and [842]. Interior postholes should have been detected in [34], the soil and rubble of the A2 floor. T2 had one centrally placed posthole [472] in its uphill end; its only other postholes, [436] and [438], form a pair 2m apart well off-centre. (Traditionally the [436]/[438] pair and the [840]/[842] pair in Z2 would be interpreted as loom supports.) The floor of T2 is well-preserved, adding weight to the absence of postholes.

However House T2 provides another form of possible evidence for roof support, six postholes [471A], [471B], [471C], [453A], [453B], and [453C] set in its inner wall face. These postholes were cut about 0.2m below the base of the wall, deep enough to have survived the removal of the wall had they continued in a regular spacing around the interior. The six postholes have a symmetrical layout. Postholes [471C] and [453A] oppose each other on the House long axis; [471B] and [453B], [453C] and [471A] then are evenly spaced out from them, leaving a straight length of wall-line 6.5m long opposite the doorway.

No postholes in any other building had a demonstrable relationship with a wall face. However a ground-set series in House Z1a may relate to a wall which no longer survives. The postholes provide a reasonably regular pattern from [884], which may have formed one side of a door-frame — [884], [855], [867], [866], [883], [870], [856], and [954]. Another group form a rough arc inside the upper part of the House, and may just possibly have held roof supports — [871], [853], [880], [879A], [879B], [886], and [850A]. Posthole [865] may relate to paving [949] laid in the remodelling of the House as Z1b.

A1 and X1-4 have the greatest number of internal postholes among the structures discussed here. The common factor is their position on the well-drained shelf at the top of the site which allowed the bases of posts to remain drier than elsewhere. The interior of A1 was sealed by soil [34A] which preceded A2 and so all the postholes found relate to one structure. This structure, however, had at least one rebuilding phase, indicated by the replaced door postholes. The A1 interior postholes which are not part of the suggested screens or partitions lie on the entrance side of the building's long axis. They form two rough arcs, [299], [55], [59]/ [59A], and [347], [334], [162]. Additional strengthening, or fittings, may have been required on the side of the building with the doorway. By contrast there was no way of attributing postholes in X1-4 to any specific structure such as the stone oval X4 House.

The roofing material is unknown. Roofs may have been composite, of both thatch and turf, as was common in many Irish buildings; strips of turf about 50mm thick were used to line thatch (Evans 1957, 51). The range of materials available for thatch/roof covering is indicated by analysis of pollen and of charred plant remains at Penhale Round (Scaife 1998/9). Here both wheat and barley could have provided straw. There also fragments of sedge (Cyperaceae). Heather and ling were represented both by pollen and by charcoal and bracken and fern by spores. Penhale is the only Cornish round site for which both pollen and macrofossil data is so far available. Examination of macrofossils from Reawla (Straker 1992) provided supporting evidence for the cereal range, and for ling and sedge (*Carex*). Grasses from both sites could relate to the use of cut turves.

10.2 Other oval buildings in Cornwall

Buildings similar to those at Trethurgy were first recognised at Grambla, Wendron, SW 693283, during excavations in 1972 (Saunders 1972). Since the Trethurgy excavations in 1973, it has become apparent that large oval buildings replaced roundhouses in Roman Cornwall, and that these formed a regional building tradition. Details from other buildings in this tradition may supplement those from Trethurgy and help to inform the process of determining the overall form of the structures and their roofs. Conversely, any proposals put forward about the superstructure of the Trethurgy buildings should be appropriate for similar buildings elsewhere in Cornwall.

Details for Grambla are only available in the interim published report (Saunders 1972, including a plan fig 16). Two buildings described as 'boat-shaped' were partly excavated. Both had parallel straight sides and symmetrical, pointed rather than oval, ends. About half of Building 1 was excavated and was about 18m long and 9m wide internally. The floor was levelled and the walls were 'mainly of granite blocks'. There were no interior postholes, but a 'large central hearth with nearby the remains of an oven' was probably a hearth pit. About a third of Building 2 was excavated; this was about 20m long and 9m wide. There were in the interior 'seven small pits, one of which showed signs of having been subjected to heat', again probably a hearth pit. It is to be presumed that the excavator would have commented had any of these pits appeared possible postholes. The Grambla buildings therefore appear to have been slightly larger than those at Trethurgy but, even so, to have had no interior post supports for the roof. The interiors of both buildings appear to have been well sealed by collapse and dumping and levelling material and so to have preserved the interior details well. There were surface indications of two more similar buildings. Dating for the excavated buildings appears to have been from the 2nd century onward. Post-Roman import sherds were only found postdating the collapse of Building 1 and so at Grambla it is not possible, at present, to suggest the continuance of the buildings into the Post-Roman period.

A single oval building, 12m long and 5.8m wide internally, has been identified at Castle Gotha, St Austell (SX 02764964; Saunders and Harris 1982, 123-5, fig 78) where about 7% of the 0.5ha interior was excavated between 1957 and 1962 under the direction of Andrew Saunders. The oval building was not recognised during the excavation which covered about three quarters of its site in a series of grid squares and trenches. The published account of the stratigraphy was prepared in the late 1970s by Daphne Harris who identified the building from the excavation archive.

The Castle Gotha house had slightly curved sides and irregularly rounded ends and was about 12m by 6m internally. Figure 3 in Quinnell (1986) presents its overall plan, although the internal details shown are only tentative. Its site was levelled at least 0.2m into the slope and most of the line of the inner wall face, surviving three courses high on the uphill side, was set in a slight foundation trench. No comment can be made on the wall core, its width, or outer face. The wall was constructed largely (possibly entirely) of blocks of Pentewan stone which occurs locally in dykes in the shillet. (At Grambla granite blocks were used in the walls in preference to material from the local Mylor beds; granite outcrops close to the site. Evidently even-grained solid rock was sought for use in oval buildings.) An entrance at Castle Gotha is suggested roughly central to the downhill long side, its width is uncertain. A floor level of 'small shillet set in brown soil' covered much of the interior and was much worn with several successive hearth pits and hearths. There were some postholes, not all contemporary, amongst which there appears no significant pattern. The evidence suggests that, as at Trethurgy and Grambla, roofing was constructed without the use of internal post supports. The finds associated with the Castle Gotha house and in its infill are all of the Roman period, and loosely datable to the 2nd to 3rd centuries AD.

The structure partly investigated at the trial excavations inside the round at Shortlanesend (Harris 1980, 67) and dated to the 2nd/early 3rd centuries was described as circular. Its plan (*ibid*, fig 27) however shows a sub-rectangular or oval shape with the ghost of a thick wall at the uphill end indicated by a scarped ridge of subsoil. At Crane Godrevy Round (Thomas 1969, fig 32) Structure Y *c* 6m long may have been an oval house of Roman date. The Round was occupied during the Roman period and, although the interim report describes Structure Y as a robbed building of the earliest phase of the Medieval reoccupation, there appears no reason why the early Medieval finds should not relate to the robbing out of a much earlier structure. The Round at Reawla, Gwinear, with occupation ranging from the Iron Age through the Roman period (Appleton-Fox 1992), had suffered very badly from plough erosion. The combined magnetic susceptibility and phosphate surveys (*ibid*, fig 13) strongly indicate the presence of both round and oval structures. The small sector of the interior excavated contained parts of three Roman-period houses (*ibid*, fig 4) which are better described as oval than as round; structural details are unclear.

The geophysical surveys of the round at Penhale, Indian Queens (Nowakowski 1998, fig 24), indicate several oval rather than circular structures in the interior. The 1993 excavations investigated an oval building Structure 2045/5405 just inside the entrance. In its first phase, this appears to belong to the 4th century (*ibid*, II, 50, fig 53) and was 12m long and 6m wide; this building *did* have a reasonably regular series of postholes around its perimeter. It was reconstructed in the late 4th or 5th centuries, and was then 8m long and 4m wide (*ibid*, fig 54), with a wall of the local shillet revetting a levelling cut but with no interior postholes. Full comment on this structure awaits its final report. Further excavations at Penhale in 1996, on one of the sectors furthest from the entrance, uncovered part of a building, with an external drainage gulley and interior postholes, dated to the 3rd or 4th centuries; while details of its plan are not clear it was interpreted as 'an oval enclosure surrounding post-built structures of more than one phase, at least one of which may have been an oval building' (Johnston *et al* 1998/9, 115). The data from both excavations at Penhale suggest a tradition of oval building in which timber formed a significant factor. The site provides the clearest indication so far available of a variation in construction methods for oval buildings to that appropriate for Trethurgy, Grambla, and Castle Gotha and discussed in Section 10.4.

Survey of the existing data indeed demonstrates that no circular houses, especially those with interior post-rings of the classic prehistoric type, belong to the Roman period in Cornwall. In the past, before the recognition of an oval building tradition, it was natural that partially excavated structures should be loosely described as 'hut circles' but re-examination of the published reports, of which the more significant have been reviewed above, shows that all partly excavated structures can be reinterpreted as oval.

Courtyard houses have now been demonstrated to belong to the Roman period rather than the Iron Age (Quinnell 1986, 120). Many courtyard house groupings include, as well as obvious courtyard houses with round and long rooms, simpler buildings which are oval rather than round. Most of the data come from unexcavated sites such as Bosullow Trehyllys (Weatherhill 1982). However excavations at Carn Euny (Christie 1978, fig 17) showed House A to be an oval building about 9m by 6m internally, with very thick walls straight on the longer sides; the only three postholes formed a line across one corner. Only a small 'room' in thickened walling adjacent to the entrance distinguishes Carn Euny House A from the general run of Roman-period oval houses discussed above. The integration of oval buildings with courtyard house complexes of Roman date further demonstrates the extent of changes in building traditions in Cornwall during this period.

It might be expected that an oval house-building tradition lasting at least four centuries, from the 2nd to the 6th centuries AD, would leave some trace on the Cornish moors. The 1980s survey of Bodmin Moor revealed that oval buildings, generally small, are present. A large oval building, with internal dimensions of 20m by 9m, has been located at Stannon on the north side of the moor (Johnson and Rose, 1994, 53, fig 35, no 6). This at present appears to be the only building comparable with the Trethurgy houses identified as a field monument, apart from those connected with courtyard house complexes.

At present it is not possible to establish whether large oval buildings were built in Devon as too few sites of the Romano-British period have been sufficiently investigated. A scant scatter of rectangular, Roman-style buildings are known from East Devon, but enclosure sites are common throughout the county. A useful summary of the extent of excavation of these and of their dates is presented by Griffith (1994, fig 2). The interiors of only three have been extensively excavated. At Hayes Farm near Exeter (Simpson *et al* 1989) plough erosion over gravel subsoil had removed any evidence for structures. At Stoke Gabriel in South Devon the limestone bedrock provided difficulties in interpretation although a small stone oval or sub-angular building, better considered in relation to the smaller Trethurgy structures discussed in Chapter 11, was found outside the enclosure (Masson Phillips 1966, 16). At Rudge in mid-Devon a spread of postholes was interpreted as a timber structure, oval rather than circular in that the suggested diameter varied from 10m by as much as 1m (Todd 1998, 142, fig 5); the site was considered tightly dated to the late 1st century AD.

It is possible that oval houses had their roots in the local Iron Age. Only a limited range of clearly defined house plans are known and most of these come from hillforts. Structures at the Rumps cliff castle (Brooks 1974) are double-ring circles as is the single, stone-walled house at Penhale cliff castle (Smith 1988). A double-ring circular house, House A1, was found beneath courtyard house levels at Carn Euny (Christie 1978, fig 22). At St Mawgan-in-Pydar most of the defined structures, extending in date from the Later Iron Age until the early 2nd century AD, have good interior timber supports but the plans of both these and the outer walls tend to be more sub-rectangular than circular. The most interesting site is Threemilestone round near Truro (Schwieso 1976), where the ceramic sequence ends in the Later Iron Age with a little Cordoned ware. Well over half the interior was excavated and a range of circular gullies and postholes were found. Also found were two oval features, Nos 2 and 3, apparently drainage ditches, enclosing areas 14m by 10m and 15m by 12m respectively within which no postholes were found. The site had suffered from plough erosion and low walls constructed, for example, of shillet-revetted soil could easily have been removed. Stratigraphic relationships were not clear but close examination of the published plan (*ibid*, fig 20) suggests that the oval ditches may be the latest features on the site. The structures at Threemilestone and St Mawgan-in-Pydar suggest some degree of experimentation with buildings dating back to the last century or so of the Iron Age.

Cornish oval houses appear to form a group unique in Britain during the Roman and early Post-Roman periods. The predominance of oval plans is reinforced by their use in smaller structures explored in Chapter 11. In rural Wales, geographically close with large areas devoid of villas, parallels might, if anywhere, be expected. Here however circular houses continued to be built, especially in the North West, or simple rectangular structures in either stone or timber are found on rural sites. Some of the buildings on Gateholm, Pembs, (Davies *et al* 1971), appear from their surface plan similar to Cornish oval houses, but the structures otherwise are rectangular not circular; limited excavations show Gateholm to have both Roman and Post-Roman occupation. Some small irregular Roman-period structures at Stackpole Warren on the south Pembrokeshire coast may belong to the same tradition (Benson *et al* 1990). In North Wales straight-sided buildings with oval ends are occasionally found in the later Roman and Post-Roman periods, best exemplified at Cefn Greanog II, Caern (Fasham *et al* 1998). These buildings however have an internal width of some 4m and could easily have accommodated a ridged roof with curved, hipped ends. The data from Wales are valuable in demonstrating that regional styles of buildings developed during the Roman period but at present include nothing at all comparable to Cornish oval houses.

10.3 The problems posed by the archaeological data

10.3.1 Introduction

A tradition of oval buildings has been demonstrated to have been universal in Roman Cornwall, a tradition previously unknown in Britain. Excavation data provide a reasonable amount of information about the buildings at ground level but little indication about their superstructure. Our understanding of prehistoric circular structures has been greatly enhanced by a range of experimental reconstructions, especially those by the late Peter Reynolds. A first step in the understanding of the superstructures of oval buildings is a consideration of what, architecturally, is possible, given the evidence which survives and this is addressed in Section 10.4. The principal points which a reconstruction on paper of oval building architecture may be expected to address are summarised here.

10.3.2 Roof structure

The data, both from Trethurgy and other sites, show that houses could be roofed without the use of internal supports, thus leaving an interior clear of posts unless needed for other purposes. The roof structure only needed the support of the external walls. Any roofing method suggested should be appropriate for a rural vernacular tradition used throughout Cornwall for many centuries. The method needs to be appropriate for buildings with both straight and slightly curved sides and with ends with symmetric or asymmetric curves or with points. The method needs to be adaptable on occasion, as with the postholes in T2, to some support by posts in the inner wall faces. The question of the possible post-circuit in Z1a may be relevant here. Whether the construction method was adaptable to external walls built solely of timber, as suggested by A3, possibly by X2 and X3, and by the first phase of Structure 2045/5405 at Penhale Round (Nowakowski 1998), cannot be addressed on the evidence from Trethurgy; this will need consideration from sites with better data against the possibility of a different construction method based principally upon timber.

It is presumed that the weight of the roof was taken by the walls. Did the eaves overhang? Traditional building methods in Ireland (Evans 1957) and in Wales (Peate 1944) seem generally to provide water run-off beyond the wall face. How does the evidence of the gullies relate? Reynolds' work at Butser (1979, 36) demonstrates that drainage gullies are not necessary if there is soil and vegetation outside the house to absorb dripping from the eaves, although other practical experience has shown that gullies are important for drainage on sloping ground (Phil Bennett pers comm).

10.3.3 Integration of the door-frames with the roofs

At Trethurgy doorways were regularly 2m wide, appropriate for double doors; the width may either indicate regular movement of large pieces of equipment or the provision of a good source of light. Door-frames were likely to have been higher than the walls to permit access without stooping. The structure of doorway carpentry needs to take account of the facts that the door might be set in various positions across the wall, centrally, or flush with the inner or outer face, and that the posts of the door-frame might or might not be ground-set. Only one side of the door-frame might be ground-set. The integration of doorway timbering with roofs needs consideration.

10.3.4 Provision of light and egress for smoke

There is minimal evidence for windows in the form of window glass. Only two small fragments were found, the only ones known from Cornwall, and, despite Professor Price's comments (Section 4.6), these need not indicate glazed windows. Circular house reconstructions usually assume no light source except the door. Would this have been appropriate here? No special vents for smoke would have been necessary in the roofs. Peter Reynolds has drawn attention to the dangers which smoke-holes cause in promoting uncontrolled draught and so the risk of buildings catching fire. It has been noted that in Stages 1-4 hearths and hearth pits were generally placed at one end of the building, normally that with the door. Medieval thatched houses frequently relied on seepage for the dispersal of smoke (Cox and Thorp 2001, 34-5). It seems reasonable to consider the possibility of half lofts above those areas without fires. Centrally placed postholes such as [742] in T2 could have provided support for half loft floors. In the later stages hearth pits tend to be set more centrally — could this indicate the provision of two half lofts, at either end, with smoke rising between?

10.3.5 Use of iron fittings in building structures

Nails found are generally 50mm or less in length and more suitable for furniture than for structures and none of the other iron objects, with the exception of a few small dogs, appear to be relevant to carpentry. Prehistoric houses did not make use of iron fittings in their roofs. The introduction of iron hinges (Manning 1985, 126) during the Roman period is well established although none has yet been found in Cornwall.

10.3.6 Why the change?

What advantages might there be in oval house construction, given the circumstances pertaining in Roman Cornwall, which could explain the change in style? Why should this change have been restricted to Cornwall? Obvious answers are that the oval houses had interiors uncluttered by roof support posts and that the absence of such ground-set posts meant avoidance of the problems of the rotting of such posts. Neither of these points appears to arise from any identifiable circumstance restricted to Cornwall.

10.4 Possible architectural solutions for large oval buildings

Stuart Blaylock

(text written 2001, revised 2003)

10.4.1 Introduction

Very little is certainly known of timber building techniques in the Roman Empire at large, still less for that of the peripheral areas of Roman Britain (Adam 1994, 205; de la Bédoyère 1991; Hingley 1989, 31). Although stone-walled roundhouses and other structures of Romano-British date are not uncommon, especially in the East Midlands (see Friendship-Taylor and Friendship-Taylor 1997 for examples), the issues of reconstruction, and of what such buildings actually looked like, have often been skirted around (with discussions of the buildings restricted to plan and function).

The many conceptual pitfalls of producing structural reconstruction drawings are ably discussed by JT Smith in an important essay on the inferences drawn from archaeological evidence (Smith 1982, 12, 17-18). Much the most useful work on the reconstruction of early timber building is that carried out on the reconstruction of Iron Age roundhouses, principally by Peter Reynolds (Reynolds 1982a; 1993). It must still be recognised that Reynolds' very useful lessons drawn from practical experimentation, as well as close observation of excavated evidence, may have limitations when applied to buildings of markedly later date and different plan form, even though they probably form part of the same building tradition. The oval building tradition in Cornwall is unique (as has already been stressed: above Section 10.2), and this may point to structural solutions that are *sui generis*. Nevertheless the fact that Iron Age roundhouses attained unsupported spans substantially greater than those required for the Trethurgy houses is taken satisfactorily to establish that it was technically possible to roof buildings of these dimensions and plan without internal support. In the last resort, the only way to prove that the Trethurgy houses could have been roofed in the way proposed is to carry out a similar reconstruction exercise to Reynolds' and this, unfortunately, was beyond the scope of the present project.

The aim of this exercise is the identification of structural solutions that are both technically possible and achievable within what is known of the building traditions of the time. The second factor is likely to be the most contentious and the solutions proposed are necessarily simplistic and generalised as a result of the paucity of available information. After preliminary evaluation of the possibilities (Sections 10.4.2, 10.4.3), a working conclusion was formed that the construction techniques and materials most likely to have been used in the Trethurgy houses would have been those drawn from the established traditions of Iron Age Britain, adapted to different plan forms, but probably not fundamentally different in techniques or materials to those of Iron Age roundhouses. One general structural solution has been adopted as both the simplest and the most in accordance with the evidence preserved. The drawings present variations on this solution in an attempt to show how individual houses might have appeared. It is accepted that other solutions are, or might be, possible.

10.4.2 The Iron Age background

During the Iron Age in Southern Britain timber roundhouses without interior supports for the roof occur quite frequently, their walls often built with stakes or less substantial timbers than are found in double-ring roundhouses, those in which the inner ring provides the main support for the roof. Single-ring roundhouses, without internal roof supports, tend to be the principal or only house type on some sites. Three sites, for which detailed consideration has been given to superstructure and roofing, serve as examples. At Little Waltham, Essex (Drury 1978), 16 houses with walls of posts set in circular, or sometimes, polygonal wall trenches varied in diameter from 10m to 14m. Drury considered that there had been some lowering of the site by ploughing and that internal postholes had been lost. He discusses possible reconstructions at length on the assumption that these houses were in fact double-ring, commenting that the 'span of rafters at 6-7m seems too great without intermediate support' (*ibid*, 120). However Cunliffe (1991, 245) remarks of these houses 'a ring beam at roof level would have been all that was required to provide the strength to carry the roof'. The difference of opinion almost certainly relates to the building of reconstruction single-ring roundhouses by Reynolds and others in the intervening period, notably those based on plans from Maiden Castle and Moel-y-Gaer (eg Reynolds 1982b).

At Danebury (Cunliffe and Poole 1991) some 73 circular structures have been identified, almost all of which lacked internal roof supports. Some of these structures had walls of timber set in ring grooves — circular wall trenches; the average diameter for this type was 6.7m but the largest was 8.7m. The majority of structures had walls of stakes driven directly into the ground. These stake-walled roundhouses averaged 7m in diameter but the largest was 9.5m. For these a construction is suggested in which the stakes are tied together at eaves level by a ring beam but continue upward to be interwoven with a curved roof (*ibid*, fig 4.9).

At Glastonbury all the houses are single stake rings, in general without internal supports (Coles and Minnitt 1995, 107). Diameters range from 5m to 8m or 9m; plans indicate that larger diameters are more common. The discussion refers to rafters of 7m in length and goes into considerable detail about the amount of materials required in such buildings. One building, House XIII, 8m in diameter, was rebuilt in 1992, and can be visited at the Peat Moors Centre. Oak and ash were used for the rafters, based on the evidence from surviving timbers at Glastonbury. The guidebook to the Centre (Cox 1993) provides considerable detail on the materials used in the reconstruction.

Overall a rapid scan of current literature suggests that Iron Age specialists accept the unsupported roofing of circular structures of 8m or slightly larger diameter. Recently this acceptance has been enhanced by work at Castell Henllys in Pembrokeshire. In 1998 a roundhouse 13m in diameter, for which excavation had shown no evidence for internal roof supports, has been successfully reconstructed (Bennett forthcoming).

10.4.3 Underlying assumptions

1. The Trethurgy buildings appear to have been roofed with structures supported on the walls, but without intervening supports, at least in their primary form. There were no systematic traces of post-rings, or settings within the buildings. Where postholes survived in the plan they were interpreted as other types of feature, and were generally not continuous enough to permit convincing interpretations as primary roof supports. The main exception (T2) is discussed separately below.

2. Although there was little evidence for the stone walls being of any great height (the maximum surviving height was *c* 0.5m in Structure U: Section 2.9.1), for purposes of reconstruction, walls averaging about 1-1.5m in height have been assumed (ie substantially higher than any surviving dimension; see also 3, below). This is because the presence of posts in T2 seems to dictate walls of a minimum height of 1-1.5m, and it was accepted that this implied a general principle of wall height in the Trethurgy houses (Section 10.4.5). There was little specific excavated evidence (such as collapsed walling) to suggest walls of greater height, although some general evidence of robbing (Section 10.1.4). Nevertheless the height of the walls remains hypothetical. It is impossible to estimate with any accuracy the amount of stone removed or recycled from individual buildings in the course of the occupation of the site, and of its subsequent history.

3. Without exception the house sites were on sloping ground and it has been suggested that some degree of slope was deliberately retained, perhaps for drainage (Section 10.1.3). It seems reasonable to assume that the walls functioned in part to level up each site for roofing (as to attempt to roof the buildings on inclined wall tops would have introduced another critical variable factor into a process already beset by difficulties). In practice this is at its most acute in House Z, where there is a fall of 0.9-1.4m along the long axis of the building; this has been applied on a basis of averaging the slope, so that the walls as reconstructed are between 1.05 and 1.95m high.

4. Although most houses appear to have possessed stone wall footings, those plans with postholes are complementary to the stone-walled plans, rather than conflicting or representing a different type of structure. The postholes are invariably on the wall lines or limits of the buildings and represent post-built structures incorporated in wall footings rather than supplementary roof supports within the buildings.

5. It is assumed that supplies of timber of necessary scantling would have been readily available in the

vicinity of the site, and that this would have been wholly or mainly of oak (see also Section 10.5).

6. Thatch is assumed, as the most easily available, and locally produced, roofing material (as well as the lightest: Clifton-Taylor 1972, 340); to more-or-less standard specification (Section 10.4.4).

10.4.4 General factors

Dimensions

Typical internal spans of up to 8-8.5m (Houses Z2, T2), and possibly as much as 9m (House Z1b), show that the roofs of the Trethurgy houses were substantial constructions. The comparative evidence of Iron Age roundhouses (above) shows that unsupported spans of these dimensions were not unusual in the late prehistoric period. Since it is accepted that this study is dealing with a development of the late-prehistoric building tradition in the Cornish Romano-British oval houses, it should not be surprising to find that the Trethurgy houses are of such substantial dimensions: up to maximum dimensions averaging 8.5x14m and a floor area of 80-120m^2 (excepting the unusually long lengths of the early phases of House Z).

Given a span of 8.5-9m and assuming a roof pitch of 45° (below), the roofing of the Trethurgy houses would have required timbers of a maximum length of 6.5-7m (21 feet 4 inches - 23 feet) for the main rafters. Such a length is perfectly possible, but the large number of timbers required again emphasises the large scale and imposing character of the buildings. In his studies of the reconstruction of the Pimperne Iron Age roundhouse at Butser (some 12.5m in diameter, and thus with a floor area of 122m^2), Reynolds explored the question of size and status of such houses, and assessed the large quantities of timber and thatching materials required for proper roofing of houses of such a size (amounting in total to at least 10 tonnes of timber, and 7 tonnes of thatch: Reynolds 1993, 99). Notwithstanding the large scale of the house, Reynolds suggested that the job of erecting such a building could be carried out by two people (*ibid*, 100). Reynolds rightly emphasised that (whatever the agricultural yields) such large quantities of materials imply buildings of high status (Reynolds 1982a, 189-90). At Trethurgy, with buildings of slightly smaller, but still comparable dimensions and floor areas, there were generally at least three substantial oval houses standing at a given phase of the site, as well as other smaller buildings (cf Figs 80-88). Rough calculations of building materials required on the basis suggested by Reynolds have substantial implications for the yield capacity and sheer area of land at the disposal of the Trethurgy builders (Section 12.7).

To put the scale of these buildings into perspective, it is instructive to compare the dimensions of the Trethurgy houses with some groups of later, Medieval buildings. The collection of comparative plans of Medieval Dartmoor longhouses compiled by Henderson and Weddell (1994, figs 7-9), provides a typical group of Medieval building plans, one that is significantly smaller in average dimensions: averaging between 3-4.5m in internal span (and 6-18m in length). The remarkable consistency in width of these houses must surely have been conditioned by the size and availability of roofing materials. To find a group of buildings of comparable dimensions to the Trethurgy houses in the later Middle Ages one must go to the open halls of the late-Medieval clergy houses of the Cathedral Close at Exeter (Blaylock forthcoming). These buildings are clearly very different in construction and in the sophistication of their roofing techniques, but they do have broadly comparable dimensions in plan — the Law Library: 6.95x9.15m (63.5m^2); the Deanery: 7.45x14.3m (106.5m^2); the Archdeacon of Exeter's house: 8.65x14.5m (125.4m^2); and the Bishop's Palace: 14.75x23m (339m^2). Of these the first three examples were roofed in one uninterrupted span, although the hall of the Bishop's Palace was aisled.

Probable roof pitch and covering

There are many arguments in favour of a pitch of around 45°, most persuasively that it provides the optimum combination of economy of materials with effective dispersal of water (Reynolds 1982a, 180; 1993, 108; Drury 1978, 120). Forty-five degrees represents the generally accepted minimum angle for a thatched roof adequately to shed water according to modern thinking (Reynolds 1982a, 180; Mitchell 1943, 262; English Heritage 2000, 5-6, 16; some authorities recommend a steeper pitch: Clifton Taylor 1972, 340; Fearn 1995, 11), and the optimum dispersal of the lateral thrust of the roof; any lesser or greater angle increases the pressure on the walls unnecessarily (Reynolds 1982a 193). In view of this consensus, a pitch of approximately 45° has been accepted throughout.

Nature and function of the stone wall footings

The wall construction is described as faces of rubble masonry with tightly-packed cores of smaller stones in a matrix of rab/growan and/or earth (Section 10.1). Reynolds' experimental work on the Conderton house made three important observations:

1. That careful construction of the core of the wall is important if it is to withstand thrust from the roof,

and this forms a crucial part of the construction process; walls composed of two faces and a static fill will collapse quickly under the thrust of the roof (Reynolds 1982a, 192).

2. Roof timbers must bear on the inner third of the thickness of the wall; the remaining thickness acts as a buttress to counter the pressure from the roof (*ibid*, 193).

3. The load exerted by roof timbers needs to be spread by wall plates. Thus timber wall plates are proposed for the Trethurgy houses. Where posts at irregular intervals appear in the walls, these have been interpreted as providing support for wall plates around the round ends of the buildings rather than direct support for the rafters (eg House T2).

Timber and fixings

Such evidence as there is for 'native' Romano-British timber building techniques suggests that, in common with late-prehistoric buildings, structural timber was mainly unconverted 'round' timber, used more-or-less in a rough-trimmed state, with the bark stripped off, but without further shaping. It goes without saying that any carpentry and fixing techniques applied to such timber would necessarily be crude. This has been termed, in a later context, 'primitive' timber building, defined as a construction with 'unsawn timber of uneven lengths and quality, and assembled without the use of mortise-and-tenon joints' (Beresford 1975, 36), although it should be noted that a limited repertoire of simple mortice-and-tenon and scarf joints is attested in waterlogged timbers (Reynolds 1993, 97). At Trethurgy, too, there is some positive evidence for squared timber posts in the main gateway of the site (Section 2.5; Fig 10). But by and large unsquared/unconverted timber is assumed for the roofs, with slighter material throughout for bracing and strengthening purposes. Oak would always have been the ideal, although whether it would have been available in sufficient quantities and lengths to be used throughout for the rafters is uncertain. A mixture of whatever timber was available is most probable. For the slighter laths or 'purlins' hazel may have been preferred, because of its flexibility (Forestry Commission 1968, 44), although, given the use of oak for larger timbers, there would have been plenty of oak brushwood suitable for the production of cleft or split laths. Notwithstanding the queries over the use of mortise-and-tenon joints (above), it is probable that the main timbers would have been joined using simple halved joints: the apex of rafter couples, junction of collar and rafter, etc. Although nails were found on the site, the overwhelming evidence in early carpentry is for fixing either by binding with organic materials of various sorts, or by the use of wooden pegs. These methods are therefore proposed throughout, in the absence of positive evidence for fixing with iron nails.

Structural aspects of the roof trusses and the sequence of erection

Given the basic assumption that the structures represent an adaptation of, or a development from, construction techniques already established in the British Iron Age roundhouse building tradition to an elongated plan form, how might the roof structures have been assembled? Two basic premises are: (i) That the roof needed to be structurally self-supporting during erection, given the length of the timbers and width of the span. (ii) That the basic structural element was the rafter, probably of unconverted timber, supplemented as necessary by lateral (horizontal) ties and longitudinal bracing.

The first premise presupposes construction in a combination of paired rafter and tripod assemblies to cope with the variable plan form. Whereas the roof of a roundhouse can be assembled by erecting a series of rafters joining at the apex, that of an oval house must progress in a more complicated sequence, either by the erection of one or more paired trusses (presumably braced) over the central parallelogram, followed by tripod-type assembly at the hips, or rounded ends, of the building; or by the initial construction of a tripod-type rafter construction over one end of the building (ie effectively a sort of 'semi-roundhouse' roof). This would have been followed by the progressive erection of paired rafter trusses along the length of the building, and finally the construction of another hip or 'semi-roundhouse' at the further end. Both sequences must necessarily have been braced as they were erected. Lateral bracing was most probably provided by a collar in the paired rafter trusses (a horizontal timber, generally about one third of the way down the rafters from the apex), and by a 'composite collar' or a series of 'purlins' — referred to as a 'ring beam' by Reynolds (1993, 98-9), a term that will be used hereafter — at an equivalent level to the collar around the curved ends of the roof. This could be fixed by half joints and pegged or lashed to the rafters. Once the main radial rafters, stretching from the wall plate to the apex of the roof, were in place, shorter rafters supported by the wall plates and the ring beam (and not reaching the apex) would have been added to complete the roof structure of the round end as necessary.

Further longitudinal bracing would have been provided by the laths (termed 'purlins' by Reynolds 1993, 98-9) which would have played an important cumulative role in the bracing of the rafter structure, and which doubled as the support for the thatched roof covering. In the experimental Iron Age houses this was found to give a strong construction with the added advantage of providing easy access around the roof, via the ladder-rung-like laths, for both construction and thatching (*ibid*, 108). Roofs survive in the vernacular building stock in Devon where the longitudinal bracing is provided by thatching laths or battens, without purlins (Beacham 1990, 31). The Iron Age roundhouse experiments have shown that the hazel laths approximately 200mm apart that are necessary for fixing thatch provide enough bracing, and thus effectively do double as purlins. In the Pimperne house these were fixed in axe-cut notches in the rafters by lashing with twine (Reynolds 1993, 108-9). A similar mode of fixing could have been used here, or the laths could have been fixed by small pegs (as later cleft thatching laths were fixed). Fixing by lashing is preferred, marginally, in view of the theoretical danger of splitting uncleft laths by pinning (although lashed fixings are prone to loosening if the rope stretches). From this stage the addition of rafters over the central part of the building could have proceeded with the running addition of laths as longitudinal bracing as each truss was raised although a two-stage solution involving temporary bracing is also possible.

Reynolds observed that the structure of tripod rafters, braced with concentric purlins/laths achieved an equilibrium on completion, making it a very strong structure, and one to which quite major repairs can be carried out without threat to the structure as a whole (1993, 102). Aspects of this reasoning can be applied to the Trethurgy houses, especially the cumulative strengthening influence of the laths/purlins attached to the rafters (which could have facilitated the construction of doorways and dormers). Although there is greater initial capacity for movement, especially longitudinal movement or racking, in the paired-rafter construction than in that of the 'wigwam' construction of the roundhouse, once braced and lathed this is likely to be just as resilient a structure.

An alternative to the paired-rafter system of construction proposed here was suggested in comments on an early draft by Phil Bennett (pers comm). The ring beams proposed for the round ends would be continued through the 'straight' sides of the houses as purlins, supported from time to time by paired rafters. This would allow for shorter rafters to be used in intermediate positions (very much as proposed for the rounded ends of the buildings). Although such a system remains a possibility I have preferred to retain the original system of paired rafters for the greater stability of structure that they confer on the roof. To cut out every other rafter, or two out of three, would also necessitate closer rafter intervals, cancelling out any saving in timber.

The question of a ridge

The elongation of the plan, from round to oval, immediately suggests that a ridge member might be introduced to span the gap at the apex, and to provide support for rafters over the central section of the buildings (Innocent 1916, 11-15). But a ridge is almost certainly unnecessary so long as longitudinal bracing was supplied by other means. The rafters could be 'braced' as they were reared, and would not need fixed support at their upper ends. The thatch could have been supported on a ridge roll of straw or brushwood (Moir and Letts 1999, 115-16). Innocent pointed out that the role of the ridge as a fundamental support of the roof has been misunderstood (a role reflected in the early etymology of the term: Innocent 1916, 13-14), rather than simply a convenient point to attach the apexes of rafters in some types of roof construction (*ibid*, 11). Nevertheless a ridge remains as a possible alternative, and the technique was certainly known in the Roman period (Vitruvius IV.ii.1: Morgan 1960, 107).

The evidence of postholes

Where convincing structural postholes survive, they can generally either be related to internal features of the buildings (the partition in House A1 or the 'loom' in House Z2), or there are stratigraphic reasons for thinking that they belong to wholly separate phases (earlier than the stone-walled building in the case of House Z1, later in the case of House A3). There is even a case to be made for the apparently integral postholes of House T2 belonging to an earlier phase than the stone walls (although the contemporaneity of timber and stone walls has been accepted for purposes of reconstruction in Section 10.4.5). The absence of convincing evidence for interior post supports in the Trethurgy houses only strengthens the case for regarding the roof structures as freestanding, supported only by the walls. Where posts do occur they are always positioned on the perimeter of the buildings, normally on the inside face of the walls. The possibility that the roof structures received primary internal support from posts looks distinctly unlikely. Postholes such as those in A3 are more likely to represent propping of decaying roof structures than independent structures in their own right.

Doorways

Full discussion of the possible reconstruction of the doorway of House A1, for which there is good excavated evidence, appears below (Section 10.4.5). There are a number of alternative possibilities for doorways in the houses where no postholes were observed. Sills, or threshold timbers, could theoretically have been positioned across the doorways and provided support for the superstructure of door frames, but no specific evidence for this system has survived. If doors were hung on iron hinge pivots as is proposed elsewhere (Section 10.4.5), then there is no need for pivots or other fixed provision at ground level. Frames supported on posts that failed to penetrate the underlying ground are also possible, if it is accepted that the adjacent roof and wall structures provided sufficient stability without earth-fast bases. Again the evidence for a conclusive interpretation is absent. A further possibility is that the stone walls were built up to a higher level around the doorways, to accommodate the doors, and at a height that could be spanned by lintels without the need for a supporting frame. This possibility is explored in the reconstruction drawing of House T2 (Fig 95). The arrangement involving a transverse (dormer) roof (as suggested in Figs 94-5) would be obviated by this solution. In some ways this is a persuasive theory, if only for its simplicity; but there is nothing in the recorded evidence to support it, and it must remain as one hypothetical solution among others. The main objection is that, with wall heights as proposed, the available height would not always be sufficient to accommodate this arrangement. The actual form of the doorways in the majority of the Trethurgy houses remains obscure (with the exceptions of A1 and A2), and none of the possible solutions proposed has much to recommend it over another.

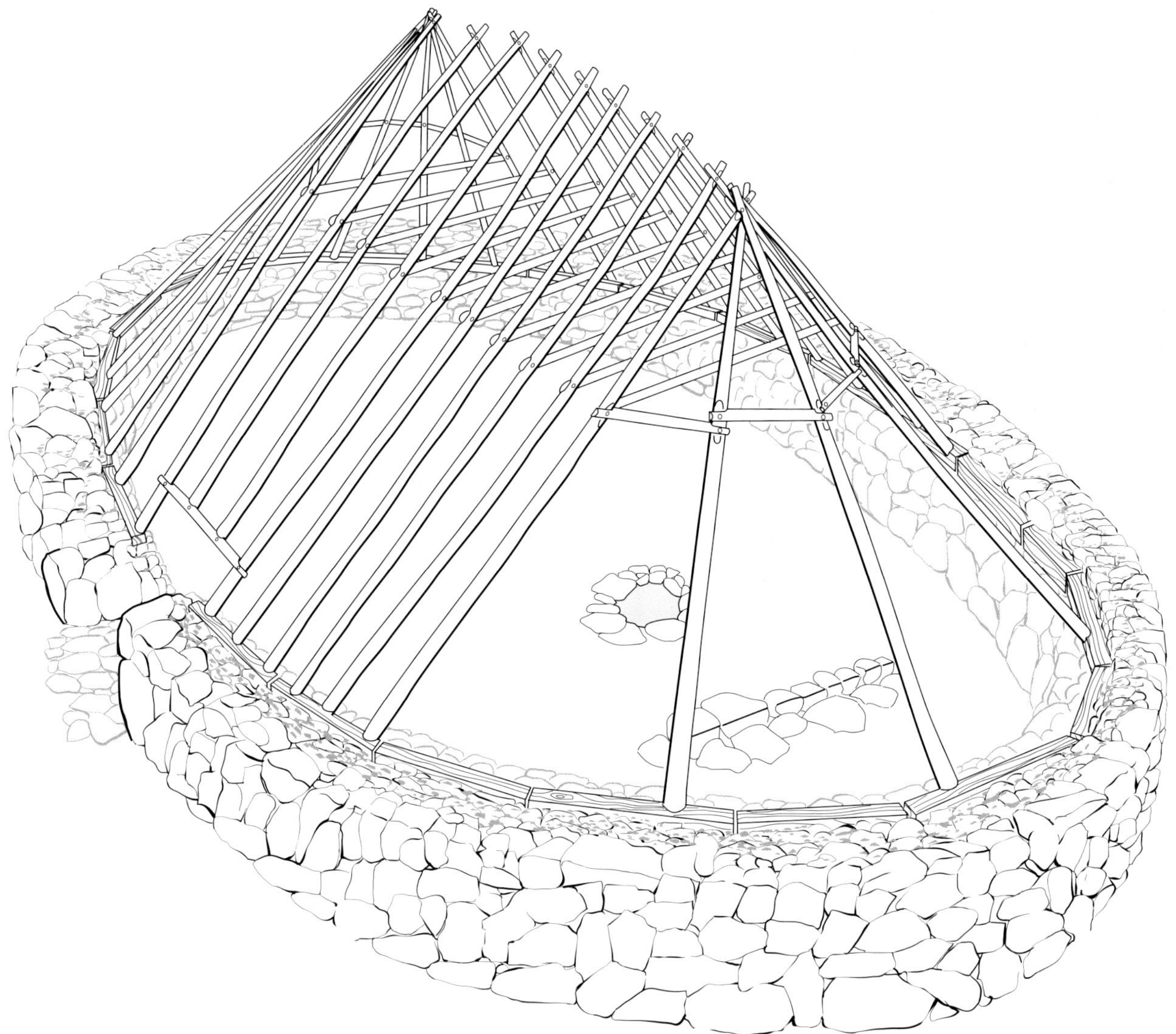

Fig 90 Conjectural reconstruction of House Z2 from the south-east, showing proposed rafter construction and outline structure at east end. NB for clarity laths are omitted in this view, although (as the text shows) laths would have been added cumulatively as the paired rafter trusses were raised, to prevent racking. Illustration Rosemary Robertson

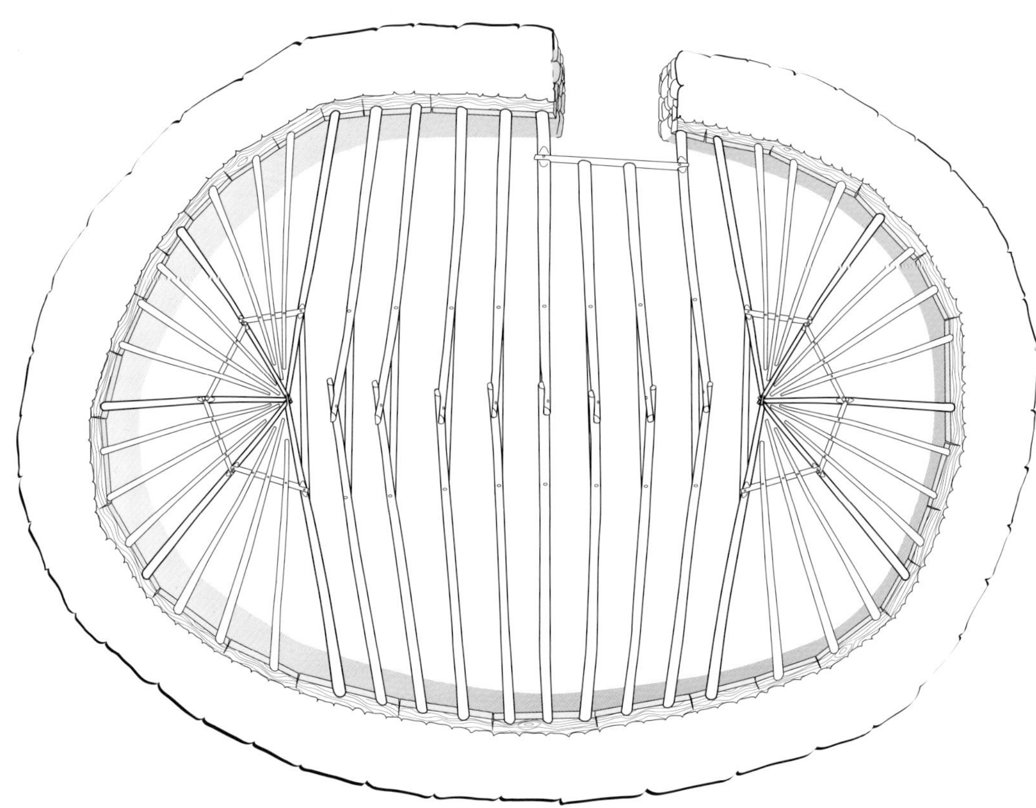

Fig 91: Conjectural reconstruction of House Z2 in plan view, showing proposed layout of main rafters. Illustration Rosemary Robertson

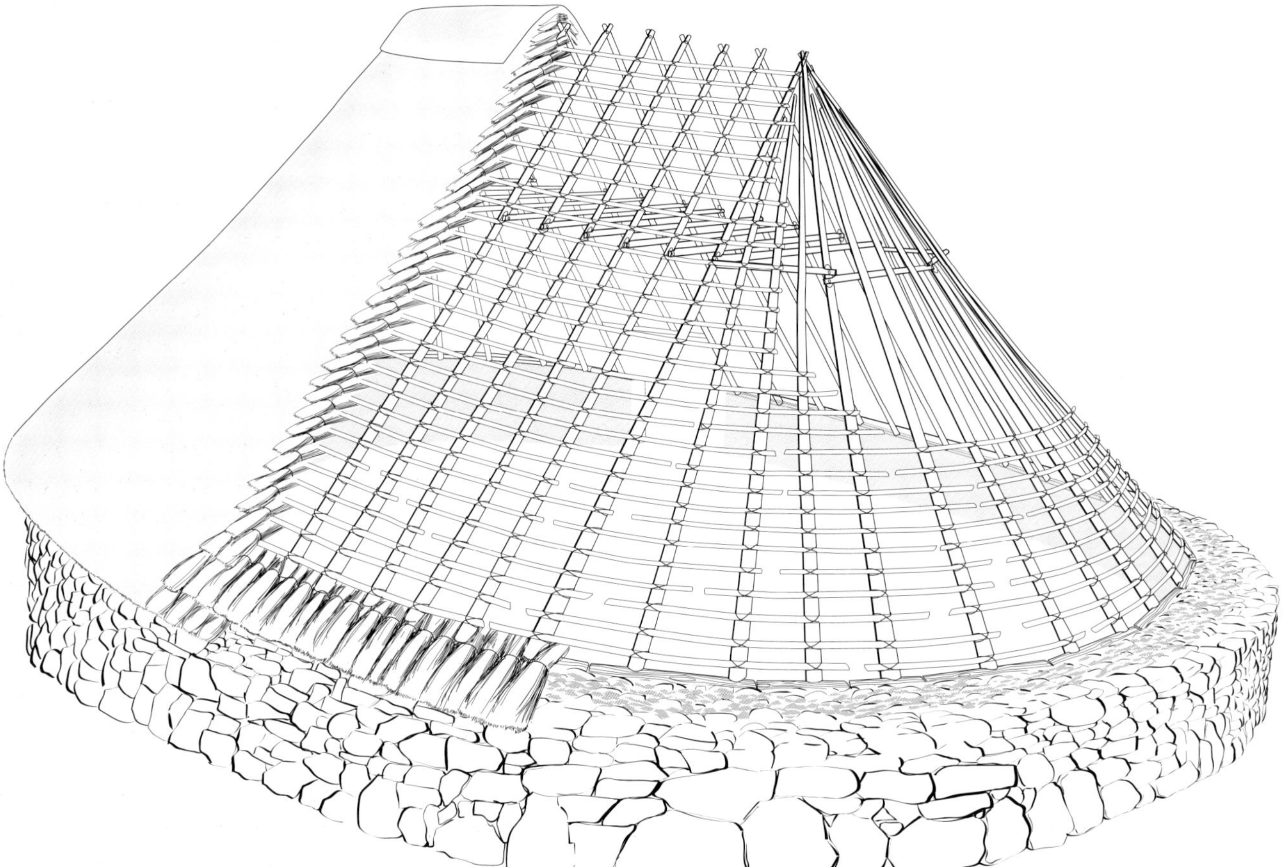

Fig 92: Conjectural reconstruction of House Z2 from the north-west, with radial rafters complete, the majority of laths in position, and thatched roof over the east end. Illustration Rosemary Robertson

(a)

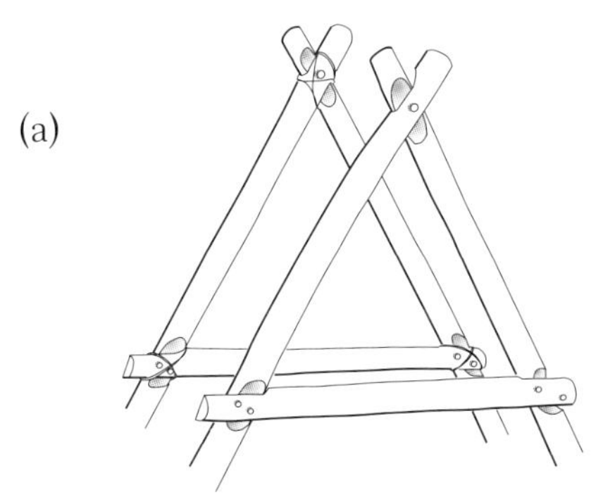

(b)

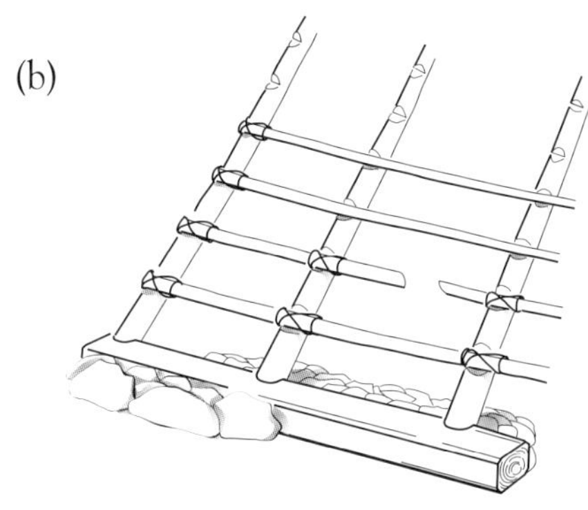

Fig 93: Conjectural reconstruction of structural details of House Z2: (a) apex of rafter trusses showing proposed methods of fixing; (b) proposed methods of fixing laths to rafters (note also the rafters bearing on the wall plates with birds-mouth joints). Illustration Rosemary Robertson

10.4.5 Specific commentary on individual drawings

Choice of plans on which to base reconstruction drawings was conditioned mainly by survival, in that poorly preserved plans could not sustain the necessary level of scrutiny. House Z2 was selected as the first 'prototype' plan for a reconstruction drawing (with the caveats that whatever solutions were adopted would need to be applicable to substantially longer houses and that the solutions proposed were not incompatible with any of the excavated evidence from the site). The general principle has been to take the preferred structural solution outlined above, and produce drawings based upon the variety of plans to illustrate the range of possible techniques and details. Thus House Z2 (Figs 90-3) served for the basic plan, explored in perspective view, plan, and in details; A1, another relatively complete plan, was selected mainly for its doorway (Fig 94); T2 explores the possible reconstruction of wall posts and, taking advantage of the higher walls, the possible support of door lintels wholly within the stone walls (Fig 95). Structure U, although well preserved, was not certainly domestic in character, and was not certainly completed; it was thus excluded as a model, although the plan has much to recommend it as comparative evidence.

House Z2 (Figs 90-93)

This plan retains a well-preserved outside wall over much of its perimeter and a continuous stone pavement within, so it can be reasonably certain that the structure had no interior postholes or settings at this phase. The main limitations of the plan (as opposed to, say, Houses A1 or A2/3) are the lack of structural evidence for a doorway, and the relatively large drop in level from one end of the building to the other. The basic internal dimensions of House Z2 are a length of 12m and a width of 8m with the floor area c 81m^2. The fall in the floor level along the long axis of the building from west to east is c 1.05m, according to section n-o (Fig 21). The wall height at the west (uphill) end survived as c 0.2m — one course of facework. To accommodate the fall in floor level west to east, the walls must therefore have been at least 1.2m high at the east end; presumably 5-6 courses of facework, depending on exact size of stone used. In fact, for reconstruction purposes, taking into account the discussion of the probable minimum height of walls elsewhere (above), the wall height is taken to range from approximately 1.05m at the uphill end to 1.95m at the downhill end. The maximum width is 8m, although the width/radius of the rounded ends is more like 7.5m/3.75m. The bowed sides to the plan mean that the ridge line of the roof was probably slightly higher in the centre than at the ends (compare many thatched buildings in Devon today).

An interval of c 900mm for the rafter trusses was originally proposed; this was reduced to c 650mm after further thought and sketch experimentation, giving eight pairs of rafters over the central part of the roof. At the ends the same spacing at the eaves would give 12 radial rafters around the curved ends of the building. This spacing is not inconsistent with that used in the Butser rebuilding exercises (judging by the published photographs, there being no specific references to this dimension in the texts). To avoid congestion three radial rafters extending as far as the apex are proposed; the remaining rafters were supported on the ring beam and did not necessarily reach the apex.

No evidence was recorded for posts or other fittings, and the position of the doorway cannot be fixed with precision. There are advantages in placing the door as far to the east as possible to enable the westernmost rafter truss to be supported on solid walling. But the southern ends of at least two and possibly three rafter trusses beyond that would probably have been without support because of the doorway opening. The obvious structural solution to this is the use of a trimmer spanning the first to the fourth or fifth rafter trusses to support the southern ends of the second/third/?fourth trusses. Because of the uncertainty, the drawing of House Z2 omits a

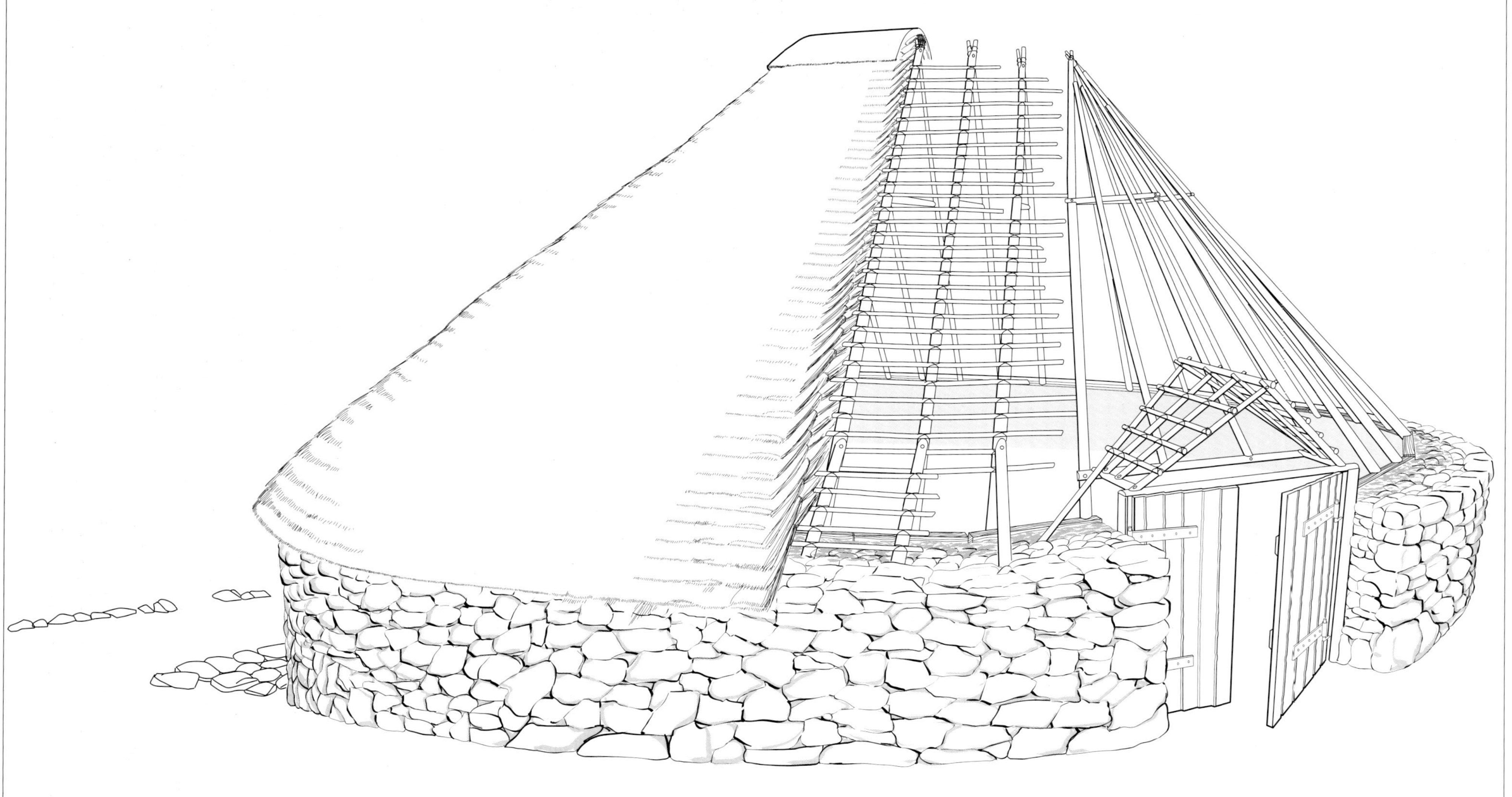

Fig 94: Conjectural reconstruction of House A1 from the north, showing rafter structure, the doorway structure, laths (centre), and thatch (left). Illustration Rosemary Robertson

doorway in detail, showing only the trimmer and general position of the doorway.

House A1 (Fig 94)

The structural techniques, details, finishes, and visual appearance proposed for House Z2 are largely transferable to A1. The good evidence for the position and form of the doorway is the exceptional aspect of this plan.

With maximum dimensions of 11.5m and 8.5m on longitudinal and lateral axes respectively, this plan (Fig 34) is more truly oval than either Z2 or T2 (which tend to have straight sides and semi-circular ends). Ignoring the terracing for the west wall [33], section x-xx shows a drop of *c* 0.4m in the floor level on the long axis of the building (Fig 35). The west wall, [33], survived as one course plus the terracing cut, about 0.3m in total above internal floor level. The east wall survived to one course, about 0.2-0.25m, above the natural subsoil. This suggests a minimum original height for the wall on the east, downhill side of *c* 0.7m, or 3-4 courses of facework; the conjectural full height of the walls would thus vary between 1.3m and 1.7m. Section w-ww (Fig 35) shows that there is a negligible fall across the building of perhaps 80-100mm. The surviving walls/footings of A1 average about 1m wide.

A distinctive aspect of the plan is the partition cutting across the eastern end of the house, clearly a substantial structure, with large posts (although interrupted by later hearth pits), and probably with a hearth immediately to the west of it (Sections 2.17, 10.1.9; Fig 34). The orientation of the partition offers an insight into the internal layout of the building, and possibly also its structure, since it establishes an orientation within the house, which would otherwise remain elusive. Moreover it suggests a way around the problem of accommodating the entrance into the roof structure. If the orientation of the screen is taken as indicative of that of a roof truss above, a second parallel truss can be proposed *c* 3.5m to the west, which would represent the west end of a short central roof section, and fall slightly short of the eastern post of the doorway. The doorway could thus be accommodated between this truss and the first radial rafter of the west end of the building (obviating the problem encountered in Z2, where some of the main rafters had to be trimmed to make room for the doorway). The greatest fall in level is more or less at 90° to the line of the partition, giving another clue as to the perceived axis of the building.

Intervals for the rafter trusses and radial rafters of each end are similar to those used for the drawing of House Z2: an interval of 700mm for the trusses in the central section, and *c* 0.9-1m for the feet of the radial rafters. This gives three 'principal ' radial rafters (ie those supporting the ring beam at collar level), and 11 radial rafters in all, with a spacing of about 1m at wall-top level. At the west end a slightly wider 'bay' would make room for the entrance, spanned by two secondary rafters supported by a trimmer above the doorway.

One additional detail of roof construction shown here is the use of extension rafters or 'kickers' at the base of the roof to span the wall and support the base of the thatch. It is proposed that the lathing was fixed to these timbers and omitted from the feet of the main rafters, thereby providing storage space in the eaves, accessible from within.

The plan is open to other interpretations, and it remains a possibility that this house could have been roofed with a centralised 'roundhouse' type roof, although this would have been substantially higher than the solution proposed to attain a 45° pitch on the long axis.

The entrance, despite clear evidence of substantial postholes flanking the doorway, poses some problems. The width (centre to centre) is 2m, probably wide enough for two door leaves, yet there is no evidence of how they might have been mounted. Framed door leaves of overlapping planks have been suggested, although with some concern that these might imply a different carpentry tradition from that represented by other aspects of the structures. Sawn planks are not necessarily implied, however, as doors could as easily have been made of radially split or adzed planks. The doors are shown hung on iron hinge pivots (or pintles) fixed into the main posts of the frame: these fixings are known in quantity from Roman Britain (Manning 1985 and pers comm), although none was found on the site. A sill beam/threshold, laid on the ground surface (because there seems to be no archaeological evidence for a below-ground structure or, for that matter, stone pivot blocks), and accommodating holes for the lower ends of door pivots, is another possibility. Some form of dormer roof over the doorway/porch assembly would have been necessary, given a maximum wall height substantially less than 2m in this part of the circumference. The simplest possible structure has been proposed in the drawing (Fig 94): a trimmer spanning the area of the doorway on the line of the main pitch of the roof; a trabeate frame and 45° gable above (1m in height to balance the 2m width of the porch) on the front facade of the doorway; ridge and eaves timbers running back to the main pitch of the roof, and short rafters to support the slope of the roof. Diagonal timbers may have marked the line of the valley and could have continued to the wall top, thereby providing some additional bracing. Reynolds has pointed out that a pitch of 45° in a porch roof

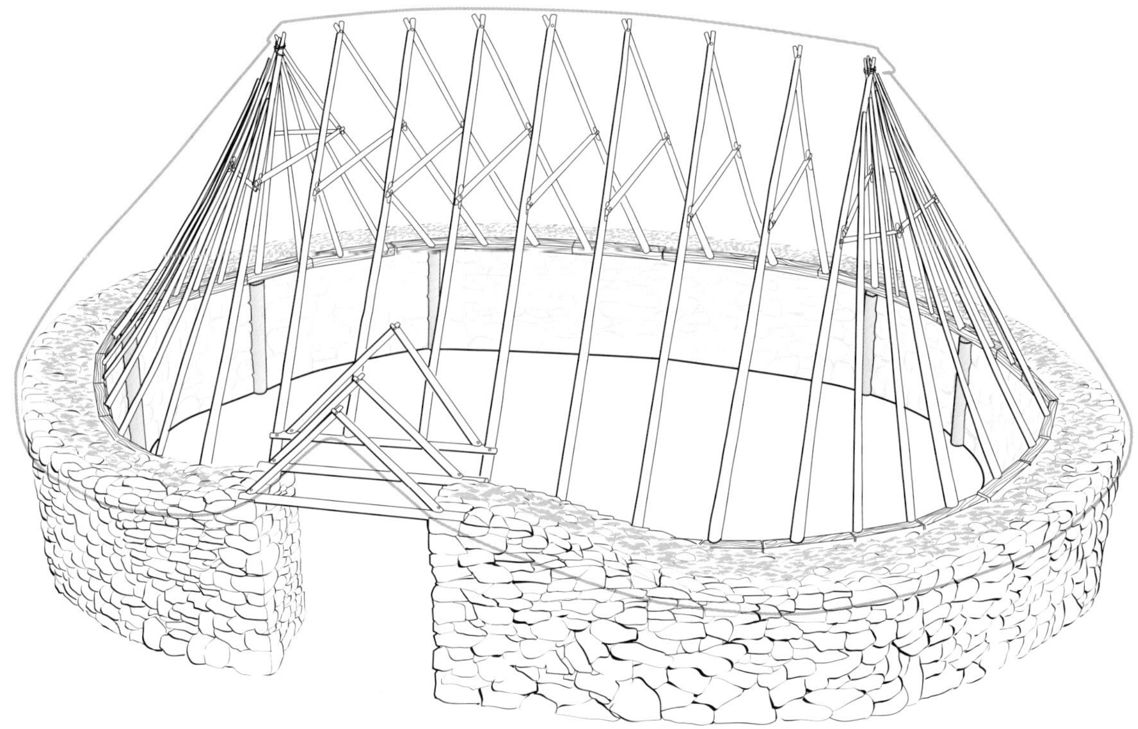

Fig 95: Conjectural reconstruction of House T2 from the north, showing outline rafter structure and proposed doorway arrangement. All longitudinal bracing is omitted. Illustration Rosemary Robertson

dictates a shallower pitch for the valley at the junction of the two roofs, and virtually guarantees that the valley will leak (Reynolds 1993, 108); a pitch of 60° would be necessary in the porch roof to ensure a watertight valley. There are, however, plenty of vernacular examples of dormers and other projecting roofs treated in this way at a pitch of around 45°; perhaps the thatch was thick enough to reduce leakage to a minimum; perhaps leakage was tolerated.

House T2 (Fig 95)

The house was 12.5m long, and up to 8.5m wide, although 7.5-8m is more typical. The walls averaged 1m thick, increasing to between 1.1m and 1.3m at the curved ends. The ground to the west was terraced for House T by up to 0.3m (Section 2.18). The interior was virtually level, with a drop of only 0.2m along its long axis, and the floor also virtually level across the building. Walls of approximately 1.5m throughout are proposed (from 1.4-1.6m at maximum variation), increasing to 2m at the doorway.

House T2 is the one plan to have retained unequivocal evidence of posts within its walls, although their distribution is confined to the curved ends of the building, and is not consistent or continuous. The dilemma in the interpretation of the posts is that those for which there is evidence surviving cannot have formed a coherent system of support for any aspect of the roof; yet they form a relatively consistent aspect of the evidence for House T, and thus demand some explanation. This raises two issues relating to a reconstruction:

1. Postholes survive at each end of the building, in line with the inner wall face, three each around the southern side of the curved ends. They do not survive on the northern side of either end (where preservation was good enough to ensure their observation had they penetrated the subsoil), nor on the long sides of the building. If they are to be taken as part of the structural evidence for roofing, then some missing elements have to be accepted. The simplest addition would be to complete the postholes at either end, but not to posit any on the long sides, where trusses would have been supported only by the wall plates.

2. The posts must have been substantial timbers, to warrant their inclusion in the structural concepts of the house (where other houses were satisfactorily constructed without them); this implies that they were either vertical wall posts (in which case the walls must have been of a sufficient height to justify their incorporation), or are in some way related to the roof timbers, perhaps holding the feet of the main rafters (in which case the opposite would be true, implying no standing walls of any height).

I have opted for the interpretation as wall posts, embedded in the wall to a certain height, carrying wall plates around the rounded ends of the building. The irregular intervals imply the use of wall plates to support the roof (Charles 1982, 102-4). Although it is also possible to propose an irregular rafter plan for House T2 in which radial rafters were directly supported by the wall posts, the irregular spacing of the posts is more likely to indicate wall plates. An irregular disposition of timbers could easily be accommodated by spacing the paired rafters more widely on the south side than the north (0.85m and 0.75m respectively), and by skewing the west end in relation to the geometric layout of the building. This would increase the pitch of the roof at the ends of the house.

No firm evidence for the position of the doorway was recorded, although general probability suggests that it would have been east of centre on the north side of the building, opposite the various hearth features (in common with most of the Trethurgy plans, Section 10.4.3). There is a convenient gap in the surviving walling in this area (where the line of the wall/limits of the building are indicated by the extent of floor [436]). The position of the door was probably at the west limit of the gap, where the floor extends slightly over the projected line of the wall. This accounts for the apparent deviation in the wall line at this point.

The conjectural reconstruction of the doorway has explored a lintel-type construction supported on raised walls to each side of the opening. This has been kept deliberately skeletal (with the position of the finished surface of the roof shown in outline).

10.5 Brief comment on the implications of the proposed reconstructions

The reconstructions proposed for the Trethurgy houses involved substantial quantities of timber. The roof of House Z2 would have required some 48 straight and substantial poles up to 7m in length, in addition to the timber required for purlins, wall plates, and for architectural details such as doorways. Traditionally Cornwall, especially those parts to the west of Bodmin Moor, has been regarded as having little woodland resource. However Henderson (1935, 135-51) has assembled data that indicate that woodland, though never comparable in area to that in many counties to the east, was more extensive in the Medieval period than at the time he was writing; he makes particular reference to the effect of mining on the depletion of timber resources (*ibid*, 151) which of course is relevant to the Trethurgy area. Unfortunately at present we lack the information which would allow us to provide a reasonably detailed environmental history of mid-Cornwall. The situation has scarcely changed since the paucity of data for the environmental history of the whole of Cornwall was highlighted by Bell in 1984. The one small-scale study of pollen connected with the round at Penhale (Scaife 1998/9) does show oak as the most frequent tree species.

The reconstructions propose the use of coppiced timber, especially oak. Long traditions of woodland management in Britain dating back to the Neolithic period are now well established (eg Rackham 1980, *passim*) and these include extensive use of coppicing of a variety of trees. Oak was regularly coppiced to provide a range of products from bark stripped from short growth for use in tanning to long poles for building (Peterken 1981, 11-41). Henderson (1935, 137) comments that, for the manor of Idless in Kenwyn for which 40 acres of woodland are recorded in Domesday Book, extensive woods of oak coppice remained in the 1930s. Recently Bennett (forthcoming) has recorded that the 9m poles of oak coppice used in the reconstruction of the Castell Henllys roundhouse took some 25 years to grow. He links this to an exploration of the implications for the late-prehistoric landscape of managed woodland being more extensive than is traditionally assumed, in a coastal area in many ways very much like Cornwall. The Trethurgy houses too make it necessary for reasonable stretches of woodland to have been present in the landscape of Roman Cornwall. The size of timbers used indicates that this woodland must have been managed on a long-term basis, drawing on centuries of traditional expertise. However it is highly likely that long-grown and sizeable coppiced timber was a valued, even limited, resource. The use of this resource in the large oval houses adds to the general impression of the status of their occupants in the local community.

There appear to have been two obvious benefits from the development of the oval houses, with the adaptations from Iron Age construction methods that their roofs imply. The first is that of an interior free of the presence of uprights; such an interior would have potential for greater flexibility in the way its space was used, while internal uprights must have been regarded as some impediment to movement. The second is much more important and relates to the prevention of damp rot among structural timbers. Bennett (forthcoming) provides comment on the difficulties caused by the rotting of ground-set internal posts in the several reconstructions at Castell Henllys which have used these, a difficulty also commented upon by Reynolds (1993) with regard to Butser. If a timber and thatched roof can be constructed based only on a wall, without any ground-set supports, then the durability of that roof is greatly enhanced and if thatching is properly maintained the building can have a long life. The proposed lives of the Trethurgy houses (Table 12.2) vary from 50 to 150 years, a span in accordance with Bennett's comment that 'there is every reason to suggest that large roundhouses could have survived for generations'.

11 Structures other than the large oval buildings

The large oval buildings form only one of the structural types in the Round. As very distinctive structures which may have been high-status dwellings they have provided the focus for interim discussion of Trethurgy building traditions (eg Quinnell 1986) and the wide range of other types present has been largely neglected. These are often incomplete in plan and difficult to interpret, and have not formed the focus of discussion at any other site.

11.1 Rectangular timber building X1

House X1 (Figs 25, 28) may represent the only rectangular timber building on the site. Details of structural features are given in Section 2.13.2 — slots [652], [731], [685], [727], and possibly [681], postholes [655A], [665B], [658A], [658B], [699], [770], [768], and [804]. Maximum size, if all these features were part of one building, would have been some 9m by 8m. Construction cannot have been easy as the ground slopes about 1m in each direction across the suggested plan. A hearth pit such as [674] early in the stratigraphic sequence may have belonged in the building. On the suggested chronology (Table 9.2), X1 may have stood for 50 to 60 years (see Stage 1 and 2 plans Figs 80, 81).

Area X, well drained and directly uphill from the Entrance, was an obvious site for any major residence within the Round. No definite structure similar to X1 has been found in Roman Cornwall or elsewhere in Britain. The one possibility is that connected with contexts 209, 114, 115, and 137 at Castle Gotha (Saunders and Harris 1982, fig 5, 118); these were described as sleeper-beam trenches, produced no dating material, and were considered possibly Post-Medieval, but their stratigraphic position is unclear. If the Castle Gotha building is Roman in date, it is much smaller than X1, some 2m by 5m. In Devon a series of irregular, post-built, rectangular structures were found beneath the later masonry building at Holcombe (Pollard 1974, fig 3) and dated to the late 1st and 2nd centuries. Also in Devon, at Topsham, a late 1st century three-roomed building with veranda was built in timber (Jarvis and Maxfield 1975, fig 4) but this belongs to a widespread tradition of buildings of recognizable Roman plan in the early centuries of Roman Britain. Trethurgy X1, and perhaps Holcombe, appear to relate to a much less well-studied tradition, in which Roman rectangular timber buildings were being adapted to much less regular ground plans. The date of X1 can only be placed very early in the use of the Round in the 2nd century, the period of experimentation with architecture in Cornwall in which the large oval buildings finally evolved.

11.2 Four-posters E1, E2, and Structure E3

The four-posters E1 and E2 seem best interpreted as storage buildings; while grain may have been a significant commodity, the term granary is better avoided as it has implications for the importance of grain over other foodstuffs, materials, and equipment which cannot be assessed (see Cunliffe and Poole 1991, 115 for discussion). A wide range of other functions for such structures has been suggested by Ellison and Drewitt (1971). An interpretation of Structure E as a watch-tower was put forward in the interim report (Miles and Miles 1973a, 26), largely on the basis of its siting on the highest part of the site, an interpretation which, of course, cannot be entirely refuted. Four-posters were not found in South West Britain until the 1970s, possibly because they were seen as part of a chalkland agricultural economy and were not expected (Miles 1977, 113). They have now been found in Cornwall at Killibury in the Later Iron Age (*ibid*, fig 43) and interpreted as present at Castle Dore from a re-examination of the excavation report (Quinnell and Harris 1985). So far they do not appear to have been recognised within rounds other than Trethurgy. In Devon they have been recognised on the 1st-century AD settlement at Topsham (Jarvis and Maxfield 1975) and probably at the Iron Age hillfort of Woodbury Castle (Miles 1975b). Recently they have been found at a series of enclosure and open sites excavated along the line of the new A30 between Honiton and Exeter, sites ranging in date from the Middle Bronze Age until the Late Iron Age (Fitzpatrick *et al* 1999).

In Wales four-posters are a common feature on both hillfort and enclosure sites during the Iron Age (eg Williams and Mytum 1998) and continue to be used on a reduced scale through the Roman period. Four-posters which may belong to the mid or late-Roman centuries have been found at Collfryn, Powys (Britnell 1989, 121), a reference which provides a useful summary; a group were dated to the 4th century in the reoccupied hillfort of Dinorben (Guilbert 1979).

The phasing and duration of Structures E1-3 is very uncertain. The main chronological argument is the central position of E between the two major uphill house sites A and X, indicating that E1 formed part of the primary layout. Structure E3 was suggested as Stage 5 simply because it had stone paving inside a possible sill-beam construction and the use of stone paving appeared greatly to increase from Stage 5 onward. The use of Structures E1 and E2 through Stages 1 to 4 would indicate each was in use for perhaps as much as a century. In Chapter 9 arguments for the different Stages present E being replaced by G in Stage 6. However in Section 11.12 an alternative case is made for G being a primary feature on the site and rebuilt in Stage 6. E and G could have existed together, and E could have continued throughout the use of the Round. The only problem here is the likely duration of each phase of E. More than a century might seem unlikely for the timber-built E1 and E2; however the ground-set E3 could have been rebuilt without leaving distinctive traces.

The chronological relationship between pit [78] and Structure E and the deliberate deposit of a quern in the pit which relates to the interpretation of E as a granary is discussed in Section 12.14.

11.3 Irregular rectangular stone structure T5

T5 (Fig 42), assigned to Stage 8 (Fig 87) late 5th century, was the only possible remnant of a rectangular stone structure. The east side was formed by wall [330] which extended for some 5m from the Rampart which had been used as its south side. The extent of the structure is indicated by paving [28]/[254], roughly rectangular and some 10m by 8m. There was no trace of a wall on the north or the west. These may have been robbed out as may the north end of wall [330]. Assuming the paving to have been enclosed by walling, there is no indication that T5 was roofed and it may have simply been a compound. It contained no features indicative of use such as hearths or hearth pits. Nothing comparable appears to have been identified in Roman or Post-Roman Cornwall although something similar might have existed amongst the Post-Roman jumbled rough masonry inside Chun Castle (Leeds 1926).

11.4 Large oval structures X2 and X3

Structure X2 is represented by the possible slot [665] and X3 by [754] (Section 2.13.2; Figs 25, 82, 84). Both X2 and X3, although surviving only partially, are in the general range, both in size and shape, of the stone oval houses, and suggest a slightly different tradition of building using only timber (Table 11.1). This may have been an adaptation of the Iron Age circular tradition in which a single timber wall supported the roof (Reynolds 1979; 1982b); the structural principals involved differ a little from that proposed for the large oval stone houses in which the stone wall buttressed the weight of the roof. Whether such adaptation involved interior supported postholes is unclear. The area of the X Houses contains far more postholes than any other House interior, and while none of these can be sorted into sensible patterns which relate to X2 or X3, it seems likely their presence is related to the rather different forms of building used here. Any further elucidation of these buildings will only be possible if a more complete plan in this timber tradition is recovered on another site. Both X2 and X3 may have stood for something over 100 years, which would indicate that the construction method used was durable; durability of construction is especially relevant in X2 which had its long axis down slope with a drop of 1m.

If Structures X2 and X3 are not accepted as together covering much of Stages 3 to 8, then some reason must be found for one of the prime uphill house sites in the Round being left unused for long periods. The possibility that a whole building phase or phases was missed or misinterpreted during excavation must be taken into account. However the use of timber for the buildings, presumably houses because of the frequency of hearth pits, on this prime site could be connected to the high status and value of timber which its extensive use in the stone oval house roofs implies.

	Internal length	Internal width	Floor area	Drop along length	Drop along width	Entrance width	Hearth pits	Hearths
X2	11m	8m	70m^2	c 1.0m	c 0.1m	n/a	663A ?	none
X3	10m	7m	60m^2	c 0.1m	c 0.9m	n/a	662B ? 689B ?	none

Table 11.1: Details of possible large oval timber structures

There are no close comparanda for these Houses. House D at Reawla (Appleton-Fox 1992, 75, fig 3) comprised an irregular circular slot enclosing an area some 13m across; this was interpreted as having held posts but the nature of the structure involved was not determined as no internal postholes or other features were found. Reawla House D probably dated to the 2nd century AD. At Trevinnick, S3 was defined by an oval gulley enclosing an area some 7m by 8m (Fox and Ravenhill 1969, 93, fig 36). The description specifies the gulley as silt-filled with a 2m entrance gap defined by postholes. The interior, as with Reawla House D, was devoid of features and S3 was interpreted as a stock pen despite the absence of any trampling on its floor. Part of a second enclosure S5 was also located. The general date of Trevinnick is late 1st or early 2nd century. It is possible that at Reawla and Trevinnick there were structures similar to X2 and X3 which were not well understood when excavated. No other Roman site in Cornwall appears to have produced possible comparanda. However there were oval gulley enclosures in the later Iron Age at Threemilestone Round (Schwieso 1976, 55), the relevance of which to the Roman oval building tradition is discussed in Section 10.1. The possibility of a timber tradition of large oval houses, especially perhaps in the earlier centuries, is stressed here to ensure that this is considered by future excavators of enigmatic structural features and also to highlight the potential variety of building traditions present in Roman Cornwall.

11.5 D1 small oval timber building

House D1 (Figs 33, 81), the earliest structure in Area D and assigned to Stage 2 in the late 2nd century, was represented by two lengths of similar slot [168] and [292], presumably all that survived from one continuous feature. It was c 5m by 6m in size, with an interior space of some 25m^2. Nothing can be said about interior arrangements because of later disturbance but enough of the area outside on the west, uphill side survived for it to be certain that, surprisingly, there was no external drainage gulley. Roofing for a building so little removed from circular would have required little adaptation from the Iron-Age traditions. There are no comparanda so far from Roman Cornwall or indeed locally from the preceding Iron Age. However circular or sub-circular structures set in slots, often described as ring grooves, are a recurrent part of the national Iron-Age structural tradition represented for example at Danebury (Cunliffe and Poole 1991, 43). The interpretation of D1 as a house is strictly based only on the good identifiers for domestic activity in the latest structure here D4; it might easily have been a store or have provided ancillary accommodation to the adjacent House A. D1 is suggested to have belonged entirely within Stage 2 which would give a probable maximum length of use of some 40 years; this might well have been much shorter.

11.6 Sub-circular stone buildings

House T4 (Figs 41, 84) had a regular sub-circular or oval shape formed by wall [410] 8m by 7m across with internal floor space of some 47m^2 covered by rab [422] and paving [254] in the 3m wide entrance. It had a central flat hearth [473] but no other internal features. It is assigned to Stages 5 and 6 which would allow some 75 years for use. The other two structures possibly comparable to T4 are D2 and D4. D2 (Figs 31, 81), suggested for Stage 3, is only represented by internal drain [232], the remainder removed by features of D4. D2 was about 6m across and had an internal area of some 28m^2. As with its successor D4, it could either have been an independent domestic structure or ancillary to House A. Structure D4 (Figs 31, 33, 84), assigned to Stages 5 and 6 like T4, was represented by external gulley [153], internal drain [136], and a worn rab floor [90] laid on a levelled area which had removed much of the earlier structures. The floor had pits and some evidence of burning, though no obvious hearth or hearth pit, many stakeholes and a line of postholes forming a screen across one side. Its internal area was some 5m across, and 20m^2 in extent.

These three buildings are far more regular in plan than the small oval structures in Cornwall discussed in Section 11.7 and have no close parallel so far from Cornwall. They belong to the 3rd and 4th centuries AD. Locally they can be seen as a variant of the oval house tradition built without interior roof supports; nationally they are not out of place among the growing numbers of round and sub-circular buildings being recognised in rural Roman Britain (Hingley 1989, 31).

11.7 Small, irregular oval buildings

A group of oval buildings are distinguished by having one straight side. These are T3 in Stage 4 (Figs 39, 83), R2 in Stage 6 (Figs 45, 85), V1 in Stage 7 (Figs 13, 86), and V2 in Stages 8 and 9 (Figs 14, 87). T3 was constructed by building wall [419] across part of the earlier T2; it had a rab floor, hearth, and hearth pit. It was 9m by 7m, its internal area 45m^2 and is the only structure in the group for which domestic activity can be argued. R2 was built up against the Rampart with walls [375] and [396], enclosing a space 10m long and 4m wide, at least 50m^2 in area. Its only surviving feature was drain [384], which might indicate animal housing except that the top of soil [386] on which R2 was built showed no more disturbance inside than outside of it. V2 was also built against the Rampart with wall [537] enclosing a paved floor [541] 7m by 3m in size, some 15m^2 in area. The floor was provided with drain [542] which connected to the Rampart drain [199]. Interior posthole [578] may have provided roof support. A clearly defined entranceway 2m across had a post for a possible door hanging [576A]. There was no hearth. The provision of drainage might argue for animal housing but might have been built to ensure dry conditions in a building which would trap water seeping down the Round. The function of V2 appears open — animal housing, ancilliary domestic, or storage either for commodities, equipment, or even rubbish as an ash house. V1 survived in a much more fragmentary state than V2. It also had the Rampart as its east side; at least 5m by 8m in size, little is known about its interior arrangements except that it was positioned so that its interior surface [557] again made use of the [199] drain through the Rampart. In summary these irregular oval structures appear to have served a range of uses but tended to belong to the later Stages of the Round.

Examination of excavations on Roman sites in Cornwall, whether enclosed or not, indicates that a variety of irregular oval buildings are found and that, together with the large oval houses, the shape of buildings was oval and not circular or rectangular. A good example is the triangular/oval building of two phases at Porth Godrevy with maximum dimensions of 8m by 5m; pottery indicates use in the 3rd and 4th centuries (Fowler 1962, fig 7a). Porth Godrevy appears domestic, with drains, hearth, hearth pit, and artefacts such as querns. At least one phase at Porth Godrevy had internal postholes, presumably for roof support. Another building which has an irregular oval plan incorporating some straight sections is Structure 63 at the salt-working site of Carngoon Bank on the Lizard (McAvoy 1980, fig 15); this was of several phases covering the 2nd to the 6th centuries AD. The building associated with salt working at Trebarveth 3 (Peacock 1969a, fig 17) was oval, 6m by 3m with ovens in its interior, and pottery probably of the 3rd and 4th centuries. The house at Boscreege, Gulval, was more sub-rectangular than oval, 5m across, with a hearth and internal drains; pottery only indicates a date within the Roman period (Russell and Pool 1963). These four examples are all isolated buildings which were not enclosed but are in areas where building stone was readily available. Most excavated rounds have not been in such areas; the pattern of postholes found for example at Castle Gotha or Reawla does not facilitate the elucidation of irregular structures. Stoke Gabriel in South Devon, an enclosure on limestone, did not provide evidence which could be interpreted as internal structures but in a contemporary field, just outside, parts of a building 8m by 5m were investigated; this was irregular in shape and made up of short lengths of straight wall (Masson Phillips 1966, 16). There was no evidence of internal roof support and the abandonment of the building was dated to the mid 4th century by a group of coins together with pottery. The Stoke Gabriel building, given the paucity of our knowledge about rural Roman Devon, implies that oval structures were perhaps a feature of the South West peninsula beyond Cornwall.

The evidence presented suggests that circular houses ceased to be built in Devon and Cornwall during the Roman period. The only area for which this may not be true is the Isles of Scilly. A range of excavations by O'Neil revealed, apparently, a mixture of round and oval houses for the Roman period, only published so far as interim plans by Ashbee (1974).

The oval building tradition continues into the early Post-Roman period, discussed in Section 10.2 with regard to the large oval structures. Recent excavations at Tintagel (Morris and Harry 1997) have identified D-shaped or oval small buildings of the 5th and 6th centuries. The sub-rectangular or irregular oval Huts 2, 3, and 4, excavated at Gwithian in 1956, are small, some 3m across, but are dated in the interim report (Thomas 1958, fig 8, 21) to the 6th to 8th centuries. Both the buildings recently investigated at Tintagel and those found in the 1950s at Gwithian fit well within the small, irregular oval building tradition described here for Roman and Post-Roman Cornwall.

11.8 Buildings with ancillary platforms

Two examples were identified. House T3, Stage 4 (Figs 39, 83), had an ancillary platform formed of levelled rubble [36] on its west, uphill side, which may have continued in use with House T4 in Stage 5. This was roughly square, *c* 6m across, with an area of some 36m^2. There was no evidence as to roofing but the west side of the platform had been scraped by ploughing and walling could have been entirely removed. The second platform was Structure Q5 between the Rampart and House Z1b, again in Stage 4 (Figs 22, 83). Q5 was enclosed by walls — the Rampart, [722]/[907] of House Z1b, [892], and [911] — forming an irregular rectangle 6m by 5m, some 30 m^2. It had a trampled surface [905] and was provided with drains [901] and [931]. Q5 was the latest, and the best preserved, in the series of ancillary structures Q1-Q4 between House Z1 and the Rampart.

No immediate parallels for these ancillary platforms have been located in Cornwall. As with so many of the

Trethurgy structures, they are constructs only likely to survive on sites with a lot of stone for building. However examination of the plans of many courtyard house groups, for example Goldherring (Guthrie 1969, fig 1a), shows areas which might have served as raised, and possibly roofed, platforms. The function of the Trethurgy platforms was presumably storage. Q5 is reminiscent of a hay loft. Morris (1979, 38) has collected the plans of various suggested rick stands with paved or raised floors, including one at Barnsley Park villa, Glos. While hay was undoubtedly produced in parts of Britain in the Roman period (Jones 1991), Hatcher (1970, 15) points out that in Cornwall in the Medieval period the local climate allowed a long growing period for grass which allowed stock to stay out for most of the year and that little hay meadow was recorded for Duchy Manors. Storage platforms, especially if roofed, could have been used for a wide range of produce. It is perhaps surprising that, once introduced at Trethurgy, they were only used for a short period during the late 3rd and early 4th centuries.

11.9 Structures with dump walls

Dump walls, stone banks rather than faced stone walls, belonged generally in the later Stages of the Round. Wall [479] from Structure R1, in Stage 4 (Figs 44, 83), was the earliest and little of it survived. In Stage 6 Structure Y (Figs 24, 85) was constructed entirely of dump walls, except for the side formed by the Rampart. Structure Q6 (Figs 22, 85), bank [934] dividing the space between the Rampart, House Z and Structure U, was also of Stage 6. The west side of Structure U2 (Section 2.9.3; Figs 18, 87) was formed by dump wall [891] in Stage 8. Walls [421] in Structure T6 of Stage 9 (Figs 36, 88), and [382] in Structure R4 of Stage 10 (Figs 36, 89), were also scrappy but Structure X5 with dump walls [683] and [677] formed a small enclosure some 12m^2 against the Rampart in Stage 10 (Figs 25, 89). Dump walls do not appear to have been identified previously on Cornish Roman-period sites. The main problem, given that they do not survive more than *c* 0.5m high, is their function. Were they in fact just banks — low enclosing features? Even then their height appears inadequate and, while this has obviously been reduced by plough damage, much higher banks might be expected to have had broader bases. Alternately, could they have formed the base of structural elements that supported roofs? Heightening with cut turves would appear to have been more effective if stone bases were defined and revetted. However the dump walls could have supported timbers which were not ground set. Positioning timbers within stone banks, perhaps daub-covered hurdling, could have prevented some of the problems connected with damp and rot. Structure U2, with its defined entrance and drain, has very much the appearance of a roofed building in which such a composite wall would have worked well, and the same applies to R1, R4, T6, and X5. Structure Y with a span of *c* 5m to be roofed was perhaps more likely to have been open or only partly roofed. All these Structures may have provided shelter for craft activities. It may be noted that positions of timbers were looked for in these walls, such positions having been successful located in Bronze Age ring-cairn walls in the vicinity (Miles 1975a). The lack of success in locating timbers was attributed to the damaged state in which the walls survived.

11.10 Lines of posts

Two lines of posts, Structure Q2 in Stage 2 (Section 2.11.2; Figs 9, 81) and Structure D3 in Stage 4 (Section 2.16.3; Figs 31, 83), were identified. Q2 had five postholes in a line, [894] to [966], associated with surface [927] between the Rampart and House Z1a. It may have partitioned the area between the House and the Rampart but, given the sequence of structures ancillary to House Z, it is more likely to have been part of a building. As surface [927] extended on both sides of the line, Q2 might be interpreted as a line of posts beneath the apex of a pitched roof over a lightweight rectangular building *c* 8m long filling the space between House Z1a and the Rampart.

The three postholes in D3 — [269], [117] and [131] — forming a line 2.3m long are less easy to provide structural interpretations for. They are sufficiently substantial for some trace of any parallel line to have survived the levelling for the subsequent House D4. A single line could either have supported some form of rack or frame or one side of a small, lean-to structure.

The only comparable posthole line from excavated sites in Roman Cornwall is that of five postholes some 7m long inside the site of the Rampart at Penhale Round (Johnston *et al* 1998/9, figs 3, 5) which was suggested as a screen or windbreak for an outside working area (*ibid*, 116).

11.11 Paired postholes

Paired posthole structures may be assumed when the holes are similar in timber size and packing and when stratigraphic data allows contemporaneity. Conditions at Trethurgy only allowed pairs to be suggested in the earlier Stages in Area R where the gradual build-up of soil provided protection from erosion and for stratigraphic distinction. The only clear pairs elsewhere in the Round were [840] and [842] 1.2m apart in the paving of House Z2, and [437] and [438] 2m apart in House T2, possibly for looms but see Section 12.11. Six pairs are suggested for Area R: three pairs in Stage 1 [462C] and [462A] 3.8m apart, [464] and [462B] 1.6m apart and [378] and [379] 1.1m apart; two pairs in Stage 2 [466a] and [466B] 2.6m apart and [432B] and [432D] 2.4m apart; and one pair in Stage 3, [432A] and [432C] 1.8m apart. Paired postholes are regularly found on chalkland settlements of the Iron Age in Southern England, where possible functions as supports for racks for hay or fodder or for frames for drying hides have been put forward (Cunliffe and Poole 1991, 140). A pair of postholes have been used to hold a successful reconstruction of a pole lathe at Castell Henllys (P Bennett pers comm). Conditions have not favoured their identification in the Iron Age or Roman settlements of South West Britain. Many sites may in fact preserve these in somewhat eroded condition, for example the Phase 2 working area at Reawla (Appleton-Fox 1992, fig 5) or postholes 356 and 329 at Carngoon Bank (McAvoy 1980, fig 12). At Trethurgy, while the identification of posthole pairs is difficult in the later Stages, it may be relevant that the ancillary structures Q5 and [13]/[36] adjacent to T3 were available as possible fodder stores in Stage 4, the first Stage for which no paired posts are suggested.

11.12 Structure G - shrine or store?

Structure G (Figs 29, 30) was unique on the site. A small, D-shaped building, with a floor space of under $4m^2$, it had orthostatic walling [291] around the curved side and a slightly worn paved floor [258]. The Structure had been set into a large scoop levelled into the hillslope, with [255] infilling the space behind the orthstats. It is unclear whether there was a wall or screen across the straight side or whether the Structure was open fronted. The rubble heap [290] which confined the infill did not appear to be a collapsed wall and so, unless any walling had been entirely removed before infilling, either the straight side was open or it was protected by a timber screen which left no archaeological trace. The method of roofing is also unknown. No coursed stonework survived in the interstices around the tops of the orthostats and the infill [256] did not have the appearance of a collapsed, corbelled roof, being irregular in its position and insufficient in quantity. The Structure conceivably might have remained unroofed but is more likely to had a semi-conical thatched roof with rafters bedded on top of the backing [255] to the orthostat wall.

Structure G has been assigned to Stage 6. The constructional material [255] contained a Cornish flanged bowl and a stone bowl fragment S5 which suggested a 4th-century date. Apart from these finds, the high soil content of this fill suggests that the Structure did not belong to an early Stage during which packing material would have been expected to have been much cleaner rab. There is however the possibility, which was not considered until an advanced stage in the report preparation, that the Structure had been entirely rebuilt during the 4th century. Such a rebuilding could account for the disparity in size between the Structure and the cut into which it was set.

No similar freestanding structure appears so far to have been located, but in size, shape, and sometimes in the use of orthostats, G is similar to the 'alcoves' or 'small rooms' leading off the main rooms in courtyard houses. Good examples are Chysauster House 7 (Hencken 1933, 253) and the small chamber leading off the courtyard at Halangy Down (Ashbee 1996, fig 17). These small rooms have usually been assumed to have been stores. However Ashbee (1996, 136), in the most recent study published of a courtyard house complex, sets out the case for their use as small domestic shrines.

Structure G is too small for human habitation, and lacks the drainage to have housed large domestic animals; it is too substantial and carefully built to have been a dog kennel or a fowl coop. Storage is one possible function; in the Stage sequence suggested, the Structure effectively replaces the latest phase of the four-post structure and probable granary Structure E. A wide range of traditional buildings for storage are recorded in the western part of the British Isles. Hulls (Tangye 1973), mainly subterranean storage units in the west part of Cornwall, can contain D-shaped alcoves but are much larger and more complex in plan. Surviving examples appear to be Post-Medieval in date and were used for dairy produce, root crops, and, occasionally, livestock. Post-Medieval ash houses, found in Devon, and sometimes in Cornwall, are small circular structures in which ash was stored for use as fertiliser (Worth 1967, 415); the retention of ash for fertiliser would be consistent with the regular practice of processing refuse for manuring postulated for Trethurgy (Section 12.10). Numerous small circular structures used for storage, and sometimes pig-keeping, are described by Evans (1957, 114-18) for the recent centuries in Ireland. Evans' description includes a reference (*ibid*, 124) to closing a gap in walling with sods. Small circular buildings on Achill Island (*ibid*, 120) were used as soot houses, much as the Devon ash houses. (Any comparison with the small circular Irish sweat houses is irrelevant to Trethurgy as no fire was found in Structure G.) If ash or manure was regularly kept in G, the interstices of the paving should have contained black greasy soil instead of the brown soil actually found. If Structure G was a store, it is likely to have been for foodstuffs. The British ethnographic references, including hulls, indicate dairy products rather than grain for underground stores, and G should certainly be classed as at least partly underground. If G really does replace E as the main storage unit in the Round, does this indicate a greater concentration on stock and dairy products, as opposed to arable farming, by the inhabitants from the 4th century onwards?

However a very different interpretation is possible. The description of Structure G given in the interim report (Miles and Miles 1973a, 27) allowed for the possibility of a ritual function, that it was a shrine. Our understanding of the ways in which ritual activity was embedded in daily life during both the pre-Roman and the Roman Iron Age has greatly increased during the 1990s (eg papers in Gwilt and Haselgrove 1997) and makes critical examination of Structure G as the religious focus of the Round more relevant than in the 1970s. The main arguments originally advanced were the siting directly uphill, although not facing down to, the Entrance, the weakness of the case for any utilitarian function, and the presence of a double handful of sea sand in [258A], the bedding for the paving. To these might be added the orientation of the opening to the north-east and the realisation that the Structure might have existed throughout the use of the Round and have been remodelled in Stage 6.

The function of fogous is relevant here. These subterranean structures, associated with settlements, usually enclosed, in the west of Cornwall, are generally interpreted as either as ritual foci (Christie 1979) or storage units (Maclean 1992), the latter synthesis linking protection to the storage of special materials. These interpretations of fogous are based on the same broad arguments as those for ritual or storage for Structure G. The question is, and may remain, insoluble. However if fogous were ritual foci, they do not appear to have attracted deposition of artefacts of the kind to survive in the archaeological record. Therefore, if Structure G is interpreted as a shrine, it related to a tradition in which the deposition of durable artefacts did not play a part, as must fogous if given a religious interpretation. There was possible structured deposition in the 6th-century infill, particularly a remarkable range of ceramics, and this is discussed further in Section 12.14.

The author considers on balance that interpretation of Structure G as a shrine is likely and that it may have existed throughout the Round's use, rebuilt in its present form in Stage 6. It is hoped that the identification of a small ritual building on a rural site will encourage consideration of this function for other atypical structures on rural settlements in future excavations.

11.13 Structure U1 as a possible byre

Structure U1 (Figs 16, 18) has been suggested as a byre because of the lack of hearths/hearth pits and other internal features and the eroded condition of the floor. A byre implies cattle because sheep tend not to require large buildings for shelter on a regular basis. U1 has an internal area of 90m^2, larger than most of the houses in the Round. It cannot be demonstrated that it was purpose-built, rather than being an unfinished and possibly unroofed domestic structure subsequently used to pen animals. The recutting of gulley [573] by [560] leading from drain [579] across to the [199] drain through the Rampart suggests that its use was of some duration, its Stage 5 phasing allowing up to 50 years. Applebaum's figures (1972, 147) for stall size in the Roman period, an average of 4 ft 6 in to 4 ft 8in, would allow up to nine cattle to be housed down either side, a total of 18. U1 lacks the tethering posts regularly found in South Western Medieval longhouses eg at Sourton Down (Weddell and Reed 1997, fig 14) but these do not seem to have been a regular feature of those byres of Roman date which have been identified. The evidence for byres in Roman Britain was summarised by Morris (1979) who demonstrated that these were few, possibly because the climate allowed animals to overwinter outside. Byres are difficult to distinguish from barns because, although they may have drains, they lack the worn hollows which are such a distinguishing feature of Medieval longhouses. The 4th-century Building 3 at Bradley Hill, Somerset (Leech 1981, 189) illustrates the difficulty, as use as a byre for part of its existence was only identified by evidence for stall divisions. No examples have yet been recorded for Roman Cornwall; the suggested stables at Chysauster (Hencken 1933, 278) were just a tentative possibility which has become repeated (Applebaum 1972, 199). Two bipartite rectangular buildings, each with stone platforms incorporating drains in one part have been interpreted as possible 2nd-century byres at Dan-y-Coed and Walesland Rath (Williams and Mytum 1998, 48; Wainwright 1971, 81) but in Wales, as in England, byres appear to have been rare.

The levelling for Structure U1 removed any trace indicative of activity in the north-east part of the Round before Stage 5. Given that hearth pits and other features connected with houses would have been sufficiently substantial to have partly survived the levelling, it is possible that U1 replaces earlier, less substantially constructed animal housing. The positioning of drain [199] through the Rampart may indicate this area was assigned for animals from the start; if [199] were just for surface water why was no similar provision made on the other side of the Entrance? The zonation of activity within the Round is explored further in Section 12.7.

If U1 was built as a byre many questions are raised which are difficult to answer. Why was a building involving all the resources of the large oval houses thought appropriate? Was there some kind of statement of status involved? Why was such extensive provision for animal housing only made for a period which is only one eighth of the life of the Round? The answers presumably relate to local climatic, social, and taxation conditions of the mid 4th century in which the byre was used.

12 Trethurgy Round - commentaries on themes and problems presented by the data

12.1 Rounds and small enclosures - definitions, frequency and function

Small univallate enclosures in Cornwall have traditionally been called 'rounds' (Thomas 1966, 87), a nomenclature frequently reflected in field names such as 'Round Meadow'. Such enclosures are usually under 1ha in size, have ditches with depths of *c* 2m or less, and simple entrances which lack elaboration or inturns. They tend to be oval or almost circular in shape, although rectilinear forms are not uncommon, and situated on hillslopes with the entrance on the downhill side. An intensive programme of fieldwork, the Cornwall Archaeological Society's parish check-list programme, first provided the basic data for their study. Check-lists were published annually starting with St Just in Penwith in 1959, first in the *Proceedings of the West Cornwall Field Club* and from 1962 until 1982 in *Cornish Archaeology*. Their results combined evidence from all sources but relied heavily on place-names. The density of small enclosures in sample areas in West Cornwall based on parish check-lists varied between one within 2.2km^2 and one within 4.5km^2 and allowed a prediction of a possible 750 for Cornwall as a whole (Thomas 1966, fig 7; *ibid*, 95). This source, and published literature in general, has equated small enclosures with rounds. The term round has been used both for a class of field monument and for the communities inhabiting them who have been assumed to be of one distinctive kind. The disentangling of this double usage is long overdue.

Since 1994 the Cornwall and Isles of Scilly Mapping Project (COMP) has been addressing the mapping, description, and classification of all archaeological sites in the county: about two thirds of the area has now been covered with completion scheduled for 2005 (Young 2001). The project has greatly increased the numbers of small enclosures, many new sites located even in areas covered by parish check-lists. While the density of sites varies considerably, in some areas it may be as high as two sites per km^2, with the prediction that the numbers recorded may be as high as 1000 for Cornwall by the end of the project. The most recently published survey of enclosure sites in South West Britain (Arbousse Bastide 2000) unfortunately relies on data collected just before that from COMP became available and therefore may be regarded as outdated.

Trethurgy is shown on Figure 1 within an area of 623km^2 on which all the evidence for small enclosures has been plotted. This data was originally compiled in 1986 from published parish check-lists, records in the Cornwall SMR, and lists held in the SMR of all field names recorded in the Tithe Apportionment of *c* 1840. This gave a total of 75 small earthworks, both curvilinear and rectilinear, evidenced by surviving remains or aerial photographs. A further 55 possible sites were indicated by place-names; most incorporated **ker* or **dyn*, names signifying 'fort' in Old Cornish (Padel 1985, 50, 84), a few 'berry' or 'castle'. A total of 110 place-names incorporated 'round', 'round field', or 'round meadow'. It is not clear how far these 'round' names are reliable archaeological indicators. The Shortlanesend round was called 'Round Field' in the Tithe Apportionment (Harris 1980, 63) but part of 'Round Park' in Lanhydrock parish was observed with negative results during the construction of the Bodmin by-pass (Irwin 1976, 81). Only 60km^2 along the south, north-west and extreme west of Figure 1 have to date (2001) been included in COMP (Andrew Young pers comm); the areas of SW 95 and SX 05 covering the St Austell granite have not yet been covered. However 25 curvilinear and 15 rectilinear enclosures have been added from COMP aerial reconnaissance data. Four in the former category had already been mapped from field name data; one of these was 'Round Close' (Sheppard 1967, St Ewe Round Fields No 3).

Leaving out the 'round' names, the 170 sites in the 623km^2 of Figure 1 gives a density of about one site to each 4km^2, not far different from Thomas' figure of one site to each 4.5km^2 in East Penwith (Thomas 1966, fig 6). This is undoubtedly a minimal figure. Some at least of the 'round' name group may be sites, and if a notional half of these are accepted as likely sites of enclosures, this brings the number of sites to 224, and the density to one site to each 3km^2, a figure which will be increased by the completion of COMP.

Figure 1 shows variations in density of rounds and related sites, with sparse distribution over parts of the St Austell granite and the higher land in the St Wenn/Withiel area north of St Columb Major; upland areas such as St Breock Downs already covered by COMP show a similar low density (Andrew Young pers comm). Lower land, especially in the valley of the Fal, has a much greater concentration. The 25km^2 of SW 94 NE, roughly the east side of the Fal valley, shows 24 sites including two 'round' names, and the 25km^2 of

Century	4^{th}BC	3^{rd}BC	2^{nd}BC	1^{st}BC	1^{st}AD	2^{nd}AD	3^{rd}AD	4^{th}AD	5^{th}AD	6^{th}AD
Threemilestone	?	●	●	●						
Bodwen	?	?	●	●	?					
Penhale, Indian Queens			?	●	?	●	●	●	?	
Trevisker 1	?	?	●							
Trevisker 2		?	●	●	●	●				
Merther Euny	?	?	●	●	●	●				
Castle Gotha	?	?	●	●	●	●				
Carwarthen	?	?	?	?	?	?	●	●		
Porthmeor	?	?	●	●	●	●	●	●	?	
Tregilders					●					
Trevinnick					●	?				
Goldherring					●	?	●	●	?	?+
Shortlanesend						●	●			
Crane Godrevy					?	●	●	?		
Carlidnack						●	?			
Grambla						●	●	●	●	●
Trethurgy						●	●	●	●	●
Reawla				?	?	●	●	●	?	?
Killigrew						●	●			
Little Quoit Farm						●	●	●		
Kilhallon						●	●			

Table 12.1: An attempt to indicate the dates at which excavated small enclosures and rounds were occupied. Sources: Threemilestone (Schwieso 1976), Bodwen, Lanlivery (Harris 1977), Penhale (Nowakowski 1998; Johnston et al 1998/9), Trevisker (ApSimon and Greenfield 1972), Merther Euny (Thomas 1968b), Castle Gotha (Saunders and Harris 1982), Carwarthen (Opie 1939; Carlyon 1995), Porthmeor (Hirst 1937), Tregilders (Trudgian 1977), Trevinnick, St Kew (Fox and Ravenhill 1969), Goldherring (Guthrie 1969), Shortlanesend (Harris 1980), Crane Godrevy (Thomas 1969), Carlidnack (Harris and Johnson 1976), Grambla (Saunders 1972), Reawla (Appleton-Fox 1992), Killigrew, (Cole forthcoming), Little Quoit Farm (Lawson-Jones 2003), Kilhallon (Carlyon 1982; 1998/9)

SW 94 NW, roughly its west side, shows 23 including one 'round' name, about a site to each km^2.

The density of small enclosures in past landscapes depends on their likely contemporaneity. Excavation indicates that there was considerable chronological variation. Some 23 small enclosures (Table 12.1) have now been excavated in Cornwall, most on a small scale. None has yet been shown to date before the local Later Iron Age and the currency of South Western Decorated pottery (Quinnell 1986); current data indicate the introduction of this pottery in the 4th century BC but this is based on very few radiocarbon determinations and new projects such as analysis of the Trevelgue Head material (Quinnell 2003) may require some adjustments to dating of the Later Iron Age in Cornwall. An initial date of around 400 BC for the widespread practice of constructing small enclosed settlements in Cornwall may be accepted for the present. Given what has been learnt about such enclosures in Devon since the 1980s (Griffith 1994; Fitzpatrick *et al* 1999) some earlier sites should be expected. Only one Cornish enclosure, Threemilestone Round, near Truro (Schwieso 1976) appears to have its occupation confined to the Later Iron Age and only one, Penhale Round, Indian Queens (Nowakowski 1998; Johnson *et al* 1998/9), to have been in use, possibly not continuously, from the Iron Age through until at least the 4th century AD. All the others were occupied for only part of the period between the 4th century BC and the 6th century AD. Appendix 2 with its presentation of radiocarbon determinations for the Roman and Post-Roman periods in Cornwall provides useful background for all chronological discussions in this Chapter.

An attempt has been made in Table 12.1 to indicate, as accurately as the very variable data allows, the dates at which excavated small enclosures were occupied; the initial date of those with South Western Decorated pottery is speculative because no sites yet have radiocarbon determinations. The Table indicates that a minority of sites were occupied during the Iron Age, that many started or ended occupation in the 2nd century AD, and that the 2nd and 3rd centuries AD show the peak of usage with a gradual decline during the 4th century and later.

In considering this data in relation to Trethurgy and the distribution of small enclosures in its area, perhaps about two out of three sites might have been in use during the mid 2nd to the early 4th century (Period 5 Round, Stages 1-4). For the Fal valley this would be two sites in each 3km^2, dropping to something like one to each 6km^2 in the (apparently) less densely used upland areas. From the mid 4th century onwards, the number of sites likely to have been contemporary decreased, leaving few by the 6th century.

The sites included in Table 12.1 show considerable variations in plan, notably the rectilinear sites of Grambla, Tregilders, and Trevinnick. The complexities of Cornish enclosures including those termed rounds were first fully demonstrated, and well illustrated, in a now classic paper by Johnson and Rose (1982). The current COMP programme is demonstrating an even wider degree of variation (Andrew Young pers comm). It is expected that the COMP programme will conclude with guidelines on the classification of Cornish enclosures as field monuments.

The function of small enclosures can only be established by excavation, and function may change during the use of a site. Here we return to the term 'round' and the second way in which it has been used in the literature, to describe a specific type of settlement. Its field monument definition may be repeated: usually under 1ha in size, ditches with depths of *c* 2 m or less, simple entrances compared to hillforts, oval or almost circular in shape but some rectilinear forms, and on hillslopes with the entrance on the downhill side. The more fully excavated sites apart from Trethurgy — Threemilestone, Trevisker 1 and its larger replacement Trevisker 2, Castle Gotha, Reawla, Porthmeor, and Goldherring — have substantial interior buildings which would have involved considerable quantities of materials and labour to construct. This enables us to start by suggesting that a 'round' was a permanent settlement of a group which had good access to local resources. Entrances have been excavated, in addition to Trethurgy, at Trevisker 1, Porthmeor, Goldherring, Penhale, and Grambla. All these were well maintained, with gates which were regularly shut; the more recent excavations of Grambla (Saunders 1972) and Penhale (Nowakowski 1998) show evidence for elaboration and alteration of the entrance. Certainly the Trethurgy Entrance through the Rampart was remodelled and maintained even after the Ditch had been allowed to silt up. We may then add to our definition of a 'round' the presence of an enclosing circuit, the importance of which was marked by the maintenance of a working gateway which may, as at Penhale and Grambla, include elements which were architecturally imposing. An aspect of enclosures which has recently been emphasised in studies of the Iron Age is the symbolic importance of an enclosure as a barrier — whatever form it may take (eg Bowden and McOmish 1987). Putting these features together, we can suggest for an interim interpretation of a 'round' the following: *a permanent settlement with substantially built houses whose inhabitants merited the distinction of a formal bound or enclosure, which may have held significance for their status beyond its provision of protection or defence*. Of the list in Table 12.1, the sites discussed so far in this paragraph may be interpreted as rounds. Shortlanesend may be added as it contained a large oval building. There is insufficient evidence available for Bodwen, Merther Euny, Carwarthen, Tregilders, Trevinnick, Crane Godrevy, Carlidnack, and Kilhallon, either because of the limited extent of excavation or of the available published evidence. Killigrew and Little Quoit Farm appear not to be rounds but enclosures in which the principal activity was the production of tin and iron artefacts respectively (Cole forthcoming; Lawson-Jones 2003). Carvossa (Carlyon 1987) is not considered here as its substantial earthworks enclose some 2ha.

The definition of 'round' given above is that used throughout this report. In modelling developments in Cornish society it may be assumed that a majority of small enclosures were functionally rounds, but no estimate for numbers will be attempted. Killigrew and Little Quoit Farm have been interpreted as metal-production sites, while the initial phase at Trethurgy, the Period 3 Enclosure, has been interpreted as a stock pound. Further excavation will undoubtedly indicate other functions for small enclosures.

It is proposed that rounds, enclosed settlements of some status, began to be established from the 4th century BC. Rounds demonstrated to be occupied in the Later Iron Age are Threemilestone, Penhale, Trevisker 1 and 2, Castle Gotha, and Porthmeor. Their introduction marks some form of social change which may be associated with multiple-enclosure hillforts which are also linked to the currency of South Western Decorated pottery. For possibly four centuries of the Later Iron Age, rounds and multiple-enclosure hillforts appear to have shared the Cornish landscape. Traditional interpretations of the relationship of rounds to hillforts have been simple and hierarchical (eg Fox 1964) with hillforts seen as housing the aristocracy and rounds a lower order of society, even if one of some status. Recently Herring (1994, 50) has proposed an alternative. Herring sees rounds as the settlements of communities who controlled their own territories and resources, communities who developed hillforts as their communal centres; he hypothesises that the emergence of rounds in the 4th century BC may have been connected to some kind of systems collapse which led to local groups taking on responsibility for their own welfare. Looking ahead to the continuance of rounds in the Roman period, Herring says 'the proliferation of rounds in the Cornish countryside in the Later Iron Age and Romano-British periods may be seen as a symptom of stability under a sophisticated and realistic social structure, rather than as a symptom of stress in the countryside'. Herring's comments work well with the definition for rounds given above. Most hillforts may not have been maintained until the end of the Iron Age (Quinnell 1986, 121); the Later Iron Age in Cornwall as elsewhere was undoubtedly socially complex, current data is poor, and detailed analysis here would be inappropriate. But if hillforts were not maintained, rounds were, and their numbers increased in the subsequent Roman period. While the ways in which round communities functioned must have changed through the centuries, the continuance of this form of settlement suggests that it was well suited to local conditions. Indeed the small size of these largely self-sufficient communities may have contributed to flexibility in changing circumstances and so to their continuity.

Nationally, regional and temporal variation in the extent of enclosed settlements has been emphasised by recent research (eg Cunliffe 1991; Collis 1996). Some social structures implicit in round communities may have extended from Cornwall into Devon where small enclosures are common (Griffith 1994; Griffith and Quinnell 1999) but the likelihood that there was regional variation within the South-West peninsula is discussed below (Section 12.3). It would be inappropriate to discuss Devon enclosures further here because the relationship between communities, status, and enclosed settlement there may have been different to that in Cornwall. Small enclosures as field monuments are a feature of upland areas because conditions both of construction and of later land-use have ensured relatively high survival rates. There has been a tendency to link such monuments, known as raths or ringworks in Dyfed, raths, cashels or ringforts in Ireland, with Cornish rounds. In Dyfed and in Ireland these small enclosures have been demonstrated to have different chronologies to those in Cornwall, construction in Dyfed starting rather earlier in the Iron Age and not continuing, although there was in some cases occupation, into the Roman period (Williams and Mytum 1998), and in Ireland (Edwards 1990) belonging almost entirely to the Early-Christian period. Linkage of the South-Welsh and Irish sites to Cornish rounds does not now, given modern knowledge of the extent and variation among small enclosures, appear to serve any particular purpose.

12.2 The Trethurgy landscape until the 2nd century AD

The flint found during excavation indicated some activity in the vicinity and, probably, some clearance of forest cover possibly as early as the Mesolithic. The majority of the flints were probably Later Neolithic, indicating intensification of activity in the 3rd millennium BC, activity which other flint finds from the area (Section 7.3) suggest was fairly widespread, with a gradual diminution of forest cover. At Trenowah

(Fig 1), some 2km to the south-east, separate pits producing an Early Neolithic sherd and a radiocarbon determination were located in an extensive excavation on a new road line (Johns forthcoming). There were numerous barrows on the higher parts of the St Austell granite (Miles 1975a), excavation of five of which showed long-established open country by the Early Bronze Age. Finds from tin grounds in the St Austell area (Penhallurick 1986, 175-7) suggest considerable population throughout the Bronze Age, as well as the extraction of stream tin through the Bronze and Iron Ages. The Trenowah excavations located a structure with a Middle Bronze Age Trevisker assemblage (Johns forthcoming) and a series of enclosures or small fields with ceramics and radiocarbon dates ranging from the Early Iron Age onward through the 1st century BC.

In the Later Iron Age the area between the Luxulyan and St Austell Rivers was physically dominated by the multiple-enclosure hillfort of Prideaux Rings, which can be seen from Trethurgy Round. Some of the small enclosures shown on Figure 1 in this area are likely to have been established then; the Round at Castle Gotha some 6km to the south certainly was. Following the model discussed above, the Later Iron Age would have seen the construction of small enclosures, some housing round communities, between the two rivers which would have looked to Prideaux Rings as a central communal place. The postulated expanding population may well have increased clearance of trees from the St Austell granite uplands and established extensive lands for grazing. Indeed there may have been long-established open country around Trethurgy by this date.

The Period 2 field system with slight lynchets beneath both the west, uphill, and east, downhill, Round Ramparts would fit appropriately into a Later Iron Age expansion of settlement and population. As the amount of lynchetting is slight and as cultivation probably continued until up to the construction of the Period 3 Enclosure, a date for the field system before the Later Iron Age is unlikely. The lower, east lynchet is in a position to form a boundary along arable ground above the valley bottom, which had once held a small stream, just east of the Round. The concentration of phosphates (Section 8.3.2) in the OLS beneath the Period 3 Enclosure indicates the presence of stock, as well as arable farming.

The unfinished Enclosure of Period 3 remains an enigmatic episode. If the date in the 1st century BC suggested for this is correct, the Enclosure was planned at a time of population expansion, also a time when changes were occurring such as the introduction of Cordoned ware and of some increase in contacts with other areas on both sides of the English Channel. No excavated Cornish enclosure so far provides a parallel for an early unfinished phase but the complexities of the plans of some small Cornish earthworks published by Johnson and Rose (1982, figs 5, 11) suggest that this may prove to have been by no means unique. The Enclosure was built on a lesser scale than the later Round, its Bank only 2m wide and its Ditch less than 1m deep, with four or five drains or gullies running through the Bank, as opposed to one in the Round. The one building located, the insubstantial Structure N (Fig 9), has been interpreted as a shieling, suitable for intermittent shelter of those concerned with stock management. The Enclosure was never completed, and, in the light of the definition supplied above, it should not be interpreted as a Round. Given the number of its drains, it may have been intended as a stock pound, and not an abortive attempt to establish an enclosed settlement. The eroded state of its Bank and the phosphate content of the silt in its Ditch suggest that its enclosed area may have continued to be used for stock for a long time, possibly for the whole 150 years thought to have elapsed before the Round was built. The alteration of one field amongst a block of small rectangular fields to provide a focus for animal care need not indicate any shift from arable to pastoral farming, but rather a more sophisticated approach to the management of animals and their folding for manuring purposes onto adjacent fields when fallow.

Strictly speaking Period 3 relates to the construction of the unfinished Enclosure and Period 4 the 150 years of its use and erosion. A scatter of finds indicates settlement somewhere in the vicinity of the Period 3 Enclosure and subsequent Period 4 activity. These include probable South Western Decorated sherds P49, the probable Dressel 1 amphora fragment, the first-phase Cordoned ware bowl P143 (Sections 5.6.2, 5.6.3) and the second-phase Cordoned ware P83, P138, P140, and P140A. There was also smithing slag. The site at Trenowah may still have been in use during Trethurgy Period 4 as a radiocarbon date indicates activity in early centuries AD, although there was no pottery later than South Western Decorated ware (Johns forthcoming). Trenowah was located through the evaluation of works for a proposed road and is a reminder of how much unseen and unknown archaeology remains to be located.

12.3 Cornwall and the *Civitas Dumnoniorum*

The Period 5 Round at Trethurgy was constructed in the middle of the 2nd century AD at a time when present evidence indicates a substantial increase in the construction of rounds and small enclosures. This increase coincides with a shift in the occupation of rounds, with some established sites going out of use; by contrast none has yet been demonstrated to have been constructed after the 2nd century AD. The increase may be connected with the general rise in population in Britain during the Roman period but may also be related to the way in which communities living in Cornwall were integrated into the social and administrative structure of Britannia. Very little is known about the ways in which *civitates* in outlying parts of the Empire operated and of how much adjustment there may have been to the usual administrative pattern to fit local conditions (Millett 1990, 66). Here it may be useful to consider how communities in Cornwall may have been organised and how they may have been affected by the advent of Rome. Such consideration is of necessity speculative but is pertinent to any evaluation of the relationship of Cornish societies to the Roman *civitas* of Dumnonia. The data from the Trethurgy excavation provide a good opportunity for this, and for an assessment of local identity displayed by those living west of Bodmin Moor, the area for which almost all Cornish excavation data comes. Consideration of local identity will form a recurring theme throughout this Chapter.

It has already been suggested (Section 12.1) that in the Later Iron Age groups with some status used the authority provided by the rounds in which they lived to maintain stability in their areas, and that hillforts, especially those with multiple enclosures, might be seen as communal centres for these groups. There are many other forms of substantial earthwork present in Cornwall about which little is known. The four centuries of the Later Iron Age are too long a period for there to have been no social change. During this period certain communities may have achieved local dominance, reflected in the construction of distinctive earthworks which do not fall either into the round or multiple-enclosure hillfort class. The two relevant excavated examples are the very different sites of St Mawgan-in-Pydar, sometimes referred to as Carloggas (Threipland 1956) and Carvossa (Carlyon 1987).

St Mawgan-in-Pydar is situated on a hilltop in North Cornwall, its substantial univallate circuit enclosing *c* 1.5ha entered by a single entrance with a marked inturn. Siting, the nature of the earthworks, and the character of the entrance make it clear that St Mawgan-in-Pydar should be categorised as a small hillfort, although its small size has caused it on occasion in the past to be grouped with rounds (Thomas 1966, fig 5). Cordoned ware was probably present, alongside South Western Decorated ware, from the inception of the site; an initial date in the 1st century BC would be appropriate.

Carvossa, 13km south-west of Trethurgy, is a complex site not fully understood at the time of its excavation (Carlyon 1987). The main rectangular enclosure of *c* 2ha, situated on flattish land, had a ditch *c* 4m deep and an entrance with a slight inturn. Finds again would support an initial date in the 1st century BC. Multiple-enclosure hillforts may well have passed out of active use before the arrival of Rome (Quinnell and Harris 1985, 129). By contrast both St Mawgan-in-Pydar and Carvossa, although very different in character, have a rich range of finds, including Roman material such as samian and brooches, of the later 1st and early 2nd centuries AD; these sites appear to have increased in affluence after the arrival of Roman administration.

Still only one Roman military fort, Nanstallon near Bodmin (Fox and Ravenhill 1972) is known from Cornwall. In Devon, recent aerial reconnaissance has revealed a complex range of military sites (Griffith 1984) but the COMP programme has failed to identify any further Cornish sites. The ways in which the Roman military authorities initially approached and controlled the varied sections of the Dumnonian peninsula may have been very different. Cornish communities, based on rounds but with local power centred, perhaps only in some areas, in sites such as St Mawgan-in-Pydar and Carvossa, may have appeared sufficiently stable to offer no immediate threat. After initial reconnaissance, some arrangement may have been made which supported the continuance of the authority based on these sites, backed up by the network of rounds. The concentration of Roman finds at Carvossa and St Mawgan may be viewed in terms of material support for their authority. Cornwall may have been left as a largely self-administering unit, although without, as far as we can tell, one central focus of authority.

No shift in settlement sites can be linked to the arrival of Rome in the 1st century AD; this appears to have been deferred until sometime in the 2nd. Finds from St Mawgan-in-Pydar show that the site was effectively out of use by the mid 2nd century. Non-local Roman material at Carvossa drops off substantially in the early 2nd century although some occupation continued into the 3rd. The 2nd-century changes at St Mawgan and Carvossa may be connected with the changes in the pattern of rounds, both perhaps to be linked to some major review of administration in Cornwall. Such a review appears to have removed support from centres of greater power and authority than those based in rounds, and to have encouraged the increase of the latter. This would have promoted a more egalitarian spread of authority. The delay of this change into the 2nd century may be connected with the gradual development of local *civitas* administration and its adaptation to local conditions. It is unlikely to have happened until the stable society suggested for round-based communities had been demonstrated to be long-lasting.

'At *Isca Dumnoniorum*, the *ordo* or Council composed of the decurions and their elected magistrates, drawn in the first instance from the tribal chieftains, would discuss matters that concerned not only the town but the whole peninsula. The Council were responsible for the assessment and collection of taxes throughout the canton' (Fox 1964, 143). This statement expresses the orthodox view that the whole of Devon and Cornwall were administered as a single unit by the *ordo* in Exeter; members qualified for the *ordo* on the amount of land under their control. In other areas of Britannia members of the *ordo* are generally equated with the owners of villas. Villas in Dumnonia only occur sparsely in east Devon; in Cornwall we still only have the atypical site of Magor near Camborne (O'Neil 1933) despite the 70 years which has elapsed since its excavation. It has generally been assumed that *ordo* members in much of Dumnonia had their property based in rounds (eg Quinnell 1986, 122), that in effect rounds took the place of villas. However perhaps we should now question how far traditional *civitas* arrangements operated throughout the South-West peninsula, how far Cornwall — at least to the west of Bodmin Moor — was administered from Exeter. Roman Dumnonia should not be assumed to have been a single unitary authority covering Devon and Cornwall; administrative and legal arrangements may have differed in the west of the peninsula and indeed in other areas beyond South and East Devon. Our limited knowledge of the situation on the periphery of the Empire allows this suggestion. We know too little to dismiss the concept of Devon and Cornwall administered together as the *Civitas Dumnoniorum* but questioning the link can only benefit innovative interpretation of future data on the Roman South West.

If Cornwall had separate administrative arrangements, these could have worked either as a unit with links back to Exeter or to central government, doubtless with changes over the centuries. The broad outline for local administration may have been confirmed in the 2nd-century period of change discussed at the beginning of this section. The general maintenance of authority was vested in the occupants of rounds, drawing on traditions which stretched far back into the Iron Age. There must have been regional administrative centres where activities such as the collection of taxes took place and also more local centres for markets and meeting places. These are likely, in a landscape in which enclosure was still the mark of authority, to have been earthworks and these may eventually be identified in some of the more substantial rectilinear enclosures.

It is generally assumed that local law codes were applied to those who were not Roman citizens, presumably the majority in the 1st and 2nd centuries in Cornwall. With the Edict of Caracalla of AD 212 all free inhabitants of the Empire became Roman citizens and subject to the Roman *jus civile*; however a law of AD 224 both allowed governors of provinces the discretion to apply local laws and advised caution in dealing with these (Percival 1976, 139). These provisions may be indications that in peripheral areas like Cornwall local law had remained the norm. Scholars such as C E Stevens (1947; 1966) and J T Smith (1978) have explored the possibility that Hywel Dda's codification of Welsh law in the 10th centuries, and Irish law codes, contain information which may be relevant to aspects of Roman Britain. Hingley (1989, 9) has considered some of the implications of landholding by a family unit with rights extending to three or four generations. Nothing is known about landholding in Roman Cornwall, but there is no reason to suppose that there was a simple equation between a round and its surrounding land, or that the classical concept of individual ownership of land applied. Hingley (*ibid*, 6) also stresses that the structure of families may have been complex, not conforming to the nuclear family of husband, single wife, and their children. These points about law, tenure, and family emphasise that it is inappropriate to apply modern ideas of ownership of land or objects to Roman Cornwall or to consider the inhabitants of a round such as Trethurgy in terms of modern family units.

12.4 The building of the Period 5 Round and the character of its enclosure

The building of the Round demanded a moderate amount of effort. The regularity of its construction, its siting over the irregular earthworks of the Period 3 Enclosure, and its internal layout together give the impression of a venture planned by a community who were experienced in what they were doing and knew the outcome they wanted.

The circuit of the Ditch is some 210m in length, and the material to be dug out varied from fine-grained rab to large stones. The depth of the Ditch allowed loosened material to be shovelled directly onto the inner side without staging. Iron hoes, or perhaps trenching tools, and wooden shovels, perhaps with iron shoeing, could all have been used (Rees 1979, 304-32); a possible long-handled wooden shovel has now been published from Bronze-Age Cornwall (Christie 1985, 36) and one of a pair of wooden shovels from tin works at Boscarne near Bodmin has a radiocarbon determination of 1140±100 BP (Penhallurick 1986, 211). Observation of excavation of the Ditch silt in 1973 showed that a length of *c* 1.5m of Ditch fill was loosened and removed by a worker in one day (only about seven actual working hours). The removal of undisturbed ground would have taken longer, but a longer working day of perhaps *c* 10 hours might be assumed. Stones would need to have been removed from the subsoil, shovelled onto the berm and stockpiled for use in revetments; the remainder of the Ditch material was moved, with shovel or basket or a combination of both, to form the tamped flat layers of the bank. It might be reasonable to assume a support team of three for these tasks, bearing in mind the very careful layering of material in the Bank and the additional work load when upper parts of the Bank were reached. These tentative figures would suggest that a team of four, of whom some could be women or adolescents, could have taken about 140 days to dig the Ditch and build the Rampart core. The time taken for the subsequent revetment is difficult to assess because of the care needed in selection of stones to form an interlocking face. The face of the bank was trimmed front and back and then any space between the revetment stones tamped with rab and soil. A length of 2m for a skilled stone layer and a helper might be reasonable for a day's work. The total length of inner and outer revetment is some 360m, which would require some 180 days labour for teams of two. This gives a total of 920 days labour for the basic construction of the Ditch and Rampart. Additional labour must be allowed for the levelling of the interior and the building of the gateway at the Entrance, perhaps a total of about 1200 hours or 120 days for a team of ten. These figures are very speculative. They demonstrate that the construction of the Round could have been carried out by a small community, although the four months continuous work would presumably have been interleaved with periods of agricultural work. Those involved could have been the original inhabitants (see below) but the time could easily have been halved or more by the involvement of others. The scale of work does not seem a large burden on the community involved, particularly if it had been spread over more than one season.

Comparisons of the profiles of the Ditch and of the surviving Rampart show material from the former would not have allowed the latter to have been built much higher than its surviving 1.5m. The Rampart may have become higher as it widened toward the Entrance. The faces of the Rampart were not vertical and the amount of material from the Ditch would not have been adequate if they had been. Some additional material could have come from levelling of the interior. Turf from the interior would have been sufficient to have provided two layers in the Rampart, although only one layer was noted in the sections excavated. The surviving angle of the front, outer revetment is about 70° and it seems reasonable to assume a smooth-sloping face to this outer side. The surviving portions of the inner revetment were almost vertical, with a maximum height of *c* 0.75m behind House T. An inner edge vertical up to a height of *c* 0.8 m would have provided a useful backing for lean-to structures; above this the Rampart must have narrowed. If there had been a broad ledge above the vertical revetment at the base, and then two sloping steps of *c* 0.5 m each, the top of the Rampart would have been about 2m wide with a height of 1.8m. This inner stepping is of course reminiscent of Irish cashels. Some form of stone parapet is suggested by the amount of large stone in Ditch silt, especially at [568A] at the Entrance. This was sealed by surface [521] which was continuous with [188], the paving in the Entrance from Stage 5 onward on which scratches indicate the regular opening of gates. As the Round continued after the collapse of stones [568A] to be an enclosure with gates regularly shut, these stones are unlikely to have derived from the deterioration of the Rampart itself. It seems likely that the Rampart as originally built was topped with a parapet, which had collapsed by Stage 5. The parapet may have been rebuilt in the Stage 5 Round refurbishment, replaced by timber or a planted hedge. Alternately during the later Stages the Rampart may have been flat-topped (see colour reconstruction). The height of the Rampart without a parapet is suggested as 1.8m. It seems highly unlikely that it would ever have been low enough for someone immediately outside to look over it, although the positioning of the Round meant that some of the interior could have been seen from nearby, if the trees and hedgebanks of the surrounding fields did not intervene.

The original Entrance had a surface of small stones [215]. It is probable that evidence for the original gateposts was removed during the Stage 5 refurbishment. Although the gate postholes were not seen as two-phase during excavation, their sections show that the postpipes do not extend to the bottom of the holes, suggesting that material beneath is the remains of the original holes. Also it seems unlikely that even substantial timbers would have survived for four centuries without replacement. It may however be assumed, as no traces of alterations were noted, that the original gate was very much of the size and character as that of Stage 5.

The Stage 5 gateway consisted of double leaves hung on substantial squared posts. Squared posts do not appear so far to be evidenced from Roman Cornwall, apart from the fort at Nanstallon. These are likely to have been braced by a lintel between them as there was no indication in the postpipes of any lean inwards. Minimum headroom may be taken as 1.7m (5 ft 6 in); it may well have been more. The Rampart would have been heightened from the suggested 1.8m around the circumference of the Round to at least 2m to embed the lintel at the Entrance; such heightening would explain its greater width here. There is no evidence that the Entrance was covered. The gates leaves were probably hung on strap hinges, a basic form of hinging well-attested in Roman Britain (Manning 1985, 125-7). The projecting pivots of the gate leaves may have been shod with iron (Manning 1985, 127). Pivot hole [208] survived for the south gate leaf; the pivot base M15 from a context in Area R is of a suitable size to have lined a pivot hole and the Stage 4/5 dating of this find means it could have belonged to the original gate. The scratches on paving [188] caused by opening and shutting the gate leaves suggest that the outer, lower, corners of the leaves may have been protected with iron cladding. It seems doubtful whether wood would have produced these marks, even with grit trapped beneath. The outer corners of the gate leaves evidently rested on the paving. This may have been the result of the gradual sagging of the gateway timbers with time. Alternately, as the gate leaves must have been heavy, they may have been designed to have rested on the pavement when shut, and to have been lifted slightly when opened. When shut, the gate could have been fastened by baulks of timber dropped into recesses behind the gateposts, although some form of metal latch and lock would not have been improbable.

The Trethurgy entrance is much simpler than those of excavated Cornish hillforts, as is to be expected from the definition of a round given in Section 12.1. Excavated round entrances available for comparison are those at Trevisker 1, Porthmeor, Penhale, Goldherring, and Grambla; the entrance located at Crane Godrevy (Thomas 1969, 85) is omitted as it appears to have been secondary and poorly preserved. There appears to be some correlation between the elaboration of these entrances and the depths of the associated ditch circuits. The entrance to the Trevisker 1, dating to the Later Iron Age and *c* 3.5m wide, was partly excavated (ApSimon and Greenfield 1972, fig 9). The published plan is misleading because irregular amounts of stratigraphy were removed from its area and the features shown may be regarded as a minimum; these were all situated on the causeway across the ditch, the position of the entrance through the bank being little investigated. The entrance features consisted of a roadway surface, a side wall and a possible pair of gate postholes; these presumably were a forward extension of the entrance through the bank, implying that the whole arrangement may have been more elaborate than a simple gate through the bank. The Trevisker 1 ditch was 2.1m deep.

Porthmeor (Hirst 1937, 22, fig 1) has no recorded ditch, though in view of the difficulties of locating the ditch at Goldherring it is possible that one had existed. Its entrance was some 2.5m wide with a stone surface. The plan indicates that the enclosure wall terminal turned inwards, providing a passage 7m in length but the arrangement appears to have been influenced by its construction as part of a courtyard house complex. The position of the actual gate was marked by a central stop stone; against one side wall, level with the stop stone, was a pivot hole *c* 75mm across worked in a stone, with a gap where its fellow would have been adjacent to the other side wall; there were no gate postholes. The date of the Porthmeor gateway is uncertain, possibly 2nd century AD.

The Goldherring ditch (Guthrie 1969), with a depth of *c* 1.3m established in two small cuttings, compares in scale with that at Trethurgy. There is a further similarity in that it appears not to have been maintained, and was in fact probably deliberately infilled soon after construction. The entrance through the bank at Goldherring (*ibid*, fig 3) was simple and 2.6m wide. The general layout was comparable to that at Trethurgy, the gateway widening to provide recesses into which the gate leaves could fold back. Its initial stage, probably 1st century AD, was surfaced with small stones. The later stage was probably constructed in the 3rd century and remained in use until around the 6th century. The details, as at Trethurgy, are likely to relate to a late part of this period. The entrance had been paved, with a pivot hole in a stone block as at Porthmeor surviving on one side. There were no postholes so presumably the gate hangers were supported directly by the walls which were composed of substantial orthostats. The pivot stone showed two phases of wear, during the latter of which the gate leaves had swung outward leaving scratches on the pavement. At both Trethurgy and Goldherring we may be seeing gateways as used in the early Post-Roman period. The dating of Goldherring is difficult because no Post-Roman imports are published and the pottery has not been available for examination. The published range shows a concentration of late-gabbroic forms such as the Cornish flanged bowl, but also includes Gwithian Style platters. It has been usual to regard these as evidence of later, and perhaps casual, reuse, but there may have been continuity of occupation into perhaps the 7th century or later.

The rectilinear enclosure at Grambla (Saunders 1972) was probably established in the 2nd century and had a ditch 3m in depth. The site continued in occupation until the currency of Post-Roman import material but no full report has been published. The entrance was 2.6m wide and had four stone-lined postholes at the corners of the rampart terminals. A stone-packed slot linked the two outer postholes and the general arrangement was interpreted as supporting a timber tower over the gate. This implies a walkway over the gate, the only round for which this has so far been suggested. The entrance way is recorded as worn with some repaving and alterations. The sequence at the gateway at Penhale is complex (Nowkowski 1998), with a variety of arrangements covering the period from the 1st century BC to at least the 4th century AD; at some stages the round was multivallate. Ditch depths varied but at some stages were at least 3m. Details will have to await full publication but it is plain that the entrance was frequently altered in ways designed to impress. The detection of a possible ten phases in the entrance reminds us that the full complexity of stratigraphy may not have been retrieved on sites dug earlier, including Trethurgy. The data from Penhale together with Grambla do appear to support some connection between elaboration of entrances and the strength of the enclosure circuit.

Even if the enclosure and entrance at Trethurgy come at the small-scale end of the range so far demonstrated for Cornish rounds, it would still have provided an impressive facade for those approaching its entrance, especially when the gates were closed. The Rampart, some 65m in overall diameter, stood, stone-fronted, at least 1.8m high, or 2m or more with some form of parapet. This heightened at the Entrance so that those approaching would have seen a sloping stone wall face about 2m high, with a parapet on top, at least in the early Stages. Each leaf of the double gate would have been c 1.4m across and perhaps 1.7m high and was presumably made of substantial timbers. The lintel across the gateway would have be a thick piece of timber. The timber elements could have been carved. In the early Stages the Ditch would have added to the impression of height. The Rampart, with or without the Ditch, would have provided a degree of protection for those inside, whether from occasional outlaws or marauders or from wild animals. The clump of possible sling stones (Section 6.13.2) found on the ground inside the Rampart in Area E would be consistent with such general protection; no implications of major problems, warfare, or unsettled conditions need to be read into such a simple find. It may be suggested however that the greatest protection it provided was psychological. The Round was a place shut off, into which only those with the right credentials could penetrate. Its likely 'closed off' appearance supports the concept of it having formed a localised centre of authority for the immediate neighbourhood.

12.5 The grooves on Entrance paving [188] and the use of vehicles

The grooves on paving [188], although discontinuous, seem to fall into two groups, one about 1.4m, the other about 1.6m, centre to centre. These grooves were all about 200mm across and never more than 10mm deep. They were difficult to record by photography, and might be more accurately described as 'flattened areas' rather than grooves. Their presence on hard granite is most likely to have been caused by regular use of some form of conveyance, most probably in connection with agricultural transport. The marks must relate to the 5th or 6th century, otherwise they would have been obscured by use of the Entrance during this period. However the paving in which they occur is worn and this wear could have removed earlier traces of grooves. None were noted in the Stages 1-4 surface [215] although the smaller stones used would probably not have shown wear clearly. Grooves or wheel ruts have rarely been recorded in Cornwall but occur in Phase 7.7 of Penhale Round (Nowakowski 1998, fig 36).

There are several forms of agricultural transport which might have been in use. Sleds survived in use in Wales (Fox 1931, pls II-III) and Ireland (Evans 1957, 171) until this century. These tend to have been narrower than the 3ft 11in (1.4m) or 4ft 5in (1.6m) gauge indicated by the Trethurgy marks; further comparisons are more easily done in imperial measurements. More importantly, straight runners would probably not have produced the slight curves especially notable near gatepost [201]. Slide-cars also have a long history of use in western parts of Britain. However experiments in connection with the well-known Maltese 'cart-ruts', which are most commonly about 3 ft 11in apart, suggest that the ends of slide-cars produce narrow V-shaped ruts. Descriptions of flatter, shallower paired marks on Malta are reminiscent of those at Trethurgy, though deeper, and are thought to have been produced by carts (Evans 1959, 189). A wide variety of two-wheeled and four-wheeled vehicles were in use in the Roman provinces. Their prehistoric forerunners have been studied in detail by Piggott (1983) but there appears to be no similar study for the vehicles of the Roman Empire. There are likely to have been regional variations, as in more recent periods. Chapman (1982) demonstrates the presence of vehicles with side-shafts and some form of horse collar in Gaul, and thus the range of vehicles is not restricted to those drawn by paired animals with a central pole.

Wheels with iron tyres would be more likely to produce the marks than those without. Nailed-on tyres, as opposed to shrunk-on hoops, cause much greater wear — so much so that wheels 'studded with triangular pointed nails ... so destructive to macadamised roads that their use was prohibited in 1822' (letter quoted in Fox 1931, 185). Hoop tyres were one of the technological advances of the Celtic North West, but tyres of nailed strakes were widely used in the Roman Empire.

So far no stretches of metalled Roman road have been located in Cornwall and the contemporary tracks around Trethurgy may be expected to have been rutted and muddy. In these conditions some two-wheeled vehicle similar to the Radnorshire wheel-car published by Fox (1931, esp pl 1) might be appropriate; four-wheeled wagons cause much more difficulty in rough country. The Radnorshire wheel-car had a pair of spoked wheels with nailed iron tyres and a gauge of about 4 ft (1.4 m). Its advantage in rough country is the high position of the axle-tree above the main frames of the body. Fox quotes comments from those still using it around 1930 which emphasise its suitability for hill country and rough tracks. Certainly such a vehicle, regularly used, could have caused the marks found in the Trethurgy entrance, and would have been within the competence of contemporary craftsmanship to construct.

12.6 The population of the Round

Table 12.2 provides a summary of the floor area of the Houses and other Structures, the Stages at which each may have been in use and their probable life span. The problems in dating the Stages and in assigning buildings to each have been explored in Chapter 9. Hopefully the variables in both the dating and the assignation of building to Stages have been explained sufficiently clearly for the reader to produce alternative versions of Table 12.2. It has been stressed that the details presented are regarded only as interpretation of the data, intended to provide some ideas about the variations through time in the use of the Round, and not a definitive statement.

Population figures are notoriously difficult to establish, especially for societies for which there is no real information on family and kinship structure. The authorities quoted here all base their data on societies in the New World. Naroll (1962) uses a formula in which population is established by dividing the available house floor area by ten. The approach of Cook and Heizer (1968) is more complicated but allows 20 square feet for the initial six occupants with an extra 100 square feet to each additional individual. Casselberry's (1974) formula, using dwellings with multiple families, estimates population by dividing the house floor area by six. There appears to be no more recent and reliable work on occupancy figures for dwellings than that of these three authorities — all three have been included in Table 12.2 to show the substantial variations that computations based on ethnographic data produce.

Millett (1990, 185) arrives at an estimate for the population of Roman Britain of c 3.7 million for the earlier 4th century, the period at which he considers that numbers reached their highest point; for this he uses the mean, 35, of a minimum of 20 and a maximum of 50 inhabitants, for rural settlements drawn from a variety of complex data. These figures are not so different from the three groups provided for Trethurgy on the basis of the authorities quoted. The Trethurgy figures vary substantially over the four centuries that the Round was occupied and show a peak somewhere around the end of the 3rd century with a lesser peak well on in the 4th century.

12.7 The Round and its landscape in the initial, 2nd century AD, Stages

The Round was established in the mid 2nd century AD when oval houses and their architecture were already well developed. The site appears to have been designed from the first for the provision of four houses around the perimeter, which was levelled and roughly surfaced to provide a good central space for outdoor activities. This assumes that the later sites of Structures V and U were never used for domestic buildings. This assumption is based partly on the fact that no remnants of features such as hearth pits or gullies were found — the levelling connected with U in Stage 5 was only substantial for a small area along its uphill edge. The other factor is the likelihood that the area inside the Rampart to the north of the Entrance was probably needed for animals and possibly for middening. Only three houses, A1a, Z1a, and X1 were built initially, with a start being made with T which was only carried through with T2 in Stage 2. House Z1a appears to have been sited well within the Rampart so that it could be provided with an ancillary structure in the intervening space. Two aspects of the original plan are striking. The central point of the uphill side, immediately opposite the Entrance, was used to site four-poster Structure E, a probable granary. Does this central siting have any significance? The central position could highlight the value of the grain store for the community. Its placing might also emphasise its shared importance amongst the whole community. (Siting close to a particular house might have indicated special status for that house.) The siting of E might however have been practical, its

Stage	Date	1 AD 150-75	2 AD 175-210	3 AD 210-60	4 AD 260-325	5 AD 325-75	6 AD 375-400	7 AD 400-50	8 AD 450-500	9 AD 500-50+	10 AD 700-1000	Length of use
V1	$36m^2$							V1				50 yrs
V2	$15m^2$								← V2	→		100 yrs
V3	$15m^2$										V3	?
U1	$94m^2$					U1						50 yrs
U2	$17m^2$							← U2	→			100 yrs
Z1 a	$120m^2$	←	Z1a	→								110 yrs
Z1b	$140m^2$				Z1b							65 yrs
Z2	$81m^2$						←	Z2		→		175 yrs
Q1	$23m^2$+	Q1										25 yrs
Q2	$14m^2$+		Q2									45 yrs
Q3	?			Q3								40 yrs
Q4	$21m^2$				Q4							30 yrs
Q5	$21m^2$				Q5							35 yrs
Q6	?						←	Q6		→		175 yrs
Y	$32m^2$						←	Y		→		175 yrs
X1	$71m^2$	← X1	→									60 yrs
X2	$70m^2$			← X2	→							115 yrs
X3	$60m^2$					←	X3	→				125 yrs
X4	$80m^2$									X4		50 yrs
X5	$12m^2$										X5	?
E1	$7m^2$	←	E1	→								110 yrs
E2	$5m^2$				E2							65 yrs
E3	$7m^2$					E3						50 yrs
G	$4m^2$						←	G		→		175 yrs
D1	25m		D1									45 yrs
D2	$28m^2$			D2								50 yrs
D3	?				D3							65 yrs
D4	$20m^2$					← D4	→					75 yrs

Stage Date		1 AD 150-75	2 AD 175-210	3 AD 210-60	4 AD 260-325	5 AD 325-75	6 AD 375-400	7 AD 400-50	8 AD 450-500	9 AD 500-50+	10 AD 700-1000	Length of use
A1a	**80m²a**	←	A1a	→								110 yrs
A1b	**80m² b**				A1b							65 yrs
A2	**45m²**					←	A2		→			175 yrs
A3	**35m²**									A3		50 yrs
T1	-	(T1)										?
T2	**80m²**		←	T2 →								85 yrs
T3	**45m²**				T3							65 yrs
T4	**47m²**					←	T4 →					75 yrs
T5	**63m²**								T5			50 yrs
T6	**32m²+**									T6		50 yrs
R1	?					R1						65 yrs
R2	**50m²+**						←	R2	→			125 yrs
R3	?										R3	?
R4	?										R4	?
Number of houses		3	5	5	4	4	5	3	2	3	-	
Total house space		271m²	376m²	378m²	335m²	172m²	253m²	186m²	126m²	196m²		
Number of other buildings		2	2	2	3	3	4	6	7	5	4	
Total space, other buildings		30m²+	21m²+	7m²+	26m²+	101m²+	86m²+	139m²+	181m²+	84m²+		
Population Naroll (1962)		27	37	37	33	17	25	18	13	19		
Population Cook/Heizer (1968)		33	45	45	41	23	31	24	18	28		
Population Casselberry (1972)		45	62	63	56	28	42	31	21	32		

Table 12.2: Details of changing structural and population patterns through the suggested Stages of the Round. Houses shown in bold.

position being the best drained in the Round and so providing the best conditions for the survival of its substantial timbers. The second unusual aspect of the original plan is the character of House X1, an irregular but rectilinear timber building. This has been discussed in Chapter 11 against the background of experimentation with buildings in the 2nd century. The position of House X is the highest and best drained of all the house sites. Does the siting of timber-built X1 here have any meaning, in a settlement which, in general, appears to be egalitarian? If timber House X1 lasted for anything like the 60 years indicated in Table 12.2 it must have been very well built. If substantial timber for building was a valuable resource, as appears probable, the building of a house entirely of timber might indicate a family within the Round community with special rights to resources, a family of special status living on the best house site. If so, the Round community may not have been entirely egalitarian. The special, or at least different, nature of House X and its family appears to have continued through most of the occupancy of the Round if the suggestion that subsequent Houses X2 and X3 were built of timber is correct. A final feature in the uphill part of the Round may have been the suggested shrine Structure G; this is not shown on Figure 80 but the arguments for a phase earlier than Stage 6 are set out in Section 11.12.

The downhill area immediately inside the Rampart was never used for domestic buildings. Area R to the south of the Entrance may have been intended for crafts, crop-processing and storage. In the early Stages paired posts, possible drying racks, were the most prominent feature. This contrasts with the use of Areas V and U to the north, already suggested as intended for animals and perhaps for refuse. The position here of drain [199], the only drain through the Rampart, is surely relevant. In very broad terms, the left-hand side of the Round inside the Entrance was intended for 'clean' activities and the right-hand side for 'dirty', a situation which appears to have been broadly maintained throughout the occupancy of the Round. Something of the same division may have been present at Penhale Round (Nowakowski 1998) with more activity evidenced on the right-hand side of the entrance, especially a 4th-century midden deposited in the ditch terminal.

The initial community in the Round appears to have consisted of three family units, whose structure remains unknown, a population of anywhere between 27 and 45 persons. Very soon, in Stage 2, substantial oval house T2 was built and House D1 was inserted into the space between House A and four-poster E. The inhabitants increased significantly, perhaps within a generation, to an estimated range of 37 to 62. This suggested second generation Stage 2 certainly saw the most extensive provision of domestic space during the whole use of the Round. The community which moved into the Round appears to have firmly established itself.

The plan suggests that the Round was inhabited by a group of families sharing facilities like storage and working areas, a group basically egalitarian although there may be nuances in terms of status which are not clear to us, perhaps hinted at by the different character of House X. The egalitarian social structure may be presumed to extend to the land which supported the inhabitants. Unfortunately there are no plans of Cornish rounds sufficiently complete for comparison. Those rounds for which we have the most extensive interior plans are Porthmeor and Goldherring which contain courtyard houses. Courtyard houses appear to be self-contained units, each with their own storage and working space. The social structure suggested by unenclosed groups of such houses, of which the pre-eminent example is Chysauster, is rather different to that at Trethurgy. The settlements appear to be egalitarian, in that no house can be distinguished, on structure, size, or artefacts, as having superior status to the remainder. But the inhabitants appear to have carried out more activities as independently as households rather than communally as in rounds. Whether this implies a significant difference in social structure as suggested by Hingley (1989, 143) is unclear. The plans of Porthmeor and Goldherring, with courtyard houses inside round enclosures, are not sufficiently well understood to help resolution of this problem.

We do not have data for the agricultural activities of the Round's inhabitants nor for the environment in its vicinity. The later 2nd century AD falls at the end of the period during which, nationally, it appears that there was generally a continuance of Iron Age agricultural patterns (Jones 1991), a reliance on spelt with some emmer and barley, on sheep rather than on cattle. The field system around the Round, in one unit of which the Period 3 Enclosure had initially been established, may have been extensive and have provided plenty of arable land. Aerial reconnaissance in mid Cornwall is beginning to reveal remnants of fields around rounds (Johnson and Rose 1982, fig 12; Andrew Young pers comm re COMP), comparable to those well known in West Penwith where conditions have allowed the survival of their landscapes as at Goldherring (Guthrie 1969).

It is suggested by Dr Staines (Section 8.2) that the waterworn pebbles in the Ditch fill may indicate beach material brought inland to improve the quality of the soil. Such material might be sand, seaweed, or both. Bell (1981) has proposed the use of seaweed in early-

Medieval contexts at Gwithian, while there is evidence for regular sanding in Medieval Cornwall (Hatcher 1970,13); the latter source notes high yields achieved locally in the Medieval period because of such soil improvement methods. Trethurgy would only have been *c* 3km from contemporary tidal inlets. Any such activity would be in addition to animal and human manure and household refuse (Section 12.10).

Animals may have been folded on fallow fields but more extensive areas of open grazing would have been needed. Trethurgy (Fig 1) lies on the lower edge of the St Austell granite, uplands which could have provided tracts of rough grazing, perhaps held in common with other communities in the neighbourhood. In addition to arable fields and pasture, the Round community must have had rights to woodland, managed and coppiced, to provide the substantial timbers needed in the major buildings; the management of woodland would have required both specialised knowledge and the investment of time. The minimal charcoal identifications show a wide range of trees were available. Both ash and hazel would have been useful for structures and equipment; hazel when coppiced would have supplied a major component of house roofs and also fences and hurdles. The presence of hawthorn, gorse, and heather in the charcoal identifications, suggested as fuel, also indicates heath in the vicinity of the Round. The needs of the community for fuel must have been considerable.

Lloyd Jones (1984, 116-18) has attempted to summarise the evidence for various forms of early farming, yields, and land-use for Wales and has produced some interesting but tentative figures. Her work emphasises the necessity of stock keeping to provide manure, even where cereals may have formed the main staple food. She assumes a cereal diet, supplemented by milk products and some meat, and on this basis suggests 'speculative figures of 1.5 to 7.5 hectares of arable land and perhaps between 2 and 12 hectares of pasture ... to support a family of five' (calorie requirements are averaged between men, women, and children). No similar study has yet been attempted for Cornwall, where a generally milder climate and longer growing season might reduce the areas required. Lloyd Jones' maximum areas relate to the lowest returns assumed on evidence from the Medieval period, her minimum area on the high yields now being demonstrated as possible for the later prehistoric period by experimental work at Butser. The population of Trethurgy peaked in the late 2nd century, with estimates, as noted above, varying between 37 and 62 persons. For the lower estimate Lloyd Jones' figures suggest between 10.5ha and 52ha of arable land and between 14ha and 84ha of pasture, for the upper between 18ha and 90ha of arable land and between 24ha and 144ha of pasture. On Lloyd Jones' maximum figures and the maximum population of the Round, this gives 234ha of land for the provision of food. To this woodland and scrub for timber and fuel must be added.

In view of the high yields evidenced locally for Medieval Cornwall (Hatcher 1970, 14), probably an area less than Lloyd Jones' maximum should be considered appropriate for the Trethurgy community. A midway point on Lloyd Jones' figures for the maximum Trethurgy population estimate would be 44ha of arable and 84ha of pasture, totalling 128ha. If land for timber and fuel is added this might come up to 150ha. These figures are extremely tentative. However they do show that there was more than ample space available for the population resident in rounds. The estimates in Section 12.1 suggest, in the 2nd century, one enclosure or round to 1.33km^2 in the fertile areas of the Fal Valley, dropping to as little as one to 6km^2 around the St Austell granite uplands. The disparity between even generous figures for the land needed to support a round community and the number of enclosures so far demonstrated leave plenty of provision if future work indicates that more rounds were in fact present in the landscape. It also allows considerable areas for unenclosed contemporary settlements which are likely to have been present but are difficult to locate.

12.8 The Round in its later Stages during the Roman period

The Round continued into the early 3rd century, Stage 3, with little alteration. The smallest house was rebuilt as D2 and Q3 succeeded Q2 as the anciliary building to House Z1a. The main change was the rebuilding of House X1 as, apparently, a large oval timber building, X2, still with the unusual use of timber distinguishing its site. Population appears to have continued at its peak for perhaps another two generations.

Stage 4 showed the first substantial alterations. All structures appear to have been rebuilt or altered, except perhaps House X2 where the detection of changes would be almost impossible. It is not suggested that the alterations grouped together were precisely contemporary but that they occurred over a period, more than a century after the foundation of the Round, when most buildings must have been in need of renovation. Buildings were rebuilt *in situ*, rather than in different positions, a trend which is marked throughout the occupancy of the Round. This may have been because each represented the holding of a family group within the Round whose stake within it needed to be maintained; a more practical reason may have to do with the reuse of levelled areas. Working clockwise around the Round, Area R appears to have continued to provide clean working space, now with outside hearths and some scrappy structure, R1. House T was rebuilt as T3, an irregular oval shape which reused earlier walls on its downhill side; adjacent to House T3 uphill was raised platform [36], a possible fodder store. House A1b was provided with a new doorway, lost its internal screen, and may have had a new roof. The structure in D, the row of posts D3, is of unknown function and certainly not domestic. The four-poster granary was rebuilt with smaller posts as E2. No change can be shown in X. House Z seems to have been entirely rebuilt as Z1b; this House survived only scrappily but, at 140m^2, provided the most extensive accommodation of any house at any time in the Round. The ancillary structure in Q was rebuilt twice, first as Q4 and then as Q5, the latter with much of the appearance of a hay loft. No evidence survives from the 'dirty' Areas U and V.

Stage 4 saw a drop of some 40m^2 of house area, despite the large size of the new Z1b, because House D was not used and House T3 was only about half the size of its predecessor. Whether this shows a decline in the number of inhabitants is impossible to say. At the end of Stage 4 was a possible hiatus in occupation, as a thin layer of soil accumulated over the downhill part of the site. The changes in Stage 4 could presage such a hiatus. There may have been effects caused by changes in agriculture and in taxation systems which will be explored under Stage 5. Some 65 years are allowed for Stage 4, which may be too few. It could be argued that, if Houses A1a and Z1a survived without much alteration for over a century, the rebuilt versions A1b and Z1b could have stood for much the same time. The general rebuilding of Stage 4 is tied to the late 3rd century at earliest, because of the presence of conical flanged BB1 and Type 22 Cornish flanged bowls. However it may be that the duration of subsequent Stage 5 is too long, and that Stage 4 extends well into the 4th century. In Stage 4 the numbers of non-domestic structures began to increase, a marked feature in later Stages of the Round (Table 12.2). The reasons for this are obscure but might relate to climatic variation (Lamb 1982) in which slightly more rain required the provision of shelters for outside activity.

It is difficult to establish the reality of any hiatus at the end of Stage 4. No soil formed in the Entrance. The layers of soil in all Houses (except the badly damaged X), continuous across much of the lower part of the Round, could have formed very quickly. The Stage 5 rebuild however involved a substantial amount of effort and planning, bringing in more stone blocks for paving than were used earlier. There may have been no actual gap, just a general run-down state, the sort of state of affairs which a single energetic individual could rectify. Apart from the rebuilding of houses, much of the interior of the Round was paved over, making areas which had become mucky and muddy usable again. A degree of major replanning was involved in the levelling for Structure U and the cleaning off of all of the 'dirty' area to the north of the Entrance.

The Stage 5 rebuild included the improvement of the Entrance, with, probably, the hanging of new gates. The Entrance was paved over with good-sized granite slabs [188] and its surface extended to seal over the Ditch terminals [521] which were by now almost completely infilled. In the rebuild of the Entrance, the Ditch was not considered necessary, either in practical terms or as an expression of status, unlike the complex situation at Penhale Round (Nowakowski 1998). The amount of effort however put into the Entrance rebuild (see Section 12.4) certainly indicates that the Round enclosure was intended to be maintained and that the enclosure as a symbol of the status of its inhabitants was still strongly emphasised. In practical terms the enclosure and especially the Entrance appear to have worked well for another two centuries or so. The paving of the Entrance made it much more durable. Did this anticipate greater use by animals and vehicles? The repaving also helped with conditions in the interior because water could flow freely out over it, a facility made use of in the new arrangement of drains and surfaces in the interior. The extra stone used in the Stage 5 rebuild must have been brought in from the immediate area; its availability may relate to stone clearance in the surrounding fields during cultivation in the period since the Round was initially established.

Rebuilding in the interior involved the remodelling of four of the traditional house sites, the exception being Z. There are features which suggest the continuance of family traditions — the ground-set door-frame in House A2, the small size of House D4, the new wooden oval in House X3, and the probable retention of the external platform in House T4. These features militate against any extensive hiatus before the rebuild. It may be argued that the same community, indeed generations of the same families, continued to inhabit the Round.

Commenting on changes clockwise around the interior, these were significant in Area R. Here repaving [7] and [8] included areas of large blocks which became very worn and which incorporated both a saddle quern and a mortar stone. This provided an area for crop-processing and other outdoor activities which was much easier to keep clean than in the earlier Stages. There were also drains which outlet over the Entrance paving. The sizeable Structure R2 was built against the Rampart, a possible equipment storage — its lack of paving indicates that it was probably not an inside working area. House T4 was rebuilt as a small oval shape and House A2 as a smaller version of the traditional oval buildings on the site. D4 was on much the same scale as before. The final phase of Structure E, the suggested granary, appears to have been constructed on sill beams. House X3, while still probably of timber, was again slightly smaller than its predecessor. The general smaller size of the Stage 5 buildings may reflect the availability of timber, good-sized timber having become rarer. Alternately the decision to rebuild over a short period of time could mean that there was not enough timber available to the community to build on the scale they had previously done. The implications may therefore either have broader applicability or relate to local circumstances.

Outside hearths in Area Y show surviving evidence for activity here for the first time. The site of former House Z1b appears to have been disused. The north-east corner of the Round, the so-called 'dirty' area, demonstrated the most substantial alteration. Some levelling was associated with the building of Structure U1, and the whole area between it and the Entrance resurfaced over rab which appears to have been scraped clean, leaving very little trace of earlier activities. Structure U1 has been interpreted as a byre. It is the one Stage 5 building on the scale of the earlier oval houses with its internal floor space of 94m^2, and therefore would have needed more substantial timbers in its roof than the contemporary houses. It is assumed here that it did function as a byre for a while — the problems surrounding the original intention in its construction and its completion to roofing stage are rehearsed in Section 11.13. This may not have been for very long; it has been suggested above that the fifty years assigned to Stage 5 may be too many.

What was happening can only be a matter of speculation. If the Houses were traditionally linked to families, the absence of a house in Z in Stage 5 suggests that any representatives of that family were not of age, or perhaps gender, to require a separate dwelling. Part of its space was therefore available for another purpose, a purpose presumably decided upon by the other residents and intended for all their benefit. The Structure U1 byre implies that for a few years cattle were regularly brought in at night or in the winter months, a practice which was not general before or afterwards. During the 3rd and 4th centuries cattle generally in Roman Britain became more common than sheep (Jones 1991). Ploughs also improved with the addition of the coulter and the asymmetric share. Improved ploughs would have needed good traction, perhaps again an emphasis on cattle. There is no reason to assume that Cornwall was too out of touch with the rest of Britain for its inhabitants not to have been aware of changes in livestock and ploughing, and not to have wished to have experimented. There were also changes in the cereals produced, bread wheats becoming more common on good soils, oats and rye in poor conditions, quite possibly in Cornwall (Section 8.6; Watts 2003). Another reason for changes might have been taxation, the increasing practice in the later centuries of collecting taxes in kind (Millett 1990, 149). Given that eating beef, as opposed to mutton, appears to have been a trend favoured by the army, officials, and town dwellers, and that cattle would have provided tougher and larger-sized leather than sheep, there could have been pressure exerted on Cornish communities to rear cattle. The investment the Trethurgy community made in the Structure U1 byre must have been considerable. The innovation of providing animal shelter may indicate experimentation with a new type of cattle stock whose management needed special care. That no provision for regular animal shelter is found after Stage 5 suggests that stock management at this Stage was an experiment which in the long term the community did not regard as being to its benefit.

The population in Stage 5 works out at quite a low level on the indicators used in Table 12.2. For this the absence of a house in Z is partly responsible. Otherwise it relates to the general smaller size of houses but we cannot demonstrate that smaller houses necessarily means fewer people; living conditions may simply have been more crowded.

In the later 4th century Stage 6 saw the number of houses again increase to the maximum five as the byre became disused and House Z2 was built. The midden which accumulated in the disused byre, important for the archaeology of the Round, is discussed in Section 12.10. House Z2 with a floor space of some 80m^2 was larger than the Houses built in Stage 5 and still in use in Stage 6, almost exactly the same size as the main houses of Stages 1 to 4. The intricacies here of relative status of different families and of the availability of timber at the time of building may have been complex and are beyond unravelling. House Z2 had one trend in common with the main other contemporary houses, A2 and T4. The interiors were simple. Z2 had a timber screen cutting off its lower end and a pair of postholes for a possible loom but otherwise no ground-set fittings; such fittings were lacking in the other houses, in contrast to Stages 1-4 when House A1 in particular had many. (If this trend is valid, the majority of the unphased interior postholes in X will have belonged to House X1 or X2, rather than X3 or X4.) With the rebuilding of House Z2, population levels rose, but not, on the indicators used, back to the levels of the 3rd century.

Structure G suggested as a shrine appears to have been built, or rebuilt, at about this Stage; the arguments are rehearsed in Section 11.12. Structure Y, possibly a partly unroofed enclosure, was also constructed. This could have provided storage for equipment; the nature of the soil in its interior makes it unlikely that animals were regularly kept there. Indeed there was now no obvious provision for internal animal housing within the Round. If the suggestion (Section 12.5) of a horse-drawn vehicle causing the marks on the Entrance paving is correct, some internal shelter may have been provided for these animals. It is possible that small-scale animal shelters were not detected in the Round at this or any stage. It is not suggested that structures were missed, rather that insufficient detail was paid to soil variation and phosphate testing; it should be noted that even the soil in byre U was not so tested.

The space below Structure Y, between House Z2, disused byre U, and the Rampart, was divided into segments. Wall [892] may well have been standing from a much earlier Stage. Bank [934], Structure Q6, was added in Stage 6. A likely use for these segments was as garden plots. It is unlikely that any space inside the Round at any Stage was left unused. Small plots for horticulture appear to have been a feature especially of later Roman Britain (Jones 1991, 23) and there is no reason why vegetables or even herbs should not have been grown in Cornwall. The plan of the Round in Stage 6 appears very full, archaeological evidence for the use of most parts of its interior now surviving. This was the beginning of a trend, more marked in the 5th century, of an increase in non-domestic structures (Table 12.2), and more stores and workshops for activities such as small-scale smithing and carpentry (Section 12.12). This increase occurs but no obvious grain store can be identified. Grain was still a substantial component of diet; the majority of stratified querns come from late-Stage contexts and the outside working area [7] with its saddle quern and mortar was in use until the end of the Round. An alternative to granaries in the later Stages may have been the increased use of large storage jars; these could have capacities up to 30 litres (Quinnell 1995, 125).

12.9 The colour reconstruction of the Round in Stage 6

The colour reconstruction of the Round provides a clear visual image to supplement written detail. Its production has forced decisions to be made about aspects of the enclosure, its buildings, and its inhabitants and their activities beyond those addressed in the text. The end product (frontispiece) is the work of Rosemary Robertson but the decisions which informed it result from a collaborative process between the artist and the author, to which JA Nowakowski also contributed.

It was decided to use Stage 6 (Fig 85) as the basis for reconstruction because this represented one of the two Stages with the largest number of houses. Stage 6 was chosen instead of Stage 4, the Stage with maximum residential capacity, because there are data for the north-east sector of the site whereas there are none for Stage 4. In addition all the residential buildings were versions of the oval house which allowed maximum use of the house reconstructions in Chapter 10. Stage 4 included the irregular House T3 and House Z1b, with its large but uncertain plan, both of which would have required additional detailed architectural work.

A viewpoint was needed which showed detail of the Entrance and was sufficiently close for the figures of inhabitants to be clear; these factors limited the range of choices. A low bird's eye view from a little north of east was chosen by Rosemary Robertson to provide a dynamic view of activity in the interior against a setting of contemporary landscape. The only part of the interior not shown is Structure Y. To have included this would have necessitated drawing of much more of the Rampart stonework, repetitive and visually boring. The time of year is May which provides good contrast between grey and dark stone and green vegetation. The time of day is mid-morning with everyday activities in full swing.

The gate is shown open, the leaves folded back in their recesses. Its leaves are made up of a number of rough-tooled timber upright pieces held together front and back by cross-pieces and hung on uprights in the postholes. As the leaves would have been heavy, a bracing lintel is shown between the two uprights. This would have provided a very narrow walkway over the gate and so has been flanked by a second timber to make this more usable. The Rampart is shown a little over 2m high at the Entrance which provides sufficient head room under the bracing lintel and walkway. The size and width of the cart conform to the spacing of the wheel ruts imprinted upon the paved entrance.

By Stage 6 the Ditch was infilled and cobbled over on either side of the Entrance leaving a slight depression; the remainder of the ditch which is in view is shown largely silted with a gentle curve and some vegetation.

The character of the Rampart is discussed in Section 12.4. The outer, front, side has an even slope and a batter of 70°. The inner side had three steps; the first vertical and *c* 0.8m high, then two slightly sloping and *c* 0.5m high. This stepping probably provided access to the Rampart top for most of the circuit. The Rampart top was about 2m wide and flattish. The inhabitants used the Rampart top and steps as an extension of interior space for craft activity and sitting out. No parapet is shown on either side; the only evidence for an external parapet comes from stone collapse from previous Stages. No internal parapet is considered necessary.

The Round had been built within a former field. The layout of the system to which this belonged is not known, and so fields to the south of the Round have not been given the regularity of a co-axial system. They do however have the established boundaries appropriate to several centuries of use, together with a trackway leading to rough pasture on the higher ground.

The site had been used for 200 years by Stage 6 and the interior had acquired dirty soil where not paved or cobbled. This was irregular in places with slight levelling or step areas as indicated in Figure 5. The interior is not tidy; a variety of equipment lies around, and there are heaps of stones and of thatch for repairs. Each House has fuel stacks of furze and logs. There was almost certainly more activity and general clutter than depicted. Animals are shown tethered or hobbled, not free-roaming, except for dogs and chicken, so that they did not impede tasks carried out in the interior.

Moving around the interior in the order described in the text (Chapter 2), Area V is shown cobbled with no buildings at this Stage. The byre U1 was ruined and out of formal use. Its low wall with a hurdle across the entrance forms an enclosure with the midden.

House Z2 uses the reconstruction Figure 90. As with all Houses, fires for cooking would have burnt all year round. In Q the area was terraced to form three garden plots or working areas. Garden plots are indicated although House Z2 shadows these from the south. There are rows of plants coming through, the young vulnerable shoots protected by penning and tethering animals. The edge of Structure Y is just out of view, providing either storage, activity space, or just possibly housing for young animals. The long axis of House X3 is east to west. Its entrance has been assumed on the south, sunny, long side as there is no data for this.

Structure G is shown as a shrine. Its semi-circular structure has been given a thatched roof with ends coming down to ground above the levelling cut on its curved side; it may have been about 2m high at apex (see Section 12.14). As there is no evidence for its straight side, this has a lightweight timber screen of wattle and daub with a small access door in one corner. Area E above the shrine is being used for storage. House D4 is a small oval building with its entrance facing the centre of Round.

House A2 is an oval house of standard type. Wall [324] revets a rise in level behind the House, consolidating a bulge in the Rampart here. (The Rampart was becoming a little dilapidated by this Stage.) House T3 is a small version of an oval house (see Section 11.6), an irregular circle with a single point in its roof and the usual 2m wide entrance.

Area R was the main craft and activity area of the Round. One of the large flat stones in the paving was a saddle quern and another a mortar, and these have a woman and a man preparing cereals. Structure R2 was a lean-to against the Rampart probably chiefly used for storage of farm implements. Activities shown in Area R include hurdle-making; smithing, carpentry, manufacture of stone bowls, and repairs to equipment would also have been carried out here.

The population of the Round at this Stage was large and it is assumed that the whole community including children would be involved in tasks. Some non-traditional gender markers such as a man involved with food preparation emphasise our poor understanding of the roles of women and of men. Males are shown wearing trousers, with short tunics and cloaks, to make them easily identifiable; women wear long tunics and cloaks. Men's hair has a medium cut, women's hair is braided, generally suggesting Roman styles.

The overall appearance of the inhabitants and their activities is intended to convey the mix and fusion of Roman and indigenous styles which is a dominant feature of the archaeological story at Trethurgy.

12.10 Middens, manure, and the survival of artefacts

The midden on the byre floor of Structure U1 produced about one third of the pre-Medieval ceramic assemblage from the Round. If the material from the lower and upper levels, [932] and [801] is added to that from [800], which appears to be largely the disturbed top of the midden, there are 2135 sherds weighing 34,040g (Tables 5.2, 5.5). This represents 30% of the Round assemblage in sherd numbers and 36% by weight. Virtually every fabric is represented (see Appendix 1) but only small parts of any vessel were present. The size of the sherds shows some variation from those from the Round as a whole. Gabbroic sherds average 16.8g compared with 14.1g, BB1 9.6g (7.8g), other fabrics 5.5g (7.6g), and South Devon ware 10.4g (10.1g). The sherds in the midden generally were abraded rather than fresh.

The soil of the midden was almost black, largely due to fuel ash as suggested by the charcoal analysis (Section 8.5). However, given the similarity observed between this soil and those which accumulated in the animal housing in medieval longhouses in the South West, it seems likely that rubbish was dumped in on top of the detritus left by the last animals to use the byre, and that the midden started to form soon after active use of the byre ceased. The north end of the byre was demolished or altered when House Z2 was built and the remnant walls of U1 would have provided a convenient container for rubbish dumping and indeed for human excrement. The midden which survived was only a part of that originally dumped, otherwise large proportions of broken vessels would have been present. Continuous disturbance may account for the small size of the fragile fineware sherds and also for the abraded condition of the sherds in general, although this may be partly due to the chemistry of the soil with quantities of animal and human waste. If the Round was regularly shut after dark, night soil must have been collected and stored until it could be removed and the midden was the obvious place for this. The question of human waste disposal is not often addressed in the study of settlement sites. The byre was used for rubbish dumping for some time and regularly cleared out; the material which remains represents an interruption in clearance which was never resumed.

A brief consideration of formation processes in the midden may be helpful, as it is assigned to the late 4th century and yet contains 2nd-century glass and samian. The site was cleared when Structure U was built and muck from animals is presumed to have been cleaned out regularly when the byre was in use. After Structure U was disused, its wall remained standing, and little soil with residual sherds can have worked its way in. While the occasional sherd may have been scraped up with ash from hearth pits, long-term residuality in soil appears highly unlikely. Any sherds in the midden were dumped when the midden was formed.

Given the general sparcity of finds and the cleanliness of surfaces, it seems likely that an area was designated for the dumping of rubbish throughout the occupancy of the Round. This will have included food waste, ash, by-products of activities such as leather preparation, as well as broken pottery and human and animal excrement. Rubbish was then regularly removed for use as manure. No other area likely to have been used as a midden was identified. In Stages 1-4 this could have been in the postulated 'dirty' area later used by Structures U and V. There is no clue as to where this might have been subsequent to Stage 6. Only a small area would have been required, and if cleaned regularly could have left little archaeological trace. It is likely to have been downhill and close to the Entrance. Structure V, from Stage 7 onward may have functioned as an ash house although it seems elaborately constructed for such a purpose. The regular clearing of refuse and its use for manure seems likely to have been general practice in rounds and would account for the comparative sparcity of artefacts found. Pits which can be filled in with rubbish are generally rare. The few occasions when middens with a substantial range of artefacts are found on rounds probably, like Trethurgy, represent a temporary breakdown of regular practices. Such remnant middens occur in the late 3rd, or more probably 4th, century over disused houses and working hollows at Reawla (Quinnell 1992), in House 7 when disused at Chysauster (Hencken 1933, 268) probably 4th century, and on the accumulating sand dunes on the coastal site of Atlantic Road, Newquay (Quinnell forthcoming c). Dumps, which may indicate clearance separate from regular middening, occur in enclosures ditches at Kilhallon (Carlyon 1982) probably early 3rd century, at Penhale (Quinnell 1998/9) late 3rd or 4th centuries, at Carwarthen (Opie 1939) probably 4th century and at Carvossa (Carlyon 1987, 105) at different dates from the late 1st and through the 2nd centuries.

Roughly a third of all pottery at Trethurgy was found in the midden, between 150 and 200 vessels of the minimum of 550 from the Round as a whole. Further consideration of this material may show how small a proportion of the artefacts among those originally in use in the Round survived. Allen and Fulford (1996, 253) have published figures for the likely duration in use of ceramic vessels based on a variety of ethnographic evidence and have used these to estimate the likely quantities of South-East Dorset BB1 pottery produced. They distinguish between vessels for personal use such as eating bowls, with a 'characteristic median age' of 1.1 years and those for communal use with a 'characteristic median age' of 1.3 years. They suggest that a family unit in Roman Britain may have had ten vessels in communal use, and each individual two, an eating bowl and a drinking vessel. These numbers may be applied as an exercise to Cornwall. Family communal vessels will have included cooking pots, storage vessels, and quite possibly drinking cups which are rare and do not occur in gabbroic fabrics. Because of this, individuals in Cornwall may only have had a pottery eating bowl and drank from communal drinking vessels of pottery, glass, metal, or wood. If the figures in Table 12.2 are used, taking a house to equate with a family, on the minimum population figures a total is reached of 13,170 vessels to the end of Stage 6, or 17,813 for the whole occupancy. The equivalent figures for maximum population are 17,432 up to the end of Stage 6, or 23, 429 for the whole occupancy. The end of Stage 6 has been used here because, while gabbroic pottery continued in use later, the quantities available may have gradually decreased. Of course these figures are tentative and take no account of the way organic materials may have been used. Even so, they are of a very different order to the 550 vessels estimated to have been present from surviving sherds; perhaps only parts of one vessel in 40 actually used survived. A rough guess might put the amount of each vessel surviving at one tenth. This would mean that only one part in 400 of the artefactual assemblage in use survives. (A third of the assemblage is represented by the midden, some 182 vessels. Allen and Fulford's figures would give 1529 or 1915 on minimum and maximum population figures for Stage 6, the midden then representing an eighth or a tenth of the pottery in use.) This minimal survival of refuse should be prominent in considerations of the significance of the excavated artefact assemblage. As an aside, Allen and Fulford's figures could be used with advantage in estimating the likely output of the gabbroic-pottery production centres in the Roman period, in much the same way that they were used for the South-East Dorset BB1 industries.

12.11 Living in an oval house

The data from Trethurgy provide a good basis for assessing the impact of Roman ideas, artefacts, and craft skills on the indigenous inhabitants who have traditionally been regarded (eg Fox 1964, 148) as living in deprivation, a continuance of Iron Age modes due largely to geographical isolation. More recently I have suggested (Quinnell 1993a) that matters were more complex. The inhabitants of Cornwall chose what to adopt from the new artefacts and techniques which they learnt about through a network of contacts, and in doing so developed a distinctive life style that suited their needs, provided a fair degree of comfort, and expressed their own sense of identity. Daily life at Trethurgy may be approached through the inhabitants of House Z2 in the late 4th century (Stage 6). The House survives fairly well and is one of those chosen for reconstruction (Fig 90), and by the late 4th century all traits adopted from the Roman world were fully absorbed into local material culture and life style.

House Z2 may have housed a family of between 8 and 14 persons, presumably an extended family whose complexities cannot now be established. Their house was of a type which had been built for over two centuries throughout West Cornwall and had proved to be durable as well as suitable for the activities of its inhabitants. Light was provided by the double doors across an entrance 2m wide. The interior stone-paved floor sloped slightly and does not seem suitable for elaborate wooden furniture. However nails are a major feature of the ironwork assemblage (Table 3.6); these are almost unknown in pre-Roman Cornwall. Indeed the general quantity of ironwork from Roman Cornish sites is very much greater than from those of Iron Age date, indicating more iron in circulation and probably a greater variety of smithing tools. Most Trethurgy nails are of small size, 50mm median length, and so suitable for use on furnishings and equipment as were cleats such as M18. The M19 upholstery studs suggest leather-seated stools or chairs. Shelving, storage boxes, and benches are possible and it is unlikely that the stone floor was directly slept upon. All furnishings may have been specially made to fit the irregularities of the paving. Postholes [842] and [840] *may* have held an upright loom, although they are situated out of the direct path of the light from the door; they may as easily have supported some form of furnishing. Away from the door, slot [858] held a timber screen, below which drain [863] provided disposal for slops and discrete toilet facilities.

Cooking was done in a hearth pit, one of the group in the centre of the House which are assumed to be sequential. Cooking pots were supplemented by metal cooking equipment. The iron cooking pan M11 is a reasonable equivalent of the modern frying pan. Eating habits had changed since the Iron Age with the introduction of individual pottery bowls or dishes in the 1st century AD. Locally made pottery was supplemented by some valuable tableware, samian, and Oxfordshire, the former at least two centuries old. Drinking vessels were generally of wood or horn as these do not occur in gabbroic fabrics, or in the most common non-local ceramics, South-East Dorset BB1 and South Devon ware. A few drinking vessels in samian and Oxfordshire ware and a very few in glass were not everyday objects, but highly valued utensils brought out on special occasions and perhaps used to circulate wine, which scattered amphorae sherds indicate was present but not in quantity; beer is likely to have been a more common beverage. Some sherds come from Dressel 20 amphorae which were containers for olive oil. Pottery mortaria occur occasionally. Their copying in stone, as Cornish mortars and the larger Trethurgy bowls, indicate that the pounding of substances before cooking became common. The preparation of complex dishes was possible with the equipment available. For everyday, porridge or stew was prepared in cooking pots and served out into individual dishes, and the more valuable tableware used for more elaborate meals on special occasions. Personal eating equipment, cooking vessels, food preparation vessels, and fine tableware would all have been stored in the house, perhaps on shelves against the wall. By the 4th century, storage jars for grain and other commodities were also present and required storage space. All in all, cooking and eating at Trethurgy need not have differed greatly from the general standard in Roman Britain.

Cooking seems to have been done mainly in hearth pits — there was no flat hearth in House Z2 although House A2 had hearth areas either side of the hearth pit. Hearth pits appear to be a distinctively Cornish feature, not apparently occurring in Wales (Williams and Mytum 1998) nor detected so far in Devon. The earliest occurrence appears to be at St Mawgan-in-Pydar (Threipland 1956, 46) in a context which is probably 1st century AD. Hearth pits thereafter are found generally on sites in Cornwall from the 2nd century onward, the oval house at Castle Gotha containing two (Saunders and Harris 1982, 124) and that at Shortlanesend probably five (Harris 1980, 69). They also occur in courtyard houses, for example at Carn Euny (Christie 1978, 366, 373). Hearth pits at Trethurgy and elsewhere sometimes contain partial linings of burnt clay but these do not appear to be the bases of ovens. By contrast above-ground ovens do occur in the Cornish Iron Age, for example at Killibury (Miles 1977, 97). The change must relate to cooking practices. Hearth pits appear designed to provide soft seating for cooking pots beneath the level of the fire. Many pits have traces of burning on their bases which suggests that fires were first lit on the bottoms and that ash was then allowed to accumulate to the level of the floor. Others were filled with soil which gradually became mixed with charcoal from the fires lit on their tops. Pots could be safely set within hearth pits which would serve as a kind of slow cooker for stews, porridge, or even clotted cream. The extensive use of hearth pits suggests a reliance on slow-cooked dishes linked to Type 4 cooking pots which gradually increase in size through the Roman centuries (Table 5.6). Many gabbroic sherds have heavy sooting and burning up to the shoulders of jars and to the rims of bowls; often the surviving lower edge on the shoulder had crumbled, presumably as the result of repeated heating. Any increase in the growing of oats (Section 8.6) might be linked to more use of porridge as opposed to bread. If stew or porridge was made every day and the average life of a cooking pot was the 1.3 years suggested by Allen and Fulford (1996), these may have been used some 400 times before breakage. It is unclear how bread was baked. Some hearth pits, for example [294] in House A1b, had remnants of burnt clay over parts of the top, effectively small hearths at floor level for baking simple flat loaves. Bake stones have not so far been recognised.

In one respect life had not altered since the Iron Age. Water still had to be carried, probably over a distance of at least 200m unless the shallow valley below the Entrance held a usable stream. Advances in carpentry made possible large rainwater barrels to be filled by run-off from the extensive thatched roofs. However Phil Bennett comments, from his experience at Castell Henllys, that the collection of water in barrels without guttering is difficult. The latter could have been present but is not shown on the House reconstructions. Here again provision may not have been as primitive as it first appears.

Clothing is hypothetical. Spindle whorls indicate spinning and cloth may have been woven. The presence of hobnails shows an improvement in footwear on that available in the Iron Age. However there is little evidence for pins for fastening or for much in the way of general adornment. Here the brooches may have something to tell us. The two brooches found (Section 3.2) must have been some generations old when brought in by the first inhabitants of the site. Brooches in Cornwall appear not to have been generally acquired after a date in the 2nd century. Yet M2 was found in the late 4th-century midden, in circumstances which make it likely that it was a recent loss. Late 1st and 2nd-century brooches became popular, presumably acquiring status value. It is as though the kudos of brooches acquired in the early period, when they appear amongst a range of early-Roman imports, was long lasting, so that these early brooches were retained as items of value rather than being replaced with more recent ones. Were these brooches badges of status, worn perhaps by certain individuals such as family heads and passed on to their successors, only occasionally lost when pins broke? Such use of brooches encapsulates the local approach to Roman consumer goods. Items which could be worked into the local life style were adopted but then given a value, a meaning, very different to that which may have prevailed in Roman Britain as a whole.

12.12 Crafts and the production of artefacts within the Round

The single focus for corn storage, animal housing, and out-of-doors cereal preparation suggests communal work by the inhabitants. The Round is likely to have been self-sufficient in food stuffs, except for a few luxuries like wine and olive oil, and also in a variety of other ways. Agricultural equipment such as ploughs and plough shares could have been produced in the Round, though wheeled vehicles may have needed greater expertise than its residents possessed. Most stone used for grinding and food preparation artefacts was obtained locally, moorland granite and beach and stream stones. The elvan for rotary querns, Cornish mortars, and Trethurgy bowls has its closest recorded source some 6km to the south in the Sticker area, although some small local outcrop may not have been located. Six kilometres is outside the likely immediate landholding of the Round but is a distance which raises interesting questions. Trethurgy animals may have had grazing rights this distance away up on the St Austell granite. Is it not equally likely that the Round's inhabitants had rights to other commodities in the vicinity such as that to take elvan from a specified outcrop? The basis to such rights may have been rooted in the background of the inhabitants of the Round, something an individual or a group brought with them when settling at Trethurgy, possibly even a perquisite like a dowry. The occasional use of greisen from a greater distance probably involved some form of exchange, although long-distance resource rights through kinship links may have operated. Some rights to the sea shore should be considered here, for seaweed and beach sand used as fertiliser and for boulders selected as tools. The net sinker S17 hints at fishing, a further use of the sea shore and a supplement to diet as do the clump of cockle-shells (Section 8.1) which survived in the Ditch silt. That elvan artefacts were worked on site is shown by the unfinished mortar S11. This mortar was worked with an iron chisel, rather than by stone maul pecking, producing waste chips which could be found in future by using on-site soil-sieving and analysis programmes. The production of stone artefacts in the Round probably took place outside, perhaps in the 'clean' space of Area R. Structures such as R2 or Y could also have provided shelters for this activity.

One outcome of agricultural work is specialised products such as leather, cloth, cheese, and even glue, all of which could have been produced in the Round. The only direct hints are the leather-preparation slicker M7, the spindle whorls and the glossed polishing stones S24-6 probably used in cloth finishing. Cloth production is likely within houses, possibly with portable looms which could be moved outside or around in areas of good light, at least for the production of small pieces of (?high-quality) cloth. Leather production, especially in its early stages, is an outside activity, perhaps protected by shelters. If tanning pits, and indeed cloth-dying pits, were used, these must have been situated outside the Round as no appropriate examples were found inside. Such features might be sited immediately outside the Entrance but are perhaps more likely some way away from the site and close to water. All the activities mentioned could have produced surpluses to contribute to taxes or to exchange for other commodities.

Smithing has been discussed in Section 3.10. The inhabitants were making and repairing simple artefacts and recycling a lot of outworn material. Smithing would have been done away from houses, perhaps using some of the hearths found in Area R or in Y predating the Structure there. But smithing traditionally is carried out under shelter, to help with draught control and keep equipment dry. Light-weight stake-built shelters may not have been detected in the disturbed soils [751] and [386] around these hearths. Iron smelting was not carried out and so iron billets were obtained by exchange. Some working with copper alloy (Section 3.3) and silver (Section 3.4) is evidenced but on a small-scale, again with the smelted metal brought in by exchange. The greisen used for moulds was obtained by exchange, in the case of S15 just possibly from France. The likely scenario with regard to tinworking is discussed in Section 3.8, some smelting probably taking place away from the Round close to the tinground (Fig 2). Smelted tin is likely to have been worked into artefacts on site, given the presence of moulds S14 and S15. Tin, either in ingot form or as artefacts, would be a valuable contributor to exchange networks and may have played a role in the requirements for taxation. All types of metalworking, like smithing, needed some form of workshop for protection.

Individuals may have developed separate skills, in smithing, tin smelting, production of metal artefacts, the crafting of stone artefacts especially the elaborate Trethurgy bowls, leather, and carpentry. It is an intriguing thought that each of these craft skills might have been maintained by members of the family groups resident in the different houses. The scale of production is entirely unclear and so is the degree to which those with different skills needed support from the remainder of the community. Some surplus beyond the Round's requirements would be necessary to obtain those items they could not produce, from essentials like iron ingots and pottery to luxuries like wine. Surplus would also have been necessary for taxation. The extent to which skills were developed may also have related to status. The production of especially fine stone bowls or cast tin artefacts may have enhanced the reputation of the Round community as a whole and therefore have been encouraged and supported.

The weight S13, an object often found singly in rounds, shows concern with mensuration on site to a standard which had regional validity. This may have been to check grain against a taxation demand, or to weigh items such as ingots which were to be used in exchange. It may also indicate that the Round, and indeed rounds in general, were locations for small-scale trading, that its inhabitants may have hosted groups who came to them to obtain certain items, that not all exchange was carried out in market centres.

This pattern of self-sufficiency producing some surplus towards a network of exchange and the needs of taxation is seen against a landscape with a variety of resources, to which there would have been a complex system of rights, possibly with communities interlocking to some degree over a wide area.

12.13 Trade, exchange, and taxation; contact with a wider world

Three themes reoccur throughout Section 12.12, craft specialisation, exchange, and taxation and all linked the Round to the communities around it, then to a more central authority or to the *civitas* of Dumnonia, and ultimately to the rest of Britannia. We cannot tell how high a degree of craft specialisation was achieved by inhabitants of the Round but there was much they were probably not skilled enough to produce. Two enclosures now demonstrate a concentration on specialist production — Little Quoit Farm in mid Cornwall (Fig 1) for ironwork (Lawson-Jones 2003) and Killigrew near Truro for tin (Cole forthcoming) — the kind of centres likely to have supplied more complicated metalwork to Trethurgy. Such centres could have been set up by craftsmen trained up in rounds and displaying especial ability, perhaps supported and promoted by a group of round communities in their vicinity which they would in future supply. But this is only speculation and there are other crafts, in particular iron smelting and potting, which have no direct connection with rounds and for which the traditional expertise was presumably nurtured by people living in different kinds of communities.

Previous sections have discussed rounds as the homes of communities with some status and authority. This statement is only meaningful if there were other contemporary communities for rounds to exercise authority over. The assumption is that not all inhabitants of Roman Cornwall lived in rounds, or in courtyard houses in West Penwith, but this is difficult to explore given the difficulty of locating non-enclosed settlements. There would have been enough land to support other agricultural communities (see Section 12.7) but if these are assumed to have been of lesser status than, and under the authority of, communities inhabiting rounds then there must have been links between the two groups. The relevance of the information contained in 10th-century Welsh law codes to communities in Roman Britain has been considered in the past (Stevens 1966) and some may wish to pursue this line of enquiry, but it seems preferable to leave this source until we have more information from Cornwall on which to work. Much stress has been placed so far on the traditional rights of round communities to land and resources, rights which may extend back into the Iron Age. Two possible scenarios for agricultural groups living outside rounds may be suggested. Either round communities encouraged cultivation of land to which they had rights but did not have the labour to use directly themselves, in which case there would have been a lower class of agricultural community presumably paying some form of dues to the round, or there may have been land outside that traditionally controlled by round-dwelling families on which others could establish themselves; the coastal site of Atlantic Road, Newquay (Reynolds forthcoming), appears a good candidate for the second alternative.

Communities engaged in specialist production are easier to see in relationship to rounds. Each needed the other and any traditional status amongst round dwellers could have been offset by the respect afforded skilled craftspeople. Such respect is not always afforded potters but pottery produced from the gabbroic clays of the Lizard became indispensable to the inhabitants of Roman Cornwall. The scale on which these will have operated, Trethurgy alone perhaps needing 90 pots a year, suggests production at least on Peacock's workshop industry scale (1982, 25-38) which would have required enough specialisation for its workers to be able to produce little of their food. Trethurgy is sufficiently close to the coast to have been supplied from the Lizard by sea, also perhaps with salt produced along the Lizard coastline as at Trebarveth (Peacock 1969a).This would have involved a journey of at least 50km by sea and about the same by land. But water transport could not have supplied all of Cornwall, even if sea transport was supplemented by some short river passages. There is still no evidence for any roads maintained to Roman standards in Cornwall. The five upright stones with imperial dedications need not be interpreted as milestones — Thomas (1993, 82) sees them as route markers. They could, in the distinctive circumstances of Cornwall, have marked lands connected with central authority or have been religious dedications to an imperial cult; the connection of these 'milestones' with roads or trackways appears never to have been questioned in print. We have to assume in Cornwall a network of routeways, developed from those present in prehistory, perhaps given a little maintenance on much-used routes but not such as to make them archaeologically detectable.

The term exchange rather than trade was used throughout Section 12.12 because the latter term can have implications for monetary transactions. Finds of coins are generally rare on Cornish sites, not just at Trethurgy, although, as far as the evidence shows, the pattern of coinage in circulation appears to have generally followed that in use in the rest of Britain (Section 3.1.2). Roman Cornwall is generally presented (eg Thomas 1966, 92) as continuing to operate a barter, non-coinage economy, unlike the majority of Roman Britain. But it is evident that matters were not so clear cut. Millett (1995, 85) suggests that throughout Roman Britain 'most day-to-day business relied on traditional modes of barter, exchange and indebtedness' and that coinage was probably only essential when transactions involved strangers to the local community or the Roman state. This is the situation in Roman Cornwall, the difference being that there were fewer transactions between strangers unvouched for by local networks. If coins were not used in day-to-day transactions, they would need to be kept safe, thus giving rise to hoards, such as that from Trethurgy. The main point here is that scarcity of coinage in Roman Cornwall may mean scarcity of transactions with outside traders, not the lack of flourishing exchange networks. The whole of gabbroic pottery production may have been maintained by barter, as indeed it had been during the Iron Age.

Coinage was however needed for taxation, at least in the early centuries, unless unrecorded provision for tax in kind was made for peripheral administrative areas. Moreover tax had to be paid in bullion, gold and silver, which meant the accumulation of copper coinage to exchange for the appropriate metal for tax. This brings us back to the status of the inhabitants of rounds. In traditional interpretations these are seen as (Section 12.3) the main landholding class from which members of the *ordo* or council of the *Civitas Dumnoniorum* responsible for the collection of taxes were drawn, despite the difficulties presented by the elongated Dumnonia peninsula. This meant that some inhabitants of Cornish rounds travelled regularly to Exeter, providing a degree of contact with the established Roman society there. A separate administrative system for Cornwall was however suggested as a possibility. If so, round communities may have formed groups, linked by kinship, which met at an appropriate centre to deal with tax and commercial transactions; such meetings would have provided a degree of contact with authority outside Cornwall. Alternatively taxes may have been collected, with the necessary bullion exchanges, at rounds either by representatives of local groups or officials from outside the area. In the later Roman period the collection of taxes in kind throughout Britannia involved the presence of outside officials representing the procurator (Millett 1990, 141), again a situation providing contact with the province beyond Cornwall, and one which could have been adapted in earlier centuries to meet local conditions in Cornwall.

Links with outside authority and the opportunities afforded by the collection of taxes may have led to enhanced status for certain rounds. By the 4th century there was widespread disparity in wealth amongst landowners in Roman Britain, some gaining more through the workings of the Roman administrative and economic systems than others. Some differentiation may have taken place amongst Cornish communities. If there was a reasonably egalitarian system based on rounds in the 2nd century, this would have been unlikely to have continued without change for more than 200 years. This could mean that by the 4th century some round communities were more prosperous than others, that there was differentiation between families and individuals within rounds, or that a group of especially prosperous communities remain to be located, perhaps within earthworks of the rectilinear class. This increasing social disparity will become relevant as we move to the possible social situation in the 5th century AD.

The production of tin was an obvious way in which communities increased their wealth. The way this may have operated in Cornwall is explored in Section 3.8. Those communities with access to tinground and who obtained licences for operation which would have enabled them to sell metal to the state would have had an obvious advantage over those which did not. The traditional view of an increased need within Britain, and quite probably the Empire as a whole, for Cornish tin in the 3rd and 4th centuries still appears valid.

Cornwall was far from isolated from the Roman world. Small quantities of pottery came in from South Devon, from Dorset, from Oxfordshire, and from the continent, and a few glass containers and glass vessels from beyond the South West. There were Kimmeridge shale trinkets, and querns from South Wales. Market sites remain to be identified. Carvossa may have served as a focus for trade in the area in the earlier Roman period, but was abandoned by the late 3rd century. Markets might have been meeting places out in the country, unmarked by earthworks and difficult to identify; they might be expected around the coast where they would be accessible to sea contacts. However it was suggested above that most transactions involving Cornish produce or artefacts occurred directly at a round. It is quite possible that much of the non-Cornish material circulated in a similar way. Artefacts such as glass vessels may have been acquired from markets within Cornwall, brought in by sea or carried down from Exeter. They may then have entered the local exchange network in commodities between rounds, and have been used in barter. In addition, some forms of gift exchange, the presentation of valuable items for the indebtedness the donor accrued, may still have operated in Roman Cornwall. This would mean that much material sourced outside Cornwall was not directly obtained from outside traders. This would have decreased even further the need for monetary transactions.

On the one hand it is being argued that in the past the geographical isolation of Cornwall has been overemphasised, on the other that there may have been a greater survival of indigenous traditions than has been supposed. The two together imply some rejection of Romano-British ways and ideas. Cornish life was affected by Rome, but mainly in superficial ways. As far as we know no community acquired sufficient wealth to differentiate themselves from their neighbours by building in Roman fashion, except possibly at the poorly understood 'villa' site of Magor. Or did communities acquire wealth but not want the disruption from the traditional social fabric that such a building would bring? All the evidence we have to date, and which that from Trethurgy reinforces, points to the maintenance of the traditional social fabric which was highly valued, and that ideas were taken from the Roman world to reinforce this, as in the production of the Trethurgy bowls, surely statements of status. Cornish communities took what they found appropriate from the Roman world and used their borrowings to reinforce their own social framework which appears to have remained basically solid throughout the Roman centuries.

As a footnote here, the question of land held in Cornwall either by the state or by non-Cornish individuals is not addressed, a possibility which might explain Magor. Such landholdings may have occurred but cannot be demonstrated. Any consideration of their likelihood broadens too much discussion of Cornish communities based on the data provided by Trethurgy.

12.14 Religious and ritual activity

The reasons for interpreting Structure G as a shrine are presented in Section 11.12 as is the possibility that the Structure assigned to Stage 6 was a rebuild of an original feature. This is the only religious focus identified in the Round. The Structure was much used because of the wear on its paving stones and the path leading to it. Although this wear was not as intensive as that found for example on paving [777] in House Z2, it is difficult to account for in a space with a maximum dimension of 2m. It suggests activity right up against the orthostatic walls, perhaps caused by people cramming up against these. It is not known whether Structure G had an open side on the north-east as any evidence was removed in the later blocking phase. This side of G, either open or covered with a screen or insubstantial walling, did not face directly downhill to the Entrance but was turned to the north-east, a direction which could have had significance in religious practice.

The possibility of a religious function for G was not considered during excavation although the presence of a 'double handful' of quartz sea sand found under one of the paving stones was noted as unusual. The paving stones [258] do not completely cover the floor but surround a central gap. This could be accounted for by the removal of a slab after disuse but this appears unlikely in a unit so carefully infilled. The gap may have been deliberate, intended for example for the reception of liquid offerings. This is another case, like the midden in the disused byre, in which detailed soil analysis might have been helpful. It is all too easy to look back after a length of time and see meanings in the detail of the arrangement of paving and walls which might have been differently interpreted if noted during excavation.

Structured deposition as a facet of prehistoric behaviour had hardly been recognised at the time of the excavation in the early 1970s and it was only during the 1990s that its continuation into the Roman period began to be considered (see papers in Meadows *et al* 1997). Structured deposition, the deliberate placement of artefacts, whole or broken, and of animal and human remains in various stages of completeness, in buildings, pits, or ditches is now generally accepted as part of religious behaviour in the Iron Age (Hill 1995). The results of such deposition can easily be interpreted as casual rubbish disposal unless carefully examined for details such as regularity in patterning of different artefact and material types. Such behaviour is more easily detected in soils where bone survives. No discussion of this has been published for Iron Age or Roman-period sites in the South West although is beginning to be addressed in current work, for example in pits and ditches of probable 3rd-century AD date Stencoose, St Agnes (Jones forthcoming). However virtually every aspect of artefacts and buildings at Trethurgy shows a distinctive mix of indigenous Iron Age traditions with adapted Roman ideas. Given the widespread practice of structured deposition in Iron Age Britain, it would be surprising if elements of this did not survive amongst the inhabitants of Roman Cornwall. The most distinctive religious centres of Roman Britain, Romano-Celtic temples, have not so far been found in Roman Devon or Cornwall and the only religious foci so far identified are the Bosence shaft (Fox 1964, 154) and the circular building on Nornour in the Isles of Scilly (Butcher forthcoming; Thomas 1985, 164). Both Bosence and Nornour are distinctive in, and functionally principally identified from, the deposition of artefacts. There was no such deposition during the use of Structure G. However a regional tradition of deposition of perishables such as foodstuffs or bones which would not survive in the acid soil is possible and would go some way to explaining the general absence of identified religious sites in Iron Age and Roman Cornwall. The possible function of fogous as religious foci for settlements is discussed in Section 11.12, a group of structures which did not attract deposition of artefacts which survive in Cornish soils. There is also Ashbee's (1996, 136) suggestion that the alcoves in courtyard houses may have been shrines, and in only one of these, at Halangy Down in the Isles of Scilly, is there a possible votive deposit of metalwork. Three types of possible shrines in Cornish settlements can therefore be identified, the so-far unique semi-circular free standing Structure G, fogous, and alcoves in courtyard houses.

It is impossible to know what modern investigation would make of the material incorporated in [255], the backing to Structure G. It is easily dismissed as rubbish incorporated in the soil among the stone backing. However is it chance that samian, BB1, South Devon ware, and gabbroic pottery are all included as well as a piece of a Trethurgy stone bowl and of a rotary quern? (see Appendix 1) Careful recording of positions would have been essential for further deductions to be drawn. The same problem occurs with the material in the infill layers [256] and [77]. It is clear that Structure G was deliberately infilled as the rough bank [290] was built to retain the packing. But were the artefacts in the infill deliberately selected? The infill, contained 11 sherds of Post-Roman imports including Phocaean slipware and Late Roman 1 and 2 amphorae, a samian and an Oxfordshire ware sherd, and six others, two South Devon ware, one South-Western Grey storage jar, but only three gabbroic sherds including the unique incised bowl P136. The group may simply be representative of material current on the site in the 6th century, for which fills [256] and [77] provide the only securely stratified contexts, but this implies a scarcity of gabbroic forms which appears unlikely. There is also the problem of the survival of samian and Oxfordshire ware, for four and two centuries respectively. These vessels are likely to have acquired value with age, as with antique china today, but if the pieces of these wares came not from recent breakages but had been curated as sherds, the argument for unusual behaviour with regard to this infill is further strengthened. If the material in [256]/[77] was deliberately deposited, then a form of structured deposition survived into the 6th century AD. Probable evidence for the survival of this practice at this date has only otherwise been explored in connection with a probable timber shrine at Cadbury Congesbury in Somerset (Rahtz *et al* 1992, 67-71, 242-6).

Deliberate infill in Structure G strengthens the arguments for its special character. If the hollow left by the abandoned Structure was simply regarded as a hazard, it would have been filled in a much less organised fashion. Deliberate infill indicates deliberate abandonment, the decision that the Structure was no longer to be used. This could have occurred when the Round was abandoned for residential purposes in the 6th century, the infill of its religious focus formally marking the closing down of the habitation site. Unfortunately it is not possible to determine whether domestic occupancy continued after the infill. If it did, then the formal sealing of a shrine is likely to have marked a change in religious practice, most likely caused in the 6th century by the impact of Christian traditions and beliefs. The nuances of the adoption of Christianity across Dumnonia have been discussed by Thomas (1994) in great detail with Cornwall in AD 500 being described as 'barely Christian' (*ibid* 306). It is just possible that at Trethurgy we are seeing for the first time archaeological evidence of the impact of Christianity on the lives of Cornish communities.

The extent of structured deposition in Roman Cornwall should be a rewarding topic for future work. The data from many sites could be usefully reviewed, for example that from the round at Reawla (Appleton-Fox 1992). Should the middens infilling house sites and working areas be regarded simply as the result of systems breakdown or do they hold more meaning — deliberate deposition enacted to signal the end of the use of certain structures? At Trethurgy two instances stand out, pit [78] and hearth pit [294]. Pit [78] (Fig 29) contained a saddle quern, a number of sizeable waterworn stones, some sherds and a iron ring (Appendix 1); the rounded shape of pit [78] is unique on the site. Its relationship with the probable granary Structure E and its assignation to Stage 6 is discussed in Section 9.2.5. The arguments for structured deposition are the close spatial relationship with the probable granary and [78] being the only pit in the Round to contain a saddle quern and other probable grain-processing tools. This is surely more than coincidence, and the artefacts may have formed a foundation deposit, one related to the rebuilding of the granary Structure E or to the end of its use for grain storage. A reasonable parallel to pit [78] occurs at Trenowah 2km south-east of Trethurgy (Section 12.2). Here an Early Iron Age pit contained a complete and a broken saddle quern and other stone tools and could be argued to belong to the beginning of a phase of occupation (Quinnell forthcoming d).

Hearth pit [294] (Figs 34, 35) in House A1b was packed with stones at the end of its use in Stage 4, presumably at the time House A1b went out of use before rebuilding as House A2 in Stage 5. The contents of [294] contained weight S13 (Fig 63) and some pottery. The weight, while used, was in good condition and unlikely to have been discarded as no longer functional. Its inclusion in the stone packing of [294] appears deliberate, not accidental. The pit fill may be seen as a deliberate deposit marking the end of use of the House. No other termination deposit in any

House at Trethurgy can be identified from surviving artefacts, but such deposits could have contained organic material which decayed.

12.15 The Round and its regional context in the 5th century AD

The reason for suggesting that the Round was occupied through the 5th century is stratigraphic continuity, with no recognisable break or hiatus between contexts with material which can be dated to the later 4th century, here Stage 6, and those associated with Post-Roman import wares, here Stage 9, the introduction of which is probably to be placed in the late 5th century. Activity in the 5th-century Round has been presented in two Stages, 7 and 8, mainly to accommodate the complexities of the sequence in its downhill side where stratigraphy was well preserved.

There are, in Western Britain, no artefacts which are regarded as distinctively 5th century and which are of reasonably common occurrence. Once the regular circulation of new coinage ceased in the reign of Honorius, there is nothing to provide a horizon to which any continued circulation of Roman-style pottery can be tied until the arrival of Post-Roman import wares nearly a century later. Generally such wares occur on sites which were not occupied during the Roman centuries, some shift in settlement having taken place. In Britain as a whole the dating of possible 5th-century sites varies according to a writer's interpretation of the period: some consider that Roman-style buildings, market centres, and institutions were likely to have had a slow run-down from the late 4th century, others see change as much more rapid. The evidence can usually be argued both ways. Different approaches in synthetic works are illustrated by Esmonde Cleary (1989) who proposes slow run-down and change, Faulkner (2000) who sees changes as faster and more dramatic in impact, and Dark (2000) who tends to place more emphasis on continuity. Whatever interpretation is placed on changes in the late-Roman provinces, they may have had little impact on Cornwall. Even Exeter probably did not continue as a centre either of regional importance or as a concentration of population from the late 4th century onward (Bidwell 1979, 113; Holbrook and Bidwell 1991, 13-14); its coin supply appears to have ended around AD 380 (Holbrook and Bidwell 1991, 38). At present we have little data to argue from for rural Devon in the 5th as opposed to the 6th century; the same may be true of Wales (Edwards and Lane 1988, *passim*); Cornwall is rather different.

Trethurgy with its extensive excavation provides the best case in Cornwall for continuous occupation through the 5th century. However (Table 12.1) it was not alone. It has been argued (Section 12.13) that the nature of Cornish society during the Roman centuries provided stability which was little affected by changes elsewhere in Roman Britain. This stability was based on two factors, on a social network which relied on indigenous traditional values of authority and kinship, derived ultimately from those which had been present in the Iron Age, and on an economic system based on exchange, barter, and perhaps indebtedness, but not, to any extent, on a monetary system. If this interpretation for the Roman centuries is correct, then there seems no reason to expect rapid or major changes after AD 400, although generally unsettled conditions may have caused gradual alterations. Some form of continuity in Cornwall has been argued for from the late 1950s (Thomas 1958, 19) although only recently (eg Quinnell 1993b) has it been realised how important and extensive this was, at least west of Bodmin Moor; the continued scarcity of excavated sites around, and to the east of, Bodmin Moor limits what can be said about Cornwall as a whole. One result of the proposed stability in west Cornwall is the continuance of the potting centres using gabbroic clays on the Lizard (Section 5.6.2) without changes in style. Devon by contrast, and possibly East Cornwall, appears to have become largely aceramic with few local potting centres which could have continued production on an exchange or barter basis. It will be interesting to see the situation on any 5th-century settlements identified in future in South Devon, where ceramic production somewhere in the vicinity the Dart valley could have continued. The complexity of settlement at Bantham continues to increase (Griffith and Reed 1998; Horner 2001) with both Romano-British and Post-Roman midden deposits. It seems highly probable that there was continuous activity in the area and that some of the pottery there which is typologically late 3rd or 4th century could date to the 5th.

At Trethurgy in the 5th century the general pattern of life is assumed to have continued much as in the previous century with a similar range of pottery and distinctive worked stone artefacts. However the excavation data put forward for Stages 7 and 8 (Table 12.2) indicate that the number of occupied houses may have dropped first to three (Z2, X3, and A2) and then to two (Z2 and A3), with the population in the late 5th century at the lowest level for the whole occupancy of the Round. At the same time the provision of non-domestic structural space appears to have continued its rise from the 4th century. The main changes from Stage 6 are the building of U2 across the ruined end of the former byre U1, probably as an animal shelter, and the provision of the large but poorly preserved Structure V1 just inside the Entrance. Whatever the function of the latter — storage, workshop, or animal shelter — this does not appear to have been domestic. In Stage 8, V is rebuilt as the smaller V2, with good paving and drains, a structure very well suited to animal housing and again certainly not domestic. The other change in Stage 8 was the replacement of Structure R2 with Structure T5 just to its south; both appear to have provided sheltered working space and perhaps storage using the Rampart as one side, and it seems reasonable to see one as the replacement for the other.

The difficulties in dealing with the data from Stages 7 and 8 are discussed in Chapter 9. The problems presented by the poor preservation of House X are particularly relevant here. If House X did not drop out of use during Stage 7, if the chronology of the surviving structures is readjusted or another building phase existed which survived so poorly as to be unrecognised, the population figures would be higher. The problems here are emphasised because diminishing numbers during the 5th century are an attractive hypothesis for a period perceived as one of turbulence and change. The figures in Table 12.2 for Stages 7 and 8 may be broadly correct, but they have a less sound foundation than those for any other Stage. Decreased habitation of rounds, if not an overall drop in population, is not inconsistent with continuance of the general pattern of life from the 4th century already suggested. It is likely that social structures were changing through the 5th century. Any links to authority based outside Cornwall ceased, including payment of taxes. It has been suggested above (Section 12.2) that some differential amongst the wealth of round communities might be expected during the 4th century. This differential may have continued to grow during the 5th century, with the more successful rounds gradually becoming completely independent and taking authority over larger areas, the social background for the emergence of status centres such as Tintagel.

Table 12.1 shows several rounds which may have been occupied during the 5th century. The situation at Grambla (Saunders 1972) appears to have been comparable with Trethurgy, structural continuity with both late-Roman and Post-Roman artefacts. Porthmeor (Hirst 1937) has structural sequence and complexity which probably indicate occupation after the 4th century although the presence of Post-Roman import wares has now been rejected (Thomas 1981). Goldherring (Guthrie 1969) is more difficult because the dating here is reliant on Gwithian Style platters, the date of which has yet to be clearly established; there might have been a gap in occupation. The difficulties with Reawla will be discussed under Section 12.16. The main excavations at Penhale with possible some 5th-century activity await full publication (Nowakoswki 1998, II, 55); nothing in the plough-damaged segment published by Johnston *et al* (1998/90) indicates use which need extend beyond the 4th century. The author views the case for 5th-century occupation of rounds set out in Table 12.1 as a likely underestimate. Excavators have been understandably reluctant to suggest continuance of sites into the Post-Roman period without very good evidence, and evidence for continuance was not as well understood in the past as it is now, let alone as it will be in the future. The potential of radiocarbon dating for the identification of 5th-century sites is only beginning to be grasped. Open settlements too will have continued. Carngoon Bank (McAvoy 1980) with both Roman and Post-Roman material should have been in use in the 5th century and as should sites at Gwithian (Thomas 1958; 1976).

It is now clear (Morris and Harry 1997, 120) that Tintagel was occupied from a date late in the Roman period and that, at least on Site C, for which recent excavations have been published, there were several structural phases before the arrival of Post-Roman import wares in the later 5th century. The clarity of dating here has been greatly assisted by an extensive range of radiocarbon dates. While the report does not put a precise initial date on the beginnings of occupation on Site C, close reading suggests a possible century between initial occupation and the first Post-Roman material. Throughout this period ceramics in the local tradition appear to have been in use.

In Somerset radiocarbon dating has had a significant impact on the 5th-century chronology of the cemetery at Cannington (Rahtz *et al* 2000, 392) and demonstrated that use continued without any obvious break from the late 3rd until the late 7th centuries. Without radiocarbon dating, this long date-range could not have been put forward with confidence nor its late-Roman pottery regarded as definite evidence for a phase predating that with Post-Roman imports. Another site at which radiocarbon dating has greatly helped to established 5th-century chronology is the settlement below the former hillfort at Poundbury just outside the Roman town of Dorchester (Green 1987, 91). Here there was greater stratigraphic detail than at Cannington, but assigning settlement phases within which some late Roman artefacts were still used to the 5th century would have been difficult without radiocarbon determinations.

In some ways Cannington complements Trethurgy — a cemetery and a settlement site. Both were extensive rescue excavations investigating the types of site common in the late-Roman and immediate Post-Roman landscape. In both, close study of all the data available demonstrated continuity between the Roman and Post-Roman periods and the use of late-Roman material into the 5th century. The Cannington dates used bone which does not survive at Trethurgy. The details of the 5th century at Trethurgy could only have been illuminated by AMS radiocarbon dating of charred grain and seed retrieved from the processing of bulk soil samples, processing which had not been introduced in 1973. It is urged that in the future extensive radiocarbon dating is used for sites in the West Country which appear likely to have had activity from the late 4th century onward into the Post-Roman period. It is obvious that far more 5th-century settlement survives to be located than was thought likely even a decade ago.

12.16 The Round and its regional context in the 6th century AD

The 6th century as used here refers to the period during which Post-Roman import wares were in use, both at Trethurgy and throughout South West Britain. It is likely that some imports were available from *c* AD 475; their general currency in Britain was probably until around AD 550/575 but the recent radiocarbon dates from Tintagel (Morris and Harry 1997, 120) raise the possibility that the terminal date should be extended until the end of the 6th century or even into the 7th. At Trethurgy these Post-Roman imports are used to define Stage 9 and, while this is almost certain to have covered the first half of the 6th century, it may well have begun in the late 5th with an uncertain end date; it may have lasted at least a century rather than the 50+ years shown on Tables 9.2 and 12.2.

The range of Post-Roman imports at Trethurgy is extensive and represents most of the types common at Tintagel. For the first time probable sherds of Post-Roman East Mediterranean coarse wares, Fabrics 1 and 5, have been recognised in Cornwall elsewhere than Tintagel. The imported pottery is accompanied by glassware, Gl 1, a 6th-century trail-decorated conical beaker probably from South West France, Gl 2, a 6th to 7th-century decorated bowl either from South West France or Iberia, as well as a few pieces of less certain date (Section 4.5). Vessels of Gl 1 type have a widespread distribution in Western Britain and tend to occur on sites with Post-Roman import wares. On Figure 88 the positions of the pottery are shown, spread right across the Round and immediately outside it. This distribution is taken at its simplest to indicate activity throughout the Round during Stage 9. This presentation of the pottery was initially suggested by Ewan Campbell because of the situation at South Cadbury. There the distribution of finds was interpreted (Alcock 1995, 94) as closely connected to the buildings in which they were used, but the South Cadbury buildings had wooden floors allowing broken sherds to filter down through cracks and remain *in situ* unlike Trethurgy where the buildings had stone paved or hard-packed floors.

Only small sherds of pottery and fragments of glass survived, a small proportion of the vessels once in use. This was probably due to continuing dispersal of refuse as fertiliser which had accounted for the small proportion of Roman-period vessels found. To what extent Roman-style gabbroic pottery was still either being manufactured or used is uncertain. In the few reasonably secure Stage 9 contexts gabbroic sherds were not noticeably abraded. Some gabbroic pottery was probably being manufactured and reaching exchange networks in West Cornwall in the 6th century, but on a substantially reduced scale. If the principal forms, Type 4 cooking pots and Cornish flanged bowls, were still being produced and used, then basic patterns of cooking and eating continued through from the Roman centuries, different to those associated with the later, grass-marked shapes. It is assumed here, in absence of evidence to the contrary, that most types of locally made artefact, especially stonework, also continued.

The buildings of Stage 9 also continued the traditions of past centuries. House Z2 is thought to have been in use until this latest residential Stage because otherwise its comparatively well-preserved walls might be expected to have been robbed for other building. The close association of House X4 with Post-Roman import sherds is discussed in Chapter 9 and presumably means that the House was built after this pottery had been in circulation for some little time. This remarkable new oval stone building had floor space similar to that of House Z2. The building of House X4, probably the first oval stone house on Area X, shows that this site continued the distinctive character its buildings had displayed since the commencement of the Round. Sizeable and good quality timber must still have been available in some quantity. It was argued above in Sections 12.7 and 12.8 that the different house sites in the Round showed a continuance of distinctive characteristics throughout their use and that this might have been linked to families and, perhaps, to ranking among them. The building of the only large stone oval house in Stage 9 in Area X may indicate that its occupants were the ranking family within the community. The third Stage 9 house, House A3, is very different to X4 as it had a small floor space of *c* 35m^2 and may have been built entirely of timber. The oval shape links A3 to the general building tradition in the Round but its function is difficult to demonstrate. It had no hearth pit but its floor surface was plough-disturbed and could well have contained a flat hearth. Tentatively therefore three households are suggested for Stage 9, with a possible rise in inhabitants from the 5th-century Stages. Non-domestic structures begin to decrease, the principal shelters, stores, and workshop areas being provided by V2, Y, and the very damaged T6. The suggested shrine G was in use for at least part of the Stage. There was still considerable structural diversity. A recent comment on Tintagel (Morris and Harry 1997, 122) contrasts the irregular stone-walled structures there with the large ovals of Trethurgy but it is now clear that Trethurgy, and other rounds, built structures in a wide variety of traditions and that broad comparanda can be found at Trethurgy for the structures described from Tintagel.

Several rounds appear to have continued into the 6th century. Grambla has Late Roman amphorae and probably Phocaean Red Slip ware and a piece of conical glass beaker. The interim report refers to this material among the rubble infill of the large oval, or rather 'boat-shaped', buildings there (Saunders 1972) but there seems no reason why the small pieces recorded could not reflect a situation similar to that at Trethurgy. Reawla has a possible piece of 6th-century conical beaker (Section 4.5); it also has three radiocarbon dates which suggest activity after the Roman period (Appendix 2). Reawla was badly plough-damaged (Appleton-Fox 1992), only partly excavated, and surviving details are difficult to understand. One of the radiocarbon dates comes from low down in its Ditch, below apparent deliberate infill, indicating the possibility of a 5th to 7th-century recut. The most likely interpretation, given the absence so far of Post-Roman import wares, is a low level of activity through the 5th and 6th centuries, at least in the parts excavated and a reinstatement of the enclosure, perhaps short lived, possibly towards the end of the main Post-Roman pottery import phase. Goldherring (Guthrie 1969) again is difficult. The case for Post-Roman activity is based on a few Gwithian Style platters, reported as coming from the surface, effectively unstratified. But a good deal of the published pottery appears to be late Roman, of the general kind likely still to be in circulation in the 5th or 6th centuries. The case for continuity of occupation at Goldherring is certainly unproven; the most likely interpretation on present evidence is that it continued into the 5th century and then was reused, perhaps casually, at a later date.

There appears to be something of a paradox in present approaches to Post-Roman import wares in Western Britain and their interpretation. A glance through Thomas' (1981) list shows a wide variety of sites, many like Gwithian connected to small groups drawing heavily on food resources available on the coast; material from Perran Sands or from the Kelsies may fall into this class. Yet much of the literature (eg Dark 1994a) regards this pottery as indicative of status and draws heavily on its links with the reinvestment of hilltop enclosures as at Cadbury Castle in Somerset. Undoubtedly settlements of high status did exist. Thomas' model of such a status settlement at Tintagel, where the large quantities of Post-Roman import wares have been increased by recent work (Morris and Harry 1997), presents the site as a focus from which high-value artefacts may have spread, perhaps highlighting archaeologically the area under the control of, or some obligation to, the community or individual living at Tintagel itself (Thomas 1993, 98, fig 76). It has been argued above (Section 12.13) that conditions in the 4th century would have allowed differential wealth accumulation amongst communities in rounds (Section 12.15) and that this differential could have led eventually to the emergence of a local elite which took control once the legal and tax networks of Roman Britain were no longer effective. By the late 5th century, there may have been a structured system of settlements with centres such as Tintagel at the top, some round communities with sufficient resources to retain local authority as the next tier, and below this a wide range of unenclosed settlement which will have included the descendants of those who could no longer maintain rounds. This scenario presents communities in rounds like Trethurgy as a middle tier in society, with a degree of prosperity and authority which drew on a millennium of tradition.

The importance of Trethurgy is as an extensively examined example of this middle social tier. This is not the place to review those settlements of higher status. One point however is of great importance. Tintagel has been recognised as outstanding in the quantities of its Post-Roman pottery imports ever since their first recognition (Radford 1956) and many of the arguments regarding its high status relate to this. It might be thought that a situation which has appeared valid for nearly half a century is as near certain as archaeological evidence allows. But recent work at Bantham in South Devon may change matters. Bantham has long been known as a settlement, probably a port, with some Post-Roman import material (Fox 1955) and work over the last few decades has indicated that it was more extensive than first supposed (Silvester 1981a; Griffith and Reed 1998). However recent investigations have produced this pottery in quantity, with broken pieces of a size rarely matched at Tintagel (Horner 2001). Our knowledge of the early Post-Roman centuries is still overall so scanty that long-accepted interpretations can be overset by a single new investigation. The data from Bantham points up how little we really know about the period and certainly calls into question Thomas' arguments (1993, 96) about a limited number of voyages providing Post-Roman imported pottery.

The interpretation of the distribution of Post-Roman import wares may in fact be generally similar to that of samian. The latter occurs on most sites of the Roman period in Cornwall but does not carry with it implications for the status of the inhabitants; status and samian only become an issue when the latter occurs in quantity and in association with other non-local artefacts as at Carvossa (Carlyon 1987). Communities using small quantities of samian or Post-Roman import wares both had the appropriate contacts and the means for their acquisition. Samian may have been exchanged by land or by water. Its wider distribution may simply be due to the longer period, possibly four centuries, during which it was in circulation and during which it may have formed part of local exchange networks. Post-Roman import wares came directly into the South West by sea, and any coastal community could on occasion have had contact with trading vessels. Communities living near the coast, including Trethurgy, may have been more likely to acquire non-local artefacts than those living inland.

We cannot tell how widespread Post-Roman import wares really were, whether for example the round at Reawla could have been occupied in the late 5th or 6th century and not possessed some of these ceramics. We also cannot tell how widespread gabbroic pottery was at this date, but its manufacture was on a smaller scale than in the Roman centuries and it was probably exchanged over a less extensive area. Whatever the date of the Gwithian Style and subsequent grass-marked wares, these need not be contemporary with any class of Post-Roman import except the late E ware. It is quite possible that there were settlements of the 6th century, even in Cornwall which is perceived as having a strong ceramic tradition, which had little or no pottery. Here the value of radiocarbon dating is again apparent. Appendix 2 includes, apart from the round at Reawla, three sites with dates which cover the 6th century. At Lanhainsworth, in the area of Little Quoit Farm (Fig 1), dates of cal AD 430-600 and 420-540 were associated with gullies which may have held sub-circular structures (Lawson-Jones 2001); there was only a single gabbroic sherd, probably of later Roman period type, in association. At Ruthvoes in the same area a hearth pit or oven with no associated ceramics (*ibid*) produced a determination which calibrated to AD 430-600. At Stencoose, south of St Agnes, a probable oval sheiling (Jones forthcoming) produced dates of AD 380-670 and 420-770; later Roman ceramics were thought to be redeposited.

These recently excavated sites suggest that the situation in Cornwall may be more similar to that in Devon than previously supposed. Apart from Bantham, there is the 'status' earthwork at High Peak with import wares (Pollard 1966) but these wares do not appear to have been widespread. However radiocarbon dating has demonstrated the probable use of recently investigated sites in the early Post-Roman centuries. These are a plough-damaged enclosure without detectable internal structures at Hayes Farm just east of Exeter (Simpson *et al* 1989), the newly identified hillfort at Raddon north of Exeter (Gent and Quinnell 1999a), and the hilltop at Haldon well known for Neolithic occupation (Gent and Quinnell 1999b). A ditch circuit at Raddon may have been recut but the nature of internal activity is uncertain, as is that investigated on a very small scale at Haldon. Other work in Devon, investigating the environmental sequence in peat and the extraction of iron, is also producing dates of this period without artefactual associations (G Juleff and A Brown pers comm).

This review of the extent of settlement in the immediate Post-Roman centuries is confined to Cornwall and Devon. Other parts of Western Britain present rather different problems. In Somerset and Dorset many of these are connected with the continuance of artefacts from the Roman centuries (see eg Rahtz *et al* 2000). In Wales the artefactual record in general is sparser than in Devon and Cornwall (eg Edwards and Lane 1988), and in South West Wales (Williams and Mytum 1998, 144-5) data are beginning to accumulate based on radiocarbon dating. Eventually we may expect to be able to detect regional patterning amongst the populations in these areas which supported status sites such as Dinas Powys, Cadbury Castle, or Cadbury Congresbury. The general standard of life for the majority of inhabitants across Western Britain is at present not ascertainable. Dark (1994b) presents a fairly optimistic picture of high standards of craftsmanship and literacy with regard to the status centres and the religious establishments connected with the advent of Christianity. It can only be speculation as to how far such standards might have affected the inhabitants of Trethurgy or those of other middle-status settlements across Western Britain.

The degree of population decline in the 5th and 6th centuries cannot be assessed at present. The situation is currently based on archaeological evidence from settlement sites of different types; this would be greatly assisted were environmental studies available for the region which showed changes in agricultural land and pasture, woodland, and scrub. The broad picture from Britain as a whole does not indicate any major decrease in the use of productive land (Dark 1996). The general pattern, and character, of settlement in Cornwall appears to have continued through from the Roman centuries until the 6th century.

12.17 End note: the move away from rounds

When did the settlement tradition demonstrated by Trethurgy Round finally end and why? After Stage 9 at Trethurgy, the Round appears to have ceased as a settlement and fallen into disrepair, with less substantial gates, probably serving a stock enclosure, only being put in across the Entrance after some lapse of time. No round can yet be demonstrated to have continued as a functioning settlement after the currency of Post-Roman import wares and the date at which these ceased to be used cannot be established with certainty.

What is certain is that by the time of Domesday Book much of the present pattern of rural settlement in Cornwall located in small hamlets denoted by *tre* place-name elements had become established. No *tre* hamlet has yet been demonstrated to be located within a round, although round-type enclosures may on occasion have been reused as Christian centres, for example at Merther Euny (Thomas 1968b) and St Buryan (Preston-Jones 1987). The few excavations of deserted *tre* sites, such as Treworld, Lesnewth (Dudley and Minter 1966), have proved of limited value to the study of their origins. Two important studies of the development of *tre* settlements have been published (Preston-Jones and Rose 1986; Rose and Preston-Jones 1995) and the change from **ker* to *tre* place-names has been extensively discussed by Padel (1985, 50-2, 223-32). Padel concludes that **ker* names could still be established in the 6th and 7th centuries but that *tre* names were formed after the 5th century and before *c* AD 1100.

Rose and Preston-Jones (1995) see a retraction in the pattern of settlements through the 5th and 6th centuries with some communities based in rounds moving a short distance to *trefs*, some disappearing but with subsequent expansion filling out the landscape with *trefs* in the following centuries. The abandonment of rounds is discussed (*ibid*) against the changing circumstances of the 5th and the 6th centuries, cross-sea movements from Ireland and to Brittany, the introduction of Christianity, and the emergence of a local British kingdom which provided a degree of political stability and authority to replace that held by round communities.

With the rounds in the 6th century ended a settlement tradition which had continued through the Roman period from the Later Iron Age. High-status sites such as Tintagel and Cadbury Castle go out of use at much the same time. There were changes in ceramic traditions, with Romano-Cornish styles replaced by the Gwithian Style and grass-marked wares. There was a change in external contacts, from those with the Mediterranean which brought wine, olive oil, and fine pottery, to shorter links to South West France producing some tableware and perhaps wine in wooden barrels. The interrelationship between all these factors cannot be determined but the 6th century is generally accepted as the pivot for a whole series of changes.

Baillie (1995; 1999) has made the case for some widespread natural disaster around AD 540, which caused some years of extremely restricted growth in tree rings and reduced the growth of crops, linked to plague which is well documented at this time in the Mediterranean. This 'AD 540 event' is now too well established to be left out of discussions of the 6th century although the dramatic headlines about comets and destruction have been academically counterproductive. A mid 6th-century disaster which acted as a catalyst for change fits the Cornish evidence very well: some drop in population due to crop failure, and possibly plague and abandonment of settlements. As communities subsequently begin to re-establish themselves they chose, as at Trethurgy, sites within their traditional landholdings but not in the old enclosures. Former authority, vested in a millennium of tradition and supported by the symbolism of enclosure, had been finally discredited by a sequence of disasters, and rounds were no longer considered appropriate places to live. In bringing the 540 event into discussion of 6th-century change however, it is stressed that its effects have not been recognised further east in England and its impact was only such as to tip the balance in some areas where change was already under way.

However a 6th-century end for round occupation and authority is far from established. It is based only on the dating of Post-Roman import wares found at two rounds, Trethurgy and Grambla, which has been accepted so far in this report. In retrospect this dating may need review in that it assumes a limited time for the use of these ceramics, either as vessels or as sherds, after the cessation of their import from the Mediterranean. It is quite possible that, as vessels or sherds, they were present for several centuries, in much the same way as samian ware has been demonstrated to have been. The situation may have been different on different types of site; imported ceramics may have been in use longer in rounds than at a major centre such as Tintagel, and even at Tintagel the radiocarbon determinations may indicate that the conventional length of occupation is too short (Morris and Harry 1997, 120). The changes in Post-Roman South West Britain are so poorly understood that major developments in data may be expected from future research. Trethurgy and Grambla are only two sites out of some 12 small enclosures here identified as rounds and it might be argued that, if rounds really continued as settlements beyond the 6th century, more sites would have been identified. But the evidence is going to come from the latest levels most subject to agricultural disturbance, and our understanding of ceramics — late Romano-Cornish, Post-Roman imports, and grass-marked wares — is very imperfect. There are radiocarbon dates from Reawla and Gwithian Style platters from Goldherring which may double the number of rounds occupied in the Post-Roman centuries from two to four, so small is the current sample. The move away from rounds, and from the social structure they represented, may have occurred in perhaps a century or through a very much longer period. It would be unfortunate if this report, the first on a round with Post-Roman occupation, is used in too definitive a way to provide an end date for rounds and the traditions they represented.

At Trethurgy, the Round was deserted as a dwelling place in the 6th century or some time later, but activity continued in the area. A sherd of E ware was found in the lynchet which accumulated uphill of the Round; there were a few grass-marked sherds of uncertain date. The Entrance served for a while as a temporary smithy. Before or after this, it was re-gated and the site became a stock pen. Later, ploughing is the likely cause of interior disturbance linked with occasional sherds of Sandy Lane type. There is some evidence that strip fields, linked to the emergence of *tre* communities, were laid out around the present settlement of Trethurgy (Chapter 9). The end of domestic occupation of the Round is not the end of its story. The site yields information about settlement in the vicinity right up to the present day, and about the link between the Round and the landscape within which it was set.

As an end note to an end note, Trethurgy happens to be the most fully excavated of the numerous rounds which existed in the late-Roman Cornish landscape. Its excavation was the result of circumstances, both local and national, in the early 1970s and may remain the most fully investigated round interior for some time to come. This report, with all its shortcomings, is likely to become a reference work on Roman and Post-Roman Cornwall. Yet we have no means of knowing how far the results it presents were typical. It is far from being a definitive report on Roman and Post-Roman Cornwall. In addition the author has placed certain interpretations which are bound to be personally biased and must be far from certain. It is hoped that overall the report will provide the stimulating basis for future work but, as with all archaeological reports, *caveat lector!*

Appendix 1
List of contexts with brief description, figure references, Stage numbers, and associated finds

The list is intended to assist identification of context numbers with references to the principal illustrations on which each occurs. Measurement in m refers to depth where this is not given in Chapter 2. Contexts are assigned to Stages where possible, some to a single Stage, others to several successive Stages. Where a context such as wall collapse intervenes between Stages, it is shown as eg Stages 4/5. Stage 4+ means that Stage 4 or any successive Stage is possible.

The list also collates the finds from each context. A finds number in bold type indicates an artefact illustrated or individually enumerated in the text; numbers in ordinary type indicate objects similar to the enumerated examples. Numbers in brackets eg (2) indicate the quantity where more than one is present. For pottery BB1 indicates South-East Dorset BB1, SD South Devon ware, G gabbroic; sherd numbers are not given for BB1, SD, or G wares and the use of BB1, SD, or G without find number simply means the presence of the fabric. For Post-Roman imports Bi, Bii etc have been retained for Late Roman amphorae. M/PMED indicates Medieval or Post-Medieval pottery without quantification. Flints, and stone artefacts not enumerated, are not included.

[Ploughsoil, whole site] South-Western Grey storage jar, M/PMED. Saddle querns (3).

[Ploughsoil, in north-east of Round] Samian (3), Dressel 30, P6 white ware import, G P44 P51 P114, M/PMED. S8 Cornish mortar.

[Ploughsoil, in south-east of Round] M/PMED.

[Ploughsoil, in north-west of Round] Exeter fabric 101, M/PMED.

[Ploughsoil in Entrance] M/PMED.

[Ploughsoil over Structure Q] Dressel 20 amphora, G P44 P48 P113 P115 P123 P126 P130 P143 P148, M/PMED. S44 rotary quern.

[Ploughsoil over House Z] Phocaean Red Slip ware, BB1 P16, G P108, M/PMED.

[Ploughsoil over House X] SD P22, G **P49** P72 P103 P108. **S32** spindle whorl.

[Ploughsoil over House D] M/PMED.

[Ploughsoil over G] South-Western Grey storage jar, M/PMED.

[Ploughsoil over House A] **P6** white ware import, Dressel 20 amphora (2), South-Western Grey storage jar (10), G P29 **P41** P44 P53 P58 **P85** **P98** P100 P110 P141, M/PMED.

[7] Paving — large pieces in surface [8] Area R. Fig 45. Stage 5+. Smithing slag.

[8] Surface in Area R, contemporary with Entrance paving [188]. On/among, Figs 5, 7, 41, 42, 45. Stage 5+. *Unguentarium* import, Dressel 20 amphora, Post-Roman coarse ware fabric 5?, Bi?, BB1, G P59 P62 P71 P86 P96 P104 P133, M/PMED. Slate disc, saddle querns (2).

[9] Soil on cobbles [173]. Area R. Not illus. Stage 4/5. **M11** iron pan, **M15** iron pivot base, iron upholstery stud. **Gl 20.** **P6** white ware import, Dressel 20 amphora (2), Bii (2), BB1 P17, SD P25, G P33 P40 P62 P74 P77 P93 P100 P106 P112 P116 P121 P131, M/PMED.

[10] Drain contemporary with surface [8], Area R. Fig 45. Stage 5+.

[11] Soil over Structures D & E. Fig 32. Silver small fragments from casting. **M2** brooch. Copper alloy casting globule. **Gl 21**. Samian Dr 18, Phocean Red Slip ware, Bi, BB1, South-Western Grey storage jar, SD P22 P27, G P30 P32 P40 P52 P79 P97 **P100** **P106** P111 P117 **P129**, M/PMED. **S11** unfinished Cornish mortar, **S17** net sinker, **S29** spindle whorl, **S42** rotary quern, saddle quern.

[13] Revetment of platform adjacent to House T3. Fig 39. Stage 4+.

[14] Soil and stones covering slope east of House D. Not illus.

[15] Period 5 Round Rampart Inner Revetment. Figs 7, 10, 14, 32, etc.

[16] Period 5 Round Rampart Outer Revetment. Figs 7, 11, 15 etc.

[20] Gulley possibly predating House A1. Fig 34. 0.20m.

[24] House A1 flags. Figs 34, 35. Stages 1-4. G.

[25] Structure E3 paving. Fig 29. Stage 5.

[26] Structure E1 posthole. Fig 29. Stages 1-3.

[26A] Structure E2 posthole. Fig 29. Stage 4.

[28] House T5 paving. Figs 42, 43. Stage 8. Samian Dr 18/31, Bi? **S2** Trethurgy bowl, **S16** slate disc, saddle quern.

[29A] Probable posthole in House A2 gulley [97]. Fig 37. Stages 5-6.

[29B] Probable posthole in House A2 gulley [97]. Fig 37. Stages 5-6.

[33] House A1 walling. Figs 34, 35. Stages 1-4. G P29.

[34] Infill between House A 2 and 3. Fig 35. Stage 8/9. **C10** - unworn coin of Tetricus AD273+. Iron loop. Hearth lining and smithing slag. **Gl 8 Gl 23**. Dressel 20 amphora, South Spanish Globular amphora (2), BB1 P18, South-Western Grey storage jar, G P56 P62 (2) P76 P78 P104 P142. **S1** Trethurgy bowl frag, **S45** rotary quern, saddle querns (3).

[34A] Soil on House A1 floor. Fig 35. Stage 4/5. South-Western Grey storage jar (3).

[36] Rubble revetted by [13], platform adjacent House T3, Fig 39. Stage 4+. Vitrified clay. **Gl 10**. BB1 P17, G P44 **P53** P93 P110 **P111** P112. **S27** spindle whorl.

[39] Rubble of House A1. Fig 35. Stage 4/5.

[46] Soil and late revetment collapse, Area R. Fig 7. Stage 9/10. Samian Dr 27, Lezoux colour-coat, Bi, G **P138**.

[48] Patchy cobbling in central area. Fig 5. Stage 1+.

[52] Cut for Period 5 Rampart Inner Revetment. Figs 7, 32, 43.

[53] House A1, later door posthole. Fig 34. Stage 4.

[53A] House A1, earlier door posthole. Fig 34. Stages 1-3. G.

[54] House A2, later door posthole. Fig 37. Stages 7-8.

[55] House A1 posthole. Figs 34, 35. 0.20m. Stages 1-4. **M19** upholstery stud.

[56] House A2, earlier door posthole. Fig 37. Stages 5-6. G.

[56B] House A1, later door posthole. Figs 34, 35. Stage 4. G P76.

[56C] House A1, earlier door posthole. Figs 34, 35. Stages 1-3. G.

[57] House A2, earlier door posthole. Fig 37. Stages 5-6.

[58] House A2, later door posthole. Fig 37. Stages 7-8.

[59] House A1, posthole. Fig 34. 0.20m. Stages 1-4.

[59A] House A1, posthole. Fig 34. 0.15m. Stages 1-4.

[60] House A1, posthole on division line across floor. Fig 34. Stages 1-3.

[61] House A1, posthole on division line across floor. Fig 34. Stages 1-3.

[65] House A2 wall. Figs 35, 37. Stages 5-8. Bii, G P46 P47. **S46** rotary quern.

[66] Posthole outside Structure G. Fig 29. 0.15m.

[68] Stone-hole/sump, connected with gulley [167]. Fig 29. Stages 1-2.

[70] Pit east of House D. Fig 31. 0.20m.

[71] House A2, drain. Fig 29. Stages 5-8.

[74] House A external paving. Fig 34. Stage 1 onward. Bi (on).

[77] Upper infill of Structure G. Fig 30. Stage 9. Schorl. **Gl 9**. Phocean Red Slip ware, Bi **P9** (5), Bii (3), **P1** Oxfordshire, South-Western Grey storage jar, SD, G **P136**, M/PMED. **S23** whetstone, **S31** spindle whorl.

[78] Pit north of Structure E. Fig 29. Stage 6. **M20** iron ring. G **P36 P60 P76**. Saddle quern.

[79] House A1, walling. Figs 34, 35. Stages 1-4.

[84] House A1, posthole on division line across floor. Fig 34. Stages 1-3.

[85] House A1, posthole on division line across floor. Fig 34. Stages 1-3.

[86] House A, posthole. Fig 34. 0.12m. Stages 1-4.

[87] Posthole possibly predating House A1. Fig 34. 0.2m.

[88] House A1, posthole on division line across floor. Fig 34. Stages 1-3.

[89] House A1, posthole on division line across floor. Fig 34. Stages 1-3.

[90] House D4 floor. Figs 31, 32. Stages 5-6.

[90A] Posthole House D4. Fig 31. 0.15m. Stage 6.

[90B] Pit House D4. Figs 31, 32. 0.20m. Stage 6.

[92] Posthole in central area. Fig 5. 0.10m.

[93] Posthole in central area. Fig 5. 0.10m.

[94] Posthole in central area. Fig 5. 0.05m.

[95] Posthole in central area. Fig 5. 0.08m.

[97] House A2, external gulley. Figs 35, 37. Stages 5-6.

[99] Posthole in central area. Fig 5. 0.18m.

[100] House A2, later external gulley. Figs 35, 37. Stages 7-8. Iron loop. **Gl 1**. G P34 P50 **P62 P71 P78 P92**.

[104] Posthole in central area. Fig 5. 0.25m.

[108] Posthole, House D. Fig 31. 0.20m.

[111] Small stones continuing surface [188] onto Ditch causeway. Fig 10. Stage 5+. **Gl 24**.

[115] Posthole House D4. Fig 31. 0.25m. Stage 6.

[116] Posthole near Structure E. Fig 29. 0.10m.

[117] Posthole in line across House D. Fig 31. Stage 4. G.

[119] Gulley north of Structure E. ?Relates House X. Fig 29.

[120] Gulley north of Structure E. ?Relates House X. Fig 29.

[120A] Gulley north of Structure E. ?Relates House X. Fig 29.

[122] Posthole House D4. Fig 31. 0.16m. Stage 5.

[123] Posthole House D4. Fig 31. 0.19m. Stage 5.

[124] Drain associated with wall [156], Structure R3. Fig 45. Stage 10. G.

[128] House A2 hearth pit. Figs 35, 37. Stages 5-8. G P142.

[128A] House A2, hearth. Fig 37. Stages 5-8.

[129] House D, stakeholes outside. Fig 31.

[131] Posthole in line across House D. Fig 31. Stage 4.

[132] Posthole House D4. Fig 31. 0.19m. Stage 5.

[133] Posthole House D4. Fig 31. 0.11m. Stage 5.

[134] Posthole House D4. Fig 31. 0.25m. Stage 6.

[135] Posthole House D4. Fig 27. 0.40m. Stage 6.

[136] House D4 internal drain. Figs 31, 32. Stages 5-6.

[137] Gulley, possibly continuation of [119], cut by pit [78]. Fig 29. Stages 1-2.

[138] Stakeholes in House D4 floor 90. Fig 31. Stages 5-6.

[140] Soil over Main Entrance paving [188]. Fig 11. Stage 9/10. **M6** iron binding. Bii **P10** (5), G, M/PMED.

[141] House A2, rubble levelling for floor. Fig 37. Stage 5. **M14** iron knife.

[145A] Structure E1 posthole. Fig 29. Stages 1-3.

[145B] Structure E2 posthole. Fig 29. Stage 4.

[149] Posthole House D4. Fig 31. 0.25m. Stage 6.

[150] House A2 internal drain. Figs 35, 37. Stages 5-8. G.

[153] House D4 external gulley. Figs 31, 32. Stages 5-6. G **P33**.

[154] Gulley cut by pit 78. Fig 29. Stages 1-2. G.

[155] Posthole in central area. Fig 5. 0.40m.

[156] Wall in Structure R3. Fig 45. Stage 10.

[161] House A1 internal drain. Figs 34, 35. Stages 1-4. Samian Dr 37, Dressel 20 amphora, G P56.

[162] House A1 posthole. Fig 34. 0.13m. Stages 1-4.

[167] Gulley, continuation of [137]. Fig 29.

[168] House D1 slot. Fig 31. Stage 2.

[169] Late drain in Area R. Fig 45. Stage 10.

[173] Scrappy cobbles on soil [386], Area R. Fig 44. Stage 4.

[174] Paving associated late wall [156], Structure R3. Fig 45. Stage 10.

[175] Cobble patchings on surface [8]. Fig 7. Stage 8. Hearth lining. Samian Dr 27 + 1, G P29 **P37** **P42** P46 **P63** P67 P73 P107. **S15** stone mould cover.

[182] Rampart revetment, south terminal. Fig 10.

[183] Rubble in Entrance, below latest gate. Figs 10, 11. Stage 9/10. Iron slag. Bii(5), Bv (7), G **P80** **P93** **P99** **P109**, M/PMED.

[185] Robber trench for outer Rampart revetment at Entrance. Fig 7. M/PMED.

[187] Rampart revetment, north terminal. Fig 10.

[188] Second surface, of large stones, in Main Phase Entrance. Figs 10, 11. Stage 5+. Bii, M/PMED.

[191] Pit in latest phase of gate. Fig 10. Stage 10. Smithing slag and ? hearth lining.

[193] North post setting for latest gate. Fig 10. Stage 10.

[194] South post setting for latest gate. Fig 10. Stage 10.

[196] Walling across north edge of entrance causeway. Fig 10. Stage 1+.

[197] Walling across south edge of entrance causeway. Fig 10. Stage 1+.

[199] Drain set within north Entrance terminal. Figs 10, 11. Stage 1+. ?Bv, G P56.

[200] North gate posthole in Main Phase Entrance. Figs 10, 11.

[201] South gate posthole in Main Phase Entrance. Figs 10, 11.

[202] Material backing revetment [187] and over drain [199] in north Rampart terminal. Figs 10, 11. G.

[205] Packing of cut for south terminal revetment [182]. Not illus. Smithing slag. G.

[207] Period 2 posthole outside Period 3 Enclosure Ditch but sealed by OLS [371]. Fig 8. 0.20m. UB-3254 2123±47 BP.

[208] Pivot-hole for south side of gate. Fig 10. Stages 5-9.

[213] Deliberate infill in south Ditch terminal. Not illus. Predates Stage 5.

[215] First surface inside Main Phase Entrance. Fig 11. Stages 1-4. SD, G P69, M/PMED.

[216] Period 4 posthole. Fig 8.

[219] Period 4 posthole. Fig 8. Bii.

[220] Period 4 posthole. Fig 8.

[221] Period 4 posthole. Fig 8.

[222] Period 4 posthole. Fig 8.

[225] Period 4 posthole. Fig 8.

[232] House D2 drain. Figs 31, 32. Stage 3.

[234] Posthole in central area. Fig 5. 0.10m.

[236] Makeup of Period 7 field hedge. Fig 7. M/PMED **P24**.

[241] Posthole in central area. Fig 5. 0.30m.

[254] House T4 paving. Figs 41, 43. Stages 5-8.

[255] Backing to Structure G. Figs 29, 30. Stage 6. Smithing slag. **M17** iron double-spiked loop. Samian Dr 31, BB1 P14, SD, G P55 P56 P69 P125, M/PMED. **S5** Trethurgy bowl, **S42** rotary quern.

[256] Infill of Structure G. Figs 29, 30. Stage 9. Iron cleat, **M21** iron collar ferrule. Samian, **P7** Phocean Red Slip ware, Bii, SD with cordon, G P34 P60. Saddle quern.

[258] Paving in Structure G. Figs 29, 30. Stage 6.

[258A] Layer on base of Structure G. Figs 29, 30. Stage 6.

[259] Posthole associated late features [156] [174] Structure R3. Fig 45. Stage 10.

[258] Paving in Structure G. Figs 29, 30. Stage 6.

[261] Posthole near Structure E Figs 5, 29. 0.15m.

[262] Posthole near Structure E. Fig 31. 0.10m.

[263] Posthole near Structure E. Fig 31. 0.10m.

[267] Posthole near Structure E. Fig 29. 0.15m.

[267A] Posthole near Structure E. Fig 29. 0.10m.

[268] Structure E1 posthole. Fig 29. Stages 1-3.

[268A] Structure E2 posthole. Fig 29. Stage 4.

[269] Posthole in Structure D3. Fig 31. Stage 4. G.

[272] Posthole south of House D. Fig 31. 0.15m.

[273] Posthole south of House D. Fig 31. 0.15m.

[276] Posthole south of House D. Fig.27. 0.15m.

[277] Posthole south of House D. Fig 31. 0.15m.

[279] Posthole south of House D. Fig 31. 0.15m.

[281] Posthole near Structure E. Fig 29. 0.35m.

[282] Structure E1 posthole. Fig 29. Stages 1-3.

[284] Posthole outside Structure G. Fig 29. 0.15m. G.

[290] Blocking across Structure G. Figs 29, 30. Stage 9. SD, G P117.

[291] Orthostatic component of Structure G. Figs 29, 30. Stages 6-9.

[292] House D1 slot. Fig 31. Stage 2.

[294] House A1 hearth pit. Figs 34, 35. Stage 4. South-Western Grey storage jar, G P142. **S13** stone weight.

[294A] House A2 paving. Figs 35, 37. Stages 5-8.

[295A] House A1 posthole in division across floor. Fig 34. Stages 1-3. G.

[295B] House A1 posthole in division across floor. Fig 34. Stages 1-3.

[295C] House A1 posthole in division across floor. Fig 34. Stages 1-3.

[296] House A1 posthole in [345]-[296] line. Fig 34. Stages 1-4.

[297] House A1 posthole in [345]-[296] line. Fig 34. Stages 1-4. G.

[299] House A1 posthole. Fig 34. 0.10m. Stages 1-4.

[300] House A1 stakehole. Fig 34. Stages 1-3.

[301] House A1 stakehole. Fig 34. Stages 1-3.

[302] House A1 stakehole. Fig 34. Stages 1-3.

[303] House A1 stakehole. Fig 34. Stages 1-3.

[304] House A1 internal drain. Figs 34, 35. Stages 1-4.

[308A] to [308G] Postholes of House A3. Figs 35, 37. Stage 9.

[310] Structure E2 surface. Fig 29. Stage 4.

[311] House A1 rab floor. Figs 34, 35. Stages 1-4.

[312] House A1 posthole in [345]-[296] line. Fig 34. Stages 1-4.

[313] House A1 posthole in [345]-[296] line. Fig 34. Stages 1-4.

[314] House A1 internal drain. Figs 34, 35. Stages 1-4. Dressel 20 amphora, BB1, G P32 P99.

[315] Stakeholes in House A1 floor. Fig 34. Stage 4.

[316] House A1 hearth pit. Figs 34, 35. Stages 1-3.

[318] Pit predating House A1. Fig 34. 0.40m. G.

[320] Structure E1 posthole. Fig 29. Stages 1-3.

[320A] Structure E1?posthole. Fig 29.

[321] Structure E2 posthole. Fig 29. Stage 4.

[322] Period 3 Enclosure Bank interior revetment behind House A. Fig 34.

[323] Period 3 Enclosure Bank behind House A. Fig 34. Smithing slag.

[323A] Rubble from Period 3 Enclosure Bank cut by House A. Figs 34, 35. G.

[324] Walling connecting House A2 to Rampart. Fig 37. Stage 5+.

[325] Posthole within area levelled for House T. Fig 34.

[326] Posthole within area levelled for House T. Fig 34.

[330] House T5 wall. Fig 42. Stage 8. Saddle quern.

[331] House A1 internal drain. Figs 34, 35. Stages 1-4.

[334] House A1 posthole. Fig 34. 0.25m. Stages 1-4.

[335] House A1 posthole in division across floor. Fig 34. Stages 1-3.

[336] Hearth associated House A1 hearth pit [294]. Fig 34. Stage 4.

[337] Pit associated House A1 hearth pit [294]. Fig 34. Stage 4.

[338A] House A1 narrow slots. Fig 34. Stages 1-4.

[338B] House A1 narrow slots. Fig 34. Stages 1-4.

[339] Period 4 posthole. Fig 8.

[340] Drain through Period 3 Enclosure Bank. Fig 8.

[341] Posthole predating House A1. Fig 34. 0.30m. G.

[344] House A1 internal drain. Fig 34. Stages 1-4.

[345] House A1 posthole in [345]-[296] line. Fig 34. Stages 1-4. G.

[347] House A1 posthole. Fig 34. 0.10m. Stages 1-4.

[348] House A1 posthole. Fig 34. Stages 1-3. 0.1m.

[349] House A1 stakeholes. Fig 34. Stages 1-3.

[354] Burnt clay feature associated hearth pit [294]. House A1. Fig 34. Stage 4.

[357] House A1 gulley. Fig 34. Stages 1-4.

[359] Recent lynchet over Round Ditch to west. Fig 7. Bi (4), E ware **P13**, M/PMED.

[360] Period 5 Round Ditch Secondary Silt (except in terminals). Fig 7. Stages 1-4 +. Bi, G **P137**, M/PMED. **S6** Trethurgy bowl, **S18** whetstone.

[361] Period 5 Round Ditch Primary Silt (except in terminals). Stage 1? Fig 7.

[363] Period 3 Enclosure Bank. Figs 4, 7, 8. Hearth lining. G **P32** (2), M/PMED.

[366] Period 3 Enclosure Bank exterior revetment. Figs 4, 7, 8.

[368] Period 3 Enclosure Bank exterior revetment slumped into ditch. Figs 7, 8.

[369] Silt (? Period 4), in Period 3 Enclosure Ditch silt. Figs 7, 8, 9, 11. Samian, Bii (2), G.

[371] Old Land Surface beneath Rampart and Period 3 Enclosure Bank. Figs 7, 14, 35.

[373] Period 3 Enclosure Bank interior revetment. Figs 4, 7, 8.

[375] Part of Structure R2, with [396], associated surface [8]. Fig 45. Stage 5-7.

[378] Posthole in R beneath surface [8]. Fig 44. Stage 1.

[379] Posthole in R beneath surface [8]. Fig 44. Stage 1.

[380] Extension of Old Land Surface [371] into Area R. Figs 7, 8, 44. Bv (2), SD, G P32 (2) P37 P67 P111, M/PMED. **S43** rotary quern.

[382] Wall, Structure R4. Fig 45. Stage 10. G.

[384] Drain contemporary with surface [8] and wall [396] in R. Fig 45. Stage 5+.

[385] Hearth on soil [386] under [8] in R. Fig 44. Stage 4.

[386] Soil in R, forming during T1-3. Fig 7. Stage 1-4. ?Bv, SD, G P47 P55 **P70** P71 **P73** **P77** **P83** **P84** P108.

[387] Drain contemporary with [8] in R. Figs 7, 8, 45. Stage 5+. Saddle quern.

[389] Cut for Period 5 Round Rampart Outer Revetment. Figs 7, 12, 17.

[390] Period 5 Round Rampart. Figs 7, 11, 17, 32, 35, 43. Smithing slag. Hearth lining.

[395] Latest soil level over T. Fig 43. Stage 10? Hearth lining. Samian, P6 white ware import, Oxfordshire WC7.

[396] Part of Structure R2, with [375], contemporary surface [8]. Fig 45. Stages 5-7.

[397] Revetment for additional Rampart material [398] behind T4. Figs 41, 43. Stage 5+.

[398] Strengthening of Round Rampart retained by [397] behind T4. Figs 41, 43. Stage 5.

[399] Revetment collapse post-T5. Fig 43. Stage 9/10. BB1 P17, SD, G P41 P91 P109 **P127** P133. **S1** Trethurgy bowl frags (2), saddle quern.

[400] Soil over T5 continuous with [140] in Entrance. Figs 7, 43. Stage 9/10. **Gl 2**. Samian Dr 37, **P6** white ware import, SD, G P30 P32 P34 **P39** P96 P107 P129 **P133 P147**, M/PMED.

[401] T4 wall. Figs 41, 43. Stages 5-6.

[403] Soil over T4. Fig 43. Stage 7. Smithing slag. **P6** white ware import (2), BB1, SD, G P29 P50 P73 **P89** P102 P134.

[409] Spread of stones, ? connected with Period 3 Enclosure drain [587], but continuing as surface with [215] in Round Stages 1-4. Fig 8.

[414] Drain contemporary with surface [8] in R. Fig 45. Stage 5+.

[415] Drain contemporary with surface [8] in R. Fig 45. Stage 5+. G P90 P101.

[419] T3 wall. Fig 39. Stage 4.

[420] External hearth T4. Fig 41. Stage 5.

[421] Dump wall, T6. Figs 42, 43, 45. Stage 9.

[422] Soil between T3 and T4. Fig 43. Stages 3/5. Smithing slag. **P6** white ware import, ?Bv, G P40 P75 P86 **P146**.

[423] T2 external drain. Fig 39. Stages 2-3. G.

[427] T3 floor. Figs 39, 43. Stage 4. Hearth lining. G **P86**. UB-3252 1806±52.

[429] Soil on platform [13]/[36] accumulating during T4. (Not illus.) Stage 4+. **P6** white ware import (2), BB1 P16.

[432A] Posthole in R beneath surface [8]. Fig 44. Stage 3.

[432B] Posthole in R beneath surface [8]. Fig 44. Stage 2. Saddle quern.

[432C] Posthole in R beneath surface [8]. Fig 44. Stage 3.

[432D] Posthole in R beneath surface [8]. Fig 44. Stage 2.

[434] Stakehole in R beneath surface [8]. Fig 44. Stage 4. G.

[435] Pit beneath surface [8] in R. Fig 44. Stages 1-4. G.

[435A] Pit beneath surface [8] in R. Fig 44. Stages 1-4.

[436] T2 floor. Figs 39, 43. Stages 2-3. G **P112 P140. S33** spindle whorl.

[437] T2 posthole. Fig 39. Stages 2-3.

[438] T2 posthole. Fig 39. Stages 2-3.

[440] Hearth on soil [386] under [8] in R. Fig 44. Stage 4.

[441] Pit in R beneath surface [8]. Fig 44. Stage 4.

[442] Soil on T2 floor. Fig 43. Stage 3. **Gl 13**. SD, G P29 P53 P65 P99 **P116**.

[446] Subsidiary layer in Round Rampart retained by A2 wall. Figs 35, 37. Stage 5.

[447] Drain through Period 3 Enclosure Bank, area of House T. Figs 4, 39. G.

[448] T2 wall. Figs 39, 43. Stages 2-3.

[449] T1 gulley. Figs 39, 43. Stage 1.

[450] ?Hearth pit in T3 floor. Fig 39. Stage 4.

[451] Material filling scoop beneath Round Rampart behind House A. Figs 34, 35. Stage 4.

[452] Stone setting, line of inner revetment [15] behind House A. Figs 34, 35. Stage 1.

[453A] Posthole in T2 wall. Fig 39. Stages 2-3.

[453B] Posthole in T2 wall. Fig 39. Stages 2-3.

[453C] Posthole in T2 wall. Fig 39. Stages 2-3. G **P145**.

[455] Soil between T1 and T2. Fig 43. Stages 1/2.

[456] T2 hearth pit. Figs 39, 43. Stages 2-3.

[458] T1 gulley. Figs 39, 43. Stage 1. G P60. Saddle quern.

[459] Drain through Period 3 Enclosure Bank under House T. Fig 4, 39.

[462A] to [462E] Postholes in R beneath surface [8]. Fig 44. Stage 1.

[463] Stakeholes in R beneath surface [8]. Fig 44. G.

[464] Posthole in R beneath surface [8]. Fig 44. Stage 1.

[465] Pit beneath surface [8] in R. Fig 44. Stage 4?

[466A] Posthole in R beneath surface [8]. Fig 44. Stage 2. G.

[466B] Posthole in R beneath surface [8]. Fig 44. Stage 2.

[467] Stakeholes in soil [386] in R. Fig 44. Stage 2.

[468] T2 pit. Fig 39. Stages 2-3.

[469] ?Hearth pit in T3 floor. Fig 39. Stage 4.

[471A] Posthole in T2 wall. Fig 39. Stages 2-3.

[471B] Posthole in T2 wall. Fig 39. Stages 2-3.

[471C] Posthole in T2 wall. Fig 39. Stages 2-3. Hearth lining. Dressel 20 amphora.

[472] House T2 pit/posthole. Fig 39. Stages 2-3.

[473] House T4 hearth. Fig 41. Stages 5-6.

[474] House T2 stakeholes. Fig 39. Stage 2.

[475] House T2 stakeholes. Fig 39. Stage 2.

[476] House T2 stakeholes. Fig 39. Stages 2-3.

[478] House T2 hearth and stakeholes. Fig 39. Stages 2-3.

[479] Wall, Structure R1. Fig 44. Stage 4.

[517] Soil infilling Structure X5. Fig 26. Stage 10. Hearth lining. Cassiterite. Bi, Bii, BB1 **P28**, SD, G **P91**, M/PMED.

[518] Soil around collapsed outer revetment rubble [519]. Fig 7. Stage 9+. Samian (2), M/PMED.

[519] Outward collapse of outer revetment. Fig 7. Stage 9 onward. Copper alloy stud frag.

[520] Upper cobbles in Ditch terminals. Fig 7. Stage 7 onward. Slate disc.

[521] First layer of cobbles over Ditch terminals and berm. Figs 7, 10. Stages 5-6. Exeter fabric 451, G P56 **P64**.

[523] Soil over upper Ditch cobbles [520], continuous with soil [140] in Entrance. Fig 7. Stage 9+. **Gl 16**. Phocean Red Slip ware **P8**, Dressel 20 amphora (2), Amphora Gauloise 4, Bii, SD, G P67 **P143**, M/PMED **P24A**. **S19** whetstone, **S36** pottery disc.

[524] Soil over V3, probably disturbed. Stage 10. Cassiterite, pebble. **M5** iron punch. Bii(5), P2 Oxfordshire, SD, G P32 P55 P67(2) **P94** P99 P101 P116 P118 P132, M/PMED.

[527] Round Ditch. Fig 7. Stage 1

[528] Paving outside entrance to Structure U. Fig 16. Stage 5.

[532] Soil over cobbles [521] in Ditch terminals. Fig 7. Stage 6. Brick/tile with vitrified surface. G cordoned body sherd.

[535] Late phase drain in Structure U. Fig 16. Stages 7-8. **Gl 3**. SD, G P109.

[537] Wall Structure V2. Figs 13, 14. Stages 8-9. Samian. Saddle quern.

[538] Wall of Structure V1. Figs 13, 14. Stage 7.

[541] Structure V2 paving. Figs 13, 14. Stages 8-9. BB1, SD P29, G P30.

[542] Structure V2 interior drain. Figs 13, 14. Stages 8-9. SD P22, G P76 P144.

[545] Pit associated with latest surface [546] in Structure V. Fig 13. Stage 10. G. **S12** stone trough.

[546] Structure V3 surface. Fig 14 (not on plan). Stage 10. **P4** Oxfordshire, SD, G **P32 P56** P134.

[546A] Soil on surface [541] Structure V2. Fig 14. Stages 9/10.

[548] Structure V1, soil inside wall [538]. Fig 14. Stages 7/8. SD P22, G P29.

[551] Late phase cobbling between Structures U and V2. Fig 13. Stage 8.

[553] Surface in entrance of late phase Structure U. Fig 16. Stages 7-8.

[555] Surface outside Structure V2. Figs 13, 14. Stage 8. Samian Dr 31 + 1, Lezoux colour-coat. Exeter fabric 125, SD P22 P25 P27, G P30 P58 P65 P101 **P106** P118, P134. **S14** stone mould, **S20** whetstone, **S40** shale bracelet.

[557] Surface beneath Structure V contemporary with Entrance paving [188]. Stage 5. Figs 10, 14, 16. **Gl 19**. SD, G. **S41** shale bracelet.

[560] Gulley, later outlet for drain [579], Structure U. Figs 8, 16. Stage 5. Samian, Lezoux colour-coat, G P48 P96.

[567] Secondary Ditch silts in terminals. Fig 7. Stages 2-4? Samian Dr 27, SD, G **P30** P48 P101, M/PMED. **S9** Cornish mortar.

[568] Primary silt in Ditch terminals. Fig 7. Stage 1? Smithing slag. G **P29 P31**.

[568A] Deliberate infill in Ditch terminals. Fig 7. Predates Stage 5.

[573] Gulley related to drain [579], Structure U. Figs 8, 14, 16. Stage 5. SD, G.

[574] Pit outside Structure V, probably late phase. Fig 13. Stage 10.

[575] Pit associated with V Phase 1. Fig 13. Stage 7.

[576] Posthole beneath cobbles [557]. ?Period 3 Enclosure. Figs 8, 14.

[576A] Entrance posthole to Structure V2. Fig 13. 0.20m. Stages 8-9.

[577] Posthole beneath cobbles [557]. ?Period 3 Enclosure. Fig 8.

[578] Central posthole in Structure V2. Fig 13. 0.30m. Stages 8-9.

[579] Drain through Structure U. Fig 16. Stage 5.

[581] Posthole beneath cobbles [557]. ?Period 3 Enclosure. Fig 8. G.

[582] Posthole beneath cobbles [557]. ?Period 3 Enclosure. Fig 8.

[584] Stakeholes associated with V1. Fig 13. Stage 7.

[587] Drain through Period 3 Enclosure Bank. Fig 8.

[588] Posthole beneath cobbles [557]. ?Period 3 Enclosure. Fig 8.

[589] Drain through Period 3 Enclosure Bank. Figs 7, 8, 14.

[590] Period 4 posthole between Period 3 Enclosure and Round. Fig 8.

[591] Posthole beneath cobbles [557]. ?Period 3 Enclosure. Fig 8.

[652] House X1 slot. Fig 25. Stages 1-2.

[654] House X posthole. Fig 25. 0.10m.

[655A] House X1 posthole. Figs 25, 28. 0.15m. Stage 1?

[655B] House X1 posthole. Figs 25, 28. 0.10m. Stage 2?

[656] House X narrow slot. Fig 25.

[657] House X posthole. Fig 25. 0.15m.

[658A] House X1 posthole. Figs 25, 28. 0.25m. Stage 1?

[658B] House X1 posthole. Figs 25, 28. 0.20m. Stage 2?

[659A] House X posthole. Fig 25. 0.10m.

[659B] House X posthole. Fig 25. 0.12m.

[660] House X posthole. Fig 25. 0.28m. G.

[661] House X posthole. Fig 25. 0.10m.

[661A] House X narrow slot. Fig 25.

[662A] House X posthole. Fig 25. 0.20m.

[662B] House X hearth pit. Fig 25. Stage 5.

[662C] House X posthole. Fig 25. 0.25m.

[663A] House X hearth pit. Fig 25. Stages 3,4.

[663B] House X posthole. Fig 25. 0.15m.

[664A] House X posthole. Fig 25. 0.30m. G **P105**.

[664B] House X posthole. Fig 25. 0.10m.

[664C] House X posthole. Fig 25. 0.20m.

[664D] House X posthole. Fig 25. 0.25m.

[664E] House X posthole. Fig 25. 0.10m.

[665] House X2 slot. Figs 25, 26. Stages 3-4.

[666] Walling House X4. Fig 25. Stage 9. Schorl. Bii, G.

[667] Drain ?connected with House X4. Fig 25. Stage 9.

[668] Paving outside House X. Fig 25. G.

[669] Walling House X4. Figs 25, 26. Stage 9.

[670] House X stakehole. Fig 25.

[671] House X narrow slot. Fig 25.

[673] House X posthole. Fig 25. 0.19m.

[674] House X hearth pit. Figs 25, 26, 27. Stages 1-2. G.

[675] House X hearth pit. Figs 25, 26. Stage 9.

[676] House X posthole. Fig 25. 0.20m. **S3** Trethurgy bowl.

[677] Structure X5 bank. Fig 25. Stage 10.

[678] Soil under paving [933] and outside House X. Fig 25. M/PMED. S1 Trethurgy bowl, **S22** whetstone, **S41** shale bracelet.

[679] Paving outside House X entrance. Figs 25, 26. Stage 9. SD, G.

[680] Walling House X4. Fig 25. Stage 9.

[681] House X1 slot. Figs 25, 26. Stages 1-2.

[682] House X posthole. Fig 25. 0.15m.

[683] Structure X5 bank. Figs 25, 26. Stage 10.

[685] House X1 slot. Fig 25. Stages 1-2. G **P135**.

[686] House X narrow slot. Fig 25.

[687] Soil over House X, predating Structure X5. Fig 26. Stages 9/10. BB1 **P15**, South-Western Grey storage jar, SD.

[689A] House X posthole. Fig 25. G.

[689B] House X hearth pit. Fig 25. Stages 6-7. G.

[690] House X posthole. Fig 25. 0.10m.

[692] House X posthole. Figs 25, 26. 0.25m.

[693] House X posthole. Fig 25. 0.21m.

[694] House X posthole. Fig 25. 0.21m.

[695] House X posthole. Fig 25. 0.24m. G.

[696] House X posthole. Fig 25. 0.24m.

[697] House X posthole. Fig 25. 0.08m. SD.

[698] House X posthole. Fig 25. 0.08m.

[699] House X1 posthole. Figs 25, 28. 0.15m. ?Stages 1-2

[700] House X stakehole. Fig 25.

[701] House X posthole. Fig 25. 0.10m.

[702] House X posthole. Fig 25. 0.15m.

[703] House X posthole. Fig 25. 0.10m. ?Stage 1.

[706] House X posthole. Fig 25. 0.08m.

[707] House X narrow slot. Fig 25.

[708] House X narrow slot. Fig 25.

[709] House X posthole. Fig 25. 0.15m.

[710] House X posthole. Fig 25. 0.10m.

[711A] House X posthole. Fig 25. 0.10m.

[711B] House X posthole. Figs 25, 26. 0.10m.

[712] House X narrow slot. Fig 25.

[712A] House X posthole. Fig 25. 0.15m.

[713A] House X posthole. Fig 25. 0.20m.

[713B] House X posthole. Fig 25. 0.20m.

[714] House X. Scoop with stakeholes. Fig 25. 0.10m.

[715] House X stakehole. Fig 25.

[716] House X posthole. Fig 25. 0.10m.

[717] House X posthole. Fig 25. 0.10m.

[718] House X posthole. Fig 25. 0.15m.

[719] House X posthole. Fig 25. 0.17m.

[720] House X1 posthole. Figs 25, 28. 0.10m.

[721] House X posthole. Fig 25. 0.10m.

[722] House Z2 wall. Figs 20, 21. Stage 4?, Stages 6-9. BB1 P20, SD (oblique lattice), G P35 P37 P44 P65 P73, M/PMED. Saddle quern.

[723] House Z, soil and tumble over. Fig 21. Stages 9 onwards. **M8** iron rake prong. **Gl 7, Gl 22**. Samian spindle whorl, Dressel 1, Dressel 20 amphora, P2 Oxfordshire, BB1, SD P22, G P38 P43 P56 P57 P59 P108 **P131 P139**. Slate disc, **S26** rubbing stone, **S34** spindle whorl, **S40** shale bracelet.

[724] House X posthole. Fig 25. 0.15m.

[725] House X1 posthole. Figs 25, 28. 0.10m.

[727] House X1 slot. Figs 25, 28. Stages 1-2.

[728] Surface in Structure Y. Fig 24. Stages 6-9. Samian, Palestinian amphora (20), Bi, Bii **P11**, Biv **P12, P5** Oxfordshire, G P40 P55 P81 P83 P99, M/PMED. **S35** slate disc.

[729] House X stakehole. Fig 25.

[730] House X posthole. Fig 25. 0.12m.

[731] House X1 slot. Figs 25, 28. Stages 1-2.

[732] Posthole north of House X. Fig 25. 0.16m. G.

[733] Posthole north of House X. Fig 25. 0.10m.

[734] House X3 slot. Figs 25, 27. Stages 5-7. G.

[735] House X posthole. Fig 25. 0.10m.

[736] House X posthole. Fig 25. 0.05m.

[738] House X posthole. Fig 25. 0.09m.

[740] Posthole north of House X. Fig 25. 0.18m.

[741] Stakehole north of House X. Fig 25. 0.10m.

[742] House X narrow slot. Fig 25.

[743] House X4 gulley. Figs 25, 27, 28. Stage 9. Samian, ?Post-Roman coarse ware fabric 1, Bii, **P28** (BB1 copy), M/PMED.

[744] House X stakehole. Fig 25.

[745] Posthole beneath gulley [665], House X. Fig 25. 0.12m.

[747] House X stakehole. Fig 25.

[749] Tumble from Structure Y. Fig 12. Stage 9 onward.

[751] Soil surface between Structure Y and wall [892]. Figs 11, 19, 20, 21. Stage 6+. Samian Dr 31 Dr 45, BB1 P18, Exeter fabric 101, SD P22, G P30 P46 **P50** P69 P72 **P95** P96 P113 **P128** P130 P141, M/PMED.

[751A] Soil beneath Structure Y. Figs 11, 20. Up to Stage 6. **C1, 2, 3, 6, 7, 9** coins of mid 3rd-century hoard. BB1 **P18**, SD with cordon, G **P46** P93 P142.

[752] House Z2, surface of soil [808] used as floor. Figs 17, 18. Stages 6-9. BB1 P16.

[753] House X posthole. Figs 22, 23. 0.20m.

[757] House X posthole. Fig 25. 0.22m.

[758] House X posthole. Fig 25. 0.18m.

[761] House Z1, external gulley. Figs 11, 16, 18. Stage 3. G **P35** **P68** P101 **P102** **P124**.

[762] Wall of Structure Y. Fig 24. Stages 6-9. **S42** rotary quern.

[763] Wall of Structure Y. Figs 11, 21. Stages 6-9.

[764] House Z1, external gulley. Figs 11, 16, 18. Stage 2. G.

[765] House Z1, earliest external gulley. Figs 16, 18. Stage 1.

[768] House X1 posthole. Figs 25, 28. 0.25m.

[769] House X1 posthole. Figs 25, 28. 0.24m.

[770] House X1 posthole. Figs 25, 28. 0.17m. Stages 1-2.

[771] House X posthole. Fig 25. 0.15m.

[773] House X posthole. Figs 25, 26. 0.25m.

[774A] Hearth on soil [751A] predating Structure Y. Fig 24. Stage 5.

[774B] Hearth on soil [751A] predating Structure Y. Fig 24. Stage 5.

[776] House Z2 hearth pit. Figs 20, 21, 27. Stage 6. G P44 P96.

[777] House Z2 paving. Figs 20, 21. Stages 6-9. Saddle quern.

[777A] House Z2 entrance paving. Fig 20. Stages 6-9.

[780] Spread Period 3 Enclosure Bank material. Fig 12. Samian (2), ?Bii (2), Biv, BB1, SD, G P29 P34 P48 P49 P58 **P107** P118, M/PMED. **S31** spindle whorl, **S35** slate disc.

[781] House X stakehole. Fig 25.

[782] House X stakehole. Fig 25.

[783] House X, posthole outside. Fig 25. 0.10m.

[784] House X, posthole outside. Fig 25. 0.15m.

[785] Soil over Structure Y. Fig 12. **C4, 5, 8** coins from mid-3rd century hoard. Phocaean Red Slip ware (2) , Palestinian amphora, Bii, BB1, SD, G P34 P49 P56(2) P64 **P79** P81 P82 P96 **P97** P110, M/PMED. **S4** Trethurgy bowl, slate disc, **S30** spindle whorl.

[787] Internal feature Structure Y. Fig 24. Stages 6-9.

[790] Posthole in exterior paving [679] of House X. Fig 25. 0.20m. ?Stage 9

[792] House X posthole. Fig 25. 0.30m.

[793] House Z2, cut for wall [722]. Figs 20, 21. Stage 4 or 6. **Gl 18**. M/PMED.

[794] Internal feature in Structure Y. Fig 24. Stages 6-9.

[796] House X posthole. Fig 25. 0.30m.

[800] Soil over Structure U. Fig 17. Copper alloy stud fragment. **M10** ?iron candlestick, **M22** iron spearhead. **Gl 12**. Samian (9), P2 **P3** + other Oxfordshire, Bii (6 + ?2), BB1 P21, SD P22 P27, G P48 P56 P96(4) P101(2) P104(2) P142 + 20 jar rims 8 Cornish flanged bowl rims, M/PMED. **S7** Cornish mortar, **S10** Cornish mortar, **S21** whetstone, **S37, S39** shale bracelets. **S44** rotary quern **S47** rotary quern.

[801] Upper soil/midden, interior of Structure U. Fig 17. Stage 6. **M7** iron slicker, **M12** iron handle, iron cleat, **M24** iron fork. **Gl 4, Gl 15**. Samian Dr 31 Dr 45(2) + 8, Lezoux colour-coat, P6 white ware import, Dressel 20 amphora, Bii, Oxfordshire P2 P4, Exeter fabric 451, BB1 P14 P16 P17 **P21**, SD **P23**(2) P26 **P27**(4) G P38 **P45** **P47** **P55** **P57**(2) **P58** **P65** **P74** **P75** **P96** P101(6) P102 **P103** P104(2) **P117** **P118**(2) **P119** **P120** **P122** P123 P125 **P126** P132, M/PMED. **S38** shale bracelet, **S49** rotary quern.

[804] House X1 posthole. Figs 25, 28. 0.20m. Stages 1-2.

[805] House Z clearance stonehole. Fig 19. Stage 6. G.

[808] Soil between Z1 and Z2. Figs 21, 23. Stages 4/6. Smithing slag. Samian Walters 81 + 2, Dressel 20 amphora (4), BB1 P18 P21, SD **P22 P26**, G P30 P44 **P59** P65 P116 **P144. S43** rotary quern.

[808] Continuation in Q of soil between Z1 and 2 but not sealed. Fig 23. Stages 4/6. **M4** iron stock, **M13** iron knife, **M23** iron cleaver. Samian, BB1, SD, G P35 P45 P47 P54 P74 **P81** P93 P101 P110 **P113**(2) P139 P144, M/PMED. **S4** Trethurgy bowl (2).

[810] Post socket in House X1 slot. Figs 25, 28. 0.25m. Stages 1-2.

[811] Post socket in House X1 slot. Figs 25, 28. 0.25m. Stages 1-2.

[812] Post socket in House X1 slot. Figs 25, 28. 0.25m. Stages 1-2.

[815] House Z1, posthole outside. Fig 19. 0.10m.

[816] House Z1, posthole outside. Fig 19. 0.10m.

[817] Stakehole outside House Z1. Fig 19. 0.10m.

[818] Pit/sump in House Z1 floor [949]. Fig 19. Stage 4. **Gl 17**. BB1, G P66.

[819] House Z clearance stonehole. Fig 19. Stage 1.

[820] House Z clearance stonehole. Fig 19. Stage 1.

[821] House Z clearance stonehole. Fig 19. Stage 1.

[826] Posthole related to Structure Y. Fig 24. Stage 6.

[827] Posthole related to Structure Y. Fig 24. Stage 6.

[828] House Z2 external drain. Fig 20. Stages 6-9. G.

[832] House Z1, posthole outside. Fig 19. 0.10m.

[833] House Z1 stakehole. Fig 19. Stages 1-4.

[834] House Z1 stakehole. Fig 19. Stages 1-4.

[835] House Z1 stakehole. Fig 19. Stages 1-4.

[836] House Z1 stakehole. Fig 19. Stages 1-4.

[837] House Z1 stakehole. Fig 19. Stages 1-4.

[838] Posthole outside Structure Y. Fig 24. ?Stage 5

[839] Posthole outside Structure Y. Fig 24. Stage 5.

[840] House Z2 posthole. Fig 20. Stages 6-9. G.

[842] House Z2 posthole. Fig 20. Stages 6-9. G.

[844] House Z1 posthole. Fig 19. 0.25m. Stages 1-4.

[846] House Z1 hearth pit. Fig 19. Stages 1-4.

[847] House Z2 hearth pit. Fig 20. Stage 9.

[849] House Z2 hearth pit. Figs 20, 21. Stage 7. G. UB-3251 1641±60 BP.

[850] House Z2 hearth pit. Fig 20. Stage 8. SD, G P44, P65.

[850A] House Z1 posthole. Fig 19. 0.30m. Stages 1-4.

[852] House Z1 drain. Figs 19, 21. Stages 1-4. Copper alloy bracelet fragments. **Gl 14**. BB1 P21, SD P22, G P48 P67 **P73** P101(2) P104 P121.

[853] House Z1 posthole. Figs 19, 21. 0.10m. Stages 1-4.

[854] House Z1 floor, west part. Figs 12, 19, 21. Stages 1-4.

[855] House Z1 posthole. Fig 19. 0.10m. Stages 1-3.

[856] House Z1 posthole. Fig 19. 0.20m. Stages 1-3.

[858] House Z2 slot in paving [777]. Figs 20, 21. Stages 6-9. SD, G P126.

[859] House Z1 drain. Fig 19. Stages 1-4.

[860] House Z2 continuation of drain [878]. Fig 20. Stages 6-9.

[861] House Z2 bedding for paving [777]. Fig 21. Stage 6. BB1, G P34 **P54**.

[863] House Z2 drain. Fig 20. Stages 6-9. G P57 P64. **S25** rubbing stone, **S28** spindle whorl.

[864] House Z1 drain. Fig 19. Stages 1-4.

[865] House Z1 posthole. Fig 19. 0.15m. Stages 1-3.

[866] House Z1 posthole. Fig 19. 0.25m. Stages 1-3.

[867] House Z1 posthole. Fig 19. 0.30m. Stages 1-3.

[870] House Z1 posthole. Fig 19. 0.15m. Stages 1-3.

[871] House Z1 posthole. Fig 19. 0.15m. Stages 1-4.

[873] House Z2 external drain. Fig 20. Stages 6-9.

[874] Soil in cut [951] outside Structure U. Fig 23. Stages 5+. G P37 **P40**.

[876] Stakeholes in House Z1. Fig 19. Stages 1-4.

[878] House Z2 internal drain. Figs 12, 20, 21. Stages 6-9. G.

[879A] House Z1 posthole. Fig 19. 0.15m. Stages 1-4.

[879B] House Z1 posthole. Fig 19. 0.15m. Stages 1-4.

[880] House Z1 posthole. Fig 19. 0.10m. Stages 1-4.

[881] House Z1 stakeholes. Fig 19. Stages 1-4.

[883] House Z1 posthole. Fig 19. 0.15m. Stages 1-3.

[884] House Z1 posthole. Fig 19. 0.30m. Stages 1-3. UB-3255 1768 ± 47 BP.

[886] House Z clearance stonehole. Fig 19. Stage 1.

[887] Structure Q1 gulley associated levelling [903]. Fig 9. Stage 1.

[889] House Z clearance stonehole. Fig 19. Stage 1.

[890] Structure U wall. Figs 16, 17, 18. Stage 5. Dressel 20 amphora, BB1 **P20**, G P101 **P108**.

[891] Structure U2 wall. Figs 16, 17. Stages 7-8.

[892] Wall in Structures Q3-5, associated with levelling cut [916] in Q3. Stages 3-6. Figs 22, 23.

[894] Structure Q2 posthole on surface [927]. Fig 9. 0.25m. Stage 2.

[903] Structure Q1 levelling. Figs 9, 23. Stage 1.

[904] Soil on levelling [903]. Fig 23. Stage 1.

[905] Soil dumped and revetted by walls [907]/[911] in Structure Q5. Figs 22, 23. Stage 4. Cassiterite pebble. Samian, G P29 P31 P58 P66 **P72** P113 P130.

[906] Cobble patch on surface [905] in Structure Q5. Fig 22. Stage 4.

[907] Wall making platform with [911] in Structure Q5. Also ?part of House Z1. Figs 22, 23. Stage 4.

[907A] Tumble from wall [907] in Q. Fig 23. Stages 4/5. Samian, Phocean Red Slip ware, South-Western Grey storage jar, SD P27, G P37 P80. **S48** rotary quern.

[910] Drain associated with wall [911] in Structure Q5. Fig 22. Stage 4. BB1 P21, G **P52** P142.

[911] Wall making platform with [907] in Structure Q5. Fig 22. Stage 4.

[912] Drain in wall [892] in Structure Q3. Fig 22. Stage 3. G P47.

[914] Structure Q2 posthole on surface [927]. Fig 9. 0.20m. Stage 2.

[916] Structure Q3 levelling cut associated with wall [892]. Figs 22, 23. Stage 3.

[917] Drain set within Period 3 Enclosure Ditch. Figs 8, 17.

[920] Drain through Period 3 Enclosure Bank, fill ?Period 4. Fig 8. **M18** iron cleat. SD, G.

[922] Paving in Q (probably extension of [949] Z). Figs 22, 23. Stage 4.

[923] Dump on levelled surface [916] in Structure Q4. Figs 22, 23. Stage 4. Iron upholstery stud. G **P30a** P55 **P142**. UB-3253 1842±46 BP.

[924] Gulley in Periods 3/4 Structure N. Figs 9, 12, 23. BB1, G **P87**.

[924A] Levelling associated with Periods 3/4 Structure N gulley [924]. Figs 9, 12.

[925] Infill of Periods 3 /4 Structure N [924A]. Fig 12.

[926] Trampled soil on Periods 3/4 levelling [924A], Structure N. Figs 9, 12.

[927] Structure Q2 surface associated with post line [894] - [914]. Figs 9, 23. Stage 2.

[929] Structure Q2 posthole. Fig 9. 0.20m. Stage 2.

[930] Structure Q2 posthole. Fig 9. 0.20m. Stage 2.

[931] Gulley delimiting dump [923] in Structure Q4. Figs 22, 23. Stage 4. Samian, G **P88** **P90** P99.

[932] Lower soil/midden, interior of Structure U. Figs 17, 23. Stage 6. **M1** brooch, **M3** tin ingot. Iron loop, **M9** iron pin, **M16** iron double-spiked loop. **Gl 5, Gl 6, Gl 11**. Samian Dr 37 Dr45 + 4, Lezoux colour-coat, **P2** Oxfordshire (3) & 4 other, Exeter fabric 101, BB1 **P16 P17 P19**, SD P22 P27, G **P34 P38 P47 P48 P49 P57 P61 P66 P69** P71 **P74** P99 **P101**(3) **P102**(2) **P103**(2) **P104**(2) **P110 P118 P120 P121 P123 P125 P126 P132 P134. S7** Cornish mortar, **S24** rubbing stone, **S39** shale bracelet, **S43, S50** rotary querns. UB-3250 1683±45 BP.

[933] Paving outside House X. Fig 25. ?Stage 9 or earlier.

[934] Bank between Z and Rampart, Structure Q6. Fig 22. Stages 6-9. **S17** net sinker.

[936A] Posthole in Periods 3/4 Structure N. Fig 9.

[936B] Posthole in Periods 3/4 Structure N. Fig 9.

[937A] Posthole in Periods 3/4 Structure N. Fig 9.

[937B] Posthole in Periods 3/4 Structure N. Fig 9.

[938A] Posthole in Periods 3/4 Structure N. Fig 9.

[938B] Posthole in Periods 3/4 Structure N. Fig 9.

[938C] Posthole in Periods 3/4 Structure N. Fig 9.

[938D] Posthole in Periods 3/4 Structure N. Fig 9.

[939] Pit ?associated with Period 3 Enclosure Bank on north-west. Figs 4, 24. 0.30m.

[939A] Posthole in levelled area [916], Structure Q3. Fig 22. 0.15m. Stage 3.

[940] ?Drain through Period 3 Enclosure Bank. Figs 4, 24.

[943A] Period 3 Enclosure Ditch upper silt on north west. Fig 12.

[944] Period 3 Enclosure Ditch primary silt on north west. Fig 12.

[945] Period 3 Enclosure Ditch, layer of deliberate infill on lip in north west. Fig 12.

[946] Stonehole on edge of Period 3 Enclosure Ditch. Fig 9.

[948] House Z1 soil beneath paving [949]. Fig 21. Stages 3/4. G P29 P69 P71 **P130**.

[949] House Z1 secondary floor in east part. Figs 19, 21. Stage 4.

[950] Paving inside Structure U. Figs 16, 17. Stage 5. G P72.

[951] Levelling probably connected with construction of Structure U. Fig 22. Stage 5.

[952A] Stakehole in Q. Fig 22. Stage 5.

[952B] Stakehole in Q. Fig 22. Stage 5.

[954] House Z1 posthole. Fig 19. 0.15m. Stages 1-3.

[957] Structure Q2 stakehole on surface [927]. Fig 9. Stage 2.

[958] Levelling for paving [949] in House Z1. Figs 19, 22. Stages 3/4.

[960] Two stakeholes sealed by Structure U. Fig 14.

[961] Stakehole sealed by Structure U. Fig 14. 0.10m.

[962] Door posthole in Structure U. Fig 14. Stage 5.

[962A] Door posthole for Structure U. Fig 14. Stage 5.

[963] Posthole sealed by Structure U. Fig 14. 0.15m.

[964] Stone-hole in Period 3 Enclosure Ditch. Figs 9, 12. 0.25m.

[965] Stakeholes associated with Periods 3/4 Structure N. Fig 9.

[966A] Posthole in Periods 3/4 Structure N. Fig 9.

[966B] Posthole in Periods 3/4 Structure N. Fig 9.

[966C] Structure Q2 posthole. 0.15m. Fig 9. Stage 2.

[966D] Structure Q2 posthole. Fig 9. 01.5m. Stage 2.

[967] House Z1 posthole. Figs 19, 21. 0.10m. Stages 1-4.

Appendix 2
Radiocarbon dates from Roman and Post-Roman Cornwall

Peter Marshall (text written 2001)

Results

The results, given in Appendix 2, are conventional radiocarbon ages (Stuiver and Polach 1977), and are quoted in accordance with the international standard known as the Trondheim convention (Stuiver and Kra 1986). Brief information on related ceramics has been compiled by Henrietta Quinnell: here C has been used to indicate the century AD, eg C2 the 2nd century AD. Sites are presented in alphabetical order. Principal references are: Atlantic Road (Reynolds forthcoming), Carn Euny (Christie 1978), Duckpool (Ratcliffe 1995), Killigrew (Cole forthcoming), Lanhainsworth (Lawson-Jones 2001), Little Quoit Farm (Lawson-Jones 2003), Penhale Round (Johnston *et al* 1998/9), Ruthvoes (Lawson-Jones 2001), Reawla (Appleton-Fox 1992), Shortlanesend (Harris 1980), Stencoose (Jones forthcoming), Tintagel (Morris and Harry 1997).

Calibration

The radiocarbon determinations have been calibrated with data from Stuiver *et al* (1998), using OxCal v3.5 (Bronk Ramsey 1995; 1998). The date ranges have been calculated according to the maximum intercept method (Stuiver and Reimer 1986), and are cited at both one sigma (68% confidence) and two sigma (95% confidence). They are quoted in the form recommended by Mook (1986), with the end points rounded outwards to 10 years if the error term is greater than or equal to 25 radiocarbon years, or to 5 years if it is less. The results are also presented graphically in Figs 96 - 97.

Laboratory Number	Material	Context	Radiocarbon Age (BP)	$\delta^{13}C$ (0)	Calibrated date range (68% confidence)	Calibrated date range (95% confidence)	Comments
Atlantic Road							
AA-39952	Bone: cattle tibia (C Ingrem)	From midden [14] around the outside edge of building [130]. Likely to be a rubbish dump created following the abandonment of the building	1785±35	-19.8	cal AD 210-330	cal AD 130-350	Ceramics end of Cordoned ware, mid-C2
AA-39953	Bone: cattle tibia (C Ingrem)	From fill of cut [27] of building hollow [108]. Possibly a levelling layer within the structure to facilitate the creation of the cultivation soil	1815±40	-21.0	cal AD 130-320	cal AD 80-340	Ceramics probably C3
AA-39954	Bone: cattle (C Ingrem)	From [30] Romano-British cultivation soil containing domestic rubbish	1640±40	-17.7	cal AD 380-440	cal AD 260-540	Ceramics late C3 - C4 including Type 22 Cornish flanged bowls; some possible continuation beyond C4
AA-39955	Bone: horse mandible (C Ingrem)	From [34] Romano-British occupation layer	1610±40	-20.9	cal AD 410-540	cal AD 340-550	Ceramics late C2 - early C3 with Type 20 bowl

AA-39956	Bone: cattle humerus (C Ingrem)	From shell midden [50]	1760±40	-20.7	cal AD 230-440	cal AD 130-400	Ceramics not closely dateable
AA-39957	Bone: cattle femur (C Ingrem)	From fill [91] of structure hollow [130]	1730±40	-18.0	cal AD 240-390	cal AD 220-420	Ceramics end of Cordoned ware with Type 20 bowl
AA-39958	Bone: various animals (C Ingrem)	From wall [130] packing within edge of building hollow	1830±40	-18.0	cal AD 120-350	cal AD 80-330	Type 20 bowls
AA-39959	Bone: cattle (C Ingrem)	From the fill of ditch [150]. Appears to be deliberate infilling using domestic refuse	2010±40	-19.3	50-cal BC-cal AD 60	110 cal BC-cal AD 80	Ceramics late C1 - early C2 ?
AA-39960	Bone: cattle (C Ingrem)	From the fill of pit [165]	2135±40	-21.7	350-90 cal BC	360-40 cal BC	No ceramics, broad context as [167]
AA-39961	Bone: various animal (C Ingrem)	From [167] the upper fill of a pit	2060±40	-22.0	160-1 cal BC	200 cal BC-cal AD 50	SW Decorated ware
AA-39962	Charcoal: elder	From fill [118] of a stone-lined hearth. Residue of *in-situ* hearth fire	2365±40	-25.2	410-390 cal BC	760-380 cal BC	No ceramics but stratigraphically over [34]

Laboratory Number	Material	Context	Radiocarbon Age (BP)	$\delta^{13}C$ (0)	Calibrated date range (68% confidence)	Calibrated date range (95% confidence)	Comments
Carn Euny							
HAR-335	Charcoal: *Quercus* sp. (S Limbrey)	From the brown earth fill of bell-shaped pit [34]; sealed by a rab floor	1860±100	-23.4	cal AD 20-320	cal AD 40-410	Pit with SW Decorated ware probably precedes Courtyard House IV
HAR-237	Charcoal: *Quercus* sp. (G C Morgan)	From the base of a thick charcoal layer below soil/stones, in pit [1] *c* 0.53m deep, sealed by *c* 0.5m accumulation of soil	1740±100	-25.3	cal AD 230- 400	cal AD 120- 440	Pit cuts surface postdating construction of Courtyard Houses II and III
Duckpool							
OxA-5069	Charcoal: *Salix/Populus* sp. (R Gale)	From the ash lining [50] of a pit which was only partially excavated but was at least 0.3m deep	1760±60	-25.2	cal AD 220- 390	cal AD 90-420	Pit relates to single activity phase, S Devon pottery tied to mid C4 group of coins. Estimated date range cal AD 130-343 (95% confidence)
OxA-5070	Charcoal: *Quercus* sp., sapwood (R Gale)	From the ash lining [50] of a pit which was only partially excavated but was at least 0.3m deep	1740±100	-24.3	cal AD 230-390	cal AD 130- 430	Pit relates to single activity phase, S Devon pottery tied to mid C4 group of coins. Estimated date range cal AD 14-344 (95% confidence)

Killigrew							
Wk-8333	Charcoal: Salicaceae *Salix/populus* (R Gale)	From charcoal deposit [93] in funnace [82]	2140±60	-26.0±0.2	350-50 cal BC	380-1 cal BC	No ceramics but range of those from site C2 to mid C3
Wk-8334	Charcoal: *Ulex/ Cystisus* (R Gale)	From thick burnt deposit [85] in funnace [82]	2040±70	-24.5±0.2	170 cal BC-cal AD 60	350 cal BC-cal AD 130	No ceramics but range of those from site C2 to mid C3
Lanhainsworth							
AA-36500	Charcoal: *Corylus* sp. (heartwood + nutshell), *Quercus* sp. (roundwood), *Prunus* sp. and *Ulex/Cytisus* sp. (J Jones)	From context [243] the fill of [242] a curvilinear or ring ditch	1530±45	-25.2	cal AD 430-600	cal AD 420- 640	Single Late Variant gabbroic sherd
AA-36501	Charcoal: *Betula* sp., *Corylus* sp., *Fraxinus* sp., *Quercus* sp. (heartwood) and *Ulex/Cytisus* sp. (J Jones)	From context [245] the fill of [244] a curvilinear or ring ditch	1575±45	-25.4	cal AD 420-540	cal AD 390- 610	Single gabbroic sherd either atypical collared urn or just possibly unique post-Roman
Little Quoit Farm							
AA-36503	Charcoal: *Quercus* sp. (sapwood) and *Ulex/Cytisus* sp. (J Jones)	From context [326] a pale bluish grey re-deposited natural clay/ decaying shillet from ditch [319]. Represents the upper or surviving layer of rampart [329]	1735±45	-25.5	cal AD 240-390	cal AD 170- 420	Phase 2 context without ceramics. Phase 2 has Type 22 Cornish flanged bowls, Type 16 storage jar.

Laboratory Number	Material	Context	Radiocarbon Age (BP)	$\delta^{13}C$ (0)	Calibrated date range (68% confidence)	Calibrated date range (95% confidence)	Comments
AA-36504	Charcoal: *Corylus* sp. (roundwood), *Quercus* sp. (roundwood), *Sambucus* sp. (roundwood) Pomoideae and *Salicaceae* (J Jones).	From context [381] the fill of a fire pit [337]	1750 ± 50	-25.8	cal AD 230-390	cal AD 130-420	Phase 2 context
AA-36505	Charcoal: *Alnus* sp. and *Quercus* sp. (sapwood) (J Jones)	From context [286] a burnt loamy clay with many charcoal flecks, the fill of [496], a rectangular feature	247 0 ± 45	-23.7	770-420 cal BC	800-400 cal BC	Phase 2 context which must contain redeposited material
Penhale Round							
AA-27530	*Corylus* charcoal (R Gale)	Context [45], part way up fill of inner ditch recut	1715 ± 55	-27.5	cal AD 240-410	cal AD 180-440	Dump of pottery late C3 or C4 with Type 22 Cornish flanged bowls
AA-27531	Salicaceae charcoal (R Gale)	Context [64], posthole in area of hut gulley [038]	1755 ± 55	-26.7	cal AD 230-390	cal AD 120-420	Type 16 storage jar sherds, most likely late C3 or C4
AA-27532	*Corylus* charcoal (R Gale)	Context [32], isolated pit	1850 ± 55	-28.0	cal AD 80-240	cal AD 20-330	Type 1 jar rim, early C2 or earlier

Ruthvoes							
AA-36499	Charcoal: *Alnus* sp., *Corylus* sp. (roundwood), *Betula* sp. and *Prunus* sp. (J Jones)	From context [407] the basal fill of [409] a fire pit/oven	1530±40	-25.6	cal AD 430-600	cal AD 420- 640	No ceramics but probable C4 material unstratified from site
Reawla							
UB-3180	Fragment of large wood	Lowest fill of hearth [324] in House B, derived from last use of hearth	1744±46	-25.8±0.2	cal AD 240-390	cal AD 130- 420	Type 16 storage jar late C3 to C4
UB-3181	Fragment of large wood	Midden [307] within House B		-26.2±0.2	cal AD 250-410	cal AD 240- 430	SE Dorset BB1 conical flanged bowl, eroded, late C3 or C4
UB-3182	Fragment of large wood	Midden deposit [148]	1619±46	-26.6±0.2	cal AD 400-540	cal AD 260-550	Eroded Oxfordshire, SE Dorset conical flanged bowls etc. Ceramics early C4 ?
UB-3183	Small branches	Fill [23] of depression left by abandonment of House A	1523±41	-29.1±0.2	cal AD 440-610	cal AD 420- 640	Ceramics include Oxfordshire, plain-rimmed S Devon bowl late C3+
UB-3184	Fragment of large wood	From[35] first backfill of outer defensive ditch	1496±42	-26.0±0.2	cal AD 530- 640	cal AD 430- 650	Deliberate demolition or collapse of rampart, no related ceramics

Laboratory Number	Material	Context	Radiocarbon Age (BP)	$\delta^{13}C$ (0)	Calibrated date range (68% confidence)	Calibrated date range (95% confidence)	Comments
Shortlanesend							
HAR-3428	Charcoal: *Quercus* sp. mainly from mature wood, but with some twig-sized fragments; also *Betula* sp. from mature timber and Leguminosae; *c* 50% identified (C A Keepax)	From pit [9], probable hearth pit	1830±80	-25.0	cal AD 80-330	cal AD 1-410	Pottery from site late C2 to early C3 including Type 20 bowls
HAR-3429	Charcoal: *Quercus* sp. and *Betula* sp. from mature timber with Leguminosae (eg *Ulex* sp.); *c* 50% identified (C A Keepax)	From pit [9], probable hearth pit	1780±90	-26.3	cal AD 120-390	cal AD 20-440	
HAR-3427	Charcoal: *Quercus* sp. mainly from mature timber and Leguminosae (eg *Ulex* sp.) and *Betula* sp. twigs; *c* 50% identified (C A Keepax)	From pit [10], probable hearth pit	1800±70	-25.7	cal AD 120-340	cal AD 60-410	
HAR-3424	Charcoal: *Quercus* sp. mainly from mature timber but with some twigs, with *Corylus/Alnus* sp. twigs; *c* 50% identified (C A Keepax)	From pit [10], probable hearth pit	1840±70	-26.5	cal AD 80-320	cal AD 20-390	

HAR-3430	Charcoal: *Quercus* sp. from twigs (less than 15-years-old) and mature wood, and Leguminosae (eg *Ulex* sp.) from twigs, and ?*Salix* sp. from twigs (less than 15-years-old); *c* 50% identified (C A Keepax)	From pit [11], probable hearth pit	1780±70	-25.9	cal AD 130-380	cal AD 70-420	
Stencoose							
Wk-5547	Charcoal: not *Quercus* sp.	From context [40], the middle of the fill of ditch [39]	1982±72	-25.1	50 cal BC- cal AD 120	170 cal BC-cal AD 220	Single sherd atypical SW Decorated - but ditch could be part of Later IA/Early RB system
Wk-5546	Charcoal: not *Quercus* sp.	From layer [52], an ashy deposit from behind Structure [60]	1520±81	-25.7	cal AD 420- 640	cal AD 380- 670	Occupation of Structure 60. Pottery dumped into Structure includes Type 22 Cornish flanged bowl
Wk-5548	Charcoal: not *Quercus* sp.	From wall [33] which formed the southern side of structure [60]	1445±80	-25.6	cal AD540-670	cal AD 420- 770	
Wk-5545	Charcoal: *Quercus* sp.	From context 47, the upper layer of burning within pit [45]	1000±80	-26.2	cal AD 980-1160	cal AD 880-1220	Hearth pit in Structure 60. Note no ceramics
Wk-5544	Charcoal: not *Quercus* sp.	From layer 5, the lowest fill in pit [2]	900±69	-25.5	cal AD 1020-1220	cal AD 990-1280	Used after Structure 60. Note no ceramics

Laboratory Number	Material	Context	Radiocarbon Age (BP)	$\delta^{13}C$ (0)	Calibrated date range (68% confidence)	Calibrated date range (95% confidence)	Comments
Tintagel							
UB-3795	Charcoal: 64.6g identified out of 176g: *Corylus* sp. (59g); *Prunus* sp. (0.7g), *Salix/Populus* sp. (2.8g), *Quercus* sp. (2.1g) (R Gale)	Charcoal from a burnt deposit [123]. [123] was overlying hearth setting [124], a flat stone surrounded by thin upright slates	1617±18	-26.4±0.2	cal AD 415-430	cal AD 400-535	Phase U2 local Roman wares and Post-Roman imports
UB-3796	Charcoal: 64.6g identified out of 176g: *Corylus* sp. (59g); *Prunus* sp. (0.7g), *Salix/Populus* sp. (2.8g), *Quercus* sp. (2.1g)	Charcoal from a burnt deposit [123]. [123] was overlying hearth setting [124], a flat stone surrounded by thin upright slates	1605±20	-26.3±0.2	cal AD 420-530	cal AD 405-540	Phase U2 local Roman wares and Post-Roman imports
UB-3797	Charcoal: 64g identified out of 168.6g; *Corylus/Alnus* sp. (29.1), *Quercus* sp. (17.8g), *Prunus* sp. (4.9g), Rosaceae, subfamily Pomoideae (0.7g), *Ulex/Cytisus* sp. (0.9g), *Salix/Populus* sp. (0.9g) (R Gale)	Charcoal from a burnt deposit [126]. [126] was overlying hearth setting [127], a depression in the scree lined by stones and clayey earth	1569±18	-26.6±0.2	cal AD 430-540	cal AD 425-560	Phase U2 local Roman wares and Post-Roman imports

UB-3798	Charcoal: 64g identified out of 168.6g; *Corylus/Alnus* sp. (29.1), *Quercus* sp. (17.8g), *Prunus* sp. (4.9g), Rosaceae, subfamily Pomoideae (0.7g), *Ulex/Cytisus* sp. (0.9g), *Salix/Populus* sp. (0.9g) (R Gale)	Charcoal from a burnt deposit [126]. [126] was overlying hearth setting [127], a depression in the scree lined by stones and clayey earth	1607±20	-25.4±0.2	cal AD 420-530	cal AD 405-540	Phase U2 local Roman wares and Post-Roman imports
UB-3883	Charcoal: 63g of which 10.7g (17%) identified, *Prunus* sp. (6.3g), bark (1.9g), *Pomoideae* (1.1g), *Corylus* sp. (1.0g), *Ulex/Cytisus* sp. (0.3g), *Sambucus* sp. (0.1g) (R Gale)	From fire pit [171/173]	1595±18	-25.8±0.2	cal AD 425-535	cal AD 415- 540	Phase Q2 late C4 or C5 glass
UB-3799	Charcoal: 13.8g identified out of 56.4g; *Corylus* sp. (5.6g), *Betula* sp. (2.2g), *Quercus* sp. (2.0g), *Ulex/Cytisus* sp. (2.2g), *Prunus* sp. cf. *P. spinosa* (1.2g), *Rosa/Ruba* sp. (0.1g), Rosaceae, subfamily Pomoideae (0.5g) (R Gale)	Charcoal from a burnt deposit [113]. [113] was contained within a possible floor deposit [111]	1645±22	-26.0±0.2	cal AD 395-430	cal AD 340-435	Phase W Post-Roman imports
OxA-6002	Charcoal: *Prunus* sp. (R Gale)	Charcoal from a burnt deposit [113]	1490±50	-26.2	cal AD 530-640	cal AD 430- 660	Phase W Post-Roman imports

Laboratory Number	Material	Context	Radiocarbon Age (BP)	$\delta^{13}C$ (0)	Calibrated date range (68% confidence)	Calibrated date range (95% confidence)	Comments
OxA-6003	Charcoal: *Prunus* sp. (R Gale)	Charcoal from a burnt deposit [113]	1550±45	-25.0	cal AD 430-600	cal AD 410- 620	Phase W Post-Roman imports
OxA-6004	Charcoal: *Betula* sp. (R Gale)	Charcoal from a burnt deposit [113]	1430±45	-26.1	cal AD600-660	cal AD 540- 680	Phase W Post-Roman imports
OxA-6005	Charcoal: *Ulex/Cytisus* sp. (R Gale)	Charcoal from a burnt deposit [113]	1705±50	25.5	cal AD 250-420	cal AD 230- 440	Phase W Post-Roman imports
OxA-6006	Charcoal: *Corylus* sp. (R Gale)	Charcoal from a burnt deposit [113]	1565±45	26.2	cal AD 420-560	cal AD 400- 620	Phase W Post-Roman imports

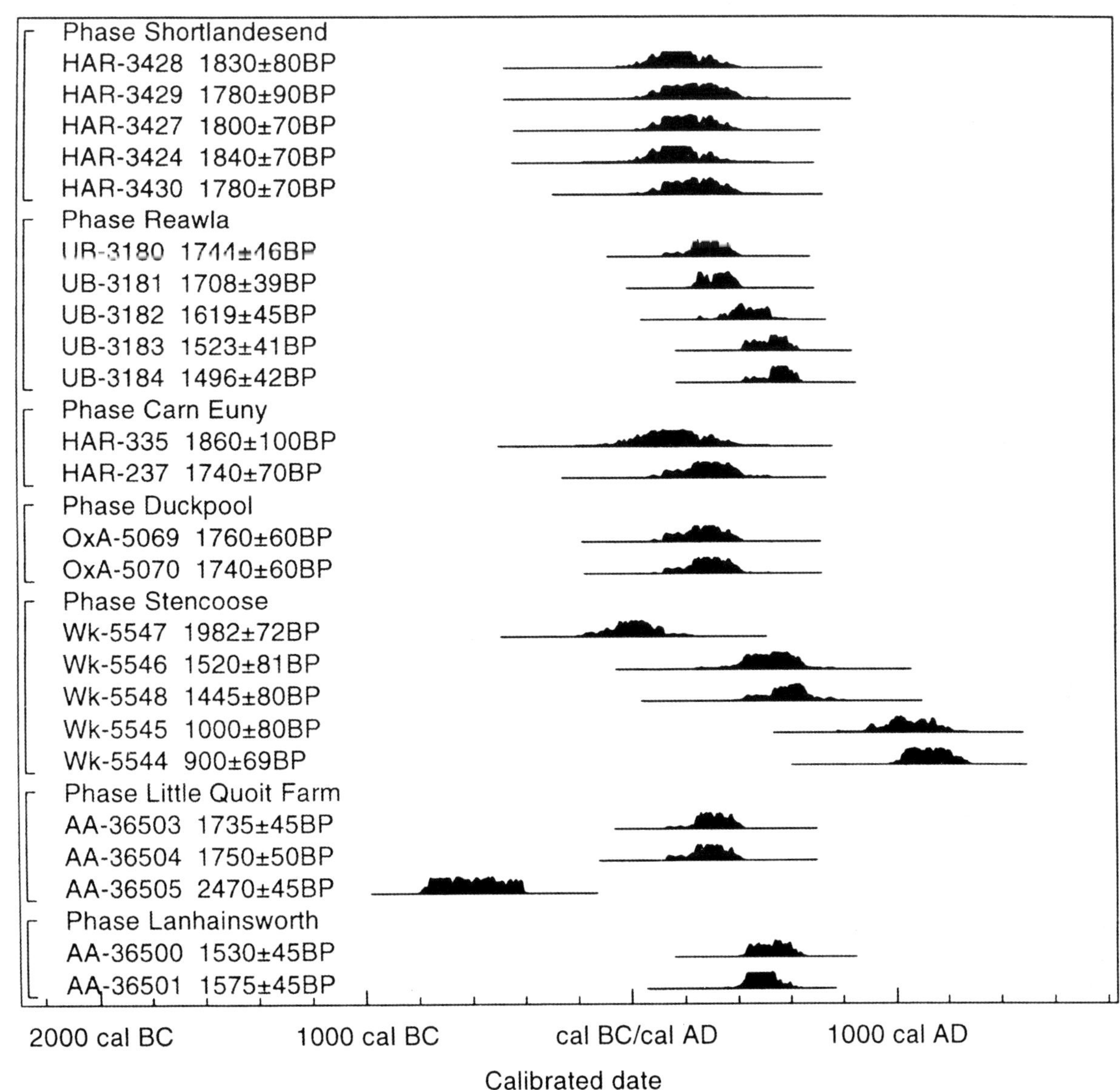

Fig 96: Probability distributions for radiocarbon dates for Roman and Post-Roman Cornwall (continued over)

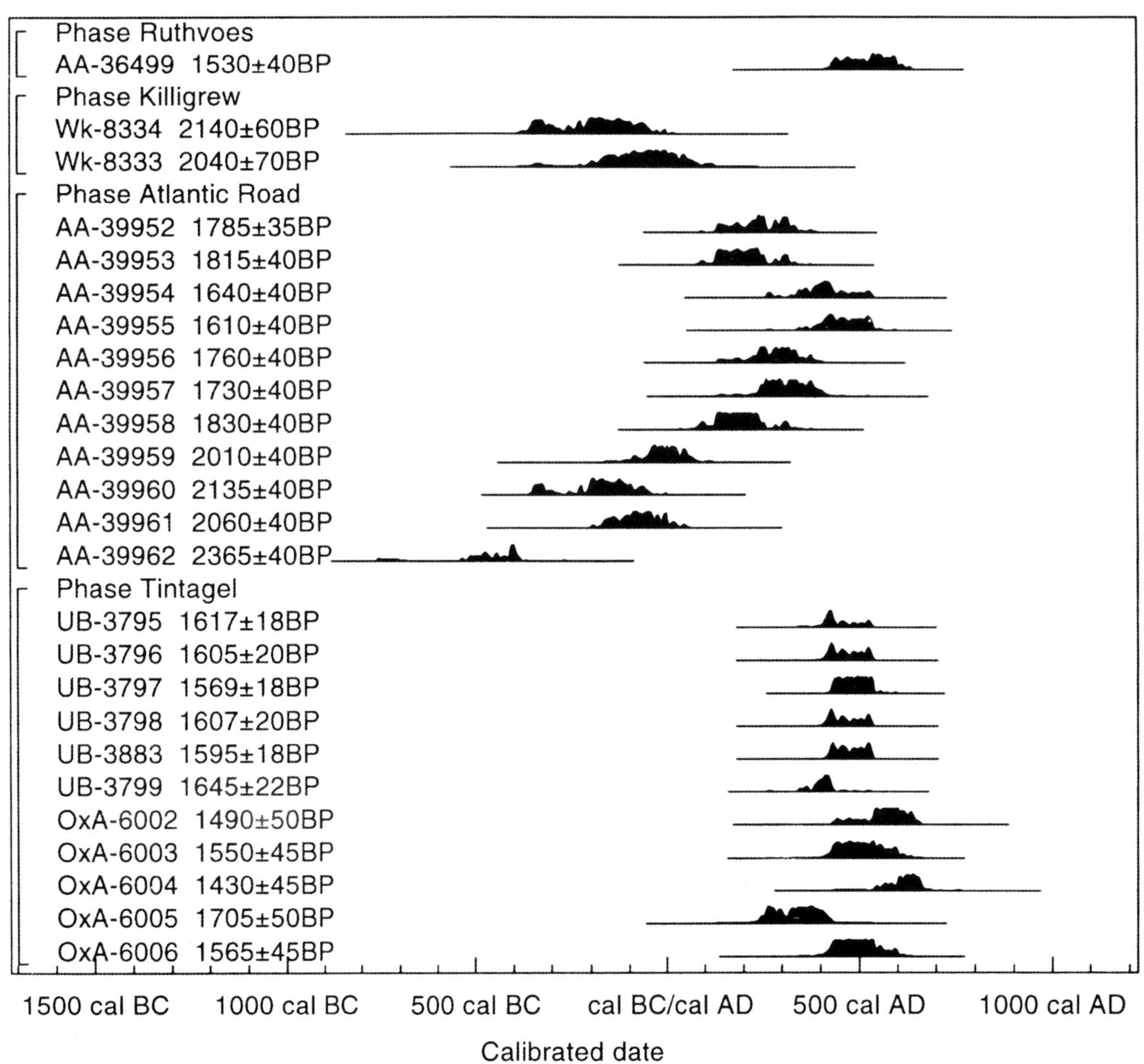

Fig 97: Probability distributions for radiocarbon dates for Roman and Post-Roman Cornwall continued

Bibliography

Adam, J-P, 1994. *Roman Building: Materials and Techniques*, London

Adkins, L, and Adkins, R, 1992. The glass, in Appleton-Fox 1992, 113

Alarcão, J, Delgado, M, Mayet, F, Moutinho Alarcão, A, and Ponte, S da, 1976. *Fouilles de Conimbriga, VI. Ceramiques Diverses et Verres*, Paris; Boccard

Alcock, L, 1963. *Dinas Powys*, Cardiff

Alcock, L, 1971. *Arthur's Britain*, London

Alcock, L, 1987. *Economy, Society and Warfare among the Britons and Saxons*, Cardiff

Alcock, L, with Stevenson, SJ, and Musson, CR, 1995. *Cadbury Castle, Somerset: The Early Medieval Archaeology*, Cardiff

Allason-Jones, L, 1991. Objects of amber, shale and jet, in Holbrook and Bidwell 1991, 271-4

Allen, D, 1991. The glass, in Holbrook and Bidwell 1991, 220-9

Allen, JRL, and Fulford, MG, 1996. The distribution of South-East Dorset Black Burnished category 1 pottery in South-West Britain, *Britannia* **27**, 223-82

Annis, MB, 1975. Amphora sixti, *Festoen Opgedragen aan A.N. Zadoks-Josephus Jitta bij haar zeventigste verjaardag*, Scripta Archaeological Groningana, **6**, 29-40

Appleton-Fox, N, 1992. Excavations at a Romano-British round: Reawla, Gwinear, Cornwall, *Cornish Archaeol*, **31**, 69-123

Applebaum, S, 1972. Roman Britain, in *The Agrarian History of England* (ed HPR Finberg), **1**, 3-282, Cambridge

ApSimon, AM, and Greenfield, E, 1972. The excavation of Bronze Age and Iron Age settlements at Trevisker, St Eval, Cornwall, *Proc Prehist Soc*, **38**, 302-81

Arbousse Bastide, T, 2000. *Les structures de l'habitat rural protohistorique dans le sud-ouest de l'Angleterre et le nord-ouest de la France,* BAR Int Ser **847**, Oxford

Ashbee, P, 1974. *Ancient Scilly*, Newton Abbot

Ashbee, P, 1996. Halangy Down, St. Mary's, Isles of Scilly, Excavations 1964-1977, *Cornish Archaeol*, **35**, 5-201

Baillie, M, 1995. *A Slice Through Time*, London

Baillie, M, 1999. *Exodus to Arthur*, London

Bayley, J, 1982. Castle Gotha, Cornwall: A metalworking site?, in Saunders and Harris 1982, 147-9

Bayley, J, 1985a. Brass and brooches in Roman Britain, *Masca Journ* 3 (**6**), 189-91

Bayley, J, 1985b. *Clay moulds from Compton Dando,* Ancient Monuments Laboratory Report No 4639

Bayley, J, 1992. Slag and other technological finds, in Appleton-Fox 1992, 114-16

Bayley, J, Dungworth, D, and Paynter, S, 2001. *Centre for Archaeology Guidelines: Archaeolometallurgy*, English Heritage

Bayley, J, and Butcher, S, forthcoming. *Roman brooches from Britain; a technological and typological study*, London, Society of Antiquaries

Bayliss, A, 1999. On the taphonomy of charcoal samples for radiocarbon dating, in *Actes du 3ème congrès international* 'Archéologie et 14C', Lyon, 6-10 Avril 1988 (eds J Evin, C Oberlin, J P Daugas, and JF Salles), *Revue d'Archéométrie Suppl 1999 et Soc Préhist Fr Mémoire* **26**, 51-6

Beacham, P, (ed), 1990. *Devon Building: An Introduction to Local Traditions*, Exeter

Beagrie, N, 1983. The St Mawes ingot, *Cornish Archaeol*, **22**, 107-11

Beagrie, N, 1985. Some early tin ingots, ores and slags from Western Europe, *J Hist Metal Stud*, **19:2**, 162-8

Beavis, J, 1970. Some aspects of the use of Purbeck Marble in Roman Britain, *Dorset Natur Hist Archaeol Soc Proc*, **92**, 181-204

Bell, M, 1981. Seaweed as a prehistoric resource, in *Environmental Aspects of Coasts and Islands* (eds D Brothwell and G Dimbleby), 117-26, BAR Int Ser **94**, Oxford

Bell, M, 1984. Environmental archaeology in South West England, in *Environmental Archaeology. A Regional Review* (ed HMC Keeley), 43-133, Directorate of Ancient Monuments Historic Buildings Occasional Paper **6**

Bennett, P, forthcoming. Roundhouses in the landscape, *Archaeol Wales*, (Currently at www.castell.henllys.com)

Benson, DG, Evans, JG, and Williams, GH, 1990. Excavations at Stackpole Warren, Dyfed, *Proc Prehist Soc*, **56**, 179-246

Beresford, G, 1975. *The Medieval Clay-land Village: Excavations at Goltho and Barton Blount*, Soc Medieval Archaeology Ser **6**, London

Bidwell, PT, 1979. *The Legionary Bath-house and Basilica and Forum at Exeter*, Exeter Archaeological Reports, **I**, Exeter

Bidwell, PT, 1982. The non-Cornish wares, in Carlyon 1982, 159-61

Bidwell, PT, and Silvester, R J, 1988. The Roman pottery, in Cunliffe 1988, 42-9

Biek, L, 1994. Tin ingots found at Praa Sands, Breage, in 1974, *Cornish Archaeol*, **33**, 57-70

Blaylock, SR, forthcoming. *Bowhill, Exeter, Devon: The archaeological study of a building under repair, 1977-1995*, English Heritage

Borlase, WC, 1870. Carn Euny, *Proc Soc Antiq London*, **2 ser 4**, 161-70

Borlase, WC, 1872. *Naenia Cornubiae*, London

Bowden, M, and McOmish, D, 1987. The required barrier, *Scottish Archaeol Review*, **4**, 84-97

Branigan, K, and Dearne, MJ, 1990. The Romano-British finds from Wookey Hole: a re-appraisal, *Somerset Archaeol Nat Hist*, **134**, 57-80

Britnell, WJ, 1989. The Collfryn hillslope enclosure, Llansantffraid Deuddwr, Powys: excavations 1980-1982, *Proc Prehist Soc*, **55**, 89-134

Bronk Ramsey, C, 1995. Radiocarbon calibration and analysis of stratigraphy:The OxCal Program, *Radiocarbon*, **37**, 425-30

Bronk Ramsey, C, 1998. Probability and dating, *Radiocarbon*, **40**, 461–74

Bronk Ramsey, C, 2000. Comment on 'The use of Bayesian statistics for 14C dates of chronological ordered samples: a critical analysis', *Radiocarbon*, **42**, 199-202

Brooks, RT, 1966. The Rumps: second interim report on the 1965 season, *Cornish Archaeol*, **5**, 4-10

Brooks, RT, 1974. The excavation of the Rumps, Cliff Castle, St Minver, Cornwall, *Cornish Archaeol*, **13**, 5-50

Brown, L, 1984. Objects of stone, in Cunliffe1984, 407-25

Brown, PDC, 1970. A Roman pewter mould from St Just in Penwith, Cornwall, *Cornish Archaeol*, **9**, 107-10

Buck, CE, Cavanagh, WG, and Litton, CD, 1996. *Bayesian Approach to Interpreting Archaeological Data*, Chichester

Burrow, ICG, 1979. Roman material from hillforts, in Casey 1979, 212-29

Burrow, I, 1981. *Hillfort and Hill-top Settlement in Somerset in the First to Eighth Centuries AD*, BAR Brit Ser **91**, Oxford

Butcher, S, forthcoming. The Roman period at Nornour, *Cornish Archaeol*

Campbell, E, 1996, Glass, in An early church and medieval farmstead site: excavations at Llanelen, Gower (A Schlesinger *et al*), *Archaeol J*, **153**, 125-7

Campbell, E, 1997. The Early Medieval vessel glass, in *Whithorn and St Ninian. The excavation of a monastic town, 1984-91* (P Hill), 297-314

Campbell, E, 2000. A review of glass vessels in western Britain and Ireland AD 400-800, in Price 2000d, 33-46

Carlyon, PM, 1982. A Romano-British site at Kilhallon, Tywardreath: Excavation in 1975, *Cornish Archaeol*, **21**, 155-170

Carlyon, PM, 1987. Finds from the earthwork at Carvossa, *Cornish Archaeol*, **26**, 103-141

Carlyon, PM, 1995. *Romano-British Gabbroic Pottery: a Summary of the Available Evidence in 1985*, Private desktop publication deposited at CAU and Royal Institution of Cornwall Library

Carlyon, PM, 1998/9. Kilhallon - an update, *Cornish Archaeol*, **37-8**, 132-6

Casey, PJ, 1979. *The End of Roman Britain*, BAR Brit Ser **71**, Oxford

Casey, PJ, and Hoffman, B, 1999. Excavations at the Roman Temple in Lydney Park, Gloucestershire in 1980 and 1981, *Antiq J*, **79**, 81-144

Casselberry, S, 1974. Further refinement of formulae for determining population from floor area, *World Archaeol*, **6:1**, 117-22

Chapman, H, 1982. Roman vehicle construction in the North West Provinces, in *Woodworking Techniques before AD1500* (ed S McGrail), 187-93, BAR Int Ser **129**, Oxford

Charles, FWB, 1982. The construction of buildings with irregularly-spaced posts, in Drury 1982, 101-12

Charlesworth, D, 1968. The glass, in Dudley 1968, 25-6

Charlesworth, D, 1979. Glass, in Bidwell 1979, 222-31

Charlesworth, D, and Price, J, 1987. The Roman glass, in Green 1987, 108-9, mf2 E11- F4

Christie, PM, 1978. The Excavation of an Iron Age souterrain and settlement Carn Euny, Sancreed, Cornwall, *Proc Prehist Soc*, **44**, 309-434

Christie, PM, 1979. Cornish souterrains in the light of recent research, *Bull Inst Archaeol Univ London*, **16**, 187-213

Christie, PM, 1985. Barrows on the North Cornish Coast: Wartime excavations by C K Croft Andrew 1939-44, *Cornish Archaeol*, **24**, 23-122

Clarke, G, 1979. *The Roman Cemetery at Lankhills,* Winchester Studies **3**

Clifton-Taylor, A, 1972. *The Pattern of English Building*, London

Coleman-Smith, R, and Pearson, T, 1988. *Excavations in the Donyatt Potteries*, Chichester

Cole, R, forthcoming. Excavations at Killigrew Round, Trispen, *Cornish Archaeol*

Coles, J and Minnitt, S, 1995. *Industrious and Fairly Civilised: The Glastonbury Lake Village*, Taunton.

Collins, JH, 1912. *Observations on the West of England Mining Region*, Plymouth

Collis, J, 1996. Hill-forts, enclosures and boundaries, in *The Iron Age in Britain and Ireland: Recent Trends* (eds TC Champion and JR Collis), 87-94, Sheffield

Cook, SF, and Heizer, RF, 1968. Relationships among houses, settlement areas and population in Aboriginal California, in *Settlement Archaeology* (ed KC Chang), 79-116, Palo Alto, California

Cool, HEM, 2000. The parts left over: material culture into the fifth century, in *The late Roman Transition in the North* (eds T Wilmott and P Wilson), BAR Brit Ser **299**, 47-65

Cool, HEM, and Price, J, 1995. *Roman Vessel Glass from Excavations in Colchester, 1971-85,* Colchester Archaeol Rep **8**, Colchester Archaeological Trust

Cox, J, and Thorp, JRL, 2001. *Devon Thatch: An Illustrated History of Thatching and Thatched Buildings in Devon*, Devon Books, Tiverton

Cox, M, 1993. *The Peat Moors Visitor Centre*, Taunton

Cunliffe, B, 1975. *Excavations at Porchester Castle*, **II**, Soc Antiq London Res Rep **33**

Cunliffe, B, 1984. *Danebury. An Iron Age Hillfort in Hampshire. Vol 2 The Excavations 1969-1978: the finds*, CBA Res Rep, **52**

Cunliffe, B, 1988. *Mount Batten, Plymouth: a Prehistoric and Roman Port*, Oxford University Committee for Archaeology Monograph **26**

Cunliffe, B, 1991. *Iron Age Communities in Britain*, 3rd edn, London

Cunliffe, B, and Poole, C, 1991. *Danebury. An Iron Age Hillfort in Hampshire. Vol 4 The Excavation 1979-1988: the site*, CBA Res Rep, **73**

Curle, J, 1911. *A Frontier Post and its People*, Glasgow

Curwen, EC, 1937. Querns, *Antiquity*, **11**, 133-51

Dark, KR, 1994a. *Discovery by Design: The identification of secular elite settlements in western Britain AD 400-700*, BAR Brit Ser, **237**, Oxford

Dark, KR, 1994b. *Civitas to Kingdom: British Political Continuity 300-800*, Leicester

Dark, KR, 2000. *Britain and the End of the Roman Empire*, Stroud

Dark, SP, 1996. Palaeoecological evidence for landscape continuity and change in Britain c AD 400-800, in *External Contacts and the Economy of Late Roman and Post-Roman Britain*, (ed KR Dark), 23-51, Woodbridge

Davies, JL, Hague, DB, and Mogg, AMA, 1971. The hut-settlement on Gateholm, Pembrokeshire, *Archaeol Cambrensis*, **120**, 102-10

Davies, W, 1982. *Wales in the Early Middle Ages*, Leicester

Davies, W, 1987. The ironwork, in Green 1987, 98-101

Dehling, H, and van der Plicht, J, 1993. Statistical problems in calibrating radiocarbon dates, *Radiocarbon*, **35**, 239-44

de la Bédoyère, G, 1991. *The Buildings of Roman Britain*, London

Dines, HE, 1956. *The Metalliferous Mining Region of South-West England*, HMSO, London

Dore, J, and Greene, K, 1977. *Roman Pottery Studies in Britain and Beyond*, BAR Int Ser **30**, Oxford

Drury, PJ, 1978. *Excavations at Little Waltham 1970-71*, CBA Res Rep **26**, London.

Drury, PJ, (ed), 1982. *Structural Reconstruction: Approaches to the interpretation of the excavated remains of buildings*, BAR Brit Ser **110**, Oxford

Dudley, D, 1956. An excavation at Bodrifty, Mulfra, near Penzance, *Archaeol J*, **113**, 1-32

Dudley, D, 1968. Excavations on Nornour in the Isles of Scilly 1962-66, *Archaeol J*, **124**, 1-64

Dudley, D, and Minter, EM, 1966. The excavation of a medieval settlement at Treworld, Lesnewth, 1963, *Cornish Archaeol*, **5**, 34-58

Edwards, N, 1990. *The Archaeology of Early Christian Ireland*, Batsford, London

Edwards, N, and Lane, A, 1988. *Early Medieval Settlement in Wales*, University Colleges of Bangor and Cardiff

Eggers, HJ, 1966. Römische Bronzegefasse in Britannien, *Jarbuch Römisch - Germ Zentralmus Hainz*, 67-164

Eidt, RC, 1984. *Advances in Abandoned Settlement Analysis*, University of Wisconsin-Milwaukee

Eldridge, D, 1978. *A Survey of Stone Mortars in Roman Britain*, Unpublished Dissertion Weymouth College of Further Education

Ellison, A, and Drewitt, P, 1971. Pits and post-holes in the British Early Iron Age: some alternative explanations, *Proc Prehist Soc*, **37**, 183-94

Elsdon, SM, 1978. The pottery, in Christie 1978, 396-424

Empereur, J-Y, and Picon, M, 1989. Les regions de production d'amphores imperiales en Méditerranée orientale, in *Amphores Romaines et Histoire Economique: Dix ans de Recherche,* Coll. De L'École Francaise de Rome, **114**, 223-48

English Heritage, 2000. *Thatch and Thatching: a guidance note*, London

Esmonde Cleary, AS, 1989. *The Ending of Roman Britain*, London

Evans, EE, 1957. *Irish Folk Ways,* London

Evans, JD, 1959. *Malta*, London

Fasham, PJ, Kelly, RS, Mason, MA, and White, RB, 1998. *The Graenog Ridge: The Evolution of a Farming Landscape and its Settlements in North-West Wales*, Cambrian Archaeological Monographs **6**

Faulkner, N, 2000. *The Decline and Fall of Roman Britain*, Stroud

Fearn, J, 1995. *Thatch and Thatching*, Princes Risborough

Fitzpatrick, AP, 1985. The Distribution of Dressel 1 Amphorae in North-West Europe, *Oxford J Archaeol*, **4:3**, 305-40

Fitzpatrick, AP, forthcoming. Roman Amphorae from pre-Roman Cornwall: pre-Roman, Roman or post-Roman?, *Cornish Archaeol*

Fitzpatrick, AP, Butterworth, CA, and Grove, J, 1999. *Prehistoric and Roman Sites in East Devon: the A30 Honiton to Exeter Improvement DBFO Scheme, 1996-9,* **1**, Wessex Archaeology

Forestry Commission, 1968. *Know Your Broadleaves*, Forestry Commission Booklet **20**, HMSO

Fowler, PJ, 1962. A Native Homestead of the Roman Period at Porth Godrevy, Gwithian, *Cornish Archaeol*, **1**, 17-60

Fox, A, 1955. A Dark Age trading site at Bantham, S Devon, *Antiq J*, **35**, 55-67

Fox, A, 1964. *South West England* (1st edn), London

Fox, A, 1966. The pottery, in Masson Phillips 1966, 17-23

Fox, A, 1995. Tin ingots from Bigbury Bay, *Proc Devon Archaeol Soc,* **53**, 11-24

Fox, A, and Ravenhill, WLD, 1969. Excavations of a rectilinear earthwork at Trevinnick, St Kew, 1968, *Cornish Archaeol*, **8**, 89-97

Fox, A, and Ravenhill, WLD, 1972. The Roman fort at Nanstallon, Cornwall, *Britannia*, **3**, 56-111

Fox, C, 1931. Sleds, carts and waggons, *Antiquity*, **5**, 185-99

Foy, D, 1995a. Le verre de la fin du IVe au VIIIe siècle en France méditerranéenne, premier essai de typo-chronologie, in Foy (ed) 1995b, 187-242

Foy, D (ed), 1995b. *Le verre de l'Antiquité tardive et du haut Moyen Age: typologie – chronologie – diffusion.* Guery en Vexin; Association Française pour l'Archéologie du Verre/Musee Archéologique du Val d'Oise

Foy, D, and Hochuli-Gysel, A, 1995. Le verre en Aquitaine du IVe au IXe siècle, un état de la question, in Foy (ed) 1995b, 151-76

Friendship-Taylor, RM, and Friendship-Taylor, DE (eds), 1997. *From Round House to Roman Villa*, Upper Nene Archaeological Society, Northampton

Fulford, MG, 1989. Byzantium and Britain: a Mediterranean perspective on post-Roman Mediterranean imports in western Britain and Ireland, *Medieval Archaeol*, **33**, 1-6

Fulford, MG, and Peacock, DPS, 1984. *The Avenue du President Habib Bourgiba, Salambo; The pottery and other ceramic objects from the site,* Excavation at Carthage: the British Mission, **1:2**, Sheffield

Gamo Parras, B, 1995. Vidros de época visigoda en Espana, una aproximación, in Foy (ed) 1995b, 301-17

Gent, TH, and Quinnell, H, 1999a. Excavation of a causewayed enclosure and hillfort on Raddon Hill, Stockleigh Pomeroy, *Proc Devon Archaeol Soc*, **57**, 1-76

Gent, TH and Quinnell, H, 1999b. Salvage Recording on the Neolithic Site at Haldon Belvedere, *Proc Devon Archaeol Soc*, **57**, 77-104

Gerrard, S, 2000. *The Early British Tin Industry*, Stroud

Gillam, JP, 1970. *Types of Roman Coarse Pottery Vessels in Northern Britain*, 3rd edn, Newcastle

Gover, JE, 1948. *The Place Names of Cornwall*, ms at RIC, Truro

Green, CS, 1987. *Excavations at Poundbury. Volume I: The Settlements*, Dorset Natur Hist Archaeol Soc Monogr Ser **7**

Green, HS, 1980. *The Flint Arrowheads of the British Isles*, BAR Brit Ser **75**, Oxford

Greene, JP, and Greene, KT, 1970. A trial excavation at Clanacombe, Thurlestone, *Proc Devon Archaeol Soc*, **28**, 130-6

Griffith, FM, 1984. Roman Military Sites in Devon: Some Recent Discoveries, *Proc Devon Archaeol Soc*, **42**, 11-32

Griffith, FM, 1994. Changing perceptions of the context of prehistoric Dartmoor, *Proc Devon Archaeol Soc*, **52**, 85-100

Griffith, FM, and Quinnell, H, 1999. Settlement, *c.* 2500 BC to *c.* AD 600, in *Historical Atlas of South-West England* (eds R Kain and WD Ravenhill), 62-8, Exeter

Griffith, FM, and Reed, SJ, 1998. Rescue recording at Bantham Ham, South Devon, in 1997, *Proc Devon Archaeol Soc*, **56**, 109-32

Guthrie, A, 1969. Excavation of a settlement at Goldherring, Sancreed, 1958-1961, *Cornish Archaeol*, **8**, 5-39

Guilbert, GC, 1979. Dinorben 1977-8, *Current Archaeology*, **65**, 182-8

Guido, M, 1968. The glass beads from Nor'nour, Isles of Scilly, in Dudley 1968, 26-7

Guido, M, 1978. *The glass beads of the prehistoric and Roman periods in Britain and Ireland*, Soc Antiq London Rep Res **35**, London

Guido, M,1979, Glass beads, *The Roman cemetery at Lankhills. Winchester Studies* **3**: *Pre-Roman and Roman Winchester* (Clarke, G), 292-300, Oxford

Guido, M, 1987. The glass beads, in Green 1987, 109, mf2 F5-7

Gwilt, A, and Haselgrove, C, 1997. *Reconstructing Iron Age Societies*, Oxbow Monograph **71**

Hammond, J, 1897. *A Cornish Parish: being an Account of St Austell, Town, Church District and People*, Truro

Harden, DB,1952. Glass, in Fox 1952, 93

Harden, DB, 1956a. The glass found at Tintagel, in Harden 1956b, 70

Harden, DB, 1956b. *Dark Age Britain*, London

Harden, DB, 1963. Glass, in Alcock 1963, 178-88

Harden, DB, 1987. Glass in Carlyon 1987, 130-1

Harding, DW, Blake, IM, and Reynolds, PJ, 1993. *An Iron Age Settlement in Dorset: Excavation and Reconstruction*, University of Edinburgh, Dept Archaeology Monograph Ser **1**, Edinburgh

Harrad, L, forthcoming. The petrography of the pottery from Atlantic Road, Newquay, in Reynolds forthcoming, *Cornish Archaeol*

Harris, D, 1977. Bodwen, Lanlivery: A multi-period occupation, *Cornish Archaeol*, **16**, 43-60

Harris, D, 1980. Excavation of a Romano-British round at Shortlanesend, Kenwyn, Truro, *Cornish Archaeol*, **19**, 63-75

Harris, D, and Johnson, N, 1976. Carlidnack Round, Mawnan, *Cornish Archaeol*, **15**, 73-6

Hartley, KF, 1987. Mortaria, in Carlyon 1987, 119-21

Hatcher, J, 1970. *Rural Economy and Society in the Duchy of Cornwall 1300-1500*, Cambridge

Haverfield, F, 1924. Romano-British remains, *Victoria County History*, *Cornwall*, **V**

Hawkes, CFC, 1966. Amphora, in Brooks 1966, Appendix

Hayes, JW, 1972. *Late Roman Pottery*, London

Hayes, JW, 1980. *A Supplement to Late Roman Pottery*, London

Hencken, HO'N, 1928. An excavation at Chysauster, 1928, *J Brit Archaeol Ass*, **34**, 145-64

Hencken, HO'H, 1933. An excavation by H M Office of Works at Chysauster, Cornwall, 1931, *Archaeologia*, **82**, 237-84

Hencken, HO'N, 1950. Lagore Crannog: an Irish Royal Residence of the 7th to 10th centuries AD, *Proc Roy Irish Acad*, **LIII Section C2**, 1-247

Henderson, A, 1949. The small finds, in *Fourth Report on the Excavations of the Roman Fort at Richborough* (JP Bushe-Fox), 106-59, Soc Antiq London Rep Res **16**, London

Henderson, C, 1935. *Essays in Cornish History*, Truro, 1963 reprint

Henderson, CG, and Weddell, PJ, 1994. Medieval settlements on Dartmoor and in West Devon: The evidence from excavations, *Proc Devon Archaeol Soc*, **52**, 119-40

Henwood, WJ, 1874. On the detrital tin-ore of Cornwall, *J Roy Inst Cornwall*, 191-254

Herring, P, 1994. The cliff castles of West Penwith in the light of recent research at Maen Castle and Treryn Dinas, *Cornish Archaeol*, **33**, 40-56

Herring, P, 1998. *Cornwall's Historic Landscape: Presenting a method of historic landscape character assessment*, Cornwall Archaeological Unit

Herring, P, 2000. *St Michael's Mount: Archaeological Works, 1995-8*, Cornwall Archaeological Unit

Hill, JD, 1995. *Ritual and Rubbish in the Iron Age of Wessex*, BAR Brit Ser **242**, Oxford

Hingley, R, 1989. *Rural Settlement in Roman Britain*, London

Hirst, FC, 1936. Stone mortaria in West Cornwall, *Proc West Cornwall Fld Club*, **1:1**, 11-16

Hirst, FC, 1937. Excavations at Porthmeor, Cornwall, 1933, 1934 and 1935, *J Roy Inst Cornwall*, **24**, Appendix II

Holbrook, N, and Bidwell, P, 1991. *Roman Finds from Exeter*, Exeter Archaeological Rep **4**

Horner, W, 2001. Secrets of the sands, *Devon Archaeol Soc Newsletter*, **79**, 1, 8-9

Hull, MR, forthcoming. *Corpus of Ancient Brooches in Britain* (ed G Simpson)

Hutchinson, G, 1979. The Bar-lug pottery of Cornwall, *Cornish Archaeol*, **18**, 81-104

Ingemark, D, 2000. Roman glass from non-Roman contexts in Scotland and north Northumberland, *Annales du 14e Congrès de l'Association Internationale pour l'Histoire du Verre* (Venezia-Milano 1998), 175-7

Innocent, CF, 1916. *The Development of English Building Construction*, Cambridge

Irwin, MM, 1976. The Bodmin Bypass; 1975, *Cornish Archaeol*, **15**, 77-86

Irwin, MM, 1987. The stones, in Carlyon 1987, 135-9

Jarvis, K, and Maxfield, VA, 1975. The excavation of a first-century Roman farmstead and a late Neolithic settlement, Topsham, Devon, *Proc Devon Archaeol Soc*, **33**, 209-66

Johns, C, 2000. *St Austell North-East Distributor Road: Excavations at Trenowah - The Archaeological Recording - Archive Report*, Cornwall Archaeological Unit

Johns, C, forthcoming a. Excavations at Trenowah, St Austell North-East Distributor Road, *Cornish Archaeol*

Johns, C, forthcoming b. Hillside Farm, Bryher, Isles of Scilly: An Iron Age sword and mirror burial and Iron Age/Romano-British settlement, *Cornish Archaeol*

Johnson, N, and Rose, P, 1982. Defended settlements in Cornwall - an illustrated discussion, in *The Romano-British Countryside* (ed D Miles), BAR Brit Ser **103**, 151-208, Oxford

Johnson, N, and Rose, P, 1994. *Bodmin Moor. An Archaeological Survey. Volume* **1**: *The Human Landscape to c 1800,* English Heritage

Johnston, DA, Moore, C, and Fasham, P, 1998/9. Excavations at Penhale Round, Fraddon, Cornwall, 1995/6, *Cornish Archaeol,* **37-8**, 72-120

Jones, A, 2001. *A Report to Imerys: Par to Trebal Archaeological Assessment,* Cornwall Archaeological Unit

Jones, A, forthcoming. The excavation of a multi-period site at Stencoose, Cornwall, *Cornish Archaeol*

Jones, M, 1991. Food production and consumption - plants, in *Roman Britain: Recent Trends* (ed RTJ Jones), 21-8, Sheffield

Jope, EM, and Threfall, RI, 1958. Excavation of a medieval settlement at Beere, North Tawton, Devon, *Medieval Archaeol,* **2**, 112-40

Keeley, HCM, 1981. Recent work using soil phosphorus analysis in archaeological prospection, *Revue d'archaeometrie*, **5**, 89-95, University of Rennes

Keeley, HCM, 1983. *The use of soil phosphorus analysis in archaeological prospection,* Ancient Monuments Laboratory Report No 3851

Lang, M, 1955. Dated jars of early Imperial times, *Hesperia*, **24**, 277-85

Lamb, HH, 1982. Reconstruction of the course of postglacial climate over the world, in *Climatic Change in Later Prehistory* (ed A Harding), 11-32, Edinburgh

Laubenheimer, F, 1985. *La Production des Amphores en Gaule Narbonnaise*, Paris

Lawson-Jones, A, 2001. *Bear's Down to Ruthvoes. Archaeological watching brief Cornwall. A Report for South West Water,* Cornwall Archaeological Unit

Lawson-Jones, A, 2003. *Little Quoit Farm, St Columb Major, Cornwall: Excavation of a Romano-British smithing site. A Report for South West Water,* Cornwall Archaeological Unit

Leach, P, 1982. *Ilchester I: Excavations 1974-75,* Western Archaeol Trust Monograph **3**

Leech, R, 1981. The excavation of a Romano-British farmstead and cemetery on Bradley Hill, Somerton, Somerset, *Britannia*, **12**, 177-252

Leech, R, 1982. *Excavations at Catsgore 1970-73: A Romano-British Village*, Western Archaeological Trust

Leeds, ET, 1926. Excavations at Chun Castle, in Penwith, Cornwall, *Archaeologia*, **76**, 205-40

Lloyd Jones, M, 1984. *Society and Settlement in Wales and the Marshes 500BC - AD1100*, BAR Brit Ser **121**, Oxford

Longley, D, Johnstone, N, and Evans, J, 1998. Excavations on two farms of the Romano-British period at Bryn Eryr and Bush Farm, Gwynedd, *Britannia*, **29**, 185-246

Lynn, CJ, 1982. The excavation of Rathmullin, a raised rath and motte in County Down, *Ulster J Archaeol*, **45**, 65-171

Maclean, R, 1992. The Fogou: an investigation of function, *Cornish Archaeol,* **31**, 41-64

Manning, WH, 1974. Iron and lead objects, in Pollard 1974, 144-7

Manning, WH, 1976. Blacksmithing, in *Roman Crafts* (eds D Strong and D Brown), 143-54, London

Manning, WH, 1985. *Catalogue of the Romano-British Iron Tools, Fittings and Weapons in the British Museum,* London

Manning, WH, with Price, J, and Webster, J, 1995. *Report on the Excavations at Usk 1965-1976. The Roman Small Finds,* Cardiff

Masson Phillips, EN, 1966. Excavation of a Romano-British Site at Lower Well Farm, Stoke Gabriel, Devon, *Proc Devon Archaeol Soc,* **23**, 3-34

Mattingly, H, and Sydenham, EA, 1923-94. *The Roman Imperial Coinage*, London

McAvoy, F, with Morris, EL, and Smith, GH, 1980. Excavation of a multi-period site at Carngoon Bank, Lizard, *Cornish Archaeol*, **19**, 31-62

Meadows, K, Lemke, C, and Heron, J, 1997. *TRAC96: Proceedings of the Sixth Annual Theoretical Roman Archaeology Conference, Sheffield 1996*, Oxbow Books

Mercer, RJ, 1970. The Excavation of a Bronze Age hut-circle settlement, Stannon, Devon, St Breward, Cornwall, *Cornish Archaeol*, **9**, 17-46

Mercer, RJ, 1981. Excavations at Carn Brea, Illogan, *Cornish Archaeol*, **20**, 1-204

Miles, H, 1975a. Barrows on the St Austell Granite, *Cornish Archaeol*, **14**, 5-82

Miles, H, 1975b. Excavations at Woodbury Castle, East Devon, 1971, *Proc Devon Archaeol Soc*, **33**, 183-208

Miles, H, 1977. Excavations at Killibury Hillfort, Egloshayle 1975-6, *Cornish Archaeol*, **16**, 89-121

Miles, H, and Miles, T, 1973a. Excavations at Trethurgy, St Austell: Interim Report, *Cornish Archaeol*, **12**, 25-30

Miles, H, and Miles, T, 1973b. Trethurgy, *Curr Archaeol,* **40**, 142-7

Millett, M, 1990. *The Romanization of Britain*, Cambridge

Millett, M, 1995. *The English Heritage Book of Roman Britain,* London

Mitchell, GA, 1943. *Building Construction and Drawing: Part 1 - Elementary Course*, 15th edn, London

Moir, J, and Letts, J, 1999. *Thatch: Thatching in England 1790-1940*, English Heritage Research Transactions **5** (Research and Case Studies in Architectural Conservation), London

Mook, WG, 1986. Business meeting: recommendations/resolutions adopted by the Twelfth International Radiocarbon Conference, *Radiocarbon*, **28**, 799

Mook, WG, and Waterbolk, HT, 1985. *Radiocarbon Dating*, European Science Foundation handbook for archaeologists **3**, Strasbourg

Morgan, MH (trans), 1960. *Vitruvius: The Ten Books on Architecture*, Dover, New York

Morris, CD, and Harry, R, 1997. Excavations on the Lower Terrace, Site C, Tintagel Island 1990-94 *Antiq J*, **77**, 1-144

Morris, P, 1979. *Agricultural Buildings in Roman Britain*, BAR Brit Ser **70**, Oxford

Munn, MLZ, 1985. A late Roman kiln site in the Hermionid, Greece, *American Journ Archaeol*, **89**, 342-3

Mutz, A, 1972. *Die Kunst des Metalldrehens bei den Romern*, Birkhauser Verlag, Basel and Stuttgart

Naroll, R, 1962. Floor area and settlement population, *American Antiquity,* **27**, 587-99

Newberry, J, forthcoming. Devon inland flint sources, *Proc Devon Archaeol Soc*

Norman, C, 1977. A Flint Assemblage from Constantine Island, North Cornwall, *Cornish Archaeol*, **16**, 3-9

Nowakowski, J, 1998. *A30 Project, Cornwall - Archaeological Investigations along the route of the Indian Queens Bypass 1992-1994. Assessment and Updated Project Design,* Cornwall Archaeological Unit

Nowakowski, J, 2003. *Trevelgue Head, Cornwall. Excavations by CK Croft Andrew in 1939: Design for Analysis and Publication,* Cornwall Archaeological Unit

O'Mahoney, C, 1989a. The medieval pottery from Tintagel Castle, *Institute Cornish Studies Special Rep* **8**

O'Mahoney, C, 1989b. The pottery: Bunnings Park, in Tin, and agriculture on medieval and early modern Bodmin Moor: landscape archaeology in St Neot Parish, Cornwall (D Austin, GAM Gerrard and TAP Greeves), *Cornish Archaeol,* **28**, 133-47

O'Mahoney, C, 1994. The pottery, in Lammana, West Looe; CK Croft Andrew's excavations of the chapel and Monks House, 1935-6 (L Olson), *Cornish Archaeol*, **33**, 11-125

O'Neil, BH St J, 1933. The Roman villa at Magor Farm, near Camborne, Cornwall, *J Brit Archaeol Ass*, **39**, 117-75

O'Neil, BH St J, 1934. The Roman villa at Magor Farm, near Camborne, Cornwall, *J Roy Inst Cornwall* **24**, Supp

O'Neil, BH St J, 1936. Excavations at Caerau Ancient Village, Clynnog, Caernarvonshire, 1933 and 1934, *Antiq J*, **16**, 295-320

Opie, SA, 1939. *Excavations in the Roseland Peninsula,* Truro

Orton, C, Tyers, P, and Vince, A, 1993. *Pottery in Archaeology,* Cambridge

Padel, O, 1985. *Cornish Place - Name Elements,* English Place Name Society, Nottingham

Panella, C, 1973. Appunti su un gruppo di anfore della Prima, Media e Tarda Eta Imperiale, *Ostia* **III**, 460-633

Peacock, DPS, 1969a. A Romano-British salt-working site at Trebarveth, St Keverne, *Cornish Archaeol,* **8**, 47-65

Peacock, DPS, 1969b. A contribution to the study of Glastonbury Ware from South-Western Britain, *Antiq J,* **49**, 41-61

Peacock, DPS, 1969c. Neolithic pottery production in Cornwall, *Antiquity,* **43**, 145-9

Peacock, DPS, 1971a. Roman amphorae in pre-Roman Britain, in *The Iron Age and its Hillforts* (eds M Jesson and D Hill), 161-88, Southampton

Peacock, DPS, 1971b. Imported pottery, in Excavations on Glastonbury Tor, Somerset, 1964-6 (P Rahtz), *Archaeol J,* **127**, 65-7

Peacock, DPS, 1975. The grass-marked sherd, in *Excavations in Medieval Southampton, 1953-1969* (C Platt and R Coleman-Smith), Leicester

Peacock, DPS, 1977. Late Roman amphorae from Chalk, near Gravesend, Kent, in Dore and Greene 1977, 295-300

Peacock, DPS, 1982. *Pottery in the Roman World: an ethnoarchaeological approach*, London

Peacock, DPS, 1988. The gabbroic pottery of Cornwall, *Antiquity,* **62**, 302-4

Peacock, D, and Thomas, C, 1967. Class E Imported post-Roman pottery: a suggested origin, *Cornish Archaeol,* **6**, 35-46

Peacock, DPS, and Williams, DF, 1986. *Amphorae and the Roman Economy*, London

Pearson, GW, 1984. The development of high precision ^{14}C measurements and its application to archaeological time-scale problems, unpubl PhD thesis, Queens University, Belfast

Peate, IC, 1944. *The Welsh House*, Liverpool

Penhallurick, RD, 1986. *Tin in Antiquity*, Institute of Metals

Pennington, RR, 1973. *Stannary Law*, Newton Abbot

Peterken, GF, 1981. *Woodland Conservation and Management,* London

Percival, J, 1976. *The Roman Villa,* London

Piggott, S, 1983. *The Earliest Wheeled Transport*, London

Pirling, R,1974. *Das römisch-fränkische Gräberfeld von Krefeld-Gellep, 1960-1963,* Berlin, Gebr. Mann verlag

Pollard, S, 1966. Neolithic and Dark Age settlements on High Peak, Sidmouth, Devon, *Proc Devon Archaeol Soc,* **23**, 35-59

Pollard, S, 1974. A Late Iron Age settlement and a Romano-British villa at Holcombe, near Uplyme, Devon, *Proc Devon Archaeol Soc*, **32**, 9-162

Potter, TW, 1979. *Romans in North-West England: excavations at the Roman forts of Ravenglass, Watercrook and Bowness on Solway*, Cumberland & Westmorland Antiq Archaeol Soc Res Ser **1**

Preston-Jones, A, 1987. Road widening at St Buryan and Pelynt churchyards, *Cornish Archaeol*, **26**, 153-60

Preston-Jones, A, and Rose, P, 1986. Medieval Cornwall, *Cornish Archaeol*, **25**, 135-85

Price, J, 1982. Glass, in Carlyon 1982, 163-4

Price, J, 1987. The glass fragments from the Lower Ward, in Excavations in the Lower Ward, Tintagel Castle, 1986 (S Hartgroves and R Walker), *Cornish Studies*, **16**, 25-6

Price, J, 1992. The Glass, in Rahtz *et al* 1992, 131-43

Price, J, 2000a. Roman and post-Roman vessel and window glass, in Rahtz *et al* 2000, 305-9

Price, J, 2000b. Late Roman glass vessels in Britain and Ireland from AD 350 to 410 and beyond, in Price 2000d, 1-31

Price, J, 2000c. Glass vessels, objects and window glass, in *Frocester - a Romano-British settlement, its antecedents and successors.Volume 2: the finds* (EG Price), Gloucester District Archaeol Res Group, 103-22

Price, J (ed), 2000d. *Glass in Britain and Ireland AD 350-1100*, British Museum Occasional Papers **127**, London

Price, J, and Cottam, S, 1995. Late Roman and Early post-Roman glass, in Alcock *et al* 1995, 99-103

Price, J, and Cottam, S, 1997. Roman glass, in *Birdoswald. Excavations of a Roman fort on Hadrian's Wall and its successor settlements: 1987-92* (T Wilmott), 272-4, 283, 341-55, English Heritage Archaeol Report **14**

Price, J, and Cottam, S, 1998a. *Romano-British glass vessels: a handbook*, CBA Practical Handbook in Archaeology **14**, York

Price, J, and Cottam, S, 1998b. Glass, in *Great Witcombe Roman Villa, Gloucestershire* (P Leach), BAR Brit Ser **266**, 73-84, 91, 93, 105-6, Oxford

Pritchard, AC, 1983. *An analysis of the distribution of Roman coinage in Cornwall, the Scilly Isles and the Plymouth area*, BA Dissertation, Department of Archaeology, University of Reading

Quinnell, H, 1986. The Iron Age and the Roman period in Cornwall, *Cornish Archaeol*, **25**, 111-34

Quinnell, H, 1987. Cornish gabbroic pottery: the development of a hypothesis, *Cornish Archaeol*, **26**, 7-12

Quinnell, H, 1992. The pottery and the stone artefacts, in Appleton-Fox 1992, 94-113

Quinnell, H, 1993a. A sense of identity: distinctive Cornish stone artefacts in the Roman and post-Roman periods in *In Search of Cult: Essays for Philip Rahtz* (ed M Carver), 69-78, Woodbridge

Quinnell, H, 1993b. A sense of identity: distinctive Cornish stone artefacts in the Roman and post-Roman periods, *Cornish Archaeol*, **32**, 29-46

Quinnell, H, 1995.The pottery, metalwork and stone objects, in Ratcliffe 1995, 120-36

Quinnell, H, 1998. Ceramics, in Nowakowski 1998, **III**, 58-64, 232-6

Quinnell, H, 1998/9. The artefacts, in Johnston *et al* 1998/9, 85-93

Quinnell, H, 2003a. Iron artefacts, in Lawson Jones 2003, 50-5

Quinnell, H, 2003b. Ceramics, in Nowakowski 2003, 107-19

Quinnell, H, forthcoming a. Prehistoric and Roman pottery, in Jones forthcoming

Quinnell, H, forthcoming b. The artefacts, in Cole forthcoming

Quinnell, H, forthcoming c. The Iron Age and Roman period pottery, in Reynolds forthcoming

Quinnell, H, forthcoming d. The prehistoric pottery, in Johns forthcoming a

Quinnell, H, forthcoming e. The pottery, in Johns forthcoming b

Quinnell, H, and Harris, D, 1985. Castle Dore: the chronology reconsidered, *Cornish Archaeol*, **24**, 123-32

Rackham, O, 1980. *Ancient Woodland, its history, vegetation and uses in England,* London

Radford, CAR, 1951. Report on the excavations at Castle Dore, *J Roy Inst Cornwall,* **n ser 1**, Appendix

Radford, CAR, 1956. Imported pottery found at Tintagel, Cornwall, in Harden 1956b, 59-70

Rahtz, P, and Watts, L, 1979. The end of Roman temples in the west of Britain, in Casey 1979, 183-201

Rahtz, P, Hirst, S, and Wright, S, 2000. *Cannington Cemetery*, Britannia Monograph Ser **17**

Rahtz, P, Woodward, A, Burrow, I, Everton, A, Watts, L, Leach, P, Hirst, S, Fowler, P, and Gardner, K, 1992. *Cadbury Congresbury 1968-73. A late post-Roman hilltop settlement in Somerset*, BAR Brit Ser **223**, Oxford

Ratcliffe, J, 1995. Duckpool: a Romano-British metal-working site and early medieval industrial site and harbour, Morwenstow, *Cornish Archaeol*, **34**, 81-171

Rees, SE, 1979. *Agriculture Implements in Prehistoric and Roman Britain,* BAR Brit Ser **69**

Reynolds, A, forthcoming. Excavations at Atlantic Road, Newquay, *Cornish Archaeol*

Reynolds, PJ, 1979. *Iron Age Farm: the Butser Experiment,* London

Reynolds, PJ, 1982a. Substructure to superstructure, in Drury 1982, 173-98

Reynolds, PJ, 1982b. *The Butser Ancient Farm Demonstration Area*, Butser Ancient Farm Project Trust

Reynolds, PJ, 1993. Part Two: experimental reconstruction, in Harding *et al* 1993, 93-113

Riley, JA, 1981. The pottery from the cisterns 1977.1, 1977.2 and 1997.3, in *Excavations at Carthage conducted by the Univ. of Michigan* (ed JA Humphrey), Vol **6**, 85-124, Ann Arbor

Robinson, HS, 1959. *The Athenian Agora*, **V**, Princeton

Roach Smith, C, 1850. *Richborough, Reculver and Lymne,* London

Robertson, AS, 2000. *An Inventory of Romano-British Coin Hoards* (eds R Hobbs and TV Buttrey), Royal Numismatic Society Special Publication **20**, London

Rose, P, and Preston-Jones, A, 1995. Changes in the Cornish Countryside, in *Landscape and Settlement in Britain AD 400-1066* (ed D Hooke and S Burnell), 51-68, Exeter

Rundle, S, 1887. Tregonning Hill and its surroundings, *J Roy Inst Cornwall,* **9**, 358-63

Russell, V, and Pool, PAS, 1963. Excavations of a Romano-British hut at Boscreege, Gulval, *Cornish Archaeol,* **2**, 19-22

Saunders, A, and Harris, D, 1982. Excavation at Castle Gotha, St Austell, *Cornish Archaeol*, **21**, 109-53

Saunders, C, 1972. The excavations at Grambla, Wendron, 1972: interim report, *Cornish Archaeol*, **11**, 50-2

Scaife, R, 1998/9. The charred seed remains and pollen analysis, in Johnston *et al* 1998/9, 94-106

Schwieso, J, 1976. Excavations at Threemilestone Round, Kenwyn, Truro, *Cornish Archaeol*, **15**, 50-67

Schwartz, GT, 1964. GalloRomische Gewichte in Aventicum, *Schweiszer Munsblatter,* **13-14**, 150-7

Serocold, OP, and Maynard, G, 1949. A Dark Ages Settlement at Trebarveth, St Keverne, Cornwall, *Antiq J*, **49**, 169-82

Sheppard, P, 1967. Parochial check-lists of antiquities; St Ewe, *Cornish Archaeol*, **6**, 98-101

Sheppard, P, 1972. Parochial check-lists of antiquities; St Austell, *Cornish Archaeol*, **11**, 72-80

Silvester, RJ, 1981a. An excavation on the post-Roman site at Bantham, South Devon, *Proc Devon Archaeol Soc*, **39**, 89-118

Silvester, RJ, 1981b. Excavations at Honeyditches Roman Villa, Seaton, in 1978, *Proc Devon Archaeol Soc,* **39**, 37-88

Simpson, SJ, Griffith, FM, and Holbrook, N, 1989. The prehistoric, Roman and early post-Roman site at Hayes Farm, Clyst Honiton, *Proc Devon Archaeol Soc,* **47**, 1-28

Smith, GH, 1980. The Pottery, in McAvoy 1980, 40-9

Smith, G, 1987. The Lizard project: Landscape survey 1978-1983, *Cornish Archaeol* **26**, 13-68

Smith, G, 1988. Excavation of the Iron Age cliff promontory fort and of Mesolithic and Neolithic flint-working areas at Penhale Point, Holywell Bay, near Newquay, 1983, *Cornish Archaeol,* **27**, 171-99

Smith, JT, 1978. Villas as a key to social structure, in *Studies in the Romano-British Villa* (ed M Todd), 149-85, Leicester

Smith, JT, 1982. The validity of inference from archaeological evidence, in Drury 1982, 7-19

Smith, RA,1905. The ancient British iron currency, *Proc Soc Antiq London,* **20**, 179-95

Staines, S, 1979. Envronmental change on Dartmoor, *Proc Devon Archaeol Soc,* **37**, 21-47

Steier P, and Rom, W, 2000. The use of Bayesian statistics for ^{14}C dates of chronological ordered samples: a critical analysis, *Radiocarbon,* **42**, 183-98

Sternini, M,1995. Il vetro in Italia tra V e IX secoli, in Foy 1995b, 243-89

Stevens, CE, 1947. A possible conflict of laws in Roman Britain, *J Roman Studies,* **37**, 132-4

Stevens, CE, 1966. The social and economic aspects of rural settlement, in *Rural Settlement in Roman Britain* (ed C Thomas), 108-28, CBA Res Rep **7**

Straker, V, 1992. Charred plant macrofossils, in Appleton-Fox 1992, 89-92

Straker, V, 1995. Plant macrofossils, in Ratcliffe 1995, 155-8

Straker, V, 1997. The ecofactual assemblage: charred plant macrofossils, in Morris and Harry 1997, 83-101

Stuiver, M, and Kra, RS, 1986. Editorial comment, *Radiocarbon,* **28**(2B), ii

Stuiver, M, and Polach, HA, 1977. Reporting of ^{14}C data, *Radiocarbon,* **19**, 355-63

Stuiver, M, and Reimer, PJ, 1986. A computer program for radiocarbon age calculation, *Radiocarbon,* **28**, 1022-30

Stuiver, M, and Reimer, PJ, 1993. Extended ^{14}C data base and revised CALIB 3.0 ^{14}C age calibration program, *Radiocarbon,* **35**, 215-30

Stuiver, M, Reimer, PJ, Bard, E, Beck, JW, Burr, GS, Hughen KA, Kromer, B, McCormac, G, van der Plicht, J, and Spurk, M, 1998. INTCAL98 Radiocarbon age calibration, 24,000-0 cal BP, *Radiocarbon,* **40**, 1041-83

Swan, VG, 1984. *The Pottery Kilns of Roman Britain,* RCHM (E) Sup Ser **5**

Tangye, M, 1973. Hulls in Cornwall: a survey and discussion, *Cornish Archaeol,* **12**, 31-52

Thomas, C, 1956. Evidence for post-Roman occupation of Chun Castle, Cornwall, *Antiq J,* **36**, 75-8

Thomas, C, 1958. *Gwithian: Ten Years Work,* West Cornwall Field Club, Gwithian

Thomas, C, 1963. Trial excavations at Mulfra Vean, 1954, *Cornish Archaeol,* **2**, 23-8

Thomas, C, 1964. Minor sites in the Gwithian area Iron Age to recent times, *Cornish Archaeol,* **3**, 37-62

Thomas, C, 1966. The character and origins of Roman Dumnonia, in *Rural Settlement in Roman Britain* (ed C Thomas), 74-98, CBA Res Rep **7**

Thomas, C, 1968a. Grass-marked pottery in Cornwall, in *Studies in Ancient Europe* (eds JM Coles and DDA Simpson), 311-32, Leicester

Thomas, C, 1968b. Merther Euny, Wendron, *Cornish Archaeol,* **7**, 81-2

Thomas, C, 1969. Excavations at Crane Godrevy, Gwithian, 1969, *Cornish Archaeol,* **8**, 84-8

Thomas, C, 1981. *A Provisional List of Imported Pottery in Post-Roman Western Britain and Ireland,* Institute of Cornish Studies, Camborne

Thomas, C, 1985. *Exploration of a Drowned Landscape: Archaeology and History of the Isles of Scilly,* London

Thomas, C, 1990. 'Gallici Nautae de Galliarum Provinciis' - A sixth/seventh century trade with Gaul reconsidered, *Medieval Archaeol,* **34**, 1-26

Thomas, C, 1993. *Tintagel: Arthur and Archaeology*, London

Thomas, C, 1994. *And Shall These Mute Stones Speak? Post-Roman Inscriptions in Western Britain*, Oxford

Thorpe, C, 1997. Ceramics, in Morris and Harry 1997, 74-82

Thorpe, C, 2000. Early medieval ceramics and pebbles (*c* 400-1066), in Herring 2000, 47-61

Threipland, LM, 1956. An Excavation at St Mawgan-in-Pyder, North Cornwall, *Archaeol Journ*, **113**, 33-81

Tingle, M, 1998. *The Prehistory of Beer Head*, BAR Brit Ser **270**, Oxford

Todd, M, 1987. *The South-West to AD 1000*, Harlow

Todd, M, 1998. A hillslope enclosure at Rudge, Morchard Bishop, *Proc Devon Archaeol Soc*, **56**, 133-52

Trudgian, P, 1977. Excavation at Tregilders, St Kew, 1975-6, *Cornish Archaeol*, **16**, 122-8

Tylecote, RF, 1962. *Metallurgy in Archaeology*, London

Tylecote, RF, 1966. The history of the tin industry in Cornwall, *Cornish Archaeol*, **5**, 30-3

Tylecote, RF, 1978. Early tin ingots and tinstone from Western Europe and the Mediterranean, in *The Search for Ancient Tin* (eds AD Franklin *et al*), 49-5, Washington DC

Tylecote, RF, 1986. *The Prehistory of Metallurgy in the British Isles*, Institute of Metals

van Alfen, PG, 1996. New light on the 7th-C. Yassi Ada shipwreck: capacities and standard sizes of LRA1, *J Roman Archaeol*, **9**, 189-213

van der Plicht, J, 1993. The Gröningen radiocarbon calibration program, *Radiocarbon*, **35**, 231-7

Wainwright, GJ, 1971. The Excavation of a fortified settlement at Walesland Rath, Pembrokeshire, *Britannia*, **2**, 48-108

Warner, RB, 1967. The Carnanton tin ingot, *Cornish Archaeol*, **6**, 29-31

Watts, S, 2003. *The Form and Function of Querns and Mortars in Iron Age and Roman Cornwall*, Undergraduate dissertation, Department of Archaeology, Exeter University

Weatherhill, C, 1982. *The Courtyard Houses of West Penwith: a Survey*, Cornwall Committee for Rescue Archaeology

Weddell, PJ, and Reed, SJ, 1997. Excavations at Sourton Down, Okehampton 1986-1991: Roman road, deserted medieval hamlet and other landscape features, *Proc Devon Archaeol Soc*, **55**, 39-147

Wedlake, WJ, 1958. *Excavations at Camerton, Somerset*, Camerton Excavation Club

Welfare, AT, 1985. The milling stones, in PT Bidwell, *The Roman Fort of Vindolanda at Chesterholm, Northumberland*, 154-64, English Heritage

Williams, DF, 1977. The Romano-British black burnished industry: an essay on characterization by heavy mineral analysis, in *Pottery and Early Commerce* (ed DPS Peacock), 163-220, London

Williams, DF, 1978. Petrological analysis of the pottery, in Christie 1978, 405-6

Williams, DF, 2001. Late Roman amphora 1: a study of diversification, *Halicarnassian Studies*, (forthcoming)

Williams, DF, and Peacock, DPS, 1983. The importation of olive-oil into Roman Britain, in *Produccion Y Comercio Del Aceite en la Antiguedad. II Congresso* (eds J Blazquez and J Remesal), 263-80, Madrid

Williams, G, and Mytum, H, 1998. *Llawhaden, Dyfed. Excavations on a small group of defended enclosures, 1980-4*. BAR Brit Ser **275**, Oxford

Woodward, PJ, Davies, S, and Graham, A, 1993. *Excavations at Greyhound Yard, Dorchester 1981*, Dorset Natur Hist Archaeol Soc Monograph **12**

Worth, RM, 1967. *Worth's Dartmoor* (eds GM Spooner and FS Russell), Newton Abbot

Young, A, 2001. *The National Mapping Programme. Cornwall and Isles of Scilly Mapping Project: Annual Progress Report 2000/2001*, Cornwall Archaeological Unit

Young, CJ, 1977. *Oxfordshire Roman Pottery*, BAR Brit Ser **43**, Oxford

Index

compiled by *Susan Vaughan*

Illustrations are denoted by page numbers in *italics.*

540 AD event 243
agriculture 10, 224–5, 227, 233
Alseveor 180, 181
amethyst, lump of 152
ancillary platforms 36, 61, 206–7, 226
antler fragments 157
architecture
  large oval buildings 183
    architectural solutions 190
      background 190–1; general factors 192–5; reconstructions *195–8*, 199, *200*, 201; underlying assumptions 191–2
    compared 186–9
    features described
      drains 184; entrances 184; floors 185; hearths/hearth pits 185; internal divisions 185; levelling, degree of 183–4; roof support 185–6; size and shape 183; walls 184
    problems posed by archaeology 189
      door frames 189; iron fittings 190; light/smoke 189; roof structure 189; style change 190
  other buildings 203
    buildings with ancillary platforms 206–7
    byre 209–10
    four-posters 203–4
    irregular stone structure 204
    large oval structures 204–5
    posthole lines 207
    posthole pairs 207–8
    rectangular timber 203
    shrine 208–9
    small irregular oval buildings 205–6
    small oval timber building 205
    structures with dump walls 207
    sub-circular stone buildings 205
archive 8
Area R
  chronology 167, 169, 171, 172, 175, 178
  discussion 224, 226
  excavation evidence 62, 63, 64–5
  reconstruction *frontispiece*, 229
army, Roman 76, 146–7; *see also* fort
arrowheads, flint 153, *154*, 156
ash (*Fraxinus*) 158, 160, 225
ash houses 206, 208–9, 230

ballauns 151
bank, Enclosure 10, *11*, *12*, 13, 15; *see also* Rampart
Bantham (Devon), Post-Roman period 82, 238, 241–2
Barnsley Park villa (Glos), rick stand 207
beads, glass 85, 86, 89, 92
Beer (Devon), flint 153
Beere (Devon), pottery 107
Bigbury (Devon), ingots 75
binding, iron 77, *79*
Birdoswald (Cumbria), glass 89
Bodrifty (Cornwall), Iron Age settlement 81, 109
Bodwen (Cornwall), round 212, 214
bone fragments 157
Bordeaux (France), glass 88
Boscarne (Cornwall), shovels/ingot 75, 218
Boscreege (Cornwall), house 206
Bosence (Cornwall)
  shaft 236
  weight 140
Bosullow Trehyllys (Cornwall), courtyard houses 188
bracelets
  copper alloy 72
  shale *144*, 145
Bradford Peverel (Dorset), brooch 71
Bradley Hill (Somerset)
  byre 209
  mortar 138
  pottery 99
Breage (Cornwall), coin hoard 69
brooches, copper alloy *70*, 71–2, 232
Budock (Cornwall), coin hoard 69
buildings *see* architecture; Houses; Structures
burnt clay 22, 36, 42, 55, 61, 128
Butser (Hants) 192, 194
byre *see* Structure U

Cadbury Castle (Somerset)
  desertion of 243
  finds distribution 240
  glass 86, 88
  ironwork 78
  status 241, 242
Cadbury Congresbury (Somerset)
  glass 86, 87, 88, 90
  ironwork 78, 82
  Post-Roman period 242
  pottery 99
  querns 151
  shrine 237
Caerau (Caern), mortar 138
Calartha (Cornwall), Trethurgy bowl *136*
Camborne (Cornwall), coin hoard 69
Camerton (Somerset), ironwork 79
candlestick, iron 77, 78, 79, 80

Cannington (Somerset)
  chronology 239–40
  glass 87, 88
  ironwork 78, 81, 82
  pottery 127
Carlidnack (Cornwall)
  ironworking 83
  pottery 114, 115
  site type and date 212, 214
Carn Euny (Cornwall)
  dates 266, 275
  hearth pits 232
  house 188
  ironwork 78
  mortar stone 152
  pottery
    amphorae 101
    gabbroic 114, 117, 123, 124, 125
    publication 93
    South Devon ware 107
  querns 146, 148, 151
  tinworking 76
Carnanton (Cornwall), ingot 74–5
Carngoon Bank (Cornwall)
  5th-century occupation 239
  postholes 208
  pottery 98, 118, 127
  structure 206
Carvossa (Cornwall)
  brooches 71
  dump 230
  function and status 214, 216, 235
  glass 85, 87
  ironwork 78
  metalworking 76, 83
  mortaria 138
  mould cover 142
  pottery
    black-burnished ware 105
    Exeter Grey wares 106
    gabbroic 108
      bowl with foot-ring 117; Type 1 111; Type 4 112, 114; Type 9 117; Type 11 118; Type 12 118; Type 13 118; Type 16 121; Type 19 121; Type 20 123; Type 21 123; Type 22 124; Type 23 125; Type 26 125; Type 28 126
    imported wares 101, 242
    Oxfordshire ware 104
    publication 93
    South Devon ware 107
  shale bracelet 144
Carwarthen (Cornwall)
  date 212
  dump 230
  pottery
    black-burnished ware 105
    gabbroic
      bowls, other 125; Type 4 112, 113, 114, 115; Type 6 117; Type 9 117; Type 16 121; Type 19 121; Type 20 123; Type 21 123; Type 22 124, 125; Type 23 125; Type 28 126
    publication 93
  site type 214
cassiterite 73, 75, 76
Castell Henllys (Pembs)
  pole lathe 208
  roundhouse 191, 201
  water collection 232
casting waste
  copper alloy 72, 76
  silver 73, 76
Castle Dore (Cornwall)
  four-poster 203
  ingot 74, 75
  pottery 101, 110
  querns 145
  shale objects 144
Castle Gotha (Cornwall)
  buildings 187, 203, 206, 213
  date 212, 214, 215
  disc 142
  hearth pits 232
  metalworking 76, 83
  mould 142
  pottery
    amphorae 101
    black-burnished ware 105
    gabbroic
      Type 1 111; Type 4 114; Type 6 117; Type 8 117; Type 9 117; Type 11 118; Type 12 118; Type 19 121; Type 20 123; Type 21 123; Type 22 124; Type 23 125
    publication 93
  quern 151
Castle Pencaire (Cornwall), mould cover 142
Castle-an-Dinas (Cornwall), weight 140
Catsgore (Somerset), mortar 138
Cefn Greanog II (Caern), buildings 188–9
cereal processing *see* crop-processing
charcoal 73, 158, 159–60; *see also* radiocarbon dates
Christianity 237, 242, 243
chronology and phasing 9–10, 164, 165
  Period 1 165
  Period 2 165
  Period 3 165
  Period 4 165–6
  Period 5 166–7
    Stage 1 *167*, *168*, 169
    Stage 2 *169*, 170–1
    Stage 3 *170*, 171–2
    Stage 4 *171*, 172–3

Stage 5 *173*, 174–5
Stage 6 *174*, 175–8
Stage 7 *176*, 178
Stage 8 *177*, 178
Stage 9 178, *179*, 180
Stage 10 180, *181*
Period 6 180
Period 7 180–2
Period 8 182
Chun Castle (Cornwall)
pottery 109
structures 204
tinworking 75, 76
Chysauster (Cornwall)
buildings 208, 209, 224
middens 230
pottery 93, 98, 117, 123, 124
shale bracelet 144
stone basins 151
tinworking 76
weight 140
Civitas Dumnoniorum 215–17, 235–6
Clanacombe (Devon), pottery 107, 120
clay pipes 127–8
cleats, iron 77, 78, 80, 81
cleaver, iron 77, *82*
clothing 232
coin hoards
Cornwall 67–70
Trethurgy 38, 67–70, 175, 235
coinage, use of in Cornwall 234–5
Colchester (Essex), glass 85, 87
Collfryn (Powys), four-poster 203
Compton Dando (Somerset), moulds 71
conductores 76
Condurrow (Cornwall), coin hoard 69
Constantine (Cornwall), coin hoard 69
cooking 231–2
copper alloy objects *70*, 71–2
copper alloy working 72, 76, 233
Cornwall Archaeological Society 3, 108, 211
Cornwall Archaeological Unit (Cornwall Committee for Rescue Archaeology) 3
Cornwall and Isles of Scilly Mapping Project 211, 213, 216
counters, ceramic/stone *143*, 144
courtyard houses 183, 188, 224, 232, 237
crafts 232–4
Crane Godrevy (Cornwall)
building 187
date 212
entrance 219
site type 214
crop-processing 152, 226
Dan-y-Coed (Dyfed), byre 209
Danebury (Hants)
structures 191, 205
weights 140
dating *see* chronology and phasing; radiocarbon dates
daub 128
Department of the Environment 3
diet 233; *see also* cooking
Dinas Powys (S Glam)
function/status 242
glass 86, 87, 88
ironwork 78, 79, 81, 82
pottery 99
Dinorben (Clwyd)
four-poster 203
mould cover 142
discs
ceramic *143*, 144
stone *141*, 142, *143*, 144
ditches
Enclosure 10, *11*, *12*, *13*, 15
Round
chronology 172
discussion 217–18
excavation evidence *11*, *15*, *16*, 17, *18*, 19, 22
see also drains/gullies
doorways, buildings 184, 189, 195
reconstructions *195*, *198*, 199, *200*, 201
Dorchester (Dorset)
brooch 71
pottery 106
see also Poundbury
double-spiked loops, iron 77, *80*, 81
drains/gullies 184
Period 3 *13*, 15, *17*
Period 4 14, 15
Period 5
Area R 63, 65, 175
House A *44*, 51–3, 55, 56, 57, 169, 175, 178
House D 48, 49, 50, 172, 175
House T 60, 61, 170
House X 38, 41
House Z 29, *31*, 33–4, *35*, 167, 168, 170, 171, 172
rampart *16*, 18–19, 22, 174, 224
Structure E 46, 168–9
Structure Q 35, *36*
Structure R 63, 65, 175, 180
Structure U 27, *29*, 174, 175, 178
Structure V 24, 25, 178
drying racks 169, 172, 224
Duckpool (Cornwall)
ironwork 78, 81
metalworking 76
plant macrofossils 160

pottery 93, 107, 118
radiocarbon dates 266, 275

East India Company 75
Enclosure (Period 3)
chronology 165
discussion 215
excavation evidence 10, *12–13*, 14–15, 215
English China Clays Ltd (Imerys) 3
Entrance, Round
chronology 167, 174, 180
discussion 213, 218–20, 226
excavation evidence 17, 18–22, 184
reconstruction *frontispiece*, 228
see also doorways
excavation
background 3–5
contexts, listed and described 245–62
method 5–7
stratigraphy 9–10
Period 1 10
Period 2 10
Period 3 10, *12–13, 14*, 15
Period 4 6, *12*, 13, *14*, 15
Period 5 *7*
Area Q *34, 35–6*, 37–8; Area R *62, 63, 64–5*; central area *23*; earthworks *15–22*; House A 50, *51–6*, 57; House D *48–50*; House T *57–60*, 61–3; House X 38, *39–44*; House Z 29, *30–3*, 34, *35*; Structure E 44, *45–6*; Structure G *45*, 46, *47–8*; Structure U 25, *26–9*; Structure V *23–5*; Structure Y *37*, 38
Period 6 66
Period 7 66
Period 8 66
see also chronology and phasing
exchange *see* trade and exchange
Exeter (Devon)
Cathedral Close, clergy houses 192
glass 85, 86, 87, 89–90
mortar 138
pottery
amphorae 102
black-burnished ware 105, 106
gabbroic 120, 121, 124
publication 97
South-Western Grey ware 107
unguentaria 99
Roman administration 217, 235, 238
shale objects 145

Fal valley 211, 213
ferrule, iron 77, *82*
field hedge, 16th-century 17, 181, 182
field systems
Period 2 10, 165, 215, 224
Round, reconstruction *frontispiece*, 229
Medieval–Post-Medieval 17, 66, 180–2, 244
finger ring, glass 85, 86, 89, 92
fishing 233
flints
St Austell area 156, 214
Trethurgy 10, 153, *154–5*, 156, 214
fogous 209, 237
fork, iron 77, *82*
fort, Roman *see* Nanstallon
foundation deposit 237
four-poster structures
chronology 168–9, 172, 175
discussion 203–4, 221–4, 226, 227, 237
excavation evidence *44–6*
Frocester Court (Glos), glass 89
fuel 73, 160, 163, 225
furnishings 231

garden plots 172, 228, 229
Gare (Cornwall), coin hoard 69
Gateholm (Pembs), buildings 188
gatepost settings 19, 20, *21*, 22, 180, 218
Gears 3
geology 1–3
glass objects 85–9, *90*, 91, *92*, 128
Glastonbury (Somerset)
pottery 102, 103
roundhouses 191
Goldherring (Cornwall)
buildings 207, 213, 224
dating 212, 239, 241, 244
entrance 213, 219
field system 224
ironwork 78, 81
pottery
gabbroic 109
Type 4 114; Type 9 117; Type 12 118; Type 13 121; Type 19 121; Type 20 123; Type 21 123; Type 22 124, 125; Type 23 125; Type 26 125
publication 93
samian 98
slag 83
gorse (*Ulex*) 158, 160, 225
Grambla (Cornwall)
buildings 183, 186–7
date 212, 239, 241, 243, 244
entrance 213, 219–20
glass 86, 87
ironwork 78
plan 213
shale bracelet 144

toggle 139
Trethurgy bowl 136
granaries, 228; *see also* Structure E
Great Witcombe (Glos), glass 89
gullies *see* drains/gullies
Gwinear (Cornwall), coin hoards 69
Gwithian (Cornwall)
buildings 206
Post-Roman occupation 239, 241
pottery 101, 109
seaweed, use of 225
weight 140

haematite 3, 83
Halangy Down (Scilly)
glass 85, 86, 89
mould 142
post-socket 152
querns 135, 151
shrine 208, 237
Haldon (Devon) 242
handle, iron 77, 80, 81
hawthorn (*Crataegus*) 158, 160, 225
hay loft 207, 226
Hayes Farm (Devon), enclosure 78, 188, 242
Hayle (Cornwall), coin hoard 69
hazel (*Corylus*) 158, 160, 193, 225
hearths/hearth pits 185
Area R 63, 172, 233
Area Y 38, 227, 233
House A 53, 55, 56, 172, 175, 237
House T 61, 171, 172, 175
House X *40*, *41–2*, 175, 203, 204
House Z *32*, 34, 168, 175, 177–8, 231, 232
heather (*Calluna*) 158, 160, 225
High Peak (Devon), earthwork 242
hillforts 214, 215, 216, 219
Hillside Farm (Scilly), pottery 125
hobnails, iron 76, 77, 78, 232
Holcombe (Devon), villa 78, 120, 203
Holme Pierrepont (Notts), glass 88
hornbeam (*Carpinus*) 160
House A
architecture
A1 183, 184, 185, 186, 195
A2 183, 184, 185, 186, 195
A3 183, 189
chronology
Stage 1 167, *168*, 169
Stage 2 *169*, 171
Stage 3 *170*, 172
Stage 4 *171*, 172, 173
Stage 5 *173*, 175
Stage 6 *174*, 176
Stage 7 *176*, 178
Stage 8 *177*, 178
Stage 9 *179*
Stage 10 180
discussion 221, 226, 227, 240–1
excavation evidence *52*
A1 *51–2*, 53, 55, 56
A2 *44*, *53*, *54*, 55, *56*, *57*
A3 *54*, *57*
reconstruction
A1 *198*, 199–200
A2 *frontispiece*, 229
ritual deposit 237
House D
architecture 185
chronology
Stage 1 167
Stage 2 *169*, 170–1
Stage 3 *170*, 172
Stage 4 *171*, 172
Stage 5 *173*, 175
Stage 6 *174*, 176
Stage 7 178
discussion 205, 224, 225, 226, 227
excavation evidence *46*, *48*
D1 48, 49
D2 49
D4 *44*, *49–50*
reconstruction, D4 *frontispiece*, 229
see also Structure D3
House T
architecture
T2 183, 184, 185, 186, 189
T3 206–7
T4 184, 185
chronology
Stage 1 167, *168*, 169
Stage 2 *169*, 170, 171
Stage 3 *170*, 172
Stage 4 *171*, 172, 173
Stage 5 *173*, 174, 175
Stage 6 *174*, 176
Stage 7 178
Stage 8 *177*, 178
Stage 9 *179*
discussion 205, 221, 224, 226, 227
excavation evidence 60
T1 *57*, 60
T2 *57*, *58*, 60–1
T3 *57*, *58*, 61
T4 *59*, 61
paired postholes 208
reconstruction
T2 *200*, 201
T3 *frontispiece*, 229
see also Structure T
House X
architecture 183, 184, 185, 186, 189, 203, 204–5

chronology
Stage 1 167, *168*, 169
Stage 2 *169*, 170
Stage 3 *170*, 171–2
Stage 4 *171*, 172
Stage 5 *173*, 175
Stage 6 *174*, 175
Stage 7 *176*, 178
Stage 8 *177*, 178
Stage 9 178, *179*
discussion 221, 224, 225, 226, 227, 239, 240
excavation evidence 38, *39–43*
reconstruction *frontispiece*, 229
see also Structure X5
House Z
architecture 183, 184, 185, 186, 189
chronology
Stage 1 167, *168*, 169
Stage 2 *169*, 170
Stage 3 *170*, 171, 172
Stage 4 *171*, 172, 173
Stage 5 *173*, 174
Stage 6 *174*, 175, 176
Stage 7 *176*, 178
Stage 8 *177*, 178
Stage 9 *179*, 240
Stage 10 180
discussion 221, 225, 226, 227
excavation evidence *33*
Z1 29, *30–1*, 32–3
Z2 *31*, *32*, 33–4, *35*
living in 231–2
paired postholes 208
reconstruction *frontispiece*, 195–7, 199, 201, 229
houses, living in 231–2; *see also* architecture
hulls 208, 209
Hywel Dda 217

Idless manor (Cornwall) 201
Ilchester (Somerset), brooch 71
ingots, tin *72*, 73, 74–6, 233
iron ore *see* haematite
iron smithing
evidence for 22, 73, 78, 83, 233
tools 78, *79*
ironwork 76–8, *79–80*, 81, 82

joiner's dogs, iron 79, *80*, 190

ker place-names 243
Kilhallon (Cornwall)
brooch 71
date 212
dump 230
glass 85, 86, 87
pottery
black-burnished ware 105
gabbroic 114, 121, 123, 124, 125
grey wares 106, 107
publication 93
samian 98
South Devon ware 107
site type 214
Killibury (Cornwall)
four-poster 203
ovens 232
pottery 111, 116
Killigrew (Cornwall)
dating 212, 267, 276
pottery 121
site type 214
tinworking 76, 234
weights 140
knives, iron 77, 78, *80*, 81

landholding 217, 235, 236
Lanhainsworth (Cornwall) 242, 267, 275
Lanyon (Cornwall), coin hoard 69
laws, local 75–6
leather working, evidence for 79, *80*, 233
Lelant (Cornwall), weight 140
Leswyn (Cornwall), mould 142
liming, evidence for 157
Little Quoit Farm (Cornwall)
dating 212, 267–8, 275
ironwork 78, 79, 81
ironworking 83, 214, 234
site type 214
Little Waltham (Essex) roundhouses 190–1
livestock, changes in 227
Llanelen (Swansea), glass 89
location 1, *2*, *4*
loft floors 189
London, Trethurgy bowl 139
longhouses, Medieval 192, 209
loom bases 33, 208, 227, 231
looms 233
loomweights 128
Lostwithiel (Cornwall), coin hoard 69
Ludgvan (Cornwall), coin hoard 69
Lydney (Glos), Trethurgy bowl 136, 139
lynchets 10, 17, 181–2, 215

Maen Castle (Cornwall), weight 140
Magor villa (Cornwall) 217, 236
brooch 71
coins 70
ironwork 81, 82
pottery 93, 98, 107, 125
Maiden Castle (Dorset), roundhouses 191
Malpas (Cornwall), coin hoard 69
manuring 157, 175, 224–5, 230, 233

markets 235
Mawgan-in-Meneage (Cornwall), coin hoard 69
Mawnan (Cornwall), coin hoard 69
mensuration 140–2, 233
Merther Euny (Cornwall), enclosure 212, 214, 243
metalworking *see* copper alloy working; iron smithing; silver working; tinworking
midden
  chronology 175, 176–8
  discussion 229–31
  excavation evidence 25, 27, 29
milestones 234
Moel-y-Gaer (Clwyd), roundhouses 191
mortar stone 63, 151–2
mortars, Cornish 133, *134–5*, 136–9
Morvah (Cornwall), coin hoard 69
Morval (Cornwall), coin hoard 69
mould and mould cover, stone 76, *141*, 142, 233
Mount Batten (Devon)
  brooch 71
  shale roughout 145
Mulfra Vean (Cornwall), pottery 93, 118
Mullion (Cornwall), coin hoard 69

nails, iron 76, 77, 78, 190, 193, 231; *see also* hobnails
Nanstallon fort (Cornwall) 216
  coins 70
  gate 219
  pottery 93, 98, 111, 112
  quern 146
  silver working 76
  weight 140
National Mapping Programme 3
net sinkers, stone *141*, 142, 233
Newquay (Cornwall), Atlantic Road
  dates 264–5, 276
  midden 230
  pottery 109
  relationship with round 234
  weight 140
Nijmegen (Neths), bowl *136*
Nornour (Scilly)
  brooches 72
  building 236
  glass 85, 89
  ironwork 78
Nowakowski, JA 228

oak (*Quercus*) 193, 201
Old Land Surface 10, 63, 157, 158, 215
Ospringe (Kent), amphora 103

Par Beach (Scilly), ingot 74
parapet 218
path 47
paving 167, 226
  Area R 63, 65, 175
  Entrance *20, 21*, 41, 174, 220, 226
  House A 51, 53, *56, 57*, 169, 185
  House T 61, 175, 178, 185
  House Z 32, 33, 34, 35, 172, 175, 185
  Structure E 44, 45, *46*, 175
  Structure G 47
  Structure Q 36
  Structure R 65, 180
  Structure U 26, 27, 174
  Structure V *24, 25*, 178
pebbles 151, 152
Penhale Point (Cornwall), cliff castle 188
Penhale Round (Cornwall)
  bracelet 144
  dating 212, 213, 214, 239, 268
  distribution of activity 224
  dump 230
  entrance 213, 219, 220, 226
  glass 85, 87
  ironwork 78
  mould 142
  plant macrofossils 152, 160, 186
  pollen 201
  posthole line 207
  pottery 121, 124
  querns 146, 151
  structures 187, 189
Perranarworthal (Cornwall), coin hoard 69
phasing *see* chronology and phasing
phosphate analysis 15, 158, 159, 215
pin *see* ring-headed pin fragment
pits
  Area R 63
  entrance 22, 83
  House A 50
  House D 50
  Structure E 45, 46, 176
  Structure V 24, 25
  structured deposition 237
  see also hearths/hearth pits; postholes/post pits
pivot base, iron 77, 80, 81
pivot setting 20, *21*, 219
place-names 1, 211–13, 243
plant macrofossils 160
plate fragments *see* sheet fragments
ploughing, changes in 227
ploughs 232
polishing stones *see* rubbing and polishing stones
pollen analysis 159
Polperro (Cornwall), coin hoard 69
population 221, 222–3, 224, 225, 227
Porth Godrevy (Cornwall)
  boulder mortar 151
  buildings 206
  pottery

gabbroic 109
Type 4 114; Type 6 117; Type 8 117; Type 13 118; Type 16 121; Type 21 123; Type 22 124; Type 23 125; Type 26 125
publication 93
rubbing and polishing stones 143
Porthmeor (Cornwall)
basin querns 151
buildings 213, 224
date 212, 214, 239
discs 144
entrance 213, 219
ingots 75
pottery
black-burnished ware 105
gabbroic
bowl with foot-ring 117; bowls, other 125; Type 4 112, 113, 114, 115; Type 8 117; Type 9 117; Type 13 118; Type 16 121; Type 20 123; Type 21 123; Type 22 124; Type 23 125; Type 26 125
Oxfordshire ware 104
publication 93
South Devon ware 107
querns 151
rubbing and polishing stones 143
spindle whorls 143–4
Trethurgy bowl 136
weight 140
postholes/post pits
discussion
Period 4 166
Period 5
four-posters 203–4, 226; internal divisions 185; lines of 207, 226; paired 207–8, 224, 227; roof support 185–6, 191, 194, 200–1
excavation evidence
Period 1 10
Period 2 10
Period 4 13, 14
Period 5 23
Area R 63, 65; House A 50, 51, 53, *55*, *56*, 57; House D 49, 50; House T 60, 61; House X 38, 41, *42*; House Z 30, 31, 33; Structure E 44, *45*, *46*; Structure G 47–8; Structure Q 36; Structure U 26; Structure V 24, *25*; Structure Y 38
see also gatepost settings; stakeholes
pot lids, stone *141*, 142
pottery
assemblage 93
methodology 93–7
quantification 94–5, 96–8
British wares
BB1 & BB2 *100*, 104–5
BB1 & BB2, fabric imitating *100*, 106
Exeter Gritty Grey ware 106
Exeter Micaceous Grey ware 106
flagons 106
Medieval–Post-Medieval 127–8
Neolithic 215
Oxfordshire wares *100*, 104–5
South Devon ware *100*, 107–8
South-Western Grey ware storage jars 106–7
miscellaneous 108
see also Cornish gabbroic pottery
Cornish gabbroic pottery 108
chronological summary 109–11
fabric, petrography and sourcing 108–9
forms
Late Iron Age Cordoned ware 111, *126*; South-Western Decorated ware 111–12, *113*; bowl with foot-ring *116*, 117; bowls, other 125, *126*; grass-marked sherd 126–7; Type 1 111, *113*; Type 2 112, *113*; Type 3 112, *113*; Type 4 *113*, 114, *115*, 116; Type 6 *115*, *116*, 117; Type 8 *116*, 117; Type 9 *116*, 117; Type 11 *116*, 117–18; Type 12 *116*, 118; Type 13 118, *119*; Type 16 *120*, 121; Type 19 121, *122*; Type 20 121, *122*, 123; Type 21 *122*, 123–4; Type 22 *122*, 124–5, *126*; Type 23 125, *126*; Type 26 125, *126*; Type 28 *126*
imported wares
amphorae *100*, 101–4
Lezoux colour-coat 99
Phocaean Red Slip ware 99, *100*
Post-Roman imported coarsewares 101
Post-Roman imported E ware *100*, 101
samian 98–9
unguentarium 99
white slipped ware 99, *100*
pottery production 234, 235, 238
pottery use 230–1
Poundbury (Dorset), Post-Roman settlement 81, 89, 239
Prah Sands (Cornwall), ingots 75
Prideaux Rings (Cornwall), hillfort 156, 215
Pritchard, Alison 67
punch, iron 77, *79*

quartz pebbles/flake 151, 152, 153
querns 129, *145–50*, 151, 152, 232
find spots 45, 46, 61, 63, 65

Raddon hillfort (Devon) 242
radiocarbon dates 161–5, 263–76
rake prong, iron 77, 78, 79, 80
Rampart
chronology 175, 180
discussion 218–19
excavation evidence *11*, *15–17*, *18*, 19, *22*

  reconstruction 228–9
  see also bank
Reawla (Cornwall)
  buildings 187, 205, 206, 213
  dating 177, 212, 241, 242, 244, 269, 275
  glass 85, 86, 87
  ironwork 78, 79
  metalworking 76, 83
  middens 177, 230
  plant macrofossils 160, 186
  postholes 208
  pottery
    black-burnished ware 105, 106
    gabbroic 108
      Type 11 118; Type 12 118; Type 13 118; Type 16 121; Type 21 123; Type 22 124; Type 23 125; Type 28 126
    Grey wares 106
    Oxfordshire ware 104
    publication 93
    South Devon ware 107
  quern 146
  rubbing and polishing stones 143
  spindle whorl 144
  structured deposition 237
  weight 140
reconstruction
  buildings *195–8*, 199, *200*, 201
  Round *frontispiece*, 228–9
recycling, iron 78, 83, 233
Redruth (Cornwall), coin hoards 69
regional context, 5th–6th century 238–43
religion 236–8
Restineas (Cornwall), round 3
revetment
  Enclosure *12*, 13, 15
  Round *15, 16, 17*, 18, 19, 22, 65, 218
Reynolds, Peter 189, 190, 191, 192, 193, 194, 199–200
Richborough (Kent)
  Trethurgy bowl 136, *138*, 139
  weight 140
ring, iron 77, 81, *82*; *see also* finger ring
ring-headed pin fragment, iron 77, 79, *80*
roads 234
robber trench 22, 182, 184
Roberts, Samuel 181
Robertston, Rosemary 228
Rock (Cornwall), brooch 71
Roman administration 215–17, 235–6
roofs
  architecture/reconstruction 190–4, *195–8*, 199, *200*, 201
  integration with door-frames 189
  roofing material 186, 192
  support 185–6
round barrows 156, 215
roundhouses, Iron Age 190–1, 192, 193–4
rounds
  administrative background 215–17
  definition and function 211–14
  distribution *2*
  Trethurgy
    living in 231–2
    middens/artefacts 229–31
    population 221
    reconstruction *frontispiece*, 228–9
    regional context 238–43
    summary
      building of 217–20; 2nd-century Stages 221–5; later stages 225–8; end of 243–4
    trade and exchange 234–6
rubbing and polishing stones *141*, 143, 152, 232
Rudge (Devon), structure 188
The Rumps (Cornwall)
  discs 142
  pottery 101
  querns 145
  structures 188
Ruthvoes (Cornwall), dates 242, 269, 276

St Agnes (Scilly), Trethurgy bowl 136
St Austell area (Cornwall)
  flints 156
  rounds 211
  stone from 129, 146
St Blazey (Cornwall), flints 156
St Breock Downs (Cornwall), rounds 211
St Buryan (Cornwall), enclosure 243
St Ewe (Cornwall), Round Close 211
St Ives (Cornwall), weight 140
St Just in Penwith (Cornwall)
  check-list 211
  coin hoard 67, 69
St Just in Roseland (Cornwall), coin hoard 69
St Mawgan-in-Pydar (Cornwall)
  brooches 71
  buildings 188
  coin hoard 69
  discs 142, 144
  hearth pits 232
  ingot/tinworking 74, 76
  ironwork 78, 81
  pottery
    amphorae 101
    black-burnished ware 105
    gabbroic 110
      bowl with foot-ring 117; Late Iron Age Cordoned ware 111; South Western Decorated ware 111; Type 4 112, 114; Type 6 116; Type 8 117; Type 9 117; Type 11 118; Type 13 118; Type 19 121;

Type 23 125; Type 26 125; Type 28 126
publication 93
South Devon ware 107
site type 216
spindle whorls 143
St Michael Carhayes (Cornwall), coin hoard 69
St Michael's Mount (Cornwall), pottery 102, 103
St Paul (Cornwall), coin hoard 69
salt supply 234
Samson (Scilly)
coin hoard 69
pottery 127
Sancreed (Cornwall), coin hoard 69
sand 157, 224–5, 233, 236
schorl 73–4, 75, 76
seashore, rights to 233
Seaton (Devon)
knife 81
pottery 120
seaweed 157, 224–5, 233
Sennen (Cornwall), coin hoard 69
shale objects *144*, 145
Sharrow Point (Cornwall), coin hoard 69
sheet fragment
copper alloy 72
iron 76, 77
shells 157, 233
Sheppard, Peter 3
shieling 215
Shortlanesend (Cornwall)
dates 212, 270–1, 275
field name 211
hearth pits 232
pottery
gabbroic 114, 118, 121, 123, 124, 125, 126
publication 93
site type 213–14
structure 187
shrines
courtyard houses 208, 237
Trethurgy *see* Structure G
silver working 76, 233
slag 73, 74, 76, 83
slate 50, 51, 152
sleds 220
slicker, iron 77, 79, *80*, 233
slide-cars 220
sling stones 152, 220
slots
House A 53
House D 48–9, 50, 170, 205
House X 38–9, *42*, 168, 171–2, 175, 203, 204
House Z 33, *35*, 231
soils
described 1–3, 157
phosphate analysis 158, 159
pollen analysis 159
see also Old Land Surface
Sourton Down (Devon), longhouse 209
South Shields (S Tyne), glass 89
spearhead, iron 77, *82*
spindle whorls 232, 233
ceramic 98, *143*, 144
stone 129, *143*, 144
Stackpole Warren (Dyfed), mortar 138
stakeholes
Period 4, Structure N 1
Period 5
Area R 63
House A 53, *55*, 56, 185
House D 50
House T 60, 61
House X *41*, 42
House Z 32, 34
Structure Q 36, 37
Structure V 24
Stannon (Cornwall), building 188
Stanwick (N Yorks), glass 90
status, indications of 224, 232
Stencoose (Cornwall)
dates 242, 271, 275
pottery 104
structured deposition 236
Stithians (Cornwall), coin hoard 69
stock, iron 77, 78, *79*, 83
Stoke Gabriel (Devon)
ironwork 78
pottery 107, 120
structures 188, 206
stone clearance 226
stone objects *129–36*, 137, *138–9*, 140, *141*, 142, *143–50*, 151–2
stone supply 232–3
stone working 233
strap fragments, iron 76, 77, 78
stratigraphy *see* excavation
Stratton (Cornwall), coin hoard 69
Structure D3
chronology *171*, 172
discussion 207, 226
excavation evidence 49
Structure E
chronology
Stage 1 167, *168*, 169
Stage 2 *169*
Stage 3 *170*, 172
Stage 4 *171*, 172
Stage 5 *173*, 175
discussion 203–4, 221–4, 226, 227
excavation evidence *44–6*
foundation deposit 237

Structure G
  chronology
    Stage 6 *174*, 175–6
    Stage 7 *176*, 178
    Stage 8 *177*
    Stage 9 *179*, 180
  discussion 208–9, 224, 228, 236–7, 241
  excavation evidence *45*, 46, *47–8*
  reconstruction *frontispiece*, 229
Structure N
  chronology 165
  discussion 215
  excavation evidence 13, *14*, 15
Structure Q
  chronology
    Stage 1 *168*
    Stage 2 *169*, 170
    Stage 3 *170*, 171
    Stage 4 *171*, 172, 173
    Stage 5 *173*, 174–5
    Stage 6 *174*, 175
    Stage 7 *176*
    Stage 8 *177*
    Stage 9 *179*
  discussion 206–7, 225, 226, 228
  excavation evidence 35, *36*, 37–8
Structure R
  chronology
    Stage 4 *171*, 173
    Stage 5 *173*, 175
    Stage 6 *174*, 176
    Stage 7 *176*, 178
    Stage 8 178
    Stage 10 180, *181*
  discussion 205–6, 207, 226–7
  excavation evidence *62*, 63, *64*, 65
  reconstruction *frontispiece*, 229
Structure T
  chronology *177*, 178, 179
  discussion 204, 207, 239
  excavation evidence 59, 61, 63, *64*
Structure U
  architecture 183, 184, 186, 197, 207
  chronology
    Stage 5 *173*, 174
    Stage 6 *174*, 175
    Stage 7 *176*, 178
    Stage 8 *177*, 178
    Stage 9 179
    Stage 10 180
  discussion 209–10, 221, 226, 227, 229–30, 238–9
  excavation evidence 25, *26–9*
Structure V
  chronology
    Stage 7 *176*, 178
    Stage 8 *177*, 178
    Stage 9 *179*
    Stage 10 180, *181*
  discussion 205, 206, 221, 230, 239
  excavation evidence *23–5*
Structure X5
  chronology 180, *181*
  discussion 207
  excavation evidence *39*, 42, *44*
Structure Y
  chronology
    Stage 6 *174*, 175
    Stage 7 *176*, 178
    Stage 8 *177*, 178
    Stage 9 *179*
  discussion 207, 228
  excavation evidence *37*, 38
structured deposition 46, 236–8
studs *see* upholstery studs

taxation 227, 233, 235, 239
textile working 143, 232, 233
Threemilestone Round (Cornwall)
  date 212, 213, 214
  structures 188, 205, 213
timber 191–2, 193, 201, 224, 225, 227
timber screens 185
  House A 53, 55, 169, 172, 185
  House D 185
  House Z 185, 227, 231
Tintagel (Cornwall)
  buildings 206, 241
  dates 239, 240, 243, 244, 272–4, 276
  glass 86, 87, 88
  ironwork 78
  plant macrofossils 160
  pottery
    gabbroic 121, 124
    imported wares 97, 99, 101, 104, 240, 241, 244-5
  status 239, 241, 243
tinworking 73, 75–6, 233, 235; *see also* ingots, tin
Topsham (Devon), building 203
trade and exchange 86, 233, 234–6, 238
transport *see* roads; vehicles
Traprain Law (Scotland), glass 88, 90
tre settlements 180, 243, 244
Trebal (Cornwall), flints 156
Trebarveth T1 (Cornwall), pottery 93
  gabbroic 111, 117, 118, 121, 123, 124
  samian 98
Trebarveth T3 (Cornwall)
  building 206
  pottery
    gabbroic 109
      bowls, other 125; Type 2 112; Type 4 114;
      Type 6 117; Type 9 117; Type 11 118;
      Type 13 118; Type 20 123; Type 22 124;

Type 26 125
publication 93
samian 98
salt production 206, 234
Tregerthen (Cornwall), weights 140
Tregilders (Cornwall)
bracelet 144
date 212
site type 213, 214
Tregonning (Cornwall), stone from 129, 139, 142, 146
Treloy (Cornwall), tin bowl *137*, 138
Trenowah (Cornwall), excavations 156, 214–15, 237
Trereife (Cornwall), ingot 75
Treryn (Cornwall), coin hoard 69
Trethurgy, present settlement 180
Trethurgy bowls *129–33*, 135, *136*, 137, *138*, 139
Trevelgue Head (Cornwall), pottery 109, 213
Treverbyn manor 1
Trevinnick (Cornwall)
date 212
site type 213, 214
structure 205
Trevisker (Cornwall)
buildings 213
date 212, 214
entrance 213, 219
ironwork 78
mortar 138
pottery
gabbroic 109
bowl with foot-ring 117; Type 1 111;
Type 20 123; Type 21 123; Type 22 124;
Type 23 125
publication 93
quern 148
slag 83
Treworld (Cornwall), deserted site 243
trough, stone 134–5
turf 15, 16, 186, 218
Tywardreath (Cornwall), coin hoard 69

upholstery studs 77, 78, *80*, 81, 231

vehicles 220–1, 226, 228, 232
vessel fragments
glass 85–9, *90*, 91–2, 128, 235
iron 76, 77, 78, *80*, 81
stone *129–36*, 137, *138*, 139
villas 217
votive deposition *see* structured deposition

Walesland Rath (Pembs), byre 209
walls 184, 191, 192–3, 207
watch-tower 203
water supply 232
wear marks, entrance *21*, 22, 219;
see also wheel tracks
weights, stone *134*, *139*, 140–2, 233, 237
roughout *141*, 143
Wendron (Cornwall), coin hoard 69
Wheal Ruby 3, 83
wheel tracks 22, 220–1, 228
wheel-car (Radnorshire) 221
whetstones *141*, 142–3
Whithorn (Dumfries & Galloway), glass 86, 88, 89
Widemouth Bay (Cornwall), pottery 105
Winchester (Hants), Lankhills 89
windbreaks 207
window glass 85, 86, 89, *90*, 92, 189
Woodbury Castle (Devon), four-poster 203
woodland clearance 215
woodland management 201, 225
Wookey Hole (Somerset), brooch 71

Zennor (Cornwall), coin hoard 69